AMERICAN WINE

AMERICAN WINE

The ultimate companion to the wines and wine producers of the USA

JANCIS ROBINSON
AND
LINDA MURPHY

MITCHELL BEAZLEY

American Wine
by Jancis Robinson and Linda Murphy

First published in Great Britain in 2013 by Mitchell Beazley, an imprint of Octopus Publishing Group Ltd, Endeavour House, 189 Shaftesbury Avenue, London WC2H 8JY
www.octopusbooks.co.uk

An Hachette UK Company
www.hachette.co.uk

Copyright © Octopus Publishing Group Ltd 2013
Text copyright © Jancis Robinson & Linda Murphy 2013

All rights reserved. No part of this work may be reproduced or utilized in any form or by any means, electronic or mechanical, including photocopying, recording, or by any information storage and retrieval system, without the prior written permission of the publishers.

The publishers will be grateful for any information that will assist them in keeping future editions up to date. Although all reasonable care has been taken in the preparation of this book, neither the publishers nor the author can accept any liability for any consequence arising from the use thereof, or the information contained therein.

The authors have asserted their moral rights.

ISBN: 9781845335281

A CIP record for this book is available from the British Library.

Set in Garamond.

Printed and bound in China.

Editorial Consultant: Gill Pitts
Senior Production Controller: Lucy Carter

PRODUCED FOR OCTOPUS PUBLISHING GROUP LTD. BY SMALLWOOD & STEWART, NYC

Managing Editor: John Smallwood
Design: Alexis Siroc
Image Research: Maria M. Zerafa
Cartographic Editor: Charlotte Miller
Editorial Research: Katherine Camargo
Cartography: Cosmographics
Index: Pharos Indexing

CONTENTS

Preface	viii	**OREGON**	146
		Willamette Valley AVA	149
American Winemaking		Southern Oregon	154
Comes of Age	1	**WASHINGTON**	160
		Columbia Valley AVA	164
		Puget Sound AVA and Seattle	178
The West		**IDAHO**	182
CALIFORNIA	18	**COLORADO**	185
Mendocino County	22	**OTHER MOUNTAIN STATES**	190
Lake County	26	South Dakota, North Dakota, Montana,	
Sonoma County	28	Utah, Nevada, Wyoming	
Los Carneros AVA	50	**HAWAII AND ALASKA**	194
Napa Valley AVA	54		
Bay Area	90		
Monterey County	102	The Southwest	
San Benito & Mount Harlan AVAs	108	**ARIZONA**	198
San Luis Obispo County	110	**NEW MEXICO**	202
Santa Barbara County	119	**TEXAS**	204
Sierra Foothills	130	**OKLAHOMA**	210
Central Valley	136		
South Coast	140		

The Midwest

MISSOURI	214
OTHER WEST CENTRAL STATES	219
Kansas, Iowa, Minnesota, Nebraska	
MICHIGAN	222
OTHER EAST CENTRAL STATES	226
Illinois, Indiana, Ohio, Wisconsin	

The Southeast

VIRGINIA	232
CENTRAL APPALACHIA	240
Kentucky, North Carolina, South Carolina, Tennessee, West Virginia	
LOWER SOUTH	244
Georgia, Florida, Alabama, Mississippi, Louisiana, Arkansas	

The Northeast

NEW ENGLAND	248
Connecticut, New Hampshire, Rhode Island, Vermont, Massachusetts, Maine	
NEW YORK	250
Long Island AVA	252
Hudson River Region AVA	256
Finger Lakes AVA	258
Niagara Escarpment AVA	264
Lake Erie AVA	265
PENNSYLVANIA	266
MID-ATLANTIC STATES	268
New Jersey, Delaware, Maryland	

Index	270
Acknowledgments/Credits	278

Preface

It's hard to believe today that as recently as twenty years ago American wine producers felt they were under siege. Talk was all of neoprohibitionists, warning labels, and even more regulatory constraint than that following The Noble Experiment (national prohibition) in the 1920s. Today, however, whenever I spend time in an American city, I feel as though wine as a subject for study and enjoyment is red hot. There's an energetic enthusiasm for experiencing its pleasures and nuances and a genuine curiosity about the complexities of how it is grown and made that I sense nowhere else in the world (with the possible exception of China's fastest-growing cities). It is hardly surprising that all wine graphs in the United States seem to be heading in one direction, so much so that the States recently overtook the effete major wine producers of Europe, such as France and Italy, where wine has no more novelty value than potatoes, to become the world's biggest wine market.

This urban love affair has been matched by a great groundswell of vinous activity in the American countryside. Grapevines were once grown seriously for wine in just a handful of states—predominantly in California's viticulturally ideal climate, as well as in upstate New York, close to major conurbations, and in parts of the Midwest, notably Ohio and Missouri, where vines historically put down roots in American soil. During the second half of the twentieth century, another array of wine-producing states, including Washington, Oregon, Virginia, Pennsylvania, and New Jersey, burgeoned and prospered. Today there is not a state in the union, even in such unlikely outposts for the vine as Hawaii and Alaska, that is not home to a winery. The total number of officially licensed wine producers in the United States has mushroomed from not much more than two thousand at the turn of the millennium to more than seven thousand today.

Admittedly, some of these wineries are located in places so inhospitable to the vine—certainly for the European grapevine *Vitis vinifera*—that they often have to depend on grapes, or sometimes wine, shipped in from other more vine-friendly states. But there can be no doubt of the sincerity with which so many Americans, wherever they live, have now embraced wine.

This book is a celebration of this delicious and delightful phenomenon, and of just how many Americans have conquered an area of expertise once regarded as quintessentially European. We hear a great deal about the big-points-scorers from California's most famous regions, but that is only one part of the inspiring patchwork that is the story of American wine today.

To pick just a few wines that either are or should be regarded as American classics: the best Cabernets and Bordeaux blends from California, Washington, Virginia, and Long Island; the finest Pinot Noirs from Pacific-cooled California and Oregon; sumptuous Chardonnays from all over the country; subtle Syrah and other Rhône grape varieties from eastern Washington; admirably precise Rieslings from New York's Finger Lakes and, increasingly, Michigan. These are being joined by bright-fruited Tempranillo from Texas and southern Oregon; and uniquely characterful Nortons from the Midwest. There is, as well, a host of other all-American varieties especially adapted to their particular state, not least a new generation of cold-hardy hybrids such as Brianna, La Crescent, and Traminette for white wines and Frontenac, Marquette, and St. Croix for reds. These represent literally thousands of reasons for Americans to feel proud that they have established their very own exuberant wine styles to match the exuberance of today's American wine enthusiast.

Jancis Robinson
2013

American Winemaking Comes of Age

Over the past three decades, a wine revolution has been taking place across the country, as Americans increasingly enjoy a glass of wine with their meals, vacation in "wine country," and take immense pride in their regions' vineyards and wineries. There are now more than 7,000 wine producers in the United States—up from 440 in 1970—and the boom has been heard around the world. America's best bottles are every bit as good as the finest wines of Europe.

Although the United States is a relative toddler as a winemaking and wine-drinking nation, hitting its stride in the mid-twentieth century while its European counterparts have been at full sprint for hundreds of years, the timeline of this relatively short enological development is surprisingly complex. The fifty states may be united as a nation, but when it comes to winemaking history, culture, and viticulture, each may as well be its own country.

People were making wine here long before the nation even existed. French Huguenots built bases in Florida in the mid-1500s and produced wine from the native Scuppernong grape (an acquired taste even today). Around 1607, English immigrants seeking religious freedom landed on the Eastern seaboard of what would become America. Accustomed to drinking wine with their meals, the Pilgrims were pleased to find native grapevines, *Vitis labrusca* and *Vitis rotundifolia*, growing wild in their new home, but they were dismayed to discover that when fermented, these grapes made musky, unsavory wines—French clarets they were not.

So the settlers sent for *Vitis vinifera* cuttings from Europe—traditional varieties such as Cabernet Sauvignon and Riesling—and planted them in the cold, wet, and often humid conditions of their new home. These noble vines were ill suited to the climate and soils of Virginia, Maryland, New York, Massachusetts, and other early colonies, and most died within a few years of planting.

Around the same time, Spanish missionaries began moving northward from Mexico into New Mexico and later into the

"Queen of the Missions"
Santa Barbara, the tenth of the twenty-one missions established by Spanish monks in California more than two hundred years ago, includes a vineyard from which the missionaries produced wine for sacramental purposes.

On the crowded wine trail
The population of wineries in some regions has become so dense that visitors can spend a week in one area and still not have time to visit all the tasting rooms (opposite).

Missouri winemaking
Stone Hill is the oldest winery in Missouri, founded in 1847 by German immigrants, who were making 1.25 million gallons of wine per year by 1900. Abandoned during Prohibition, the winery was restored by the Held family in 1965 (Betty and Jim Held are shown here), and today it is one of the state's most important producers.

territory that was to be known as California. Between 1769 and 1824, Franciscan monks established twenty-one missions in that territory, planting the Mission grapes they had brought with them from Spain to make wine for communion purposes. California's Mediterranean-like climate proved conducive to successful Mission grape growing and winemaking.

East Coast vintners, however, continued to be destined for failure. Thomas Jefferson, the nation's first secretary of state and third president, was a great admirer and collector of Bordeaux wines. In the mid- to late-1700s, he attempted to grow European varieties at his Monticello estate in Virginia. But he, and other Eastern statesmen with cravings for claret, failed to grow and vinify Cabernet Sauvignon, Merlot, and Cabernet Franc, varieties that were then unsuited to the East Coast climate and soils. In Pennsylvania, German immigrants were experiencing similar disappointments with Riesling and Gewürztraminer plantings. There James Alexander, exasperated by his vinifera-based wines, converted to the native *Vitis labrusca* in the 1730s. Others followed, loading the wines with sugar to offset the musky aromas and flavors inherent in the grapes.

The country's first commercially successful winery was established in Cincinnati, Ohio, in the mid-1800s by banker Nicholas Longworth. Sparkling wines made from the native Catawba grape were his specialty, and the wines were so competently made that they became popular in England as well. But in the 1860s, disease decimated his vines, and Ohio winemakers scattered to New York and Missouri to begin again.

A real turn came in 1849, when Italian and French immigrants began to flood Northern California to seek their fortunes in gold mining. And they began to cultivate wine grapes, including Zinfandel and Carignane, in the Sierra Foothills to make wines to slake their European thirst.

In the 1850s and '60s, European vintners faced a crippling crisis. Phylloxera, a root louse that saps the strength from vines, had made its way into Europe, most likely on cuttings from the United States, where native vines tolerated the bug and those planted on St. George rootstock—primarily Zinfandel, Petite Sirah, and Carignane—were resistant to it. When vines from America were propagated in France, the country that would be hardest-hit by phylloxera, the infestation exploded, killing vines at alarming rates.

At the same time, Americans were increasing their plantings of *Vitis vinifera,* using cuttings imported from Europe. These species were not resistant to phylloxera, so they, too, began to die. The remedy—grafting European varieties onto resistant American rootstock—slowly brought the vineyards back to life. (In the 1970s and '80s a rootstock believed to be phylloxera-proof was developed to produce large yields of high-quality grapes consistently. But it, in fact, proved susceptible to phylloxera, and California growers were forced to rip out their vines and replant with other rootstocks.)

While California and Europe struggled, vineyards in the east, planted in labrusca, continued to thrive, and researchers realized that by grafting French vinifera onto native labrusca rootstock, grape growers could have disease-resistant vines that produced drinkable wines in a more European style. These grafted vines, also planted throughout Europe, became common on the East Coast and in the South—a happy medium between disease-prone vinifera and the funky wines produced from labrusca.

When the gold ran out in California in the late 1850s, the miners moved to San Francisco, Sonoma, Napa, Mendocino, Southern California, and other warm areas, planting wine grapes on the sections of their properties that could not sustain such crops as tomatoes, peppers, squashes, orchard fruits, and nuts. These largely Italian and French settlers put wine grapes into ground that would later be deemed as hallowed by winemakers. The existence today of intense, characterful old-vine California red wines can be traced to the immigrants who planted and then maintained those first vines through Prohibition and beyond.

For the next few decades, the wine industry in the United States was largely local; nationally, interest in wine and its consumption was limited, and those who enjoyed wine often chose European bottles. The advent of Prohibition didn't help matters any.

Prohibition was spurred by a decades-long temperance movement, whose advocates held that intoxication led to crime, debauchery, and the ruination of society. Their initial calls for moderation in the consumption of wine, beer, and spirits evolved into demands for a total ban on the production, transportation, and sale of "demon drink," and their wishes were granted by the 1919 ratification of the 18th Amendment to the Constitution and the implementation of the law via the Volstead Act in 1920.

THE LEGACY OF PROHIBITION

Since Colonial times, America has had temperance periods, some national, others limited to specific states or regions within states. Various government, religious, and public health leaders have voiced their concerns about the effects of alcohol on the populace, viewing such drinks as threats to physical and spiritual health.

When Prohibition began in 1920, approximately one-half of the states already had laws prohibiting or limiting alcohol manufacture. Upon Repeal in 1933, several of those states continued to ban booze—some until as late as 1966, when "farm winery acts" began to be put into place, granting farmers the right to produce and sell wines made from their own crops. Not only had alcohol consumption become less objectionable in these straggler states (most of them in the Midwest and South), agricultural economics were also at play, with state officials seeing additional revenues from wine excise and sales taxes, as well as the money to be made from wine-based tourism.

Kansas was the first state to actively prohibit alcoholic beverage production, in 1881 (at the time, Maine had such a law on its books, but rarely enforced it). Kansas didn't end its state prohibition until 1948; Oklahoma (1959) and Missouri (1966) were the last to lift such laws and put farm winery regulations in place. One can only imagine the advanced state of the grape growing and winemaking in America today, had Prohibition not stalled progress.

And remnants of Prohibition remain. The 21st Amendment guarantees that states can retain the authority to control alcoholic production, distribution, and sales within their borders. Thus, some states, counties, and even cities have a crazy quilt of regulations specific to them, often contradictory and archaic.

Several counties in the Bible Belt are "dry" to this day, with virtually no alcohol sales permitted. In 2011, there were nearly two hundred dry counties in Tennessee, Arkansas, Mississippi, and Alabama alone. So-called moist counties allow wine and beer to be sold, but not spirits. Across the country, some regions prohibit alcohol sales on Sundays; others limit the number of hours in a day that alcohol can be sold. In New York State, groceries and higher-strength alcoholic beverages are still strictly separated: grocery stores cannot sell wine or spirits, and liquor stores cannot sell beer or food. And, it is illegal for anyone relocating to Utah from out of state to drive his or her wine collection across the border unless they've first paid taxes on the value of the bottles.

Gotham goes dry

Although religious objections to alcohol consumption played a part, Prohibition was largely a result of the belief that a reduction of inebriation would effect a decrease in crime, marital unfaithfulness, and health issues. In actuality, it allowed mobsters to control liquor sales and establish an estimated 100,000 speakeasies in New York City alone.

AMERICAN WINEMAKING COMES OF AGE

Judgment of Paris, triumph of American wines
In 1976, the stunning victory of California wines over French in a blind tasting put America on the world winemaking map. The tasting was conducted by, from right, Steven Spurrier and Patricia Gallagher. Visible beyond them are judges Pierre Tari, Pierre Brejoux, and Christian Vanneque of La Tour d'Argent.

For nearly fourteen years, commercial production of wine and other alcoholic beverages was illegal, although wineries could bottle wine for sacramental and medicinal purposes. But drinking didn't stop, and demand increased. Bootleggers flourished, underground speakeasies were packed, and mobsters such as Al Capone controlled the transport and sale of illicit beverages. At the same time, Americans learned to ferment and brew their own in bathtubs or hidden stills.

It is difficult to know exactly how much Prohibition affected the amount of alcohol consumed in the United States, because without taxes collected on the sale of alcohol, the government had no way of tracking the volume produced and consumed. One thing is certain: Prohibition stopped winemaking dead in its tracks throughout the country. By 1933, when President Franklin D. Roosevelt ushered the 21st Amendment repealing Prohibition through Congress, only a handful of farmers had kept their vineyards in production, and few others were eager to plant anew. And some states continued to make alcohol production illegal long after national Prohibition ended (see box p. 3).

Starting in the 1930s, California producers such as Paul Masson, Almaden, and Gallo began aggressively marketing jug wines—one-gallon bottles of slightly sweet, inexpensive wines made from blends of different grape varieties and bearing generic names such as "Chablis" or "Burgundy." They were distributed nationally in liquor and grocery stores and became popular throughout the country. Other producers, however, such as Beringer Vineyards, Inglenook, and Beaulieu Vineyard, among others, began making high-end wines as well, and with great success. By the early 1970s, a wave of newcomers, including Warren Winiarski at Stag's Leap Wine Cellars and Jim Barrett at Chateau Montelena, both in Napa Valley, had staked their success on the production of fine French-style wines. The problem was that little attention was paid to them on an international level—until they became the unexpected winners of a blind tasting of top-quality wines held in Paris in 1976. Organized by British wine merchant Steven Spurrier and his American colleague Patricia Gallagher, the "Judgment of Paris" invited British and French wine critics to rate a series of French white Burgundies and red Bordeaux against California Chardonnays and Cabernet Sauvignons. The sweep by the Americans in both categories shocked the European wine community and gave U.S. vintners a huge boost of confidence in their abilities and potential.

The 1970s were also marked by the production of inexpensive sweet wines made from California Central Valley grapes and sometimes enhanced with additional flavorings. More adult soda pop than Sancerre, these simple, fruity wines from such brands as Annie Green Springs, Boone's Farm, and Spañada became the gateway to wine for many American consumers. Giant producers based in the Central Valley, such as E. & J. Gallo and United Vintners, churned out tremendous volumes of these easy-drinking wines, using marketing magic to entice Americans to buy a bottle and thereby add a splash of culture to their lives.

Yet no one wine can claim to have won over more U.S. wine lovers than white Zinfandel, created in 1973 by Bob Trinchero of Sutter Home Winery in California's Napa Valley. A "happy mistake" in winemaking produced a pink, slightly sweet Zinfandel that was embraced by Americans unaccustomed to drinking dry wine, and white Zin remains a huge seller today.

Beginning in the 1970s, Champagne producers recognized the potential of California as a premium winegrowing area, with Moët & Chandon, G. H. Mumm, and Louis Roederer establishing vineyards and wineries for the purpose of making sparkling wine. By the early 1990s, there was so much interest in California wines that those made from hybrid and native grapes

(continued on p. 9)

Safeguarding the vines
Vines such as the head-pruned Zinfandel, Carignane, and Alicante Bouschet planted in 1895 on the Saitone Ranch in Russian River Valley are protected by California's Historic Vineyard Society.

GRAPE VARIETIES GROWN IN THE UNITED STATES

Most drinkers of American-made wines identify them by grape variety and not by the region in which the grapes are grown, as is the custom in Europe. In France's Burgundy region, for example, it is understood that Chardonnay is the predominant white grape, so "Chardonnay" doesn't appear on labels; the appellation and vineyard are the most important information, as they indicate the style of wine in the bottle.

Unlike most European wine zones, the American Viticultural Area (AVA) system places no restrictions on which varieties can be grown where, so the name of the predominant grape is what consumers look for on labels. Some vintners assign proprietary names to their wines without designating the grapes used.

While the *Vitis vinifera* wines of Europe have been models for many American makers, vintners planting grapes in climates too challenging for vinifera have found success with native American and hybrid varieties. These vines have adapted to or been bred for regions that are too cold, too humid, and/or too prone to disease for vinifera to survive. The availability of French-American and American hybrid varieties, and improved methods of growing grapes native to the United States, have led to the boom in American winemaking.

Vitis vinifera

Developed in Europe, these grape varieties need warm summers and moderate winter temperatures. In the United States, the West Coast dominates this category, although a few other states, including Michigan, New York, Texas, and Virginia, have been successful with vinifera when it is planted in suitable soil and climate.

WHITES

Chardonnay—The most-planted wine grape in California and also a star performer in Washington, Oregon, Virginia, and parts of New York state, Chardonnay is remarkably malleable and can be grown successfully in cool, warm, and hot climates. Like most vinifera varieties, however, it cannot survive Midwest deep freezes nor the rot-inducing humidity of the Deep South. There are two basic Chardonnay styles: rich, sometimes buttery, and with toast, vanillin, and spice notes from oak barrel fermentation and aging; and leaner, crisper wines that see little or no contact with oak.

Pinot Gris—A mutation of the red Pinot Noir grape, Pinot Gris tolerates warm and cold climates and is widely planted in the United States. Its name comes from the gray-ish ("gris") to pinkish-brown color of the grapes, although the juice inside is clear. It ripens early, making it a good choice for farmers in regions where the growing season is short. Some winemakers label their Pinot Gris as Pinot Grigio, which suggests a lighter, crisper, less fruity wine.

Riesling—This noble variety is one of the few vinifera types that thrives in cold temperatures during the growing season, although it is susceptible to injury in bitterly cold areas in winter and early spring. Riesling styles range from bone-dry and somewhat austere to semidry, semisweet, late-harvest dessert wines, and ice wines. Crackling acidity and minerality are hallmarks of great Riesling, and in New York's Finger Lakes region and on Michigan's Old Mission and Leelanau peninsulas, the grapes reach full maturity with their natural acidity intact. Washington, the No. 1 Riesling-producing state by volume, is a bit warmer, and its Rieslings tend to be fruitier and slightly richer.

Sauvignon Blanc—Although smatterings of Sauvignon Blanc plantings exist in the United States, California is its ground zero, with more than 15,000 acres planted. It's a vigorous plant that enjoys warm-to-hot summers, and usually produces wines with lemon, lime, grapefruit, and herbal characteristics; when grown in warm zones, Sauvignon Blanc tends to show a melon and tropical-fruit personality. Stainless-steel-fermented versions are lean and crisp; oak-fermented styles are more dense and layered.

REDS

Cabernet Franc—This vine flourishes in many soil types, and in both cool and warm regions. It's the go-to red vinifera grape along the Atlantic seaboard, as it ripens earlier than Cabernet Sauvignon and thus dodges fall rainstorms and drops in temperature that force grapevines to shut down before clusters have fully ripened. Cabernet Franc is arguably Virginia's best red grape, as well as New York State's. In the West, winemakers use Cab Franc in their Bordeaux-style blends for its aromas and freshness, and it is increasingly being bottled as a stand-alone varietal.

Cabernet Sauvignon—The variety responsible for the muscular "King of Wine" is a late ripener and is therefore limited to regions that have long, warm, dry growing seasons—California, Washington, Arizona, and Texas, in particular, with Virginia, Maryland, and New York's Long Island also suited when the grape is planted in the right spots.

Merlot—Known for producing red wines that are softer and more drinkable in their youth than Cabernet Sauvignon, Merlot typically ripens a few weeks earlier than Cabernet, and has a better chance of ripening in cool areas. Sunny California and Washington are the nation's Merlot leaders, yet Long Island in New York State is just as adept at producing high-quality Merlots, albeit in a leaner, more European style. The variety is frequently blended with other red grapes, and it's not uncommon to see Merlot in some of Arizona's and Virginia's best red wines.

Cabernet Sauvignon

Pinot Noir—The Burgundian variety prized for its precision, silky tannins, and ethereal qualities is, like Cabernet Sauvignon, a wine many vintners aspire to make, yet few have the opportunity. Pinot Noir is particular about where it is planted—it loves limestone soils and cool but not cold climates—and only Oregon and certain regions in California (Russian River Valley, Sonoma Coast, Santa Cruz Mountains, Santa Barbara County) have proved consistently adept with the grape.

Syrah—Wines made from this variety run the gamut from crisp and restrained to ripe and juicy to meaty and earthy; soils and climate largely determine the style of wine. Often blended with Mourvèdre and Grenache, Syrah wines are produced not only in California and Washington, where they have achieved some fame, but also in other warm growing regions, among them Arizona, New Mexico, Texas, and Virginia.

Zinfandel—California has a virtual monopoly on Zinfandel (although there are a few producers in Oregon and Washington). European immigrants planted Zinfandel and other varieties in California after the 1849 Gold Rush, and because the vines were on phylloxera-resistant rootstock, many have survived to this day.

Also: WHITE—Gewürztraminer, Marsanne, Muscat, Pinot Blanc, Roussanne, Viognier; RED—Alicante Bouschet, Barbera, Carignane, Grenache, Malbec, Mourvèdre, Petite Sirah, Petit Verdot, Sangiovese, Tempranillo (see box p. 157).

Native American varieties

The *Vitis labrusca* and *Vitis rotundifolia* vine species that early settlers found growing wild on the East Coast didn't produce particularly palatable wines. Varieties of these species are now grown for juice, jams, and jellies, but in skilled hands they can be transformed into rewarding wines.

Concord—Grapey and simple, this purple labrusca variety is primarily used to make juices, jams, jellies, and the popular kosher wine Manischewitz. Michigan, Pennsylvania, and New York are the major growers of Concord, with much of their production going to Welch's.

Muscadine—This group of *Vitis rotundifolia* includes the specific varieties Carlos and Scuppernong for white wines, and Noble for reds. Muscadines have a high tolerance for the humidity and fungal diseases typical in the South—in Florida, Kentucky, North Carolina, and Mississippi, to name the most prominent states—and produce mostly sweet, viscous wines that have a candied-fruit, musky aroma.

Niagara—As Concord's white labrusca counterpart, Niagara has a similar "foxy," musky character that tastes foreign to those accustomed to vinifera wines. Production is centered largely in New York State, where the wines are made in semisweet and sweet styles.

Norton—a.k.a. Cynthiana, this native *Vitis aestivalis* grape produces a full-bodied, spicy red wine. Norton is tolerant of humidity and is thus widely cultivated in Missouri and Virginia, with pockets of plantings in the Midwest and Texas. Although it's a native species, Norton/Cynthiana lacks the musky, foxy aroma of other native varieties, and is capable of making high-quality, dry red wines.

Also: Catawba (red).

Niagara

Norton

Hybrid varieties

French-American hybrids are genetic crosses of *Vitis vinifera* and native American species made by French breeders. More recently, American hybrids have been developed by the University of Minnesota and New York's Cornell University, intended to have a higher tolerance for harsh winter conditions than French-American hybrids.

WHITES

Brianna—This relatively new (introduced in 2001), cold-tolerant variety has quickly become a standout white-wine grape in the Midwest, particularly in Iowa, Minnesota, and Nebraska. Brianna can be produced in off-dry and semisweet styles, and displays rich, exotic pineapple, mango, and papaya flavors that are balanced by brisk acidity. Expect more frigid regions to embrace Brianna, as news of its potential spreads.

(continued)

GRAPE VARIETIES GROWN IN THE UNITED STATES (continued)

La Crescent—Producing white wines reminiscent of floral Rieslings, this vinifera hybrid was bred at the University of Minnesota to withstand -35°F winter temperatures, and is a popular choice for growers in the frigid Midwest and Great Lakes regions.

Seyval—This French-American hybrid produces dry and semidry, medium-bodied whites that can have an herbal accent. It's a popular grape in New York and Missouri.

Traminette—A white variety bred to withstand harsh winters, Traminette has the floral and spice character of one of its parents, Gewürztraminer. It has become one of Michigan's best white-wine varieties, and Indiana producers created a "Try on Traminette" campaign to promote the wine to consumers.

Vidal Blanc—A cold-hardy French-American hybrid, it makes full-bodied, fruity, and floral whites, and is also excellent for ice wine. New York's Finger Lakes region is the hub for Vidal Blanc production, with small volumes also produced in Missouri, Ohio, and Pennsylvania.

Vignoles—This cold-hardy French-American hybrid is similar to Vidal Blanc in its character and growing regions.

REDS

Chambourcin—This French-American hybrid produces wines with bright red-fruit flavors, herbaceous aromas, firm tannins, and crisp acidity. While it doesn't tolerate the harsh winter temperatures of the Great Lakes region, it is especially suited to the less-challenging climates of Illinois, Indiana, Ohio, and Pennsylvania.

Frontenac—This University of Minnesota hybrid makes robust red wines with palate-refreshing acidity. The vines withstand -30°F temperatures in winter and emerge in spring to pump out grapes with lively cherry and berry character. Frontenac has quickly become a superstar grape in the Midwest and New England.

Marechal Foch—A dark-skinned French-American hybrid, "Foch" makes medium-bodied wines with black cherry flavors, and also flavorful rosés. Popular with Midwest winemakers, it can handle cold winters, yet isn't as cold-hardy as Frontenac and Marquette.

Marquette—Popular with growers in the Midwest and New England, this hybrid is similar to Frontenac.

Also: WHITE—Blanc du Bois, Brianna, Cayuga White, Chardonel, Edelweiss, La Crosse, Melody, St. Pepin, Stover, Valvin Muscat; RED—Baco Noir, Black Spanish (a.k.a. Lenoir, Jacquez, Blue French), Corot Noir, Léon Millot, Noiret, St. Croix.

La Crescent

Chambourcin

east of the Rockies had taken a backseat. Today, the state is the overwhelming leader in U.S. viticulture, with around 80 percent of American grapevines (many of them for raisin production and the table), followed by Washington, New York, Oregon, Texas, New Jersey, Virginia, Michigan, and Pennsylvania. California's influence, however, is now being countered by the emergence of quality wines from other states, with consumers becoming interested in wines from their own backyards, whether made from native grapes, French-American hybrids, or *Vitis vinifera* or from fruits such as raspberries, cherries, and apples.

In these other regions, vintners are discovering which varieties perform best in their terroir. In Virginia, Viognier and Cabernet Franc stand out. Norton is a star in Missouri. Finger Lakes Rieslings from New York State can be stunning, and Michigan's Rieslings, Gewürztraminers, and Pinot Blancs shine. Cabernet Franc and Merlot from New York's Long Island can be splendid, and Gruet in New Mexico makes serious sparkling wines using Champagne techniques and grapes (Chardonnay and Pinot Noir). Certain American and French-American hybrid grapes such as Seyval, Chambourcin, and Marquette flourish in challenging climates.

Growing the Grapes

It's a cliché much used by vintners, but it's absolutely true: Great wines are made in the vineyard. Without perfectly ripened, high-quality grapes, winemakers have zero chance of producing outstanding wine. To that end, whether with *Vitis vinifera*, native vines, or hybrids, grape growing in America has made tremendous strides in a relatively short period of time. Trial and error, research by university agricultural departments, and advice from international consultants have put American viticulture on the fast track to success. Following the lead of the University of California at Davis, which for decades has been the primary training ground for U.S. winemakers as well as for many foreign vintners, other universities throughout the country have established viticulture and winemaking departments to address the specific needs of their regions and to train future growers and winemakers. The industry has also taken on a greenish hue, as growers increasingly implement sustainable, organic, and biodynamic practices, both to increase wine quality and to reduce environmental impacts.

Each growing region has its own issues, related to climate, soils, elevation, pests, disease, availability of irrigation and frost-protection water, and cultural factors that affect grape growing. For example, while farmers without access to reliable well, river, lake, or stored rainfall water must dry-farm their vines, others with available water choose to dry-farm, believing that it produces more intense fruit character in the grapes and conserves a valuable natural resource.

Pierce's Disease
This Merlot vine shows the effects of Pierce's disease, a bacterium transferred to vines by winged sharpshooter insects. The infection causes blockage of the water-conducting system of the plant; without sufficient water, a vine's leaves dry out and become discolored (called scorching), and grape clusters shrivel or raisin. Although quality wines can be produced from them, affected vines typically die within five years.

In the East, multicolored Asian lady beetles can hitchhike from grapes to fermenters and impart a surprisingly strong, and undesirable, peanut-buttery aroma and taste to wines. In the West, however, the beetle's cousin, the ladybug, is a farmer's friend, devouring aphids and other insects that damage vines and grapes without imparting any foreign flavor.

Growers throughout the United States continue to battle two nasty vine destroyers: phylloxera, the root louse that wiped out European grapevines in the 1860s and many California vineyards in the 1980s and 1990s, and Pierce's disease (PD), a bacterial infection. Phylloxera is a tiny aphid-like insect that feeds on vinifera roots, slowly sucking the sap out of them until the vine dies. The PD bacteria are spread by leafhoppers called glassy-winged sharpshooters; infected vines can die within one to five years, and entire vineyards have been lost to PD.

In the case of both pests, there are no cures, only preventive measures. PD- and phylloxera-resistant rootstocks have been developed and continue to evolve. To prevent PD, growers plant vines far away from sharpshooter feeding and breeding areas, such as riverbanks and citrus groves. Because the phylloxera louse has been known to travel on farm equipment and workers' boots, thorough cleaning is mandatory to prevent its spread. Most states have Integrated Pest Management (IPM) programs to educate and assist farmers with these and other vineyard pests.

The increasing availability of grapevine selections, or clones, has had a major impact on the quality gains made in U.S. winemaking. California's Foundation Plant Services and programs such as France's ENTAV (Etablissement National Technique pour l'Amélioration de la Viticulture) and Geisenheim Research Institute in Germany continue to make new clones available, and the benefits are twofold: Growers have much more choice in selecting

AMERICAN WINEMAKING COMES OF AGE | 11

United States of America

The map shows the relative extent of grape growing and wine production as of 2012. Vineyard acreage is given for states with significant plantings.

the best clones for their growing conditions, and winemakers can tweak quality and increase complexity in their wines.

However, there is little doubt that contraband cuttings helped establish some of America's greatest vineyards. Tales are rife of vintners tucking vine cuttings from Bordeaux and Burgundy into their boxer shorts or suitcases and bringing them into the United States illegally, circumventing five-year quarantines on foreign plant material, in place to prevent the introduction of diseased vines and other plants into the country. (Such illicit efforts are largely impossible today because of the intense scrutiny passengers and their bags get at airports.)

Mechanical harvesting, pruning, and canopy management have been introduced in areas where hands-on labor is unavailable or unaffordable. Viticulturists continue to learn more about how much water their vines need, and when they need it. Research is ongoing in such areas as trellising and canopy management, crop load, pruning, and cover crop rotations, all part of how vineyard practices are constantly being adapted to improve wine quality.

And momentum is building for the practice of sustainable winegrowing, which includes organic and biodynamic methods. By replacing synthetic pesticides, herbicides, and fertilizers with natural alternatives, growers and vintners are being kinder to the

New York State Ice Wine
Frigid weather conditions in upstate New York in late fall allow Leonard Oakes Estate Winery, in the Niagara Escarpment AVA, to harvest Vidal Blanc after the grapes have frozen on the vines. The frozen grapes will be pressed to make ice wine.

land and their neighbors. Some are erecting owl boxes and raptor perches to host insect- and gopher-hungry birds. Cover crops prevent soil erosion and host beneficial insects. Sheep grazing on weeds between vine rows eliminate the need for chemical herbicides. Compost replaces harsh fertilizers. While the climate in some regions limits growers in their response to fungal disease, the trend across the country is to have as little chemical impact on the land as possible.

By far the most laudable development is the acknowledgment by growers and winemakers that certain grape varieties do well in some places but are unsuited to others. Everyone wants to produce Cabernet Sauvignon and/or Pinot Noir, France's most important wines, but few regions here have the soil and climate to support these grapes. Many have learned this the hard way; savvy growers have done their homework and now plant varieties suited to their climate and soil conditions.

The Letter of the Law

Where a particular vineyard is located greatly influences the style of wine in the bottle. Determining a wine's precise geographical origins is the job of the American Viticultural Area (AVA) system, administered by the U.S. Treasury Department's Alcohol and Tobacco Tax and Trade Bureau (TTB), which does what its name implies—collects taxes on production and sales of alcohol and tobacco and sets federal alcohol policies for wine label certification, varietal and alcohol content of U.S. wines, and more. Winemakers must also adhere to laws within their own states on the production, labeling, and sales of their wines.

AVAs, patterned after France's Appellation d'Origine Contrôlée (AOC) system, recognize specific winegrowing areas for their climate, soil, elevation, exposure, and historical significance. Loosely, an AVA is defined as "a viticultural area for American wine as a delimited grape-growing region distinguishable by geographical features, the boundaries of which have been recognized and defined.... These designations allow vintners and consumers to attribute a given quality, reputation, or other characteristic of a wine made from grapes grown in an area to its geographic origin. The establishment of viticultural areas allows vintners to describe more accurately the origin of their wines to consumers and helps consumers to identify wines they may purchase."

If only this were entirely true. The diversity of varieties planted within any AVA (growers can plant any grape types they choose, not the case in French AOCs), the varied viticultural and winemaking practices conducted within it, the abilities of winemakers to blend several varieties into one wine, and the emergence of sub-AVAs within larger AVAs complicate things so much that consumers have no solid guarantees of quality or character from AVA alone when they purchase a bottle of wine they haven't tried before.

Alexana Winery
Oregon's Dundee Hills AVA, where Alexana is located, was established in part on the basis of its topography and unique soil types.

The AVA system is also very young. Europeans have had centuries to sort out their appellations, but the first AVA was established only in 1980, for the Augusta region of Missouri (California's Napa Valley AVA was approved eight months later). It has been suggested by some that the United States should produce wine for another fifty years, then begin to draw appellational boundaries, but the horses are already out of the barn. Today there are more than two hundred AVAs, plus innumerable state and county political appellations that appear on wine labels.

The AVA approval process is based on petitioners stating their reasons for acceptance; if they're persuasive, their request is opened to public comment on the TTB website. Unless there are strenuous objections, most AVAs pass muster. TTB doesn't inspect the regions, look at the soils, determine the climate, or taste the wines.

The New Winemaking

Old-time U.S. winemakers grew grapes, crushed them with their feet or in buckets, put the juice and skins into redwood tanks, tossed in some yeast, and let nature do the rest. Voilà—wine!

WHAT'S IN A LABEL?

All labels affixed to commercial wines made in the United States must be approved by the Alcohol and Tobacco Tax and Trade Bureau (TTB) and adhere to precise standards. A COLA (Certification of Label Approval) is issued only to labels that meet numerous criteria for specific characteristics, including varietal (or breakdown of grape varieties), appellation, vintage, alcohol percentage, and mandatory health/sulfite warnings.

Varietal makeup of wines varies by AVA and appellation, as well as state to state. In most cases, a wine must be made from a minimum of 75 percent of a particular grape in order to be labeled by that grape variety name (Cabernet Sauvignon, Chardonnay, Riesling, etc.).

A wine must contain at least 85 percent of grapes from the AVA stated on the label, or 100 percent if the wine is estate designated. A minimum 95 percent of the wine must come from a vineyard designated on the label.

Wines with proprietary, rather than varietal, names—such as Opus One in Napa Valley and Col Solare in the Red Mountain AVA of Washington State—typically don't list their varietal content, and when they do, this information is usually on the back label.

TTB requires an alcohol-by-volume (abv) listing on all labels, though such labeling is not always precise. For wines with 14 percent abv or less, TTB allows the percentage stated to vary by as much as 1.5 percent from the actual alcohol content. Thus, a wine labeled "Alcohol 12.5 percent by volume" can have an actual alcohol content of as little as 11 percent or as much as 14 percent. Wines at 14.1 percent and above have a label tolerance of 1 percent. However, once a wine reaches 14.1 percent actual alcohol, the label variance can only go up; it cannot go down. That means that a wine with 14.5 percent abv cannot be labeled 13.5 percent, but it can actually be as high as 15.5 percent.

In 2001, TTB began the lengthy process of updating its rulemaking regarding approved wine grape varietal names for U.S. wines. At the time, fifty-five varieties were approved for use on labels; many others will likely be added as producers experiment with a growing number of grape types in an attempt to match varieties with their soil and climatic conditions. Who would have thought ten years ago that California would produce Grüner Veltliner?

TTB has also sought more precise definitions for such terms as "Estate Bottled," "Reserve," "Barrel Select," and "Old Vine" among others, which have traditionally been marketing terms with little legal clout. One grower's "old vines" may be only ten years old (though they are "older" than the vines he planted five years ago). It's easy to find $4 bottles of wine with "Reserve" in the brand name, making the term meaningless. TTB has cracked down in recent years on the use of wine names "borrowed" from European wine regions. U.S. winemakers who want to label their fortified red wines as "Port" can no longer do so unless they were grandfathered in before the new regulation became official. "Burgundy," "Chablis," "Sherry," "Champagne," and other terms are prohibited from use unless wineries have a long history of using these terms. Korbel's "California Champagne" will continue to live a long life, even though no wine connoisseur would ever confuse Korbel with Krug.

Since 1987, "Contains Sulfites" labels have been required on alcoholic beverages containing at least 10 parts per million of sulfites, which are used as preservatives. In 1989, the government began requiring all wine bottles to include this statement, in capital letters:

GOVERNMENT WARNING:
(1) ACCORDING TO THE SURGEON GENERAL, WOMEN SHOULD NOT DRINK ALCOHOLIC BEVERAGES DURING PREGNANCY BECAUSE OF THE RISK OF BIRTH DEFECTS.
(2) CONSUMPTION OF ALCOHOLIC BEVERAGES IMPAIRS YOUR ABILITY TO DRIVE A CAR OR OPERATE MACHINERY, AND MAY CAUSE HEALTH PROBLEMS.

There is talk within the U.S. Food and Drug Administration that wines should have two additional labels beyond what is already required: for ingredients (yeast, egg whites used for fining, etc.) and nutritional content (calories, carbohydrates, etc.), so that consumers know exactly what they're getting. Vegans and those with certain allergies might want to know if egg whites or isinglass (fish bladder) were used to filter a wine, for example.

Such regulations have not yet been put into place, but in 2009, renegade Randall Grahm, proprietor of Bonny Doon Vineyard in the Santa Cruz Mountains of California, began listing the ingredients of his wines on the back labels. Grahm also details the amount of sulfur dioxide (SO_2) used at bottling for consumers concerned about its use. These are noble gestures to be sure, but Grahm is also tweaking the noses of those who set wine label policy, by providing information voluntarily before the government tells him he must. A handful of other producers have followed his lead, among them Shinn Estate on Long Island.

Bonny Doon label
Proprietor Randall Grahm includes ample information on his labels, specifying not only the planet the grapes were grown on but also technical information, such as exact winemaking ingredients, that most other wineries don't provide.

Such rudimentary techniques are long gone, replaced by methods that apply science and technology to the vinous gifts nature provides. Among recent trends: White grapes are no longer crushed, they're gently pressed (some red grapes are too) so that the skins and seeds impart as little harshness as possible. Before the grapes reach the press or crusher, they are meticulously sorted, mechanically and/or by hand, to remove unripe berries and shriveled raisins.

Once the grapes are crushed or pressed, the resulting grape must is inoculated with special yeasts or allowed to ferment on its own with the native yeasts present on the grapes and in the winery. Though red wines meant for long-term cellaring need tannic structure, the tannins should be integrated with the intensity of the fruit and the natural acidity in the grapes. The tannin level can be controlled by adjusting elements of the maceration—soaking the juice with the skins and sometimes stems before and/or after fermentation. In some regions, it's legal to add acid during winemaking; in others, it's prohibited. The same is true for the technique of adding sugar during fermentation, called chaptalization, which can increase a wine's alcohol content and body. In California, it's illegal; in Oregon, it's acceptable.

French oak barrels for the fermentation and aging of wine, which cost upward of $1,000 each depending on the exchange rate, are fabulous for certain wines, giving them toast and vanilla aromas and flavors and layered texture. American oak barrels from Missouri, Minnesota, and other states cost half as much and are useful for wines for which the winemaker desires stronger characteristics, such as dill or coconut. Inner staves, chips, tea bags, and other "oak products" are available to those who can't afford oak barrels or who make inexpensive wines for which barrels are out of the financial question.

Micro-oxygenation (bubbling air into wine) is a trick to transform high-tannin wines into softer, more accessible ones that can be enjoyed the day they're purchased. Filtration, reverse osmosis, and spinning-cone technology can lower the alcohol content in wines, remove wildfire smoke taint, and reduce volatile acidity.

Yet for all this new technology, the most accomplished winemakers prefer to use as little of it as possible. By sourcing high-quality grapes, picking them at ideal ripeness, handling them carefully, fermenting and/or aging the wine in the appropriate vessels (often with ambient, rather than commercial, yeasts), and keeping a constant watch in the cellar, they save money—and create a finer, more natural wine.

Our Love Affair with Wine

America has become a nation of wine drinkers. In 2011, it moved ahead of Italy and France to become the No. 1 wine-consuming country, purchasing 311.3 million 12-bottle cases (the equivalent of 3.735 billion bottles) that year, according to a report from VinExpo/International Wine & Spirit Research. The report also predicted that U.S. wine consumption would increase 10 percent between 2011 and 2015.

In the last two decades or so, wine has moved from the fringes of American culture—the drink of elites and immigrants—to the center of the table. Better marketing and wider availability has something to do with it: Globalization has been a friend to the food and wine industry, whetting American appetites for new tastes. But so does improvement in American winemaking. In addition, discount retailers have expanded their selections, making fine wine within reach of more people, and hundreds of Internet wine bloggers have spread their knowledge and passion.

The United States has also become a nation of winemakers—the world's fourth-largest wine producer, trailing only France, Italy, and Spain. California was once the only state in the game, but in 2002, Pointe of View Winery was established in North Dakota, its first commercial winery, making that state the fiftieth to climb aboard the country's fast-moving wine production train. According to WinesVinesDATA, there were 7,345 wineries in America in 2012, an increase of 450 from the previous year; in 1970, just 440 wineries crushed grapes in this country.

Production has soared in regions outside the traditional California-Oregon-Washington triumvirate, thanks in part to the availability of hybrid grape varieties developed to withstand cold temperatures, humid conditions, and/or certain plant diseases and pests. Every year, new winegrowing areas are being discovered by vineyardists and winemakers who understand that planting specific varieties in specific places can lead to quality wines. Young maverick winemakers without deep pockets can enter the business by purchasing grapes and processing them at custom-crush wineries or co-ops, where they can lease space and equipment. Such facilities have also given rise to small-scale wineries located in the centers of big cities.

Nationally, several major wine and food festivals draw thousands of wine and food lovers to tastings, seminars, and winemaker dinners—among them the *Food & Wine* Classic in Aspen, Colorado; the Sun Valley Center for the Arts Wine Auction in Idaho; and the Naples (Florida) Winter Wine Festival.

Wine tourism is booming, and not just in Napa, Sonoma, Willamette Valley, and Walla Walla. Wineries throughout the United States draw visitors for the chance to taste their wines, as well as for vineyard and cellar tours.

Important changes in the law have also made buying wine easier. A groundbreaking U.S. Supreme Court decision in 2005, *Granholm v. Heald*, struck down laws in Michigan and New York State that made it a crime for out-of-state producers to ship wine to consumers in those two states while

In celebration of food and wine
Americans' booming interest in wine has led to a proliferation of tasting and educational events, such as the venerable *Food & Wine* Classic in Aspen, Colorado, as well as more intimate regional affairs that showcase local wines and foods.

permitting in-state wineries to ship to locals. The Court ruled that such discrimination violated the U.S. Commerce Clause, which serves to ensure a level playing field for businesses throughout the country. But the Court didn't endorse direct shipping per se; it merely said that states had to treat in- and out-of-state producers the same way when it comes to shipping wines to consumers. As a result, a few states that previously allowed their own wineries to ship to state residents have banned such deliveries altogether, while others opened the floodgates to wine shipments.

Today most states allow at least some shipping of wine from producer to consumer, thereby bypassing wholesalers and retailers, although some have restrictions, require special permits, and/or charge fees to wineries and those who order from them. In 2012, seven states had outright bans on shipping wine and other alcoholic beverages: Alabama, Arkansas, Mississippi, Oklahoma, Pennsylvania, South Dakota, and Utah.

The law in this area remains a moving target, but in most states, consumers can now purchase U.S. wine online and have it delivered to their door, circumventing the post-Prohibition model of the "three-tier" system, which requires producers to sell their alcoholic beverages to wholesalers, who sell to retailers/restaurateurs, who sell to consumers.

American wine lovers now have access not only to the locally produced wines of their own regions, but also to those from other states and around the world. With "local" and "artisanal" the catchwords of a rising cultural movement, the boom in U.S. wine production increasingly offers something for everyone, from collectors of the highest-profile bottlings to visitors who want to sample the specialties of a region and learn more about wine.

A NOTE ON OUR "SNAPSHOTS"

Throughout the book Snapshot boxes present capsule information about major winegrowing regions. AVAs and figures for vineyard acreage and wineries reflect industry information at the time this book went to press. Where states do not separate wine grape acreage from table and juice-grape acreage, this is noted. In regions with low vineyard acreage and/or few wineries, Snapshot categories may vary for practical reasons.

Most-planted varieties are listed in descending order of acreage; where appropriate, best varieties are singled out. For most regions, we have selected key wineries in the categories Trailblazers (historic/early wineries in the region), Steady hands (consistently reliable), Superstars (some of the most sought-after names), and One to watch (up-and-coming, new, or particularly innovative producers). Not all Snapshots have examples in all four categories.

An evolving aspect of winemaking in the United States is the establishment of AVAs, which recognize wine regions for their specific soils, climates, elevations, exposures, and histories. As this book went to press, several AVA petitions filed with the Alcohol and Tobacco Tax and Trade Bureau (TTB) were pending; they are not detailed here, as AVA approval—or rejection—can take two or more years of analysis, followed by a public comment period on petitions.

The West

California
Oregon
Washington
Idaho
Colorado
Other Mountain States
Hawaii and Alaska

California

California is the most important winegrowing state in the United States, the granddaddy of them all in both prestige and production. It produces 90 percent of the nation's wine (nearly 250 million cases per year), is home to more than half of the two-hundred-plus American Viticultural Areas (AVAs), and attracts 200 million visitors annually to its wineries and vineyards. Were it a country, California would rank number four in the world in wine production, behind only France, Italy, and Spain.

Golden Gate Bridge
Completed in 1937, the bridge spans the Golden Gate Strait, linking San Francisco with the wine regions of Marin, Sonoma, and Napa counties.

Yet the California wine industry had remarkably humble beginnings. Between 1769 and 1824, Franciscan *padres* established missions throughout what would become California, planting vines at each one and fermenting grapes into crude wines used for sacramental purposes. The 1849 Gold Rush in the Sierra Foothills drew immigrants who planted vineyards and made wine to accompany their meals, in the European tradition. The prospectors later scattered to other regions, establishing vineyards and small wineries.

Prohibition stalled commercial winemaking between 1919 and 1933, and after the Volstead Act, as it was called, was repealed, most vintners had to start all over, having replanted their land to other crops. Some growers had maintained their vines (some of which survive to this day) during Prohibition, and a few abandoned plots were rediscovered in modern times.

The 1940s were all about easy-drinking, inexpensive jug wines. The 1950s brought a welcome focus on quality, particularly in Napa and Sonoma. By the 1970s, California wines had begun to attract international attention, especially after the star-making 1976 "Judgment of Paris" tasting, at which a California Chardonnay and Cabernet Sauvignon outscored top French wines.

Long before that, however, brothers Ernest (1909–2007) and Julio Gallo (1910–93) started E. & J. Gallo Winery in the Central Valley town of Modesto, in 1933. The brothers—Ernest was the sales and marketing whiz, Julio the vineyard expert—produced simple yet crowd-pleasing wines that they sold using aggressive pricing and new marketing strategies, including television commercials. The Gallos no doubt converted countless Americans into wine drinkers, and in the mid-1970s one of their most popular wines, Hearty Burgundy (a multigrape red blend including Zinfandel and Carignane), was proclaimed to be the greatest American red-wine value by *Los Angeles Times* wine critic Robert Lawrence Balzer.

Gallo, today under the leadership of Ernest's son, Joseph, and Julio's son, Bob, leads the world in total wine production. It continues to pump out oceans of cheap supermarket wine, but it has created midpriced brands. It also plays the higher-end game, having acquired such noted producers as Louis M. Martini Winery in Napa Valley and Bridlewood Estate in the Santa Ynez Valley of Santa Barbara County. The company uses third-generation winemaking Gallos—the most visible being winemaker Gina Gallo and her grape-growing brother, Matt—as the public faces of the family.

Diversity is California's middle name, and this is as true in winemaking as in other areas. The varying climates, soil compositions, elevations, and exposures across its regions mean that the state can support more than one hundred grape varieties. In the early days, vintners produced Chardonnay and Cabernet Sauvignon—mimicking the great wines of France's Burgundy and Bordeaux—and took advantage of pre-Prohibition Zinfandel and Petite Sirah vines to craft gutsy red blends. Over time, winemakers have learned to plant the grapes best suited to local conditions.

Chardonnay, Pinot Noir, and Riesling shine in cool, coastal regions, where the Pacific Ocean provides air-conditioning with its breezes and fog. Cabernet Sauvignon and Merlot like a bit more warmth and are planted in interior valleys and on hillsides. While Zinfandel, Rhône varieties such as Syrah and Grenache, and the Portuguese grapes Touriga Nacional, Touriga Franca, and Tinta Cão can do well in cool-weather zones, California's Mediterranean-like hot spots are best suited to them.

Abundant sunshine and scant rainfall during the March–October growing season usually mean that growers and winemakers enjoy relatively easy, rote harvests. However, recent years have been unusually cool and wet, and the 2011 harvest was one of the most challenging in memory, with chilly temperatures and an October plagued by rain that caused rot

NORTHERN & CENTRAL CALIFORNIA

The most important of the state's 116 (and counting) AVAs are mapped here and on the pages outlined on this map. Southern California is mapped on p. 140.

development in the grapes. Late-ripening varieties such as Cabernet Sauvignon were picked earlier than is normal, at lower grape sugar levels than is customary.

For every American who believes in climate change, there is another who insists it's just political propaganda. Yet California's coastal areas had a string of cooler, wetter seasons from 2009 to 2011, and some interior zones have been warmer than in the past. Scientists have arrived at differing conclusions about whether or not a region such as Napa Valley will eventually become too warm for high-end viticulture, yet it is safe to say that there is no longer such a thing as a "normal" season in California. Every year brings new challenges and rewards.

Cooler years are positives for those who prefer less-ripe, understated wines, and a disappointment for lovers of ultraripe, high-alcohol versions. The latter style was popular in the mid-1990s and throughout the 2000s, fueled by endorsements from influential critics. Many (but not all) wineries produced this flamboyant style in the hope that high scores would boost sales, and they largely did. However, recent climate conditions and a consumer and media backlash against high-octane wines have returned some normalcy to the production of California wine.

The San Francisco–based Wine Institute is a powerful advocate for the state's wines, using its influence in Washington, D.C., to win protections and benefits for its members in such areas as direct-shipping legislation, taxation, preservation of place names, and international trade. In 2002, the Wine Institute joined with the California Association of Winegrape Growers to create the California Sustainable Winegrowing Alliance, which encourages the adoption of sustainable grape-growing practices. These include reducing or eliminating the use of synthetic (non-organic) pesticides, herbicides, and fertilizers; preservation of natural resources; and being responsible stewards—as opposed to owners—of the land.

Organic and biodynamic farming practices are also on the rise in California, as growers reduce vineyard inputs, such as synthetic herbicides and pesticides, and create balanced, self-sufficient systems that produce what they believe to be healthier vines and place less stress on the land.

New AVAs are popping up like prairie dogs on a Montana field as Californians explore all the nooks and crannies suitable for grape growing. Appellational marketing groups (the Napa Valley Vintners, Sonoma County Vintners, Santa Barbara County Vintners' Association, and so forth) have become vital promoters of new AVAs, and the Association of African American Vintners and the Napa Valley Mexican-American Vintners Association reach out to specific segments of the population.

Yet all is not paradise in the Golden State. Ongoing issues include decreasing availability of water for irrigation and frost protection; invasive pests such as the glassy-winged sharpshooter (a vector for vine-killing Pierce's disease), mealybugs, and moths; wildfires (such as the ones in 2008, whose smoke penetrated the thin skins of developing Pinot Noir grapes in some vineyards and affected wine quality); and a paucity of fieldworkers due to crackdowns on illegal immigration (Mexicans have long performed the bulk of California vineyard and harvest work).

Vineyard expansion has riled environmentalists who deplore the loss of wild, undeveloped lands and the creatures that inhabit them. But vintners are increasingly embracing conservationist measures, which include erosion control, fish-friendly farming, the restoration of native vegetation along waterways, and removing as few oaks and redwoods as possible when developing vineyard sites.

Los Carneros, Napa Valley
The Los Carneros region is the southern gateway to the Napa Valley, California's most iconic wine region. More than 45,000 acres of wine grapes are planted in Napa Valley, including Chardonnay and Pinot Noir in Los Carneros, and Cabernet Sauvignon and Merlot in more northerly AVAs.

CALIFORNIA SNAPSHOT

Vineyard acreage: 535,000

Most-planted varieties: Chardonnay, Cabernet Sauvignon, Zinfandel, Merlot, Pinot Noir, Syrah

AVAs: 116

Wineries: 3,365

Winery tourism
Most wineries welcome visitors, offering them a range of experiences including tours, tastings, wine and food pairings, art shows, and musical performances. Small-volume wineries sell a significant percentage of their production through their tasting rooms. Some larger wineries, such as Castello di Amorosa shown here, really court tourist traffic (see p. 60).

MENDOCINO COUNTY

To the west of Lake County and north of Sonoma County is Mendocino County, a 3,500-square-mile region that runs hot and cold when it comes to grape growing. "Mendo," as the locals affectionately call the county, is a tale of two climates, and two very different types and styles of wine are produced. Organic and biodynamic farming principles are widely employed, and wineries throughout California purchase Mendocino grapes for multi-region blends.

Mendocino's interior Redwood, Ukiah, and McDowell valleys, flanked by the coast ranges to the west and the Mayacamas Range to the east, are typically dry, sunny, and warm—often very warm, sometimes surpassing 100°F in the summer and early fall. They have a long history of producing hearty, sometimes rustic red wines, including Barbera, Carignane, Zinfandel, Syrah, Petite Sirah, and field blends of these varieties, many from vines planted in the early 1900s.

Anderson Valley AVA

In Anderson Valley, just 20 or so miles to the west (and also 20 miles closer to the air conditioner that is the Pacific Ocean), chilly morning and evening temperatures and blankets of fog during the growing season promote the production of crisp, elegant Pinot Noirs and white wines in the tradition of those of Alsace and Germany, including Gewürztraminer, Pinot Gris, and Riesling. Days can be gloriously balmy and reach 80°F, yet temperatures can plummet to 45°F or lower at night.

The Anderson Valley AVA and the smaller Yorkville Highlands AVA, on its eastern fringe, are, frankly, more fashionable than interior Mendocino County, thanks to consumers' relatively recent enthusiasm for Pinot Noir, and the ancient redwood forests and emerald-carpeted vineyards that draw oohs and aahs as travelers drive west on Highway 128 toward the coastal burg of Mendocino. The rugged Mendocino Coast, with waves crashing violently onto rocks below steep cliffs, draws thousands of tourists each year, and many go through Anderson Valley to get there. Some fifty winery tasting rooms are just a quick detour off 128.

Anderson Valley's success with Pinot Noir and Alsatian varieties is directly attributed to its climate, with soils being less important.

Navarro Vineyards
The Bennett-Cahn family grows Riesling, Gewürztraminer, Muscat, and Pinot Noir grapes in their Anderson Valley vineyard near Philo (above).

MENDOCINO COUNTY SNAPSHOT

Vineyard acreage: **17,000**

Most-planted varieties: **Chardonnay, Cabernet Sauvignon, Pinot Noir, Zinfandel, Merlot**

Best varieties: **Anderson Valley—Gewürztraminer, Pinot Noir, Riesling, sparkling wine; interior valleys—Barbera, Carignane, Petite Sirah, Syrah, Zinfandel**

AVAs: **Anderson Valley, Cole Ranch, Covelo, Dos Rios, McDowell Valley, Mendocino, Mendocino Ridge, Potter Valley, Redwood Valley, Yorkville Highlands**

Wineries: **85**

Trailblazers: **Fetzer Vineyards, Navarro Vineyards, Parducci Wine Cellars, Roederer Estate**

Steady hands: **Breggo Cellars, Claudia Springs Winery, Drew Family Cellars, Fetzer/Bonterra Vineyards, Graziano, Greenwood Ridge Vineyards, Handley Cellars, Husch Vineyards, Jeriko Estate, Londer Vineyards, Meyer Family Cellars, Parducci Wine Cellars, Patianna Organic Vineyards, Paul Dolan Vineyards, Saracina Vineyards, Scharffenberger Cellars, Yorkville Cellars**

Superstars: **Goldeneye, Navarro Vineyards, Roederer Estate**

One to watch: **Foursight Wines**

The valley is a dozen or so miles from the ocean, whose breezes and fog cool the otherwise warm area during the growing season. There is just enough sun and warmth between June and October to ripen the grapes, with moderate sugar accumulation; the cold nights and foggy mornings help the grapes maintain their acidity—which, when it's in balance, gives wine its refreshing quality.

Between the tiny towns of Boonville and Philo, steep hillsides pinch in both sides of Highway 128 that halt the flow of fog through the valley. Vines planted west of this get more fog and rain than those on the eastern side. Locals call the western portion of Anderson Valley "the Deep End"—it's a Region I (coolest) climatic zone on the UC Davis heat summation scale; from Boonville east is considered to be Region II.

Anderson Valley Pinot Noirs run the gamut from light, minerally, nuanced styles from the coldest sites to richer, more opulent styles from the warmer spots. Grower decisions on which clones and rootstocks to plant, and when to harvest the fruit, also play important roles in determining wine style. Yet if there is a signature quality of these Pinot Noirs, it's bright, crunchy acidity. It's so valued that wineries throughout California, including La Crema, Littorai, Saintsbury, Siduri Wines, Twomey Cellars, and Williams Selyem, vinify the grapes for appellation- and vineyard-specific bottlings.

Goldeneye is Duckhorn Vineyards' outpost in Anderson Valley. Better known for its Napa Valley Merlots and Cabernet Sauvignons, Duckhorn purchased the former Obester Ranch

Mendocino & Lake Counties

While Mendocino and Lake counties are situated side by side, they are very different winegrowing regions. Mendocino County's cool western area is suited for growing Pinot Noir and Alsace grape varieties, its interior valleys are hot and best for Mediterranean grapes. Lake County (see p. 26) is somewhere in between, with warm days that are cooled by Clear Lake breezes.

near Philo and transformed it into a top-flight Pinot Noir estate and winery. Acquisitions of the Floodgate and Monument Tree vineyards have strengthened Goldeneye's Pinot Noir power in the valley.

Most of the area's early vineyards were abandoned during Prohibition, replaced by apples, peaches, and grazing pastures. Donald Edmeades, a Southern California physician, reversed that development by planting wine grapes in Anderson Valley in 1964. The region was thought to be too cold, wet, and frosty for vinifera, yet Edmeades put in Gewürztraminer, French Colombard, Chardonnay, and Cabernet Sauvignon. He had some success, and he sold his grapes to others before starting to crush his own for the Edmeades label in 1972. Husch Vineyards was planted soon after the Edmeades vines were, and became the first commercial winery in Anderson Valley in 1971.

Yet the pivotal year was 1982, when the French Champagne house Louis Roederer began planting a vineyard and building a sparkling-wine facility in Philo. Roederer's Jean-Claude Rouzaud recognized that the Anderson Valley climate was conducive to growing Pinot Noir and Chardonnay grapes that could achieve the high levels of natural acidity required for traditional sparkling-wine production. Three decades later, Roederer Estate is one of America's most accomplished makers of bubbly, its cuvées tight and lemony, with striking acidity and cellarworthiness.

Mendocino Ridge AVA

Mendocino Ridge, once part of Anderson Valley, is an utter oddity of an AVA. It's the only noncontiguous AVA in the States, and it is based on the belief that vineyards planted at elevations of 1,200 feet or higher are different from those below. The ridgetops here aren't affected by fog and they get a full day of sun during the growing season. Just 75 acres are planted in the Mendocino Ridge AVA, which covers more than 250,000 acres. Greenwood Ridge Vineyards' White Riesling and Pinot Noir from here can be splendid, and its breathtaking Manchester Ridge Vineyard is emerging as a superstar producer of Chardonnay and Pinot Noir grapes that are sold to others.

Yorkville Highlands AVA

The Yorkville Highlands AVA fills the gap between Anderson Valley and Sonoma County's Alexander Valley. There is only a handful of vineyards here because frost is an ever-present threat to grapes. The solution has been to plant vines on the rocky hillsides rather than on the valley floor, where cold air settles. But hillside viticulture is expensive. Nevertheless, intrepid producers such as Maple Creek, Meyer Family, Yorkville Cellars, and Wattle Creek do a fine job with Chardonnay, Merlot, Cabernet Sauvignon, and Syrah.

Redwood Valley and Potter Valley AVAs

Drive a few miles east of Yorkville Highlands on Highway 128, and the geographic and climate differences between Anderson Valley and interior Mendocino viticulture become obvious. From Hopland, at the southern end of the county, to Redwood Valley, on the north, interior Mendocino County vines are largely planted on a broad, flat valley floor where it's quite warm in summer and fall. The majority of the county's population lives along the Highway 101 corridor between Hopland and Ukiah, so vines coexist with houses, shopping centers, and industrial parks, not giant redwoods.

Until the 1960s, Parducci Wine Cellars, in Ukiah, was the only continuously operating winery in Mendocino County. Then Barney and Kathleen Fetzer relocated from Oregon to Hopland in 1968 and launched Fetzer Vineyards, which not only became one of California's largest wine brands, but was also a pioneer in sustainable practices.

Adolph Parducci, a Tuscan immigrant, purchased a ranch near Ukiah in 1921 and planted vineyards at the height of Prohibition. The rich clay soils reminded him of his native Italy, and he made a living selling his grapes to home winemakers. His son, John, joined him in the business, traveling by himself by train to New Jersey at age fourteen to sell grapes.

After Prohibition, Parducci became the first winery to bottle wine with Mendocino County identified on the label. John became winemaker, but the business hit a rough patch and was sold in 1972. It was later sold again, to The Mendocino Wine Company. John Parducci went on to found McNab Ridge Winery in 1999 and is still involved; the wines are made by his grandson, Rich Parducci.

Fetzer Vineyards' longtime winemaker, Paul Dolan, left in 2003 to join brothers Tim and Tom Thornhill at The Mendocino Wine Company. Their first move was to buy and remake Parducci in the Fetzer sustainable mold. Today the Parducci estate vineyards and winery are certified organic and biodynamic; Parducci employs 100-percent green power; and it uses earth-friendly packaging. Its most successful wine is a Petite Sirah called True Grit—a trait the straight-talking John Parducci shares with the late actor John Wayne.

Before the Fetzers sold their business to drinks giant Brown-Forman in 1992, Dolan and the family instituted a series of programs to make Fetzer a greener grower and winemaker—steps many wineries copy today. Organic and biodynamic farming methods, carbon emission reduction, waste reduction, and solar power are among the groundbreaking practices Fetzer brought to American winemaking. According to the Mendocino Winegrape and Wine Commission—which has trademarked the slogan "America's Greenest Wine Region"—ten Mendocino County wineries are

Demeter-certified biodynamic; thirty-five are Fish Friendly Farming certified, twenty-one have certified organic vineyards; and eight others farm organically, though without certification. Twenty-two report using sustainable winegrowing practices, and Parducci is the first winery in the nation to be certified carbon neutral.

North of Ukiah is the Redwood Valley AVA, slightly cooler than Ukiah Valley (not yet an AVA) and home to full-throttle Zinfandels, Syrahs, Petite Sirahs, and Cabernet Sauvignons. Potter Valley AVA is due east of Redwood Valley, but at approximately 300 feet higher in elevation, it's cooler and has a greater diurnal temperature swing. Sauvignon Blanc and Riesling are the stars (Chateau Montelena in Napa Valley makes a terrific Riesling from here), and some good-value Pinot Noirs are made in cool years.

Mendocino residents include Pomo and other Native Americans, Italian and Greek families whose ancestors put down stakes after the Gold Rush, and 1960s hippies who fled San Francisco to find a more peaceful, agrarian lifestyle (often including the cultivation of marijuana). Logging remains a vital industry, and now wine tourism is on the upswing, particularly in Anderson Valley. Ted Bennett and Deborah Cahn of Navarro Vineyards blazed that trail.

Bennett and Cahn left the San Francisco Bay Area to found Navarro, near Philo, in 1973. They saw the area as prime for growing German and Alsatian varieties; Pinot Noir would come later. Their wines are pure, focused, and on the leaner side, yet they are big winners in competitions and among critics. Their bustling tasting room is the envy of other wineries, as is the Navarro mailing list—the only other way to buy the wines.

Stuart Bewley is another notable transplant. He farms a most intriguing vineyard, Alder Springs, tucked into the northernmost part of the county near Laytonville. It has 145 hillside and terraced acres divided into 31 blocks and planted to 30 grape types. It's a quirky patchwork of soils, mesoclimates, elevations, and exposures, where Bewley has been able to experiment intensely since selling his California Coolers brand in 1985. While in his twenties, Bewley and Lodi High School classmate Michael Crete hit on the idea of adding fruit juice to wine, creating the first commercial wine cooler in the country, and beating E. & J. Gallo Winery to the punch.

Only in the last two decades has Mendocino County won acclaim for its wines; previously it was known for selling its grapes to producers outside the county. In the early 1900s, Mendocino didn't have railroads or river systems with which to deliver finished wines to San Francisco, where they could be sold. So growers transported their fruit by wagon to the Italian Swiss Colony co-op in Asti (Sonoma County), where they were "lost" in large, inexpensive blends.

Those discouraging days are finally over.

WHERE HAVE ALL THE FETZERS GONE?

After waiting out the eight-year noncompete clause from the family's 1992 sale of Fetzer Vineyards to Brown-Forman, five of Barney and Kathleen Fetzer's eleven kids started their own brands, all based on organic and/or biodynamic viticultural methods.

The eldest Fetzer child, John (top), owns Saracina Vineyards in Hopland and produces an impressive Loire Valley–style Sauvignon Blanc, among other wines. Daniel Fetzer's Jeriko Estate, south of Saracina, makes a lively sparkling wine. Bobby, who created the Pinot Noir–focused Masút label, died in a 2006 rafting accident; sons Ben and Jacob continue the business.

Patti Fetzer (bottom) owns Patianna Organic Vineyards in Hopland, where she produces racy Sauvignon Blancs and fruity Syrahs. Her brother Jim built the vinous oasis Ceàgo Vinegarden on the north shore of Clear Lake in Lake County, where visitors can dock their boats and taste the wines.

In 2011, Brown-Forman sold Fetzer to Viña Concha y Toro, Chile's biggest wine company, along with their organically grown Bonterra brand and 1,000 acres of vineyard.

LAKE COUNTY

Lake County's evolution as a commercial winegrowing region began, as most in California did, in the late 1800s, when European immigrants abandoned the goldfields in the Sierra Nevada to start new lives elsewhere in the state. Accustomed to drinking wine, they planted vines and produced wine until Prohibition halted the industry. While some California regions restarted soon after Repeal, Lake County was slow to respond, having devoted most of its business efforts to tourism and agriculture—mainly growing pears and walnuts.

Clear Lake—the largest natural lake entirely within California, with more than a hundred miles of shoreline—became a popular spot for swimming, fishing, boating, and camping. Hikers flocked to volcanic Mount Konocti, rising 4,300 feet above the lake's southern shore. Trailer parks and inexpensive rental cottages catering to out-of-towners reproduced like Star Trek Tribbles. Lake County residents were beer-and-a-shot types, and visitors drank lagers and hard liquor at Konocti Harbor Resort and Spa, where country and rock musical acts performed under a cloud of marijuana smoke, without a carafe of Cabernet Sauvignon in sight.

Clear Lake
The majority of Lake County vineyards are planted in close proximity to Clear Lake, whose cooling breezes moderate the summer heat.

Yet the raw ingredients for making good-quality wines always have been present in Lake County, and in the last two decades, local growers and winemakers have begun to seize the opportunity.

They've had to face a high hurdle, however: the fact that Lake County has largely been a factory for inexpensive grapes sold to wineries in Napa and Sonoma. Beringer Vineyards, Cakebread Cellars, Hess Collection, and Stag's Leap Wine Cellars are among the producers who rely on Lake grapes for their lower-priced wines or for blending into their higher-tier bottlings. As recently as 2011, the Lake County Winegrape Commission estimated that 90 percent of the region's grapes were shipped to other areas, and at prices that were typically one quarter those for Napa Valley fruit.

JESS JACKSON

Jess Jackson, one of the most powerful vintners in the United States and owner of no fewer than 25 wineries and/or brands and 14,000 acres of vineyards, got his start in what was then considered "lowly" Lake County.

In 1974, Jackson and his first wife, Jane Kendall, bought an 80-acre walnut and pear orchard in Lakeport. Jackson, a San Francisco attorney, and Kendall converted the property to wine grapes, first selling the fruit to local wineries and then creating their own brand, Chateau du Lac. In 1982, they bottled the now-famous Kendall-Jackson Vintner's Reserve Chardonnay, which soon became the best-selling wine in America and continues to hold a strong sales position today.

The wine's initial success was built on a winemaking mistake: an unintended "stuck" fermentation that left some sugar in the wine. Yet consumers raised on Coke and sweetened iced tea lapped it up, and Jackson and his winemaker, Jed Steele, continued to produce this sweet style of wine for several years, although the Vintner's Reserves are drier these days.

Kendall and Jackson divorced, as did Jackson and Steele—who sued each other over Steele's alleged divulgence of the "secret formula" for KJ Chardonnay (eliciting guffaws from winemakers everywhere, who knew that leaving unfermented sugar in wines was Winemaking 101). Steele established his own company, Steele Wines, which remains a top-notch Lake County–based brand; Jackson and his second wife, Barbara Banke, grew the KJ brand from a Sonoma County base and assembled the Jackson Family Wines empire, which includes the Arrowood, Byron, Cambria, Cardinale, Freemark Abbey, Hartford Family Winery, La Crema, Lokoya, Matanzas Creek, and Stonestreet brands in California, plus others in Italy and France.

Jackson, who died in 2011, may not have stayed in Lake County for long, but his efforts here lifted the vinous image of the area.

Jess Jackson
The popular Kendall-Jackson Vintner's Reserve Chardonnay was born in Lake County in 1982, produced from grapes Jackson grew in Lakeport beginning in 1973. The wine is now made from Chardonnay grapes grown throughout California.

LAKE COUNTY SNAPSHOT

Vineyard acreage: 8,600

Most-planted variety: Cabernet Sauvignon

Best varieties: Cabernet Sauvignon, Petite Sirah, Sauvignon Blanc, Syrah, Tempranillo, Zinfandel

AVAs: Benmore Valley, Clear Lake, Guenoc Valley, High Valley, Red Hills Lake County (a part of the greater North Coast AVA)

Wineries: 30

Trailblazers: Langtry Estate (formerly Guenoc), Kendall-Jackson, Steele Wines

Steady hands: Brassfield Estate, Ceàgo Vinegarden, Gregory Graham, Shannon Ridge, Six Sigma, Snows Lake, Wildhurst Vineyards

Superstars: Derenoncourt, Obsidian Ridge Vineyard

Yet encouragement can be drawn from the fact that Lake County's winemaking stalwarts—Jed Steele of Steele Wines, the Holdenried family at Wildhurst Vineyards, and Langtry Estate (formerly Guenoc) among them—are still going strong, and they have been joined by newcomers focused on quality, including Obsidian Ridge (run by Napa Valley vintners Peter Molnar and Michael Terrien) and French interloper Stéphane Derenoncourt, a Bordeaux consultant, who began producing Red Hills Lake County Cabernet Sauvignon in 2006.

But when it comes to validation of Lake County winegrowing, look no further than Andy Beckstoffer, the largest grower in Napa Valley, in both acreage and reputation. Beckstoffer realized that the Mayacamas mountain range, which runs south to north along the western boundary of Napa County and the eastern boundary of Sonoma County, offers growing conditions similar to those of eastern Lake County's **Red Hills AVA**. In 1997, he began planting Cabernet Sauvignon in the undulating brick-red soils at the base of 4,300-foot Mount Konocti, and his Red Hills acreage since has grown to 2,000 acres.

The Mayacamas range was formed by ancient volcanic eruptions, tectonic plate shifts, and eons of water and wind erosion. The soils that helped make Napa Valley Cabernet Sauvignon so famous also exist in the Red Hills AVA, yet with an additional element: an astonishing obsidian content. At Obsidian Ridge Vineyard, planted at 2,650 feet, one is nearly blinded by sunlight reflecting off the glassy black shards that litter the site and slice truck and tractor tires to shreds. Obsidian also acts as a heating element, bouncing sunlight onto the developing grape clusters so that they can survive the chilly nights of the mountains.

The **Clear Lake AVA** is overly broad geographically speaking. It boasts one marquee producer: Jim Fetzer's Ceàgo Vinegarden. Fetzer, whose family was instrumental in developing Mendocino County's wine industry, created a *Gilligan's Island*–style tropical oasis on Clear Lake's north shore, between Lucerne and Nice. Here one can steer a boat to the dock and walk a short distance to the Ceàgo tasting room. Jim Fetzer's vineyards, olive groves, and vegetable gardens are farmed biodynamically, and while the wines are competently made and tasty, the thrill of visiting Ceàgo lies largely in the relaxed atmosphere of drinking biodynamically grown wines while munching on biodynamically grown snacks.

The **Benmore Valley AVA**, on the border of Lake and Mendocino counties, is tiny and, for now, inconsequential. The **Guenoc Valley AVA**, well south of Clear Lake and near the Napa County line, is best known for the fact that it was once British actress Lillie Langtry's estate and for Orville Magoon's winemaking efforts on it, which ended when he sold the company in 2003 to Malulani Investments Ltd.

The **High Valley AVA**, on the northeast side of Clear Lake, has volcanic soils on its hillsides and alluvial soils on the valley floor, making it conducive to producing several grape varieties, with Sauvignon Blanc being its strong suit. Yet Tempranillo also appears to have a bright future in Lake County, if Spencer Roloson's Madder Lake bottlings are any indication.

Says Andy Beckstoffer, "When I got here in 1997, Lake County wasn't quality or environmentally oriented, and most of the grapes were being sold to producers in other regions. But we're finding the sweet spots, and we'll find more as the region develops."

SONOMA COUNTY

For the longest time, Sonoma County played second fiddle in the California winemaking orchestra conducted by Napa Valley. Napa's triumph at the 1976 "Judgment of Paris" tasting and acclaim from critics ever since have made its Cabernet Sauvignons famous throughout the world. Napa Valley doesn't just produce great Cabernet; its enological identity is Cabernet. Sonoma, however, has emerged with an opus all its own, and consumers are listening.

Unfortunately for Sonoma County, much of its image has been tied to Zinfandel, a wine the world doesn't drink, and a "We grow everything" claim, which is true, yet hardly a forceful marketing message. That Sonoma produces wine from more than fifty grape varieties has implied that it is a jack-of-all-trades, yet master of none.

Those days began to fade fast, however, as Sonoma County sorted out which varieties grow best in which sites within its vast 1,600 square miles. In doing so, it discovered that its cool-climate Chardonnays and Pinot Noirs can do for the county what Cabernet Sauvignon has done for Napa Valley. In fact, Sonomans are proud that many Napa producers have crossed the county line to plant Burgundian varieties in cold, windy, foggy western Sonoma, with conditions that don't exist in Napa. In the early 1970s, Napa Valley's Chateau Montelena, the Chardonnay winner at the "Judgment of Paris," used grapes for that wine from Alexander Valley in Sonoma County.

Hirsch Vineyards
In 1980, David Hirsch became one of the first to cultivate Pinot Noir on ridges overlooking the Pacific Ocean, in the Sonoma Coast AVA.

Sonoma County's topographical mélange includes the rocky Pacific coastline, dense redwood forests, gently rolling hills, pastoral valleys, dry flatlands and the Mayacamas Mountains, where madrone and manzanita trees stand sentinel over narrow, winding roads. Soils can be volcanic in one vineyard, gravel-run alluvial in one down the road, sandy loam in another, heavy clay in yet another. Healdsburg in the north can get 50 inches of rain a year; Santa Rosa, Sonoma County's largest city, just 14 miles to the south, gets only 35 inches. On a 100°F afternoon in the Sonoma Valley, it can be 75°F on the coast.

Unlike most California wine regions, Sonoma County does not owe its grapevine history to Spanish missionaries. Russians came to the area in 1812, working their way south from Alaska to trap sea otters, whose plush pelts commanded top ruble in Moscow. They built Fort Ross near the mouth of the Russian River, where it empties into the ocean, and planted grapevines. When the otter population declined, the Russians moved on, but the seeds for winegrowing were sown.

The establishment of Mission San Francisco de Solano in 1823, in what is now the city of Sonoma, marked the arrival of

SONOMA COUNTY SNAPSHOT

Vineyard acreage: **60,300**

Most-planted varieties: **Chardonnay, Cabernet Sauvignon, Pinot Noir, Merlot, Zinfandel, Sauvignon Blanc**

Best varieties: **Cabernet Sauvignon, Chardonnay, Merlot, Pinot Noir, Sauvignon Blanc, Zinfandel**

AVAs: **Alexander Valley, Bennett Valley, Chalk Hill, Dry Creek Valley, Fort Ross-Seaview, Green Valley of Russian River Valley, Knights Valley, Los Carneros, Northern Sonoma, Pine Mountain-Cloverdale Peak, Rockpile, Russian River Valley, Sonoma Coast, Sonoma Mountain, Sonoma Valley**

Wineries: **350**

NORTHERN SONOMA & SONOMA COAST

Sonoma County's fifteen AVAs are spread across its 1,600-square-mile area and cannot be shown in any great detail on one map. Southern Sonoma and Los Carneros on mapped on p. 45. The Mendocino County portion of the Pine Mountain–Cloverdale Peak AVA is mapped on p. 23.

Sonoma vineyards in the fall
After the harvest in early November, leaves turn from green to orange gold in Sonoma vineyards as the grapevines go dormant.

the Franciscan fathers, who had started their colonization efforts and winemaking in San Diego in 1769. After Mexico seceded from Spain, General Mariano G. Vallejo came to own the Sonoma mission, and he planted vineyards. Once the 1849 Gold Rush in the Sierra Foothills had petered out, Italian, French, and German miners headed to Sonoma County, lured by the bountiful agricultural and fishing opportunities there. Coming as they did from wine-drinking cultures, they too planted vineyards and began making wine.

The Hungarian "Count" Agoston Haraszthy (the title is suspect) planted some of California's first European grape varieties in 1857 in Sonoma and began building Buena Vista Winery. In 1861, Haraszthy was appointed to a commission to improve agricultural methods in the state. He traveled to Europe to collect vines and fruit stock, returning with more than 100,000 vines and thus laying the foundation for the California wine industry. Haraszthy later moved to Nicaragua, where he reportedly was eaten by a crocodile.

In San Francisco, Tuscans Giuseppe and Pietro Simi founded Simi Winery in 1876, after leaving the gold mines. The rolling hills of Alexander Valley reminded them of home, and they moved there in 1881. In 1904, both brothers died and Giuseppe's daughter, Isabelle, took over the winery, at age eighteen. She and her husband, Fred Haigh, kept Simi going through Prohibition until 1970, when she turned eighty-four. Isabelle sold Simi in that year, although she continued to work there for years afterward.

There are now 350 wineries, more than 60,000 acres of vines, and 15 AVAs within Sonoma County. It's also home to several large producers, most notably Geyser Peak Winery, Gallo Family Wines, Kendall-Jackson/Jackson Family Wines (see p. 26), and Korbel Champagne Cellars.

By January 1, 2014, any wine with one of Sonoma County's thirteen AVAs on its label must also include the phrase "Sonoma County." This requirement, known as conjunctive labeling, is also used in Napa Valley and Paso Robles, and is intended to advise consumers of the provenance of the wines, hammering home Sonoma's identity. The Rockpile AVA, for instance, could be anywhere—San Quentin State Prison, perhaps—but it's in Sonoma County, and conjunctive labeling will give buyers that information.

Alexander Valley and Knights Valley AVAs

It's not the first thing Alexander Valley vintners want people to know, but the area was once "the Buckle of the Prune Belt." Prunes—now more delicately called dried plums—were the valley's most profitable crop during Prohibition and for years thereafter. As late as the 1960s, an annual Prune Blossom Tour was conducted in spring to draw tourists to the region. Healdsburg's baseball team was named the Prune Packers.

Yet wine grapes preceded prunes there, beginning in 1841, when Cyrus Alexander arrived to manage the Sotoyome Rancho, a Mexican land grant. Alexander received 9,000 acres as payment, built a house and grain mill, and planted a vineyard. In the three decades following the Gold Rush, the population of Alexander Valley grew quickly, as did its vineyard acreage. Prohibition scuttled the industry in 1920, and prunes had their heyday. It took time for winegrowing to return after Repeal in 1933.

The Alexander Valley is twenty-two miles long and varies in width from two to seven miles. The Russian River wends its way from Mendocino County through the valley before bending west south of Healdsburg and heading to the Pacific. Wine grapes take up 15,000 of the appellation's 77,000 acres, interspersed with cattle ranches, fruit and walnut orchards, houses, and businesses.

Vines planted near the Russian River (upstream of the Russian River Valley) get some cooling effect from it, and Chardonnay does well in these locations, but most of Alexander Valley is warm and arid, optimal conditions for Cabernet Sauvignon and Merlot. Grapes grown on the hillsides typically produce more complex, structured wines; those from valley-floor fruit are softer and fruitier.

In 1935 Robert Young, who died in 2009 at age ninety, took over his family's ranch near Geyserville and began converting the prune orchards to vineyards. A Sonoma County farm advisor, Robert Sisson, encouraged him to plant varieties destined for high-quality wines, not generics such as "Burgundy," so in 1963, Young rooted 6,500 vines on 14 acres. UC Davis was advocating Cabernet Sauvignon, so that's what Young planted first; it also helped that the late-ripening Cabernet grapes could also be harvested by the prune-picking crew.

Young planted his first Chardonnay grapes in 1967, and eventually propagated what's now called the Robert Young Clone from a Wente selection. The quality of Young's grapes caught the attention of Richard Arrowood, then winemaker at Chateau St. Jean in Sonoma Valley, and for more than three decades, St. Jean has bottled a single-vineyard Chardonnay from Robert Young's vines. His children, JoAnn, Jim, Susan, and Fred, now run the business, which includes Robert Young Estate Winery.

Alexander Valley Vineyards produced its first vintage in 1975, after Maggie and Harry Wetzel purchased a large portion of a homestead that had been built by Cyrus Alexander and then planted wine grapes. The third generation of Wetzels is now involved in the winery; its flagship is a Cabernet Sauvignon–based blend called Cyrus.

In 1972, oilman Tom Jordan founded Jordan Vineyard & Winery. At the time, most Sonoma vintners grew their grapes on the valley floors, where they could get a high-yielding, rewarding crop. In response to the phylloxera outbreak in the late 1980s, many growers began replanting on the benchlands and hillsides, which gave their grapes more intensity and complexity. Jordan, now steered by Tom's son, John, eventually made the move to hillsides for Cabernet Sauvignon, and to Russian River Valley for Chardonnay. Rob Davis, the only winemaker Jordan has had (if one doesn't count consultant André Tchelistcheff, who introduced Davis to Jordan) has used these new plantings to add an extra layer of interest to the winery's famously long-lived wines.

The most spectacular vineyard in the valley is Jackson Family Wines' Alexander Mountain Estate. Previously the Gauer

Jordan Vineyard & Winery
Ivy covers the walls of the Alexander Valley winery, built in an eighteenth-century French château style by Tom and Sally Jordan in 1976.

Alexander Mountain Estate
Cabernet Sauvignon and Chardonnay are planted as high as 2,400 feet above sea level; most of the grapes go to Stonestreet Winery.

ALEXANDER VALLEY AND KNIGHTS VALLEY AVAS SNAPSHOT

Vineyard acreage: Alexander Valley 15,000; Knights Valley 2,000

Most-planted varieties: Chardonnay, Cabernet Sauvignon, Merlot, Zinfandel

Best varieties: Cabernet Sauvignon, Chardonnay, Merlot, Zinfandel

Wineries: 50

Trailblazers: Alexander Valley Vineyards, Beringer Vineyards, Jordan Vineyard & Winery, Peter Michael Winery, Robert Young Estate Winery, Simi Winery

Steady hands: Anakota, Clos du Bois, Geyser Peak Winery, Hanna Winery, Knights Bridge, Lancaster Estate, Sausal Winery, Stuhlmuller Vineyards

Superstars: Jordan Vineyard & Winery, Peter Michael Winery, Ridge (Geyserville Zinfandel), Seghesio Family Winery, Silver Oak Cellars, Stonestreet Winery

One to watch: Captûre Wines

Ranch, this 5,100-acre dramatic, diverse property was purchased by Jess Jackson in 1995, saving it from likely residential development. Vines are planted as high as 2,400 feet above sea level, mostly in red volcanic soil, and are stressed in their search for water and nutrients. As a result, the Chardonnays and Cabernet Sauvignons from the property, bottled under the Stonestreet label (Stonestreet was Jackson's middle name) are firmly structured, often taut, and with a minerally edge. All benefit from bottle age.

One cannot talk about Alexander Valley, which became an AVA in 1988, without mentioning Seghesio Vineyards, known for its marvelous old-vine Zinfandels. Seghesio is often thought to be in Dry Creek Valley, and while it does have vineyards there, its home is in Alexander Valley, as are two of its most important vineyards: San Lorenzo, planted in the early 1890s, and Home Ranch, purchased by Edoardo Seghesio in 1895. Seghesio was sold to the Crimson Wine Group in 2011, with most family members staying on.

Pine Mountain–Cloverdale Peak AVA

High elevation (1,600 to 2,600 feet), steep hillsides, and rocky red soils distinguish the county's newest AVA, Pine Mountain–Cloverdale Peak, nested within the northern Alexander Valley AVA. Approved in late 2011, Pine Mountain–Cloverdale Peak, which also includes a portion of Mendocino County, is primarily vineyard land—too rugged for winery construction—and Cabernet Sauvignon is its flagship variety.

Captûre Wines, a partnership between Ben and Tara Sharp and former Château Latour cellarmaster Denis Malbec and his wife, May-Britt, is the standout producer of wines made from grapes grown in the AVA. Their Cabernet Sauvignons, red blends, and Sauvignon Blancs are superb.

Knights Valley AVA

Knights Valley, an AVA since 1984, borders Alexander Valley and connects Sonoma and Napa counties at their northernmost point. All the vineyards within the AVA are on the Sonoma side, snuggled against the base of Mount St. Helena and spilling down to the valley floor. Highway 128 threads its way through Alexander Valley north from Healdsburg, the road narrowing, twisting, and turning over the Mayacamas Mountains, then dropping into Knights Valley, a sea of vines and cattle pastures.

The 37,000-acre valley is named for Thomas Knight, who purchased the former Rancho Mallacomes after California

Peter Michael Winery
The harvest in Knights Valley typically begins in early September with the picking of Sauvignon Blanc, and concludes in late October/early November with the later-maturing reds including Merlot and Cabernet Sauvignon. Peter Michael harvests its grapes by hand, so that they arrive at the winery in pristine condition.

FROM FRENCH TO ITALIAN

The late Leland "Lee" Stewart, who founded the Souverain winery in Napa Valley in 1944 and oversaw its relocation to Alexander Valley in 1973, wouldn't recognize the place today. His French-styled and -named winery has been taken over by an Italian, and a well-known one, movie director/producer Francis Ford Coppola, who has turned it into a day resort for adults and kids alike.

Stewart sold Souverain but remained a consultant when the new winery was constructed near Geyserville. Designed by John Marsh Davis, Souverain blended French château and Sonoma hop kiln architecture, and it won an American Institute of Architects Design of Excellence Award in 1974. In 1986, Nestlé, one of many owners of Souverain over the years, added "Chateau" to its name.

Now everything French is gone, replaced by Coppola's version of Italy-meets-Hollywood. The main hop kiln tower at Francis Ford Coppola Winery is now a pyramid with a tip that glows at night. The fountain has been replaced by a large swimming pool and changing cabins. The restaurant, which once featured California-French cuisine, now sends out pizzas, hearty servings of spaghetti and meatballs, and Mrs. Scorsese's Lemon Chicken. Visitors can also view Coppola movie memorabilia, including Don Corleone's desk from *The Godfather*. Coppola produces his everyday wines in quantity here. They are said to finance his much more serious winemaking ambitions for his Inglenook estate in Napa Valley.

The Souverain brand, once again sans "Chateau," has also gone Italian. The grapes are now grown and the wines made at the former Italian Swiss Colony in Asti, an agricultural community created by immigrant Andrea Sbarbaro in 1881. ISC became one of the largest wine producers in the country, and in the 1950s was the No. 2 tourist attraction in California, after Disneyland. The facility had fallen on hard times, but Nestlé's Wine World Estates renovated the winery in the 1990s, and Souverain's wines are now produced there.

Francis Ford Coppola Winery
Visitors have many family activities to choose from, among them viewing movie memorabilia, swimming, bocce, and dining.

became a state in 1850. He planted vines, peaches, and wheat; built a sawmill on Kellogg Creek, and drew other settlers to the area. Wine grapes became a major crop, with most of the fruit sold to Charles Krug Winery in St. Helena. But phylloxera and Prohibition stalled vineyard development, and wildfires wiped out the town of Kellogg.

Knights Valley is Sonoma County's warmest AVA, its narrow shape trapping daytime heat, with nightly breezes cooling vineyards planted on the hillsides. The soils are minerally, rhyolitic material washed down from Mount St. Helena. Beringer Vineyards, in Napa Valley, planted vines here in the late 1960s and bottled its first wine from Knights Valley in 1974. It continues to produce a Cabernet Sauvignon and two blends, Alluvium (red) and Alluvium Blanc, from its 600 acres in the valley.

In 1982, British electronics magnate Sir Peter Michael, who first visited Knights Valley while working in Silicon Valley, purchased land in the valley and began developing an eponymous winery estate. His wines have been produced by a succession of talented winemakers: Helen Turley (Marcassin), Mark Aubert (Aubert Wines), Vanessa Wong (Peay Vineyards), and brothers Luc and Nicolas Morlet (Morlet Family Vineyards).

The wines—Sauvignon Blanc, Chardonnay, Merlot, Cabernet Sauvignon, and Pinot Noir—hail not only from Knights Valley but also from vineyards on the Sonoma Coast and in Napa Valley, and the Pinot Noir has been sourced from as far south as Santa Lucia Highlands in Monterey County. Most of the wines are unfiltered, boldly flavored, ripe, and potent. Knowing French pronunciation is helpful when ordering a Peter Michael wine, as they have proprietary names such as Mon Plaisir (Chardonnay) and Les Pavots (a Bordeaux-variety red blend).

Kendall Jackson/Jackson Family wines' Anakota brand Cabernet Sauvignons are sourced entirely from the company's extensive Knights Valley plantings.

Captūre Wines
The team for this up-and-coming brand includes (left to right), Dave Komar, Tara Sharp, May-Britt and Denis Malbec, Benjamin Sharp, Glenn Alexander, and Carol and Mike Foster.

Dry Creek Valley and Rockpile AVAs

The Pedroncellis, Teldeschis, Rafanellis, and other Italian families get most of the credit for establishing Dry Creek Valley's winegrowing credentials in the late 1800s. Yet, as Preston of Dry Creek owner Lou Preston points out, many who arrived in the valley in the nineteenth century had names like Bourdens, Glaser, Patten, Petersen, or Reilly—English, German, Irish, French, and Danish immigrants who also farmed the land now known as Dry Creek Valley.

The first documented vineyard in Dry Creek Valley was French immigrant George Bloch's, planted in 1869. Countryman Alex Colson joined Bloch to found the area's first winery. European varieties had made their way to the valley by the early 1880s, and by the end of the decade, there were fifty-four vineyards, mainly planted to Zinfandel. In this era, wineries sold their production in bulk and earned little recognition.

Yet the Italians persevered through Prohibition, the Great Depression, and phylloxera. Drinking wine is ingrained in Italian culture, so why would they stop making it in California just because of a few hurdles? Other growers converted their vineyards to wheat, walnuts, plums, and livestock pastures, yet many Italians kept their vineyards going, even if their only income came from selling grapes to home winemakers (demand, of course, soared during Prohibition).

Only two Dry Creek wineries remained in business after Prohibition: J. Pedroncelli Winery (still very much alive) and Frei Brothers Winery (now Gallo's Sonoma winemaking outpost). Thanks to the Italian families who kept their vines in the ground—planted on phylloxera-resistant St. George rootstock—Zinfandel, Petite Sirah, and Carignane cultivated in the late 1800s still exist today, producing extremely low yields of intensely flavored grapes.

Pedroncelli and others continued to produce wine through the 1960s, but it was newcomers to the valley in the 1970s who invigorated the scene. One of those, East Coast native David Stare, founded Dry Creek Vineyard in 1972, the first new winery in the valley since Prohibition. Not only did Stare pursue his love of Loire Valley white wines by planting Sauvignon Blanc and Chenin Blanc in his vineyard, he also embraced old-vine Zinfandel, and he was, amazingly, among the first to put the term "old vine" on labels.

Following the lead of Robert Mondavi in Napa Valley, Stare labeled his Sauvignon Blancs as Fumé Blancs, although the wines were anything but smoky, as the word *fumé* would suggest. They were then, and are remarkably so now, racy and fresh, with lemon, lime, and lemongrass flavors and streaks of minerality. A 2008 retrospective tasting of Dry Creek Vineyard

DRY CREEK VALLEY AND ROCKPILE AVAS SNAPSHOT

Vineyard acreage: **Dry Creek Valley 9,300; Rockpile 160**

Most-planted varieties: **Cabernet Sauvignon, Zinfandel, Merlot, Chardonnay, Sauvignon Blanc**

Best varieties: **Cabernet Sauvignon, Petite Sirah (in field blends), Sauvignon Blanc, Zinfandel**

Wineries: **65**

Trailblazers: **Dry Creek Vineyard, Pedroncelli Winery**

Steady hands: **Bella Vineyards, Carol Shelton Wines, Dashe Cellars, Dry Creek Vineyard, Ferrari-Carano Vineyards & Winery, Gallo Family Vineyards, Nalle Vineyards, Papapietro Perry Winery, Pedroncelli Winery, Sbragia Family Wines, Unti Vineyards**

Superstars: **A. Rafanelli Winery, Lambert Bridge Winery, Ravenswood Winery (Teldeschi Vineyard Zinfandel), Ridge Lytton Springs**

One to watch: **Mauritson Family Wines/Rockpile Winery**

Lambert Bridge Winery
Once a Merlot house, this Dry Creek Valley winery now produces elegant, cellar-worthy Cabernet Sauvignons and polished Zinfandels.

Fumé Blancs demonstrated how remarkably well they age—the 1977 was still in fighting form.

But Cabernet Sauvignon is the most-planted grape in Dry Creek Valley, with Zinfandel just a nudge behind. Cabernets from this region can have a dusty, rustic edge to them, although Lambert Bridge Winery is setting the bar high for Napa-caliber Cabernet Sauvignons and refined Zinfandels. A bit less polished yet nonetheless elegant, A. Rafanelli's Zinfandels and Cabernet Sauvignons have an almost cultlike following.

Ray and Patti Chambers acquired Lambert Bridge in 1993, after founder Jerry Lambert closed the facility in 1992. The Chambers have slowly transformed a steady yet unexciting producer specializing in Merlot into a real thriller. Their 2005 hiring of winemaker Jill Davis, an alumna of Beringer, William Hill, and Buena Vista wineries, and their commitment to giving her all the resources she needs, including vineyards and equipment, have turned Lambert Bridge into a shining star. A new vineyard planted in the hills above Sonoma Valley has all the right stuff: volcanic soils, good drainage, and a southwestern exposure.

Zinfandel loves a warm climate, and it finds it in Dry Creek Valley, with the wines typically showing jammy, wild-berry character, with a dash of black pepper. Yet the grape is a notoriously uneven ripener, with one cluster sometimes bearing raisins, perfectly ripe grapes, and green ones at the same time, which makes a decision on when to pick the fruit challenging. Old vines, often virused and diseased, tend to be "self-regulating," slowing ripening so that the grapes achieve maturity at the same time. Young vines are sugar machines, eager to develop sweetness in their clusters before the grapes are physiologically mature.

Alcohol levels of California Zinfandels—Dry Creek Valley included—have gone as high as 16.5 percent on labels in recent years, many wines resembling port more than table wine. But potency appears to be dropping to more moderate levels of 14.5 to 15.5 percent in the wines of many producers. Nalle Vineyards and A. Rafanelli have always had a less-is-more mindset, their wines consistently balanced and with alcohol levels of between 13.5 and 14.5 percent.

Ridge Vineyards' Lytton Springs winery, perched above Highway 101 on the eastern edge of Dry Creek Valley, is a benchmark for California Zinfandel–based wines; its vines planted as early as 1901. The Ridge Lytton Springs bottling shows the slightly wild, brambly side of Zinfandel, yet in well-mannered fashion. Ridge's Geyserville bottling also comes from old plantings, although the vineyard is Alexander Valley, just across Highway 101 from Lytton Springs.

Both wines are field blends of Zinfandel with lesser amounts of Petite Sirah, Carignane, Mourvèdre, Grenache, or Alicante Bouschet. Zinfandel is always the primary component, but Ridge uses proprietary, rather than variety, labeling to account for the varying percentages of grapes used in the wines from year to year.

Rockpile AVA

There are no wineries in this sub-AVA of Dry Creek Valley, just vineyards. The area, west of Lake Sonoma, is so remote that building wineries is foolhardy. The AVA's total acreage is 15,000, although only 160 acres are planted to vineyards, at elevations of 800 to 2,100 feet. At these heights, there are long periods of intense sunlight during the growing season, and no fog—rare for a zone that is just 15 miles from the Pacific Ocean.

The average temperature in Rockpile is 10 to 15 degrees cooler than in Dry Creek Valley, due to elevation and gusty breezes. The soils are a vivid copper brown, mostly oxidized clay loam, and support a range of red grapes, including Zinfandel, Petite Sirah, Syrah, and Portuguese varieties. Most Rockpile grapes are sold to other vineyards, among them JC Cellars in Alameda (Syrah) and Carol Shelton Wines in Santa Rosa (Zinfandel).

A sixth-generation farming family, the Mauritsons, produces Dry Creek and Alexander Valley Sauvignon Blanc, Chardonnay, Zinfandel, and Cabernet Sauvignon for their Mauritson Family Wines label. They introduced a companion brand, Rockpile Winery, for wines made from their Rockpile Ridge Vineyards: Zinfandel, Petite Sirah, Syrah, and a Portuguese variety–based blend, Independence Red (Tinta Cão, Touriga Nacional, Sousão, Tinta Madeira, and Tannat).

PROTECTING THE OLD-VINE HERITAGE

Old vines are as much a part of California's winegrowing history, and its future, as the latest in clones, rootstocks, trellis systems, and irrigation techniques are. A Sonoma County–based group of winemakers and grape growers has formed the nonprofit Historic Vineyard Society, working to ensure that old vines are preserved and appreciated.

The founding team (David Gates of Ridge Vineyards, Mike Officer of Carlisle Vineyards, Tegan Passalacqua of Turley Wine Cellars, Morgan Twain-Peterson of Bedrock Vineyards, and Mike Dildine, plus this book's coauthor, Jancis Robinson) has compiled a comprehensive directory of California's heritage vineyards (www.historicvineyardsociety.org). They qualified because they currently contribute to California wines, none of their vines were planted later than 1960, and at least one-third of the producing vines can be traced back to the original planting date. The registry lists more than two hundred vineyards, a significant portion of them in Dry Creek Valley and Sonoma County, but others are in Napa Valley, Paso Robles, Livermore, Lodi, Amador, Contra Costa, Lake, and Mendocino counties, or elsewhere.

Pagani Ranch Vineyard
Four generations of Paganis have farmed their Sonoma Valley vineyard, which includes one-hundred-plus-year-old Zinfandel, Alicante Bouschet, Petite Sirah, and Carignane vines. Pagani is on the Historic Vineyard Society register.

As vineyards age, their production drops markedly, although the grapes they do produce tend to be intensely concentrated. Growers are tempted to replace old vines with new to achieve higher, more economically feasible yields, but just as buildings are preserved for their historic value, the society hopes to do so with grapevines.

Russian River Valley AVA

This important region, known for its Chardonnays and Pinot Noirs, also carries some baggage: a compulsion to tweak its AVA boundaries; a cumbersome name for one of its sub-AVAs (Green Valley of Russian River Valley); and the inclusion of an area better suited to Cabernet Sauvignon and Merlot.

Despite the drama, however, and the competition from Anderson Valley, Santa Barbara County, Santa Cruz Mountains, and the Sonoma Coast for Chardonnay and Pinot supremacy, Russian River Valley remains the mother ship for Burgundian varieties in California.

The boundaries of the Russian River Valley AVA are defined by the daily intrusion of fog, which, along with the Russian River itself, shields the region's grapes, morning and night, from dry daytime warmth and bright sunlight May through October. The AVA, established in 1983, attempted to expand in 1999 but it was denied. In 2003, new boundaries were approved by TTB that grew the AVA by 767 acres when the Russian River Valley Winegrowers group chased the fog and found previously overlooked areas that were indeed cooled by maritime mists.

E. & J. Gallo asked to expand the appellation by 14,000 acres in 2008, to include its Two Rock Vineyard in Cotati—an area within the Sonoma Coast AVA, where a break in the coastal mountains allows marine fog and winds to intrude unimpeded. Opposition stalled Gallo's expansion petition, but it was approved by TTB in late 2011, once again redrawing the AVA lines of Russian River Valley.

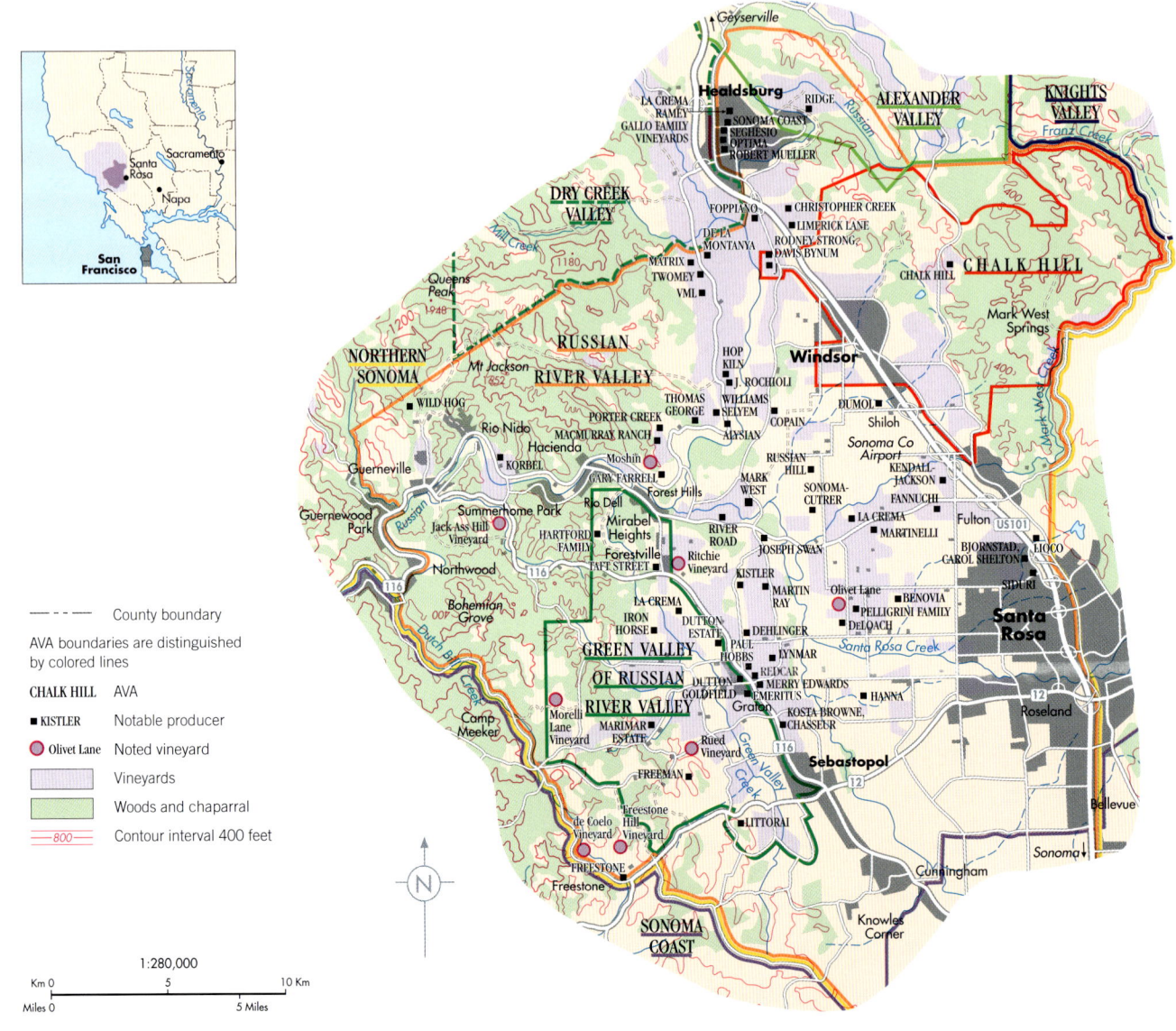

RUSSIAN RIVER VALLEY AVA SNAPSHOT

Vineyard acreage: **20,000**

Most-planted varieties: **Chardonnay, Pinot Noir, Zinfandel, Merlot, Sauvignon Blanc**

Best varieties: **Cabernet Sauvignon (Chalk Hill), Chardonnay, Pinot Noir, Sauvignon Blanc, Zinfandel**

Sub-AVAs: **Green Valley of Russian River Valley, Chalk Hill**

Wineries: **120**

Trailblazers: **Davis Bynum, Dutton Ranch, Foppiano Vineyards, Joseph Swan Vineyards, Korbel Champagne Cellars, J. Rochioli Vineyards, Pellegrini Family Vineyards, Williams Selyem**

Steady hands: **Chasseur, Copain, Dehlinger, DeLoach Vineyards, DuMOL, Freeman Vineyard & Winery, Gary Farrell Wines, Iron Horse Vineyards & Winery, J Vineyards & Winery, Joseph Swan Vineyards, Lynmar Estate, Marimar Torres, Moshin Vineyards, Rodney Strong Vineyards**

Superstars: **Alysian Wines, Dutton-Goldfield, J. Rochioli, Kistler Vineyards, Dutton Ranch, Kosta Browne, Merry Edwards Wines, Paul Hobbs Winery, Williams Selyem**

One to watch: **Thomas George Estate**

The Russian River gets its name from a colony of Russians who built Fort Ross in 1812 near Jenner, where the river empties into the Pacific Ocean. The river begins in northern Mendocino County and takes a southerly direction for 115 miles, with a westward turn near Healdsburg as it heads to the sea. The Russian American Company sent Russian settlers from Alaska to Fort Ross to grow produce, harvest redwoods, and trap sea otters and seals, whose pelts and skins were used for clothing and boots. The Russians stayed at Fort Ross until 1841, when the last of their ships left the harbor.

When the get-rich-quick dreams of most Gold Rush miners faded in the Sierra Foothills in 1850, some headed west to what is now Russian River Valley, where they became farmers. The Russians had planted grapevines among their crops, and by the 1870s, European immigrants had planted wine grapes as well. In 1891, the California State Viticulture Commission reported that more than 300 growers were farming 7,000 acres of wine grapes in the valley and producing half a million gallons of wine a year.

When Prohibition reared its head in 1920, apple orchards replaced most vineyards in the valley—deliciously sweet/tart Gravensteins for pies and eating out of hand, Romes for applesauce and baby food. After Prohibition ended, apples, as well as other orchard fruits, remained important crops. But by the 1960s, apple orchards were barely profitable, as Washington State was able to grow the fruit much more cheaply. University of California farm advisor Bob Sisson urged farmers to plant cool-climate Chardonnay and Pinot Noir grapes, advice taken by pioneers such as Warren Dutton, Joe Rochioli, Joe Swan, and Davis Bynum.

Dutton Ranch, planted by the late Warren Dutton, is not one contiguous vineyard, but rather eighty individual vineyards and blocks within vineyards, scattered throughout the Russian River Valley, Green Valley, and Sonoma Coast. More than two dozen wineries put Dutton Ranch on their labels, including the Steve Dutton–Dan Goldfield brand, Dutton-Goldfield Winery, and Joe and Tracy Dutton's Sebastopol Vineyards.

Dutton-Goldfield wines, many of which are sourced from the coolest parts of Sonoma and Marin counties—Goldfield has discovered several vineyards on backroads bicycle rides—are elegant and on the leaner side, with alcohol levels a reasonable 13.5 percent. The Freestone Hill (Russian River Valley), McDougall (Sonoma Coast), and Devil's Gulch (Marin County) Pinot Noirs are highly recommended, as is the Rued Vineyard Chardonnay (Green Valley). Sebastopol Vineyards' Kyndall's Reserve Chardonnay (Russian River Valley) and Thomas Road Vineyard Pinot Noir (Green Valley) are also exceptional.

Joseph Swan made his first Pinot Noir in 1973, getting advice from André Tchelistcheff of Beaulieu Vineyard fame. Swan's son-in-law, Rod Berglund, has been the Joseph Swan Vineyards winemaker since 1987; Swan died in 1989. Berglund continues to produce the old-vine Zinfandels that Swan loved so much.

Westside Road, in the Middle Reach area of Russian River Valley, is the AVA's most famous address. San Francisco newspaperman Davis Bynum built his eponymous winery—the first on Westside Road—in 1973 and produced Pinot Noir from Joe Rochioli's first crop, grown just up the road. The following year, Gary Farrell took a cellar job at Bynum, where he first worked with Rochioli grapes.

Rochioli and his banker son, Tom, started their own brand in 1982; Farrell produced the wines for them at Davis Bynum until 1985, when he helped the Rochiolis build their own winery. Also in 1982, Farrell started Gary Farrell Wines, producing Chardonnay and Pinot Noir from Rochioli grapes crushed at Davis Bynum, where he continued to serve as winemaker until 2000.

Meanwhile, Ed Selyem, a grocer, and a newspaper pressman, Burt Williams, began making Pinot in a garage in Forestville in 1979. By 1981, they had their first commercial vintage, first calling the brand Hacienda del Rio ("farm by the river"), and later changing it to Williams Selyem. After winning a torrent of acclaim for their wines, Williams and Selyem sold the brand to John and Kathe Dyson, owners of Millbrook Winery in New York and Villa Pillo in Tuscany, in 1998. Bob Cabral has been the Williams Selyem winemaker ever since, continuing to purchase fruit from Rochioli and multiple other A-list vineyards. Selyem and Williams never had their own vineyards; the Dysons and Cabral planted the Drake Estate Vineyard near Guerneville in 1998, and in 2011, the Williams Selyem Estate Vineyard on Westside Road, with a sparkling new winery.

Farrell sold his eponymous winery in 2004 and restarted with Alysian Wines, for which he continues his stellar work.

Merry Edwards made wine for others for a quarter century (Mount Eden Vineyards, Matanzas Creek, Domaine Laurier) before she was able to plant her own vineyards in Russian River Valley beginning in 1998. She now has five estate Pinot Noir vineyards. Edwards, one of the first female winemakers in California's modern winemaking age, has had a remarkably long relationship with Pellegrini Family Vineyards' Olivet Lane Vineyard, from which she has made wine since the mid-1980s. The company began life as Pellegrini Wine Company in 1933, founded by Italian immigrants. In 1973, an apple and plum orchard on West Olivet Road was replanted to Pinot and Chardonnay by Vincent and Ida Pellegrini, and their son Bob oversees it today.

Two wineries not usually associated with Chardonnay or Pinot Noir are among Russian River Valley's oldest, Korbel Champagne Cellars (1882) and Foppiano Winery (1896). Foppiano became known for Petite Sirah, although Louis M. Foppiano, whose father and grandfather made wine at the site, has recently put just as much emphasis on Pinot Noir. Korbel, founded by three Czech brothers in 1882, was purchased by Adolph Heck in 1954; his son, Gary, has been in charge since 1974, overseeing production of 1.5 million cases a year of inexpensive bubbly.

On a higher quality level, Iron Horse Vineyards & Winery, established in 1978 by the Sterling family, and J Vineyards & Winery, founded in 1987 by Judy Jordan and her father, Jordan Vineyard & Winery owner Tom Jordan, produce some of the best sparkling wines in California, using the painstaking traditional method that is de rigueur in France's Champagne region. Judy became sole owner of J Vineyards & Winery in 1995, and like most sparkling winemakers, she, as well as Iron Horse, also produce still Chardonnay and Pinot Noir wines.

Davis Bynum retired in 2008 and sold his property to Jeremy Baker, a Toronto restaurateur and wine buyer, and his family. Baker spent more than a year upgrading the winery and tasting room, adding an 8,000-square-foot wine cave. An admitted Viognier nut, he produces three different bottlings,

DAVID RAMEY'S TERROIR

David Ramey has made wine at Simi, Matanzas Creek, and Chalk Hill wineries in Sonoma County, and Dominus and Rudd Estate in Napa Valley, and worked at Château Pétrus in Bordeaux. He is a much-sought-after California consultant (his collaboration with Rodney Strong Vineyards has had a hugely positive impact on quality in recent years) and he also runs Ramey Wine Cellars.

Ramey's winery is in Russian River Valley, in the city of Healdsburg, yet he doesn't let that confine him in the vineyards from which he sources grapes for his world-class Chardonnays, Syrahs, and Cabernet Sauvignons. The Cabs are produced from Napa Valley grapes; the Syrah comes from the Rodgers Creek Vineyard in the Petaluma Gap area of the Sonoma Coast AVA; and his Chardonnays—among the best in America—are made from Hudson and Hyde vineyards in Napa Carneros and the Ritchie Vineyard in Russian River Valley.

Whole-cluster pressing, native yeast fermentation in Burgundian barrels, lees stirring, and no filtration are standard, yet each of his Chardonnays is distinctive, expressing terroir in a way few other Chardonnays do. They have a hedonistic richness, along with nervy acidity and solid structure. "This is neo-classical white Burgundy," Ramey says with a laugh. "I want to balance classic elegance with California fruit. Texture is what I want. How does the wine feel in your mouth? That's the pleasure quotient."

Iron Horse Vineyards
Named for the train that stopped at a nearby station at the turn of the twentieth century, Iron Horse is located in the chilly Green Valley of Russian River Valley AVA, and bottles solid sparkling wines, Chardonnays, and Pinot Noirs.

in addition to Pinot Noir, Chardonnay, and Grenache. This new producer, named Thomas George after Baker's father and grandfather, has tons of potential.

Green Valley and Chalk Hill AVAs

The Green Valley of Russian River Valley sub-AVA, wholly contained within the southwestern edge of Russian River Valley, is cooler and foggier than the rest of Russian River Valley, due to its proximity to the Petaluma Gap. The "Sonoma County–Green Valley AVA" was approved in 1983, the county reference differentiating the region from the Green Valley AVA in Solano County. In 2008, the name was changed to "Green Valley of Russian River Valley," making it clear that it is a subregion of Russian River Valley.

Green Valley, bounded by the towns of Sebastopol, Forestville, and Occidental, includes more than one hundred growers and seven key wineries: Dutton Estate, Dutton-Goldfield, Emeritus Vineyards, Hartford Family Winery, Iron Horse Vineyards, Marimar Estate, and Orogeny. Multiple other wineries purchase Green Valley grapes, prized for their bracing acidity and structure (especially noticeable in Iron Horse sparkling wines); the Chardonnays in particular sport a steely, stony, citrusy character.

The tiny Chalk Hill sub-AVA (1,600 acres), adjacent to Alexander Valley, is also within the Russian River Valley AVA. When the appellation borders were redrawn in 2003, with fog intrusion as the key parameter, petitioners were shocked to see just how far east the fog travels from the Pacific Ocean into the Chalk Hill area, as far as the Mayacamas hillsides west of the city of Windsor. Rocky volcanic soils strewn with white ash (not chalk) predominate, deposited eons ago by eruptions in Lake County to the northeast. Chardonnay was the early leader in wine quality in the Chalk Hill AVA, but today, Cabernet Sauvignon is just as important.

Fred Furth, a prominent antitrust attorney in San Francisco, purchased what would become Chalk Hill Estate in 1972 with his then-wife Peggy. He planted grapes and began making wine ten years later. The Furths expanded the estate to 1,236 acres, 280 of them in grapevines, and built the winery, a residence and guesthouses, a hospitality center, a culinary garden, athletic fields, ponds, and an equestrian center. Their wines, made by a series of winemakers over the years, were well received although pricey; the Chardonnays and Cabernet Sauvignons have shown a proclivity for improving in the cellar. William Foley purchased Chalk Hill Estate Vineyards & Winery in 2010.

Sonoma Coast AVA

Sonoma Coast is one of the most confounding AVAs in California. It is so large and diverse that its listing on a wine label tells the consumer almost nothing. The appellation stretches from Marin County north to the Mendocino County line, 80 miles, and includes parts of the Sonoma Valley, Russian River Valley, Sonoma Mountain, and Carneros AVAs—more than 800 square miles in total—with dozens of soil types, climates, elevations, and exposures throughout.

But the AVA is held in high regard, the words *Sonoma Coast* conjuring images of Pinot Noir and Chardonnay vineyards planted within sight of the Pacific Ocean; a rugged landscape; chilly climate; fresh, slightly salty air; and bracing, pure-fruit wines. Such settings and wines exist, in what locals call the "true" or "real" Sonoma Coast. Yet wineries near the town of Sonoma, some 40 miles east of the ocean, can still fall within the Sonoma Coast AVA, despite the fact that their average summertime temperatures can be 25°F higher than on the true coast.

To reduce the confusion this convoluted AVA causes, an association of growers and wineries, the West Sonoma Coast Vintners, formed in 2011 to advocate for wines of balance, varietal integrity, and character that their cool-climate conditions can produce. Among the members are Flowers Vineyard & Winery, Failla Wines, Freestone Vineyards, Cobb Wines, Littorai Wines, Martinelli, Patz & Hall, Peay Vineyards, Ramey Wine Cellars, Hirsch Vineyards, Benovia, Freeman, Red Car, and Evening Land Vineyards. In January 2012, after this group's founding, TTB approved a long-gestating request for the formation of the Fort Ross–Seaview AVA, a 27,500-acre area within the existing Sonoma Coast AVA. Vines here are planted between 900 and 1,800 feet elevation, above the fog line, and receive more sun than lower-elevation sites. Vineyards in the Fort Ross–Seaview AVA include Fort Ross, Flowers, Hirsch, Marcassin, Martinelli, and Wild Hog.

The true Sonoma Coast, where vineyards cling to ridges three to eight miles from the ocean, is centered around the towns of Annapolis, Cazadero, Freestone, and Occidental. Wild Hog Vineyard owners Daniel and Marion Schoenfeld have made Zinfandel and Pinot Noir from grapes grown in the hills between Cazadero and Fort Ross since 1977. David Hirsch planted Pinot Noir in the area in 1980, and others followed.

Joseph Phelps Vineyards in Napa Valley launched its Freestone Vineyard in 1999, just five miles from the ocean. The site is chilled by marine winds and a daily blanket of fog during the growing season, with just enough afternoon sun to ripen the grapes. Phelps's vineyards are partly in Russian River Valley, partly in the Sonoma Coast AVA.

The Occidental Vineyard, planted by the Dutton family for Steve Kistler of Kistler Vineyards, was sold in 2005 to a partnership with roots in New York and France. Sashi Moorman, winemaker for Stolpman Vineyards and Piedrasassi in Santa Barbara County, makes Evening Land's California-grown Pinot Noirs from the Occidental Vineyard and plantings in the Sta. Rita Hills AVA of Santa Barbara County; another winemaking team produces the brand's wines from Oregon's Willamette Valley.

Benziger Family Winery in Glen Ellen joined the crowd of wineries growing Pinot Noir in the true Sonoma Coast in the mid-2000s. Its de Coelo ("day-CHAY-low"), which in Latin means "that which is from heaven," is a 25-acre certified-biodynamic estate just five miles from the Pacific Ocean and planted entirely to Pinot Noir.

A preponderance of vineyards in the true Sonoma Coast are above the fog line. Because the Pacific Ocean generates so much cold air, grapes shrouded in fog would never ripen; vines planted between 1,000 and 2,000 feet enjoy brisk breezes from the ocean yet get enough sunlight to fully ripen grapes, and without disease threats such as mildew. Temperatures can drop from 80°F in midafternoon to 45°F at night.

Sonoma Coast winemakers have been at the forefront of a movement to produce more-restrained, less-alcoholic wines of late. California's generally warm climate, and U.S. consumers' embrace of intensely fruity wines, has dictated wine styles in the last two decades. Yet a growing number of wine drinkers seek

Ted Lemon, Littorai Wines
After working in Burgundy, Lemon produces understated, sense-of-place wines from grapes grown in the true Sonoma Coast region, Russian River Valley, and Mendocino's Anderson Valley.

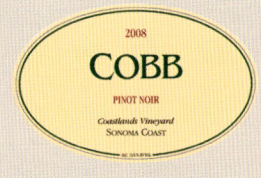
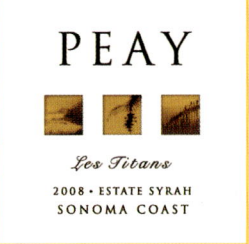

SONOMA COAST AVA SNAPSHOT

Vineyard acreage: **3,600**

Most-planted varieties: **Pinot Noir, Chardonnay, Syrah**

Best varieties: **Chardonnay, Pinot Noir, Syrah**

Sub-AVA: **Fort Ross–Seaview**

Wineries: **20**

Trailblazers: **Hirsch Vineyards, Wild Hog Vineyard**

Steady hands: **Fort Ross Vineyard & Winery, Hartford Family Winery, Keller Estate, Lioco, Martinelli Winery, Red Car Wine Company, Sonoma Coast Vineyards**

Superstars: **Cobb Wines, Evening Land Vineyards, Failla Wines, Flowers Vineyard & Winery, Freestone Vineyards, Littorai Wines & Estate Winery, Marcassin, Peay Vineyards**

One to watch: **Benziger Family Winery's de Coelo**

Pinot Noir cluster
The Sonoma Coast AVA excels at growing Pinot Noir, which thrives in the cool springs and summers but gets enough sunshine to ripen fully.

Fort Ross Vineyard
Just one mile from the Pacific Ocean and at a top elevation of 1,800 feet, this vineyard is typical of those in the Fort Ross–Seaview AVA: dramatic and prime ground for producing pure Pinot Noirs and Chardonnays.

delicacy over power, and earthy nuance over full-on fruitiness. Sonoma Coast winemakers feel the same way.

There is Ross Cobb, winemaker for his family's Cobb Wines. His six Pinot Noirs from the true Sonoma Coast, including the family's Coastlands Vineyard, are all 13.5 percent alcohol or lower, yet they have plenty of flavor. Jamie Kutch, a former Wall Streeter who moved to Northern California to make wine, began producing high-alcohol wines to appeal to certain critics; he has since had a change of heart, and palate, and his Sonoma Coast Pinots are elegant and under 13 percent alcohol. Wells Guthrie of Copain is another high- to low-alcohol convert.

The Petaluma Gap region, while not currently an AVA, might become one soon. Named for the break in the coastal mountain range that allows marine winds and fog to flow unimpeded into the region, this Sonoma Coast area, centered in Petaluma, has numerous vineyards planted largely to Pinot Noir, Chardonnay, and Syrah. Clary Ranch, Keller Estate, Pfendler Vineyards, Ridgeway Family Vineyards, Terra de Promissio Vineyards, and Sonoma Stage are the most promising, although few wineries exist here, at least for now.

Sonoma Valley, Sonoma Mountain, and Bennett Valley AVAs

The Sonoma Mountain and Bennett Valley AVAs are nestled within the larger Sonoma Valley AVA, which was federally recognized in 1981, with its boundaries amended in 1985 and 1987. Parts of the Carneros and Sonoma Coast AVAs also overlap in Sonoma Valley, causing consumers and cartographers much confusion, particularly since wineries with vineyards in overlapping areas can choose which appellation to print on their labels. One vintner's Sonoma Valley is another vintner's Sonoma Coast.

The region is steeped in winemaking history. Franciscan *padres* first planted grapevines near the Sonoma mission in 1823, and after Mexico gained independence from Spain, Mariano G. Vallejo arrived in Sonoma in 1834 to transform the mission into a pueblo and expand vineyard plantings. Famously, Agoston Haraszthy brought European vine cuttings to Sonoma in 1857 and founded Buena Vista Winery. Yet none of this is as important as the existence of old-vine Zinfandel and field-blend plots that continue to survive today: Kunde's Shaw Vineyard (1880s), Old Hill Vineyard (1880s), Pagani Ranch (1880s), Casa Santinamaria (1890s), and Barricia Vineyard (1890s) are among them.

No Sonoma Valley winemaker has seized upon such treasured ancient assets more zealously than Joel Peterson of Ravenswood Winery. His passion for patches of gnarly Zinfandel vine plantings, Petite Sirah, Carignane, and Alicante Bouchet in Sonoma Valley (Barricia, Old Hill), Alexander Valley (Big River Vineyard), Dry Creek Valley (Teldeschi Vineyard), Russian River Valley (Belloni Vineyard), and Napa Valley (Dickerson Vineyard) led him to capture the character of each in small-production, single-vineyard bottlings.

Ravenswood also produces a popular, value-priced Vintners Blend Zinfandel and other varietals, and a midtier County Series, which includes bottlings from Sonoma County, Napa Valley, and Lodi. Ravenswood's "No Wimpy Wines" motto, fun-loving tasting-room staff, and famous weekend barbecues have earned

Shaw Century Vines
Sonoma Valley is home to some of the oldest Zinfandel vines in California; Kunde Family Estate in Kenwood owns the Shaw Century Vines vineyard, planted in 1882.

THE WEST | CALIFORNIA | SONOMA COUNTY | Sonoma Valley, Sonoma Mountain and Bennett Valley AVAs | 45

SOUTHERN SONOMA & LOS CARNEROS

The Sonoma Valley, Sonoma Mountain, and Bennett Valley AVAs are mapped here, as well as the Los Carneros AVA to the east. The Sonoma and Napa county portions of Carneros have similar soil and climate characteristics.

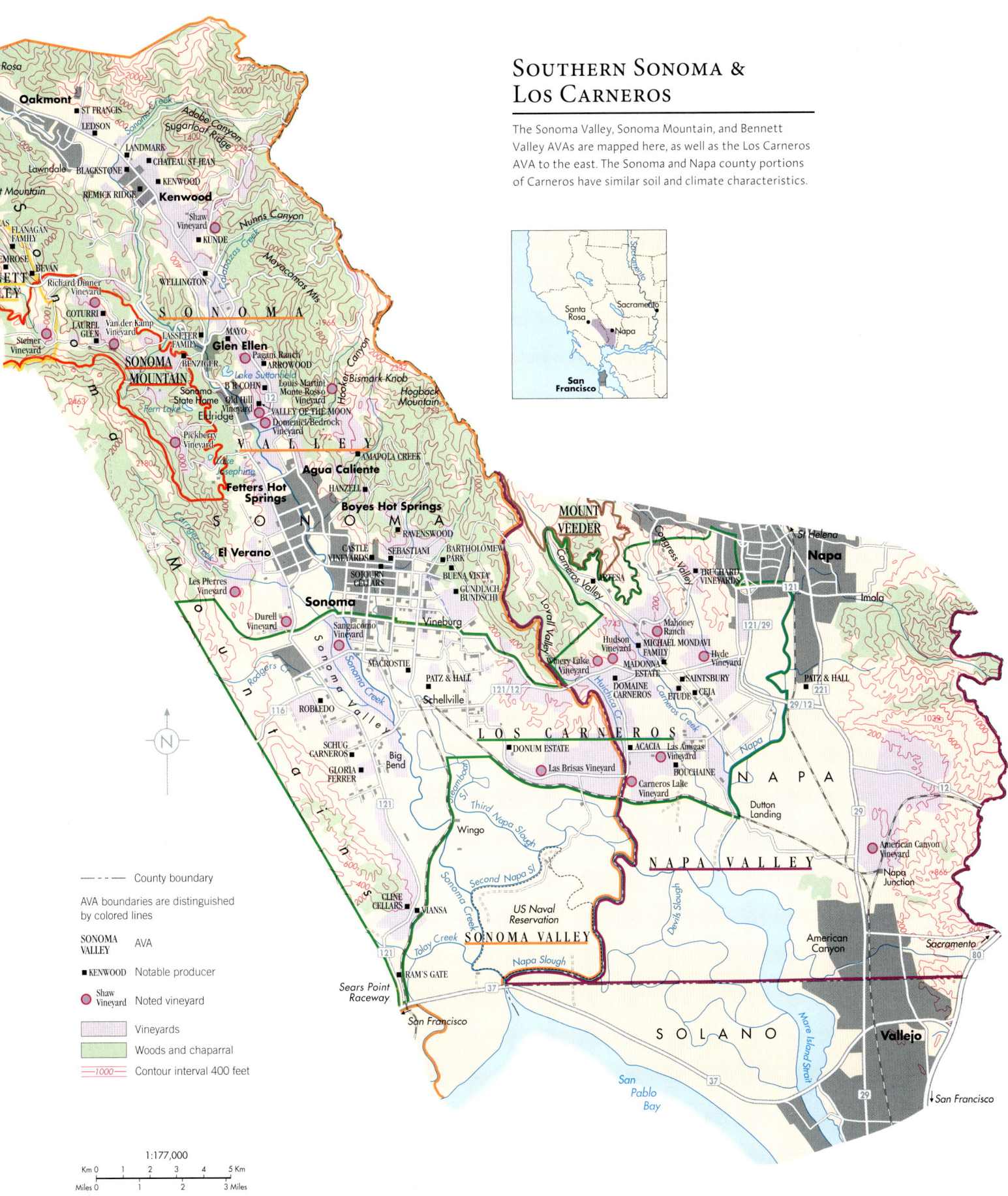

SONOMA VALLEY, SONOMA MOUNTAIN, AND BENNETT VALLEY AVAS SNAPSHOT

Vineyard acreage: **15,000**

Most-planted varieties: **Chardonnay, Cabernet Sauvignon, Merlot, Zinfandel, Syrah**

Best varieties: **Cabernet Sauvignon, Merlot, Sauvignon Blanc, Syrah, Zinfandel**

Wineries: **75**

Trailblazers: **Hanzell Vineyards, Laurel Glen Vineyard, Louis Martini Monte Rosso Vineyard, Sebastiani Vineyards**

Steady hands: **Arrowood Vineyards & Winery, Benziger Family Winery, Chateau St. Jean, Kenwood Vineyards, Kunde Family Estate, Matanzas Creek Winery, St. Francis Winery, Sebastiani Vineyards**

Superstars: **Hanzell Vineyards, Laurel Glen Vineyard, Louis M. Martini Monte Rosso Vineyard, Paul Hobbs Wines (Richard Dinner Vineyard Sonoma Mountain Chardonnay), Ravenswood Winery**

Ones to watch: **Bedrock Wine Co., Sojourn Cellars**

Joel Peterson
Mr. "No Wimpy Wines" of Ravenswood Winery and his son, Morgan Twain-Peterson, are intent on preserving historical-vineyards grapevines in California.

it cult status among Zin fans—some of whom got winery logo tattoos long before body ink was cool.

Peterson, who remains as chief Ravenswood winemaker even though the winery has been owned by Constellation Brands since 2001, instilled a reverence for old vines in his son, Morgan Twain-Peterson. After college, Twain-Peterson worked as a wine salesman before returning to Sonoma in 2005 and becoming a winemaker. Following in his father's footsteps, he seeks out old vines and vineyards interplanted with heirloom varieties such as Alicante Bouschet, Carignane, Mourvèdre, Petite Sirah, Valdiguié, Peloursin, and others for his Bedrock Wine Co.

Twain-Peterson is a founder of the Historic Vineyard Society (see p. 37), which maintains a registry of old-vine California vineyards and promotes their importance as historical landmarks. He's doing his part as a grower, having purchased, with partners of like mind, the Domenici family's 152 acres in Sonoma Valley, formerly known as Madrone Ranch. The site is steeped in history; it was founded in 1854 by two men who would become Civil War generals, William "Tecumseh" Sherman and "Fightin' Joe" Hooker. By the 1880s it was owned by Senator George Hearst, a mining baron whose son, William Randolph Hearst, became the newspaper and magazine publishing magnate, and owner of Hearst Castle in San Simeon.

The overall climate of Sonoma Valley is influenced by two cooling forces: the Petaluma Gap, which funnels marine air into the northern part of the valley, and, in the south, breezes from San Pablo Bay, the same ones that give Carneros its morning and afternoon refresher. In the heart of the valley, the soil types, like most in Northern California, are myriad. At their most basic, valley-floor soils are usually loamy and fertile and retain water easily—not always desirable with certain grape varieties. Hillside and mountain soils are rockier, much lower in nutrients, and well drained, typically composed of volcanic material.

Also known as the Valley of the Moon—the title Glen Ellen resident Jack London gave to one of his novels in the early 1900s—Sonoma Valley is bordered by the Mayacamas Mountains to the east and Sonoma Mountain to the west, which protects the valley from rainstorms and bitter Pacific Ocean winds and fog.

Louis M. Martini's winery was in Napa Valley, but that didn't stop him from planting vineyards in Sonoma County. He purchased the Goldstein Ranch in 1838 and planted 250 acres of vines on what he would call Monte Rosso ("red mountain"), in the Mayacamas Mountains above Agua Caliente in Sonoma Valley. Named for its brick-red, iron-rich soils, Monte Rosso is planted predominantly to Zinfandel and Cabernet Sauvignon, at elevations of 700 to 1,240 feet.

Monte Rosso Vineyard
The Louis M. Martini Winery is in Napa Valley, but the producer's famed vineyard, Monte Rosso, is on the Sonoma side of the Mayacamas mountain range.

It's a grand cru–quality vineyard, with a distinctive rocky-earth minerality and wild raspberry/blackberry character in the wines produced from the site. Monte Rosso, overseen by Louis M. Martini's grandson Michael Martini, supplies grapes not only to the namesake winery (now owned by Gallo) but also to Richard Arrowood's Amapola Creek Winery, Charter Oak, Paradise Ridge, Robert Biale, Rosenblum Cellars, and Sbragia Family Wines. Monte Rosso grapes have high acidity and low pH, which helps the wines made from them age beautifully.

Not very far from Monte Rosso is Hanzell Vineyards. While its history goes back "only" to 1948, when the industrialist and U.S. ambassador to Italy, James D. Zellerbach, acquired 200 acres in the Mayacamas Mountains, Hanzell's importance is on par with Monte Rosso's.

Zellerbach planted 6 acres in 1953, including possibly the oldest Pinot Noir vines in the United States. His first vintage was 1957. The property was sold twice, the second time in 1975 to the de Brye family, Hanzell's current owner. The original 6 acres have grown to 42, allowing Hanzell to produce 6,000 cases of wine a year: 75 percent Chardonnay, 25 percent Pinot Noir. The wines are meant to be aged before consumption;

> ### SONOMA STAR POWER
>
> Napa Valley doesn't own the franchise on celebrity vintners; Sonoma has its share too, an eclectic mix of musicians, actors, and film producers.
>
> Pixar Animation chief creative officer John Lasseter (*Cars*, *Toy Story*, *Finding Nemo*) and his wife, Nancy, who have lived in Sonoma Valley since 1993, evolved into vintners (Lasseter Family Wines) at the encouragement of their neighbor, comedian and yo-yo master Tommy Smothers, owner of Remick Ridge Vineyards. Sonoma Valley vintner Bruce Cohn, the longtime manager for rockers the Doobie Brothers, grew up on a Russian River Valley goat dairy farm, went into the music biz, and returned to Sonoma to found B. R. Cohn Winery in 1984.
>
> In Russian River Valley, Primus bass guitarist Les Claypool owns Claypool Cellars and bottles a Pinot Noir called Purple Pachyderm. Jonathan Cain, keyboardist for the band Journey, resides in Marin County and produces a Sonoma Coast Pinot Noir, Chanconne ("slow dance"), at De La Montanya Winery in Russian River Valley.
>
> *Perry Mason* and *Ironside* TV star Raymond Burr and partner Robert Benevides moved their orchid-growing business to Dry Creek Valley and planted wine grapes on the property in 1986; their first vintage was 1990. Burr died in 1992, and Benevides honored his friend by naming the property Raymond Burr Vineyards. The winery produces an exemplary Cabernet Franc.

Hanzell Vineyards
James D. Zellerbach, a former U.S. ambassador to Italy, planted what is now named Ambassador's 1953 Vineyard in Sonoma Valley in 1953. It is believed to be the oldest Pinot Noir vineyard and the oldest continuously producing Chardonnay vineyard in North America.

a new-release Hanzell Chardonnay or Pinot Noir is tightly wound and subdued, needing five years or more in the bottle to blossom.

Sonoma Valley's Gundlach Bundschu Winery, whose vineyards were planted in the late 1850s, boasts a long history both troubled and blessed. On April 18, 1906, its winery in San Francisco was flattened by the earthquake that devastated most of the city and the Gundlachs and Bundschus were forced to relocate production to their Rhinefarm vineyard in Sonoma Valley. That turned out to be an advantage, as it gave them a greater respect for their grapes and how they were transformed into wine, and it enabled them to become a small family estate winery, producing only 25,000 cases of estate-grown wine a year to this day.

Sebastiani Vineyards is a granddaddy of Sonoma Valley wineries, started by Tuscan immigrant Samuele Sebastiani in 1904. He quarry-mined the Sonoma hills for cobblestones that were used to lay the streets of San Francisco, but he saved his money, purchased acres of land in Sonoma Valley, planted grapes, and began making wine. His son, August, took over in 1952 and turned Sebastiani into one of California's most important wineries, largely because of its huge volume, and August's convincing "Aw-shucks, we're just a small family winery" routine (he dressed in denim overalls and a weathered straw hat).

Much has changed since Sebastiani's heyday, enough fodder for a book on the squabbles, power plays, and business decisions of the Sebastiani family. Its members are no longer involved in the winery, having sold it to William Foley in 2008. In 2011, Foley leased unused space in Sebastiani's cellar to Crushpad, a business that allows hobbyists and small commercial vintners to have their wines made with others' equipment. Crushpad began, to great huzzahs, in San Francisco, the first of several urban wineries to crop up in the city.

The northern end of Sonoma Valley, in and around the town of Kenwood, is a wine-tourist haven, with a half-dozen established quality-minded producers all in a row, including St. Francis Winery (founded in 1971), Landmark Vineyards (founded in Windsor in 1974, relocated to Kenwood in 1989, and sold to Fiji Water in 2011), Chateau St. Jean (1973), Kenwood Vineyards (1970), and Kunde Family Estate (Louis Kunde planted vines there in 1904).

Just down the road, on the outskirts of Glen Ellen, is Arrowood Vineyards & Winery, started by Richard Arrowood and his wife, Alis, in 1986, after he left his job as Chateau St. Jean winemaker. Arrowood is now a Jackson Family Wines property; its production was moved to a company winery in Napa Valley in 2010, and Arrowood retired as winemaster there, to concentrate on his Amapola Creek vineyard and winery. The wines of Arrowood Vineyards & Winery continue to be produced from Sonoma County grapes, and the tasting room on Highway 12 is still open.

Kenwood Vineyards
The Lee and Sheela families purchased Pagani Winery in 1970, changed its name to Kenwood, and turned it into a seminal Sonoma producer. They sold to Gary Heck of Korbel in 1999, and in summer 2012 New York-based Banfi Vintners was poised to purchase the property, but the deal fell through.

A most impressive newcomer in Sonoma Valley is Sojourn Cellars, a partnership between winemaker Erich Bradley and sales and marketing whiz Craig Haserot. Their Pinot Noirs, made from grapes from Sonoma Coast growers, are pure and precise, with refreshing acidity. Cork taint is never a problem at Sojourn: Haserot's Red Fox Labrador, Ziggy, was trained to sniff out TCA (Trichloroanisole), a compound that forms in corks and other materials, which can impart musty aromas to wines.

Sonoma Mountain AVA

Only a handful of wineries operate on the mountain, but three of them are important: Benziger Family Winery, Coturri Wines, and Laurel Glen Vineyard.

In the mid-1980s, Bruno Benziger moved his large family from New York to Sonoma Mountain and established Glen Ellen Vineyards and Winery. Their Proprietors' Reserve Chardonnay, which sold for less than four dollars a bottle, won over new wine drinkers in the U.S. for its easy-drinking taste and because of consumers' misinformed belief that "Reserve" meant a top-end wine. The brand was so successful that the Benzigers sold it and poured the proceeds into the higher-end Benziger Family Winery and their 85-acre Sonoma Mountain Estate, now certified biodynamic. Along with 42 acres of vines, the property has cow and sheep pastures, a biodynamic preparation house, three insectaries, bat and owl houses, water-reclamation wetlands, a composting station, olive groves, and vegetable gardens.

The Coturri family has grown grapes organically, without pesticides or herbicides, since 1979, long before the practice became fashionable in California. Red Coturri and his sons, Phil and Tony, planted 2 acres of vines on Sonoma Mountain in 1967 and another 5 acres in 1975. The vineyard is composed primarily of the Martini Monte Rosso Zinfandel clone on phylloxera-resistant St. George rootstock. The wines tend to be late-harvest in style, rich and jammy—just the way the Coturris like them. Phil Coturri is much in demand as a consultant to others on organic farming.

Patrick Campbell established Laurel Glen Vineyard in 1977 after spending time at a Sonoma Mountain Zen retreat. For thirty-five years, he produced elegant, nuanced Cabernet Sauvignons until selling the winery and vineyard in 2011 to Bettina Sichel; she is a former director of marketing for Quintessa in Napa Valley and daughter of Peter M. F. Sichel, who once owned Château Fourcas Hosten in Bordeaux. Sichel's work at Laurel Glen will be put under the microscope by fans of Campbell's Laurel Glen wines; she plans to convert the vineyard to certified organic winegrowing.

The van der Kamp Vineyard on Sonoma Mountain supplies Pinot Noir to several top-notch Sonoma County wineries, including Bjornstad Cellars, La Follette Wines, and Siduri Wines. The Richard Dinner Vineyard has been the source of grapes for Paul Hobbs Winery's celebrated Chardonnays.

Bennett Valley AVA

Grapevines were planted in Bennett Valley in the early 1900s, but they were abandoned during Prohibition. The AVA is only a baby, established in 2003, its vines averaging just fifteen years of age. Bennett Valley is markedly cooler than the Sonoma Valley AVA, with Pacific Ocean winds shooting through the Petaluma Gap in the coastal mountain range. There are only 700 acres of vines in the 8,100-acre AVA. Soils are diverse, but most are rocky and volcanic in nature. Elevations range from 250 to 1,850 feet.

Merlot has been a star performer in Bennett Valley, aided by great play in the media during Sandra and Bill McIver's ownership of Matanzas Creek Winery from 1977 to 2000, when the couple sold the property to Jackson Family Wines. The Kendall-Jackson Highland Estates Taylor Peak Merlot joins Matanzas Creek as a one-two punch by the same company.

In the early 2000s, new vineyard owners planted Syrah and Grenache and they have produced wines with the distinctive spiciness, deep color, and brisk acidity of wines from grapes grown in cold climates. Jemrose Vineyards, Flanagan Family, and Bevan Cellars are emerging stars in Bennett Valley; Grey Stack Vineyard's Rosemary's Block Sauvignon Blanc is one of the finest in California, scintillating and spicy.

LOS CARNEROS AVA

Los Carneros once was considered cool—and it still is, from a hipness standpoint. Yet this AVA, shared by Sonoma and Napa counties, is no longer climatically the coolest, as it was once thought to be. The western Sonoma Coast, Russian River Valley's Green Valley, Marin County, and other more southerly regions have emerged as chillier, foggier, wetter, and/or windier than Carneros, as it's also called, and they have stolen some of the region's thunder as a producer of racy cool-climate wines.

Carneros is still on the cool side for California, with chilly mornings and breezy late afternoons, though summer days are warm before the winds return. There is little difficulty here to ripen grapes, so fruit maturity and alcohol levels become stylistic choices, not growing-condition shackles. Try ripening Merlot in the chilly northwest Anderson Valley in Mendocino County, or in the Sta. Rita Hills AVA of Santa Barbara County! Carneros can do that, in addition to producing juicy and often minerally Chardonnays; plump, spicy Pinot Noirs; and traditionally made sparkling wines that undergo a second fermentation in the bottle, just as in Champagne.

The 37,000-acre Los Carneros region (its name means "the rams" in Spanish) became an American Viticultural Area in 1983, one in a wave of early AVAs. It's perched north of San Pablo Bay, the northernmost reach of San Francisco Bay, in a series of gently rolling hills covered with grapevines or sheep pastures (hence its name). Goat ranches became popular after Laura Chenel made her namesake Sonoma chèvre from goats raised in Carneros and sold her cheeses to local chefs, including Alice Waters at Chez Panisse in Berkeley. Today Sonoma goat cheese is everywhere, made by multiple artisan producers.

Vineyards and wineries in Sonoma Carneros use that term on their labels; Napa Valley Carneros is the corresponding label language. In addition to sharing its allegiances with two county appellations, Carneros also has the confusing feature of overlapping with two other AVAs, Sonoma Valley and Sonoma Coast. There are a handful of vineyards whose owners can choose any one of the three AVAs for their labels.

Los Carneros is the first AVA one reaches when driving north from San Francisco or Oakland, each some 40 miles away. The most visible winery in Carneros is on the Napa side, Domaine Carneros. The spitting image of Taittinger's own Château de la Marquetterie in Champagne, it is situated prominently on Highway 12/121, the southern connector between Sonoma and Napa.

The winery's original raison d'être was to produce sparkling wine for Champagne Taittinger, beginning in 1987. But, like many other bubbly producers in California, Domaine Carneros has added still wines in recent years, Chardonnay and Pinot Noir, to diversify its offerings. Most Americans continue to consider Champagne a special-occasion-only drink; Domaine Carneros and other serious makers of traditional-method sparkling wines in California cannot live by weddings and New Year's Eves alone.

Count Gloria Ferrer, on the Sonoma side of Carneros, in that fizz-plus-flat world. Owned by Spanish cava producer Freixenet, Gloria Ferrer added still Chardonnay and Pinot Noir to its roster to complement, but not supplant, the sparkling wines it produces from those same two grapes.

For years, it was easy for the trade and consumers to describe Carneros Pinot Noir as tasting of red fruits and made in a light, elegant style, while Russian River Valley Pinots were black fruit–flavored, fleshy, and intense. That may have been somewhat true twenty years ago, but as Carneros has been replanted with Dijon clones from Burgundy and more compatible rootstocks,

Los Carneros
The open rolling hills of Los Carneros expose vines to cooling breezes from San Pablo Bay (above).

Domaine Carneros
Champagne Taittinger established its Carneros sister winery in 1987; it includes a striking hospitality center modeled after Taittinger's château in France.

it's difficult to pick out either region's wines in a blind tasting. Specific sites mean so much more than AVAs these days.

The U.S. market has skewed toward darker, bigger wines, motivated in large part by influential critics' preferences for this style. In years past, Carneros Pinots have been faulted for lacking the oomph of those from Russian River Valley, Santa Lucia Highlands, and Sta. Rita Hills, yet the AVA is in a position to make that style of wine if it wants to.

The Sonoma and Napa halves of Carneros are strikingly similar; county boundaries are all that truly separate them, not soils, weather, or exposure. Attitude and real estate prices are another matter. Carneros is rated Region I, the coolest on the UC Davis heat summation scale (see p. 53), and its chill comes more from San Pablo Bay winds and fog than from low temperatures.

Starting in the late 1980s, large wine companies seized the opportunity to purchase inexpensive Carneros pastureland and plant wine grapes. Constellation Brands (owner of Robert Mondavi Winery), Diageo (owner of Sterling Vineyards), and Treasury Wine Estates (formerly Fosters, owner of Beringer Vineyards and Etude Winery) continue to be major landholders in Carneros, and a number of independent wineries have their own vineyards in the area.

It became abundantly clear in the late 1990s that many Napa Valley wineries were growing Chardonnay in sites too warm for the grape; their wines were soft and lacked the acid structure of those from grapes cultivated in cooler climates. By 2003, there was a mass exodus to Carneros for Chardonnay grapes by those determined to produce high-quality Napa Valley Chardonnay.

Dick Ward and David Graves had figured all that out long before. They met in 1977 at UC Davis and founded Saintsbury in 1981, two years before Carneros was approved as an AVA. They realized the benefits of this cooler climate for Chardonnay and Pinot Noir and have produced consistently

Dick Ward and David Graves
In the early days of Saintsbury, the fun-loving Ward and Graves marketed themselves as the "Dick and Dave Show," telling consumers their wines were "Beaune in the USA." But Saintsbury's owners are serious about their Pinot Noirs and Chardonnays.

outstanding, long-lived wines that are wonderfully balanced and nuanced, with supple tannins, crisp acidity, and moderate alcohol levels.

Of course, the wines Ward and Graves made in the 1980s aren't at all like those of the 2000s. Improved winemaking techniques, replanting, and wider choices in clones and rootstocks have resulted in more concentrated Saintsbury wines in recent vintages, yet they remain firmly on the elegant and, dare it be said, Burgundian end of the spectrum. Ten years in bottle adds a patina of complexity.

Three famous independently owned vineyards, Hyde and Hudson in Napa and Sangiacomo in Sonoma, have succeeded by custom-farming for select clients, such as David Ramey, whose winery is in Russian River Valley but who produces

LOS CARNEROS AVA SNAPSHOT
Vineyard acreage: **9,000**
Most-planted varieties: **Chardonnay, Pinot Noir**
Best varieties: **Chardonnay, Merlot, Pinot Noir**
Wineries: **45**
Trailblazers: **Acacia, Bouchaine, Carneros Creek, Saintsbury**
Steady hands: **Artesa Winery, Bouchaine, Ceja Vineyards, Gloria Ferrer, MacRostie Winery, Schug Carneros Estate, Truchard Vineyards**
Superstars: **Domaine Carneros, Donum Estate, Etude Winery, HdV, Saintsbury**
One to watch: **Buena Vista Carneros**

three beautiful Carneros Chardonnays each year (one each from Hyde and Hudson, and a regional blend). Patz & Hall, a company with a winery in Sonoma and a tasting salon in Napa, also makes single-vineyard Chardonnays and Pinot Noirs from Hyde and Hudson.

Sangiacomo Vineyard, founded in 1969, is composed of more than 1,600 acres, the majority of them in Carneros, with additional plantings in Sonoma Valley and the Sonoma Coast. The Sangiacomos sell grapes—mostly Chardonnay and Pinot Noir—to seventy-five wineries, nearly half of whom vineyard-designate their wines as Sangiacomo Vineyard.

Hyde Vineyard has 150 planted acres that include Semillon, Chardonnay, Sauvignon Blanc, Merlot, Pinot Noir, Cabernet Sauvignon, and Cabernet Franc. Hyde is also a partner in a most unusual relationship with a Burgundian winemaker, one that does not involve Pinot Noir.

Larry Hyde's cousin Pamela is married to Aubert de Villaine, director of Domaine de la Romanée-Conti, Burgundy's most famous wine producer. Pamela put the two men together, and they created a brand called HdV for the production of Chardonnay, Syrah, and a Bordeaux blend made from Hyde Vineyard fruit. The wines are impeccably made by Burgundy native Stéphane Vivier and are among Carneros's finest. There's no Pinot Noir, which would only invite comparisons that neither partner wishes to be made.

Gloria Ferrer Caves & Vineyards
Spain's Freixenet Group, under Ferrer family ownership, purchased Sonoma Carneros land and planted it for the production of sparkling—and now still—wines.

Hyde has long been a proponent of Merlot in Carneros, and HdV's Belle Cousine blend is Merlot-dominant. Truchard Vineyards produces a cool-climate Carneros Merlot that puts to rest the idea that the variety is always soft and plummy. Their Merlots are crisp and refreshing, with firm backbones, but they also are rich in plum and black cherry flavors, with a gentle herbal character that lends interest.

Several of Robert Sinskey Vineyards' wines, including Pinot Noir, Pinot Blanc, and Cabernet Franc, are made from Carneros fruit, although the winery is in Napa's Cabernet Sauvignon–centric Stags Leap AVA.

Anne Moller-Racke came to Carneros from Germany in 1981 and still farms some of the same ground. She became vineyard manager for Buena Vista Carneros Winery in 1983 and eventually rose to be vice president of vineyard operations, in 1997. She oversaw the expansion of Buena Vista's Carneros estate, with acreage reaching 935.

Through a series of transactions involving Buena Vista, Moller-Racke found herself in possession of the Tula Vista Ranch in 2001, a part of the Buena Vista holdings. She's turned it into Donum Estate, farming 70 acres of vines at the home ranch, plus 20 acres of the Ferguson Block in Carneros, and the Nugent Vineyard in the Russian River Valley, which she planted in the mid-1990s. From those sources, she produces immensely complex and deep Pinot Noirs under the Donum label and its sibling, Robert Stemmler.

Wine quality at Bouchaine Vineyards has gone up and down, although the winery has history in its favor. Bouchaine is the oldest continually operating winery in Carneros: it was

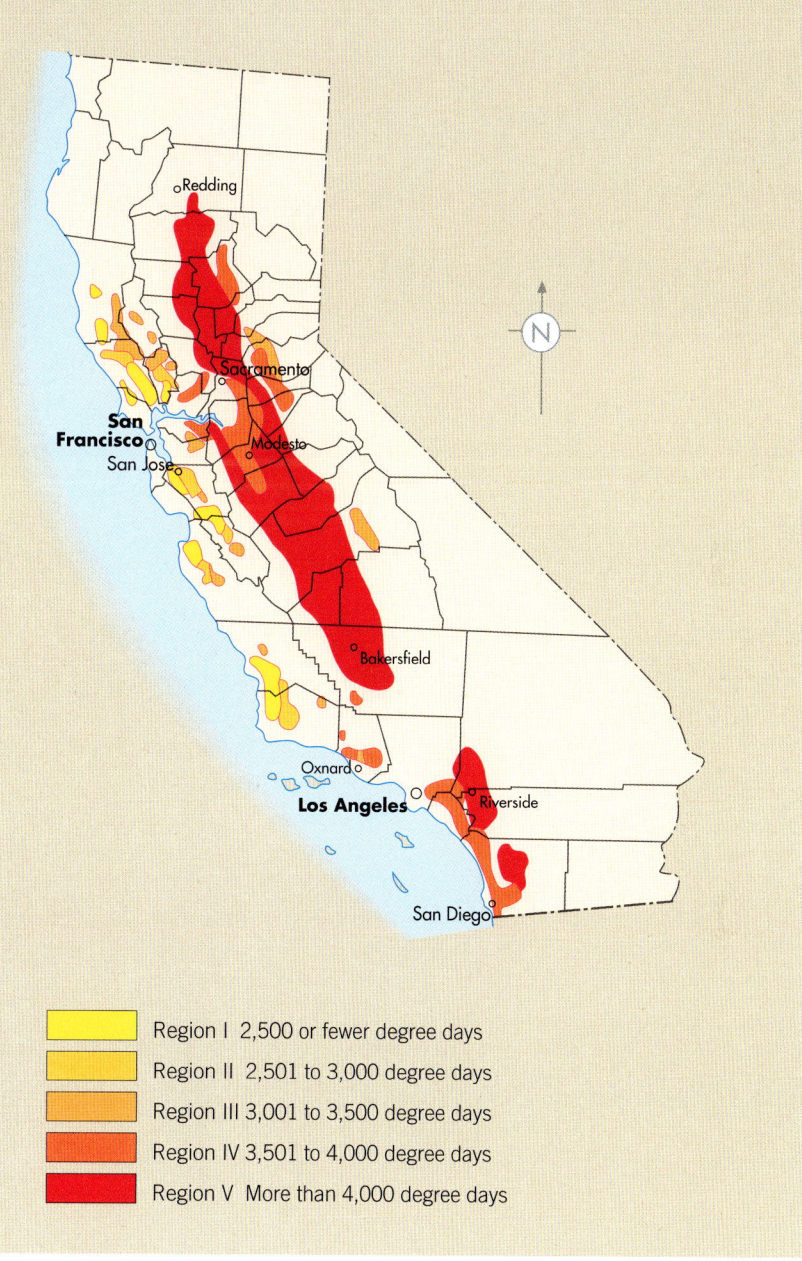

HEAT SUMMATION SCALE

The UC Davis Heat Summation Scale, also known as the Winkler Scale (it was created by professors Albert Winkler and Maynard Amerine), places California wine regions in one of five tiers based on heat accumulation during the growing season, April through October.

It's a rather complicated system based on "degree days," for which they subtracted 50 degrees—vines don't grow in temperatures colder than that, they had determined—from each day's average temperature and then assigned it a value. For example, 50 degrees would be subtracted from an average daily temperature of 60 degrees, resulting in 10 degree days. Winkler and Amerine added up all the degree-day values for each day from April through October, then defined the regions as follows:

- **Region I: 2,500 or fewer degree days:** best for Chardonnay, Pinot Noir, Gewürztraminer, Riesling
- **Region II: 2,501 to 3,000 degree days:** Cabernet Sauvignon, Merlot, Sauvignon Blanc
- **Region III: 3,001 to 3,500 degree days:** Zinfandel, Barbera, Gamay
- **Region IV: 3,501 to 4,000 degree days:** Malvasia, Thompson Seedless
- **Region V: More than 4,000 degree days:** Table grapes

The scale is a rough one and does not take into account vintage conditions, mesoclimates within regions, or climate change. Yet in the absence of a more precise method of assessing suitability for planting specific grape varieties in various regions, it remains a useful, if much-debated, tool that has been used around the world.

---

first planted to vines in the mid-1800s by Boon Fly, one of the great (and memorable) names in California viticulture. Just before the end of Prohibition, an Italian immigrant, Johnny Garetto, purchased the vineyard, and after Repeal, he opened the first winery with a tasting room in Los Carneros.

Garetto sold the ranch to Beringer Brothers in 1951. Beringer, with a home base in St. Helena in Napa Valley, used the facility for thirty years, until Gerret and Tatiana Copeland bought it in 1981.

And then there is Francis Mahoney, a Carneros pioneer who founded Carneros Creek Winery in 1972. He stepped away from winery management in 2001 to concentrate on growing an eclectic mix of grapes in his Las Brisas Vineyard. The 110-acre site in southern Sonoma Carneros supports not only fifteen Pinot Noir clones on six rootstocks, but also Montepulciano, Vermentino, and Tempranillo grapes.

Boisset Family Estates, based in Burgundy and owner of Raymond Vineyards in Napa Valley and DeLoach Vineyards in Sonoma County, purchased the historic Buena Vista Carneros brand in 2011, adding to this producer's serpentine history. The winery, established by Agoston Haraszthy in 1857 just south of the town of Sonoma, was relocated to Carneros in more modern times, but the original winery building continues to host Buena Vista's tasting room and museum. Jean-Charles Boisset, president of Boisset Family Estates, said at the time of his purchase that Buena Vista would continue its focus on Carneros Pinot Noir, Chardonnay, Merlot, and Syrah.

NAPA VALLEY AVA

The Napa Valley AVA, which includes nearly all of Napa County, is the king of the U.S. wine realm; those arguing against that fact are sentenced to the Castello di Amorosa winery dungeon for being out of touch with reality. No wine region in America has a finer reputation around the world for high-quality grapes and wines. None draws more visitors, has more Michelin-starred restaurants and posh hotels, and has more eclectic and sometimes ostentatious architecture than Napa Valley.

This is not to say that Napa Valley makes the best wines in America. But based on the quality and cachet of its Cabernet Sauvignons, it has achieved global recognition as a top-tier wine region, on par with France's Bordeaux, Burgundy, and Champagne regions; Italy's Piedmont and Tuscany; Spain's Rioja; and Germany's Mosel.

The revelatory 1976 "Judgment of Paris" tasting, at which the 1973 Chateau Montelena Chardonnay and the 1973 Stag's Leap Wine Cellars Cabernet Sauvignon finished ahead of top French wines in a blind tasting by European experts, vaulted Napa Valley into the world theater, and since that moment it has not given up an inch of stage space.

The Napa Valley AVA is within the only slightly larger Napa County appellation, and is composed of sixteen sub-AVAs: Atlas Peak, Calistoga, Chiles Valley District, Coombsville, Diamond Mountain District, Howell Mountain, Los Carneros, Mount Veeder, Oak Knoll, Oakville, Rutherford, St. Helena, Spring Mountain District, Stags Leap, Wild Horse Valley, and Yountville. Napa Valley was the first in California to require conjunctive labeling for its wines, in 1989. This means that every label that designates a sub-AVA (such as Rutherford, for example) must also state "Napa Valley" on the label. More recently adopted by Paso Robles and Sonoma County producers, conjunctive labeling gives consumers a bit more information on where the grapes were grown.

As powerful and prominent as Napa Valley is, it encompasses just 44,000 vineyard acres and produces only 4 percent of California's wine. Yet the valley accounts for 25 percent of the state's wine sales revenue, and more than four million people visit each year, largely to taste wine and dine. Where great wines are made, great restaurants tend to follow, and Napa has more than its share—including Thomas Keller's French Laundry in Yountville, one of the world's finest restaurants.

Napa Valley also has the highest-priced Cabernet Sauvignons in America. Price tags of $75 to $150 are the norm, and Cabs

Napa Valley mustard
Vibrant yellow mustard growing between vine rows is a signature sight in Napa Valley. Mustard helps control erosion, yet growers are increasingly replacing mustard with legumes, barley, radishes, and perennial grasses, which limit erosion and also add more nitrogen to the soil than mustard.

NAPA VALLEY AVA SNAPSHOT

Vineyard acreage: 46,000 (includes Napa Carneros)

Most-planted varieties: Chardonnay, Cabernet Sauvignon, Sauvignon Blanc, Merlot, Pinot Noir

Best varieties: Napa Valley—Cabernet Sauvignon, Merlot, Sauvignon Blanc; Carneros—Chardonnay, Pinot Noir

Sub-AVAs: Atlas Peak, Calistoga, Chiles Valley District, Coombsville, Diamond Mountain District, Howell Mountain, Los Carneros, Mount Veeder, Oakville, Oak Knoll, Rutherford, St. Helena, Spring Mountain District, Stags Leap, Wild Horse Valley, Yountville

Wineries: 420

NAPA VALLEY

The Napa Valley AVA (and its sixteen sub-AVAs) encompasses almost all of Napa County. Vineyards and a handful of wineries are also located in American Canyon, in Napa County yet outside Napa Valley.

Legend:
- ––– County boundary
- AVA boundaries are distinguished by colored lines
- **NAPA VALLEY** AVA
- ■ LONG — Notable producer
- ⬣ Hudson Vineyard — Noted vineyard
- Vineyards
- Woods and chaparral
- —1000— Contour intervals: below 100 feet every 20 feet, above 100 feet every 200 feet
- 58 Area mapped at larger scale on page shown

Scale: 1:175,000

Charles Krug
The St. Helena winery, more than 150 years old, was the first commercial wine producer in the Napa Valley. This is Krug's Home Vineyard.

over $150 are numerous. Like art and antiques, wine is worth whatever people are willing to pay for it and, thanks to the high scores of America's most influential wine critics, Robert Parker Jr. (*Wine Advocate*) and James Laube (*Wine Spectator*), Napa Cabernet Sauvignon has soared in price since the late 1980s, with consumer and collector demand driving the increases.

The best-quality Napa Cabernet grapes can command $10,000 per ton, and sometimes more for very special vineyard sites. The formula for pricing wines from purchased grapes is called the rule of 100: If a vintner pays $100 per ton of grapes, he or she needs to charge $1 for a bottle of wine. Thus, a $10,000-per-ton wine will likely be priced at $100.

Vintners who grow their own grapes have more latitude in wine pricing than those who don't, but they also have vineyard mortgage payments and farming costs. Most have invested in skilled hands who will be in the vineyard year-round, carefully tending each vine from pruning through picking. Such meticulous labor is expensive. When workers cut undesirable or surplus grape clusters from vines in spring and summer to allow the vines to concentrate their energies on ripening the remaining fruit, that's money on the ground, and this loss is factored into the price of the wine.

The start of the 2008 recession sent many Napans scrambling to sell their pricey wines. Some reduced their prices; others made deals with retailers and restaurateurs that moved cases while preserving the higher tasting-room price. Some maintained sales volumes thanks to loyal customers and direct-to-consumer marketing, but others found themselves in financial peril, having based their business plans on selling expensive wines forever.

More positively, less-expensive Napa Cabernet Sauvignons, priced at $50 or less, found eager buyers, and *négociants* purchased high-end producers' extra wine and bottled it under new labels, selling them at very attractive prices. By late 2011, the economy showed signs of a rebound, but pricing of Napa Cabernet and other high-end wines remained in flux.

Single-vineyard (vineyard-designated) wines command some of the highest prices in Napa Valley. In the 1970s and 1980s, most wines were labeled simply as being from Napa Valley. The Napa Valley AVA was established in 1983, with sub-AVAs to follow, and as certain vineyards stood out for their exceptional grapes—To Kalon, Martha's, and Eisele, to name a few—wineries that produced wines from them began stating so on their labels. The vineyards certainly benefited from this acknowledgment, making their grapes more desirable to others (and more expensive). Today vineyard designations are so prevalent on Napa Valley wines that blocks, hillsides, and sometimes even clones within vineyards are identified on some labels.

Napa Valley is 30 miles long north to south and from 1 to 5 miles across. The Mayacamas Mountains and the Vaca Range flank the Napa River on the west and east, respectively, with vineyards planted on both sides of the river, creeping up the benchlands, on hillsides, and on mountain elevations as high as 2,600 feet. Mount St. Helena is the northern boundary; the Carneros region on San Pablo Bay is the southern boundary.

In general, the southern end, near Napa and Yountville, is the coolest, as it's exposed to winds and fog from San Pablo Bay. The northern end is the warmest, although there is some evening cooling from Pacific Ocean breezes that waft across northern Sonoma County and through a gap in the Mayacamas range near Calistoga. Vines planted at higher elevations typically get less heat than those on the valley floor, although they get plenty of intense sunlight to promote photosynthesis and grape ripening.

Soils are particularly diverse, with some thirty-three soil types identified by researchers. This mosaic of volcanic, ancient seabed, river-run, and sedimentary deposits formed millions of years ago by volcanic eruptions, massive tectonic plate shifts, floods, and winds—as well as meso- and microclimates, elevations, aspect, irrigation, rootstocks, clonal selections, trellising systems, and more—have a profound impact on the quality and character of grapes grown in Napa Valley.

Despite Cabernet Sauvignon's dominance, the AVA is not a one-grape wonder. Some sixty varieties grow here, with a bit of Albariño here, a patch of Carignane there, and a few acres of Riesling and Touriga Nacional scattered about. Still, Cabernet Sauvignon is the grape of Napa, even though when Napa's Carneros vineyards are included in the total, there is more Chardonnay planted in the valley (27,250 acres) than

Cabernet Sauvignon (19,600). Add in the acreage for the four other grapes often used as complexity-builders for Cabernet Sauvignon—Merlot, Cabernet Franc, Malbec, and Petit Verdot—and the 28,100 acres of red Bordeaux varieties surpasses the acreage of Chardonnay.

The Wappo Indians, who first inhabited the valley, called it Napa, meaning "land of plenty": salmon, waterfowl, elk, bears, and wildcats—and wild grapes too. Settler George Calvert Yount is recognized as the first to plant wine grapes in the valley, in what is now Yountville, in 1836. Early pioneers also included John Patchett, who planted the first commercial vineyard, and Hamilton Walker Crabb, who experimented with more than four hundred grape varieties.

German immigrants played an enormous role in laying the foundation for Napa Valley winemaking. Charles Krug established the valley's first commercial winery in 1861, near what is now St. Helena. By 1889, more than 140 wineries were scattered throughout the valley, among them Schramsberg (1862), Beringer (1876), Inglenook (1879), and Spottswoode (1882), all started by Germans.

Overproduction and vine damage by phylloxera wreaked havoc on the young industry, and in 1920 Prohibition dealt a near-fatal blow that, coupled with the Great Depression, would sting for thirteen years. By the time Repeal came in 1933, most vineyards and wineries had closed, although an intrepid few remained in business by selling sacramental wines.

The 1940s brought newcomers to the valley to plant grapes and make wine on land previously committed to plums and walnuts, or on the raw, rugged foothills. But the real boom came in the 1960s and early '70s, when a wave of icons-to-be hit Napa Valley, restoring derelict wineries or starting their own businesses. Among them were Heitz Wine Cellars (1961), Robert Mondavi Winery (1966), Chappellet Vineyard & Winery (1967), Sterling Vineyards (1967), Diamond Creek Vineyards (1968), Spring Mountain Vineyard (1968), Cuvaison (1969), ZD Wines (1969), Stag's Leap Wine Cellars (1970), Smith-Madrone Vineyards & Winery (1971), Joseph Phelps Vineyards (1972), Caymus Vineyards (1972), Raymond Vineyard & Cellar (1971), Cakebread Cellars (1973), and Franciscan Oakville Estate (1973).

This was Napa Valley's golden era, when vintners worked and learned together. They had Inglenook and Beaulieu Vineyard to show them the ropes, and the American can-do spirit that told them Europeans weren't the only ones who could produce excellent wine. In 1960, a mere dozen wineries existed in the valley; by 1975, there were forty-five. The winery number hit the century mark by 1980, and today there are more than four hundred producers and 45,000 acres of vineyards in Napa Valley, plus a handful of outliers in Napa County.

To many, Robert Mondavi is synonymous with Napa Valley wine. He left his family's Charles Krug Winery in St. Helena in 1965 to start Robert Mondavi Winery in Oakville, and from that moment, his name and winery were recognized throughout the world. Not only did Mondavi produce good-quality wine, he sold it with unforgettable passion and verve. He spoke on behalf of all California wineries when he extolled the pleasures of drinking wine with meals—a concept somewhat foreign to Americans raised to drink iced tea, milk, and carbonated drinks with dinner. It's said that people tire of their own message long before it's been heard; Bob Mondavi, who died in 2007, would be pleased to know that today his message is being heard all across the United States.

Shafer Vineyards, Stags Leap District
Stags Leap District is one of sixteen sub-AVAs in Napa Valley, bounded by the Vaca Mountains on the east and the Napa River on the west.

Calistoga AVA

Calistoga, once considered "the other side of the tracks" by southern Napans, has gained cachet with wine lovers but remains casual and quirky. Known for its 1950s-era resorts, mud baths, mobile-home parks, Old Faithful Geyser, and the annual holiday tractor parade, Calistoga has now taken on a sheen of sophistication. Producers such as Araujo Estate, Carter Cellars, and Chateau Montelena draw high-end buyers, and Montelena is also a fine place for novices to get a firm grasp on Napa Valley wine and history—as well as view a display devoted to the 2008 movie *Bottle Shock*, which takes Hollywood liberties in portraying Chateau Montelena's role in the "Judgment of Paris" tasting.

Late to come to the AVA party, the Calistoga appellation was approved only in 2009, after years of wrangling over how to deal with two existing wine brands that had "Calistoga" in their names yet did not use the mandated 85 percent Calistoga grapes in their wines. The AVA petition was finally approved, with a grandfather clause that allowed the two brands to phase out their use of the word *Calistoga*. The celebration that followed

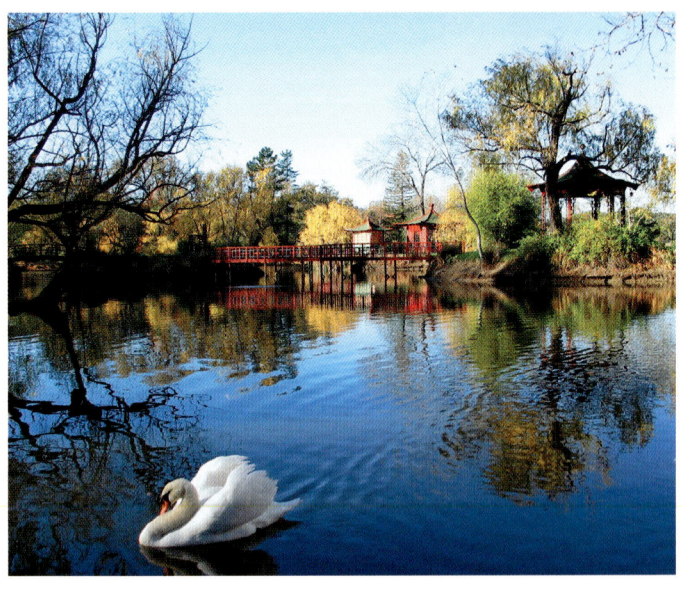

Jade Lake at Chateau Montelena
Weeping willows, Chinese pagoda–like gazebos, and a territorial white swan make a picturesque setting at Chateau Montelena's historic winery.

Calistoga & Diamond Mountain

The Calistoga AVA was established in 2009 after years of effort. For the adjoining Diamond Mountain District AVA see p. 61.

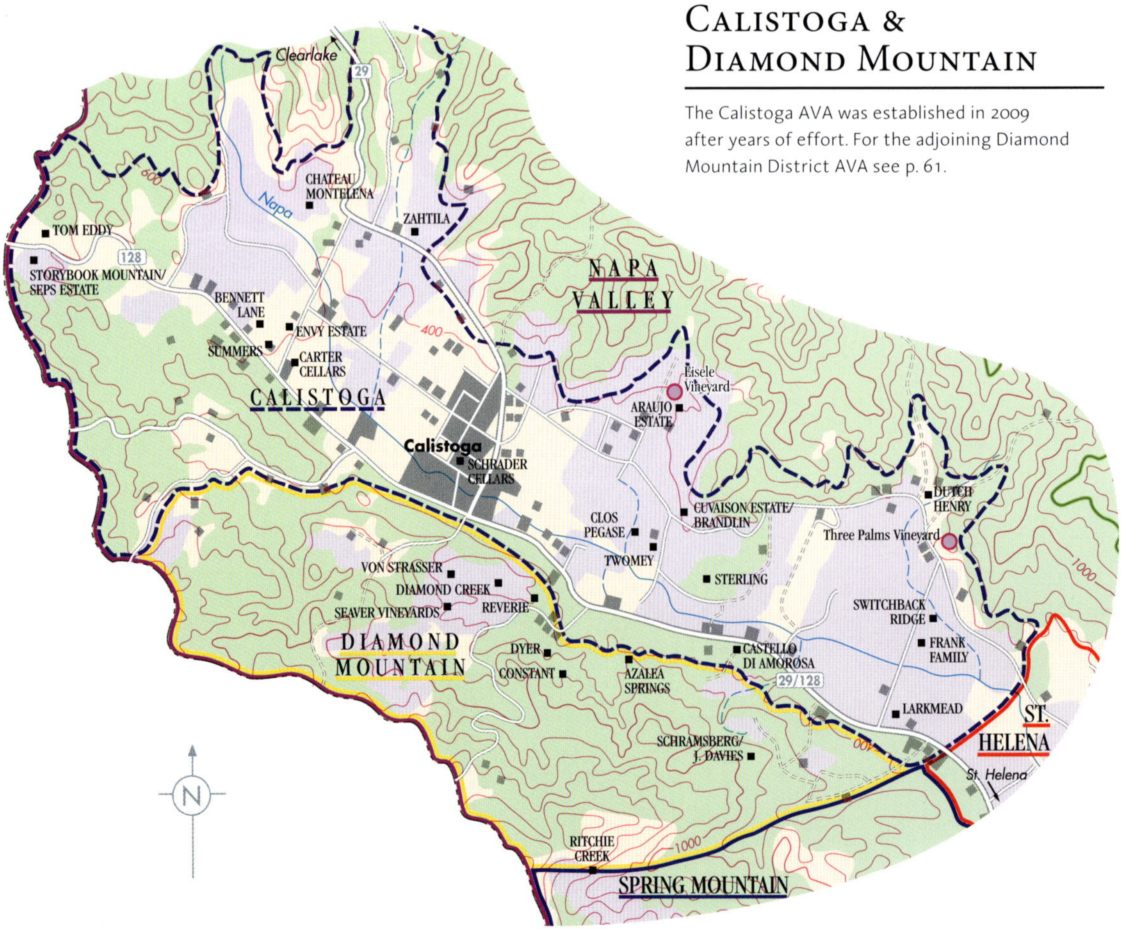

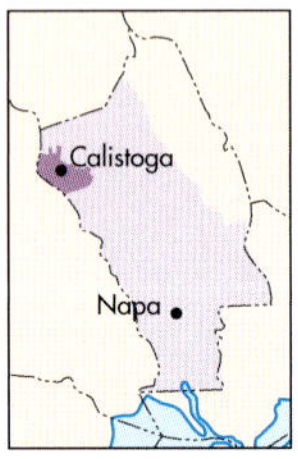

County boundary
AVA boundaries are distinguished by colored lines
CALISTOGA AVA
■ TWOMEY Notable producer
Three Palms Vineyard Noted vineyard
Vineyards
Woods and chaparral
400 Contour interval 200 feet

1:85,000
Km 0 1 2 Km
Miles 0 1 Mile

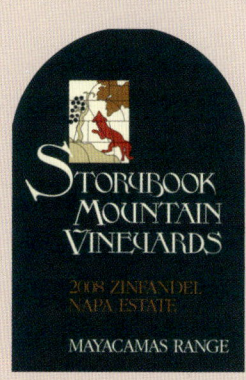
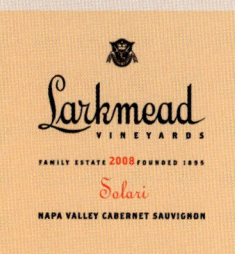

CALISTOGA AVA SNAPSHOT

Vineyard acreage: **2,500**

Most-planted varieties: **Cabernet Sauvignon, Zinfandel**

Best varieties: **Cabernet Sauvignon, Petite Sirah, Zinfandel**

Wineries: **25**

Trailblazer: **Chateau Montelena**

Steady hands: **Bennett Lane, Clos Pegase, Cuvaison Estate Wines/Brandlin, Frank Family Vineyards, Larkmead Vineyards, Sterling Vineyards, Storybook Mountain/Seps Estate, Summers Winery, Tom Eddy Wines, Twomey Cellars, Venge Vineyards, Zahtila Vineyards**

Superstars: **Araujo Estate Wines, Carter Cellars, Chateau Montelena, Switchback Ridge**

---

could not have come soon enough for Jim and Bo Barrett, proprietors of Chateau Montelena and major supporters of the AVA petition.

Their winery was started in 1882 by San Francisco businessman Alfred Tubbs, who purchased 254 acres and planted grapevines. He came up with the winery name by contracting the words in Mount St. Helena, the 4,300-foot peak that overlooks Calistoga. Winemaking ceased during Prohibition, but the Tubbs family continued to tend the vineyard until 1958, when they sold it to Yort and Jeanie Frank. They loved the Old World–style stone winery and added Jade Lake and Chinese gardens to the property.

In 1972, attorney Jim Barrett bought Chateau Montelena and invested heavily in renovating the winery and the 100 acres of vineyards on the estate—a task finally completed almost forty years later, in time for the 2011 harvest. The end of the project was quite a turnabout for Jim and his winemaker son Bo, because in 2008 they had been on the verge of selling Montelena to the owner of Bordeaux's Château Cos d'Estournel. The deal collapsed, and instead of looking for another buyer, the Barretts recommitted themselves to their estate.

Chateau Montelena wines—Chardonnay, Zinfandel, and Cabernet Sauvignon, with a splash of Riesling made from grapes purchased from Potter Valley in Mendocino County—are famed for their minerality and longevity. Often angular and closed in their youth, they begin to open at about five years after vintage. The Chardonnays are a wonder, made, surprisingly, from grapes grown in Napa Valley's warmest region and still impeccable after fifteen or more years in bottle.

Trivia fans note: The judgment-winning 1973 Montelena Chardonnay included grapes from Sonoma County's Alexander Valley. The winemaker, Miljenko "Mike" Grgich, went on to found his own winery, Grgich Hills Cellar, in Rutherford.

The AVA is warm to hot, depending upon the time of year. During the growing season (April through October) temperatures peak at around 90°F and fall to the low 50s at night. While rain is plentiful—38 to 60 inches per year—most of it falls in winter; spring through fall are typically dry.

Calistoga AVA elevations range from 300 to 1,200 feet, and the soils are nearly all volcanic, deposited there by ancient volcano eruptions in Lake County, to the north. Rocks, stones, and cobble-littered loam soils are found on the hillsides; heavier clay and silt soils are found in the alluvial fans on the valley floor.

Bart and Daphne Araujo's 1990 purchase of the 38-acre Eisele Vineyard east of Calistoga established them as major players in the Napa Valley wine game. Eisele Vineyard Cabernet Sauvignon grapes had previously gone to Joseph Phelps Vineyard for a vineyard-designated Cabernet, but now Araujo Estate Wines, wisely, uses all the fruit itself.

The vineyard, first planted to Riesling and Zinfandel in the nineteenth century, is located on an alluvial fan, protected by

Castello di Amorosa
Dario Sattui's replica of a thirteenth-century Italian castle includes a moat, dungeon, and torture chamber, in addition to the winery and vineyards.

palisades to the north and cooled by breezes from the Chalk Hill Gap to the west. The vineyard is very rocky and well drained, so high yields aren't a problem. Meticulous farming has helped adjust for the warmth of the region, and the Araujos have called upon consultant winemakers Tony Soter and Bordeaux's Michel Rolland to fine-tune their wines in the past. Araujo, which uses organic and biodynamic viticultural techniques, also produces a Viognier and a crisp, grassy Sauvignon Blanc.

Carter Cellars, owned by Mark Carter of Carter House Inn in Eureka, makes his luxe Cabernet Sauvignons, including one from grapes from Beckstoffer To Kalon Vineyard in Oakville, at Envy Estate Winery in Calistoga. His Envy partner, Nils Venge, is one of Napa Valley's most experienced winemakers; he is also owner of Saddleback Cellars in Oakville.

The Peterson family's Calistoga vineyard in Dutch Henry Canyon is the sole source of grapes for its Switchback Ridge Wines. The Petersons' Cabernet Sauvignons, Merlots, and Petite Sirahs are heady and rich, produced by Bob Foley in a modern style that resonates with the winery's avid mailing-list customers and those critics who embrace opulence.

Two Calistoga wineries raised eyebrows when they first opened. Since 1973, Sterling Vineyards' aerial tram has transported visitors from the parking lot to the winery atop a knoll overlooking northern Napa Valley, drawing references to "Napa's Disneyland." Founded by British businessman Sir Peter Newton (who went on to found Newton Vineyard) in 1969, Sterling has changed hands several times and, like the tram, has had its ups and downs.

However, the Sterling skyway turned out to be rather ho-hum compared to Castello di Amorosa, Dario (formerly Daryl) Sattui's thirteenth-century-style castle/winery in the western hills above Calistoga. Sattui, who also owns V. Sattui Winery in St. Helena, reportedly spent $40 million during a period of fourteen years to build the Tuscan castle replica, which includes 107 rooms on seven levels. Opened to the public in 2007, Castello di Amorosa is so over-the-top that it could be relocated to Disneyland and be a fine fit.

Diamond Mountain District AVA

Like the Spring Mountain, Howell Mountain, and Mount Veeder AVAs, Diamond Mountain is defined by its elevation, which ranges from 400 to 2,200 feet. Vines planted at high elevations—generally 800 feet and above—tend to stay cooler in the afternoons and warmer at night than those on the valley floor, although they get plenty of sunshine. Yet they capture marine breezes and are significantly cooler than, say, Calistoga, on the flatland east of Diamond Mountain.

The uplifted soils are typically reddish and very fine-grained, even gritty, in texture, composed of weathered sedimentary and volcanic material. Red wines are solidly structured and tannic when young, with a graphite/mineral character. They're neither supple nor generous in the first few years, but they develop beautifully for up to twenty years.

Schramsberg celebrated its 150th birthday in 2011. In the year 1861, German Jacob Schram purchased the property and began developing a vineyard and winery. After several changes of hands, Jack and Jamie Davies purchased the dilapidated Schram Victorian house, winery, and vineyards in 1965 and transformed the property into Schramsberg Vineyards, producer of arguably the finest sparkling wines in the United States today.

The Davies were the first to make blanc de blancs, blanc de noirs, brut rosé, and a prestige cuvée in California, using the traditional sparkling winemaking method in which the wines undergo a second fermentation in the bottle and are aged from two to ten years, with the spent yeast cells remaining in contact with the wine, adding brioche-like complexity.

In the mid-1990s, the Davies ripped out their Chardonnay and Pinot Noir vines on Diamond Mountain and replanted with Cabernet Sauvignon. They had reached two conclusions before replanting: one, regions much cooler than Diamond Mountain—Carneros, Marin County, Anderson Valley in Mendocino County, and Monterey County—produced better sparkling-wine grapes with energetic fruit character and higher acidity; and, two, making Cabernet Sauvignon in the heart of Cab Country was a no-brainer. Since the first vintage in 2001, J. Davies Cabernet Sauvignons have shown flashes of diamondlike brilliance, and they are becoming more consistent as the vines mature.

Jack, who was a leader of the Napa Valley Agricultural Preserve, which keeps overdevelopment of the valley at bay, died in 1998. Jamie, who passed away in 2008, was known for, among other things, bringing the world's top chefs to Schramsberg for showcase dinners and demonstrations. Their youngest son, Hugh, is now the winery president and winemaker.

Jack and Jamie Davies and their consultant, André Tchelistcheff, gave Al Brounstein the encouragement he needed to begin developing Diamond Creek Vineyards in 1967. The property he chose was dramatically beautiful, but fraught with boulders, trees, wild vegetation, and other obstacles that made vine cultivation difficult. Yet Brounstein felt blessed because his property had four separate and distinct terroirs: Rock Terrace, a 7-acre north-facing outcropping of iron-rich, deep, reddish-brown volcanic soil; Volcanic Hill, 8 acres facing south, with a white volcanic ash soil; Gravelly Meadow, 5 acres of mostly sand

DIAMOND MOUNTAIN DISTRICT AVA SNAPSHOT

Vineyard acreage: 500

Most-planted varieties: Cabernet Sauvignon, Cabernet Franc, Chardonnay

Best varieties: Cabernet Sauvignon, Grüner Veltliner (von Strasser)

Wineries: 10

Trailblazers: Diamond Creek Vineyards, Schramsberg Vineyards

Steady hands: Azalea Springs Vineyards, Constant, Diamond Terrace, Dyer Vineyard, Reverie

Superstars: Diamond Creek Vineyards, J. Davies, Schramsberg Vineyards, von Strasser

One to watch: Seaver Vineyards

and gravel; and Lake Vineyard, a tiny (0.75-acre) plot of gravel and sand in the coldest part of the estate.

The wines are bottled separately, and each displays subtle flavor, aroma, and tannin differences. Diamond Creek Cabernet Sauvignons are textbook Diamond Mountain, with saturated color, ripe extracted fruit, chewy texture, and big yet smooth tannins.

Brounstein is legendary for smuggling vine cuttings from Bordeaux into the United States by way of Mexico. The practice was common back in the day, although vintners ran the risk of introducing diseased plants into the country. Brounstein, who died in 2006 after a long struggle with Parkinson's disease, delighted in driving visitors through his vineyard in a deluxe golf cart, pretending not to have total control of the vehicle—in a manner reminiscent of Mr. Toad's Wild Ride at Disneyland. He also was fond of saying, "My Volcanic Hill Cab will live for a hundred years, easy. If it doesn't, I will personally refund your money." Brounstein was in his eighties when he made that promise. His wife, Boots, continues to manage the vineyards and winery.

In 2005, Rudy von Strasser was the first in California to produce a commercial version of the Austrian white variety Grüner Veltliner. Better known for his fine hillside Cabernet Sauvignons, von Strasser planted Grüner Veltliner in homage to his Austrian father, and he was rewarded with a gold medal at the AWC Vienna competition for his 2010 bottling.

Von Strasser, whose mother is Hungarian, studied winemaking at UC Davis and worked at Bordeaux's Château Lafite-Rothschild and at Trefethen Family Vineyards and Newton Vineyard in Napa Valley before starting von Strasser Winery in 1990. His Cabernet Sauvignons are dense, with chewy tannins, and there is an elegance to them that suggests skilled winemaking handled the rugged terroir.

One to watch: Hall of Fame baseball pitcher Tom Seaver and his wife, Nancy, produced their first Cabernet Sauvignon in 2005 from Seaver Vineyards, a 3.5-acre plot on a south-facing slope on Diamond Mountain. Tom Terrific, as Seaver was called during his hugely successful baseball career, grew up in California's Central Valley, the son of a raisin broker. After baseball, Seaver eventually made his way to Diamond Mountain to grow grapes—a fitting location for a man who spent twenty years on diamonds as a professional pitcher. Now that the vines are mature, the Seavers call upon sought-after consultant winemaker Thomas Rivers Brown to make their GTS Cabernet Sauvignon, which is remarkably polished.

Schramsberg Vineyards
Ramon Viera has riddled—hand-turned—bottles of Schramsberg sparkling wines for nearly forty years at the Calistoga winery.

Howell Mountain AVA

Growing conditions on Howell Mountain are similar to those on Spring Mountain, even though Howell is on the eastern side of Napa Valley, in the Vaca Range. Vineyards are planted above the fog line, between 600 and 2,200 feet, in volcanic soils that are remarkably shallow and infertile, forcing vines to struggle to sink their roots deep enough to find water and nutrients. This struggle results in grapes with thick skins and forceful tannins. Managing those tannins in the cellar is the key to producing Cabernet Sauvignons that are drinkable in their younger years.

Randall Dunn, though, of Dunn Vineyards, doesn't give a hoot about early enjoyment. His dense, tannic Cabernet Sauvignons are meant for long-term aging. While he worked as winemaker at Caymus Vineyards, Dunn and his wife, Lori, established Dunn Vineyards on Howell Mountain, releasing their first Cabernet Sauvignon in 1982. He continued as the Caymus winemaker until 1985. Dunn is a forceful opponent of high-alcohol wines—he picks his grapes at lower sugars than any of his neighbors do—and an avid proponent of extracting tannins not just from grape skins, but also from the leaves and seeds that most other winemakers eliminate before fermentation. Dunn wines are ones for the ages.

Betty O'Shaughnessy left the frozen winters of Minnesota to live in Napa Valley in 1990. She purchased a vineyard in Oakville, then expanded to acreage on Howell Mountain

O'Shaughnessy Estate Winery
Minnesota transplant Betty O'Shaughnessy grows 26 acres of Cabernet Sauvignon, Cabernet Franc, Malbec, Merlot, Petit Verdot, Carmenere, and St. Macaire on Howell Mountain; her wines, like others from the mountain, are bold and rich, with sturdy tannins.

HOWELL MOUNTAIN AVA SNAPSHOT
Vineyard acreage: **600**
Most-planted varieties: **Cabernet Sauvignon, Sauvignon Blanc**
Best variety: **Cabernet Sauvignon**
Wineries: **50**
Trailblazer: **Dunn Vineyards**
Steady hands: **CADE, Ladera, La Jota Vineyards, Lamborn Family Vineyards, Robert Craig Winery**
Superstars: **Dunn Vineyards, O'Shaughnessy Estate Winery, Robert Foley Vineyards**

and Mount Veeder. The talented Sean Capiaux makes the O'Shaughnessy wines—Sauvignon Blanc, Chardonnay, Syrah, Merlot, and Cabernet Sauvignon—at the Howell Mountain winery. The most intriguing are the Cabernets from the Howell Mountain Rancho del Oso Vineyard, named for a grape-feasting bear (*Oso*), and from Mount Veeder. The former offers graphite minerality, dark black fruit, and hefty tannins; the latter has supple texture, rich cassis fruit, and floral aromatics.

A relative newcomer to Howell Mountain is CADE, a spinoff of PlumpJack Winery in Oakville. Opened in 2007, the CADE winery is LEED (Leadership in Energy and Environmental Design) Gold certified by the U.S. Green Building Council and is organically farmed. Two Howell Mountain Cabernet Sauvignons are produced, as well as a brisk Napa Valley Sauvignon Blanc.

Bob Foley, who cut his winemaking teeth at Markham Vineyards and vaulted Pride Mountain Vineyards to the top of the quality wine pile in his fifteen years there, now consults for others and produces his own Robert Foley Vineyards wines from Howell Mountain grapes. His claret, a Cabernet Sauvignon/Merlot mix, is the flagship, and Foley also has a soft spot in his vinous heart for muscular Petite Sirahs and Charbonos.

Corry Dekker and Dino Dina's Cimarossa ("red hilltop") vineyard, at 2,100 feet, has a 360-degree view and sells Cabernet Sauvignon grapes to top producers TOR and Sbragia Family Wines. Consulting winemaker Mia Klein also produces two Cabernets for the couple, and at their early stage of production, the wines show racy briar and exotic spice notes.

Ladera Vineyards
Snowfall is uncommon in Napa Valley, but Ladera's vines, at an 1,800-foot elevation on Howell Mountain, get an occasional dusting.

Spring Mountain District AVA

This mountain AVA totals 8,600 acres, although only 1,000 are in vines. Vineyards, most of them small and difficult to cultivate, cling to terraces and slopes, surrounded by stands of pine, fir, and oak. Although the city of St. Helena is at the base of Spring Mountain, few vintners have a view of it by day or night, so thickly forested is the region. On a winter night in a rainstorm (the AVA can get as many as 85 inches of rain in a wet year), Mussorgsky's *Night on Bald Mountain* would be a fittingly haunting musical accompaniment.

The appellation sits on the eastern slopes of the Mayacamas Mountains, which separate Napa and Sonoma counties. One of the AVA's finest wineries, Pride Mountain Vineyards, has contiguous vines planted in both counties, and it must be careful how it handles the grapes from both sides of the county line and how its Cabernet Sauvignons, Merlots, and Viogniers are labeled. When grapes from both counties are used in one wine, Pride labels them by the percentage of grapes from each county.

Su Hua Newton has no such issues. The widow of Peter Newton, who sold Sterling Vineyards to Coca-Cola in 1977 and used the proceeds to plant Newton Vineyard, oversees the estate's 120 acres of Merlot, Cabernet Franc, Cabernet Sauvignon, and Petit Verdot, planted in 112 separate blocks. Chardonnay grapes are sourced from Carneros, and Newton's unfiltered Chardonnays are collector's items.

The Newton estate is one of California's most beautiful, merging Peter's and Su-Hua's personal tastes, with a pagoda, Chinese red gate, lanterns, English gardens, and a London phone booth. It's a spectacular property and well worth a visit.

Terra Valentine
Angus and Margaret Wurtele acquired the abandoned Yverdon Winery on Spring Mountain in 1999 and painstakingly restored it.

The Spring Mountain AVA is named for its numerous springs and is drained by several small streams. Elevations range from 400 to 2,600 feet, and most vineyards have eastern exposures. The best way to view Spring Mountain plantings is not from the mountain itself, but from the major Napa Valley thoroughfare, Highway 29, on the valley floor, looking west.

Vineyards are planted largely in soils derived from Franciscan sedimentary rocks—weathered sandstone and conglomerates—and the Sonoma volcanic series. To the north, Diamond Mountain's soils are almost all volcanic; to the south, on Mount Veeder, they're mostly sedimentary.

SPRING MOUNTAIN DISTRICT AVA SNAPSHOT

Vineyard acreage: **1,000**

Most-planted varieties: **Cabernet Sauvignon, Merlot, Chardonnay, Cabernet Franc**

Best varieties: **Cabernet Sauvignon, Chardonnay, Merlot, Riesling**

Wineries: **30**

Trailblazer: **Smith-Madrone**

Steady hands: **Barnett Vineyards, Behrens Family Winery/Erna Schein, Cain Vineyard & Winery, Hollywood & Vine, Paloma Vineyards, Smith-Madrone Vineyards & Winery, Spring Mountain Vineyard, Terra Valentine**

Superstars: **Newton Vineyard, Pride Mountain Vineyards**

Smith-Madrone Vineyards
An alley of olive trees separates vineyards planted to Riesling, Chardonnay, Cabernet Sauvignon, Cabernet Franc, and Merlot, each on ideal slopes and exposures.

Growing-season temperatures swing from 50° to 90°F; the cool nights help the grapes retain their bracing acidity.

Spring Mountain Vineyard's Victorian mansion was in the opening shot of *Falcon Crest*, and for a time, the winery produced a Falcon Crest label to capitalize on the publicity. Spring Mountain Vineyard is a source of seriously produced Sauvignon Blancs and Cabernet Sauvignons from its 845 acres. Its flagship wine is Elivette, a cellar-worthy Cabernet Sauvignon–based blend.

Thanks to the German immigrants who started wineries in and near St. Helena in the mid- to late 1800s (Jacob Schram of Schramsberg, Charles Krug, and the Beringer brothers were among them), Riesling was once widely planted in Spring Mountain before being supplanted by Cabernet Sauvignon and other grapes. One holdout, Smith-Madrone Vineyards & Winery, perched atop Spring Mountain, makes dry, aromatic Rieslings that have a reputation for aging beautifully.

Brothers Stu and Charles Smith of Smith-Madrone also produce commendable Chardonnays and Cabernet Sauvignons, although their Rieslings attract most of the attention. The Riesling vines are planted on an east-facing slope and thus aren't subjected to intense afternoon sun during the growing season. The winery, which turned forty in 2011, occasionally releases older-vintage Rieslings for sale, demonstrating the ageworthiness of the wines.

St. Helena AVA

St. Helena's growing season is warm, and there is little fog or wind incursion—both are impeded by the Mayacamas Mountains to the west and the Vaca Mountain Range to the east. The AVA pinches down to just 3 miles across at one point, but it widens to the north and south, in an hourglass shape. Midsummer temperatures hit the mid- to high-90°F range, and there is less diurnal temperature difference here than in most Napa AVAs.

In 2011, two St. Helena wineries celebrated mega-anniversaries: Charles Krug its 150th, and Freemark Abbey its 125th. Beringer Vineyards turned 135 that same year, and Spottswoode Estate celebrated its 130th birthday in 2012, making St. Helena a most important part of Napa Valley winemaking history.

The AVA is relatively small, with just under 1,000 vine acres, yet it is home to dozens of top producers, many of which source grapes from throughout the valley. Charles Krug Winery is the granddaddy of them all. It began

Charles Krug Winery
Peter Jr., Peter Sr., and Marc Mondavi (from left) produce Bordeaux-style wines at this St. Helena landmark, the oldest winery in Napa Valley.

its life in 1861, after German-born Charles Krug moved to Napa Valley following stints as a teacher and newspaper reporter in Philadelphia and San Francisco. After Krug's death in 1892, the winery was sold, then sold again to Italian immigrants Cesare and Rosa Mondavi in 1943. Their sons, Robert and Peter, would later work at the winery, with Robert famously leaving in 1965 following a punch-throwing fight with Peter. Robert found fame at his Robert Mondavi Winery in Oakville, and Peter stayed the course, taking over the winery and, in contrast to his older brother, quietly going about his winemaking business.

In 2011, as Charles Krug Winery celebrated its 150 years, Peter Mondavi turned ninety-six and continued to report to work every day. His sons, Peter Jr. and Marc, are now in charge of the winery and its 850 acres of vineyards. A capital improvement plan begun in 1999 and completed in 2011 included winery and vineyard upgrades and restoration of the historic carriage house and redwood cellar.

Freemark Abbey began life in 1886, and its co-owner at the time, Josephine Tychson, is believed to have been the first female vintner in California. She and her husband, John C. Tychson, purchased 147 acres in Napa Valley and established a vineyard. He died, but she soldiered on, tending to the vines and two children. But by 1893, phylloxera had ravaged her vineyard, and Tychson sold the property. It was sold again, four years later, to Antonio Forni, who renamed it Lombarda Cellars after his Italian birthplace.

Forni built the stone winery and then, following Prohibition, sold Lombarda in 1939 to three Southern California businessmen—Albert "Abbey" Ahern, Charles Freeman, and Markquand Foster. They renamed it Freemark Abbey, a combination of their names. Eventually acquired by seven Napa grapegrowers in 1967, Freemark Abbey began producing exceptional Cabernet Sauvignons and Chardonnays, and they held their own at the "Judgment of Paris." George Taber, the only journalist to cover the tasting, recalls French judge Raymond Oliver proclaiming, "Ah, back to France!" after mistaking the Freemark Abbey Chardonnay for a white Burgundy. The making of fine wines continues at Freemark, now owned by Jackson Family Wines.

Elegant isn't a word often used to describe modern-day Napa Valley Cabernet Sauvignon, which typically is rich and extracted and often has high alcohol. Still, there are winemakers who have stuck to their guns by producing Cabs that are refined, keenly balanced, and refreshing and have twenty-year drinking windows after release. Is it coincidence that the two wineries frequently singled out for this style are owned by females?

The women of Spottswoode Estate—Mary Novak and daughters Beth and Lindy—have maintained a refined style of Cabernet Sauvignon at their 1882-established property since Jack Novak purchased the property and moved his wife and

Kronos Vineyard
Cathy Corison farms Kronos organically and produces a vineyard-designated Cabernet Sauvignon from her forty-five-year-old vines. Her blended Napa Valley Cabernet Sauvignon is made from grapes purchased from Rutherford and St. Helena growers.

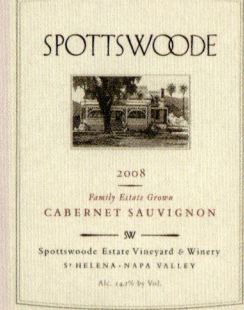
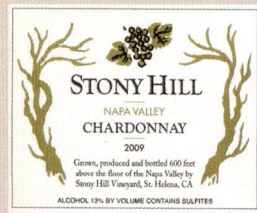

ST. HELENA AVA SNAPSHOT
Vineyard acreage: **985**
Most-planted varieties: **Cabernet Sauvignon, Sauvignon Blanc, Merlot, Cabernet Franc**
Best varieties: **Cabernet Franc, Cabernet Sauvignon, Sauvignon Blanc**
Wineries: **50**
Trailblazers: **Beringer Vineyards, Charles Krug Winery, Freemark Abbey, Heitz Wine Cellars, Louis M. Martini Winery**
Steady hands: **Benessere, Beringer Vineyards, Charles Krug Winery, Duckhorn Vineyards, Ehlers Estate, Freemark Abbey, Hall Wines, Heitz Wine Cellars, Louis M. Martini Winery, Titus Vineyards, Trinchero Napa Valley, Vineyard 29, Whitehall Lane**
Superstars: **Corison Winery, Joseph Phelps Vineyards, Spottswoode Estate**

five kids from Southern Californina to St. Helena in 1972. Jack died unexpectedly in 1977, leaving the vineyard and winery operations to Mary and her children, and thirty-five years later, Spottswoode basks in the glow of being one of California's most admired wine estates.

In 1882, George Schonewald planted the vineyard, which is just a few blocks west of downtown St. Helena at the foot of the Mayacamas Mountains. Two owners later, the Spotts family gave Spottswoode its name, and the Novaks made it stick. They were among the first in Napa Valley to farm organically (no doubt pleasing residents of the houses that surround the vineyard) and have employed such talented winemakers as Tony Soter, Pam Starr, and Rosemary Cakebread over the years. All have followed the path to refined wines, although recent vintages have been a bit more ripe and concentrated, as young, healthy vines have replaced aged, diseased ones in the last decade.

On the south side of St. Helena, Cathy Corison makes Cabernet her way. The wines are a bit reticent when young, with a gentle herbaceousness and dusty tannins that most others have bred out of their wines. Corison Cabs are a throwback to the 1970s and 1980s, when Napa Cabernet Sauvignon had moderate alcohol levels (hers are around 13.5 percent), were allowed to show the variety's classic forest-floor character, and were built to age gracefully.

Corison, who made wine for Chappellet, Freemark Abbey, and Staglin Family before starting her own brand, produced her first vintage in 1987 and broke ground on her own Corison Winery in 1999. She purchases grapes for her Napa Valley Cabernet Sauvignon from vineyards located between St. Helena and Rutherford, and she ekes out a precious few cases of Cab each year from her own Kronos Vineyard, with its crusty, decrepit-looking vines planted around 1966.

Although Robert Mondavi Winery is often given credit for building Napa Valley's first new winery after Prohibition in 1966, Fred and Eleanor McCrea actually won the race back in 1952 when they built the small Stony Hill winery and began producing Chardonnay, Riesling, and Gewürztraminer from vines planted in 1947 on a northwestern slope of Spring Mountain. The wines were then, and are today, pure, precise, and minerally, with amazing longevity.

The McCreas' son, Peter, and his wife, Willinda, manage the property—which is in the St. Helena AVA despite being located on Spring Mountain—with winemaker Mike Chellini, who arrived in 1972. Not until 2009 did they begin making red wine, a Cabernet Sauvignon–Merlot blend from young vines.

Until the 1970s, the wines of Louis M. Martini Winery were the choice of many Americans—good, honest, hearty Cabernet Sauvignons and Zinfandels that sold for a song (in 1968, Martini was among the first in California to bottle Merlot as a varietal wine). Founded in 1922 by Louis M. Martini, the winery was operated by his son, Louis P., from 1954 to 1977, and is now overseen by Louis P.'s son, Michael Martini. The winery struggled financially in the 1980s and 1990s, mostly because it was not large enough (150,000 cases per year) to gain traction with wholesalers, but not small enough to be viewed by consumers as special in the Napa Valley scheme of things.

Enter E. & J. Gallo, which in 2002 acquired Martini, renovated the cellars and visitor center in St. Helena, and put its massive sales force to work on the brand. The results have been impressive: wine quality is rising, packaging is smarter, and Mike Martini continues to oversee winemaking, maintaining the family connection. While Martini produces Napa Valley wines, its finest come from grapes grown in Sonoma County, including its own Monte Rosso Vineyard (meaning "red mountain," named for its crimson volcanic soils) in Sonoma Valley.

Duckhorn Vineyards is a Napa brand built on Merlot. After visiting Bordeaux's Pomerol region, Dan and Margaret Duckhorn founded Duckhorn Vineyards in 1976 and bottled their first Merlot in 1978. "We liked the softness, the seductiveness, the color, the fact that it went with a lot of different foods," Dan Duckhorn said. "It wasn't as bold as Cabernet and didn't need to age so long, and it had this velvety texture to it."

Consumers agreed, and Duckhorn became synonymous with Merlot. Sauvignon Blanc and Cabernet Sauvignon were added to the lineup, with grapes sourced from estate vineyards and purchased, including Merlot from John and Sloan Upton's Three Palms Vineyard, in Calistoga. The Uptons claim to have heard party laughter and the tinkling of glasses in the vineyard, once the site of a residence of San Francisco socialite Lillie Hitchcock Coit, who hosted spirited parties there. She died in 1929, and the house no longer exists, so if the Uptons indeed hear a party in progress, it must be Lillie's spirit that's raising the ruckus.

One of Napa Valley's greenest wineries is Hall Wines in St. Helena. Kathryn Hall, former U.S. ambassador to Austria, and her husband, Craig Hall, have earned LEED (Leadership in Energy and Environmental Design) Gold status for their winery, equipped with solar power panels, radiant floors, and other ecofriendly building elements. The grapes are farmed organically and tractors use biodiesel fuel.

For its philanthropical activities, Ehlers Estate is a wonder, as well as an outstanding producer of Sauvignon Blanc, Merlot, Chardonnay, and Cabernet Sauvignon. Frenchman Jean Leducq purchased the property in 1985, which included a stone winery built by Bernard Ehlers in 1886. In 1996, Leducq and his wife, Sylviane, started the Leducq Foundation, devoted to raising funds to research and combat cardiovascular disease.

Rutherford AVA

Oakville may be more glamorous (Screaming Eagle, Harlan Estate, and Robert Mondavi Winery), and Yountville claims George Yount as the first to plant wine grapes in Napa Valley, but Rutherford has, along with the St. Helena AVA, the richest, most layered history of all of Napa Valley's appellations. It also has enormous star power in movie producer/director Francis Ford Coppola (*The Godfather I, II,* and *III, Apocalypse Now*), who has, since his 1975 acquisition of the original Inglenook property, made a succession of offers that could not be refused in his intent to reunite the Inglenook name with the original vineyards and winery.

The AVA is named for Thomas Rutherford, who grew grapes and made wine here from 1850 to 1880. A Finnish sea captain and West Coast fur trader, Gustave Niebaum, who retired in 1880, established Inglenook Winery in Rutherford, constructing the massive stone winery that Coppola has obsessively restored.

John Daniel, Niebaum's great-nephew, became the Inglenook owner-winemaker in 1939. His string of great wines—including the 1941 Cabernet Sauvignon, considered one of the greatest wines ever produced in California—spurred others to come to Napa to make wine. Daniel, however, hit tough financial times and sold Inglenook in 1964. It soon came to be owned by drinks giant Heublein, and to make a very long story very short, Heublein sentenced the wines to imprisonment in jugs and boxes.

Coppola purchased part of the Inglenook estate in 1975, naming it Niebaum Coppola, because the Inglenook trademark was held by a series of corporations, including Constellation Brands and The Wine Group. In 2011, Coppola and his wife, Eleanor, were able to purchase the Inglenook trademark, and they restored the property name to Inglenook.

In advance of this trademark purchase, Coppola had hired winemaker Philippe Bascaules from Bordeaux first-growth Château Margaux to manage the estate. Coppola announced that Bascaules would be "invigorating the vineyards, planning a new state-of-the-art winemaking facility and focusing on what it would take to achieve his goal of restoring this property into America's greatest wine estate."

Georges de Latour, a French immigrant whose first Napa Valley business was the production of cream of tartar, purchased land adjacent to Inglenook in 1900 and called it Beaulieu, or "beautiful place" in French. De Latour imported rootstock from France, including St. George rootstock, which was resistant

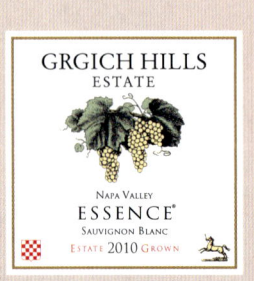

RUTHERFORD AVA SNAPSHOT

Vineyard acreage: 3,518

Most-planted varieties: **Cabernet Sauvignon, Sauvignon Blanc, Merlot**

Best variety: **Cabernet Sauvignon**

Wineries: 48

Trailblazers: **Beaulieu Vineyard, Inglenook**

Steady hands: **Beaulieu Vineyard, Cakebread Cellars, Flora Springs, Frog's Leap Winery, Hewett/Provenance Vineyards, Mumm Napa, Peju Province Winery, Quintessa, Round Pond Estate, Sequoia Grove, St. Supéry Vineyards & Winery**

Superstars: **Caymus Vineyards, Grgich Hills Estate, Rubicon/Inglenook, Staglin Family Vineyards**

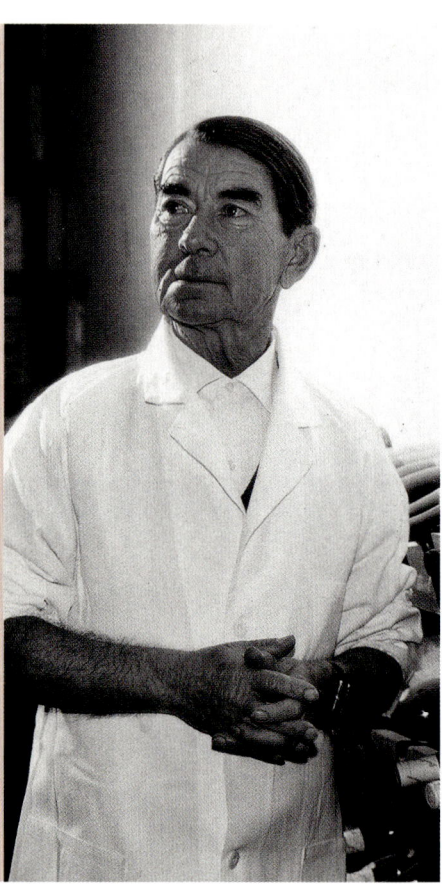

André Tchelistcheff
The Russian enologist arrived in Rutherford in 1938 to work for Beaulieu Vineyard; he remained for five decades and counseled many others in the winemaking craft around the world.

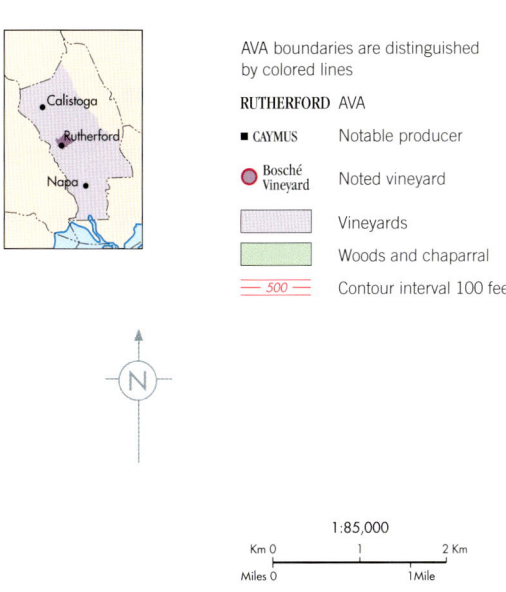
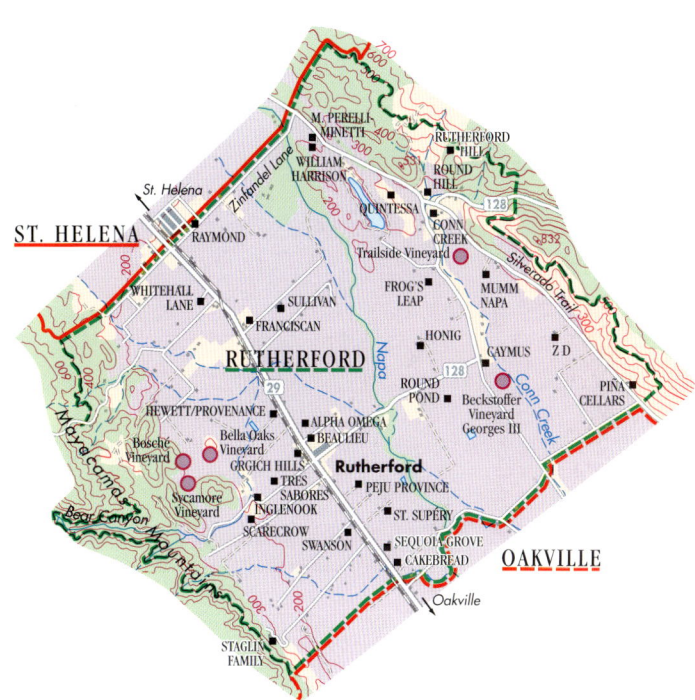

to the root-destroying insect phylloxera. He supplied grafted vines from his nursery for use in other California vineyards. De Latour outlasted Prohibition (1920–33) by producing sacramental wines for the Catholic Church, and he won a Grand Sweepstakes award for his Cabernet Sauvignon at the 1939 Golden Gate Exposition in San Francisco.

Before he died, de Latour hired Russian-born, French-trained André Tchelistcheff as the Beaulieu Vineyard enologist. The diminutive, bushy-browed, chain-smoking Tchelistcheff proved to be a master taster and intuitive winemaker, and he taught many a Californian the benefits of cold-temperature fermentations, controlled malolactic fermentations, choosing the best sites for particular grape varieties, and, most important of all, allowing the character of the vineyard to show itself in the wine.

Tchelistcheff, who died in 1994 at age ninety-two, consulted for dozens of wineries, but he is best known for leading Napa Valley and Rutherford wineries in their restart efforts after Prohibition. He is famous for saying, "It takes Rutherford dust to grow great Cabernet." Tasters have searched for a "dusty" character in Rutherford Cabernet Sauvignons ever since, but Tchelistcheff likely used the term not as a sensory descriptor, but rather as a statement on Rutherford as a high-quality Cab-growing region.

Beaulieu Vineyard, now owned by the multinational corporation Diageo, has a recent track record for producing a vast range of solid, quality wines. Its flagship, the Georges de Latour Cabernet Sauvignon, is one of Napa Valley's finest wines, with a separate winery facility devoted to its production.

"Famous Caymus" Vineyards has long been a favorite American producer of Cabernet Sauvignon. Charles "Charlie" Wagner founded the winery in 1972, with Randy Dunn becoming his winemaker. They created Caymus Special Selection Cabernet from the 1975 vintage, a wine that received lengthy barrel aging and had a toasty character that many adored. Dunn left in 1986 to start Dunn Vineyards, and Charlie's son, Chuck, took over the winemaking. The Special Selection and Caymus's lower-priced Napa Valley Cabernet Sauvignon are immensely drinkable on release, with soft textures and lush fruitiness.

While Chateau Montelena basked in the glory of having its Chardonnay chosen the best at the 1976 "Judgement of Paris,"

Wagner Family of Wine
Chuck Wagner (second from right) and his family, shown in their Caymus Vineyard in Rutherford, produce one of Napa Valley's most acclaimed Cabernet Sauvignons. Their Mer Soleil (Chardonnay) and Belle Glos (Pinot Noir) are made from out-of-Napa grapes by Wagner's sons, Charlie and Joe, respectively.

Grgich Hills harvest
Workers at Rutherford's Grgich Hills cut grape clusters from the vines and drop them into small plastic bins. They hand-carry their bins to larger containers mounted on trucks, and gently dump the grapes to ensure that the berries are not broken or crushed before they are delivered to the winery.

kudos also went to its then-winemaker, Miljenko "Mike" Grgich. Grgich, a Croatian immigrant who arrived in Napa Valley in 1958, had worked for Souverain, Christian Brothers, Beaulieu Vineyard, and Robert Mondavi Winery before joining Montelena in 1972. He had a five-year contract at Chateau Montelena, and when it expired, he founded his own winery, Grgich Hills Cellar, with Austin Hills and Hills's sister, Mary Lee Strebl, of Hills Bros. coffee fame.

Since then, Grigch Hills Fumé (Sauvignon) Blancs, Chardonnays, Merlots, Cabernet Sauvignons, and Zinfandels have been consistently good, and often excellent, made in a fruit-driven style with refreshing acidity. Grgich's daughter, Violet, and his winegrowing nephew, Ivo Jeramaz, oversee the day-to-day operations of what has grown into a 365-acre vineyard estate, farmed biodynamically since 2006.

Mumm Napa, the California sparkling-wine outpost established by Champagne producer Mumm in 1985, has its winery and tasting salon in Rutherford, though most of the grapes are grown in cooler regions, mainly Carneros. Mumm Napa's Brut Prestige and Brut Rosé are outstanding values; the premier bottling is DVX, named for founding winemaker Guy Devaux.

Garen and Shari Staglin of Staglin Family Vineyards not only produce highly sought-after Cabernet Sauvignons from their Rutherford estate, they host the annual Staglin Family Music Festival, which has raised more than $135 million for mental health research since 1994. The event features a tasting of wines rarely available to the public, an auction, and performances by the likes of Gladys Knight, Dionne Warwick, Dwight Yoakam, and Pat Benatar.

Heitz Wine Cellars is best known for its Martha's Vineyard Cabernet Sauvignons from Oakville, but its Bella Oaks and Trailside Vineyard Cabs from Rutherford are no slouches either. Following in their father Joe's footsteps, winery president Kathleen Heitz Myers and winemaker David Heitz continue to produce Martha's, Bella Oaks, and Trailside from their St. Helena winery, although the wines have not reached the "Heitz" they did in Joe's prime. Heitz Cellars, for better or worse, did not keep up with Napa winemaking trends and clung to Joe's old-fashioned ways. However, recent vintages have shown a plumper fruit personality, although with a lower-alcohol, leaner profile than most modern Napa Cabernet Sauvignons.

The AVA is moderately warm and receives some cooling from early-morning fog. The majority of vines are planted on benchlands—shoulders that separate the valley floor from mountain slopes—at elevations of approximately 500 feet. The western benches are cooler than the eastern, as they receive less late-afternoon sun. Western soils are gravelly-sandy and alluvial, with moderate fertility; eastern soils are volcanic, moderately deep, and more fertile, so growers there must limit both vine vigor and crop load in order to harvest concentrated grapes.

The AVA's winery/grapegrower association, the Rutherford Dust Society, is working with Napa County and the Napa County Resource Conservation District to restore the Napa River on the 4.5-mile stretch that runs through the appellation. To date, the Rutherford Dust Restoration Team (RDRT, or "our dirt") has opened fish passages, removed nonnative plants and replaced them with natives, and stabilized riverbanks to prevent erosion.

Oakville AVA

Oakville is in the heart of Napa Valley, and in the hearts of many California Cabernet Sauvignon admirers. Although vintners in other Napa Valley AVAs might protest, Oakville is a sweet spot for Cabernet, and Robert Mondavi certainly thought so when he built Robert Mondavi Winery there in 1966.

One hundred years earlier, the area was a water stop for a steam train owned by Samuel Brannan, which shuttled visitors between ferry boats that docked in Vallejo and Brannan's resorts in Calistoga. In 1868, Hamilton W. Crabb purchased 240 acres of land and established a vineyard and winery named To Kalon ("the highest beauty" in Greek). By 1880, Crabb owned some 430 acres.

When Robert Mondavi acquired his Oakville property in 1966, it included a section of Crabb's To Kalon Vineyard. Mondavi trademarked the vineyard name, even though he didn't own all of it; at the time, 89 acres were in the possession of Beaulieu Vineyard.

Enter Andy Beckstoffer, a native Virginian who was hired by drinks giant Heublein—owner at the time of Inglenook and Beaulieu Vineyard—to establish the Vinifera Development Corporation in 1970. In the manner of drinks giants, Heublein put the division up for sale in 1973, and Beckstoffer bought it. In 1978, he renamed the company Beckstoffer Vineyards, and today he owns 1,000 acres of some of Napa Valley's most prized vineyard land, as well as significant plantings in Lake and Mendocino counties.

Far Niente Chardonnay room
Far Niente stores red wines, which slowly mature under the naturally cool conditions, in excavated caves. As is done at many Napa Valley wineries, the Chardonnay fermentation takes place in a separate room, where temperatures are precisely controlled.

In 2002–2003, Beckstoffer, owner of Beaulieu's portion of To Kalon, and Robert Mondavi Winery, owner of 250 acres of To Kalon, went through various legal wranglings before reaching a compromise: Beckstoffer could use the name To Kalon for wines produced from his property and clients who purchased grapes could use the name as long as they attached 'Beckstoffer' to the vineyard name. Robert Mondavi Winery could use To Kalon for

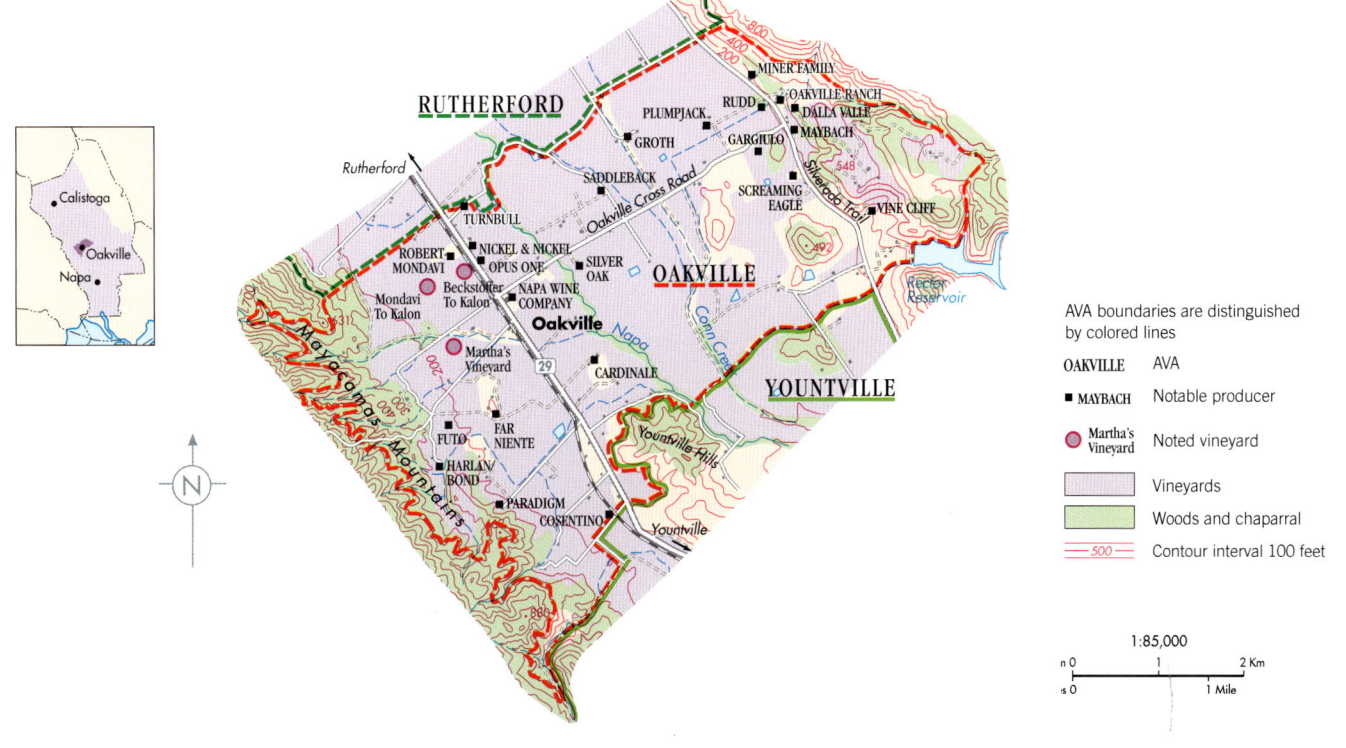

Robert Mondavi Winery
Robert Mondavi founded his namesake winery in 1966, employing Cliff May to design the facility to reflect the missions of early California winemaking history.

wines made from grapes grown on its property, primarily Cabernet Sauvignon and I Block Fumé Blanc.

In the background was UC Davis, the university that has trained hundreds, if not thousands, of winemakers, grape growers, and other wine industry professionals. It owns a small piece of To Kalon, its 40-acre Oakville Experimental Vineyard adjacent to Robert Mondavi Winery. The vineyard supplies the enology and viticulture department with Cabernet Sauvignon, Merlot, Petite Sirah, Syrah, and Zinfandel grapes and hosts viticultural trials, the results of which are shared with the industry. The Oakville site is also home to the Zinfandel Heritage Vineyard, where old-vine Zin cuttings from throughout California are maintained in a vinous museum.

With some exceptions, most of the original To Kalon vines have been replanted, thanks to the destruction caused by phylloxera infestations and the simple march of time. Humans run out of life, and so do grapevines.

The To Kalon trademark negotiations may have been heated, but the Oakville AVA is only moderately warm, with temperatures commonly in the low 90s in high summer—gentler than those in Calistoga and St. Helena. And the region is

OAKVILLE AVA SNAPSHOT

Vineyard acreage: **4,700**

Most-planted varieties: **Cabernet Sauvignon, Merlot, Sauvignon Blanc, Cabernet Franc, Chardonnay**

Best variety: **Cabernet Sauvignon**

Wineries: **40**

Trailblazers: **Robert Mondavi Winery, To Kalon Vineyard**

Steady hands: **Flora Springs Winery, Gargiulo Vineyards, Groth Vineyards & Winery, Miner Family Vineyards, Nickel & Nickel, Oakville Ranch Vineyards, PlumpJack Winery, Rudd Estate, Swanson Vineyards & Winery**

Superstars: **Dalla Valle Vineyards, Harlan Estate/BOND, Opus One, Far Niente, Robert Mondavi Winery, Screaming Eagle Winery and Vineyards**

positively affected by nighttime and early-morning fog, which helps to maintain acidity levels in the grapes. Sedimentary, gravelly, and alluvial-loam soils dominate the western side of the AVA, with volcanic matter and heavier soils on the eastern side. Some may disparage valley-floor vineyards as being too fertile and the wines made from them as lacking complexity and structure, but Oakville, whose elevation ranges from 75 to 500 feet, proves otherwise.

Far Niente is a textbook example. Its estate Chardonnays and Cabernet Sauvignons, made in a gloriously restored pre-Prohibition stone winery, are on the rich, sumptuous side, yet have a tannic backbone and natural acidity not always found in low-elevation wines. Oklahoma natives Gil and Beth Nickel purchased Far Niente in 1979 and began restoring the abandoned winery and vineyards. In 1989, they added a second label, Dolce, for the production of unctuous dessert wines. And when single-vineyard wines became popular in the 1990s, the Nickels and their partners developed the Nickel & Nickel winery, also in Oakville, for the production of Cabernet Sauvignons, Merlots, Zinfandels, Syrahs, and Chardonnays from single sites (including a few in Sonoma County).

In 2008, Far Niente became the first winery to be a 100-percent net-zero user of electricity by going solar in an interesting way. Instead of installing solar panels on valuable vineyard ground, Far Niente placed them on its irrigation pond, originating the term *flotovoltaic*—floating photovoltaic panels.

Dalla Valle Vineyards is an Oakville leading light, founded by Gustave Dalla Valle in 1986 and now managed by his widow, Naoko. They planted 25 acres of Cabernet Sauvignon and Cabernet Franc on an eastern slope of the Oakville AVA, above the Silverado Trail, and Dalla Valle's Maya blend is highly sought after.

Yet nothing in Oakville compares to the current-day successes of Screaming Eagle Winery and Vineyards and Harlan Estate. These most cultish of Napa Valley wines deserve their place of prominence not only for the demand consumers have created for their wines, but also, and more important, for the quality in the bottles. Bill Harlan is the closest thing the Napa Valley has to a squire. His name is best known to wine consumers for his eponymous wine, made (and sold, or, rather, allocated) with more attention to detail than even a Bordeaux first-growth in a lavishly equipped estate on the western hills of the appellation. But he is also responsible for the glamorous Meadowood resort, scene of the annual Auction Napa Valley; he dreamt up Napa Valley Reserve, a sort of wine club for plutocrats; and he produces BOND, a series of wines from individual locations around the valley. All of these wines have in their time taken Napa Valley Cab's signature richness and velvety texture to the limit, but they continue to evolve, so minutely are they, and the techniques responsible for them, analyzed.

The arrestingly named Screaming Eagle, grown on a bowl of much lower land just off the Silverado Trail on the eastern edge of the valley floor, has had a more checkered history. St. Helena realtor Jean Phillips owned and lived on a substantial vineyard here, selling most of the grapes. But she decided to develop her own label for the cream of the crop, with help from her winemaker friend Heidi Peterson Barrett. The wine established such a following at the annual auction that in 2000 one generous collector paid half a million dollars for a 6-liter bottle of its debut vintage, 1992. Volumes were always low, which helped keep prices high and meant that it has been sold strictly on allocation, generally just three bottles per name on the all-important mailing list. But production recently has been shrunk by the incursion of fanleaf virus from a neighboring vineyard. Rather than oversee the massive replanting program herself, Phillips sold the property, with its 54 acres of vineyard, to sports entrepreneur Stan Kroenke, who is underwriting a whole new winery and vineyard design. There have been considerable personnel changes as well, so it will be interesting to see how the team manages to retain the particularly subtle character of the best wines the red volcanic soils here can produce.

Far Niente solar panels
As part of its "green" efforts, Far Niente installed solar panels on its irrigation pond.

ROBERT MONDAVI

No single person did more to promote wine—particularly California wine—than the late Robert Mondavi.

In addition to founding the nation's most iconic winery, the Spanish mission–styled Robert Mondavi Winery in Oakville, Mondavi and his sons, Michael and Tim, pioneered cutting-edge winemaking techniques, including low-temperature fermentations, stainless steel tanks, and aging wine in French oak barrels, all widely used today. He shared the results of his enological and viticultural research with other winemakers, and he quickly became the global ambassador for California and Napa Valley wine, a constant and energetic promoter who was always eager to compare his wines, side by side, to the greats of Europe.

Opus One winery, across Highway 29 from Robert Mondavi Winery, is the result of Robert's partnership with Bordeaux's Baron Philippe de Rothschild of first-growth Château Mouton-Rothschild. They joined forces in 1979 to produce a proprietary Cabernet Sauvignon–blend wine, made from Napa Valley grapes by Mondavi winemaker Tim Mondavi and Château Mouton-Rothschild winemaker Lucien Sionneau. Despite its initial cachet, Opus One took time to find its footing, as the grapes were first sourced from Mondavi vineyards undergoing post-phylloxera replanting. The wine is now consistently excellent, with reliable fruit sourcing.

Also in 1979, Mondavi purchased a winemaking cooperative near Lodi, named it Woodbridge, and began producing value-priced wines that suited consumers who couldn't afford the far more expensive wines made at the Oakville mother ship. He also partnered with Italy's Frescobaldi family and Eduardo Chadwick of Viña Errázuriz of Chile in joint ventures. In his final years, Robert; his wife, Margrit; winemaker son Tim; and daughter Marcia Mondavi Borger launched Continuum, a Cabernet Sauvignon–based wine that, as its name suggests, continues to be family-made today.

Mondavi, who died in 2008 at age ninety-four, championed the enjoyment of wine with meals and the importance of music and art in life, and he contributed generously to programs that supported both. A visit to Robert Mondavi Winery became de rigueur thanks to its tours,

To Kalon Cellar
Mondavi's To Kalon Cellar features gravity-flow movement of grapes, juice, and wine and 11-foot-tall oak tanks for fermentation of red wines.

educational programs, concerts, and Great Chefs series, all of which set the bar high for Napa Valley marketing and hospitality.

At time of his death, Mondavi was chairman emeritus of the Robert Mondavi Corporation. In order to expand his business, Robert and his family had taken the company public in 1993; in 2004, it was sold to multinational drinks company Constellation Brands, which continues to operate the winery and has maintained the Opus One joint venture with Baron Philippe's daughter Philippine.

After Mondavi's death, many asked, "Who will be the next Robert Mondavi?" There likely won't be another individual in California with Mondavi's combination of passion, energy, drive, ego, international contacts, spirit of inclusiveness, and willingness to promote twenty-four hours a day, seven days a week. But California might not need another Mondavi, given the growth of the industry since he began his campaign, and the consolidation of brands by major companies. Still, it's exciting to consider who might be the next Bob Mondavi in another state, someone ready and willing to elevate an emerging wine region to lofty heights and set it on the world stage.

Stags Leap District AVA

In Napa Valley, the word *stag* has caused confusion for consumers and instigated litigation between two vintners. Even locals get their tongues twisted when it comes to talking about wineries and AVAs with *stags* and *leap* in their names.

The native Wappo tribe told of a stag evading hunters by leaping magnificently over a huge chasm in the steep cliffs that form the region's eastern boundary. The area came to be known as the Stags Leap Palisades, which overlook the Silverado Trail.

In the early 1970s, both Warren Winiarski and Carl Doumani launched wineries at the base of the Palisades, each using "Stag" and "Leap" in their branding—Winiarski's Stag's Leap Wine Cellars and Doumani's Stag's Leap Winery. Winiarski sued, seeking to force Doumani to change the name of his winery. Doumani countersued, and they went to court. In 1986, the State Supreme Court ruled that the two men could keep their winery names, but with Doumani moving his apostrophe to make it Stags' Leap. The vintners later became friends and jointly released a 1985 Cabernet Sauvignon named Accord to show they'd kissed and made up.

The Stags Leap District AVA was approved in 1989, sans apostrophe—and sans support from Winiarski and Doumani, who wanted to protect their hard-won names (both wineries have since joined the Stags Leap Winegrowers association). The Stags Leap District, adjacent to the eastern edge of the Yountville AVA, is Napa Valley's smallest appellation, at 1,700 acres, with just half of those planted to wine grapes. This is

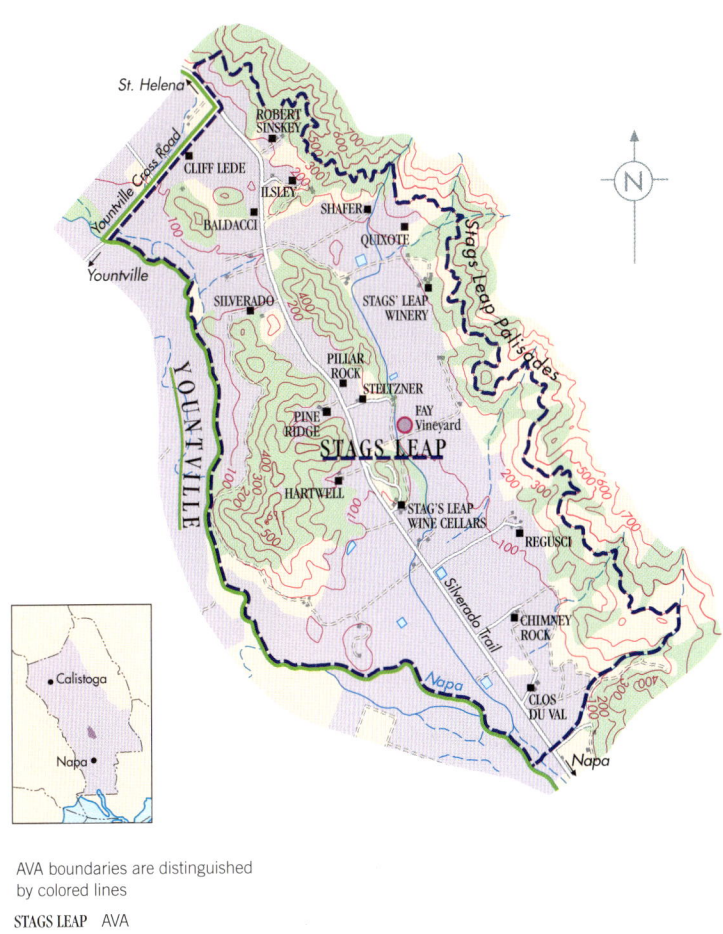

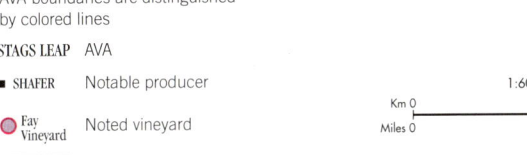

STAGS LEAP DISTRICT AVA SNAPSHOT

Vineyard acreage: **850**

Most-planted varieties: **Cabernet Sauvignon, Merlot, Sauvignon Blanc**

Best varieties: **Cabernet Sauvignon, Merlot**

Wineries: **20**

Trailblazer: **Stag's Leap Wine Cellars**

Steady hands: **Chimney Rock, Cliff Lede, Clos du Val, Hartwell Vineyards, Ilsley Vineyards, Pine Ridge Vineyards, Quixote, Robert Sinskey Vineyards, Silverado Vineyards**

Superstars: **Shafer Vineyards, Stag's Leap Wine Cellars, Stags' Leap Winery**

Stag's Leap Wine Cellars FAY vineyard
Warren Winiarski chose what is now the Stags Leap District as the home for his Stag's Leap Wine Cellars based in part on the temperature-moderating benefits of the Palisades rock formation that towers above the vines.

overwhelmingly red-wine country, producing "Goldilocks" Cabernet Sauvignons and Merlots that are just right, with tannins that aren't too hard, acidities and structures that aren't too soft, and blackberry fruit character that is neither warmly ripe nor coolly herbaceous. The St.-Julien of Napa Valley, perhaps?

Soils in Stags Leap District are primarily of eroded volcanic matter on the eastern elevations of the Vaca Mountains, and old Napa River sediments that are gravelly blends of clay and loam elsewhere. The Palisades reflect daytime heat onto the vineyards below, yet by late afternoon, they also help funnel brisk marine air flowing north from San Pablo Bay through the district. This nightly cooling allows the grapes to maintain their natural acidity—a signature of Stags Leap District Cabernet Sauvignon and Merlot.

Doumani eventually sold the Stags' Leap Winery brand (now owned by Treasury Estates) and relaunched with the Petite Sirah–driven Quixote brand, although he labels it as Petite Syrah. He retained the wacky winery building designed by Viennese architect Friedenreich Hundertwasser, with its onion dome covered in gold leaf, embedded glass tiles, painted columns, and uneven floors.

The inimitable Winiarski's first commercial vintage, 1973, of Stag's Leap Wine Cellars Cabernet Sauvignon stunningly finished first in the 1976 "Judgement of Paris" tasting, and, with Chateau Montelena's Chardonnay, put California wines in the international spotlight. An academic from Chicago, Winiarski—his name means "son of winemaker" in Polish—made good on his moniker by moving to Napa Valley in 1970 with his family. Impressed with vineyard owner Nathan Fay's homemade Cabernet, Winiarski purchased property next door and began planting Stag's Leap Vineyard, later shortened to S.L.V.

In 1986, he acquired Fay's property and added Stag's Leap Wine Cellars FAY Cabernet Sauvignon to the lineup. Cask 23 is a proprietary red that is now a blend of grapes from FAY and S.L.V. Winiarski is famous for describing his red wines, which include Merlot, as "an iron fist in a velvet glove" and for touting the effects of fire (soils from ancient volcanic eruptions) and water (alluvial soils) on the balance and elegance of his wines and their ability to mature gracefully over time. In 2007, a few months shy of his eightieth birthday, Winiarski and his family sold the winery to the partnership of Ste. Michelle Wine Estates of Washington State and famed Tuscan vintner Piero Antinori. While the new owners have upgraded the winery with the latest equipment, the Stag's Leap wine style remains one of restraint and finesse.

Bernard Portet, who worked with his father at Château Lafite in Bordeaux, came to California to join John Goelet in producing Bordeaux-like Cabernet Sauvignons at Clos du Val. Their first vintage, 1972, was among the wines chosen for the "Judgment of Paris" tasting, and since then, their leaner, more herbal style has largely continued. Portet retired from Clos

Ilsley Vineyard
The Ilsley family has grown Cabernet Sauvignon for Robert Mondavi Winery and other Napa Valley producers for fifty years. In 1999, the Ilsleys began using a portion of their Stags Leap District grapes for their own wine brand, Ilsley Vineyards.

du Val in 2010, leaving things to COO/chief winemaker John Clews, who also produces Chardonnay, Merlot, Pinot Noir, and Ariadne, a Semillion–Sauvignon Blanc blend. But Portet missed winemaking, and in 2011, he established Polaris Wines in Napa Valley with Don Chase.

Founded in 1972 as a grape grower, and in 1978 as a wine producer, Shafer Vineyards is one of California's most beloved wine brands. Its Cabernet Sauvignons, Merlots, Carneros-grown Chardonnays, and field blend of Syrah with Petite Sirah called Relentless are ripe, intense, and not shy on alcohol, but they have great staying power in the cellar. Fans are legion, although there are detractors—most of them in the Old World.

John Shafer left the publishing industry in Chicago to purchase a 1920s-era vineyard in what would become the Stags Leap District in 1972 and immediately replanted its steep slopes. In 1983, his son, Doug, a UC Davis enology and viticulture graduate, became the winemaker. Today Doug's assistant, Elias Fernandez, is the winemaker; Doug is the president; and John is the proud papa who remains closely connected to the business.

The Hillside Select Cabernet Sauvignon is Shafer's flagship: 100 percent Cabernet Sauvignon, aged 32 months in new French oak barrels, typically weighing in at 15.5 percent alcohol. The grapes are so intensely flavored and their tannins so firm that they can handle new oak, and the wines are balanced so remarkably that despite their potency, they don't taste "hot."

Yountville AVA

George Yount planted the first commercial vinifera vineyard in Napa Valley in 1836, on the former Spanish land grant Rancho Caymus, near what would become the town of Yountville. The pancake-flat AVA (20 to 200 feet in elevation) has a patchwork of soil types dominated by gravelly silt loams and alluvial sediments, and a coolish climate similar to that of Carneros, with early-morning and late-afternoon fog and breezes from San Pablo Bay that temper midsummer temperatures in the 90s.

The Champagne house Moët & Chandon was the first to recognize that high-quality sparkling wines could be produced in the United States by combining the winemaking techniques of Champagne with ripe, vibrant Napa Valley grapes. In 1973, Moët-Hennessy (a partnership formed in 1971 between Moët & Chandon and Cognac producer Hennessy) found suitable vineyard land on Mount Veeder, in Carneros, and in the Yountville location that is home to their Domaine Chandon winery.

The first sparkler was released in 1976, and in 1977, a visitor center opened that would later include an upscale restaurant, now named Étoile. Yountville became a tourist destination with the opening of Chandon, where guests could learn how sparkling wine is produced and upgrade their wine-drinking habits from the simple bulk-process bubblies and sweet Cold Duck widely available at the time. Over time, Yountville developed into Napa Valley's "restaurant row," with a dozen top-notch eateries, including The French Laundry, Mustards Grill, Bottega, Bouchon, Bistro Jeanty, Ad Hoc, and Redd.

Domaine Chandon also broke ground on another front: the hiring of a female winemaker, Dawnine Dyer, who in twenty-four years rose from assistant winemaker to vice president of winemaking. Her Chandon career began in 1976 and ended in 2000, when she left to join her husband, Bill Dyer, at Dyer Vineyard on Diamond Mountain. That a Champagne house would entrust its wines to a woman was so, well, un-French, but it spoke volumes about Domaine Chandon's determination to break the mold. Its lower-tier bubblies are expertly made, if unexciting, and the top-of-the-line Étoile Brut is elegant and precise, gaining depth and complexity with aging.

Christian Moueix didn't arrive in Yountville until 1981, by which time the locals had already become accustomed to having French folks in the neighborhood. On a visit to Napa Valley, Moueix, whose family owns or runs many Bordeaux properties, including the prestigious Château Pétrus in Pomerol, met Robin Lail and Marcia Smith, daughters of the late John Daniel Jr. Daniel, the former owner of Inglenook

Dominus Estate
The architecture of Christian Moueix's winery includes gabion walls—steel cages filled with basalt stones quarried from nearby American Canyon.

Domaine Chandon
Grapes grown at its Yountville estate contribute to the wines of Domaine Chandon. It was the first French-owned sparkling wine producer in the United States, established in 1973 by Moët & Chandon.

YOUNTVILLE AVA SNAPSHOT

Vineyard acreage: 4,000

Most-planted varieties: **Cabernet Sauvignon, Merlot, Cabernet Franc**

Best variety: **Cabernet Sauvignon**

Wineries: 15

Trailblazer: **Domaine Chandon**

Steady hands: **Blackbird Vineyards, Domaine Chandon, Goosecross Cellars, Hill Family Estate, Jessup Cellars, Keever Vineyards, Lail Vineyards**

Superstars: **Dominus, Kapcsandy Family Winery**

Winery, had kept the 140-acre Napanook Vineyard in Yountville after Inglenook was sold in 1964.

Lail and Smith welcomed Moueix, who had studied at UC Davis, into their fold in 1982, calling their partnership the John Daniel Society. They named their wine Dominus—"god" in Latin. Moueix purchased Napanook from the sisters in 1985 and spent the next twenty years understanding the vineyard, replanting aging vines, determining the best blocks (used for Dominus), and allocating grapes from younger vines to the Napanook label.

The Dominus winery, built in 1997, was designed by Swiss architects Jacques Herzog and Pierre de Meuron. Its walls are constructed of galvanized cages, called gabions, that are filled with basaltic rocks quarried in American Canyon in southern Napa County. The small gaps between the rocks allow light and air to enter the winery, making it a breathing building that stays cool in summer.

In the last decade, the Cabernet Sauvignon–dominant Dominus wines have had unusually muscular tannins that plead for ten years of bottle age before they start to round out, though the center core of juicy black fruit and graphitelike minerality tempts some to uncork Dominus upon release.

Lou Kapcsandy, a former Seattle commercial developer, purchased the State Lane Vineyard in Yountville in 2000, a vital cog in Beringer Vineyards' single-vineyard and Private Reserve Cabernet Sauvignon programs. With advice from Helen Turley and her viticulturist husband, John Wetlaufer, Kapcsandy replanted the vineyard to Cabernet Sauvignon, Merlot, and Cabernet Franc; the winery was completed in 2005.

Turley and Rob Lawson of Napa Wine Company produced the first few vintages. Since 2007, Denis Malbec, formerly of Bordeaux first-growth Château Latour, has made the wines, and they are supremely balanced and layered, straddling the line between European elegance and California richness.

Lou Kapcsandy
The Yountville vintner's wines, made by former Chateau Latour cellarmaster Denis Malbec, are rich yet beautifully balanced.

Oak Knoll District of Napa Valley AVA

Although there are only a dozen wineries in the Oak Knoll AVA, the region is a source of grapes for producers throughout Napa Valley. Sandwiched between Yountville and the city of Napa, and greatly influenced by breezes and fog from San Pablo Bay, Oak Knoll is an all-things-to-all-people AVA, with climatic conditions warm enough to ripen Cabernet Sauvignon, but cool enough to grow Chardonnay and Pinot Noir. Winemakers whose estates are in warm areas of Napa Valley might blend in some higher-acid Oak Knoll juice to add more refreshment to their wines; those in colder regions can get more richness and softer tannins with the addition of Oak Knoll fruit.

Temperatures are commonly in the mid-90s in high summer, but night and early-morning fog helps to keep acidity levels up and the grapes refreshed. Most vineyards are on the valley floor, with some reaching 500 feet in elevation. Sedimentary, gravelly alluvial loam soils prevail on the western side of the AVA; the east has heavier, more volcanic composition.

Listed on the National Register of Historic Places, Trefethen Family Vineyards was founded in 1968 by the late Eugene and Catherine Trefethen, whose son John and daughter-in-law Janet now run the business. Eugene and Catherine purchased six small farms and a nineteenth-century "ghost" winery in what is now the Oak Knoll District of Napa Valley AVA. The abandoned winery, originally named Eshcol, was built in 1886 by Captain Hamden McIntyre, a civil engineer brought to Napa Valley by Gustave Niebaum of Inglenook. McIntyre also designed Inglenook, Far Niente, and Greystone wineries. Eshcol survived Prohibition by producing sacramental wine, but went dormant in 1940. The Trefethens painstakingly restored the winery, keeping its gravity-flow design in place.

Trefethen's reserve Cabernet Sauvignons are most noteworthy, and it is one of the handful of Napa Valley wineries to produce Riesling—it's crisp and dry, with solid structure.

The Corley family of Monticello Vineyards & Winery has grown grapes and produced wine since Jay Corley arrived in Napa from Southern California in 1969. His sons, Stephen, Chris, and Kevin, manage the winery and farm the vineyards, taking advantage of the cool conditions in the Oak Knoll AVA for Chardonnay, Pinot Noir, Syrah, Merlot, and Cabernet Franc, and the warmer Yountville, Rutherford, and St. Helena AVAs for Cabernet Sauvignon.

Its starting wine tier is the Monticello Vineyards line. The Corley and Corley Reserves line offer the best wines, and Chardonnay and Cabernet Sauvignon are the strengths. The family's roots are in Virginia, so the winery name was a natural, underlined by various street names and parks referencing Thomas Jefferson. The architecture of its Jefferson House tasting room was influenced by Jefferson's Monticello home (see p. 230-31).

Robert Biale Vineyards has grown and produced Zinfandel in the Oak Knoll region since 1937. Bob Biale, his father, Aldo, and his brothers grew the grapes, which were sold to others until the family created its own label. Its Black Chicken and Aldo's Vineyard Zinfandels are favored by those who love ripe, fleshy wines.

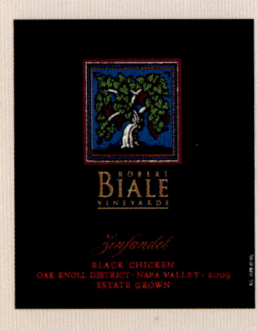

OAK KNOLL DISTRICT OF NAPA VALLEY AVA SNAPSHOT

Vineyard acreage: 3,500

Most-planted varieties: **Merlot, Chardonnay, Cabernet Sauvignon, Pinot Noir**

Best variety: **Cabernet Sauvignon**

Wineries: **12**

Trailblazer: **Trefethen Family Vineyards**

Steady hands: **Monticello Vineyards & Winery, Robert Biale Vineyards, Trefethen Family Vineyards**

Trefethen Vineyards
The plan of the Oak Knoll District vineyard allows wildlife to move freely about the property; this coyote ventured deep into the vineyard.

Atlas Peak AVA

It has taken the power of Atlas—or dynamite—to blast out plantable vineyard locations in the Atlas Peak AVA, approved in 1992. The region is so isolated in the Vaca Mountain Range that just two roads service the 11,400-acre appellation: Soda Canyon Road, off the Silverado Trail, and Atlas Peak Road, off Hardman Lane. Dynamite helped in the creation of these thoroughfares too.

Although grapes are grown and wines are made in the AVA, the location is not conducive to tourist traffic, so several producers have tasting rooms in Napa or St. Helena. A few do host visitors by appointment only, but don't expect a meal nearby; it's a twenty-minute drive back to town.

Cabernet Sauvignon dominates Atlas Peak, with much smaller amounts of Merlot, Cabernet Franc, Petit Verdot, Zinfandel, Syrah, and Chardonnay. Atlas Peak itself is 2,671 feet high, and vineyards are planted from 700 feet to nearly its summit. Winters are wet, summers dry and warm, and irrigation is necessary during the growing season. Most vines are planted above the fog line, so they soak up lots of summer and early-fall sunshine, then are refreshed by nighttime mountain breezes.

The soils are volcanic in origin, iron-rich and red in color, and tend to be shallow and well drained. To say Atlas Peak is rocky is an understatement: More than one billion pounds of rock were dynamited and removed from Stagecoach Vineyard to make room for vines. The property gets its Wild West look from groupings of boulders that might have given Wells Fargo stagecoach robber Black Bart (Charles Boles) his cover in the late 1800s.

Antinori daughters
Piero Antinori's daughters, Albiera, Alessia, and Allegra (left to right), have been groomed to take over the Antinori business, including Antica Napa Valley on Atlas Peak.

Stagecoach Vineyard is owned by retired internist Dr. Jan Krupp. It's a massive property, 1,200 acres, and covers portions of the Atlas Peak AVA and Pritchard Hill to the northwest. Some 600 acres are planted to fifteen varieties, at elevations of between 1,200 and 1,750 feet, and are divided into 175 separate blocks. Cabernet Sauvignon comprises more than half of the plantings, with a jaw-dropping twenty-two Cab clones matched to specific soil types, soil depth, mesoclimates, and exposures. Sixty wineries purchase Stagecoach fruit, and Krupp produces his own wine under the Krupp Brothers and Krupp Estate labels.

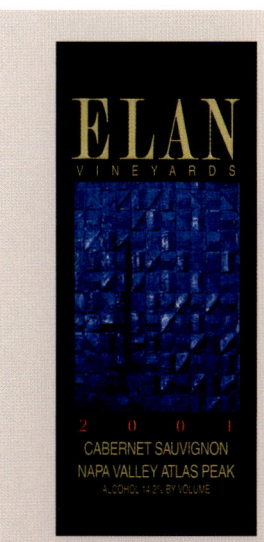

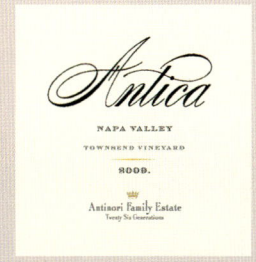

ATLAS PEAK AVA SNAPSHOT
Vineyard acres: **1,500**
Most-planted varieties: **Cabernet Sauvignon, other reds**
Best variety: **Cabernet Sauvignon**
Wineries: **7**
Steady Hands: **Astrale e Terra, Bialla Vineyards, Elan Vineyards, Vin Roc Wine Caves**
Superstars: **Antica Napa Valley, Stagecoach Vineyards**

Bialla Vineyards
Behind the redwood doors is a naturally cooled wine-aging cave, dug into an Atlas Peak hillside. Vito and Linda Bialla sold their property in mid-2012 to a Chinese businessman, who is expected to ship the winery's Cabernet Sauvignons to China.

An Italian, however, is making Atlas Peak's most exciting wines, a fellow by the name of Piero Antinori. Make that Marchese Antinori, a title conferred to Italians who are of higher status than a count, but just a notch below prince. His family has produced wine in Italy for twenty-six generations, and this internationally respected vintner is involved in two Napa Valley wineries: Atlas Peak Winery and Stag's Leap Wine Cellars (the latter in partnership with Ste. Michelle Wine Estates in Washington State). In the early 1980s, Antinori began developing Atlas Peak Vineyards on a 1,200-acre site. By 1993, his partners had lost interest, and Antinori became sole owner of the land, which by then had approximately 450 acres of vines, 100 of them Sangiovese. Allied Lyons (which became Allied Domecq) acquired the Atlas Peak brand and began producing wines from the estate under a fifteen-year lease agreement with Antinori.

The brand bounced around from owner to owner as though it were trapped in a pinball machine. In 2008, the lease expired, and Antinori moved back in. Most of the Sangiovese had been grafted over to Cabernet Sauvignon (U.S. consumers never truly embraced the Tuscan Chianti–style wine), so Antinori began refining the vineyard, renaming it Antica—a contraction of Antinori and California—Napa Valley. Antica also means "ancient" in Italian, which is appropriate, since ancestor Giovanni di Piero Antinori joined the Florentine Guild of Winemakers in 1385.

Antica's focus is Cabernet Sauvignon, and its flagship Cab is pure and extraordinarily sophisticated for a mountain-grown wine. It is also one of Napa Valley's best buys, selling for $55 per bottle when some wines costing twice as much aren't nearly as good or interesting. Antica also has a remarkably fresh and minerally Chardonnay—among Napa Valley's best of that variety.

Jayson Pahlmeyer's Waters Ranch is on Atlas Peak, supplying his Pahlmeyer brand with the Cabernet Sauvignon, Merlot, Cabernet Franc, Petit Verdot, and Malbec grapes used in his Merlot and proprietary red wines.

Mount Veeder AVA

From their vineyard on Mount Veeder, Stephen Lagier and Carole Meredith can see San Francisco Bay and feel its breezes in the early evening. Mount Veeder is Napa Valley's coolest mountain AVA, and that is a major reason why Lagier, a former Robert Mondavi Winery winemaker, and Meredith, a now-retired UC Davis enology and viticulture professor who led the research teams that used DNA profiling to untangle the origins of the grape varieties Cabernet Sauvignon, Chardonnay, Syrah, and Zinfandel, planted their Lagier Meredith Vineyard there.

Going against type, the couple planted not Cabernet Sauvignon, but Syrah, a wine they wanted to drink, with a vineyard site that afforded a cool climate, shallow sandstone soils, a 1,300-foot elevation, and east-facing exposures. They planted the first vines on this rugged, remote location in 1994 and released their first commercial Syrah in 2000.

Fewer than 5 acres on the 84-acre property are given over to vines; the rest remains in its natural state—redwoods, Douglas firs, black oaks, madrones, and bay laurels. The closest neighbors are deer, raccoons, skunks, coyotes, and bobcats. The Syrahs Lagier and Meredith produce from this hard-yard vineyard are full-bodied, floral, meaty, and spicy.

Guitarist/Singer Boz Scaggs also planted Syrah and other Rhône Valley grapes on his Mount Veeder property, though without much forethought. He and his wife, Dominique, were planting fruit trees one day when they were offered Syrah vines left over from another vineyard. Today their Scaggs Vineyard wines include a rosé of Syrah as well as Montage, a Mourvèdre-Grenache-Syrah blend made by Ken Bernards of Ancien Wines.

However, Cabernet Sauvignon is the most-planted grape, with 64 percent of the variety plantings on Mount Veeder, and here it produces a wine that can be every bit as good as any first-growth Bordeaux. Bob and Elinor Travers have owned Mayacamas Vineyards since 1968, and Bob is still the winemaker, producing Cabernet Sauvignons that are as dramatic as the surroundings. The wines are beautifully balanced, with layers of complexity—red fruits, cedar, forest floor, and tobacco—and have great cellaring potential. Steven Spurrier placed the 1971 Mayacamas in his 1976 "Judgment of Paris" tasting, and while it finished ninth out of ten, it should be noted that Bob Travers hesitated before giving Spurrier the unreleased 1971, saying it hadn't had enough time in bottle. (It was tied for third in the rerun of the 1976 tasting in London in 2006.)

The 1889 stone winery is perched on the edge of a dormant volcano crater near the top of Mount Veeder, at approximately 2,400 feet. Fifty-two acres of vines are planted, including Chardonnay, Merlot, and Sauvignon Blanc. Jack and Mary Taylor, the winery's third set of owners, bought the property in 1941 and restored it, turning an old stone distillery into their home. They called the estate Mayacamas Vineyards, a name the Travers have continued to burnish during their stewardship.

The appellation, west of the cities of Napa and Yountville, is named for a German Presbyterian minister, Peter Veeder, who lived in Napa during the Civil War era. He enjoyed hiking on the mountain—perhaps to get closer to God or because the area reminded him of home, with its redwood and fir trees.

In 1973, Arlene and Michael Bernstein planted the first Petit Verdot in Napa Valley and shared cuttings with other growers. Their 1977 Mount Veeder Winery Cabernet Sauvignon was California's first wine composed of all five red Bordeaux varieties, though it didn't say so on the label.

At 15,000 acres, Mount Veeder is the largest AVA within Napa Valley, but its dense forestation and steep, rocky hillsides limit vineyards to just 1.3 percent of Napa Valley's total yearly tonnage. Most vineyards are planted above the fog line, at 600 to 2,100 feet

Dave Guffy
The Hess Collection director of winemaking uses a pneumatic punch-down system to keep the wine and skins mixed during red-grape fermentations.

Carole Meredith and Stephen Lagier
While at University of California at Davis, Carole Meredith unraveled the genealogy of Cabernet Sauvignon. But when she and Steve Lagier planted their Mount Veder vineyard they chose Syrah, not Cabernet. It's one of Napa Valley's finest.

MOUNT VEEDER AVA SNAPSHOT

Vineyard acreage: **1,000**

Most-planted varieties: **Cabernet Sauvignon, Malbec, Merlot, Syrah**

Best varieties: **Cabernet Sauvignon, Syrah**

Wineries: **22**

Trailblazer: **Hess Collection**

Steady hands: **Hess Collection, Lokoya, Mount Veeder Vineyards, Scaggs Vineyard, Sky Vineyard**

Superstars: **Lagier Meredith, Mayacamas Vineyards**

Mayacamas Vineyards
Since 1968, Bob Travers has made Cabernet Sauvignon, Merlot, Chardonnay, and Sauvignon Blanc in this stone winery, built atop Mount Veeder in 1889.

above sea level, where they enjoy cooling breezes from San Pablo Bay. This translates to warmer nights and cooler days than on the valley floor; summer daytime temperatures can be 10 to 15 degrees cooler on the mountain than in the city of Napa below. The soils are uplifted former seabed and sedimentary types, very shallow and low in fertility.

Mount Veeder is almost always the last AVA to start and end harvest. Hess Collection winemaker Dave Guffy tells of crushing grapes in late November in some years while the rest of his family prepared Thanksgiving dinner, while his peers in St. Helena had finished harvest three weeks before. The lateness of the pick puts grapes at risk from fall rainstorms.

The first recorded wines on Mount Veeder were made in 1864 by Captain Stelham Wing, from what is today's Wing Canyon Vineyard. The first commercial-scale winery was Theodore Gier Winery, built in 1903 of locally quarried stone and now home to the Hess Collection.

Despite a long drive up a winding road, Hess Collection is one of the most-visited wineries in Napa Valley. The wines are excellent: Hess Collection Cabernet Sauvignon and Chardonnay are the top tier; Hess Napa Valley is the middle; and the third tier is Hess Select, a North Coast brand. Founder Donald Hess, who retired in 2011, installed a large portion of his contemporary art collection at the winery, and the public is welcome to visit at no cost.

The Swiss-born Hess made his fortune by building his family's Valser Water Company into the largest mineral-water producer in Switzerland. In 1978, he founded the Hess Collection Winery by purchasing land that included the Gier Winery. Hess renovated the original building, which previously had been the Mont La Salle Winery, run by the Christian Brothers.

A number of out-of-region wineries produce wines from Mount Veeder fruit, among them Atlas Peak, Renteria Wines, Robert Craig, and Y. Rousseau. Betty O'Shaughnessy, owner of O'Shaughnessy Wines, on Howell Mountain, uses the Progeny Winery label for her Mount Veeder Cabernet Sauvignon.

Other Napa Valley Regions

Coombsville AVA

One of the coolest areas in Napa Valley, Coombsville has displayed a gift for producing Cabernet Sauvignons with freshness and verve. The infant AVA, formalized in December 2011, is just east of the city of Napa. Its neighbors include the Oak Knoll District of Napa Valley AVA, to the northwest; Los Carneros, to the southwest; the Wild Horse Valley AVA, to the east; and the Solano County Green Valley AVA, to the southeast.

Of Coombsville's 11,000 acres, 1,360 are planted to grapevines, at elevations from 300 to 500 feet. Volcanic ash, debris, and lava from ancient eruptions of nearby Mount George, just south of the Stags Leap District, contribute to the soil profiles.

Hillsides are exposed to wind and fog from San Pablo Bay, creating cool mornings and evenings and pleasantly warm afternoons—ideal conditions for long ripening of red grapes.

Producers in this AVA include Ancien, Buoncristiani Family Winery, Caldwell Vineyards, Frazier Winery, Farella Vineyard, Marita's Vineyard, Meteor Vineyard, Sodaro Estate Winery, Whetstone Wine Cellars, and Palmaz Vineyards.

Chiles Valley District AVA

The Chiles Valley District AVA produces Zinfandel and red Bordeaux varieties that benefit from its elevation (800 to 1,300 feet), summer fog, and chilly temperatures (below 50°F) at night during the growing season. These conditions create wines with linear structure and refreshing acidity. Just seven wineries are located in the valley. Brown Estate and Green & Red Vineyard bottle noteworthy Zinfandels, and Volker Eisele does a fine job with Cabernet Sauvignon blends. Nichelini Winery is a blast from the past, established by Italian-Swiss immigrant Anton Nichelini in 1884. Fifth-generation Nichelinis operate the winery today, making wines from a few remaining plantings by Anton in 1890, plus more recent cultivations. Zinfandel is the flagship wine.

Wild Horse Valley AVA

Southeast of the Oak Knoll District, the Wild Horse Valley AVA is a remote Napa Valley sub-AVA that most ignore because there are just 40 acres of vineyards here. Elevations range from 400 to 1,500 feet, and vineyard irrigation is essential, due to the limited

Chappellet Vineyard & Winery
Pritchard Hill, above St. Helena in eastern Napa Valley, is home to Chappellet and several other outstanding producers, but it is not an AVA, and there is no rush to make it one.

Continuum Estate Vineyard
Tim Mondavi and Marcia Mondavi Borger, son and daughter of Robert Mondavi, chose Pritchard Hill as the site for their Continuum Estate Vineyard.

water retention of its shallow soils. The important grapes are Cabernet Sauvignon and Sangiovese. The most notable winery to date is Kenzo Estate. Established by Japanese video game tycoon Kenzo Tsujimoto of Capcom Entertainment Inc., Kenzo is a serious producer in an AVA given little respect otherwise. Its entire inaugural 2005 vintage was exported to Japan, but Kenzo is now available in the United States. No expense has been spared in establishing the vineyards on Mount George, or in hiring consulting winemaker Heidi Peterson Barrett and vineyard manager David Abreu. The wines—a Sauvignon Blanc, Cabernet Sauvignon, and Bordeaux-style blend—are high-quality carrots that might lead others to invest in Wild Horse Valley.

Other Napa Valley Areas

There are also areas within Napa Valley that produce superior grapes and wines, but don't fall into sub-AVA categories. **Pope Valley** is a potential Napa Valley sub-AVA. Situated approximately 25 miles from the Silverado Trail, east of Chiles Valley and south of Howell Mountain, Pope Valley is home to St. Supéry's Dollarhide Ranch, a major contributor to the Rutherford winery's production. Flora Springs, among many others, also has plantings in Pope Valley, where land costs and grape prices are lower than in most Napa Valley AVAs. The jury is out on grape quality.

Although it's not an AVA, the **Pritchard Hill** area, east of St. Helena, is home to some of the biggest names in Napa Valley—Bryant Family, Chappellet, Colgin, Ovid, and Continuum (the latter developed by Robert Mondavi and family). The folks on Pritchard Hill don't seem to care much about AVA status, figuring that their sought-after wines speak for themselves, and simply use "Napa Valley" on their labels.

Donn and Molly Chappellet were the first vintners on the hill, arriving in 1967 from Southern California. Over the years, they have planted 65 acres of Cabernet Sauvignon, Merlot, Malbec, Cabernet Franc, Petit Verdot, and Chenin Blanc on their 100-acre property, which ranges in elevation from 800 to 1,800 feet. Their six adult children are all involved in the business in some fashion, and the wines are admirable, the best being the Chappellet Pritchard Hill Estate Vineyard Cabernet Sauvignon.

Continuum is a relatively new wine, a Cabernet Sauvignon–based proprietary blend first made in 2005 by Robert Mondavi; his wife, Margrit; younger son, Tim; and daughter, Marcia Mondavi Borger. Robert died in 2008, but not before sipping the wine that fills the family void after the sale of Robert Mondavi Winery to Constellation Brands. The Mondavis (minus older son Michael) produced the 2005 and 2006 vintages from purchased grapes, and in 2008 began planting Continuum Estate Vineyard at Pritchard Hill. For the 2008 vintage, 70 percent of the fruit came from the vineyard.

Bryant Family Vineyard and Colgin Cellars are two of Napa Valley's first-wave cult brands, and their Pritchard Hill wines are still difficult to find for anyone not on their mailing lists and unwilling to pay a few hundred dollars per bottle. Like other Pritchard Hill wineries, Cabernet Sauvignon is the predominant grape, liking the high elevations and rocky, red volcanic soils.

CULT OF PERSONALITY

To some wine drinkers certain American wines have achieved cult status. Often, such wines are either difficult to acquire, receive scores in the mid- to high-90s from critic Robert Parker Jr., are produced in tiny quantities, are sold only via a mailing list, and/or are ultra-expensive—usually all of these.

Certain Pinot Noirs (Helen Turley's Marcassin Sonoma Coast tops the list) and Manfred Krankel's quirky Sine Qua Non qualify as cult brands, although the majority of California's most sought-after wines are Napa Cabernet Sauvignons. In the early 2000s, one had to know the secret handshake to get hold of a bottle of Bryant Family, Colgin, Harlan Estate, Schrader, or Screaming Eagle Cabernet Sauvignon, at prices in the hundreds of dollars. In the late 1970s and 1980s, the handshake scored Heitz Martha's Vineyard Cab; in the 1990s, Silver Oak and Caymus Special Selection. There will no doubt be a clutch of new cult Cabs to come in the 2010s.

However, the latest generation of limited-production wines with high scores and prices and limited volume—Futo, Kenzo, Maybach, and Ovid, to name a few—emerged at the worst possible time, with the economy in the tank and even the wealthiest cutting back. Add to that Parker's 2011 baton-passing of California wine evaluation to *Wine Advocate* colleague Antonio Galloni—will his scores carry as much weight as Parker's?—and new cult-wine producers have their work cut out for them. Screaming Eagle and Harlan Estate show no signs of letup and will likely be coveted gems for ages. But those about to launch a $250 Cabernet Sauvignon had best think twice, or have deep—very deep—pockets.

Sodaro Estate Winery
Don and Deedee Sodaro purchased land east of the city of Napa in 1996 and planted vines in what would become the Coombsville AVA in 2011.

NAPA VALLEY VINTNERS

The Napa Valley Vintners (NVV), a 408-member nonprofit association of wineries, has zealously promoted Napa wines and protected the Napa Valley name. It is the California leader in advocating the importance of place names, and in 2007, Napa Valley wine became the first non–European Union agricultural product to receive geographical indication protection throughout the EU.

A year prior to that, NVV won a long court battle against Fred Franzia and his Bronco Wine Company, which has used "Napa" on some of its labels even though the wines did not contain the federal minimum of 85 percent of the grapes grown within that AVA to allow for such labeling. NVV has also pursued foreign wine producers as far away as China that have, in NVV's view, fraudulently used the Napa name on labels.

NVV is a powerful and united organization, heavily involved in lobbying and domestic- and foreign-market promotion. It also sponsors the Napa Green program (which encourages growers and wineries to adopt environmentally conscious practices) and Fish Friendly Farming. Its signature

event, Auction Napa Valley, had raised more than a hundred million dollars by 2011, which has gone towards providing health care, youth programs, and affordable-housing initiatives for the largely Hispanic vineyard workers and their families in Napa Valley.

In 1968, vintners and others in the community had the forethought to preserve open space and prevent overdevelopment of Napa Valley by enacting the nation's first Agriculture Preserve. Since its adoption, not one acre of land has been lost from the preserve. This land-zoning ordinance established agriculture and open space as the "best use" for the land in the "fertile valley and foothill areas of Napa County." Initially the ordinance protected 23,000 acres of agricultural land stretching from the city of Napa to Calistoga. Today, more than 30,000 acres are preserved from nonagricultural development.

BAY AREA

Bargetto
Bargetto Winery grows a dozen grape varieties on its 40-acre Regan Estate Vineyards, in the Corralitos area of southern Santa Cruz County (see p. 97).

There are myriad "bay areas" in the United States, but just one Bay Area—shorthand for the San Francisco Bay Area. This broad and mostly densely populated region includes the cities of San Francisco, Oakland, and San Jose, and several counties surrounding the Bay: Alameda, Contra Costa, Marin, San Francisco, San Mateo, Santa Clara, Santa Cruz, and Solano. These counties all have their own "wine country," or are very close to one. Napa and Sonoma counties are also considered to be in the Bay Area; they are detailed separately in this book.

SAN FRANCISCO BAY AREA

San Francisco Bay and its interconnected bays have a moderating effect on the mesoclimates of this multicounty region.

Marin County

Marin is where many of Northern California's wealthy live: they sail off Sausalito, go antiquing in San Anselmo, and call their BMWs "Basic Marin Wheels"—starter cars for teenagers turning sixteen. A fifteen-minute drive south on Highway 101, over the Golden Gate Bridge, puts Marinites in San Francisco, mecca of restaurants, chic lounges, theaters, and the symphony. Marin offers a respite from big-city energy and tension. That's why *Star Wars* movie mogul George Lucas, actor Sean Penn, singer/guitarist Bonnie Raitt, and other celebrities and well-heeled individuals live there, the southernmost wine region in the North Coast AVA.

While many Marin residents enjoy wine, and make quick trips to Sonoma and Napa for the wine country experience, some aren't aware that there is an evolving and exciting wine industry in their own backyard. Pinot Noir just might make Marin famous for something other than its upper-class lifestyle and a chance to spot rocker Sammy Hagar at Whole Foods. It will never be a quantity producer, because suitable land is scarce and grape yields are dismayingly small, yet Marin is establishing itself as a prime Pinot Noir producer.

Wine has been made in Marin on and off for nearly two centuries, beginning with the intrepid *padres* who built Mission San Rafael Arcángel in 1817 and made sacramental wine. In the 1890s, Frenchman Jean Escalle planted a 23-acre hillside vineyard in Larkspur, built a brick winery that still exists today, and famously threw an annual "Vintage Festival" at which he poured his wines for San Francisco's social elite.

Mark Pasternak
Pasternak's Devil's Gulch Ranch in Nicasio grows Pinot Noir grapes for several wineries and raises rabbits, quail, pork, and lamb for area restaurants.

Prohibition and phylloxera stalled winemaking in Marin until the early 1970s, when the locals, seeing the phenomenal success experienced by vintners in Napa and Sonoma counties, asked, "Why not us?" Encouragement came indirectly from Schramsberg Vineyards in Napa Valley, which sought out high-acid Marin County grapes to make its sparkling wines.

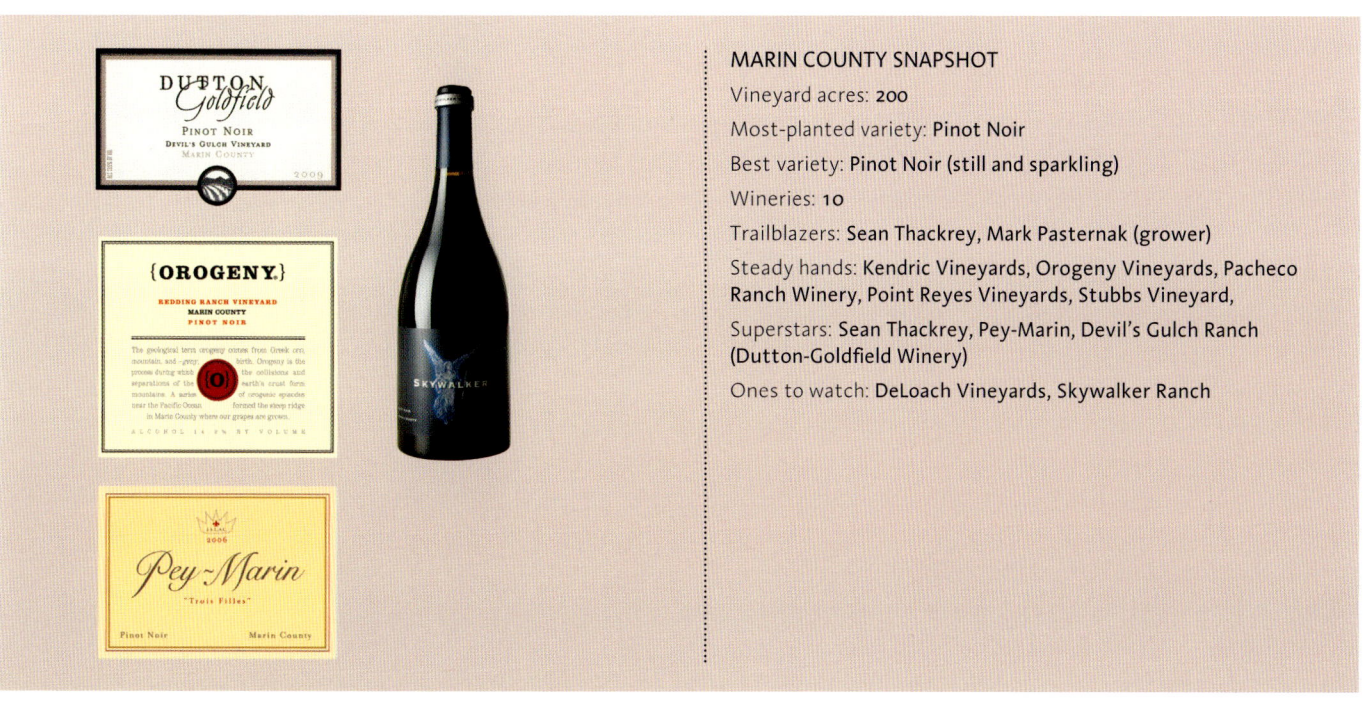

MARIN COUNTY SNAPSHOT

Vineyard acres: **200**

Most-planted variety: **Pinot Noir**

Best variety: **Pinot Noir (still and sparkling)**

Wineries: **10**

Trailblazers: **Sean Thackrey, Mark Pasternak (grower)**

Steady hands: **Kendric Vineyards, Orogeny Vineyards, Pacheco Ranch Winery, Point Reyes Vineyards, Stubbs Vineyard,**

Superstars: **Sean Thackrey, Pey-Marin, Devil's Gulch Ranch (Dutton-Goldfield Winery)**

Ones to watch: **DeLoach Vineyards, Skywalker Ranch**

Skywalker Ranch
The wine force is with George Lucas, the *Star Wars* director/producer who makes Pinot Noir from grapes grown on Skywalker Ranch in Marin County.

Mark Pasternak was one grower who sold his grapes to bubbly producers after planting Chardonnay and Pinot Noir in the 1970s on his Devil's Gulch Ranch, overlooking Nicasio Reservoir in western Marin County. In the early 1990s, his grapes caught the attention of Dan Goldfield, then winemaker at La Crema in Russian River Valley (and now partner-winemaker at Dutton-Goldfield, also there); eventually Devil's Gulch became a single-vineyard bottling for Dutton-Goldfield.

There are ten producers in Marin, and a few outsiders buy grapes from Pasternak, Mary and Tom Stubbs, and other growers. Susan and Jon Pey produce a well-filled, wild-berry Pey-Marin Trois Filles Pinot Noir and a dry, minerally Pey-Marin Shell Mound Riesling from their Marin vineyards. Sean Thackrey, equal parts winemaker, philosopher, and archivist (he owns, and shares online at www.wine-maker.net, more than six hundred old wine texts), achieves remarkable intensity in his Andromeda Devil's Gulch Vineyard Pinot Noir. Orogeny and George Lucas's Skywalker Ranch Pinot Noir projects also produce positive results from very young vines. Most wineries use the Marin County appellation on their labels; their other option is the vast North Coast AVA.

The wet winters, dry summers, diverse soils, and abundant sunshine are positives in Marin, but bud break begins in February, a month earlier than in Sonoma County (with which Marin shares a border), and harvest can start as late as October. This long hang time is of tremendous benefit for the slow, even ripening of grapes, but it also puts immature clusters at risk for damage and fungal disease from fall rainstorms.

San Francisco Bay AVA

This far-flung AVA (1.5 million acres), the northernmost within the Central Coast AVA, covers the counties of Alameda, Contra Costa, Santa Clara, San Francisco, San Mateo, and Santa Cruz. It's a catchall AVA for areas that have not demonstrated, or don't yet care to, that they have distinctive-enough conditions to merit a more precise AVA status. "San Francisco Bay" lends marketing cachet to the wines, even though there is wide variation in the types of soil and climate conditions. The U.S. AVA system is far from perfect, and this appellation demonstrates that fact. "San Francisco Bay" is simply too broad a term to have much meaning.

The most important wine regions in San Francisco Bay are Livermore Valley in Alameda County; Contra Costa County; and the Santa Cruz Mountains in San Mateo, Santa Clara, and Santa Cruz counties. Very little, if any, grape growing is done near San Francisco itself (there isn't enough sunlight or warmth), although a handful of winemaking facilities and tasting rooms are located in the city, as well as in Oakland, Berkeley, and Alameda. Among the first urban wineries in California was Crushpad, a make-your-own facility that outgrew its San Francisco space and relocated to Napa, then Sonoma.

In the East Bay, clusters of small urban wineries have emerged, and they have demonstrated that fancy buildings and gardens aren't requirements for making and selling fine wine. Tracey and Jared Brandt of Donkey & Goat have a lot of no-nos at their Berkeley winery, housed in a 105-year-old former ink factory. They don't use any commercial yeasts, fining, filtration, new oak, or machines for crushing, and they keep sulfur to a minimum at bottling (sulfur is a preservative that helps to keep wine stable). The Brandts, who lived in France's Rhône Valley for one year, focus on Syrah, Grenache, Mourvèdre, and other Rhône grapes. They harvest much earlier than most in California, so their wines are nervy and high in acid. "No cocktails disguised as wine," as they like to point out.

Wente Vineyards
The cornerstone of Livermore Valley winemaking, Wente also offers fine dining, a golf course, a concert series, and myriad hospitality events.

ALAMEDA COUNTY SNAPSHOT

Vineyard acreage: **6,000**

Most-planted varieties: **Cabernet Sauvignon, Chardonnay, Petite Sirah, Syrah**

Best varieties: **Cabernet Sauvignon, Petite Sirah**

AVAs: **Livermore Valley, San Francisco Bay**

Wineries: **60**

Trailblazers: **Concannon Vineyards, Wente Vineyards**

Steady hands: **Concannon Vineyards, Dashe Cellars, Edmunds St. John, Fenestra Winery, JC Cellars, La Rochelle Winery, Thomas Coyne Winery, Wente Vineyards**

Superstars: **Rosenblum Cellars, Steven Kent Winery, Donkey & Goat**

One to watch: **Rock Wall Wine Company**

Donkey & Goat
Jared and Tracey Brandt's winery may be in urban Berkeley, but their grapes are grown in Mendocino County, Monterey County, and the Sierra Foothills.

Jeff Cohn at JC Cellars (Syrah, Zinfandel) and Mike Dashe of Dashe Cellars (Zinfandel, Riesling) cut their winemaking teeth in Alameda, at Rosenblum Cellars, founder Kent Rosenblum's winery at a ship-repair facility on the former Alameda Naval Base. Beginning in 1978, Rosenblum and his cohorts made up to twenty different Zinfandels a year, mostly from old vines in Mendocino, Sonoma, Napa, and Contra Costa counties.

Rosenblum Cellars still produces these wines, although Kent and his partners sold the company to Diageo in 2008. The global drinks giant moved production to Napa Valley, but it left the tasting room in Alameda. Rosenblum and his daughter, Shauna, have a new brand, Rock Wall Wine Company, located in an airplane hangar at the Alameda naval base. Rock Wall gets its name for the perimeter wall built during World War II to protect the base from Japanese torpedoes. Rosenblum father and daughter source Zinfandel, Petite Sirah, and Cabernet Sauvignon grapes from throughout the North Coast AVA for their wines.

Emeryville is home to former postal carrier Steve Edmunds's Edmunds St. John wines. Edmunds was one of the first Californians to produce Rhône Valley varietals, and he is one of the last to make Gamay Noir, the major grape of France's Beaujolais region.

Livermore Valley AVA

An Englishman, Robert Livermore, planted the first vineyard in Livermore Valley in 1846. Then in the 1880s Carl H. Wente, James Concannon, and Charles Wetmore made a real, and indelible, winemaking impact on this region, which is less than an hour's drive from San Francisco, and just as close to the farmlands of the Central Valley.

Livermore Valley is where many big-city workers live, commuting to jobs in more expensive San Francisco and San Jose. It's known as much as a science and technology center—Lawrence Livermore National Labs and Sandia National Laboratory are here—as wine country. But long before Napa Valley's wines became well known, Livermore was the Northern California wine region. It was the first in California to bottle varietally labeled Chardonnay and Sauvignon Blanc. The majority of Chardonnay vines in the state can be traced back to the original Wente clone. In the late 1890s, there were a reported 6,000 vineyard acres, and there were more than fifty wineries when Prohibition began in 1920.

Prohibition sent many vintners off to find work in other regions, and upon Repeal, Livermore Valley land was far more valuable for houses and shopping centers than it was for wine grapes. Vineyard acreage dropped by nearly half, but the Wentes and Concannons, who founded their vineyards and wineries in 1883, stayed the course and are Livermore's largest wineries today. Wente Vineyards produces 300,000 cases of wine per year, with one-third of that bottled for export markets; Concannon Vineyard's annual case volume is 425,000.

According to Wente, it is the country's oldest continuously operated, family-owned winery, with the fifth generation now holding the reins. The wines, produced from 2,800 acres of Livermore Valley and Monterey County grapes, are amiable and well made. The finest, bottled under the Nth Degree label, are the responsibility of Karl Wente, and are composed of small lots of Chardonnay, Merlot, Cabernet Sauvignon, Syrah, and Pinot Noir.

Visiting Wente is a full-on experience. In addition to its four tasting rooms and vineyards, it has a high-end restaurant (supplied with produce from a garden current-CEO Carolyn Wente planted in the mid-1980s), a concert pavilion that hosts big-name acts, and a golf course, complete with an affiliation with former top-ranked professional golfer Annika Sorenstam, for whom Wente produces Annika-branded Chardonnay and Syrah.

David Kent has made Concannon a huge player in Livermore Valley. As chief executive officer for The Wine

Steven Kent Mirassou
After his family's sale of Mirassou Vineyards to E. & J. Gallo in 2002, Steven Mirassou established the Steven Kent Winery brand; Lineage is his top-shelf label.

Ghielmetti Vineyard
Established in 2001, the 64-acre Ghielmetti Vineyard in the upper Livermore Valley is planted to five different clones of Cabernet Sauvignon and nine other varieties. Ghielmetti uses drip irrigation, as do the majority of California vineyards.

Group, Kent has had a hand in growing the wine company into the world's third-largest by volume. TWG began with boxed wines, moved up to fighting varietals, and, in 2002, a year after Kent became CEO, purchased Concannon and turned it into a 425,000-case winery.

Concannon claims its own list of firsts: Along with Wetmore's Cresta Blanca winery, begun in 1882, it was one of the first in California to produce Sauvignon Blanc (labeled "Sauterne" at the time). In 1950, it was the first to hire a female professional winemaker, Katherine Vajda. And in 1964, Concannon released the first varietally labeled Petite Sirah, now its signature wine.

Steven Kent Mirassou's family (no relation to David Kent) has an even longer California winemaking history, dating to 1854. At his Steven Kent Winery (the Mirassous sold their brand to Gallo and cannot use their last name on their own labels) he produces arguably Livermore's best Cabernet Sauvignon and he has achieved remarkable success in producing wines comparable to those from Napa Valley. His 2007 Lineage, a blend of Cabernet Sauvignon, Cabernet Franc, Petit Verdot, Malbec, and Merlot, is superb, the target more Livermore vintners could shoot for as far as quality and complexity are concerned. No other vintner in Livermore can command $125 per bottle, as Steven Kent does for Lineage.

Most of the grapes come from his Ghielmetti Vineyard, planted in 2001–02. Because of the youth of the vines, the vineyard is just now hitting its stride. Lanny and Fran Replogle's Fenestra Winery has had great success with Ghielmetti Petite Sirah. Steven Mirassou's reach also extends to Pinot Noir; he produces several AVA-designated Pinots from outside Livermore Valley.

Livermore Valley is quite warm in summer—Region III on the UC Davis scale, similar to the northern section of Napa Valley. Even though Livermore is 25 miles east of San Francisco Bay, it gets some fog and breezes that temper the heat. The valley is an ancient riverbed composed of rocky, gravelly soils and a thin layer of fertile topsoil, making for excellent drainage. Livermore's winemaking history is long and rich, and it has the potential to resume a place of importance in California winemaking.

Contra Costa County

Oakley is still the hub of Contra Costa County winegrowing, yet it is a mere semblance of its old self. Approximately 1,500 acres of Carignane, Mourvèdre, and Zinfandel vines planted as long as a century ago still remain, though housing developments have wiped out what once was a thriving farming community. The few remaining vines supply Rosenblum Cellars for its Carla's Vineyard San Francisco Bay Zinfandel and give Fred Cline of Sonoma-based Cline Cellars the grapes he needs to continue his old-vine program.

Cline's grandfather Valeriano Jacuzzi and his brothers emigrated from Italy to Southern California in the early 1900s. They established an aviation equipment–manufacturing business, Jacuzzi Brothers, where they designed and built propellers and the first enclosed-cabin monoplane, which was used by the U.S. Postal Service and to fly passengers from San Francisco to Yosemite National Park. Unfortunately Valeriano's brother Giocondo and several others died when the plane crashed near Modesto. The family abandoned that business, diverting their energy into building hydrotherapy pumps. The Jacuzzi whirlpool bath was born, and the family sold the business for $70 million in 1979.

Valeriano had a small farm in Oakley, and his grandchildren, including Fred and Matt Cline, worked it during summers. The Cline boys later leased vineyards, sold grapes, and started Cline Cellars, relocating it to Sonoma, where Fred continues to produce old-vine Mourvèdres, Zinfandels, and Carignanes from Oakley, primarily the Big Break and Bridgehead vineyards. The soil is literally sand, deposited by the San Joaquin River, and is so well drained that vine roots are severely stressed in their efforts to get adequate moisture. That typically translates into concentrated grapes, and thus intense wines. Oakley is warm, Region III (out of five) on the UC Davis heat summation scale, so Zinfandel, Mourvèdre, Carignane, and Petite Sirah thrive here. Bonny Doon, Neyers, Rock Wall, Rosenblum, and Turley Wine Cellars are among those who produce wines from Oakley grapes.

In 1994, Fred and Nancy Cline added the Jacuzzi Family Vineyards label to their lineup. Grapes for Jacuzzi wines are sourced from throughout California, including rare (for California) Nero d'Avola and Montepulciano, from the Tracy Hills AVA in San Joaquin and Stanislaus counties.

Cline Cellars
Cline's tasting room (above, right), located in the town of Sonoma, pours its Contra Costa County wines, which include old-vine Mourvèdres and Zinfandels.

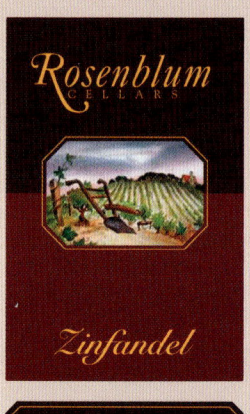

CONTRA COSTA COUNTY SNAPSHOT
Vineyard acreage: **2,000**
Most-planted varieties: **Zinfandel, Mourvèdre, Carignane, Petite Sirah**
AVAs: **Livermore Valley, San Francisco Bay**
Wineries: **15**
Trailblazers: **Cline Cellars**
Steady hands: **Bloomfield Vineyards, Hanna Nicole Vineyards, Parkmon Vineyards, Tamayo Family Vineyards, Viano Vineyards**
Superstars: **Cline Cellars,* Rosenblum Cellars,* Turley Wine Cellars***

*Denotes out-of-county wineries that produce Contra Costa County–grown wines

Santa Cruz Mountains AVA

Is it possible that one large, sparsely planted area in a remote and mountainous part of north-central California, in a region best known for earthquakes, hippies (old and new), surfers, the Santa Cruz Beach Boardwalk, and a university whose mascot is the slimy banana slug, could produce world-class wines—and from three different grape varieties?

The answer is yes: The Santa Cruz Mountains AVA is home to the magnificent Monte Bello Vineyard Cabernet Sauvignons of Ridge Vineyards; the pure, long-aging Chardonnays of Mount Eden Vineyards; and the racy wines made by several Silicon Valley vintners who put a Burgundian spin on California Pinot Noir.

The 350,000-acre AVA encompasses parts of southern San Mateo County, northern Santa Clara County, and sections of Santa Cruz County. It is not in the San Francisco Bay AVA, however, as that appellation is defined largely by climate, specifically the winds and fog that flow into the region from San Francisco Bay. The Santa Cruz Mountains, the seventh AVA established in the country, in 1982, is defined by a different soil composition than San Francisco Bay's and, more powerfully, by altitude, with most vineyards planted above the fog line, as high as 2,600 feet above sea level.

Mount Eden Vineyards
Martin Ray was producing great wine from these Mount Eden Vineyards decades before the area far below became known as Silicon Valley.

South of The Bay

This map shows the important Santa Cruz Mountains wine region, south of San Francisco, and the much smaller number of vineyards and wineries along the densely populated Highway 101 corridor, between Redwood City and just south of Gilroy.

SANTA CRUZ MOUNTAINS AVA SNAPSHOT

Vineyard acreage: 1,500

Most-planted varieties: Chardonnay, Cabernet Sauvignon, Pinot Noir

Best varieties: Cabernet Sauvignon, Chardonnay, Pinot Noir

Sub-AVA: Ben Lomond Mountain

Wineries: 70

Trailblazers: Bargetto Winery, David Bruce Winery, Mount Eden Vineyards, Ridge Vineyards

Steady hands: Bargetto Winery, Bonny Doon Vineyard, Clos de la Tech, Clos LaChance, David Bruce Winery, Kathryn Kennedy Winery, Testarossa Winery, Thomas Fogarty Winery & Vineyards, Varner Vineyards

Superstars: Mount Eden Vineyards, Rhys Vineyards, Ridge Vineyards

---

Despite its expanse, just 1,500 vineyard acres exist in the Santa Cruz Mountains. Only on the accessible ridges of steep, craggy mountain slopes at elevations above 400 feet are wine grapes planted and tended. The mountains were created by millions of years of seismic activity along the San Andreas Fault, which dissects the region along the highest ridgetops, with the Pacific Plate on the coastal side and the North American Plate inland. Soils on the Pacific Plate, an ancient seabed, are primarily sedimentary sandstone, mudstone, limestone, clay, and loam; North American Plate soils are mostly granitic. In some vineyards near the fault, soils from both plates can be found. Warm but not hot days are moderated by coastal breezes at night.

Santa Cruz Mountains winemaking began in the eighteenth century, when the Franciscan missionaries planted their sacramental wine grape, Mission. Burgundian Paul Masson later made Champagne-style sparkling wines in the Santa Cruz Mountains until 1936, when Martin Ray purchased Masson's 40-acre property. Ray planted more Pinot Noir, Chardonnay, and Cabernet Sauvignon and began producing varietal wines, rather than the generic "Chablis" and "Burgundy" popular at the time.

Ray's property is now Mount Eden Vineyards, where Jeffrey and Ellie Patterson have produced long-lived Chardonnays and Pinot Noirs for thirty years. The wines, minerally and tight when young, begin to unfold and show their personalities beginning at five years of age and continuing for up to twenty years. Mount Eden wines are the antithesis of drink-tonight supermarket wines; patience is required to fully appreciate them.

Ridge's Monte Bello Vineyard sits at 2,600 feet above sea level on the eastern side of Black Mountain, overlooking the city of Cupertino and Silicon Valley. From this perch, Ridge CEO/winemaker Paul Draper has watched a once-agricultural landscape become populated with the likes of Apple, Google, and Yahoo, and the housing and retail developments that support them. But on a clear day, Draper can also look west and see the Pacific Ocean fifteen miles away, with nary a house or office compound in sight.

Originally called Monte Bello Winery, Ridge was constructed from 1886 to 1891 by Italian doctor Osea Perrone, with quarried limestone used to build the cellar walls. The vineyard, clay-loam soil with fractured limestone underneath, has been farmed organically for forty years, and it has been replanted during that time, with dying and diseased vines replaced by new recruits.

Draper harvests earlier than most of his neighbors, and the wines are produced with as little intervention as possible. Unlike most Cabernet Sauvignon producers, he uses American oak barrels, not French. The key to U.S. oak, Draper says, is that the barrel staves must be dried outside for up to two years, with cycles of rainfall and warm weather drawing out the harsh tannins invariably found in kiln-dried American barrels.

While little marketing has been required at Ridge—the wines sell themselves, to customers who appreciate their nuance, affinity with food, and longevity—Draper had the satisfaction in 2006 of seeing his 1971 Monte Bello finish first in a reenactment of the famous "Judgment of Paris" tasting, vanquishing Châteaux Mouton-Rothschild and Haut-Brion wines of similar age. This triumph, while tremendous for Ridge, could not be shared by all California Cabernet Sauvignon makers, for many do not produce wines meant to age or to be compatible with

Ridge Monte Bello Vineyard
Ridge's famous Monte Bello Vineyard follows the Black Mountain's contours at an elevation of 2,600 feet. The vineyard was first planted in the 1880s, producing the first of its world class wines in 1892.

SHAKING IT UP

California is spared the threat of tornadoes, hurricanes, and deep freezes, but it does have earthquakes—lots of them, though most are minor and do little, if any, damage. But every decade or so, a big one hits somewhere in the Golden State, and the Santa Cruz Mountains are often the epicenter.

California quakes usually occur along the boundaries of the Pacific Plate (to the west) and the North American Plate (to the east). As the plates grind against each other, stress builds along the faults and is released as earthquakes. Faults on both sides of San Francisco Bay and Santa Clara Valley are particularly active; the San Andreas runs through San Juan Bautista, the Santa Cruz Mountains, and the San Francisco Peninsula.

The tectonic plate collision that created the Santa Cruz Mountains over millennia account for its diversity of topography and soils. But an earthquake demolished California's wine industry in 1906. In addition to taking lives and destroying much of San Francisco, the Great Quake leveled winery buildings, tanks, and barrels, spilling wine into the streets. Because California wine companies had their headquarters, shipping lines, and wine stocks in San Francisco, they were ruined. As a result, they eventually moved their businesses closer to the vineyards and farther away from major fault lines, to Sonoma, Napa, and elsewhere.

In 1989, another Santa Cruz Mountains–born quake, Loma Prieta, killed sixty-three people in the Bay Area and injured thousands, as buildings and freeways crumbled and fires raged from ruptured gas lines. Downtown Santa Cruz was destroyed and four people died there. The Pacific Plate thrust itself over the North American Plate, causing the Santa Cruz Mountains to rise 14 inches with that one jolt, again altering its landscape. Wineries and most California buildings have been or are being retrofitted to withstand earthquakes, but the Earth's natural argument with itself continues to affect much of California.

Paul Draper
Ridge Vineyards' longtime winemaker is an opponent of overly ripe grapes, which, he believes, produce wines that obliterate vineyard character.

food. Instead, they cater to critics who adore ripe, rich wines and the consumers who embrace them.

Vineyards in the Santa Cruz Mountains' higher elevations have cooler nights and warmer days than in Bordeaux. "We get more acid in our grapes than Bordeaux," Draper explains, "but we have no trouble getting the grapes ripe." Ripeness is his sticking point. Alcohol levels have increased in California since the mid-1990s (there are myriad reasons for this, chief among them influential U.S. wine critics who give their highest scores to full-throttle wines with robust alcohol). Draper calls the development "a tragedy," saying that overripeness obliterates vineyard character and shortens the cellar life of a wine. For fifty years, Ridge Monte Bello has averaged 13.2 percent alcohol by volume; 15 percent-plus is now common elsewhere in California.

A mix of old and newer vines in the 108-acre Ridge Monte Bello Vineyard helps balance fruit ripening, and Draper harvests at lower sugar accumulations than most. After graduating from Stanford University he was introduced to Ridge wines, then made by four Stanford Research Institute engineers who had bought the winery and vineyard in 1959. Finding the 1962 and 1964 Ridge Cabs more complex than anything he had previously tasted from California, Draper joined Ridge, and he has been there ever since.

In 1986, Japanese pharmaceutical baron Akihiko Otsuka purchased Ridge, but his management style is admirably hands-off, leaving the details to Draper and his day-to-day winemaker, Eric Baugher.

Flying somewhat under the radar is Ridge's estate Chardonnay, a rich and complex wine with vibrant fruit and nervy, lip-smacking acidity. Definitely in full view are Ridge's wide range of Zinfandels, including the renowned Geyserville and Lytton Springs bottlings, most made from ancient vines, many of them field blends, at its northern Sonoma County winery.

Bonded in 1964, David Bruce Winery has 16 planted acres, 9 of them to Pinot Noir. It also sources grapes from other Pinot-centric regions of California. At the Novitiate Winery in Los Gatos, built in 1888 as part of a training center for new priests, Rob and Diana Jensen lease the space for the production of Testarossa Winery Chardonnays and Pinot Noirs. The couple purchases grapes largely from cool zones in Sonoma and Monterey counties.

In 1995, Kevin Harvey, a Silicon Valley software developer with a passion for the wines of Burgundy, planted Pinot Noir in his Woodside yard, in the foothills of the Santa Cruz Mountains. He soon became what is known in France as a *garagiste*—garage winemaker—and the results of his homemade wines inspired him to go pro, seeking out vineyard sites that, while they may not be economically viable, produce the grapes for the style of wine he wants to make. His Rhys Vineyards Pinot Noirs are minerally, subtle, and almost ethereal; uncommonly restrained, they run counter to the more-is-better style of opulent California Pinot Noirs.

The lone sub-AVA in the region, **Ben Lomond Mountain**, is on the western edge of the Santa Cruz Mountains. First planted in the 1860s, it has a spotty record, with vines dying from Pierce's disease—a bacterium spread by insects known as sharpshooters, which feed on infected vegetation and inject the bacterium into the sap of the vines. A handful of wineries have sporadically bottled wines from this AVA.

Last, and certainly not least, is Randall Grahm and Bonny Doon Vineyard. Grahm was among the first to do many things in the wine business. He is an original "Rhône Ranger," producing wines from Rhône Valley varieties such as Syrah and Mourvèdre; an early adopter of biodynamic farming methods; an embracer of synthetic closures, then screw caps, as worthy substitutes for natural cork; among the first to bring affordable Riesling to the American masses, under the Pacific Rim label; and the high-bar setter for winery newsletters, written so cleverly that a grasp of the French language and preferably a little Latin and Yiddish are needed to get all his jokes.

Randall Grahm
Bonny Doon Vineyard's swashbuckling owner has embraced the challenge of growing a vineyard from seeds, not nursery plants, in San Benito County.

He's also an enigma. A UC Santa Cruz philosophy major, he began Bonny Doon in 1981, intent on making Pinot Noir from the Santa Cruz Mountains. Unhappy with the results, and plagued by Pierce's disease in his vineyards, he turned to Rhône varieties, and he has dabbled ever since with grapes and vineyards far and wide. A master marketer, Grahm has used playful labels to sell wine—Cardinal Zin for a Zinfandel, Big House Red for a wine produced from grapes grown in close proximity to Soledad State Penitentiary, and his famous Le Cigare Volant—French for "flying cigar" or "flying saucer"—a Rhône Valley varietal blend.

Yet Grahm has methodically divested himself of several brands and vineyards, dropping from 450,000 cases of wine a year to just 30,000. His flagship, Le Cigare Volante, thrives, but Grahm's attention is now on a piece of property he purchased in San Juan Bautista in San Benito County—Popelouchum he calls it—where he is planting a vineyard from seeds, literally from the ground up, rather than planting rootstock. It's a pie-in-the-sky project, yet one that Grahm says will authenticate him as a winegrower. Time will tell if he is successful.

Testarossa Winery
Rob and Diana Jensen make their fine Testarossa Chardonnays and Pinot Noirs in the renovated Novitiate Winery, built into a Los Gatos hillside by Jesuits in 1888.

MONTEREY COUNTY

In the 1980 movie *Private Benjamin*, Goldie Hawn's character joins the U.S. Army after she sees recruitment images of sailboats moored in Monterey Bay. When she reports to Fort Ord and is shown her barracks, she tells her captain, "I think they sent me to the wrong place. See, I did join the army, but I joined a 'different' army. I joined the one with the condos and the private rooms." This was one of many shocks Judy Benjamin would experience in Monterey.

Indeed, the name Monterey County evokes sapphire bays, yacht clubs, cypress trees precariously clinging to rocky outcroppings, and the dramatic Pacific Ocean coastline. Sea lions bask on the rocks, and sea otters float on their backs in the shallow waters, snacking on shellfish. The many country clubs and resorts exude an aura of wealth.

But Monterey's wine country is 15 miles, and a world, away from Monterey's rich and famous, lying in the Salinas Valley to the east. Driving from north to south on Highway 101 between the cities of Salinas and Bradley, along the Salinas River, is a 90-mile treat only for those who find beauty in vast, flat fields of lettuce and spinach, or who marvel at tractor technology. Long before it became famous for wine, the Salinas Valley was known for salad, as well as John Steinbeck's novels and Cesar Chavez's efforts to unionize the migrant workers who did, and still do, the backbreaking farmwork.

Monterey County
The widely diverse climates and soils have encouraged growers to plant forty distinct varieties in this region.

Steinbeck, the Nobel Prize–winning author, was raised in Salinas and based several of his novels there, including *Of Mice and Men* and *Cannery Row*. The latter is Steinbeck's fictionalized account of Monterey's sardine-canning factories in the 1940s. The sardines disappeared in the early 1950s, and so did the canneries, although Cannery Row was later reinvigorated with restaurants, bars, shops, and the wondrous Monterey Bay Aquarium.

Savvy wine drinkers who drive Highway 101 through Monterey County look past the valley-floor row crops and west to the terraces and hillsides, where rocky, low-vigor granitic soils are home to several grape varieties. Chardonnay, Pinot Noir, and Syrah are the rock stars of the northern hillsides; Bordeaux varieties sing in the warmer south.

It wasn't always this way. Two decades ago, large wine companies such as Mondavi and Kendall-Jackson invested in Monterey vineyards to supply Chardonnay grapes for their inexpensive blends. At that time, the Salinas Valley was considered too cold for red grapes, and those who tried produced underripe, "Monterey veggie" Cabernet Sauvignons and Zinfandels, the most popular varieties at the time.

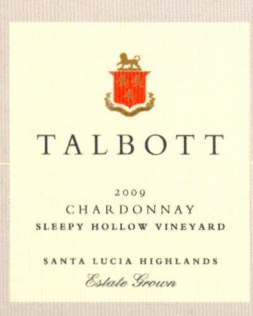

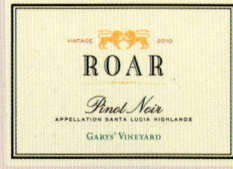

MONTEREY COUNTY SNAPSHOT

Vineyard acreage: **70,000**

Most-planted varieties: **Chardonnay, Pinot Noir, Merlot, Cabernet Sauvignon, Riesling**

Best varieties: **Chardonnay, Pinot Noir, Riesling**

Emerging varieties: **Albariño, Grüner Veltliner, Tinta Cão, Touriga Nacional**

AVAs: **Arroyo Seco, Carmel Valley, Chalone, Hames Valley, Monterey, San Antonio Valley, San Bernabe, San Lucas, Santa Lucia Highlands**

Wineries: **100**

Trailblazers: **Chalone Vineyard, J. Lohr Vineyards and Wines, Paraiso Vineyards, Ventana Vineyards**

Steady hands: **Bernardus Vineyards & Winery, Estancia, Hahn Estates, Jackson Family Wines**

Superstars: **Mer Soleil, Morgan Winery, Pisoni Vineyards & Winery, ROAR Wines, Robert Talbott Vineyards**

Yet once growers began planting cold-hardy Chardonnay and Pinot Noir on the eastern slopes of the Santa Lucia Mountains in the north, and heat-seeking Bordeaux and Rhône Valley varieties in the south, Monterey County began to earn respect for its wines. In fact, the Santa Lucia Highlands AVA has become a household name for Pinot Noir lovers, even if few are really sure how to pronounce it (loo-SEE-ah).

More than two hundred vineyards grow forty grape varieties in the county. There are nine AVAs and one hundred wineries and/or tasting rooms, the majority of them in or near the tourist-friendly city of Monterey and in Carmel Valley.

Monterey County can be downright cold and windy during the growing season, March through October, with late-afternoon gusts and evening fog blowing in from Monterey Bay, bringing temperatures that rarely rise above 57°F. The winds die down and the fog burns off by midmorning, allowing vines just enough sun to ripen their fruit. The northern part of the valley experiences this marine influence first and most strongly each day and is the last to see it subside. Southern regions such as Hames Valley and San Antonio Valley get some fog and wind, but are 20 degrees warmer on summer days. The farther south one goes in the Salinas Valley, the warmer the temperatures.

Monterey & San Benito Counties

Within Monterey County are nine AVAs, including the overarching Monterey AVA. This map also shows San Benito County and its five AVAs; text on them begins on p. 108.

Monterey AVA

Not to be confused with the Monterey County political appellation, the Monterey AVA is a large (40,000 vineyard acres) region on the eastern side of Monterey County. It encompasses the entire Salinas Valley and a segment of Carmel Valley, overlapping other AVAs (and adding to the confusion). It was approved as an AVA in 1984, before Monterey County terroirs had been sorted out.

The growing conditions vary widely, as the AVA runs 80 miles north to south. Generally, the region is coolest in the north (good for Chardonnay and Pinot Noir) and warmest in the south (Cabernet Sauvignon, Syrah). The soils are predominantly sandy, and vineyards are entirely dependent on irrigation.

Estancia, Jackson Family Wines, Robert Mondavi Private Selection, and Scheid Vineyards are among the major growers/producers in this AVA.

Santa Lucia Highlands AVA

On east-facing slopes, stitched together like a patchwork quilt, is the Santa Lucia Highlands AVA, where Chardonnay, Pinot Noir, and Syrah grow particularly well. This AVA, established in 1991, encompasses 6,100 acres of vineyards planted on the elevated terraces of the Santa Lucia mountain range in low-vigor, well-drained granitic soils; elevations range from 200 to 1,200 feet.

Monterey Bay fog and winds have a huge impact on this region. Because of them, diurnal temperature swings can be as much as 50 degrees, from a high of 85°F to a low of 35°F. In almost every vintage, while retaining their crisp natural acidity, grapes get ripe some three weeks after vintners in the North Coast have ended their harvest season. Ocean gusts called howlers can turn vine leaves nearly inside out, reducing photosynthetic efficiency. Yet there is a benefit: The grapeskins thicken as protection from the wind. Because most of a grape's flavor is in its skin, red wines from Santa Lucia Highlands tend to be tannic and firm, but generous in ripe black-fruit flavor and natural acidity.

Rich Smith and his wife, Claudia, were ahead of the curve, recognizing the potential of the Santa Lucia Highlands when they began planting the Paraiso Springs Vineyard (now Paraiso Vineyards) in 1973. They have steadily increased vineyard acreage to 400, planted mostly to Chardonnay and Pinot Noir grapes that are sold to others. The Smiths began producing their own Paraiso wines in 1988.

Swiss national Nicky Hahn, credited with the establishment of the Santa Lucia Highlands AVA, arrived in 1980, purchased the Smith and Hook Ranch, and began producing Cabernet Sauvignon from the vineyard already planted there. Later he converted almost entirely to Pinot Noir, produced under the Hahn Estates label.

Robert "Robb" Talbott moved from the East Coast to seaside Carmel in 1950, where his father, Robert Sr., and mother, Audrey, operated Robert Talbott Company, producing luxury neckties. In 1982, father and son launched Talbott Vineyards, first planting the Diamond T Vineyard in Carmel Valley, then purchasing the Sleepy Hollow Vineyard (now 565 acres) in Santa Lucia Highlands in 1994.

Chardonnay is the flagship wine at Sleepy Hollow. The wines have historically been viscous and exotically tropical, with the papaya and pineapple character common in Monterey County Chardonnay. Since 2009, Dan Karlsen, former winemaker at Chalone, has refined the winemaking, and recent Talbott Sleepy Hollow vintages show more crispness, elegance, and minerality than in previous years.

Paraiso's Smiths may have "discovered" Santa Lucia Highlands in the 1970s, but it's only since the mid-1990s that the region has held premier status. One vital cog in this star-making machine is Dan Lee, who took his first winemaking job at Jekel Vineyards in Monterey's Arroyo Seco region in 1978. By 1982, he and his banker wife, Donna, had founded Morgan Winery in Salinas, starting with purchased grapes and then planting their own Santa Lucia Highlands vineyard, Double L, in 1996.

Morgan Winery
Morgan Winery, situated in the windy Santa Lucia Highlands, specializes in the cool-climate Pinot Noir and Chardonnay varieties.

Double L is certified organic and planted to twelve Pinot Noir and six Chardonnay clones on eight different rootstocks. The wines produced from this vinous laboratory are particularly supple and elegant, and they include single-vineyard bottlings from the nearby Garys' and Rosella's vineyards.

Garys' Vineyard is a joint venture between Gary Franscioni and Gary Pisoni, who grew up together in the Salinas Valley, sons of Swiss-Italian farmers. They too made agriculture their careers, but they grew bored with beets and broccoli and began planting Pinot Noir, Chardonnay, and Syrah grapes in the Santa Lucia Highlands in the mid-1990s. Each Gary also has his own vineyards and produces his own wines (ROAR for Franscioni; Pisoni and Lucia for Pisoni). Their much-publicized partnership in Garys' Vineyard, and a shared commitment to custom-farming for choosy clients, has made them cheerleaders for Santa Lucia Highlands wine.

The shaggy-haired, irrepressible Pisoni, who describes himself as "just a big kid," tells wine-related tales (not all of which are known to be true) with a gee-whiz wonderment that makes one want to believe; Franscioni is equally amiable but more down to earth. They are yin and yang, complementary forces committed to high-quality grape growing.

Although the waiting list is long for wineries wanting to purchase grapes from Garys' Vineyard, Franscioni's Rosella's Vineyard (named for his wife), and the Pisoni Vineyards, relief is on the way for wait-listers. In 2007, Franscioni planted the Sierra Mar Vineyard in the Santa Lucia Highlands, and in 2008, the Garys collaborated again, jointly planting the 35-acre Soberanes Vineyard. If track record is any indication, the grapes from these new plantings will be as sought after as those of Garys', Rosella's, and Pisoni.

Even Napans give high-fives to the Highlands. The Wagner family of "Famous Caymus" Vineyards has vines here too. Chuck Wagner inherited Caymus, in Rutherford, one of California's most acclaimed Cabernet Sauvignon producers, from his father, Charlie. Now Chuck's older son, Charlie, operates Mer Soleil, a Chardonnay producer in the Santa Lucia Highlands. Like his father's Cabernets, Charlie's Mer Soleil wines are rich and ripe. He also produces one of California's first so-labeled unoaked Chardonnays, Silver, which is fermented in stainless steel and cement tanks, not oak barrels. Charlie's brother, Joe, is the Pinot Noir maker in the family, producing three vineyard-designated wines, including one from the Wagners' Las Alturas Vineyard in Santa Lucia Highlands.

Chalone AVA

This tiny and remote AVA is tucked into the Gavilan (sometimes spelled Gabilan) Mountains on the east side of the Salinas Valley. Grapes appear to have been first planted in Chalone's limestone- and quartz-rich soils around 1911, and

Sierra Mar Vineyard harvest
At Gary Franscioni's Sierra Mar Vineyard in the Santa Lucia Highlands, harvesting at night or at dawn keeps the fruit cool, which allows the winemaker greater control over the fermentation.

in the 1940s, fruit was sold to Beaulieu Vineyard in Napa Valley and Wente Vineyards in Livermore.

It took Richard Graff, who purchased Chalone Vineyard in 1965, to establish the 1,800-foot-elevation AVA as a high-quality producer, particularly of long-lived Pinot Noirs, Chardonnays, Pinot Blancs, and Chenin Blancs. In the shadows of the jagged peaks of Pinnacles National Monument, Graff employed such then-innovative Burgundian winemaking techniques as oak-barrel fermentation, lees aging, and malolactic fermentation to produce wines that were ahead of their time in terms of minerality, tautness, and remarkable complexity after several years of cellaring.

Graff reportedly smuggled Burgundy Pinot Noir cuttings into California and grafted them onto his existing vines—a common practice at the time, though also illegal, as foreign plant material must clear quarantine to avoid introducing vine disease into U.S. vineyards. Eventually Graff and his business partner, Phil Woodward, took on investors, and the company acquired other wineries, going public in 1984. Its annual shareholders' parties were legendary.

Graff died in a plane crash in 1998. In 2004, drinks giant Diageo bought Chalone Wine Group for $260 million, and while the small-production, estate-grown wines remain commendable, the bulk of Chalone's wines are unexceptional—grocery-store-bound, good values but uninspiring.

Chalone is one of just two wineries in the AVA, which includes only 300 planted acres. The other is Michaud Vineyard, owned by Michael Michaud, who toiled for nineteen years as a winemaker at Chalone before founding his own winery in 1998. Michaud's wines—Chardonnay, Pinot Blanc, Pinot Noir, and Syrah—bear the Chalone AVA signature of strong minerality and tight tannins. The area receives an average of just 10 inches of rainfall per year and has extremely low humidity. These factors, combined with the strong sunlight at its 1,500-foot elevation, mean that Chalone AVA grapes are typically small, with high skin-to-juice ratios, intense fruit, and structured tannins that require extended bottle-aging.

Arroyo Seco AVA

Commercial grapevines were first planted in Arroyo Seco (Spanish for "dry creek") in 1962, and now there are more than 7,000 acres planted in the 14,000-acre AVA. Most of the vineyards are owned by large companies, such as Jackson Family Wines, J. Lohr Vineyards & Wines, and Wente Family Estates. Arroyo Seco has long been a provider of Chardonnay and Pinot Noir grapes that go into multiregion blends, but some fine wines are now being made that proudly state "Arroyo Seco" on their labels.

The AVA is in the center of the Salinas Valley, and as such is the recipient of morning and evening fog and wind, but plenty of sunshine and warmth in the afternoon. The climate and the gravelly soils that contain fist-sized rocks called "Greenfield potatoes" (Greenfield is the town within the AVA) are conducive to growing not only Chardonnay and Pinot Noir, but also cool-climate varieties such as Riesling, Albariño, and Grüner Veltliner.

Eons ago, the Arroyo Seco River cut a deep channel as it flowed into the Salinas River, leaving gravel, rock, and sand in its wake. It is on this alluvial deposit that Doug Meador, just back from a second tour of duty in Vietnam as a Navy pilot, decided to plant wine grapes in 1972. In 1974, he and his wife, LuAnn, began establishing their Ventana ("window") Vineyards in what became the Arroyo Seco AVA in 1983. With little nutrients in the soil, pure water, and vines warmed, on cold mornings and evenings, by heat retained by the "potatoes," Meador's site allowed him to grow grapes and produce wines with higher natural acidities, crystalline fruit character, and minerality.

The Meadors, now retired, turned Ventana over to Greenfield native Randy Pura, and the winery continues to produce high-quality wines, the most interesting being its off-dry Riesling

J. Lohr Vineyards & Wines
J. Lohr's Chardonnay, grown on loam soil over the famous "Greenfield potato" stones, has helped bring prominence to the Arroyo Seco AVA.

and a Grenache-Syrah blend called Rubystone. Jeff Cohn, owner-winemaker of JC Cellars in Alameda, across the bay from San Francisco, has long purchased Ventana Syrah grapes, and he produces a remarkable wine from them, with notes of lavender, savory herbs, black pepper, and roasted game.

Joining Meador in the pioneer category is Jerry Lohr, who planted his first 280 acres of vines in the area in 1972–73. Over the years, Lohr has acquired more than 3,000 acres of vineyard land, focusing on Chardonnay, Riesling, and Pinot Noir in Monterey County (Arroyo Seco and Santa Lucia Highlands); Cabernet Sauvignon, Merlot, and Syrah in Paso Robles; and Cabernet Sauvignon and Sauvignon Blanc in Napa Valley. Nine hundred Lohr acres are in Monterey County, including a rare 30-acre planting of Valdiguié, which many California winemakers in the past erroneously labeled as Napa Gamay. Once popular and inexpensive, Valdiguié—"poor man's Pinot," some called it—is no longer in favor, with just 300 acres of it remaining in California.

One of the "big guys" who invested in Arroyo Seco, Jackson Family Wines in Sonoma County, doesn't bury all of its Arroyo Seco grapes in its multiregion Kendall-Jackson Vintner's Reserve wines. Its Kendall-Jackson Seco Highlands Arroyo Seco Chardonnay and Carmel Road Arroyo Seco Chardonnay are high-end and highly regarded.

Carmel Valley AVA

Carmel Valley is south of the city of Monterey and 10 miles inland from the town of Carmel-by-the-Sea—famous for its former mayor, actor Clint Eastwood. It's a small AVA—18,000 acres, just 300 of them in vines, first planted in 1968—but visitors are drawn here by the mountainous terrain, scenic roads, and handful of winery tasting rooms.

Diamond T Vineyard, sister to Talbott Vineyards' Sleepy Hollow Vineyard in the Santa Lucia Highlands, is Robb Talbott's successful attempt to grow Pinot Noir in a cold, windswept place. In 1982, while others snickered, Talbott planted vines in sparse, chalky shale soils at 1,200 feet in elevation. His yields are a measly 1 ton per acre, but the Diamond T Pinot Noirs and Chardonnays are serious, collectible wines, tight and lean when young, with brisk acidity and a pleasant earthiness.

Still, Cabernet Sauvignon and Merlot account for 70 percent of the wine grapes in Carmel Valley, and Bernardus Vineyards & Winery is arguably its top producer of Bordeaux-style wines. Owner Ben Pon's Marinus, a blend of Cabernet Sauvignon, Merlot, Malbec, Petit Verdot, and Cabernet Franc, is stylish and cellarworthy. Galante Vineyards, whose owner, Jack Galante, is the great-grandson of J. F. Devendorf, founder of the city of Carmel, specializes in restrained Cabernet Sauvignons and oak-aged Sauvignon Blancs, from grapes grown on former cattle-grazing land.

San Bernabe Vineyard
The Indelicato family's sprawling 11,000-acre vineyard in southern Monterey County has its own AVA, San Bernabe, and grows twenty grape varieties.

San Bernabe AVA

One vineyard within Monterey County has to be seen to be believed. It's the San Bernabe Vineyard, owned by the Indelicato family of Delicato Family Vineyards (DFV). At a mind-boggling 11,000 acres and encompassing 20 square miles, San Bernabe is said to be the largest contiguous vineyard on earth (the Indelicatos prefer to call it "the world's most diverse single-vineyard property"). It also has its own AVA, called, not surprisingly, San Bernabe.

DFV built its reputation on making solid, everyday-drinking wines (its largest brand is Delicato). San Bernabe Vineyard, south of King City in the southern end of the county, supplies DFV's various brands, and those of other wine companies, with more than twenty grape varieties. Its viticulturists say San Bernabe has a hundred-plus separate blocks, thirteen different soil types, and more than twenty mesoclimates, allowing for experimentation as well as varied commercial grape production.

Other AVAs

Located on the southwestern edge of Salinas Valley, the **San Lucas AVA** has alluvial fans and terraces and more than 8,000 acres of grapes, including Cabernet Sauvignon, Merlot, Chardonnay, and Sauvignon Blanc. The **San Antonio Valley** and **Hames Valley AVAs** are the warmest in Monterey County, hospitable to red Bordeaux varieties. Growers have also had recent success with the Portuguese red varieties Tinta Cão and Touriga Nacional.

SAN BENITO & MOUNT HARLAN AVAs

San Benito County was once a most important wine region, home to Almaden Vineyards, a huge producer of jug and inexpensive cork-finished wines based in Paicines. But Almaden eventually relocated to the Central Valley, its owners (there have been several) selling off thousands of vineyard acres, and San Benito County as wine country faded away—with one glaringly positive exception: Josh Jensen and his Calera Wine Company. There, from vines planted on a remote mountain, Josh Jensen produces some of California's most expressive Pinot Noir.

The Gavilan (sometimes spelled Gabilan) Range separates San Benito County from Monterey County. These mountains are home to the San Benito AVA and **Mount Harlan AVA** of San Benito County, the latter being the location of the vineyards of Calera Wine Company, a pivotal producer of California Pinot Noir. In addition to Calera, a handful of small wineries exist in these AVAs.

Mount Harlan's peak is 3,289 feet above sea level. In 1975, Calera owner Josh Jensen, after finding rare limestone deposits on the mountain, planted Pinot Noir (and later Chardonnay and Viognier) on its slopes, at elevations of between 2,200 and 2,500 feet.

Jensen's story could make a book—and it did, Marq de Villiers's *The Heartbreak Grape*. The CliffsNotes version is that this lover of Burgundy wines graduated from Yale University, studied at Oxford University, and then begged his way into working at Domaine de la Romanée-Conti and Domaine Dujac in Burgundy. While there, Jensen realized that limestone soil was the single most important ingredient in producing great Pinot Noir, and he returned to his native California to find it.

Using geological maps from the U.S. Bureau of Mines, Jensen searched for more than two years for limestone (calcium carbonate) in areas that had both hillside slopes appropriate for planting vines and enough sunlight to ripen grapes. He found his grail on Mount Harlan in 1974, and purchased 324 acres in this isolated, calcium-rich area. The Jensen, Reed, and Selleck blocks were planted to Pinot Noir in 1975, and Jensen later purchased contiguous acreage that became the de Villiers, Mills, and Ryan vineyard blocks. Chardonnay, Viognier, and the Burgundian Aligoté were added to the mix.

DeRose Vineyards
The Gavilan Range (alternate spelling Gabilan) is the backdrop for DeRose's Cabernet Franc vineyard in Cienega Valley, a sub-AVA of the San Benito AVA.

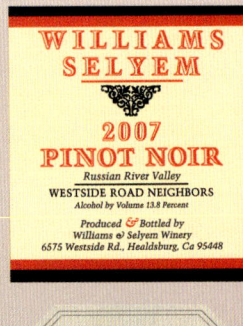

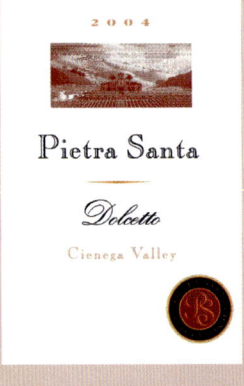

SAN BENITO & MOUNT HARLAN AVAs SNAPSHOT

Vineyard acreage: **Mount Harlan 177; San Benito 1,825**

Most-planted varieties: **Chardonnay, Pinot Noir, Merlot, Viognier**

Best varieties: **Aligoté, Chardonnay, Pinot Noir, Sangiovese, Viognier**

Sub-AVAs: **Cienega Valley, Lime Kiln Valley, Paicines (all in San Benito AVA and the Central Coast AVA)**

Wineries: **7**

Trailblazers: **Almaden Vineyards (no longer located here), Calera Wine Company**

Steady hands: **DeRose Vineyards, Enz Vineyards, Pietra Santa Winery**

Superstars: **Calera Wine Company, Williams Selyem (Vista Verde bottlings)**

Josh Jensen
Calera Wine Company founder Josh Jensen spent years searching California for limestone-rich soils in which to grow Pinot Noir, and found them on Mount Harlan in San Benito County. The winery is located in nearby Hollister.

With its elevation and exposure to marine breezes, Mount Harlan's climate is remarkably cool for an inland area (it is 25 miles from the Pacific Ocean). From April through September, temperatures rarely rise above 80°F. Although the six Calera vineyards have minor variations in soil composition, elevation, and exposure, the wines made from them share savory, spicy aromas; intensity of fruit; and a bracing acid/tannin structure. They can be backward upon release, depending on vintage, but with five years or more of aging, Jensen's Pinot Noirs typically blossom into round, integrated, approachable wines.

In 1990, Mount Harlan was recognized as an American Viticultural Area, and Calera remains the only grower within it. There is no electricity or phone service on Mount Harlan, so Jensen located his winery at a former cement plant near the city of Hollister and turned it into a multilevel, gravity-flow facility.

The Calera vineyards are 12 miles from Hollister, an epicenter of seismic activity in Central/Northern California. The San Andreas Fault runs through the middle of town, and cracks and buckles in the streets are evidence of the constant horizontal shifting of tectonic plates, called seismic creep. Most Californians worry about a major earthquake that could strike without warning, but to Hollister residents, their ongoing temblors are a part of life; "the big one" is more likely to happen elsewhere.

The **San Benito AVA** includes the Cienega Valley, Lime Kiln Valley, and Paicines AVAs. Wineries here are low-profile and small in production volume, with vineyards planted in varied mesoclimates and elevations. A majority of the grapes grown in the AVA are sold to large producers, most of whom use the fruit for Central Coast AVA-labeled wines.

The **Cienega Valley AVA** is the former home of historic Almaden Vineyards. In the 1970s, Almaden owned more than 4,500 vineyard acres in Cienega and produced thirteen million cases a year of fruity, inexpensive wines. In 1997, then-owner Heublein Inc. sold the Almaden property and moved, lock, stock, and barrels, to Madera in the Central Valley.

From the dust of the former Almaden property, Pietra Santa Winery and DeRose Vineyards have grown. The Blackburn family owns Pietra Santa, which produces several varietals. Its Sangioveses have been the most successful, and it's no wonder: they're made by Alessio Carli, former assistant winemaker at Badia a Coltibuono in Tuscany's Chianti region.

The DeRose family owns 100 acres of vines, 40 planted before 1900. The benchmark wine is the Negrette, from a grape that originated near Toulouse, France—and formerly known in California as Pinot St. George—tannic, peppery, and produced from a mere half-ton per acre of grapes. The San Andreas Fault runs through DeRose's main building, cracking floors and buckling walls; University of California equipment monitors seismic activity at the winery.

Lime Kiln Valley, a sub-AVA of Cienega Valley, has just one winery, Enz Vineyards, and 100 vine acres.

The **Paicines AVA** is mostly rolling hills, at elevations of 800 feet and lower, and is much warmer than Mount Harlan and Cienega Valley. Its most important figure is John Dyson, owner of the Williams Selyem winery in Sonoma County. His 550-acre Vista Verde Vineyard in Paicines is planted to several varieties; the best blocks of Chardonnay, Gewürztraminer, and Pinot Noir go into Williams Selyem's Central Coast bottlings.

Calera lime kiln
The Calera winery is named for a 30-foot-high lime kiln (*calera* in Spanish) located adjacent to the winery's Viognier vines in the Mount Harlan AVA. Calera's global sales manager, Marta Rich, and Jim Ryan, its vineyard manager since 1979, are shown here.

SAN LUIS OBISPO COUNTY

The Central Coast AVA is a monster, a 4-million-acre strip of appellational land running 250 miles down the California coastline, from south of San Francisco to Santa Barbara County. Nearly 100,000 acres are planted to wine grapes. Many consumers mistakenly believe that the Central Coast and Santa Barbara County are one and the same. Rather, the midsection of the Central Coast AVA, north of Santa Barbara, is home to numerous accomplished wineries and vineyards in San Luis Obispo County as well as the AVAS of Paso Robles, York Mountain, Edna Valley, and Arroyo Grande. The geography of this area includes east-west valleys that funnel coastal fog and wind to the vineyards, and soils comprised mainly of marine deposits.

San Luis Obispo County, located in the heart of the **Central Coast AVA**, is equidistant from San Francisco and Los Angeles. Residents refer to both the county and the city of San Luis Obispo as "San Luis" (LEW-is) or "SLO." The region is just far enough away from major cities to have developed slowly in wine tourism, which is reliant on day- and weekend-trippers, but other vacationers have flocked here for decades, because it's not near a major city.

Before the wine bug bit it, San Luis Obispo was known as a college town with beach benefits. Cal Poly, San Luis Obispo, draws students from all over California, enticed by the education, of course, but also the sunbathing on white sand, surfing, four-wheeling at Oceano Dunes, and hard partying. It's also a haven for refugees from the stiflingly hot Central Valley, who head west each summer to be energized by the area's Pacific Ocean breezes, saltwater taffy, strolls on piers, and chowder made from Pismo clams. Wine's role here has been a rather recent one, emerging in the Edna Valley and Arroyo Grande AVAs, just southwest of San Luis Obispo city.

Gary Eberle
Instrumental in establishing the Paso Robles AVA, Gary Eberle (above) was also the first to plant Syrah in the region. Eberle Winery produces a wide range of wines, including Syrah, Rhône blends, and Italian varietals.

Firepeak Vineyard
Baileyana Winery's estate vineyard in Edna Valley has a clay-loam-volcanic soil mix known as the Diablo series—"dirt of the devil"—but the wines are on the angelic side.

THE WEST | CALIFORNIA | SAN LUIS OBISPO COUNTY | 111

MID & SOUTH CENTRAL COAST

This map shows the portion of the large Central Coast AVA that lies south of Monterey County, including San Luis Obispo and Santa Barbara counties.

- — — — County boundary
- AVA boundaries are distinguished by colored lines
- **YORK MOUNTAIN** AVA
- ■ SAXUM Notable producer
- ● Benito Dusi Vineyard Noted vineyard
- Vineyards
- Woods and chaparral
- —2500— Contour interval 500 feet
- 116 Area mapped at larger scale on page shown

1:725,000

Paso Robles AVA

Just north of San Luis Obispo, and within San Luis Obispo County, is Paso Robles, which for years was virtually invisible to outsiders, its best grapes traditionally sold to wineries in other regions that rarely, if ever, put Paso Robles ("pass of the oaks" in Spanish) on the label. Paso is both a city of 30,000 people and an AVA, one of the largest in the country at 666,000 acres, 26,000 of them planted to vineyards. For now Paso Robles has no sub-AVAs, although they are sure to arise as this vast region sorts out its myriad terroirs.

There are 185 wineries in Paso Robles/York Mountain, and while they rely on local grapes, there is such a surplus that an estimated 58 percent of the fruit continues to go elsewhere. However, Paso's recent boom in vineyard development and winery establishment, improved grape and wine quality, developing reputation as the "Rhône Zone of the West," and effective promotion by the Paso Robles Wine Country Alliance have made it a major player in the California wine game.

Paso Robles, once rustic and remote, is one of California's last cowboy towns. Its cattle and horse ranches were its major reasons for being, and some of them are still around (as is Boot Barn, with a vast array of cowboy boots and Western wear). But vineyards have replaced acres upon acres of grazing land, and thanks to grapes and wine, Paso Robles has dusted itself off, spiffed up its downtown area to attract visitors, and become an important center of high-quality wines, restaurants, and accommodations.

The Paso Robles AVA extends from Monterey County's southern border to the Cuesta Grade, below Santa Margarita, and from the Santa Lucia Mountains on the west to Kern County on the east. Its size and head-spinning variations of soils, temperatures, rainfall, elevations, and exposures to ocean breezes and fog make the AVA designation almost meaningless.

An attempt was made in 2007 to split the Paso Robles AVA in half by creating a Paso Robles Westside AVA. The theory was that vineyards on the west side of Paso Robles (west of the Salinas River and Highway 101) were, thanks to the Pacific influence, cooler than those to the east and produced a distinctive style of wine. The implication was that Westside was better, its wines having more acidity and firmer structure.

After that proposal came a great hue and cry as opponents raised the fact that Paso's temperatures and soils vary greatly from north to south, not just east to west. "Paso Robles Westside" was far too simplistic, and inaccurate, they said. The AVA petition was withdrawn in 2009, and a committee of winemakers and grape growers hired outside experts to conduct soil analyses, study weather station data, and research

PASO ROBLES AVA SNAPSHOT

Vineyard acreage: **26,000**

Most-planted varieties: **Cabernet Sauvignon, Merlot, Syrah, Zinfandel, Chardonnay**

Best varieties: **Grenache, Mourvèdre, Petite Sirah, Roussanne, Syrah, Viognier, Zinfandel**

Sub-AVA: **York Mountain**

Wineries: **185**

Trailblazers: **Estrella River Winery/Eberle Winery, J. Lohr Vineyards & Wines, Tablas Creek Vineyard**

Steady hands: **Adelaida Cellars, Eberle Winery, Edward Sellers Vineyards & Wines, Halter Ranch Vineyards, J. Lohr Vineyards & Wines, Niner Vineyards, Norman Vineyards, Robert Hall Winery, Treana/Hope Family, Villa Creek, Vina Robles**

Superstars: **Justin Vineyards & Winery, L'Aventure Winery, Linne Calodo Cellars, Saxum Vineyards, Tablas Creek Vineyard**

Zenaida Cellars
The vineyards of this Paso Robles producer and its neighbors experience extreme temperature swings almost daily. These are created by the Templeton Gap, a break in the coastal mountain range that funnels Pacific Ocean breezes to the interior.

the historical significance of the growing areas within Paso Robles. They came up with eleven possible sub-AVAs within Paso Robles; those AVAs are pending.

The city of Paso Robles is 20 miles from the Pacific Ocean, but the AVA's westernmost boundary is just 6 miles from the coast. Temperatures and soils vary wildly here. For example, the Templeton Gap, a break in the coastal mountain range, funnels cooling breezes into an otherwise very warm region, moderating a 100°F summer afternoon with a chill-down to 50°F at night. Winemakers say this cool-down locks in intense varietal character and the natural acidity in the grapes. Other pockets of Paso that don't experience this chill-down produce riper, broader, more generously fruity wines that can also be soft and jammy.

In the decade ending 2011, Paso Robles experienced more than a fivefold increase in the number of bonded wineries, from 35 to 185. Two-thirds of its wineries produce fewer than 5,000 cases per year, and more than 95 percent of the brands are family-owned. Land is far less expensive here than it is in Napa, Sonoma, and Santa Barbara counties, so the region allows those without deep pockets to enter the industry at an affordable price.

Cabernet Sauvignon is the most-planted grape, and it can be successful when cultivated in the right places and vinified by the right hands. Adelaida Cellars, Eberle Winery, J. Lohr Vineyards & Wines, L'Aventure Winery, and Robert Hall Winery are among those who have mastered the formula.

Heat-craving Zinfandel, once thought to be Paso's best variety, remains vital, although it has been eclipsed in cachet by wines based on such Rhône Valley varieties as Syrah, Grenache, and Mourvèdre. Old Zinfandel vines planted by Italian immigrants in the late nineteenth and early twentieth centuries continue to produce intense, spicy, and often jammy Paso Zins; Ridge Vineyards in the Santa Cruz Mountains bottles a more mannered, elegant Zin from the Benito Dusi Ranch, planted during Prohibition. Local producers Castoro Cellars, Norman Vineyards, and Peachy Canyon can be counted upon to deliver high-flavor and flamboyant yet balanced Zinfandels from Paso Robles.

However, Paso's claim to fame is its Rhône-style wines, white and red. Single-variety bottlings and blends of Grenache Blanc, Roussanne, and Viognier for white wines, and Grenache, Mourvèdre, and Syrah for reds, have won applause from critics and cash-paying consumers alike. From 1992 through 2012, Paso Robles hosted the annual Hospice du Rhône, drawing thousands of attendees bent on tasting Rhône-variety wines from all over the world. After the 2012 event, organizers announced that they had shelved Hospice du Rhône in favor of holding smaller events in different areas.

Back in 1975, Gary Eberle was the first to plant Syrah in Paso Robles, using vine cuttings said to have come from the Chapoutier Vineyard in Hermitage, in the northern Rhône Valley. Eberle transplanted the cuttings on his family's Estrella River Winery property on the east side of Paso (later to become Meridian Vineyards), and after that, Syrah plantings began to spread throughout the state, with Eberle happy to supply cuttings. He also was instrumental in winning approval for the Paso Robles AVA in 1983, the same year he established his own winery, Eberle Winery.

The 1989 arrival in Paso Robles of the Perrin family of the Rhône Valley's famed Châteauneuf-du-Pape estate Château de Beaucastel, and their U.S. importer, Robert Haas, signaled Paso's potential for producing Rhône-style wines. After searching for five years for the right piece of land to plant Rhône varieties, the Perrins and Haases found it on Las Tablas Mountain, on the west side of the Paso Robles AVA. The 120-acre property was first planted to Beaucastel clones of Syrah, Grenache, Mourvèdre, Counoise, Viognier, Marsanne, Roussanne, and Grenache Blanc in clay soils mixed with high-pH limestone. Limestone was the key to their purchase, as well as the warm, sunny days with cool evenings—conditions that mirror those in Châteauneuf-du-Pape.

Tablas Creek established a nursery on its property, propagating vines for its vineyard from Beaucastel cuttings. When it found itself with a surplus of plants, it began selling them to other growers. Demand for grafted vines from Tablas Creek soared, so much so that in 2004, the winery outsourced its nursery business to a Sonoma County nursery, taking a royalty from each sale.

Tablas Creek, now managed by Robert Haas's son, Jason, arrived in Paso Robles with the mindset to grow grapes organically (as the Perrins did in France) and blend Rhône Valley varieties into single wines. The founders believed that, as in Châteauneuf-du-Pape, blends were greater than the sum of their parts, and since then, Tablas Creek's best wines have been multivariety blends: Esprit de Beaucastel (Mourvèdre, Syrah, Grenache, and Counoise) and Esprit de Beaucastel Blanc (Roussanne, Grenache Blanc, and Picpoul). The winery does bottle single-variety wines, including Syrah and Mourvèdre, but in small amounts, and they're sold only at its tasting room. Blending is the thing at Tablas, and at so many other successful Paso Robles wineries.

Consumers don't know what to expect from any given bottle of California Syrah, so they tend not to purchase from the category. Yet they are charmed by Rhone-style blends, and so are critics. Justin Smith can attest to that.

He's the owner/winemaker of Saxum Vineyards, and Paso Robles' best-known "young whippersnapper" winemaker. He's in his early forties, looks as if he's in his early thirties, and began his brand only in 2002, but his Saxum James Berry Vineyard 2007, a Grenache-driven red blend, was *Wine Spectator*'s wine of the year for 2010. Four months later, Smith was on the magazine's cover. His father, James Berry Smith, planted the Templeton Gap vineyard in the 1980s, and Justin learned the winemaking ropes so well that he now produces several bottlings a year from his dad's vineyard and sells grapes to others.

Like the Perrins and Haases, Stephan Asseo was attracted to Paso Robles by the calcareous soils and cool nighttime temperatures in the Templeton Gap region in the western hills. Asseo,

FROST DAMAGE

California's weather during grape-growing season typically has very little rain and few cold snaps between March and early November. But in spring 2011, Mother Nature threw a fit, particularly in Paso Robles, where she dealt growers a blast of bitter-cold air on two consecutive nights in April. Temperatures plummeted to the mid-20s and stayed there for ten hours each night, frost-burning tender buds just emerging from the vines.

It was the worst frost in a quarter century and destroyed as much as 75 percent of the potential crop in some vineyards. Early-budding white-wine varieties and Pinot Noir were most affected. Tablas Creek sustained nearly 100-percent damage in its Grenache, Grenache Blanc, Viognier, and Marsanne blocks. The cold temperatures in the upper and middle atmosphere meant that Tablas Creek's vineyard fans were ineffective; only those vineyards with ample water supplies could be protected against frost by overhead sprinklers and thus dodged major damage.

Water is a major issue in California, and not just for wine grapes. Years of drought conditions, growing populations that need drinking water, efforts to preserve fish habitats, and environmental regulations have prevented some farmers from drawing water from rivers and reservoirs for frost protection (water encases the buds and freezes around them, sealing in warmth), and from building lakes and ponds on their own properties to capture rainfall. Sprinklers are great for counteracting frost, but they need plenty of water.

Frost damage
New growth sprouts from a Grenache vine that was damaged by frost at Tablas Creek Vineyard in Paso Robles.

Tablas Creek crew
Robert Haas, Jason Haas, and Francois Perrin, in front, and Neil Collins and Cesar Perrin, in back, form the core of the Tablas Creek Vineyard team.

a winemaker in his native Saint-Émilion in Bordeaux, purchased 125 barren acres in "the Gap" in 1998 and began planting his vineyard, L'Aventure, after becoming "tired of all the regulations in France. If you compare this part of the Central Coast to the Rhône Valley," he says, "they have a similar Mediterranean climate, there are the same Châteauneuf mistral winds, the same vegetation, the same trees."

L'Aventure has certainly been an adventure for Asseo, as he has worked to determine which varieties grow best in the eighteen different soil types he's identified on his property. His initial plantings included Chardonnay, but he later discovered that Roussanne is the best white grape for the site. Asseo has also experimented with various red blends, letting Cabernet Sauvignon, Syrah, Grenache, and Mourvèdre comingle in various formulas. His straight-ahead Cabernet Sauvignon is arguably Paso Robles' finest.

Like many Paso reds, L'Aventure's have alcohol levels nudging 15 percent, but Asseo's remain elegant and ageworthy. This is the trick for Paso winemakers: harnessing the ripeness that comes from growing-season days that surpass 90°F, while capturing the natural acidity and backbone that can develop during 50°F nights.

One of Paso Robles' most important producers, Justin Vineyards & Winery, has devoted the lion's share of its production to Bordeaux varieties. Deborah and Justin Baldwin began the business in 1981, on the western edge of the Paso Robles AVA, and have added an elegant inn and restaurant. Their proprietary red wines, Isosceles (a Cabernet Sauvignon–dominant blend) and Justification (a Right Bank–style blend of Cabernet Franc and Merlot), have been superb over several vintages, as have other bottlings spread across several price points.

However, the Baldwins sold their winery to Roll International, owner of Fiji Water, in late 2010. Time will tell where the wines go from here.

South Dakota farm kid, Rhodes scholar, Air Force captain, and NASA engineer Jerry Lohr brought intelligence and a get-it-done attitude to Paso Robles. In the early 1970s, he planted vineyards in Monterey County, then expanded to Paso Robles in 1986, where he now owns 2,000 vine acres and bottles 500,000 cases of wine per year; his Paso wines are dedicated to Cabernet Sauvignon, Merlot, Petite Sirah, and Syrah.

Kenneth Volk founded Wild Horse Winery & Vineyards in Templeton in 1981 and built it into one of Paso Robles' finest producers. Volk sold the business in 2003 and relocated south to Santa Maria Valley in Santa Barbara County; Wild Horse has had several owners since, and it is now a member of the Constellation Brands family. Under Constellation, Wild Horse production shifted from Paso Robles grapes to a broad Central Coast sourcing.

Despite the lassos, Paso is not passé when it comes to celebrity presence. National Football League veteran defensive back Terry Hoage owns Terry Hoage Vineyards with his wife, Jennifer. For the truly starstruck, know that *American Idol* and *So You Think You Can Dance* producers Nigel Lythgoe and Ken Warrick own Villa San-Juliette Winery & Vineyards in San Miguel. Miss America 1957, Marian McKnight, owns Carmody McKnight winery with her husband, Gary Conway, an actor who starred in the 1960s–70s TV shows *Land of the Giants* and *Burke's Law* (Conway is his stage name, Carmody his birth name).

York Mountain AVA

This tiny appellation isn't within the Paso Robles AVA, although it is conjoined on the western edge of Paso Robles. It's just 6 miles from the sea, and thus cool and wet, making viticulture a challenge. The AVA only has one winery, York Mountain Vineyards, established in 1882 by Andrew York.

The winery is significant not only for its age, but also for the vineyard established there in 1913 by Polish pianist Ignacy Jan Paderewski. While on concert tour, Paderewski found relief for his rheumatism in Paso Robles' hot mineral baths. He established Rancho San Ignacio, where he planted Zinfandel and Petite Sirah. The property was sold shortly before his death in 1941, and the land went fallow until Liz and Bill Armstrong acquired it and replanted the site in 2005. In 2010, they purchased the adjacent winery as the home for their Epoch Estate Wines, producing Rhône varietals, Tempranillo, and Zinfandel.

Arroyo Grande and Edna Valley AVAs

Paso Robles may dominate the northern Central Coast region in size, yet these two small AVAs south of Paso have an extremely high per-capita wine quality ratio. Unusually for California, both the Arroyo Grande and Edna Valley AVAs are defined by valleys running east-west rather than north-south, leaving them largely unprotected from Pacific Ocean fog and breezes. As a result, these regions are much cooler during the summer than most parts of the Paso Robles AVA, and their harvests typically take place as much as two weeks later, thanks to the slow ripening process.

A gap exists in the mountain barrier where the Los Osos Valley meets the ocean at Morro Bay. Los Osos Valley serves as a wide-mouthed funnel, providing unobstructed airflow from the ocean to the Edna Valley. The hills and mountains surrounding Edna Valley capture marine air flowing in from Morro Bay, creating climatic conditions that differentiate Edna Valley from the surrounding areas. This pocket of cool air rests directly over Edna Valley Vineyard.

Edna Valley's most praised winemaker, John Alban of Alban Vineyards, has become so not only for being one of the original "Rhône Rangers"—U.S. winemakers who embrace wines made from Rhône Valley grapes, such as Syrah and Viognier—but for his total devotion to the Rhône category long before anyone else had made such a commitment. To produce Cabernet Sauvignon and Chardonnay wasn't ever a part of his plan.

Instead of following his Southern California physician father and enrolling in medical school, Alban chose Fresno State University's enology program, much to his parents' dismay. He worked four harvests at Rhône Valley wineries to study the grape varieties and their characteristics, and in 1989, with a bank loan, began Alban Vineyards in Edna Valley. Tablas Creek in Paso Robles had arrived at approximately the

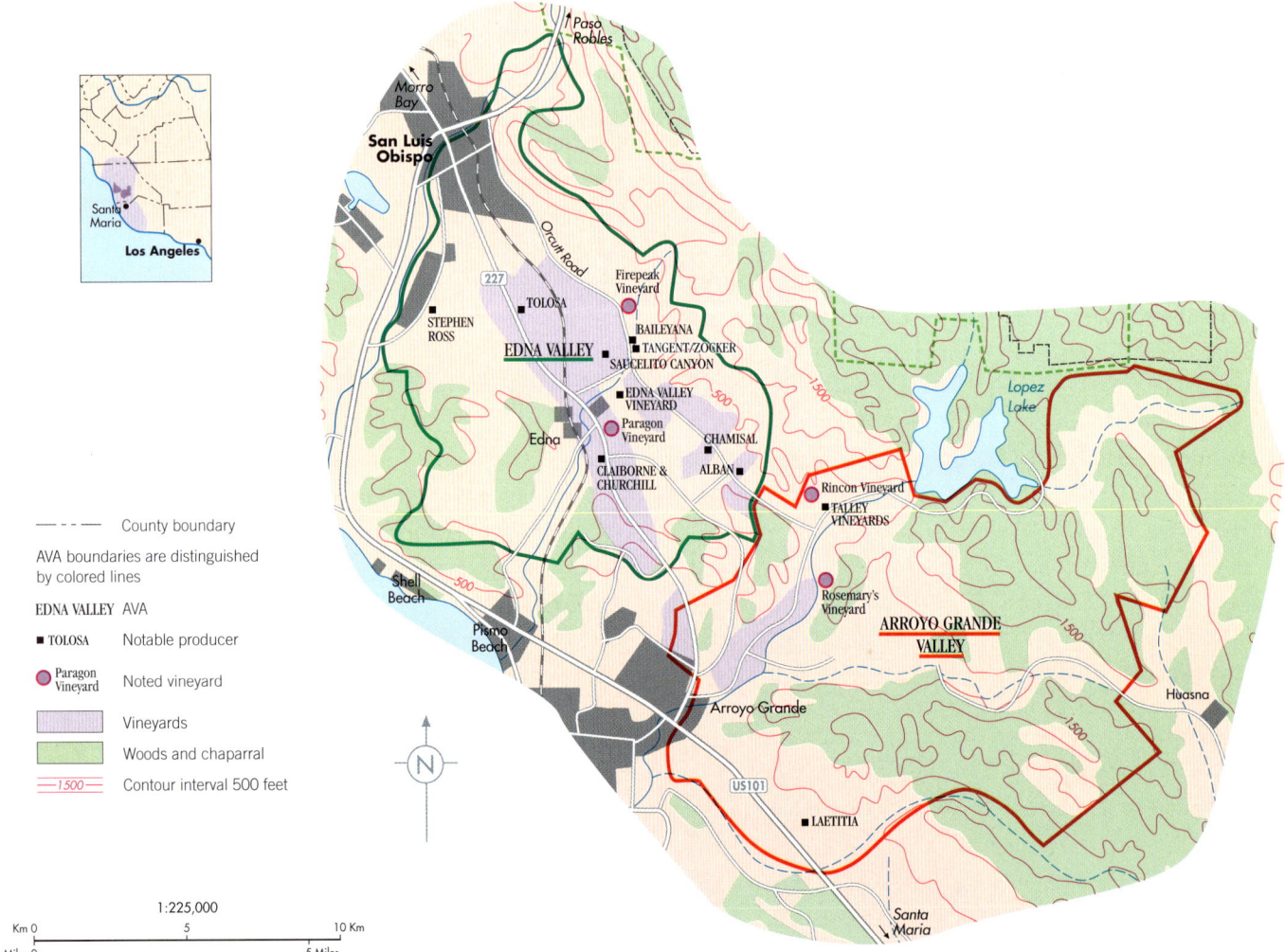

ARROYO GRANDE AND EDNA VALLEY AVAS SNAPSHOT
Vineyard acreage: **Arroyo Grande 6,500; Edna Valley 2,500**
Most-planted varieties: **Chardonnay, Pinot Noir, Syrah, Viognier**
Best varieties: **Chardonnay, Pinot Noir, Syrah, Viognier**
Emerging varieties: **Albariño, Grenache Blanc, Grüner Veltliner**
Wineries: **30**
Trailblazers: **Alban Vineyards, Chamisal Vineyards, Paragon Vineyard, Saucelito Canyon Vineyard**
Steady hands: **Baileyana Winery, Chamisal Vineyards, Claiborne & Churchill, Laetitia, Saucelito Canyon Vineyard, Stephen Ross Vineyards, Tangent, Tolosa Winery**
Superstars: **Alban Vineyards, Talley Vineyards**

same time from France, but had not yet established its nursery, so Alban began propagating his own Syrah, Viognier, and other Rhône varieties.

His first vintage was 1991, and by the mid-1990s, he had drawn the attention of important wine critics for his extracted, alcoholically potent, and utterly decadent wines, and a following of budding Rhône Rangers. The wines, the most sought after being the smoky, meaty Reva Syrah, named for Alban's mother, are made in small amounts (the highest-scoring are difficult to find) and require a deep pocketbook. Recent vintages have seen the wines dialed down a bit in terms of alcohol and density.

What attracted Alban to Edna Valley was the "dirt of the devil": shallow, well-drained soils heavy in both volcanic and ancient marine sediment—which includes sand, seashells, and whale fossils. A chain of volcanic cones, called the Nine Sisters, stretches from Edna Valley into the sea, a reminder of the violent eruptions and upheavals that formed the region.

Alban also favored the climate. The Pacific Ocean is just 4 to 6 miles from the valley, and its chilly breezes smack you in the face in the early morning and early evening, channeled by the east-west-oriented valleys that cut through the Santa Lucia mountain range. Fog during the growing season generally doesn't lift until noon, and daily highs are in the mid-70s to low-80s, resulting in a very long, dry, even growing season that's the envy of many in the warmer areas of California, except for one thing: grapes can still be ripening on vines when fall storms roll in, usually three weeks after North Coast winemakers have completed their harvest.

Franciscan missionaries planted vines in the area two hundred years ago, but modern Edna Valley/Arroyo Grande winemaking began in the early 1970s, when Norman Goss planted Chamisal Vineyard in Edna Valley, and Catharine and Jack Niven followed with the Paragon Vineyard. By 1974, the Greenough family had purchased an old-vine plot in Arroyo Grande and was making Zinfandel under the Saucelito Canyon label.

It wasn't long thereafter that the Talley family, longtime grower of peppers, cabbage, avocados, and cilantro in Arroyo Grande, began adding grapevines to their ranch. Brian Talley, whose late father, Don, started his first vineyard in 1981, has explained that his dad planted vines where vegetables wouldn't grow, attempting to make full use of his land. Little did Don know that wine grapes would bring his family far more greenbacks than cilantro. Talley's plantings later expanded to Edna Valley and Paso Robles.

Today Talley is one of the top producers of elegant, fresh-tasting Chardonnays and Pinot Noirs in the state. Its Bishop's Peak brand wines, from grapes grown throughout San Luis Obispo County, are good values and include Sauvignon Blanc, Syrah, and Cabernet Sauvignon. The Talleys own 190 acres of vineyards: The Rincon, Rosemary's, Monte Sereno, and Las Ventanas vineyard in Arroyo Grande; Oliver's and Stone Corral vineyards in Edna Valley (the latter in a partnership with Kynsi Wines and Stephen Ross Wine Cellars); and the Hazel Talley Vineyard in the Templeton Gap area of Paso Robles.

After planting Paragon Vineyard (now 832 acres), the Nivens partnered with Chalone Wine Group to build Edna Valley

Baileyana tasting room
Baileyana's tasting room is housed in a picturesque 'Independence schoolhouse,' originally built in 1909 and lovingly restored to its original one-room layout.

Vineyard in 1979 (later acquired by Diageo and now owned by E. & J. Gallo). In 1995, the Nivens established the Firepeak Vineyard in Edna Valley and hired Burgundy-born Christian Roguenant to produce Chardonnay, Pinot Noir, and Syrah from the site for their Baileyana label. Roguenant knew the region well, having served as winemaker at the Maison Deutz sparkling-wine house (now Laetitia) in Arroyo Grande.

Managing Firepeak, Paragon, and Baileyana wasn't enough for Catharine and Jack Niven's grandsons, John Niven and Michael Blaney. In 2006, they launched Tangent, a family of Chardonnay-alternative white wines, including Albariño, Sauvignon Blanc, Pinot Gris, and Pinot Blanc. With little or no oak influence, no malolactic fermentation, alcohol levels of around 13.5 percent, and a screw-cap closure, the Tangent wines, particularly the Albariño, are a crisp, vibrant answer to heavier styles of California wine.

In a huge leap of faith, Niven and Blaney planted a whopping 55 acres of Albariño in the Paragon Vineyard, as well as 16 acres of the Austrian white variety Grüner Veltliner. Roguenant, also the winemaker for Tangent, bottles the Grüner under the Zocker ("gambler" in Austrian German) label; the first vintage, 2009, was minerally, peppery, and fresh.

Claiborne and Fredericka Churchill Thompson are former University of Michigan professors who fell in love with Alsatian white wines and relocated to Edna Valley in 1981 to reproduce that aromatic style. Their Claiborne & Churchill Rieslings, Pinot Gris, and Gewürztraminers are pure and precise.

SANTA BARBARA COUNTY

First, it should be made clear: Santa Barbara County, located on the Pacific Coast between Paso Robles and Los Angeles, did not invent Pinot Noir. Some may think it did, if the 2004 movie *Sideways*, set in Santa Barbara County, is their major reference on wine. Still, *Sideways* sparked sales growth of Pinot Noir in the United States, spurring casual wine drinkers to put down their Cabernet Sauvignon and pick up a Sanford & Benedict. The Oscar-nominated film, by letting wine lovers know they didn't have to travel to Burgundy to find a fine bottle of Pinot Noir, also boosted wine tourism immeasurably in Santa Barbara.

At almost 6,500 acres, Chardonnay is still the predominant grape in Santa Barbara County, but Pinot Noir acreage, just half that of Chardonnay a few years ago, is gaining ground, with 4,260 acres. Syrah is important, too, at 1,400 acres of the total 21,000 acres of grapes planted in the county. More than one hundred wineries operate in the region; in 1980, just thirteen existed.

Relative to the North Coast (Napa, Sonoma, and all that), Santa Barbara County got a late start in commercial winemaking, although its wine history dates to before California became a state. The Golden State's wine godfather (no, not Francis Ford Coppola), Father Junípero Serra, planted the seeds for Santa Barbara County wine country more than two hundred years ago, when he and fellow *padres* began establishing California's twenty-one missions and growing grapes for sacramental purposes.

In 1786, Mission Santa Barbara, the tenth in the chain, was built in what is now the city of Santa Barbara. This "Queen of the Missions" has endured, still hosting friars who live and work there, and thousands of visitors a year who tour its magnificent grounds, admire its architecture, and steep in the historical perspective presented.

When California's commercial winemaking boomed after the 1849 Gold Rush, Santa Barbara County was hundreds of miles from the action. In Northern California, ex-miners and the businessmen who followed them to the Sierra Foothills found plenty of inexpensive land upon which to build houses, plant grapevines, and make wine; if they didn't stay in the Sierra, they typically moved down the mountains to Lodi, Mendocino County, Napa County, or Sonoma County. Santa Barbara County received little trickle-down from the Gold Rush, and it was further delayed in wine production by Prohibition and the Great Depression.

Yet the county found success in other areas: offshore oil drilling, the fishing industry, citrus fruit production, the military (Vandenberg Air Force Base is on its coast), horse husbandry, real estate for the wealthy and the retired, and beach-oriented tourism. It was only in the early 1960s, after UC Davis professors Maynard Amerine and Albert Winkler advised vintners that some areas of Santa Barbara County had outstanding viticultural potential, that grape growers and vintners went to work in earnest.

Rancho La Cuna
Jim Clendenen farms 6 acres of wine grapes and more than 5,000 olive trees at his Rancho La Cuna property. Below it is Los Alamos Vineyard, where Clendenen founded his Au Bon Climat winery in an old dairy barn.

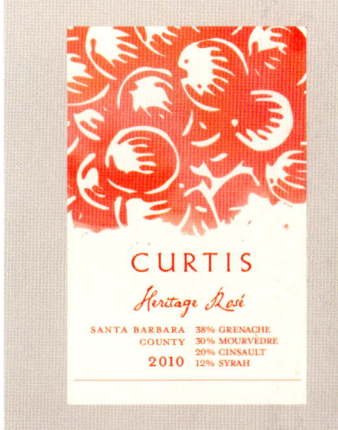

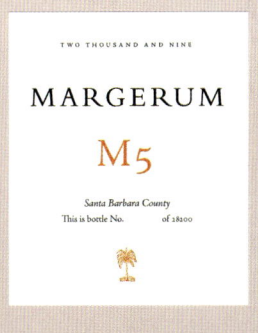

SANTA BARBARA COUNTY SNAPSHOT

Vineyard acreage: **21,000**

Most-planted varieties: **Chardonnay, Pinot Noir, Syrah, Pinot Gris, Cabernet Sauvignon, Sauvignon Blanc, Merlot**

Best varieties: **Chardonnay, Pinot Noir, Syrah, and other Rhône Valley varieties**

Emerging varieties: **Grenache (red), Grenache Blanc, Tocai Friulano**

AVAs: **Happy Canyon of Santa Barbara, Santa Maria Valley, Santa Ynez Valley, Sta. Rita Hills**

Wineries: **100-plus**

Pierre Lafond opened the first post-Prohibition winery in the county, Santa Barbara Winery, in 1962, in downtown Santa Barbara. Three years later, the first new vineyard after Repeal, now owned by Byron Vineyard & Winery, was planted by Uriel J. Nielson in Santa Maria Valley. Zaca Mesa Winery planted vines in 1973 and produced the county's first Syrah in 1978.

These wines were labeled with the Santa Barbara County appellation until 1981, when the Santa Maria Valley AVA was approved for the benchlands east of the city of Santa Maria, which produce a wide range of wines, the best being Chardonnay, Pinot Noir, and Syrah. The Santa Ynez Valley AVA, south of Santa Maria Valley and including the towns of Buellton, Solvang (a kitschy Danish village), and sleepy Santa Ynez, was established in 1983 and has proved adept at Rhône Valley varieties.

Santa Rita Hills joined the AVA club in 2001, though it changed its name to Sta. Rita Hills, in 2006, after Chilean winery Viña Santa Rita complained that consumers would be confused by the similarity in labeling. Sta. Rita Hills, which sits on the westernmost crag of the Santa Ynez Valley, earned its own AVA status for its significantly cooler, fog-driven climate and ability to produce crisp Chardonnays and deep-colored Pinot Noirs.

At the other end of the spectrum is the Happy Canyon of Santa Barbara AVA, approved in 2009 and also within the Santa Ynez Valley AVA; its distance from the ocean and warm-to-hot climate doesn't positively support high-quality Chardonnay and Pinot Noir, yet it is quite favorable to Bordeaux varieties, including Sauvignon Blanc and Cabernet Sauvignon.

Unusual in California, the winegrowing valleys in Santa Barbara County run northwest to southeast, rather than north to south, with the daily march of ocean winds and fog unimpeded by mountain ranges; think of it as an air conditioner turning on in the evening and off at midmorning. So these transverse valleys are cooled significantly, though to varying degrees. Sta. Rita Hills, the closest AVA to the Pacific Ocean, can be 15 to 20 degrees cooler in summer than the town of Los Olivos in the Santa Ynez Valley, which can be 10 degrees cooler than Happy Canyon.

Thanks to cool spring temperatures, some vintages suffer from poor fruit set, as pollination is disrupted, and yields can be low. The silver lining is that the grapes that do form are usually smaller and more intense in color and flavor, due to the higher skin-to-juice ratio. As in most California winegrowing regions, rainfall between May and early November is rare.

The soils are so diverse as to almost defy description: They include ancient seabeds, river-forged alluvial fans, limestone, diatomaceous earth, chalk, clay, and sandy loam.

Several wineries and vineyards have changed hands in recent years as large producers have sought more grapes to expand production, already-built facilities to process the fruit, and existing tasting rooms to capture Santa Barbara tourist dollars.

Bien Nacido Vineyards
Owners Marshall, Nicholas, and Stephen Miller (left to right) make small batches of wine for their own Bien Nacido label, in addition to selling grapes to some of California's most accomplished wineries.

In 1994, Gallo acquired Bridlewood Estate Winery in Santa Ynez Valley from Cory Holbrook. Illinois-based Terlato Wine Group assumed control of Richard and Thekla Sanford's Sanford Winery in Santa Rita Hills in 2005 and purchased the groundbreaking Sanford & Benedict Vineyard in 2007.

Byron "Ken" Brown, who started Byron Vineyard & Winery in 1984 after being the first winemaker at Zaca Mesa in Santa Ynez Valley, sold his business to the Robert Mondavi family in 1990 but stayed on as winemaker. However, Constellation purchased Mondavi Corporation and all of its brands in 2004, then shuffled off the Byron brand to Legacy Estates Group. Brown, a loyal soldier throughout most of the brand-flipping—it's difficult to leave a winery when one's name is on it—departed Byron in 2003 and started anew with Ken Brown Wines, for which he makes Pinot Noir, Chardonnay, and Syrah from grapes purchased from Santa Maria Valley and Sta. Rita Hills vines.

The story doesn't end there. Legacy Estates, based in Napa Valley, eventually saw its brands—Byron, Arrowood Vineyards & Winery, and Freemark Abbey—sold at bankruptcy auction to Jess Jackson and Jackson Family Wines. Mondavi had built Brown a new Byron winery and sold the original to Kenneth Volk as home for his fledgling Kenneth Volk Vineyards. Volk got the cash for that transaction by selling his high-volume Wild Horse Winery near Paso Robles to…Constellation.

In the modern-day California wine business, one needs a scorecard to track all the players.

Santa Maria Valley AVA

Long before the Santa Maria Valley was a winegrowing region, the native Chumash Indians knew it as *tepuztli*, meaning "copper coin." Later, Spanish settlers translated the word as Tepusquet. Part of an 1837 Mexican land grant, Rancho Tepusquet was home to cattle and row crops throughout the 1800s, and remained so until Uriel J. Nielson cultivated a vineyard there in 1964.

Nielson's first harvest took place in 1966—8 tons of grapes that were sold to the Christian Brothers in Napa Valley for $187 a ton. A second commercial vineyard was planted two years later, to Riesling and Cabernet Sauvignon, on the 33,000-acre Sisquoc Ranch, now home to Rancho Sisquoc Winery. The grapes were sold to others until 1972, when ranch manager Harold Pfeiffer made the first Rancho Sisquoc vintage. The winery today bottles 20,000 cases of wine per year.

Rancho Sisquoc has two most interesting features: its own chapel and Sylvaner grapes, from which it produces a crisp, citrusy varietal that is far more common in Alsace, France. So little Sylvaner is planted in California that the variety isn't included in the annual state grape acreage report. The San Ramon Chapel, built in 1875 near the entrance to the ranch, is depicted on Rancho Sisquoc's labels.

Rancho Sisquoc's neighbor in Foxen Canyon is Foxen Winery & Vineyard. Dick Doré acquired the former Rancho Tinaquaic Mexican land grant property in 1985. Now, using both Foxen's own vineyard grapes and purchased grapes, winemaker Bill Wathen fashions excellent Chardonnays, Pinot Noirs, and Syrahs, among other varieties. The most honorable bottling is the Foxen Ernesto Wickenden Vineyard Old Vines Chenin Blanc, one of the few remaining ultrapremium Chenins made in California; the vines were planted in 1966.

Santa Maria Valley typically has one of the longest growing seasons in California. Bud break can occur as early as February, and daytime highs leading into and through harvest reach only the high 70s. By comparison, the thermometer in the Middle Reach of Sonoma County's Russian River Valley, another prime Chardonnay and Pinot Noir zone, would likely show 90°F on that same day.

The granddaddy of Santa Barbara County vineyards is Bien Nacido in Santa Maria Valley, encompassing 800 acres, 300 of them under vines. Not only is it one of California's largest premium plantings, it's also among the select few in California that would earn grand cru status if the United States had such a classification system.

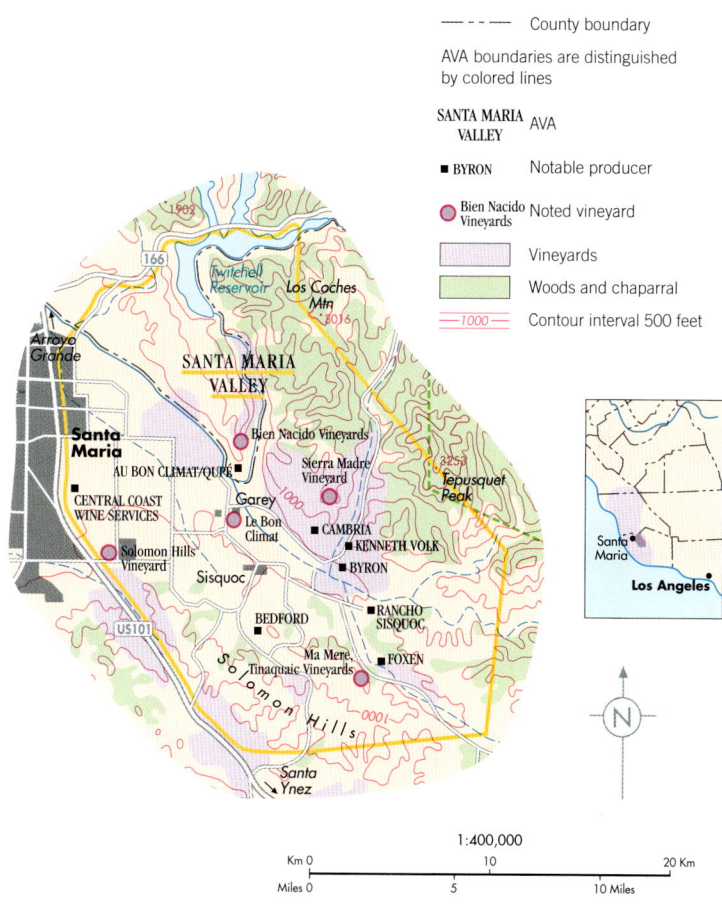

The Miller family founded Bien Nacido in 1969 and began planting it in 1972. The name is Spanish for "well born," referring to how the Mexican vineyard workers joked about the pampering they gave the vineyard. Bien Nacido, located 20 miles from the ocean, grows dozens of varieties in myriad blocks, each with its own soil characteristics, elevation, exposure, rootstocks, and clones. The Millers farm the blocks to the specifications of the wineries under contract to purchase the fruit. The vineyard's best grapes are Chardonnay, Pinot Noir, and Syrah, and there is a waiting list of wineries that hope a client will drop out, moving them up in line.

Some forty wineries use Bien Nacido on their labels, and not all of them are local. Jed Steele of Steele Wines in Lake County, Gary Farrell Vineyards & Winery in Sonoma County, and Villa Mt. Eden in Napa Valley are among the out-of-area vintners who have had a longstanding relationship with the vineyard and its grapes.

In 1998, the Millers established a second vineyard in Santa Maria Valley, Solomon Hills. The plot is closer to the ocean and has more calcareous, ocean-floor-sediment soils than Bien

Nacido; the Solomon Hills Chardonnays and Pinot Noirs tend to be a bit crisper and more minerally than those from Bien Nacido. After forty years of selling grapes to others, the Millers released their own line of wines in 2010—Pinot Noir and Syrah from Bien Nacido and Chardonnay from Solomon Hills.

The family is vital to Santa Maria Valley in another way. Winemakers just getting started and those who can't afford their own winery have the Millers' Central Coast Wine Services at their disposal; it offers crushing, pressing, fermentation, cellaring, and bottling services at its Santa Maria custom crush facility.

No producers are more closely connected to, and dependent upon, Bien Nacido than Jim Clendenen's Au Bon Climat, Bob Lindquist's Qupé, and Adam Tolmach's Ojai Vineyard. Collectively, their early wines became great advertisements for the quality of Bien Nacido grapes, and they remain loyal customers.

Clendenen was the assistant winemaker at Zaca Mesa when he met enologist Adam Tolmach. In 1982, they partnered to create Au Bon Climat ("a well-exposed vineyard," also called ABC), using significant amounts of Bien Nacido fruit for their Chardonnays and Pinot Noirs, which they made in an old dairy barn. Tolmach left ABC to construct a winery on his family's property near Ojai in Ventura County, but Bien Nacido and Solomon Hills remain major contributors to his vineyard-designated Chardonnays, Pinot Noirs, and Syrahs.

Qupé's Lindquist, another Zaca Mesa alumnus with a passion for Syrah, Marsanne, and other Rhône varieties, joined Clendenen in 1989 in assembling a ramshackle yet functional winery on the Bien Nacido property that they continue to use today. As early purchasers of Bien Nacido grapes, the leonine-maned Clendenen and the more conservatively dressed, neatly trimmed Lindquist, who often sports a Los Angeles Dodgers baseball cap, have been able to select the blocks they most want for their wines.

Jim Clendenen
The Au Bon Climat owner/winemaker has always embraced elegance and age-ability in making his Chardonnays and Pinot Noirs, even when ripeness and power became more important to some influential critics.

As different as they are in appearance, Clendenen and Lindquist share the philosophy that wines, whether they be Burgundian, Rhône-style, or any other, should be balanced, with firm acidity and tannins for long-term aging; should be compatible with food; and, most important, should express the character of their vineyard or region. ABC and Qupé rarely receive superhigh scores from U.S. critics, as their wines usually require aging before they blossom and aren't meant to be heady predinner cocktails. However, they tend to be leaner and more nuanced than many made by their neighbors, and for that, they have a wide fan base.

SANTA MARIA VALLEY AVA SNAPSHOT

Vineyard acreage: **7,500**
Most-planted varieties: **Chardonnay, Pinot Noir, Syrah**
Best varieties: **Chardonnay, Pinot Noir, Syrah**
Wineries: **25**
Trailblazers: **Au Bon Climat, Bien Nacido Vineyards, Nielson Vineyard, Rancho Sisquoc Winery**
Steady hands: **Byron Vineyard & Winery, Cambria Estate Winery, Foxen Winery & Vineyard, Ojai Vineyard (Ventura County)**
Superstars: **Au Bon Climat, Qupé**
One to watch: **Kenneth Volk Vineyards**

In 1998, Clendenen purchased 100 acres of land on the south side of the Sisquoc River, across from Bien Nacido, and planted Le Bon Climat vineyard to Chardonnay, Pinot Noir, and Viognier. The vineyard was certified organic in 2003.

Clendenen also has a love for Italian wines and Italian grape varieties, and he produces them, on and off, from Santa Barbara County, most recently under the Buon Natale label.

Barbara Banke, wife of the late Jess Jackson, acquired a large portion of the original Tepusquet Vineyard (planted in 1970 to 1971) in 1986 to serve as the site for her Cambria Estate Winery, which she owns separately from the Jackson Family Wines business. Banke's Chardonnays and Pinot Noirs have always been well made and correct, but improvements in the vineyards, including replanting of rootstocks and clones more suited to the climate and geology than those available two decades ago, have produced more exciting and interesting wines of late. Cambria's Julia's Vineyard Pinot Noir is complex and reasonably priced for California Pinot Noir.

All of Santa Maria Valley, in fact, has lifted its game, as new plant material has become available and advances made in viticultural knowledge and techniques. Replanting is an ongoing process in all of Santa Barbara County's winegrowing regions, and at a minimum of thirty thousand dollars per acre to replant, it's no wonder top bottles cost as much as they do.

In 2011, the Santa Maria Valley AVA, which includes a small portion of southern San Luis Obispo County, was expanded to the south by nearly 19,000 acres, bringing the total to 116,270. The Millers' Solomon Hills Vineyard, Addamo Estate, Goodchild Vineyard, Foxen's Tinaquaic and Ma Mere vineyards, and Clendenen's Le Bon Climat, all previously limited to "Santa Barbara County" on their labels, now can use "Santa Maria Valley."

Bien Nacido Vineyard
If the United States had a French-style quality-classification system for vineyards, wines from Bien Nacido in Santa Maria Valley would be grand crus, top of the line.

Santa Ynez Valley AVA

The Santa Ynez Valley is framed by the Santa Ynez and San Rafael mountain ranges. Its name is taken from the 1804 Mission Santa Inés, the first Spanish settlement in the area.

The long, east-west-running valley has cool temperatures and fog at its western end (best for Pinot Noir and Chardonnay) and a warmer, sunnier climate at its eastern end (best for Cabernet Sauvignon, Cabernet Franc, Sauvignon Blanc, and Rhône varieties). In the middle, north of Buellton on Ballard Canyon Road and almost into Los Olivos, is the likely next Santa Barbara AVA, Ballard Canyon. This area is a bit too warm for Burgundian grapes and slightly too cool for Bordeaux varieties, but seems just right for Rhône and Italian varieties.

Firestone Vineyard was Santa Barbara County's first estate winery, producing wines only from grapes grown on the property. Leonard Firestone, former U.S. ambassador to Belgium and a descendent of the Akron, Ohio-based Firestone Tire family, established the ranch in Santa Ynez Valley in the early 1970s. Joined by his son, Brooks,

Santa Ynez, Sta. Rita Hills & Happy Canyon of Santa Barbara

Within Santa Barbara County's Santa Ynez Valley AVA are two sub-AVAs, Sta. Rita Hills and Happy Canyon. See p.126 for more about Sta. Rita Hills, p. 129 for Happy Canyon.

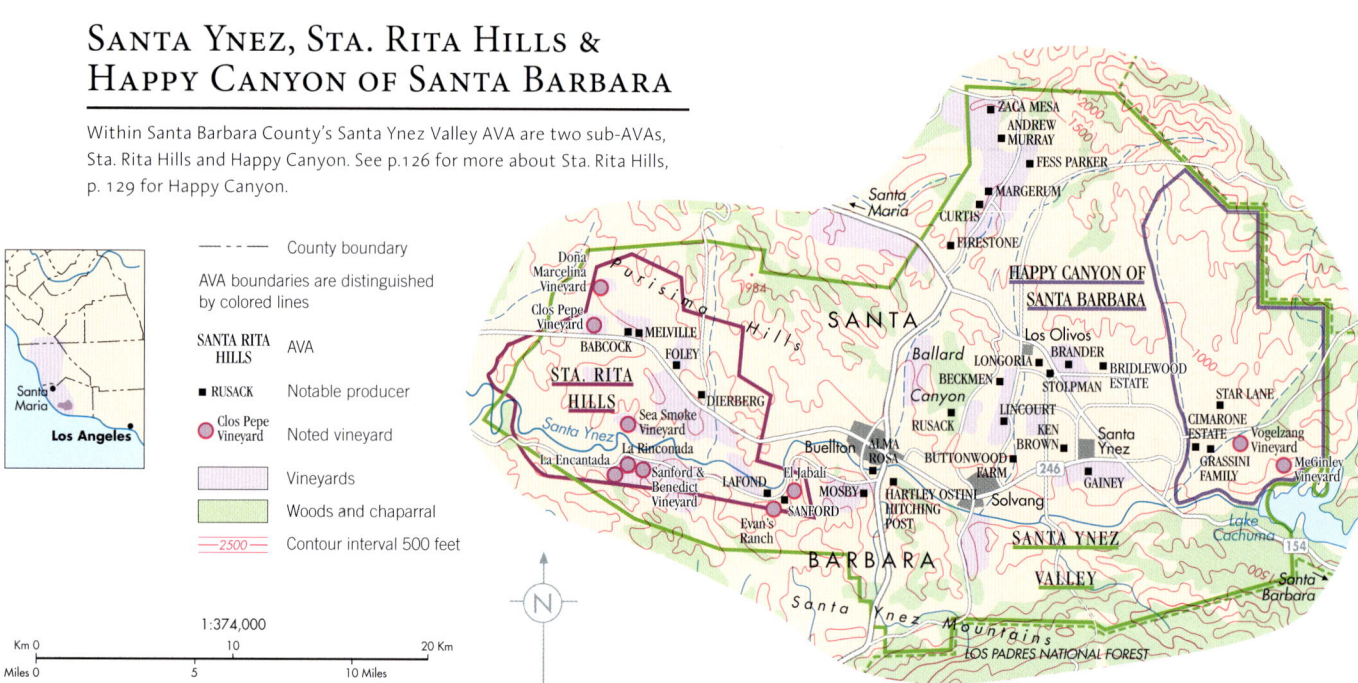

SANTA YNEZ VALLEY AVA SNAPSHOT

Vineyard acreage: 5,300

Most-planted varieties: Chardonnay, Pinot Noir, Syrah

Best varieties: Chardonnay, Grenache, Pinot Noir, Syrah

Sub-AVAs: Happy Canyon, Sta. Rita Hills

Trailblazers: Firestone Vineyard, Zaca Mesa Winery & Vineyards

Steady hands: Bridlewood Estate Winery, Fess Parker Winery, Hartley Ostini Hitching Post Winery, Star Lane Vineyard, Stolpman Vineyards

Superstars: Beckmen Vineyards, Jonata, Rusack Vineyards

Gainey Winery horses
Like many others in the Santa Ynez Valley, the Gainey family raised horses before deciding to plant grapevines and produce wine. Horse breeding is still a part of their livelihood.

and Brooks's wife, Kate, he planted a vineyard and later began producing wine under the Firestone label.

In 1995, the Firestones started Curtis Winery, a complementary producer dedicated to Rhône-style wines. Firestone Vineyard was sold to title-insurance mogul William Foley in 2007, with the Firestones retaining Curtis. Brothers Adam and Andrew Firestone operate Curtis today.

Beckmen Vineyards, founded in 1994 by Tom Beckmen and his son, Steve, is a highly developed representation of Santa Ynez Valley grape growing. Planted to eighteen blocks and seven clones of Syrah and eight blocks and five clones of Grenache, Beckmen's Purisima Mountain Vineyard also has smaller plots of Mourvèdre, Counoise, Marsanne, Roussanne, Grenache Blanc, Sauvignon Blanc, and Cabernet Sauvignon.

The vineyard, which would be included in the potential Ballard Canyon AVA, is farmed biodynamically. Its elevations, reaching upward of 1,250 feet, shape climatic factors such as moisture, temperature, exposure, and the marine air drawn up from the Pacific Ocean through the valley. Purisima experiences morning fog and afternoon breezes in the summer, which moderate temperatures and lead to a long, slow ripening—a winemaker's dream.

A limestone subsoil, similar to that found in the Côte-Rôtie and Châteauneuf-du-Pape regions of France's Rhône Valley, limits vine vigor and berry size, which helps the grapes develop deep color and dense concentration of fruit flavor.

Geoff and Alison Wrigley Rusack own Rusack Vineyards in Santa Ynez Valley/Ballard Canyon. They started their vineyard in 1995, and in 2001, hired Napa Valley veteran John Falcone to produce their wines. He advised the couple on replanting their vines to varieties best suited for the soils and climate, and fine-tuned winemaking procedures. The Rusack Chardonnays, Pinot Noirs, and Syrahs are now gorgeously supple and refined; Anacapa, its Cabernet Franc, is on par with any made in Napa Valley. The Rusacks also grow Chardonnay grapes on Catalina Island (see box p. 141).

Falcone left Rusack in spring 2012 to join the Gainey Vineyard, part of a large farming operation that has been owned by the Gainey family for the past fifty years. Along with breeding Arabian horses, growing vegetables and fruit, and maintaining rangeland that supports beef cattle, the Gaineys produce a wide mix of wines from their Santa Ynez Valley Home Ranch, and Pinot Noir and Syrah from Evan's Ranch in Sta. Rita Hills. Gainey's Limited Selection Santa Ynez Valley Sauvignon Blanc is a keeper, with 50-percent barrel fermentation lending richness and palate weight to the tangy citrus flavors and flinty minerality.

Brander Vineyard, established in 1975 by Erik Brander and his son Fred, has come to be known as the "King of Sauvignon Blanc" in Santa Ynez Valley, bottling as many as seven Sauvignon Blancs in any given vintage. Brander's Cuvée Nicolas, a partially barrel-*sur-lie*–aged Sauvignon Blanc, is California's equivalent of white Bordeaux. Achieving equal status is his Westerly Vineyards Sauvignon Blanc, a blend of grapes from three vineyards in the Santa Ynez Valley/Happy Canyon region.

Although it's not an AVA, the Los Alamos Valley, located between the Santa Ynez Valley and Santa Maria Valley, has a similar marine, cool climate.

Sta. Rita Hills AVA

Designated an AVA in 2001, Sta. Rita Hills comprises more than 30,000 acres, but just 1,700 acres of wine grapes are planted on its steep slopes above the Santa Ynez River. The appellation, east of Lompoc and west of Buellton, is a superb yet risky location for growing cool-climate, structured, bracing Chardonnays and Pinot Noirs. Sta. Rita Hills is what's known as a "nested" AVA—in this case a small appellation within the Santa Ynez Valley AVA.

Sta. Rita Hills is on the western end of the Santa Ynez Valley, with the Santa Rosa Hills to the south and Purisima Hills to the north. This east-west valley, created by the Santa Ynez River, draws cold breezes and fog from the Pacific Ocean—just 10 or so miles away—making it some 15 degrees cooler in summer than the eastern side of the valley.

The climate makes for a long, seven- to eight-month growing season, yet there is just enough warmth between May and October to ripen grapes. The soils are a mix of loams based on sand, calcified seashells, and alluvial and terrace deposits.

Richard Sanford and Michael Benedict were the pioneers here, planting the Sanford & Benedict Vineyard in 1970, despite derision from locals that the area wasn't warm enough to support grape growing. It proved to be a tremendously good source of Pinot Noir grapes—intense, steely, and structured, with deep crimson colors and plenty of natural acidity to ensure the wines enjoy long lives in the cellar.

Most of their grapes went to Richard and Thekla Sanford's Sanford Winery, established in 1981; they also sold fruit to Santa Barbara County neighbors. Sanford, a former naval officer who served in Vietnam, and Benedict, a botanist, eventually parted ways, and the 135-acre vineyard was sold to Robert and Janice Atkin; Sanford continued to purchase their grapes.

Over time, Sanford & Benedict was replanted and modernized. Today it grows Pinot Noir, Chardonnay, Viognier, and Pinot Gris and supplies grapes to Au Bon Climat, Bonaccorsi, Longoria, Foxen, Babcock, and Sanford wineries, to name a few. In 1983, the Sanfords planted Rancho El Jabalí, farmed organically, to support Sanford Winery. Their La Rinconada and La Encantada vineyards followed, and by 2000, Sanford's three estate vineyards had been certified organic by the California Certified Organic Farmers. The Sanfords sold La Encantada in the summer of 2011 but continue to buy grapes from the site.

Today Sanford Winery no longer belongs to the Sanfords. After Terlato Wine Group invested in the winery in 2005, the relationship soured, as the Sanfords and Terlato could not reach agreement on how to farm the vineyards and produce the wines. Richard and Thekla departed the business and created Alma Rosa Winery & Vineyards, a Chardonnay/Pinot Noir brand in Sta. Rita Hills.

Perhaps attracted to Sta. Rita Hills by Sanford & Benedict, Pierre Lafond, who established Santa Barbara County's first post-Prohibition winery, Santa Barbara Winery, in 1962, advanced west into Sta. Rita Hills in 1971, planting 65 acres for his new Lafond brand with winemaker Bruce McGuire. Yet the itch to make world-class wines from Sta. Rita Hills didn't get truly scratched until the 1980s, when a small swarm of producers, among them Babcock Vineyards & Winery, Richard Longoria, and ABC's Jim Clendenen, committed to its vineyards. In the 1990s, producers such as Brewer-Clifton, Melville, and Clos Pepe came to the fore.

Bob Davids was and still is a big boomer in Santa Rita. He made his money in handheld electronic games and invested

STA. RITA HILLS AVA SNAPSHOT

Vineyard acreage: **1,900**

Most-planted varieties: **Pinot Noir, Chardonnay, Syrah**

Best varieties: **Chardonnay, Pinot Noir, Syrah**

Wineries: **30**

Trailblazers: **Sanford & Benedict Vineyard, Sanford Winery**

Steady hands: **Alma Rosa, Babcock Winery & Vineyards, Brewer-Clifton, Clos Pepe, Dierberg Estate Vineyards, Foley Estates Vineyard & Winery, Lafond Winery, Loring Wine Company, Melville Vineyards & Winery, Palmina, Richard Longoria Wines**

Superstars: **Sanford Winery, Sea Smoke Cellars**

One to watch: **Evening Land Vineyards**

Sea Smoke Vineyard
Bob Davids' Sta. Rita Hills vineyard, perched above the Santa Ynez River, is named for the marine fog that the river draws into the vineyard.

chunks of it in Sea Smoke Cellars, arguably Sta. Rita Hills' most sought after Pinot Noir. Sea Smoke produces three Pinots—Botella, Southing, and Ten—from its 300-acre property overlooking the Santa Ynez River, where Davids and his general manager/director of winemaking, Victor Gallegos, planted 25 separate blocks with ten Pinot Noir clones and four different rootstocks.

Davids named his vineyard Sea Smoke after the maritime fog that rolls across its hillsides on summer evenings, slowing fruit maturation and preserving the natural acidity in the grapes. Sea Smoke and Sta. Rita Hills in general is an unlikely place to grow Pinot Noir. The area is rated Region I—the coldest—on the UC Davis heat summation scale, but it has the same latitude (34°N) as Tunisia in North Africa, with the same solar intensity and lack of rainfall. Somehow the frigid temperatures and sun power combine in yin-yang fashion to produce some of California's longest-lived, most bracing Pinot Noirs.

The long growing season produces intense flavors, great complexity, and firm acidity in Chardonnay and Pinot Noir grapes. Still, there is enough daytime warmth at the end of the season to fully ripen the fruit. The soils are a mix of loams based on dune sand, marine deposits, alluvium, and terrace deposits. Yields are low and farming costs are high, Gallegos says, making Sta. Rita Hills viticulture "borderline economical." This region is only for the fanatical and well funded.

The Pinots of Sea Smoke and nearby producers, which include Ampelos Cellars, Brewer-Clifton, Cargassachi, Clos Pepe Vineyards, Fiddlehead Cellars, Gainey, Loring Wine Company, and Melville Vineyards & Winery, tend to show juicy black fruit, mineral and tea notes, firm natural

WILLIAM FOLEY

It began as many wineries do: A wealthy businessperson decides it would be fun to start or purchase a winery…a little something to do on the weekends. In 1996, William Foley, chairman of Fidelity National Financial, a title-insurance company, purchased a small winery in Santa Ynez Valley from Firestone Vineyard and named it Lyncourt Winery—a combination of the names of his daughters, Lindsay and Courtney. Two years later, he bought a 460-acre horse ranch in the Santa Rita Hills, planted Chardonnay and Pinot Noir there, and founded Foley Estates Vineyard & Winery as a companion to Lyncourt.

Life, business, and the wines were good—so good that in 2008, Foley embarked on an aggressive buy-up campaign, acquiring, in order, the former Fess Parker Ashley's Vineyard in the Sta. Rita Hills AVA; Firestone Vineyard in Santa Ynez Valley; high-end Cabernet Sauvignon maker Merus in Napa Valley; Three Rivers Winery in Walla Walla, Washington; Sebastiani Vineyards in Sonoma County; Kuleto Estate in Napa Valley; and Sonoma's swanky 1,300-acre Chalk Hill Estate Vineyards & Winery. The *Press-Democrat* newspaper in Santa Rosa, California, said the price Foley paid Chalk Hill owner Fred Furth was as much as $100 million, making it one of the biggest single-winery sales in California history.

In 2011, Foley and his Foley Family Wines group also bought the Clifford Bay and Vavasour wineries and brands in New Zealand. His multibrand, multi-price-point strategy, very much like the one the late Jess Jackson used to build Jackson Family Wines, gives Foley clout with wholesalers that he would not have otherwise.

Lyncourt Vineyards
William Foley began his winery shopping spree in 1996, when he acquired J. Carey Cellars in Santa Ynez Valley and renamed it Lyncourt. Foley now owns a dozen wineries in California, Washington state, and New Zealand.

acidity, and youthful tannins that need bottle age to round out. Some have an exotic spiciness, others a more meaty, forest-floor savoriness.

Sea Smoke's neighbor, Evening Land Vineyards, is an unusual partnership of Paris and New York restaurateurs with Burgundy's Dominique Lafon and Sashi Moorman, a young rock-star California winemaker (Stolpman Vineyards, Piedrasassi) in Sta. Rita Hills. Evening Land produces Pinot Noir from the Eola Hills of Oregon's Willamette Valley (made by Lafon and Isabelle Meunier) and the Occidental Vineyard in the Sonoma Coast AVA of Northern California (made by Moorman). The company has since planted Pinot Noir in Sta. Rita Hills, some 40 acres, which include experimental blocks of vines grown from seeds. It will be interesting to see what comes of this effort, although the high quality of the wines made from Willamette Valley and Sonoma Coast vineyards suggest success in Sta. Rita Hills.

Going against the Pinot tide is Palmina, a brand created by Brewer-Clifton partner Steve Clifton in 1995. For Palmina, he's keen on Italian grape varieties grown in Santa Barbara County, putting a California spin on Malvasia Bianca, Arneis, Tocai Friulano, Barbera, Dolcetto, and Nebbiolo, some of them from Sta. Rita Hills. The majority of Palmina's wines are layered and intriguing.

The city of Lompoc (LAHM-poke), a temperance colony in the late 1800s that preached alcohol abstinence long before Prohibition, has become, ironically, home to the Lompoc Wine Ghetto, on Industrial Avenue and in a most industrial setting, where thirteen small yet quality-crazed wineries do their work and pour their wines.

Current-day Lompoc is a drab place, built to serve the needs of nearby Vandenberg Air Force Base workers. Its economy, once boosted by Vandenberg's role in the NASA space shuttle program, suffered when the program ended, but savvy winemakers found a silver lining, albeit a thin one, by establishing the Wine Ghetto as a low-cost place to make their wines. Their rent is low, the camaraderie high, and the wines, for the most part, excellent.

Palmina is here, along with Evening Land, Richard Longoria, Ampelos, Samsara, Fiddlehead Cellars, and Moorman's Piedrasassi/New Vineland. It's a concentration of makers of high-quality, low-volume wines that attracts knowledgeable consumers more interested in tasting individualistic wines than in soaking up architecture and gardens.

Happy Canyon of Santa Barbara AVA

This infant (2009) AVA totals 24,000 acres in the easternmost part of the Santa Ynez Valley, northwest of Lake Cachuma. It's much warmer and drier in Happy Canyon than in western Santa Ynez Valley, with average summer-day temperatures in the low 90s. This warmth, and the loam and clay soils mixed with serpentine cobblestones, allows Cabernet Sauvignon, Cabernet Franc, Merlot, Sauvignon Blanc, and Rhône varieties to grow quite happily here.

Large horse ranches, pastures, and majestic oak trees share space with hillside vineyards planted beginning in 1996. Six producers are in Happy Canyon: Cimarone Estate Winery, Grassini Family Vineyards, Happy Canyon Vineyard, McGinley, Star Lane Vineyard, and Vogelzang Vineyard.

Star Lane, owned by Jim and Mary Dierberg of Dierberg Estate Vineyards in Sta. Rita Hills, does an expert job with Cabernet Sauvignon and Sauvignon Blanc. The Vogelzang Sauvignon Blanc, at a hefty $40 a bottle, is a stunner, made by former Peter Michael (Sonoma County) winemaker Robbie Meyer; it's both minerally and rich, with a complex leesy note.

Doug Margerum, longtime owner of and wine guru at Santa Barbara's renowned Wine Cask restaurant, sold the business to become a winemaker in 2007 (and returned as an investor in 2009). He produces wine for his Margerum Wine Company brand, as well as for Cimarone and Happy Canyon Vineyard.

About the AVA name? During Prohibition, one could not legally purchase alcoholic beverages, but could make small amounts of wine, beer, or booze for personal use. A potent elixir, likely a distilled spirit, was produced in the canyon; legend has it that folks would "take a trip up Happy Canyon" to purchase the intoxicating drink, and the name stuck.

Grassini Family Vineyards
This sustainability-minded Happy Canyon producer has wine caves to ensure humidity and temperature control of its wines, is constructed of reclaimed fir wood, and is solar-powered.

SIERRA FOOTHILLS

Holly's Hill Vineyards
This El Dorado County producer excels at growing and producing Rhône Valley varieties, including Roussanne, Viognier, and Mourvèdre.

James Marshall's 1848 discovery of gold in the Sierra Nevada mountains lured thousands of miners from all over the world to seek their fortunes in a rugged region that two years later would become a part of the state of California. Marshall's spotting of glimmers of gold in the South Fork of the American River, at his business partner John Sutter's mill at Coloma, sparked not only the 1849 Gold Rush, but also an influx of European immigrants who brought their wine-drinking culture with them.

Sierra Foothills, Lodi & the Delta

This map focuses on the major wine-producing counties in the Sierra Foothills AVA (Amador, El Dorado, and Calaveras) and the Lodi and Clarksburg AVAs in the Sacramento River Delta (see p. 137).

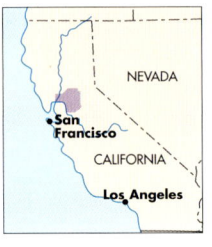

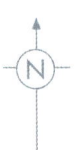

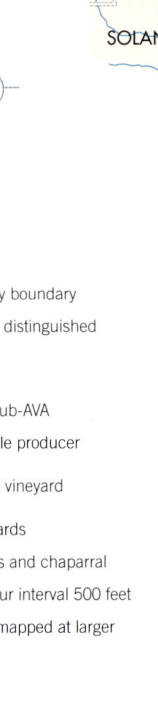

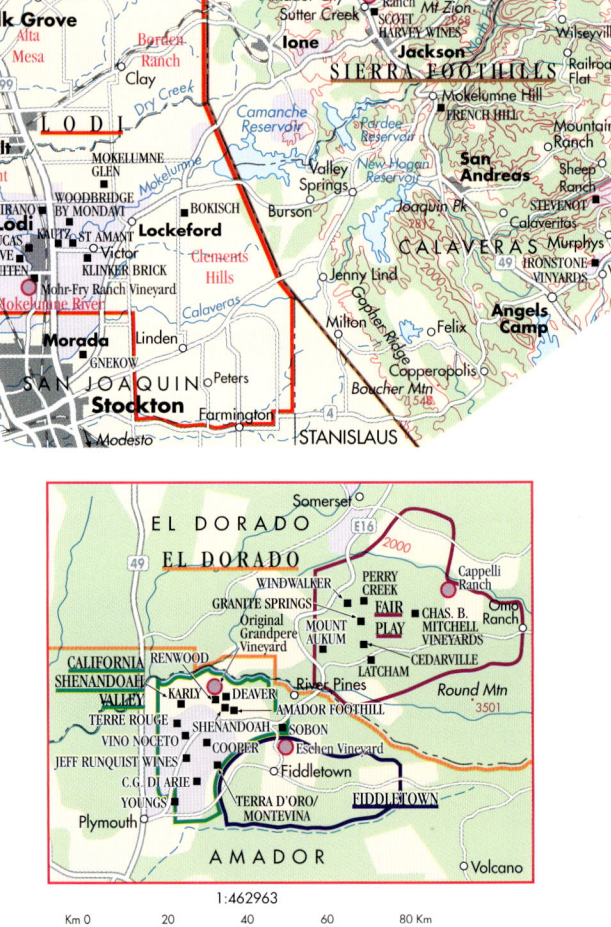

WHITE ZINFANDEL

Sutter Home Winery in Napa Valley established the pink and slightly sweet white Zinfandel style in 1975, thanks to a "fortuitous mistake" made by then-winemaker and now chairman-CEO Louis "Bob" Trinchero. Wine snobs sneer at white Zin, but Trinchero's goof led to two definitive events in U.S. wine history: the creation of a wine that won over Americans who previously thought they didn't like wine, and the salvation of hundreds of acres of old Zinfandel vineyards, many of which continue to produce today.

Between the early 1980s and the late 1990s, white Zinfandel was the most popular wine in the United States; only in 1998 did Chardonnay take the top rung. In the 1970s, traditional red Zinfandel lost some of its sizzle after the prevailing style became overripe and overly alcoholic, and Merlot and Cabernet Sauvignon rose in plantings and popularity.

Some growers ripped out their Zinfandel vines and replanted to other varieties; others were patient, and soon found buyers seeking grapes for white Zinfandel. When red Zin became fashionable again in the 1990s, those who had kept their decades-old vines were ready for action.

As for Bob Trinchero's error: In 1975, 1,000 gallons of free-run juice from a lot of Deaver Vineyard Amador Zinfandel refused to ferment to dryness, "sticking" with a substantial amount of sugar remaining in the wine. In the heat of harvest, Trinchero put the lot aside. "Two weeks later, I tasted that wine and it was sweet, had a pink color, and I thought, 'Darn, that's pretty good,'" he said. "We bottled it, and the rest is history."

Under its Sutter Home label, Trinchero continues to bottle massive amounts of white Zinfandel, competing head to head with Beringer Vineyards for white Zin sales supremacy.

White Zinfandel
Bob Trinchero "invented" white Zin at Sutter Home Winery in 1975, when a batch of Amador Zinfandel refused to ferment to dryness.

Times were hard in Europe in the 1840s, and *gold* was the only word tens of thousands of French, Italian, German, and Irish immigrants needed to jump on ships and sail to America. Once in Coloma and the surrounding gold-rich Mother Lode area of what is now the Sierra Foothills, the immigrants built camps that became towns, spent their money in saloons and bordellos that popped up seemingly overnight, and made wine, just as they had done in their native lands. Some brought vine cuttings with them, others sent home for them, and by the late 1800s, there were more than one hundred wineries in the Sierra Foothills.

However, the gold ran out, the grapevine-killing root louse phylloxera moved in, and many prospectors went west, to San Francisco, Sonoma, Mendocino, and the Central Valley. Those who remained in what would become Amador and El Dorado counties were barred from winemaking in 1919, when Prohibition rang its "last call for alcohol" bell, making it illegal to produce and sell alcoholic beverages. Vineyards were ripped out and became grazing land or were replanted to plums, apples, pears, and walnuts. The small stone wineries were abandoned, left to crumble over time—ghosts of glorious days past.

The silver lining is that the Gold Rush had lured foreigners who brought with them the rich cultural traditions of their European homelands, some forty years before New York's Ellis Island began processing newcomers into the States. The immigrants seeking El Dorado—Spanish for "the golden one"—in the Sierra Foothills would later spread their culture and customs, including winemaking, throughout the state.

The Sierra Foothills AVA, approved in 1987, is one of California's largest, at 2.6 million acres, although just 5,700 acres are planted to wine grapes. The AVA encompasses eight counties (Yuba, Nevada, Placer, El Dorado, Amador, Calaveras, Tuolumne, and Mariposa) and five sub-AVAs (California Shenandoah Valley and Fiddletown in Amador, El Dorado and Fair Play in El Dorado, and North Yuba in Yuba County).

This is red-wine country, and Zinfandel is its star grape, although Petite Sirah, Barbera, and Rhône varieties do exceptionally well here. Significant plantings of Chardonnay remain, although the wines typically achieve only average results. The future of white wines in the Foothills appears to be the Rhône varieties Grenache Blanc, Marsanne, Roussanne, and Viognier, but plantings are too new to know for certain.

Most Sierra Foothills wineries are small and family-run. They sell most, if not all, of their production in their tasting rooms, largely to Sacramento-area residents making day or weekend trips to the Foothills, and to those passing through on their way to or from Lake Tahoe. The wines traditionally have been bold, deeply flavored, a bit rustic, and excellent values.

Amador County

The Shenandoah Valley is the focal point for grape growing and winemaking in Amador County. Officially known as the **California Shenandoah Valley AVA** (to differentiate it from the Shenandoah Valley AVA in Virginia and West Virginia), the region was largely dormant from Prohibition until the 1960s. Revival came from those who recognized the region's viticultural history and potential and crunched the numbers to see how much more affordable land was in the Sierra Foothills than in Napa and Sonoma. Grape growing and winemaking became important again, and the industry continues to expand.

Vines in the Shenandoah Valley cling to hillsides at 500 to 2,000 feet in elevation. The other Amador County AVA is tiny **Fiddletown**, in which vines are planted up to 2,300 feet. Both AVAs share a preponderance of what are called Sierra Series soils—sandy clay loam with large amounts of well-drained, decomposed granite and volcanic rock. Although scientists have had a difficult time explaining whether, and how, soils impart minerality to wine, there is a definite crushed-stone nuance to many Amador and El Dorado wines, suggesting that granite has something to do with it.

Amador joins Mendocino and Sonoma counties in having more pre-Prohibition Zinfandel vines than anywhere else in the state. One of Amador's most famous Zin fields, Deaver Vineyard, was planted in 1881 by the Davis family. The Deavers inherited it in the early 1900s, and a 14-acre parcel of the original Davis Zinfandel field continues to produce for them.

Another antique Amador vineyard, Terri Harvey's Original Grandpere Vineyard, was planted in 1869 and is likely the oldest producing Zin vineyard in California. That claim is difficult to prove, as statewide records have not been kept on vine age, or on the capability of vines to produce viable crops. The Original Grandpere Vineyard has had a soap-opera-like history involving the owners' divorce and splitting of marital property, and a nearby vintner's trademarking of the Grandpere name for his own vines. But if a wine label says "Original Grandpere Vineyard," "OGP," or "Vineyard 1869," the grapes were grown in this vineyard.

Harvey's former husband, Scott Harvey, grew up in the Foothills. After college, travel to Germany, and a stint at Montevina, he became winemaker at Santino Winery, and later Renwood Winery, in Amador. The Original Grandpere Vineyard was his primary source of Zinfandel grapes, and while he is now anchored in Napa Valley, Harvey continues to make wines from Amador, under Scott Harvey Wines. Many an Amador winemaker credits him with mentorship.

Beginning in the late 1960s, outlier producers including Sutter Home Winery and Mayacamas Vineyards in Napa Valley and Ridge Vineyards in the Santa Cruz Mountains, began producing blockbuster Zinfandels from Amador County. Their success lured a new generation of vintners to the area—Walter Fields of Montevina, Leon Sobon of Shenandoah Vineyards/Sobon Wine, Buck Cobb of Karly Wines, and Ben Zeitman at Amador Foothill Winery.

In terms of establishing Amador as a modern, large-volume, premium winemaking region, the most important winery is Montevina, founded in 1973 in Shenandoah Valley. Walter Fields built it, the first Amador winery constructed after Prohibition, with

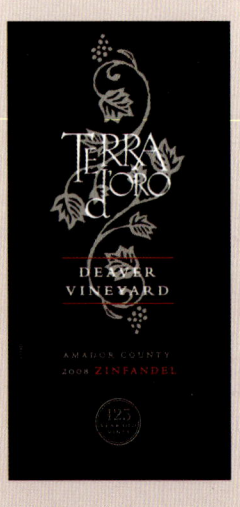
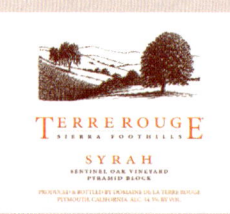

AMADOR COUNTY SNAPSHOT

Vineyard acreage: 3,500

Most-planted varieties: Zinfandel, Syrah, Barbera, Cabernet Sauvignon

Best varieties: Barbera, Petite Sirah, Sangiovese, Syrah, Zinfandel

AVAs: California Shenandoah Valley, Fiddletown

Wineries: 40

Trailblazers: Montevina, Santino

Steady hands: Amador Foothill, Domaine de la Terre Rouge, Karly Wines, Scott Harvey Wines, Shenandoah Vineyards/Sobon Estate, Terra d'Oro, Vino Noceto

Superstars: Favia, Yorba

Trinchero Family Estates
Heat-loving Amador old vines from Montevina Vineyard go into Trinchero's Montevina Zinfandel.

his son-in-law, Cary Gott, as the first winemaker. Trinchero Family Estates now owns Montevina and directs its best grapes to the Terra d'Oro ("land of gold") brand: deep, heady Zinfandels (including a Deaver Vineyard bottling) and Barberas, and sprightly Pinot Grigios. Montevina-labeled wines are value-priced but rarely have the intense, spicy character that old vines give to Terra d'Oro.

Sangiovese is also prominent in Amador, as many a miner who arrived in the Sierra Foothills from Italy sought a taste of home by planting the grape. Suzy and Jim Gullett's Vino Noceto bottlings are varietally true versions of Tuscan Sangiovese, but with a California fruit-forwardness.

A fondness for the wines of France's Rhône Valley drove Bill Easton and his wife, Jane O'Riordan, to establish Domaine de la Terre Rouge in the Shenandoah Valley. Easton, a former wine retailer, moved to Amador County in 1984, intent on producing wines in the style of those he loved from Côte-Rôtie, Hermitage, and Saint-Joseph. Their most distinctive wine, the Ascent Syrah, is meaty and spicy, with heady black-fruit flavors and crisp acidity. Under the Easton label, Easton and O'Riordan also produce Sauvignon Blanc, Zinfandel, and Cabernet Sauvignon.

Barbera is another Amador star. Dick Cooper, owner of Cooper Ranch in Shenandoah Valley, is known locally as the godfather of Barbera (although the Louis Martini and Sebastiani wineries actually beat him to the punch, as they started producing Barbera commercially in Napa and Sonoma counties in the 1960s). Cooper began planting this northern Italian variety in the early 1980s and now has 35 acres of vines. He sells most of his fruit to others, and one of the most successful with this variety is Jeff Runquist Wines.

Some 7,000 acres of Barbera are planted in California, most of them in the Central Valley, where the majority of grapes are absorbed into generic red blends. The 163 acres of Barbera in Amador County (and 81 acres in El Dorado County) are mere drops in the bucket, but new plantings hold promise, as the variety retains its firm acid backbone even in hot temperatures.

A most convincing endorsement of Amador County comes from Napa Valley viticulturist Annie Favia and her winemaker husband, Andy Erickson. She has managed vineyards for several high-end Napa wineries; his résumé sparkles with winemaking positions at Screaming Eagle, Staglin Family, and Harlan Estate. Together, they own the Favia brand, and their Amador Quarzo Syrah is a positive representation of the county's potential.

Grapes for Quarzo are grown in the 34-acre Shake Ridge Vineyard near Sutter Creek, planted in 2003 by Ann Kraemer and her family. Kraemer is an experienced Napa viticulturist who now devotes her energies to Shake Ridge, planted to several varieties—too many, she confides—on slopes between 1,500 and 1,800 feet in elevation. Loamy soils sit on a base of granite and quartz, the latter lending Quarzo its name. Favia also produces Rompecabezas, a smoky, leathery Grenache-Mourvèdre-Syrah blend, from Shake Ridge (*rompecabezas* is Spanish for "puzzle").

Kraemer's family makes small quantities of their own Yorba wines from Shake Ridge grapes.

El Dorado County

Whereas Amador County is rolling hills and oak trees, El Dorado County is mountain slopes and pines, with breathtaking backdrops of Sierra mountain peaks to the east, often covered in snow until summer. Vineyards are planted as high as 3,500 feet above sea level, so it's cooler here than in Amador wine country. Lower daytime temperatures make growing Bordeaux varieties such as Cabernet Sauvignon, Merlot, and Cabernet Franc possible, and many producers started with these grapes, but old- and not-so-old Zinfandel remains the foundation, with Barbera and Rhône Valley varieties more recent standouts.

Boeger Winery is the oldest winery in the **El Dorado AVA**, if one starts counting after Prohibition. Greg Boeger was born into the business, the grandson of Anton Nichelini, the Swiss-Italian founder of Nichelini Winery in Napa Valley. In 1857, another Swiss-Italian, Giovanni Napoleon Lombardo, planted a vineyard northeast of Placerville, which was later converted to a fruit orchard. In 1972, Boeger and his wife, Sue, purchased the former Lombardo estate, which included an 1872 house and wine cellar.

The vineyard, north of Highway 50 in an area known as Apple Hill, was first planted to Zinfandel and Mission grapes, at a 2,800-foot elevation. The Boegers replanted most of the vineyard, including the Mission vines, using cuttings from old-clone plant material from nearby vineyards. While there is a modern tasting room at Boeger, visitors can sample wines in the 1872 stone cellar by appointment—a blast from the Sierra Foothills' rich enological past.

As it is in Amador, weathered granite is the predominant soil type in El Dorado. Yet some sites, among them Lava Cap Winery, also on Apple Hill, have significant amounts of volcanic rock in the soil, which tends to produce wines that are crisp and elegant, and often with a graphite-like aroma. David Jones, a geologist at UC Berkeley, and his wife, Jeanne, purchased their Lava Cap property because of its volcanic soils. Millions of years ago, the Sierra Nevadas rumbled with eruptions, and lava flowed down the mountainsides, coating the Foothills. Over thousands of years, the hardened lava eroded, but some minerally volcanic pockets, such as at Lava Cap, remain. The winery has been particularly successful with Merlot, which struggles to produce good-quality grapes in more granitic soils.

Grape growers and winemakers point out, with pride, that summer daytime temperatures in El Dorado are similar to those in Oakville, the epicenter of Napa Valley. While coastal regions such as Napa, Sonoma, and Santa Barbara are cooled by fog and marine breezes, it's elevation that air-conditions El Dorado. Grapevines need sunlight more than they do heat to ripen their fruit, and while fog moderates warm temperatures, it cuts off sunlight. El Dorado vines get full days of direct sunlight and are chilled at night by mountain breezes, allowing grapes to develop intense color and firm natural acidity.

Fair Play is a 36-square-mile AVA within the El Dorado AVA, with 350 acres of vines. Susan Marks and Jonathan Lachs escaped the pressures of their high-tech Silicon Valley

EL DORADO COUNTY SNAPSHOT

Vineyard acreage: **2,200**

Most-planted varieties: **Zinfandel, Cabernet Sauvignon, Syrah, Merlot, Petite Sirah**

Best varieties: **Barbera, Petite Sirah, Syrah, Viognier, Zinfandel**

Emerging varieties: **Grenache, Mourvèdre, Roussanne**

AVAs: **El Dorado, Fair Play**

Wineries: **60**

Trailblazers: **Boeger Winery, Sierra Vista Vineyards**

Steady hands: **Cedarville Vineyard, C. G. Di Arie Vineyard & Winery, Holly's Hill Vineyards, Madroña Vineyard, Miraflores Winery, Mount Aukum Winery**

A NEW ANGELICA

Marco Cappelli made his mark during seventeen years as winemaker at Swanson Vineyards in Napa Valley's Oakville district. He was W. Clarke Swanson's first winemaker, hired in 1987 by the heir to the Swanson frozen-TV-dinner fortune, and won consumer and critical acclaim for the wines, particularly the Merlots, Pinot Grigios, and Alexis red blends.

Yet Cappelli longed to have his own business, and in 2002, he purchased the 42-acre Herbert Vineyard in what is now the Fair Play AVA in El Dorado. It has since been largely replanted and renamed Cappelli Ranch, with Zinfandel, Syrah, Petite Sirah, and Roussanne grapes grown and sold to local wineries. Cappelli moved to El Dorado and also began a consulting business, bringing Napa Valley expertise to a region whose winemakers are largely self-taught. His biggest impact has been on the wines of Miraflores Winery in Placerville, owned by Victor and Cheryl Alvarez.

Although no longer on the full-time staff at Swanson, Cappelli continues to produce the winery's Angelica, a fortified wine made from Mission grapes grown in an Amador County vineyard planted in 1856, one of the few remaining Mission plantings in California.

Attempting to reproduce a wine similar to one made during the Gold Rush, Cappelli and Swanson came up with Angelica. In the 1850s, it was made by adding brandy to Mission grape juice. In order to be able to label Swanson's Angelica as wine, Cappelli ferments the juice before adding a fortifying spirit. Angelica is aged in barrels for up to eight years, during which time it develops its tawny port, roasted coffee, and caramelized hazelnut aromas and flavors. Due to its rarity and limited production, it commands $140 per bottle.

Marco Cappelli
El Dorado County grower/winemaking consultant Marco Cappelli poses with a monstrous Mission vine, believed to have been planted in the mid-1850s. It contributes grapes to the Angelica wine Cappelli produces for Swanson Vineyards in Napa Valley.

---

jobs to pursue their winemaking dreams here. The granitic soils and 2,500-foot elevation of their Cedarville Vineyard allow them to produce minerally, well-mannered Zinfandels, meaty Syrahs, and juicy Grenaches.

Their neighbor, Chaim Gur-Arieh, a food scientist who created Cap'n Crunch cereal and Hidden Valley Ranch dressing, and his wife, Elisheva, excel at balanced, polished Zinfandels under the C. G. Di Arie brand, based in Fair Play and also a purchaser of Amador County grapes. Nearby Mount Aukum Winery produces first-rate Petite Sirahs and Viogniers, and it offers visitors a sweeping view to the west from its 2,615-foot perch.

Pleasant Valley, southeast of Placerville, is home to Holly's Hill Vineyards, within the El Dorado AVA. Holly and Tom Hill founded the winery in 1998, after falling in love with a Rhône Valley Châteauneuf-du-Pape on their honeymoon. Their vineyard is planted solely to Rhône grapes—Viognier, Roussanne, Grenache, Mourvèdre, Syrah, and Counoise—and the flagship is Patriarche Rouge, a blend of Mourvèdre, Syrah, Grenache Noir, and Counoise. Their daughter, Carrie Bendick, and her husband, Josh Bendick, run the show now, and the wines are suave and nuanced, with high refreshment value.

Sierra Vista Vineyards & Winery is one of the original "Rhône Rangers" in California winemaking. John and Barbara MacCready planted their 32-acre vineyard in Pleasant Valley in 1974, starting out with Chardonnay, Cabernet Sauvignon, and Zinfandel. Yet they soon realized that Rhône varieties were best suited to the mountain conditions, and in 1979 they began planting Syrah, Grenache, Cinsault, Mourvèdre, Roussanne, and Viognier. The MacCreadys have taught many an El Dorado vintner how to work with Rhône varieties, and they are widely viewed as Sierra Foothills pioneers. And, yes, the gorgeous snow-capped Sierra Nevada image on their labels is indeed what one sees from the winery until summer.

CENTRAL VALLEY

California's 400-mile-long Central Valley—the convergence of the Sacramento Valley to the north and San Joaquin Valley to the south—is America's produce basket. Almost every nontropical crop imaginable thrives in the valley's deep, rich soils and its asphalt-melting-hot summers, among them asparagus, tomatoes, lettuce, peaches, plums, sugar beets, pistachios, walnuts, alfalfa, and cotton, as well as grapes for the table and for a sizable proportion of the world's raisins.

Farmers also planted wine grapes in the flat, fertile Central Valley once U.S. wine consumption began to catch on in the 1960s. The Central Valley became infamous for growing grapes that went into inexpensive jug and boxed wines produced by such megawineries as E. & J. Gallo Winery and Franzia (the latter now owned by San Francisco–based Wine Group, which also produces boxed and bottled wines under such brands as Almaden, Corbett Canyon, and Fish Eye). An estimated 47 percent of California's wine grapes are grown in the Central Valley, although their quality cannot be considered high, with the exception of those for some port-style wines and others covered in detail below.

Daytime valley temperatures surpass 100°F and "cool" to 80°F at night in summer and early fall. Under such conditions, irrigation is essential, and wine grapes cannot help but get very ripe and lose their acid backbone. Yet these are key components in large-scale blended wines that also include underripe, high-acid grapes. The goal is to blend the two negatives and end up with a positive.

E. & J. Gallo Winery, the largest wine-producing company in the world as of 2011, was founded in 1933 by Ernest and Julio Gallo in Modesto. While Gallo has major vineyard holdings and brands based in the high-quality North Coast and Central Coast regions, its commercial clout was and is built on mass-produced wines from Central Valley grapes, including the low-end Thunderbird and André and Carlo Rossi brands. Gallo's alter ego, its more quality-oriented personality, is displayed in its Gallo Family Vineyards, Louis M. Martini, Mirassou Vineyards, MacMurray Ranch, Frei Brothers, Redwood Creek, and Bridlewood California brands, although its business remains based on cheaper Central Valley grapes.

The Franzia family's wine-in-a-box business built on valley fruit was quite successful in the 1960s and 1970s, and under The Wine Group—the third-largest global volume producer, following Gallo and Constellation Brands—Franzia boxed wines are the number-one sellers of their type in the United States.

Fred Franzia, whose family sold Franzia Brothers in 1973 to Coca-Cola (which spawned The Wine Group), started anew with Bronco Wine Company, eventually creating the insanely successful Charles Shaw brand of bottled and cork-finished wines known as "Two Buck Chuck" for their $1.99 price at Trader Joe's stores in California and other states. The wines are made from 40,000 Central Valley vineyard acres that Bronco owns or controls, plus purchased bulk juice and wine.

Today, dessert and fortified wines are a good fit for the Central Valley's hot climate, and Quady Winery in Madera is one of America's most accomplished producers of these styles. Andrew and Laurel Quady started the winery in 1977, after he'd worked at Heublein in Madera. They built a tiny winery behind their house and made "port" in their spare time. In 1980, the Quadys bottled a fortified white wine, Essensia, produced from Orange Muscat. By 1983, they'd added Elysium, from Black Muscat, and then Electra White and Red (sweet yet refreshing dessert wines), a Palomino Fino, and Vya vermouth.

Quady used "port" on its labels for several years, but when it began exporting to Europe, it had to drop the term, because true port comes only from Portugal. Other American wineries blithely put "port" on their bottles, yet the Quadys removed it from their domestic labels too, and began calling their wine Starboard—the nautical opposite of port. Since 2006, an agreement between the United States and the European Union has prohibited American wine brands from using "port," "sherry," "Burgundy," and other such European terms on their labels, with one glaring exception: Producers who used such terms before 2006 may continue to do so.

Also in Madera, Ficklin Vineyards has produced port-style wines for sixty-five years, from grapes grown in the family vineyard since 1945. Its Old Vine Tinta Port, first released in 1951, is an aged ruby style made by a solera fractional blending system initiated by David Ficklin, father of current winemaker Peter.

Unfortunately for Quady, Ficklin, and others of their ilk, Americans are not big drinkers of late-harvest and fortified wines. These remain specialty wines, though they do have some fanatical followers.

Ernest and Julio Gallo
Sales and marketing whiz Ernest Gallo (left), and his brother, viticultural expert Julio, made E. & J. Gallo a volume leader among the world's winemakers.

Lodi AVA

For decades, Lodi—situated between Sacramento and Stockton, 90 miles east of San Francisco—grew grapes that went into North Coast Chardonnays, Cabernet Sauvignons, Zinfandels, and Viogniers. In the 1990s, California's premier wine regions couldn't grow enough grapes to meet demand, so vintners looked to Lodi for low-cost replenishments. They blended Lodi's best into other wines to stretch volume, or crushed the grapes for second-label wines. Lodi rarely got label credit for its contributions.

Yet a handful of Zinfandel makers, among them Joel Peterson of Ravenswood (Lodi County Series Zinfandel) and Patrick Campbell of Laurel Glen Vineyard (ZaZin), in Sonoma, and Kent Rosenblum of Rosenblum Cellars, in Alameda, talked up Lodi after tasting the intense berry-jam flavors and black spice notes in Zinfandels made from the region. The exotic character of Lodi Zin comes largely from vines planted before Prohibition. "Old vines" is a phrase tossed about by growers and vintners everywhere, as there is no legal definition of "old." But in Lodi, the majority of Zinfandel vineyards are at least thirty-five years of age, with many topping one hundred. Jessie's Grove is the oldest still-producing Zin plot in Lodi, planted by Joseph Spenker in 1888; the grapes go to the Jessie's Grove Winery brand.

These old codgers stand alone, without trellis support. Their trunks and arms are thick, gnarled, and often covered in lichen. They dodged phylloxera when other California regions were decimated by it—the phylloxera louse doesn't like Lodi's sandy soils, and the St. George rootstock used in the original Zinfandel plantings is resistant to the bug.

The Gold Rush attracted European immigrants to work the mines in the Sierra Foothills starting in 1849, and when gold became scarce, many miners moved down the mountains to Lodi, where they planted grapevines and other crops. They weathered Prohibition by selling Zinfandel, Alicante Bouschet, and Tokay grapes to home winemakers.

When Prohibition ended, U.S. wine drinkers wanted sweet, fortified wines, and Lodi was more than willing to produce them. As consumer tastes eventually shifted to dry wines, Lodi farmers adapted again, learning how to grow higher-quality grapes for table wines. Their mentor was Robert Mondavi, who grew up in Lodi, played on the Lodi Union High School football team, and helped his father, Cesare, in the business of shipping grapes from California to amateur winemakers.

After building Robert Mondavi Winery in Oakville in 1966, Mondavi returned to Lodi in 1979 to purchase the Cherokee

LODI AVA SNAPSHOT

Vineyard acreage: 120,000

Most-planted varieties: Zinfandel, Chardonnay, Cabernet Sauvignon, Merlot

Best varieties: Petite Sirah, Syrah, Viognier, Zinfandel

Emerging varieties: Albariño, Garnacha/Grenache, Tempranillo, Verdelho, Vermentino

Sub-AVAs: Alta Mesa, Borden Ranch, Clements Hills, Cosumnes River, Jahant, Mokelumne River, Sloughhouse

Wineries: 85

Trailblazer: Woodbridge by Robert Mondavi

Steady hands: Bokisch Vineyards, Jessie's Grove, Klinker Brick Winery, Lucas Vineyards, Mettler Family Vineyards, Uvaggio, Van Ruiten Family Vineyards

Superstars: Michael-David Vineyards, Ravenswood, Rosenblum Cellars

Las Lomas Vineyard
Lodi vineyards enjoy more moderate summers than most regions in the hot Central Valley, thanks to the cooling impact of the Sacramento River Delta. In Lodi, grapevines get an overnight respite from the infamous valley heat.

Vineyard Association co-op. He wanted to process inexpensive grapes and sell wines to those unable to afford his Napa bottlings. He named the facility Woodbridge Winery; his full name would later be attached, to encompass the bargain-priced wines he produced in Lodi within the Mondavi halo.

Mondavi outfitted Woodbridge with the latest equipment, employed talented vineyard managers and enologists, and had them teach growers that they could make more money by focusing on quality, not quantity. As a result, vineyards that once produced 12 tons of grapes per acre now produce 3 to 5 tons (except for those with ancient vines, which struggle to produce 1 ton per acre).

The Lodi AVA enjoys a Mediterranean climate, with hot, dry summers and cool, wet winters. Deep, sandy soils predominate, with clay loam in some areas. Elevation averages 100 feet above sea level. Yet despite its location within the Central Valley, Lodi is a blessed oasis, because its hot daytime temperatures drop significantly at night, into the 60s, thanks to winds from the Sacramento–San Joaquin Delta. The Central Valley is an oven, hemmed in east and west by mountains. The only portal through which Pacific Ocean air can pass is the Delta, and Lodi and its neighbor Clarksburg are the lone Central Valley recipients of it.

The Lodi AVA can be a bit confusing. Two of its sub-AVAs, Mokelumne River and Clements Hills, are in San Joaquin County; the Cosumnes River, Alta Mesa, and Sloughhouse AVAs are in Sacramento County; and Borden Ranch and Jahant each have a foot in both counties. And Lodi's appellational structure has changed twice. The AVA, established in 1986, had 458,000 acres. Some 93,000 acres were added in 2002, making the total 551,000. Then, in 2006, the original 458,000 acres were split into the 7 sub-AVAs, with the remaining 93,000 acres not subappellated. They remain within the overarching Lodi AVA.

The **Alta Mesa AVA,** at 55,000 acres, is a tabletop landform built up from deposits from the American and Cosumnes rivers. The soils are red clay loam, and the word *prairie* is often used to describe the landscape. Red-wine grape varieties do well here. The AVA that borders Alta Mesa to the west, **Cosumnes River** (55,000 acres), is lower in elevation, with meadows and riverbank and woodland topography. The soils are diverse along the floodplain and sloughs, with patches of older soils on river terraces and fans. The cool, breezy conditions favor white grapes.

Sloughhouse (79,000 acres) has the elevated river terraces and low bedrock hills of the Sierra Range. It's the warmest region in Lodi, and it is planted to both white- and red-wine grapes.

Jahant is the smallest sub-AVA, at 28,000 acres, and also one of the coolest. It, too, succeeds with wines of both colors.

Borden Ranch (70,000 acres) has Lodi's oldest valley floor soils and ancient river terraces and hills. Vernal pools and prairie mounds are its primary physical features, and the growing-season climate is warmer and wetter than in other Lodi AVAs. Red varieties are its strong suit.

Clements Hills (85,000 acres), also suited to reds, has a woodland environment with higher-elevation (400 feet) river terraces, and hills with older soils and volcanic sediments.

Mokelumne River (86,000 acres) includes the city of Lodi and has the greatest concentration of old-vine Zinfandel in the region. It's cool by Lodi standards, and some Riesling and Gewürztraminer is planted here.

While Lodi may call itself the "Zinfandel Capital of the World"—it grows 40 percent of California's Zin grapes—it has also seen a modern-day explosion of Italian and Spanish varieties. If one has a Mediterranean climate, doesn't it make sense to produce Mediterranean varieties?

That's what former Mondavi winemaker Jim Moore believes, so he purchases Vermentino, Moscato (Muscat), Barbera, and Primitivo grapes from Lodi growers for his Italianate Uvaggio brand. Markus and Liz Bokisch of Bokisch Vineyards grow and produce Spanish-style Albariño, Garnacha, and Tempranillo. The intrepid Koth family of Mokelumne Glen Vineyards cultivates Germanic varieties such as Gewürztraminer, Riesling, Dornfelder, and Zweigelt. Their wine production is small, and they don't pretend to be able to duplicate the characteristics of German wines. Instead, they're interested in seeing what German varieties can do in Lodi.

E. & J. Gallo Winery and Constellation are the biggest buyers of Lodi grapes, but they typically pay rock-bottom prices. In response, many growers have morphed into vintners. Michael-David Winery is a classic example. The Phillips family has grown melons and other produce in Lodi for decades, and they were among the first in California to plant Syrah, in 1985. Brothers David and Michael Phillips manage the vineyards and winery, and their popular, well-priced wines include 7 Deadly Zins and hefty Earthquake Syrahs and Petite Sirahs. They sell grapes to others but keep the good stuff for themselves, and turn a prettier profit by bottling their own.

Lodi growers are proud of their sustainable agriculture efforts. The Lodi Rules for Sustainable Winegrowing program is California's first third-party, regionwide sustainable viticultural certification program, and it encourages farmers to reduce the use of pesticides and herbicides and to use natural remedies that have little or no impact on the environment. In 2010, some forty growers, following Lodi Rules, had 20,000-plus acres certified as sustainable.

Lodi, once disparaged in the 1969 Creedence Clearwater Revival song "Lodi" ("Oh, lord, stuck in Lodi again"), has evolved into not only a producer of serious quality grapes and wines, but also a visitor destination.

Clarksburg AVA

Just fourteen wineries exist in the Clarksburg AVA, northwest of Lodi. It, too, enjoys Sacramento River Delta breezes, but the grapes from the 20,000 vineyard acres are often lost in North Coast and California blends. Although Zinfandel and Merlot are the most-planted varieties, today the building excitement is over white varieties, including Chenin Blanc, Albariño, and Grüner Veltliner.

The AVA covers parts of three counties: Sacramento, Solano, and Yolo. It has growing conditions similar to those in Lodi, with cooling bay breezes wafting through the delta at night, tempering what can be hot days during the summer.

The list is long of wineries that purchase Clarksburg grapes, but it was a Chenin Blanc produced by Sonoma's venerable Dry Creek Vineyard that put Clarksburg on the wine map. Dry Creek has made Chenin Blanc for more than thirty years, and its current grape source is Wilson Vineyard in Clarksburg. Other wineries have taken notice and become more open about identifying the previously obscure Clarksburg AVA as a source for quality fruit.

The big dog is Bogle Vineyards, run by Warren Bogle, the sixth generation of his family to farm the region. Although some Bogle wines are blends of grapes grown elsewhere, Clarksburg fruit is the foundation for its finest wines: Chardonnay, Chenin Blanc, and Petite Sirah.

Bokisch Vineyards
Workers harvest the Spanish Garnacha (Grenache), Graciano, Monastrell, and Tempranillo varieties for Bokisch Vineyards in Lodi.

SOUTH COAST

Southern California is famous for white-sand beaches, palm trees, surfing, skateboarding, and Hollywood celebrities. Few wine lovers know that California's wine industry began here—in the heart of Los Angeles, no less, before it was a city, and before California became a state. While little winegrowing remains in Los Angeles County, and it has decreased substantially in the South Coast AVA counties of San Bernardino and San Diego, the Temecula Valley AVA in Riverside County is undergoing something of a rebirth.

Malibu Vineyards
The volcanic hills overlooking Malibu are one of the few places in Los Angeles County where wine grapes are still grown. At 1,200 feet above the Pacific Ocean, Malibu Vineyards doesn't get the morning-long fog that makes successful grapegrowing nearly impossible at lower elevations.

Southern California

The range of this map is broad and reflects the relatively sparse possibilities for wine in a region of rampant development.

GRAPES ON CATALINA

Twenty-six miles across the sea
Santa Catalina is a-waiting' for me
Santa Catalina, the island of romance,
romance, romance, romance.

When the pop group the Four Preps released the song "26 Miles" in 1957, Alison Wrigley Rusack was not yet a gleam in her father's eye. But her great-grandfather, chewing-gum magnate William Wrigley Jr. of Chicago, fell in love with the arid beauty of Santa Catalina Island, one in the chain of Southern California's Channel Islands.

He purchased the Santa Catalina Island Company in 1919, giving him ownership of most of the island, where many a Southern California couple honeymooned—and still do—traveling 22 miles southwest from Los Angeles and back by boat (the Four Preps were off on their mileage calculation). Wrigley's son Philip turned most of the land over to the Catalina Island Conservancy, a nonprofit he founded to protect the natural beauty of the area.

Fast-forward to 2009, when Alison and her husband, Geoff Rusack, who produce splendid wines at their Santa Barbara County winery Rusack Vineyards, harvested the first vintage of grapes from a 2.5-acre vineyard they planted on non-Conservancy land on Catalina in 2007. The first wines were released in 2011, Chardonnay and Zinfandel. Rusack winemaker John Falcone said the growing conditions are similar to those in the chilly, fog-shrouded Sta. Rita Hills AVA of Santa Barbara County. If that's true, expect firm, elegant, high-acid wines from Catalina.

Rusack Catalina Island Vineyards
Alison and Geoff Rusack took a risk in planting wine grapes on Catalina Island, west of San Clemente. Early winemaking results are encouraging.

Despite its long history—from the founding of the first mission in 1769 in San Diego, where Franciscan *padres* began planting the Mission grape, to the establishment of California's first commercial wineries in Los Angeles in 1820s, to the introduction of European varieties by Bordeaux transplant (and appropriately named) Jean-Louis Vignes in 1833—the region now known as the South Coast has, sadly, few quality producers left. Considering the sky-high price of real estate in sunny Southern California, it's surprising that any viticulture remains at all.

Once the largest grape-growing region in the state, the South Coast was struck by two near-fatal blows: Prohibition, from 1920 to 1933, and the end of World War II in 1945, which created a commercial and housing boom that made Southern California land far more vital for tract homes, parks, golf courses, and factories than for vineyards. Today those who still produce wine in SoCal are stubborn pioneers, hobby winemakers who turned pro, wealthy folks eager to play the wine game, or entrepreneurs who see tasting rooms as tourist draws.

Los Angeles County

After the founding of their first mission in San Diego, the Franciscans moved north along what they called El Camino Real ("the Royal Road"), which today is, roughly, Interstate 5. Commercial winemaking began at the pueblo of Los Angeles and at Mission Arcángel San Gabriel, 9 miles to the east in San Gabriel, providing jobs and refreshment for early Californians. The 1831 arrival of Jean-Louis Vignes, a failed businessman from Bordeaux, and his importation of vine cuttings from France two years later, sparked a quality movement in Southern California that encouraged others to produce European-style wines. One of them, Kentucky native William Wolfskill, had 145 acres of wine grapes and was Vignes's major competitor; he went on to grow the first lemons and oranges in California, which he sold to Gold Rush miners for a dollar apiece, a small fortune at the time. (His son, Joseph, founded the Southern California Fruit Exchange co-op, which later became Sunkist Growers.)

Prohibition dampened the LA wine party, and the end of World War II, in 1945, nearly killed it. Agriculture was soon replaced by subdivisions, manufacturing plants, and shopping centers. The estimated 6,000 acres of vines cultivated in the county were among the first crops ripped out to make way for urban growth. Now fewer than 200 vineyard acres remain.

However, through sharp business acumen, San Antonio Winery continued to produce wine in Los Angeles, and does so today. Hemmed in by freeways (the 5, 110, and 101) and surrounded by industrial development, San Antonio celebrated its ninety-fifth birthday in 2012. Founded in 1917 by Santo Cambianica, an immigrant from Lombardy, Italy, the winery is the only one remaining from pre-Prohibition days. It stayed alive during Prohibition by bottling wines for the Catholic Church, which used them for sacramental purposes. (Historians note that U.S. wine consumption increased during Prohibition, suggesting that Americans managed to get their hands on "sacramental" wines and/or produce their own using fresh grapes or dehydrated grape bricks they purchased [legally] from wineries and growers.)

Grapes for San Antonio wines are no longer grown in Los Angeles—some of the most expensive real estate in America—so the Riboli family, descendants of Cambianica, source fruit from Monterey County, Paso Robles, and Napa Valley. The Catholic Church continues to be a big customer, purchasing 10 percent of San Antonio's annual wine production.

Malibu, home to stars and beaches that are backdrops for movies and TV shows, is also home to a small clutch of wineries. In 1987, George Rosenthal began planting vineyards at his 250-acre property, Rosenthal: The Malibu Estate, is the only winery within the Malibu–Newton Canyon AVA. His Bordeaux-style red wines are produced by consulting winemaker Christian Roguenant. In 1997, Jim Palmer planted his Malibu Trancas Canyon Vineyard in Malibu to red grapes; his Cabernet Sauvignons and Syrahs are complex and satisfying.

And Tom Jones has carved out the cosseted Moraga Vineyards in a steep enclave in the luxurious residential district of Bel-Air, drawing on advice from some of Bordeaux's most experienced hands.

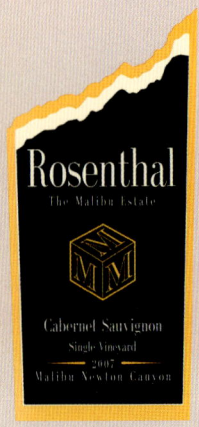
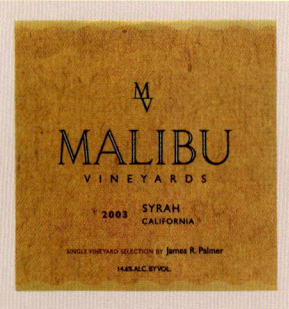
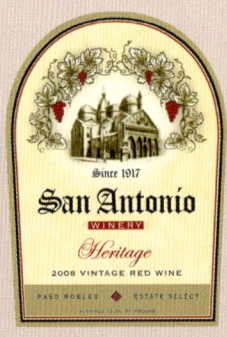

LOS ANGELES COUNTY SNAPSHOT

Vineyard acreage: **190**

Most-planted varieties: **Cabernet Sauvignon, Syrah, Merlot**

Best varieties: **Cabernet Sauvignon, Merlot, Syrah**

AVAs: **Antelope Valley of the High California Desert, Leone Valley, Malibu–Newton Canyon, Saddle Rock–Malibu, Sierra Peloma Valley**

Wineries: **10**

Trailblazer: **San Antonio Winery**

Steady hands: **Malibu Vineyards, Moraga Vineyards, Rosenthal: The Malibu Estate, San Antonio Winery**

Riverside and San Bernardino Counties

These two counties share the Cucamonga Valley AVA; the region's other AVA, **Temecula Valley**, is entirely within Riverside County. Temecula is by far the larger and better known. Cucamonga has a precious few old Zinfandel vines remaining from the time when San Bernardino County produced more wine than Napa and Sonoma counties combined.

In 1846, Pío Pico, the Mexican governor of California, granted Rancho Pauba, which included land now known as Temecula Valley, to Vicente Moraga. In 1905, cattleman Walter Vail purchased Rancho Pauba, adding it to his other three ranches, totaling 87,500 acres of grazing land. Vail Ranch changed hands again in 1964, when Kaiser Aetna purchased it for $21 million and began subdividing the property for the planned residential community Rancho California (now Temecula); other parcels were zoned for citrus groves, many of which are now vineyards.

Vincenzo Cilurzo, a Hollywood lighting director, and his wife, Audrey, bought 100 acres and were encouraged to grow grapes. Experts cautioned that the region was too warm for vinifera (it's classified as Region IV on the UC Davis scale), but the Cilurzos went ahead, planting Chenin Blanc and Petite Sirah in 1968, thereby owning the area's first commercial vineyard.

Ely Callaway, CEO of Burlington Industries (and inventor of pantyhose), visited the Cilurzos that year, picking their brains on grape growing. He planted vines that year and, in 1975, constructed Temecula's first winery, Callaway Vineyard & Winery.

Callaway Vineyard
Entrepreneur Ely Callaway established Callaway Vineyard & Winery in Temecula in 1969. After years of corporate ownership and repositioning, the Lin family now owns the winery and vineyards and has reinstated Callaway as a small family winery.

The Cilurzos and John Poole of Mount Palomar Winery followed with their own wineries in 1978.

The Temecula Valley AVA was approved in 1983, and vineyard acreage continued to climb at a steady pace. Then disaster struck. In 1996, Temecula vineyards were found to be infested with the glassy-winged sharpshooter (GWSS), a pest that spreads the bacterium *Xylella fastidiosa*, resulting in Pierce's disease, fatal for vines. But only in 1999 did growers realize they had a major problem. By May 2002, some 850 acres of diseased vines had

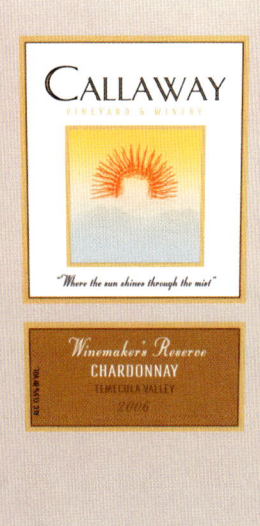

RIVERSIDE AND SAN BERNARDINO COUNTIES SNAPSHOT

Vineyard acreage: Riverside 1,500; San Bernardino 900

Most-planted varieties: Zinfandel, Cabernet Sauvignon, Chardonnay, Merlot, Syrah

Best varieties: Riverside—Petite Sirah, Syrah, Tempranillo, Viognier; San Bernardino—Zinfandel

AVAs: Cucamonga Valley, Temecula Valley (both within South Coast AVA)

Wineries: Riverside 35; San Bernardino 3

Trailblazers: Riverside—Callaway Vineyard & Winery, Cilurzo Winery, Mount Palomar; San Bernardino—Joseph Filippi Winery & Vineyards, Galleano Winery

Steady hands: Riverside—Hart Winery, Leonesse, South Coast Winery, Wilson Creek Vineyards; San Bernardino—Filippi, Galleano, Rancho de Philo

Superstar: Carol Shelton Wines

South Coast Winery
The Temecula Valley wine region got a shot in the arm when Jim Carter opened South Coast Winery & Spa—a mix of winemaking, accommodations, fine dining, and massage.

been removed, and a series of remedies developed, including quarantine, trapping of the insects, and planting new vineyards away from the sharpshooter's favored habitat, citrus groves. As other California regions suffered from Pierce's disease, the lessons learned in Temecula helped them battle the bug.

Callaway sold his vineyards and winery to distiller Hiram Walker & Sons in 1981 and turned his attentions to golf, founding Callaway Golf and giving hackers more distance off the tee with the Big Bertha driver. In an all-too-common occurrence in the modern-day wine business, another conglomerate, Allied Domecq, acquired Callaway in 1998 and began repositioning the winery as a California, rather than Temecula Valley, brand. It was renamed Callaway Coastal, and grapes grown in the Central Coast AVA replaced Temecula fruit. Locals felt betrayed; not only did they sell their grapes to Callaway to feed its 200,000-case annual production, they also feared that the Callaway facility would be abandoned, with winemaking conducted elsewhere.

But the Lin family of San Diego stepped in, buying the property and brand in 2005. The Lins have cut production drastically and sell their wines only in the tasting room and online. They've also restored the original brand name.

More than thirty grape varieties are now grown in Temecula Valley, at an elevation of approximately 1,500 feet. The valley heat, often in the 90s during the growing season (May through October), is refreshed by late-afternoon winds. Although the AVA totals 33,000 acres, just 1,300 are planted to wine grapes. Red varieties that enjoy a long, hot growing season—Syrah, Petite Sirah, Tannat, and Tempranillo—are the most promising, but some beautiful Viogniers have been produced here too.

The emergence of South Coast Winery, part of a 39-acre resort and spa owned by Jim Carter, as a producer of high-quality wines has lifted Temecula's game. Texas native Jon McPherson is the winemaker, and his wines win multiple gold medals at wine shows. They may not be threats to Napa Cabernet Sauvignon and Santa Rita Hills Pinot Noir, but they offer fine quality at affordable prices.

In 1868, San Bernardino County had 600 acres of wine grapes; the number had exploded to more than 9,000 by 1887, and had grown to 33,000 acres by 1945. However, Los Angeles's rapidly growing population needed housing and jobs at the end of World War II, and eastward the people marched, into San Bernardino and Riverside counties. Vineyards were torn out and replaced by subdivisions, shopping malls, and factories, and today, San Bernardino's vineyards have dwindled to approximately 900 acres, most of them of old-vine Zinfandel and Alicante Bouschet near the city of Cucamonga.

The dry, desertlike climate and sandy soils of the **Cucamonga Valley** successfully supported only grape varieties used in the production of sweet, fortified wines—meaning Zinfandel. One of the seminal producers, Galleano Winery, is much the same as it was in 1927, when the Galleano family purchased the land and planted grapes for port-style wines. Nearby Joseph Filippi Winery & Vineyards had its ninetieth anniversary in 2012, and it continues farming 80-plus acres of Zinfandel, Grenache, Mourvèdre, Alicante Bouschet, and Petite Sirah.

However, the most accomplished maker of Cucamonga wines is an outsider, Carol Shelton Wines in Sonoma County. Shelton's rich, mouth-coating Monga Zin Old Vine Zinfandel from the certified organic, dry-farmed Jose Lopez vineyard in Cucamonga Valley, planted in 1918, is winemaking at its best, from a region that no longer has much of it.

San Diego County

San Diego is the birthplace of California winemaking, although the wines Junípero Serra and his fellow *padres* made at Mission San Diego de Alcalá from Mission grapes were not for enjoyment, but for sacramental Communion wine. What the fathers foisted on their faithful likely would be thought undrinkable today.

After the Franciscans moved north, founding twenty other California missions between 1769 and 1823, San Diego County's winemaking role was minor at best. Citrus, avocados, and other crops proved successful and profitable in the then-rural northeastern parts of the county; the western half offered beaches and surfing, but was devoid of viticultural promise.

Yet San Diego County now offers quality wines from a handful of vintners. The best, and largest, is Fallbrook Winery. Thanks to recent replantings of Cabernet Sauvignon, Merlot, Sangiovese, and Sauvignon Blanc in the decomposed granite soils of Gracie Hill Vineyard, Fallbrook produces balanced, restrained wines that get a refreshing lift from the cooling influence of the nearby Pacific Ocean.

Mission San Diego de Alcalá
Where it all began. In 1769, Franciscan father Junípero Serra established the first mission in what would become California in San Diego, planting vines that would yield grapes for sacramental wines.

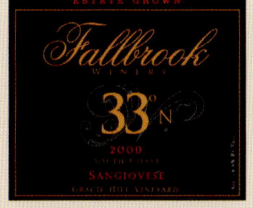

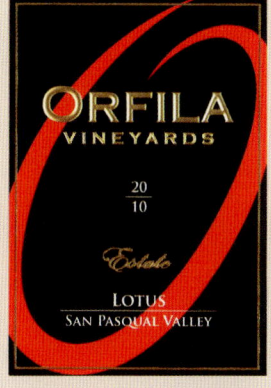

SAN DIEGO COUNTY SNAPSHOT
Vineyard acreage: **210**
Most-planted varieties: **Syrah, Cabernet Sauvignon, Merlot**
Best varieties: **Cabernet Sauvignon, Merlot, Sauvignon Blanc, Syrah, Viognier**
AVAs: **Ramona Valley, San Pasqual Valley (both within South Coast AVA)**
Wineries: **60 (many purchase grapes from outside the county)**
Steady hands: **Orfila Vineyards & Winery, San Pasqual Winery**
Superstar: **Fallbrook Winery**

Oregon

Oregon is the fourth-largest wine-producing state in America, its reputation built largely on Pinot Noir. Its first winegrowers came to Oregon specifically to produce Pinot Noir and other cool-climate varieties, and in forty years—a very short period in wine industry time—the state has evolved into a world-renowned wine region. Even the Burgundians acknowledge the excellence of Oregon Pinot Noir, and, in fact, several produce wine there, a positive affirmation if there ever was one. Pinot Gris is the state's leading white wine, and recent plantings of new clones give Chardonnay great potential.

Bounty of the land
Vineyards blend seamlessly into Oregon's rural landscape, where wine grapes are planted next to berry patches, hazelnut and pear orchards, and potato and onion fields.

Within Oregon are sixteen AVAs, three of them shared with Washington and one with Idaho. The state has more than 420 wineries and 20,500 planted vineyard acres, the majority of them in the Willamette Valley, some 30 miles southwest of Portland. There are a smaller number of accomplished producers in southern Oregon, in the Umpqua, Rogue, and Applegate valleys. For now, the three sub-AVAs that are shared with Washington State—Columbia Gorge, Columbia Valley, and Walla Walla Valley—and the Snake River Valley, shared with Idaho, are minor compared to Willamette Valley, which boasts 65 percent of the state's grapevines.

The relationship between Oregon and Washington is seemingly a paradox: The vast majority of Oregon's vineyards are west of the Cascade Mountains in wet forested areas chilled by exposure to the Pacific Ocean, while Washington's vines are on the east, in a barren, irrigated high desert. The planting decisions were based on the types of wine to be produced—Oregon's Pinot Noir and Pinot Gris crave cool conditions, Washington's Cabernet Sauvignon and Merlot require warmth and plenty of sunlight.

There are no large wine companies in Oregon, and that's just the way Oregonians like it. The biggest producer, King Estate in Lorane, bottles approximately 155,000 cases of wine annually, which would qualify it as a medium-sized winery in California. Willamette Valley Vineyards, at 71,000 cases per year, is the only publicly traded wine company in the state.

OREGON SNAPSHOT

Vineyard acreage: **20,500**

Most-planted varieties: **Pinot Noir, Pinot Gris, Chardonnay, Riesling, Cabernet Sauvignon**

Best varieties: **Chardonnay, Pinot Gris, Pinot Noir, Tempranillo**

AVAs: **Applegate Valley, Chehalem Mountains, Dundee Hills, Eola–Amity Hills, McMinnville, Red Hill Douglas County, Ribbon Ridge, Rogue Valley, Southern Oregon, Umpqua Valley, Willamette Valley, Yamhill-Carlton; Columbia Gorge, Columbia Valley, and Walla Walla Valley (shared with Washington State); Snake River Valley (shared with Idaho)**

Wineries: **420-plus**

Pinot Noir
Pinot Noir is Oregon's signature wine grape, with 12,400 of the state's 20,500 acres of vineyards planted to this Burgundian variety.

THE WEST | OREGON

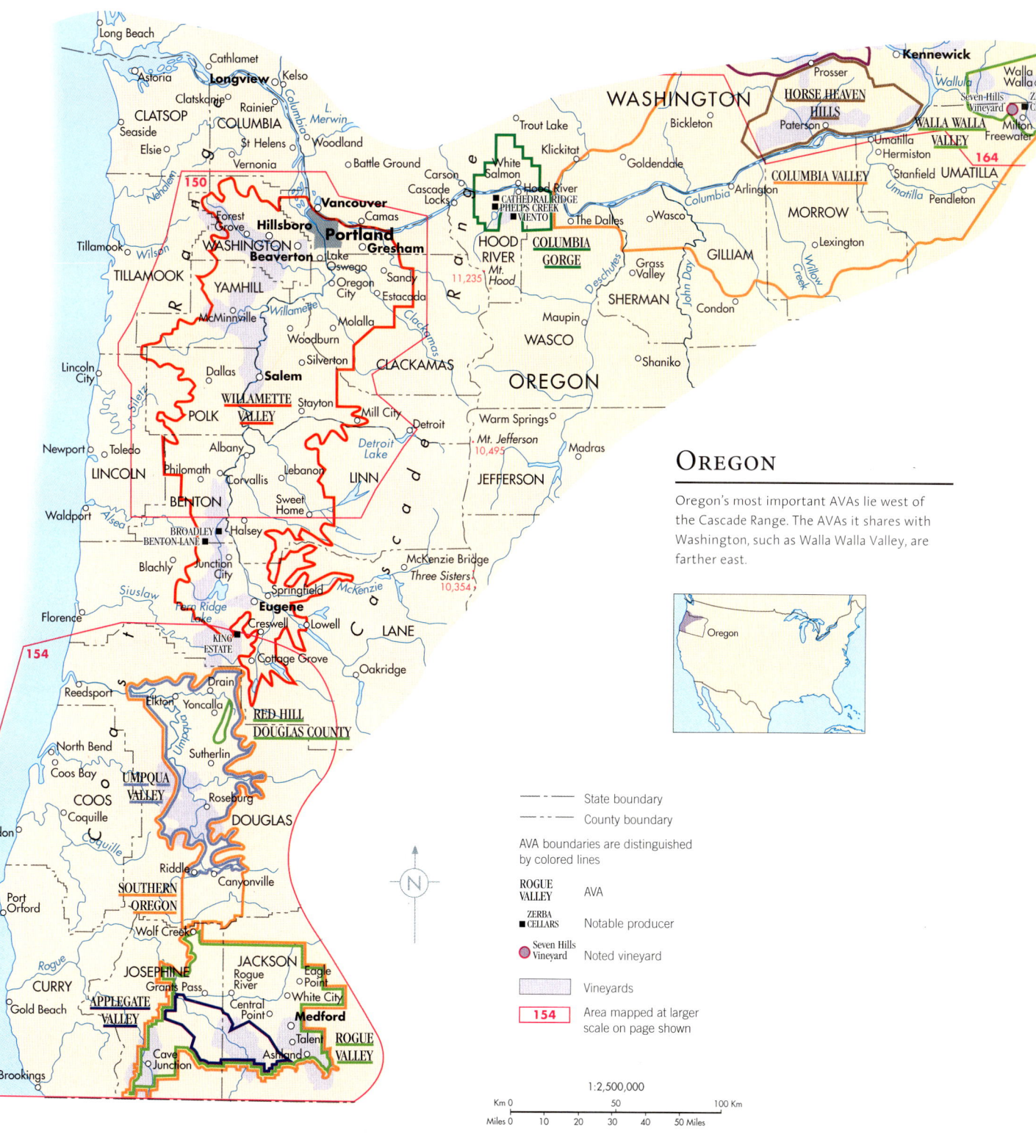

OREGON

Oregon's most important AVAs lie west of the Cascade Range. The AVAs it shares with Washington, such as Walla Walla Valley, are farther east.

International Pinot Noir Celebration
Every summer, Pinot Noir producers and passionate consumers from around the world gather at the IPNC in McMinnville in Willamette Valley for tastings, tours and seminars.

Pinot Noir continues to be the dominant grape, taking up some 60 percent of the planted acreage. Pinot Gris and, to a lesser extent (by acreage), Riesling are established as Oregon's best white-wine varieties. Chardonnay has had its ups and downs, though replacing California clones with Dijon clones from Burgundy has recently yielded some much more complex wines from those committed to the noble grape.

There were no Franciscan fathers to establish missions in Oregon and plant wine grapes, as there were in California. The first nonnative settlers began arriving in the territory in the mid-1850s via the Oregon Trail, which extended from Independence, Missouri, to Oregon City. They were more interested in beaver pelts for hats than they were in wine, and while there is evidence that a few vineyards existed at this time, they disappeared, and the budding vintners who trekked north to Oregon from California in the late 1960s and early 1970s started from scratch.

In 2011, nearly four decades after modern-day wine grapes were first planted in Oregon, the city of Forest Grove, in the Willamette Valley, caused a stir by unveiling its new slogan, "Forest Grove: Where Oregon Pinot Was Born." The claim was immediately challenged by a number of vintners, including Dyson DeMara of HillCrest Vineyard in the Umpqua Valley AVA, where HillCrest founder Richard Sommer is widely believed to have planted the first Pinot Noir in the state in 1961, and Jason Lett, son of the late David Lett of the Eyrie Vineyard, who was the first to grow Pinot Noir in Willamette Valley, beginning in 1965.

But Forest Grove hoped to attract more visitors, and the Pinot Noir connection was too delicious to pass up. Indeed, Charles Coury had planted grapes near the city at approximately the same time as David Lett planted in the Willamette Valley, though Coury had always credited Sommer as the state's Pinot pioneer. When challenged on their slogan, Forest Grove officials said that Coury was the first to recommend growing Pinot Noir and other cold-climate grapes in Oregon, and that his advice ignited the industry. Many will argue to the contrary; Sommer, Lett, and Coury are no longer alive to settle the matter.

Sommer, Lett, and Coury all attended UC Davis in California, where they studied enology and viticulture, and then made their way to Oregon. In addition to the cool growing season, the three men, and others who followed, were attracted to the low cost of land in Oregon, compared to California. Sommer saw the Umpqua Valley in central Oregon as a prime location for Riesling, and soon thereafter he embraced Pinot Noir. Lett, Oregon's "Papa Pinot," yearned to produce Pinot Noir with the same elegance, complexity, and longevity as those he'd enjoyed in Burgundy. Coury planted a vineyard and established Charles Coury Winery, but he left the industry after just a few years.

Dick Erath (Erath Vineyards) arrived in the Willamette Valley in 1968 and planted Pinot Noir, Pinot Gris, and Chardonnay. Then came fellow Californians Dick and Nancy Ponzi (Ponzi Vineyards) in 1970, Susan Sokol and Bill Blosser (Sokol Blosser) in 1971, and David and Ginny Adelsheim (Adelsheim Vineyard) in 1972. The rush was on, with most of the prospectors coming from the Golden State to seek their fortune in an all-new environment. They relocated to a state where forestry was and still is the top business dog. Oregon is the number-one grower of Christmas trees in the United States, and forestry and agriculture contribute more than $38 billion to the state's economy, a 25-percent piece of its pie.

WILLAMETTE VALLEY AVA

Oregon's largest AVA, Willamette Valley, formalized in 1984, is 150 miles long and 60 miles across at its widest; it runs from the Columbia River in Portland south through Salem to the Calapooya Mountains outside Eugene. The valley has the largest concentration of wineries and vineyards in Oregon and six sub-AVAS: Chehalem Mountains, Dundee Hills, Eola–Amity Hills, McMinnville, Ribbon Ridge, and Yamhill-Carlton.

Yamhill County is winemaking central in the Willamette AVA. Situated on the west side of the lower-middle part of the valley, Yamhill extends from about 15 miles southwest of Portland to within 11 miles of the Pacific Ocean. McMinnville is the largest city in the 728-square-mile county, with a population of 33,000, yet it's still very much a small town— except when the International Pinot Noir Celebration (IPNC) arrives each July. The first IPNC was held in McMinnville in 1987 and the conference has been here every year since, with seventy international Pinot Noir producers pouring their wines and participating in seminars for a combined consumer and trade audience. Oregonians are just as proud of their farm-to-table cuisine as they are of their wines, and everyone eats well at IPNC. It's the hottest ticket in Oregon.

Yamhill County has the most wineries in the state, 130, and close to one-third of Oregon's vineyard acreage is here, at approximately 6,500 acres—5,200 of them in Pinot Noir. The weather is relatively mild throughout the year, with cool, wet winters and warm summers. Most of the rain falls from November through March, but it's also common to see showers during harvest. Vintners tend to let the moisture roll off their backs. As Argyle Winery winemaker Rollin Soles says, "When it rains in California during harvest, winemakers get all worried; when it rains in Willamette Valley, we go fishing."

Most Oregonians love the outdoors: cycling, hiking, river rafting, mountain climbing, and, yes, fishing. Their skins are tough, their energy levels high, their minds open to adventure; growers and winemakers tend to gravitate to Willamette Valley not only for the lifestyle, but also for the camaraderie and collegial atmosphere. If a pump goes out, the winemaker down the road is usually happy to deliver a loaner.

Willamette Valley is dotted with hazelnut orchards, verdant pastures, grain elevators, and red barns; vineyards don't dominate the landscape, but instead fit in like pieces of a jigsaw

Knudsen Vineyards
This is one of the Willamette Valley's oldest Pinot Noir vineyards, planted in 1970 in what would become the Dundee Hills AVA. Knudsen is the primary grape source for Argyle Winery's Pinot Noirs, Chardonnays, and sparkling wines.

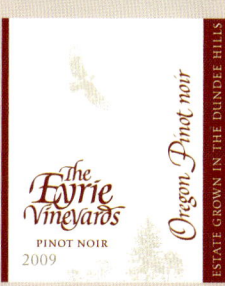

WILLAMETTE VALLEY AVA SNAPSHOT
Vineyard acreage: **15,000**
Most-planted varieties: **Pinot Noir, Pinot Gris, Chardonnay, Riesling**
Best varieties: **Pinot Gris, Pinot Noir**
Sub-AVAs: **Chehalem Mountains, Dundee Hills, Eola–Amity Hills, McMinnville, Ribbon Ridge, Yamhill-Carlton**
Wineries: **300**
Trailblazers: **Adelsheim Winery, Erath Vineyards, The Eyrie Vineyard, Ponzi Vineyards, Sokol Blosser Winery**
Steady hands: **The above, plus Archery Summit, Argyle Winery, Bergstrom, Hamacher, Maysara, Owen Roe, Penner-Ash, Rex Hill, Stoller Vineyards, WillaKenzie Estate, Willamette Valley Vineyards**
Superstars: **Beaux Frères, Brick House Vineyard, Chehalem, Cristom Vineyards, Domaine Drouhin Oregon, Domaine Serene, Eyrie Vineyard, Ken Wright Cellars, Lemelson Vineyards, Soter Vineyards**
One to watch: **Evening Land**

WILLAMETTE VALLEY

A small portion of the southern Willamette Valley AVA is not shown on this map.

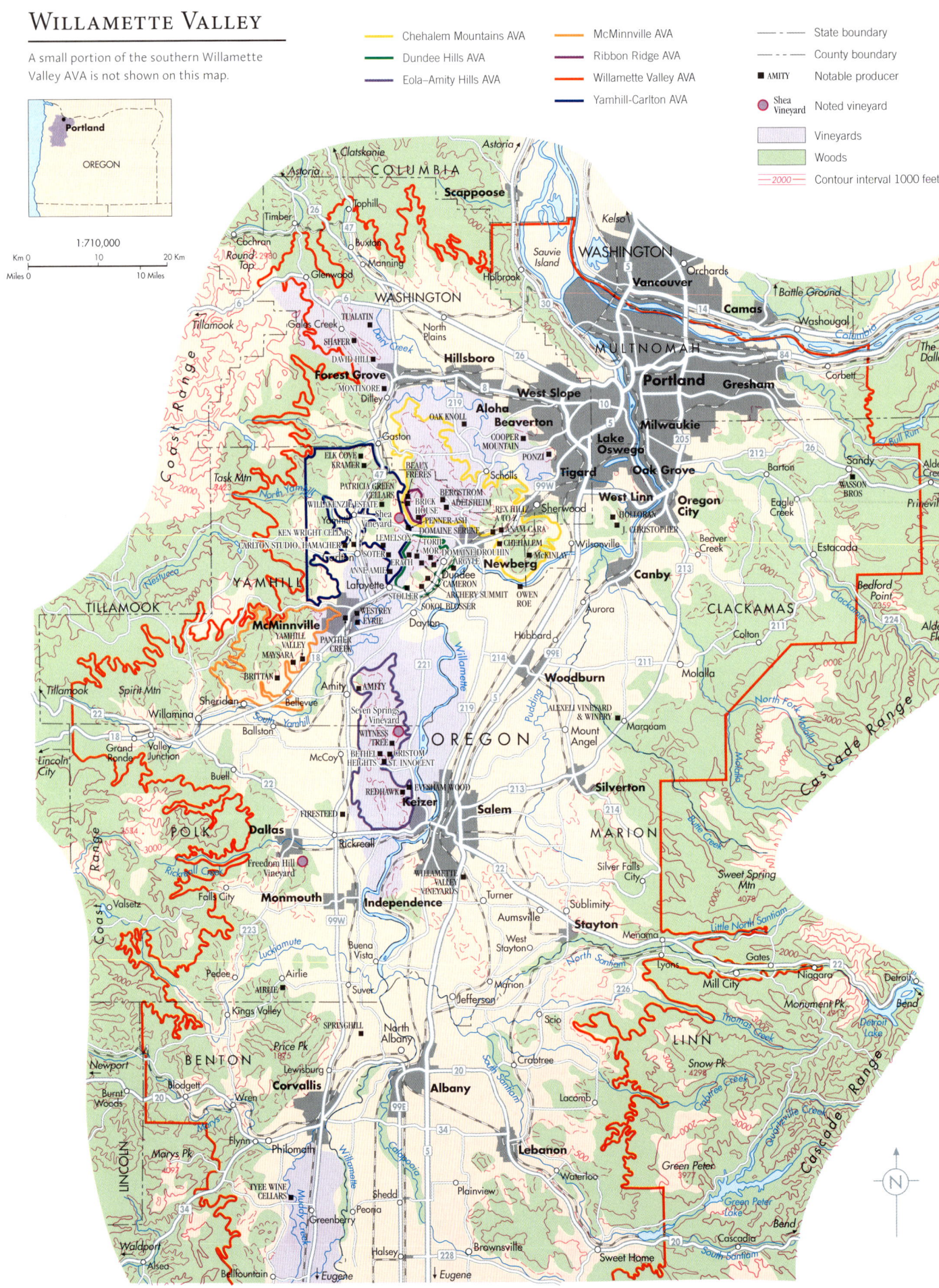

puzzle. Roadside stands sell local berries, tomatoes, corn, lettuce, and orchard fruits. The main thoroughfare, Highway 99W, links Willamette Valley with Portland. The towns along the route, the best-known being McMinnville and Newberg, are small but bustling with residents heading to work, dropping kids off at school, or hitting the local market. Highway 99W is not for those in a hurry, but then neither is Willamette Valley.

The region is an old volcanic and sedimentary seabed overlaid with gravel, silt, and rock deposited during the Missoula Floods, which raged ten to fifteen thousand years ago. The most common of the volcanic-type soils is the brick-red Jory, typically found at 300-feet elevation and above. Like all good wine grape soils, Jory provides excellent drainage—particularly important in this rainy valley. Jory is so important that it is the Official State Soil; few other states have such a thing.

Yet Jory doesn't always get the majority vote in Willamette Valley. Some winegrowers embrace the sedimentary soils on the uplifted sea floors of the region. These sandy, yellowish soils, labeled Willakenzie (a combination of two river names, Willamette and McKenzie), provide a noticeable difference in flavor from that of wines grown in Jory soils. Volcanic Jory soils typically produce Pinot Noirs with bright red-cherry fruit, similar to those of Burgundy's Côte de Beaune if one were to generalize; Pinot Noirs grown in Willakenzie soils are more Côte de Nuits in style, with dark-berry and black-cherry character.

Willamette Valley is hemmed in by the Coast Range to the west, the Cascades to the east, and a series of hills to the north. Most vineyards are west of the Willamette River, on south-facing slopes or in valleys formed by the river's tributaries. While most of the region's vineyards lie a few hundred feet above sea level, parts of the valley do reach much higher. The Chehalem Mountains are the highest in the valley, with their tallest point, Bald Peak, rising 1,633 feet above sea level.

The 1987 arrival in the valley of Domaine Drouhin Oregon—locally known as DDO—validated the instincts and efforts of Oregon's Burgundy-worshipping Pinot Noir pioneers. Robert Drouhin of Burgundy's Maison Joseph Drouhin purchased 225 acres in the Dundee Hills and began planting vines. He then turned winemaking over to his daughter, Véronique Drouhin-Boss, who has produced every vintage since 1988. The results have been dynamic: The Willamette Valley and higher-end Laurène Pinot Noirs are balanced and subtle, with only a light touch of oak in their texture, and brilliant clarity and acidity. Drouhin-Boss, who lives in Beaune but visits DDO frequently to check on the wines, also has a light touch with Chardonnay; her Arthur bottling is restrained when young and ages beautifully.

Local vinophiles even have their own glass, a machine-blown crystal stem created by Austrian glassware king Georg Riedel just for Oregon Pinot Noir. It's used mostly in tasting rooms, and Oregon vintners swear the glass makes their wines taste better than any other crystal. When the stem was

Dirt matters
Red volcanic Jory soils (shown here) and ancient-seabed sedimentary Willakenzie soils are deep, well drained, and ideal for growing Pinot Noir in Willamette Valley.

introduced, Riedel cautioned a Californian not to drink California Pinot from the glass, explaining that its shape was designed to concentrate the delicate, nuanced aromas of Oregon Pinot Noir. California Pinot, he said, was too powerful for such a vessel.

Passionate as Oregon winemakers are about Burgundy's red grape, they have been less enthused about its white companion, Chardonnay. Early attempts at producing Chardonnay in Willamette Valley were discouraging, in large part because growers planted a UC Davis clone from California that was bred to deliver maximum yields and retain natural acidity in warm climates. Chardonnays made from this 108 clone in the cooler climate of Willamette Valley were lean and flavorless and often had screeching acidity.

So growers and winemakers came to rely on Pinot Gris as their flagship white, with plantings nearly doubling in the past decade and 2,700 acres of it in the ground. It had much going for it: easy to grow, easy to drink, easy to sell, excellent yields, inexpensive to make (no barrels required) and thus highly profitable, and makes good use of soils unsuited to Pinot Noir; also its $15 to $20 price offsets the pain of pricier Pinot Noirs.

King Estate's signature wine is Pinot Gris—it bottles five versions—although it also produces Pinot Noir. The Pinot Gris wines deliver more flavor and richness than Italian Pinot Grigios, but less complexity than stellar Chardonnays—and that's just what many wine drinkers seek.

By the time French Dijon Chardonnay clones became available to Oregon growers and wineries in the mid-1990s—selections that were suited to Willamette Valley conditions—most had already given up on "white Burgundy" and replaced Chardonnay with more Pinot Noir and Pinot Gris vines.

Domaine Serene
Domaine Serene moved into its new winery in the Dundee Hills in time for the 2001 harvest; the winery's Pinot Noirs have earned high scores from critics.

Yet some brave souls replanted with the Dijon clones and began experimenting with yeasts, barrels, and other production techniques. Liking what they were tasting, they formed a group called ORCA—Oregon Chardonnay Alliance—and took their act on the road, pouring their new-style wines for trade and the media, asking them to give Oregon Chardonnay a second chance.

Rollin Soles of Argyle, Harry Peterson-Nedry of Chehalem, Véronique Drouhin-Boss of Domaine Drouhin Oregon, Dave Paige and David Adelsheim of Adelsheim, Luisa Ponzi of Ponzi Vineyards, Eric Hamacher of Hamacher Wines, and Tony Rynders (then of Domaine Serene) make vibrant, layered, elegant Chardonnays that showcase pure white-fruit flavors. Their promotional efforts hit a lull for a while, but they're on the move again, joined by new members who also believe that where Pinot Noir grows, so can Chardonnay.

Dundee Hills AVA

The Dundee Hills AVA includes 1,200 vineyard acres and twenty-five wineries. Approved in 2005, the AVA is in northern Willamette Valley, 28 miles southwest of Portland and 40 miles inland from the Pacific Ocean. It features hillside vineyards planted above the Willamette and Chehalem valley floors. Before the AVA was established, the area was known as the Red Hills of Dundee, for its volcanic red Jory soils.

Argyle Winery, founded by Australian Brian Croser, is a textbook Dundee Hills producer, with a splash of Champagne-quality sparkling wine to liven things up. Argyle's Pinot Noirs and Chardonnays benefit from the early-1990s conversions of its vineyards from California clones to Dijon clones from Burgundy. Traditional Pommard and Wädenswil clones remain in Willamette Valley, though they tend to be used more as spices, adding complexity to Dijon-dominant blends.

In 1989, Minnesota pharmaceutical company owners Ken and Grace Evenstad purchased a 42-acre piece of land near Domaine Drouhin Oregon in the Dundee Hills and established one of Oregon's most ambitious wine estates, Domaine Serene. At the time, many Oregon producers were struggling to build viable businesses and compete in the marketplace against wines from California. With their deep pockets, the Evenstads planted vineyard blocks with quality rather than quantity in mind. They hand-thinned grape clusters from the vines so that the remaining fruit would have more intensity. They built a winery with all the latest equipment, hired Ken Wright, then of Panther Creek Cellars, to make their first nine vintages, and aggressively marketed their wines to high-end restaurants. There was no compromising wine quality—a message that filtered down to other Willamette Valley winemakers.

McMinnville AVA

There are just seven wineries and 600 vine acres in the McMinnville AVA, the most westerly of all Oregon appellations, in the Coast Range foothills of Yamhill County. The soils are a combination of marine sedimentary soils and basalt, created during the Eocene epoch thirty-eight to fifty-five million years ago, the result of a combination of Cascade Mountain lava flows and tectonic plate movements that created the Coast Range. Vines planted on east- and south-facing slopes are protected from chilling winds in the unstable air conditions of the spring and fall.

Maysara Winery was established in 2001, in what would become the McMinnville AVA. In 1982, after the Shah of Iran was overthrown, Moe and Flora Momtazi made a harrowing escape from Iran on a motorcycle, with Flora eight months pregnant. They got to Pakistan and eventually to Texas, where Moe polished his engineering skills at Texas A&M University. Later they purchased an abandoned wheat farm in McMinnville and converted it to 260 acres of vineyards.

Their Momtazi Vineyard is the largest certified biodynamic vineyard in Oregon, and they grow Pinot Noir, Pinot Gris, Pinot Blanc, and Riesling. The Maysara winemaker is their daughter, Tahmiene—the child Flora was carrying when she hopped on that motorcycle in Tehran.

Robert Brittan, longtime winemaker at Stags' Leap Winery in Napa Valley, relocated to Willamette Valley and purchased a 128-acre hillside site, Brittan Vineyards, in McMinnville in 2004, planted to Pinot Noir and Syrah. Brittan has three Pinot Noir vintages under his belt and consults for other wineries.

Yamhill-Carlton AVA

North of McMinnville, the land slowly rises to the towns of Carlton and Yamhill. The landscape is dotted with orchards, vegetable gardens, grazing animals, and grain silos. The benchlands and hillsides of this region, the Yamhill-Carlton

AVA, established in 2004, are planted to grapevines, mostly Pinot Noir. The soils are sedimentary Willakenzie; the weather is slightly warmer here than in other Willamette Valley AVAs, so in seasons shortened by fall rains, Yamhill-Carlton winemakers often have their grapes safely in the cellar when others still have fruit hanging.

Longtime Napa Valley winemaker Tony Soter (Spottswoode, Etude) returned to his native Oregon to raise his family and start Soter Vineyards. His Mineral Springs Ranch Pinot Noirs from Yamhill-Carlton are among Oregon's finest. Elk Cove Vineyards dates to 1974, making founders Pat and Joe Campbell members of the Pinot Noir Pioneer Club. Their son, Adam Godlee Campbell, today oversees the winemaking and the family's 220 acres of vineyards.

Like many in Willamette Valley, Dick Shea started out as a grape grower and morphed into a winemaker. His Shea Vineyard is custom-farmed for other winemakers, and he keeps some of the best grapes for Shea Wine Cellars. Among the other top performers here are Lemelson Vineyards, Penner-Ash Wine Cellars, and WillaKenzie Estate—the latter bought by Burgundians Bernard and Ronni Lacroute in 1991. The winery's name pays tribute to the soils of the region.

With more than thirty years of winemaking to his credit, Ken Wright is the dean of Willamette Valley winemaking. After stints with Ventana Vineyards and Talbott Vineyards in California's Monterey County, and at Panther Creek Cellars and Domaine Serene in Oregon, Wright founded Ken Wright Cellars in 1994, for which he produces multiple single-vineyard wines, including one from Shea Vineyard, at his Yamhill-Carlton winery.

Chehalem Mountains and Ribbon Ridge AVAs

Adelsheim Vineyard, Chehalem, and Ponzi Vineyards are three of the most prominent producers in the Chehalem Mountains AVA and its own sub-AVA, Ribbon Ridge. An estimated 120 vineyards are planted here in a patchwork of small, family-owned plots on varying soil types and elevations ranging from 200 to 1,000 feet.

Chehalem, under the guidance of founder and winemaker Harry Peterson-Nedry, has a stellar lineup of wines, the most impressive being the unoaked INOX Chardonnay and the Corral Creek Vineyard Riesling. Chehalem sources grapes from the Chehalem Mountains, Ribbon Ridge, and Dundee Hills, and Peterson-Nedry typically bottles them separately so as not to blend away the characteristics of the vineyards.

Ponzi's Pinot Noirs, particularly its reserves, are among the best in Oregon, and the family's Italian heritage has led it to plant and successfully produce Arneis, the signature white wine of Piedmont.

One of Willamette Valley's first cult wine brands, Beaux Frères, has a celebrated co-owner in wine critic Robert M. Parker Jr. Parker and his brother-in-law, winemaker Michael Etzel, began their business in 1987, and the wines are still difficult to find and purchase because of overwhelming demand. Patricia Green of Patricia Green Cellars, also on Ribbon Ridge, is a terroiriste, a relentless pursuer of grapes grown in small blocks of vineyards in the Ribbon Ridge, Dundee Hills, Chehalem Mountains, and Eola–Amity Hills from which she can make single-site wines—as many as fifteen in any given vintage.

Doug Tunnell, a former CBS News correspondent, returned to his native Oregon to make wine at Brick House Vineyard, which he farms biodynamically, producing Pinot Noir, Chardonnay, and a lovely Gamay Noir (the grape of Beaujolais), which sells out upon release.

A relative newcomer, Anam Cara Cellars, is the effort of former Napa Valley residents Sheila and Nick Nicholas. She was a Napa wine public relations professional, he a restaurateur, and they ditched it all to plant Pinot Noir, Riesling, and Gewürztraminer in their Chehalem Mountains vineyard. The winery was founded in 2001, and its Heather's Vineyard Pinot Noir and estate Riesling are worth a search.

Eola–Amity Hills AVA

Evening Land Vineyards is a groundbreaker, a producer of Pinot Noirs from vineyards it owns in the Eola–Amity Hills AVA of Willamette Valley, Occidental Vineyard in the California Sonoma Coast AVA and Tempest Vineyard in the Sta. Rita Hills AVA, in California's Santa Barbara County. The Evening Land Oregon operation includes 120 acres of organically farmed vines grown in volcanic soils at the Seven Springs Vineyard. Burgundian winemaker Isabelle Meunier is at the controls, with consultation from Dominique Lafon of Domaine Comtes Lafon in Meursault, Burgundy.

The Eola–Amity Hills AVA is the southernmost in Willamette Valley, with the town of Amity near its northern end and the state capital, Salem, to the southeast. Some 37,000 acres in size, with 1,400 acres planted to grapevines, Eola–Amity Hills has mostly volcanic soils with some sedimentary components, and elevations of between 200 and 1,100 feet; vineyards are planted on the hillsides and valley floor. The region is home to top producers Amity Vineyards and Bethel Heights Vineyard—two more early arrivals in Willamette Valley, in 1974 and 1977, respectively—and Cristom Vineyards. After attending the International Pinot Noir Celebration in 1991, engineer Paul Gerrie decided to produce Oregon Pinot Noir and hired Steve Doerner away from California's Calera Wine Company to be Cristom's winemaker. Doerner remains in place today; his Pinot Noirs are silky and refined, and he produces a rare, for Willamette Valley, Viognier.

SOUTHERN OREGON

One can find Pinot Noir producers in Southern Oregon, though it takes some searching. The region is generally quite a bit warmer than Willamette Valley, and it is higher too, with vines planted at up to 2,000 feet. With abundant sunshine and heat, its more suited to Bordeaux and Mediterranean grape varieties than it is to Pinot Noir. This is mountainous country, sandwiched between the Coast Range and the Cascade Mountains. Slopes are studded with firs and pines, rivers draw white-water rafters and fishermen, and winter snows bring out skiers.

The huge, 2.3-million-acre AVA takes up where the Willamette Valley leaves off, south of the city of Eugene, and ends at the California border. The Southern Oregon AVA came about in 2004, to incorporate three previously established AVAs, the Umpqua, Applegate, and Rogue valleys, and the Red Hill Douglas County AVA, approved in 2005.

Vintners in Southern Oregon take great pride in their wines and have a "We're not Willamette and don't want to be" attitude.

Abacela
Owners Earl and Hilda Jones take advantage of Umpqua Valley AVA's diverse exposures and soil types to grow Spanish grape varieties that are becoming increasingly popular in warm U.S. growing areas. .

They are quick to point out that Richard Sommer, a California transplant, was the first to plant Pinot Noir in Oregon, in 1961, at HillCrest Vineyard in the Umpqua Valley.

Rogue Valley AVA

The Rogue Valley AVA (1991) is the warmest growing region in Oregon, best suited to the cultivation of Cabernet Sauvignon, Merlot, Cabernet Franc, and Syrah. There are 2,000 acres of vineyards planted in mostly sandy loam and hard clay soils; twenty wineries are located in Rogue Valley, including Bridgeview Vineyards and Winery, which is exceptionally large

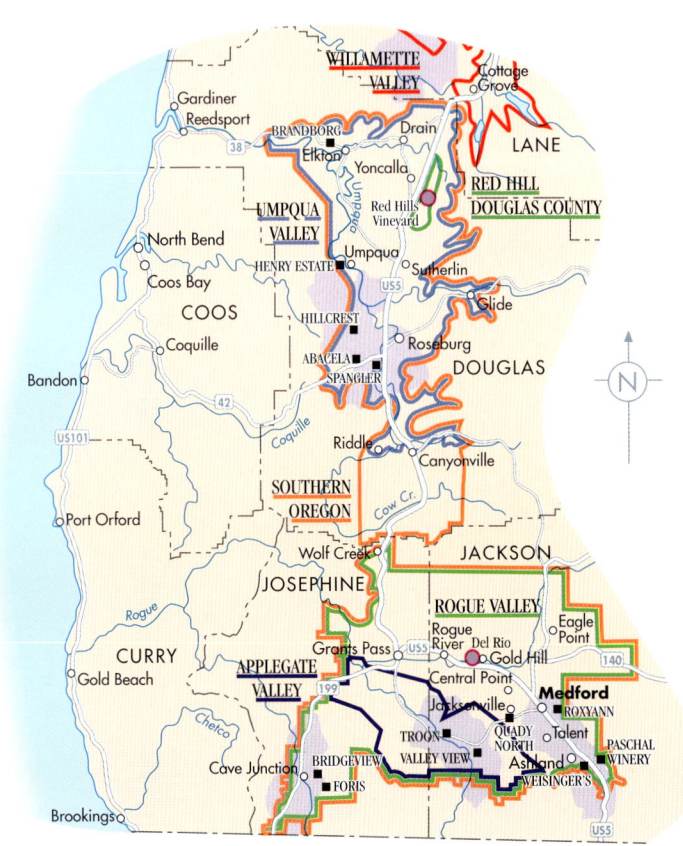

SOUTHERN OREGON

Southern Oregon is a massive (2.1 million acres) AVA with four sub-AVAs to give it more terroir-based definition: Applegate Valley, Red Hill Douglas County, Rogue Valley, and Umpqua Valley.

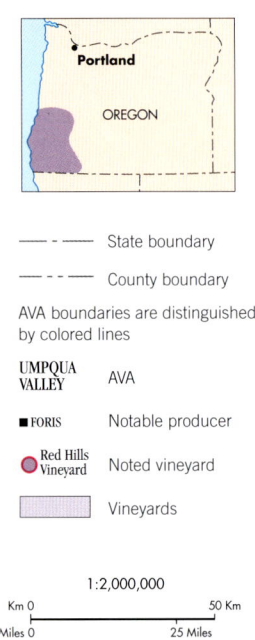

SOUTHERN OREGON SNAPSHOT

Vineyard acreage: **2,800**

Most-planted varieties: Cabernet Sauvignon, Syrah, Merlot, Chardonnay, Tempranillo, Viognier

Best varieties: Pinot Noir, Syrah, Tempranillo, Viognier

AVAs: Applegate Valley, Red Hill Douglas County, Rogue Valley, Umpqua Valley

Wineries: **60**

Trailblazer: HillCrest Vineyard

Steady hands: Bridgeview Vineyard & Winery, Foris Vineyards, Spangler Vineyards, Troon Vineyard, Quady North

Superstars: Abacela Winery, Brandborg Vineyard & Winery

---

for the area, producing 80,000 cases of wine a year. Its popularly priced, off-dry Blue Moon Riesling is a top seller, helped along by its blue glass bottle.

Foris Vineyards is one winery where Pinot Noir can be found, made in a lighter than usual style but clean, fresh, and floral. Foris's Rieslings and Gewürztraminers are Alsatian in style, with good palate weight and juicy fruit.

Del Rio Vineyards, near Gold Hill, is Southern Oregon's best-known vineyard. Rob Wallace was a farmer in the Sacramento, California, area before planting Del Rio in 1998. He added a winery in 2004 to produce Bordeaux-style red wines, Syrah, and an award-winning Reserve Pinot Gris.

Within the Rogue Valley AVA is the Applegate Valley AVA, which includes fifteen wineries and 400 vineyard acres. Its strongest suits are Cabernet Sauvignon, Merlot, and Syrah, due to the warm days and abundant sun exposure the vines receive on hillside plantings at elevations as high as 1,600 feet. Soils include decomposed granite derived from stream terraces and alluvial fans.

Troon Vineyard put Applegate on the map when Dick Troon planted his first vines there in 1972. He rooted his favorite varieties, Cabernet Sauvignon and Zinfandel, and began making his own wine in 1993. Troon sold the business to the Martin family and retired in 2003. Herb Quady, son of California port-style winemaker Andrew Quady, is the winemaker, and he continues Troon's passion for Zinfandel.

Umpqua Valley AVA

The Umpqua Valley AVA sits between the Coast Range to the west and the Cascade Range to the east, with the Willamette

Richard Sommer
In 1961, UC Davis–trained Sommer was the first to plant Pinot Noir in Oregon, at his HillCrest Vineyard in the Umpqua Valley.

Valley AVA to the north and the Rogue Valley AVA to the south. Named for the legendary fishing river that runs through it, the appellation stretches 65 miles from north to south and 25 miles from east to west. With 1,200 vineyard acres and twelve wineries, the AVA isn't large, but it is mighty important from a historical perspective.

The valley's winegrowing history dates to the 1880s, when German immigrants who had worked for Beringer Bros., the oldest continuously operating vineyard in Napa Valley, planted the first vineyard in Umpqua. Post-Prohibition, Richard Sommer established HillCrest Vineyard near Roseburg in 1961, planting Riesling and Pinot Noir—the first in Oregon to do so.

Sommer, who studied enology and viticulture at UC Davis, had been told by professors that planting wine grapes in Oregon would certainly meet with disaster. Too cold, they said. He proved them wrong, opening the doors for others to begin planting commercial vineyards in the state.

Eight years later, in 1969, Paul Bjelland of Bjelland Vineyards founded the Oregon Winegrowers Association in the Umpqua Valley. During the 1970s, more wineries opened, including Henry Estate Winery, whose winemaker, Scott Henry, developed the now internationally known trellis system bearing his name.

One of Oregon's more diverse AVAs, the Umpqua Valley can successfully grow cool- and warm-climate grape varieties. There are three distinct climatic subzones within the AVA. The northern area around Elkton has a cool, marine-influenced climate, receiving approximately 50 inches of rainfall annually, making irrigation unnecessary. Pinot Noir and other cool-climate varieties thrive here. The central part of the valley, northwest of Roseburg, has a transitional, or intermediate, climate where both cool and warm varieties do well. The region south of Roseburg is warmer and more arid, similar to the Rogue and Applegate valleys to the south, making irrigation imperative. Warm-climate varieties, including Tempranillo, Syrah, and Merlot, grow well here.

The soils are generally derived from a blend of metamorphic, sedimentary, and volcanic rock, although 150 soil types have been identified in the region. The valley floor levels have mostly deep alluvial or heavy clay materials, while the hillsides and benches have mixed alluvial, silt, or clay structures.

These conditions lend themselves well to a wide range of wine types and styles, from Pinot Noir and Chardonnay to Rhône varieties such as Viognier, Grenache, and Syrah and the Spanish grapes Tempranillo, Albariño, and Graciano.

The Joneses of Abacela had Iberian wine varieties in mind when they purchased 500 acres near Roseburg in 1992. Earl, a California physician, had developed a taste for Tempranillos from Rioja and Ribera del Duero while in medical school, as they were the least-expensive good quality wines he could afford. When he and Hilda, a medical technologist, decided that

Del Rio Vineyards
Rob Wallace farms 185 acres of grapes at Del Rio in the undulating Rogue Valley, selling them to forty wineries in Oregon, Washington, and California. He keeps some fruit for his Del Rio Vineyards brand.

TAPAS AND TEMPRANILLO

Zinfandel has its own marketing association, Zinfandel Advocates & Producers (known as ZAP, which is exactly what some of its most potent wines will do to a body). Petite Sirah's fan club, P.S. I Love You, sounds kinder and gentler, although the wines made from this variety are muscular and masculine. Now there is TAPAS—Tempranillo Advocates, Producers and Amigos Society—for those who, such as Earl and Hilda Jones at Abacela, love to drink Tempranillo and other Spanish varieties, including Albariño, Verdelho, and Graciano.

Tempranillo, the sixth-most-planted wine grape in the world and the foundation of the red wines of Rioja and Ribera del Duero in Spain, has been planted in the United States during the last two decades, with most of the acreage in California's Central Valley. But southern Oregon, Washington, Texas, and Arizona have also experienced success with the grape, and acreage is increasing in warm-to-hot regions where other more mainstream varieties don't fare well.

Earl Jones was the first president of TAPAS, encouraged to found the association after he won a sweepstakes award for his Tempranillo at the San Francisco International Wine Competition in 1998, beating a field of Spanish Tempranillos. That helped him begin to win support for a U.S. Tempranillo trade association, and there are now more than eighty members. They stage tastings and other events throughout the year to call attention to Tempranillo, and they almost always serve—you guessed it—tapas.

TAPAS estimates that there are between 1,500 and 2,000 acres of Tempranillo in the United States, with the most in California (850 acres), followed by Oregon (about 150), Washington (100), and Texas (75).

Tempranillo grapes
The flagship grape of Spain's Rioja and Ribera del Duero regions has caught fire in Southern Oregon, where it thrives in the warm summer climate.

---

they wanted to produce American Tempranillo to go with the spicy Spanish foods they loved so much, they first went to Spain to study the soils and climate, then went about trying to find U.S. real estate with similar conditions.

They found it in Umpqua Valley: cool spring; hot, dry summer; and low rainfall. A handful of wineries were already there, yet their focus was on cool-climate viticulture. To their neighbors' great shock, the Joneses began planting their vineyard to Tempranillo. Winemaking began elsewhere in 1996, and Abacela (from *abacelar*, an old Spanish/Portuguese word for "to plant a grapevine") became the first producer of varietal Tempranillo in the Pacific Northwest. Today Abacela is planted to Tempranillo, Albariño, and a host of other often-overlooked European vine varieties.

Terry and Sue Brandborg have had remarkable success with Pinot Noir in Umpqua Valley. Terry, previously a winemaker in Northern California, longed for a change of scenery. After meeting and marrying Sue, he found land for a vineyard in the northern end of Umpqua Valley, near Elkton, in 2001. They purchased grapes from southern Oregon growers until their estate vineyard came onstream in 2005.

The Pinot Noirs from Brandborg are supple and polished, reflecting the cool mountain conditions with brisk acidity and a hint of earthy minerality; alcohol by volume tends to be in the mid-13-percent range.

The Brandborgs' Ferris Wheel Vineyard is in the coastal mountains, 25 miles from the Pacific Ocean. It has southern exposures and ranges in elevation from 750 to 1,100 feet, with soil composition including sand and clay loams. The vineyard, which receives enough marine influence that only cool-climate varieties will ripen, is planted to a mix of Dijon and Pommard clones.

Red Hill Douglas County is a subappellation of the Umpqua Valley AVA, near the small town of Yoncalla. It's a single-vineyard AVA, the 220-acre Red Hill Vineyard.

Other Oregon AVAs

The Walla Walla AVA actually includes vineyards in Washington as well as Oregon. Near the town of Milton-Freewater, just south of the Washington state line, the Seven Hills Vineyard, developed by partners Norm McKibben of Pepper Bridge Winery, Gary Figgins of Leonetti Cellar, and Marty Clubb of L'École No 41 (all in Washington), provides red grapes not only to their own brands but to several others. Zerba Cellars, also in Milton-Freewater, is one of the few Oregon wineries to produce Cabernet Sauvignon from Walla Walla grapes.

The **Columbia Gorge AVA** begins 60 miles east of Portland, with the dramatically powerful Columbia River defining the boundaries between Oregon and Washington. Forty square miles in all, the AVA, approved in 2004, belongs to Oregon on the appellation's southern edge and to Washington on the north. It also includes a piece of the Columbia Valley AVA. The predominant varieties are Gewürztraminer, Chardonnay, Pinot Noir, and Syrah; Viento Wines (Gewürztraminer, Syrah) and Phelps Creek Vineyards (Pinot Noir, Chardonnay) are the stars here.

The **Snake River Valley AVA** is partially in Oregon, but Idaho dominates the wine production there.

GREEN STATE

Oregon proudly claims to be the "greenest" grape-growing and winemaking state in the Union, with the majority of its vintners using some level of sustainable, earth-friendly practices. Indeed, Monty Waldin, one of the most critical specialist writers on sustainable practices in wine production, points out in his *Biodynamic Wine Guide 2011*, "Oregon has the highest percentage of certified organic and Demeter biodynamic vineyards in the world— ahead even of Alsace in France, which is by far Europe's greenest wine region." With all these green thumbs, those who wantonly spray pesticides and herbicides, waste water, and don't rigorously recycle stick out like sore thumbs.

The term *sustainable* means different things to different people, and in different states and industries. At its simplest, it means viticultural and winemaking practices that reduce or eliminate chemical applications; create natural habitats that invite beneficial predators to control destructive ones; use recycled wastewater for irrigation, frost protection, and judicious cleaning; and encourage recycling programs and other regimes that leave as little artificial impact on the land as possible. (Sustainable also means staying in business.) Oregon has gone out of its way to create and/or embrace sustainability certification programs— some with third-party inspections— meant to keep the state green for future generations. Among them:

- Demeter Certified Biodynamic: Biodynamics is a growing, if still niche, form of superorganics dating from 1924 and predating the organic movement by more than a generation. Its main tenet, making farms, and thus vineyards, "self-sustaining living organisms," resonates with winegrowers keen to express the terroir. Cows and other livestock must be part of the vineyard to maintain soil life and fertility, and to allow vineyard and winery waste (prunings, grapeskins) to be recycled back onto the land as a compost. Biodynamic compost must also contain small amounts of six medicinal plants: yarrow, chamomile, stinging nettle, oak bark, dandelion, and valerian. Biodynamic producers also try to prune, ferment, and even bottle their vines/wines according to lunar and other celestial cycles, partly to save fossil fuels, but also to keep the vines and wines "vital." Demeter is the globally recognized biodynamic certifier. America's Demeter Association is based in Philomath, Oregon, and certifies vineyards in Chile and Argentina, as well as in other American states, including California.

- Low Input Viticulture & Enology (LIVE): This program certifies vineyards and wineries according to international guidelines for environmental stewardship, social responsibility, and economic accountability. LIVE also provides education and resources to growers interested in sustainable farming. LIVE certification is often the first step winegrowers take before going fully organic or biodynamic.

- Oregon Certified Sustainable Wine (OCSW): Launched in 2008, this program focuses on the shared principles of LIVE, Demeter biodynamic, the Food Alliance, and the National Organic Program and its certifying agencies. Its unifying platform and certification logo aim to help consumers identify and purchase sustainable wines, no matter which entity has certified them. In 2011, there were twenty-two participating Oregon wineries and 3.55 million certified bottles.

- Oregon Tilth Certified Organic (OTCO): Oregon's oldest organic organization, founded in 1974, this certifies almost every Oregon vineyard claiming organic status, as well as other farms and market gardens. Its name endorses what organic farmers strive for: fine tilth soils that contain enough worms and other beneficial organisms to nurture healthy plants. Oregon Tilth is accredited by IFOAM (International Federation of Organic Agriculture Movements), an organization whose mission is to protect organic regulations from dilution.

- Salmon-Safe: Founded in 1995 by an Oregon-based river and native fish protection organization, Salmon-Safe works with grape growers to eliminate erosion and runoff from hillside vineyards, which can dump silt into streams and reduce the ability of the native salmon to survive. Since first

certifying vineyards in the Willamette Valley more than a decade ago, Salmon-Safe has certified 110 Oregon vineyards, representing one-third of the state's wine-grape acreage. Producers affix Salmon-Safe labels on wine bottles to inform consumers of their efforts to maintain river and stream health.

- Vinea, The Winegrowers' Sustainable Trust: Vinea is a group of winegrowers that has voluntarily embraced environmentally friendly and socially responsible viticultural practices. Its mission is to develop a sustainable vineyard management program that will be internationally recognized for its strict environmental standards and high-quality farming practices.

In addition, the U.S. Green Building Council's LEED (Leadership in Energy and Environmental Design) certifications have been won by some Willamette Valley wineries. In 2002, Sokol Blosser Winery in the Dundee Hills became the first winery in the

Bethel Heights Vineyard solar panels
The winery's photovoltaic system assists in powering the facility and two family homes on the vineyard property in the Eola Hills.

Sokol Blosser barrel room
Because it's underground Sokol Blosser's cellar is cooled naturally and uses no energy for temperature control. It has been designed to blend in with the local landscape.

country to receive LEED Silver certification. It constructed a three-chambered underground barrel room that utilizes the naturally cool temperatures of the soil. Heat and carbon dioxide are dissipated by fans and fresh-air intakes called earth tubes. Water-efficient wildflowers and grasses cover the building and an adjacent field to support beneficial insects, and more than 75 percent of the materials used in building the room were sourced from within 500 miles of the winery.

Stoller Vineyards, also in the Dundee Hills, was the first winery to achieve LEED Gold status. It was certified in 2006 for its integration of gravity-flow techniques, energy-efficient heating and cooling, and waste-water reclamation to reduce negative environmental impacts.

Washington

Washington has achieved its status as the number-two wine-producing state in the nation rather rapidly, considering that its premium wine industry began only in the late 1960s, when farmers, seeing California's success with wine grapes, began replacing vegetable row crops, apples, and hops with *Vitis vinifera*. American Concord grapes were already established in Washington, for use in juices and jams, but growers could see the potential for higher profits by converting some of their land to wine grapes.

The snowy Cascade Range separates arid eastern Washington, where most of the state's vineyards are planted, and the rainy Puget Sound area to the west.

And, as in California, nearly every traditional vinifera variety grows in Washington, along with some obscure ones. Cabernet Sauvignon, Merlot, Syrah, and Riesling are the brightest lights in terms of quality and market success, with Chardonnay, Sauvignon Blanc, Pinot Gris, Semillon, Gewürztraminer, Viognier, Grenache, Cabernet Franc, and Sangiovese thriving as well. The high-acid red variety Lemberger (known as Blaufränkisch in Europe) has a small but loyal following, and it's not a shock to find a Washington Barbera, Malbec, Tempranillo, or Zinfandel on a restaurant list or in a tasting room.

Yet this marvelous diversity also hinders Washington vintners globally, because they aren't known for any one wine. Like it or not, California is viewed outside the state largely as the home to Napa Valley Cabernet Sauvignon, Oregon is defined by Pinot Noir, and New York's Finger Lakes region by Riesling. When it comes to Washington, not only do many consumers not know which varieties are its best, some don't even know that "Washington" on the label isn't D.C., the District of Columbia. Adding to that confusion: Washington State's largest AVA is the Columbia Valley. And, just to further confuse things, some of it is in Oregon.

Washington's first prime-time wine was Riesling, a variety thought to be one of the few that could withstand the cold winters. Later vintners including Gary Figgins at Leonetti Cellar, Marty Clubb at L'Ecole No. 41, and Rick Small at Woodward Canyon Winery proved that Merlot was a fine fit for the conditions, and they produced wines garnering acclaim along the lines of Napa Cabernets. Filled with confidence, Washingtonians successfully tackled Cabernet Sauvignon, and then Syrah, and now Riesling has come back strongly.

The number of AVAs in Washington has mushroomed from three in 1984—Yakima Valley (1983), Columbia Valley (1984), and Walla Walla Valley (1984)—to twelve today, and others are in the pipeline. Consumer confusion is inevitable, though the same is true in any state where multiple grape

varieties thrive, and where exploration and experimentation is ongoing as vintners work to discover which varieties should be planted where. In 2011, the Washington State Wine Commission committed $7.4 million to support construction of a Wine Science Center at Washington State University's Tri-Cities campus in Richland, to further the education of budding viticulturists and winemakers, and to fund research programs tailored to the specific needs of the state. Vintners say they expect the center to be as important to Washington as UC Davis is to California's wine industry.

Beginning in the mid-1850s, cold-hardy grapes such as Müller-Thurgau and Madeleine Angevine were brought to western Washington's Puget Sound area and planted by European immigrants. But Prohibition shut down commercial winemaking in 1920, and after its repeal in 1933, only a few wineries resumed production on the western side of the Cascade Mountains.

In the mid-1960s, Dr. Walter Clore of the Washington State University Agricultural Extension in the Yakima Valley demonstrated that vinifera had a future in eastern Washington, and his trials spurred the likes of Hinzerling Vineyard and Winery, Preston Vineyards, and E. B. Foote Winery to establish wineries in Yakima Valley.

At approximately the same time, enologist André Tchelistcheff, from Napa Valley, and wine historian/author Leon Adams explored the state. They advised Associated Vintners,

WASHINGTON

Three of Washington's AVAs spill into Oregon: Columbia Gorge, Columbia Valley, and Walla Walla Valley. It's common for wineries in one state to produce wines from grapes grown in the other.

WASHINGTON SNAPSHOT

Vineyard acreage: **40,000**

Most-planted varieties: **Cabernet Sauvignon, Merlot, Chardonnay, Riesling, Syrah**

Best varieties: **Cabernet Sauvignon, Chardonnay, Merlot, Riesling, Syrah**

AVAs: **Columbia Gorge (shared with Oregon), Columbia Valley (shared with Oregon), Horse Heaven Hills, Lake Chelan, Naches Heights, Puget Sound, Rattlesnake Hills, Red Mountain, Snipes Mountain, Wahluke Slope, Walla Walla Valley (shared with Oregon), Yakima Valley**

Wineries: **700**

Celilo Vineyard
Syncline Wine Cellars and Woodward Canyon are among the wineries that prize the Chardonnay, Gewürztraminer, and Pinot Noir grapes grown in this Columbia Gorge vineyard.

---

founded in 1962 by a group of University of Washington professors/home winemakers who would become Columbia Winery, and American Wine Growers (later to be named Chateau Ste. Michelle), that wine grapes would find hospitable conditions east of the Cascade Mountains. Thus Washington's premium industry began, spurred on by the continued expansion of the California wine industry to the south.

In 1981, there were nineteen wineries in the state; today there are more than seven hundred, a phenomenal growth in such a short time.

Yet Washington's wine story really began fifteen million years ago, when the region experienced chaotic volcanic activity. Lava flows hardened into the basalt bedrock that covers much of the Northwest today. Cataclysmic floods followed, resulting from glaciers moving south from Canada and stopping at the Clark Fork River in the Idaho Panhandle. This enormous piece of ice formed a natural dam, creating Lake Missoula. The dam eventually burst with the "Missoula Floods" depositing sand, silt, granite, and quartz throughout the region—a cycle that would repeat itself many times over. Winds spread this matter to the surrounding hills, and volcanic eruptions in the Cascades added ash to the already-complex soils.

East of the Cascades, winters are cold and often below the freezing point, although then the vines are dormant and usually unaffected. Harmful pests are destroyed in such conditions, which is why phylloxera, the root-sapping louse that has killed grapevines throughout the world, has not made a major march into eastern Washington. It simply cannot stand the cold, and it doesn't much like the sandy soils that are so common in eastern Washington.

However, every decade or so, temperatures remain below freezing—as low as 13° F—for an extended period of time, causing injury to dormant vines. The roots are usually protected by the warmth of the soil, but above-ground trunks and canes can become damaged, requiring repair or sometimes replacement.

Eastern Washington is a desert populated by sagebrush, tumbleweeds, and nothing edible—unless water is applied. It averages less than 10 inches of rain per year, as the Cascade Mountains block Pacific storms from reaching the Columbia Valley, in what is called the rain shadow effect. Tapping water from the Columbia, Yakima, and Snake rivers is imperative for agriculture, and water rights are hard to come by; legal access to water is the first consideration for anyone seeking to plant vineyards in eastern Washington.

West of the Cascades, the Seattle/Puget Sound area is quite different, being so exposed to Pacific Ocean storms, it averages 40 inches of rain per year. The wet conditions, which occur throughout the year save for a precious few months in summer and early fall, support only the humble Müller-Thurgau, Madeleine Angevine, Siegerrebe, and other early ripening grape varieties. The wines made from them may be beloved by many, but they have nothing like the following of the much more full-bodied wines produced from eastern Washington grapes.

However, the Seattle area, most specifically Woodinville, is home to Chateau Ste. Michelle, Columbia Winery, Andrew Will, McCrea Cellars, DeLille Cellars, and dozens of other top producers who source grapes from eastern Washington, but find it easier to make and sell their wines in the west. Chris Camarda of Andrew Will is a classic example: He lives on Vashon Island west of Seattle and purchases Cabernet Sauvignon, Merlot, and other red grapes that arrive by truck from the Columbia Valley and are ferried from Seattle to his Vashon winery.

ALLEN SHOUP

Chateau Ste. Michelle and many of its affiliated brands — Col Solare, Columbia Crest, Domaine Ste. Michelle, Eroica, North Star, and Snoqualmie among them— were shepherded by Allen Shoup, who headed Ste. Michelle Wine Estates (then Stimson Lane) for almost twenty years before retiring in 2000.

Shoup accomplished as much for all Washington winegrowers as he did for his own brands. As the president of the largest wine company in the state, he had tremendous input into the establishment of the Washington State Wine Commission, the state's wine marketing organization, and in the formation of the Columbia Valley AVA. He also convinced Piero Antinori, of Tuscany, and Dr. Ernst Loosen, of the Mosel region of Germany, to become Ste. Michelle's partners in Col Solare and Eroica, respectively.

Not content to play golf for the rest of his life, the "retired" Shoup cast his long shadow over Napa Valley, Bordeaux, Australia, Italy, and Germany, creating unique wines that match renowned winemakers in these areas with Washington state grapes. Long Shadows Vintners is the umbrella company for wines made by Shoup and his partners.

These include Armin Diel (Schlossgut Diel, Nahe, Germany), for Poet's Leap Riesling; former Barossa Valley Penfolds maker John Duval, for Syrah-based Sequel; Bordeaux enologist and Le Bon Pasteur owner Michel Rolland, for Pedestal Merlot; Randy Dunn of Dunn Vineyards in Napa Valley, for Feather Cabernet Sauvignon; Ambrogio and Giovanni Folonari of Italy, for Saggi (a blend of Cabernet Sauvignon, Sangiovese, and Syrah); Chilean Agustin Huneeus of Quintessa in Napa partnered with French-born winemaker

and superstar Napa Valley consultant Philippe Melka, for the red blend Pirouette; and Shoup and former Woodward Canyon winemaker Gilles Nicault, for Chester-Kidder, a Washington red blend.

Shoup is also managing partner of The Benches at Wallula Gap, a 650-acre vineyard in Washington's Horse Heaven Hills, a majority share of which his investor group purchased in 2008 from Bill and Andy Den Hoed and their father, Andres. Formerly the Wallula Vineyard, it has twenty-seven benches of land rising from the Columbia River banks to 1,450 feet elevation. Shoup sells grapes to Chateau Ste. Michelle and Pacific Rim, among others.

Shoup came to Chateau Ste. Michelle and its parent company, Stimson Lane, in 1980. While CEO, he developed the wildly successful Columbia Crest and Domaine Ste. Michelle brands, and he used Stimson Lane's financial clout to host charity auctions and other events at the "chateau" that benefited the entire Washington wine industry. Ted Baseler took over as president and CEO when Shoup retired, changing the company name to Ste. Michelle Wine Estates in 2004 and carrying on collaborations with others, including the company's purchase, with Antinori, of iconic Napa Valley winery Stag's Leap Wine Cellars in 2007.

COLUMBIA VALLEY AVA

The massive Columbia Valley AVA (11 million acres) encompasses all but two of Washington's sub-AVAs: Horse Heaven Hills, Lake Chelan, Naches Heights, Rattlesnake Hills, Red Mountain, Snipes Mountain, Walla Walla Valley, Wahluke Slope, and Yakima Valley, as well as winegrowing areas that don't (yet) have sub-AVA status. For example, Chateau Ste. Michelle's Cold Creek Vineyard is an exceptional source of older-vine Chardonnay, Riesling, Cabernet Sauvignon, Merlot, and Syrah grapes, but its location 38 miles east of Yakima and south of the Columbia River leaves it in no-man's-land as far as federally recognized growing areas go. Wines from Cold Creek are simply labeled "Columbia Valley."

Now that Riesling is rocking with U.S. wine drinkers, Chateau Ste. Michelle has made it easy for them to find affordable bottles. It is the largest single Riesling brand, producing a million cases per year, at prices starting at $9 per bottle. Ste. Michelle's Rieslings have become more complex and vibrant in recent years, thanks to the viticulture and winemaking expertise it gained by partnering with Ernst Loosen of the German Mosel producer Weingut Dr. Loosen. Together, Loosen and Ste. Michelle produce a high-end, off-dry Riesling called Eroica. In 2007, Ste. Michelle hired Australian Riesling winemaking expert Wendy Stuckey from Wolf Blass Winery, further bolstering its Riesling program.

Most Washington Rieslings are off-dry with a hint of residual sugar, but drier styles are emerging as vines planted in cool regions mature, including those in the Ancient Lakes area north of the Wahluke Slope, where ripe fruit, minerality and crisp acidity converge.

Columbia River Gorge
The Columbia Gorge AVA extends to both banks of the Columbia River, with Washington on the more elevated northern side and Oregon on the south bank.

THE WEST | WASHINGTON | COLUMBIA VALLEY AVA | 165

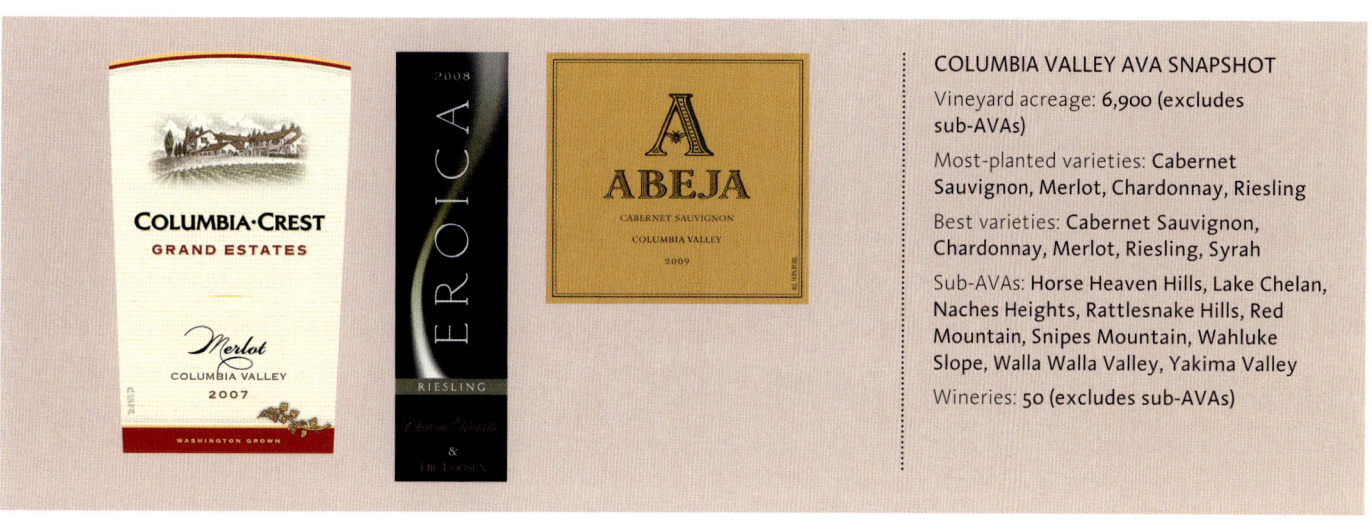

COLUMBIA VALLEY AVA SNAPSHOT

Vineyard acreage: 6,900 (excludes sub-AVAs)

Most-planted varieties: Cabernet Sauvignon, Merlot, Chardonnay, Riesling

Best varieties: Cabernet Sauvignon, Chardonnay, Merlot, Riesling, Syrah

Sub-AVAs: Horse Heaven Hills, Lake Chelan, Naches Heights, Rattlesnake Hills, Red Mountain, Snipes Mountain, Wahluke Slope, Walla Walla Valley, Yakima Valley

Wineries: 50 (excludes sub-AVAs)

EASTERN WASHINGTON

The Cascade Range blocks Pacific storms and rainfall from eastern Washington, where the vast majority of the state's vineyards are planted. Vine growth is carefully controlled by irrigation water taken from the Columbia River.

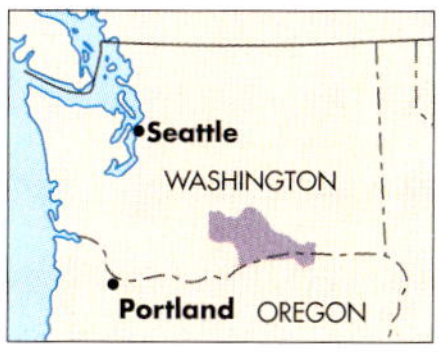

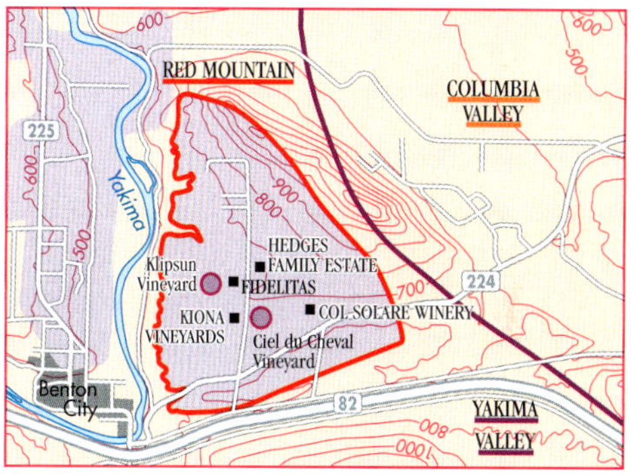

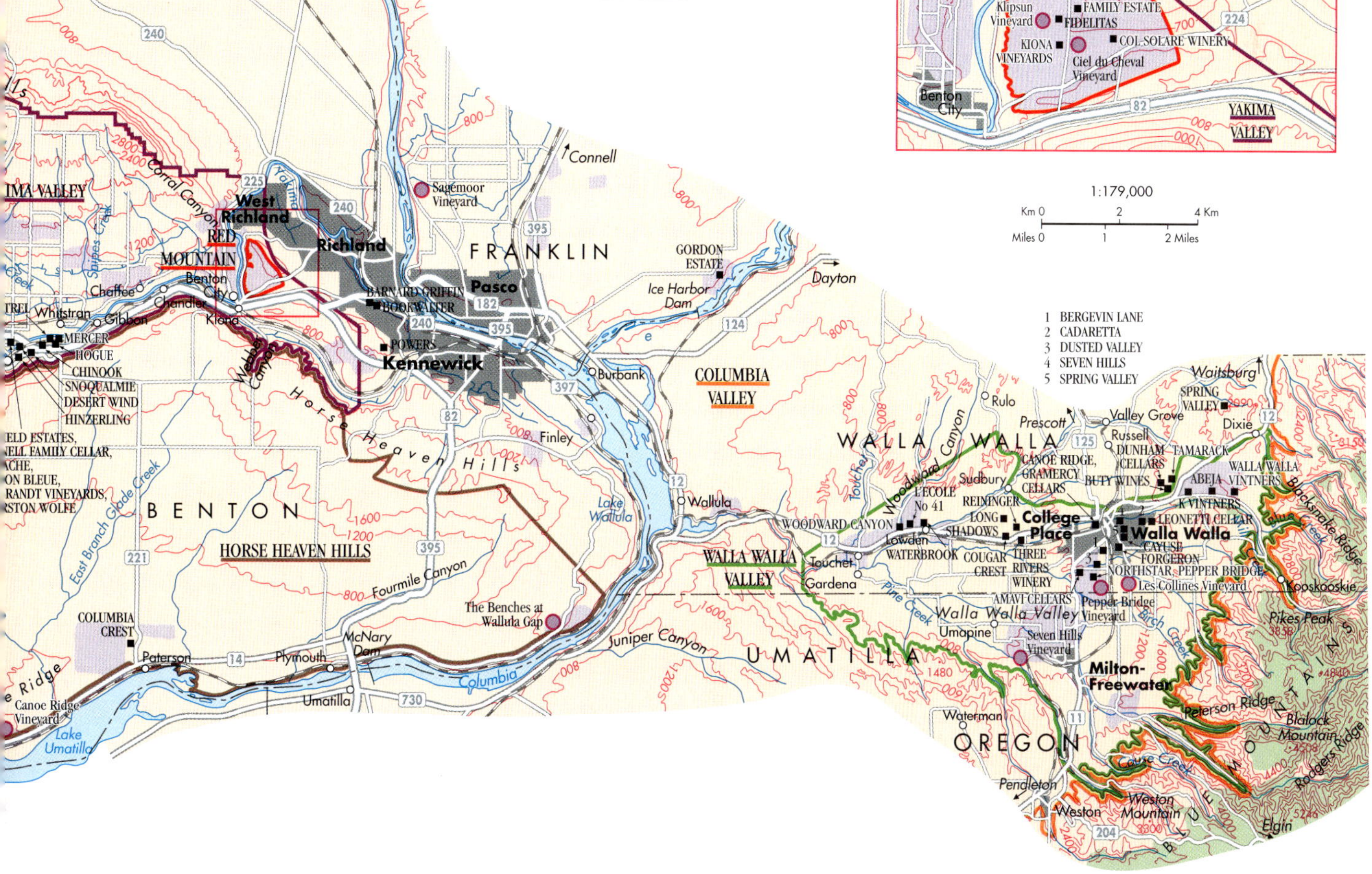

Yakima Valley AVA

The state's first AVA, Yakima Valley was established in 1983. It's home to more than sixty wineries and grows 35 percent of the state's wine grapes, on 12,000-plus vine acres. The AVA begins in the city of Yakima and extends through Benton City to the Red Mountain region, hugging the lower Yakima River before it empties into the Columbia River.

The Yakima Valley AVA contains three sub-AVAs—Red Mountain, Rattlesnake Hills, and Snipes Mountain—and wineries throughout the state source grapes from myriad combinations of these AVAs.

Winemakers here like to talk about Yakima Valley being cool, although that's relative to the surrounding AVAs. Region II on the Davis scale (see box p. 53), the valley has elevations that range from 600 to 1,300 feet. Years ago, most grapes were planted on the valley floor, but today those driving west-east along Interstate 82 won't see many vineyards, as most have been relocated to the slopes where soil is less fertile and leaf canopies can be more easily controlled.

Plantings of white grapes match those of red—rare for eastern Washington. Riesling and Chardonnay enjoy cooler conditions than they would on Red Mountain or Wahluke Slope. Syrah hasn't caught on in Yakima as it has in Walla Walla, even though two pioneering Syrah growers, Dick Boushey of Boushey Vineyards and Mike Sauer of Red Willow Vineyard, continue their success with the grape here. There appears to be an effort on the part of Yakima Valley vintners to produce less flashily potent wines in favor of ones that are crisp and balanced—the sort one would want with dinner, not as a cocktail.

There are exceptions, of course, but Yakima folks seem to take their time—just as their grapes do to ripen in the long, moderate growing season—and not continually chase the next great thing.

Actually, one of the current next great things, Riesling, has been in Yakima Valley all along, demonstrating that everything old will indeed be new again. With advice and assistance from Washington State University's then agriculture whiz, Dr. Walter Clore, Mike Hogue planted 6 acres of Riesling in 1974 on the family farm in Prosser in the heart of Yakima Valley. Awards were immediately won, and in 1982, Mike lured his brother, Gary, from his Seattle cabinetry business to establish the Hogue Cellars winery. Their Merlots took flight too, along with Cab-Merlot blends and Chenin Blanc (Hogue once made three different styles), and over the years, production eventually grew to a fat half a million cases in 2001.

It was retirement time for Mike Hogue, though, so he and his partners sold Hogue to Canadian drinks company Vincor. Now in the hands of Constellation, Hogue makes 600,000 cases of wine a year, in multiple varieties and price points ($10 to $30). Since 2011, all Hogue wines, including reserve reds intended for long-term cellaring, have been sealed with screw caps. After

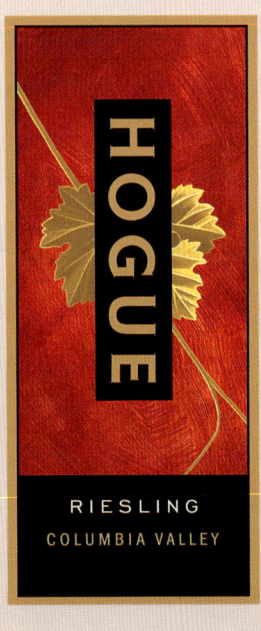
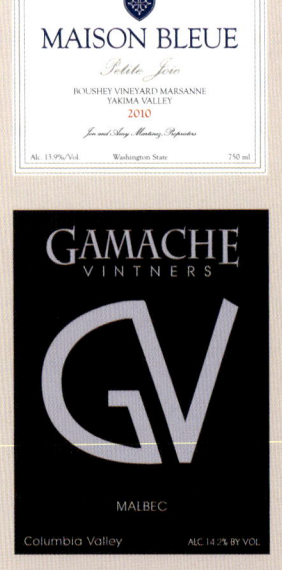

YAKIMA VALLEY AVA SNAPSHOT

Vineyard acreage: 12,000

Most-planted varieties: Chardonnay, Riesling, Merlot, Cabernet Sauvignon

Best varieties: Cabernet Sauvignon, Chardonnay, Merlot, Riesling

Sub-AVAs: Rattlesnake Hills, Red Mountain, Snipes Mountain

Wineries: 50

Trailblazer: Hogue Cellars

Steady hands: Chinook Wines, Desert Wind Winery, Fidelitas Winery, Hedges Family Estate, Hogue Cellars, Hyatt Vineyards, Kestrel Vintners, Kiona Vineyards and Winery, Mercer Estates Winery, Snoqualmie Winery, Thurston Wolfe Winery

Superstar: Col Solare

Ones to watch: Gamache Vintners, Maison Bleue Family Winery

more than a decade of testing natural corks and various versions of twist-off caps, Hogue determined that polyethylene-lined screw caps not only protect wines from possible taint from corks, they also permit a desirable oxygen exchange rate that allow the wines to maintain slow, steady development in the bottle while also preserving freshness.

Dr. Wade Wolfe knows as much about Washington State viticulture as anyone, after years of overseeing vineyards for Chateau Ste. Michelle, Hogue, and a long list of consulting clients, as well as researching and writing the Columbia Valley AVA petition, approved in 1984. He also knows a few things about winemaking. In 1987, Wolfe and his wife, Becky Yeaman, founded Thurston Wolfe Winery in Prosser, producing tiny amounts of Syrah (before it was fashionable), Zinfandel (a rare bird in Washington), and Primitivo (Wolfe is likely the first in the state to plant and vinify this Italian variety). He continues to blaze trails, introducing Malbec, Petite Sirah, Tempranillo, Lemberger, and Orange Muscat to many unfamiliar with these grapes.

Two of Washington's most skilled female winemakers, Kay Simon and Joy Anderson, are also based in Prosser. Simon, a former winemaker at Chateau Ste. Michelle, has owned Chinook Wines with her husband, Clay Mackey, since 1983. He grows the grapes and she turns out Chardonnays, Cabernet Francs, and Cabernet Sauvignons that are full-fruited yet elegant.

The Snoqualmie Winery winemaker since 1991, Anderson pays particular attention to sustainability and employs as little intervention as possible in making her wines. Her Naked Wines line (she also produces Columbia Valley, Winemaker's Select, and Reserve wines) is produced entirely from certified organically grown grapes in Snoqualmie's organic winery.

Gamache Vintners is a textbook tale of the evolution of a modern Washington winery. Roger and Bob Gamache began growing grapes north of Pasco in 1982—before the boom—selling most of their crop to Ste. Michelle Wine Estates' various brands. With an itch to produce their own wine, they recruited longtime client Charlie Hoppes of Fidelitas in 2002 to make their wines at a Benton City winery. The brothers opened a tasting room near the facility, then relocated to the sleek Vintner's Village tasting room in Prosser. The Gamaches don't have their own facility for the production of their estate Cabernet Sauvignons, Syrahs, Malbecs, and other varieties, but it could be only a matter of time.

The city of Prosser, not that long ago just a McDonalds-and-gas pit stop for drivers on Interstate 82, is blossoming into a bona fide wine visitor destination. Vintner's Village—"clustered for your convenience"—is a 32-acre center of twelve tasting rooms; also located here, among others, are Chinook, Hogue, Kestrel Vintners, Mercer Estates, Snoqualmie, and Maison Bleue Family Winery. The last is a relatively new and highly regarded producer of Syrah and

Red Willow Vineyard
Mike Sauer began planting this northwestern Yakima Valley vineyard in 1973, and in 1986 he was one of the first to grow Syrah in Washington.

Grenache wines made from grapes grown in top eastern Washington vineyards, among them Boushey.

Federal funds granted in late 2011 will allow for the construction of the Walter Clore Wine and Culinary Center in Prosser. The $4 million agritourism and education center will be built on 24 acres overlooking the Yakima River, Horse Heaven Hills, and Rattlesnake Mountain. Named for the late Clore, who began viticultural research in Yakima Valley in 1937, the center will include a tasting room/retail shop, agriculture and viticulture exhibits, conference rooms, and instructional vineyards.

Red Mountain AVA

This AVA embedded within Yakima Valley AVA is named for a mountain that is not red and isn't really a mountain—it's rather a sloping, treeless mound with soil the color of cocoa powder. Yet this appellation, located north of the Tri Cities (Kennewick, Pasco, and Richland) in Benton County, is golden for growing Cabernet Sauvignon and Merlot, and, in recent years, Syrah. Winemakers throughout Washington have long prized Red Mountain grapes, and while the AVA lacks calendar-quality scenery, plentiful tasting rooms and high-quality hotels and restaurants, it makes up for this in vinous excellence.

As part of the vast eastern Washington desert, Red Mountain gets a paltry 5 to 7 inches of rain a year, making irrigation an absolute necessity to grow any crop in its gravel and silty loam soils. Red Mountain vineyards face southwest near the Yakima River, but just far enough away from the river that accessing irrigation water requires expensive pipelines and pumps for those fortunate enough to earn water rights. Cabernet Franc, Malbec, Petit Verdot, and Sangiovese also fare well here, although Marchese Piero Antinori won't likely have anything to do with that last variety on Red Mountain.

Italian vino maestro Antinori teamed with Chateau Ste. Michelle in 1992 to create Cabernet Sauvignon–dominated Col Solare ("shining mountain"), initially produced from purchased grapes and now, increasingly, from Col Solare vines planted on Red Mountain in 2007. In Napa Valley, Antinori had a less than stellar experience growing Sangiovese, the grape from which twenty-six generations of his family have produced wine in Tuscany. Atlas Peak in southeastern Napa Valley proved to be Cabernet country, and so it is for Col Solare on Red Mountain.

The first vintage of Col Solare was 1995, blended from purchased Columbia Valley grapes; in 2005, Red Mountain fruit entered the mix. The Col Solare winery opened in 2006, with 28 acres planted in 2007. Estate grapes joined the proprietary wine with the 2010 harvest. Before investing in Red Mountain, Antinori and Chateau Ste. Michelle bought grapes from Kiona, Klipsun, and Ciel du Cheval vineyards.

In 1972, John Williams and Jim Holmes took an 84-acre plot of sagebrush and cheatgrass owned by Williams' father-in-law on Red Mountain and planted its south-facing slopes to Cabernet Sauvignon, Chardonnay, and Riesling. They spent every nickel they had to sink a well 555 feet deep to find water for irrigation. If they hadn't found water, they would have lost their shirts, but they did, and in 1980, their Kiona Vineyards and Winery produced its first wine.

Williams and Holmes later took over the Ciel du Cheval ("horse sky, or heaven") vineyard, which Holmes had helped friends plant on Red Mountain. In 1994, Holmes and Williams split their businesses, with Williams taking Kiona and Holmes becoming sole owner of Ciel du Cheval, where he now farms 120 acres, plus 40 adjacent acres in limited partnerships with Quilceda Creek and DeLille Cellars. His Cabernet Sauvignon, Merlot, Syrah, Mourvèdre, Viognier, Roussanne, and Sangiovese grapes are sold to a long list of clients, including Andrew Will, Barnard Griffin, Cadence, Januik, JM Cellars, Mark Ryan, McCrea Cellars, and Fidelitas.

Holmes's next-door neighbors, Patricia and David Gelles, planted Klipsun Vineyard beginning in 1984, on a slope overlooking the Yakima River. Their Cabernet Sauvignon, Merlot, Nebbiolo, and Syrah grapes develop thick skins that translate to structured tannins and dark-fruit flavors in the

wines made from them. Buyers include Col Solare, Betz Family Winery, L'Ecole No 41, Northstar, and Quilceda Creek.

Tom and Anne-Marie Hedges led the charge in petitioning for the approval of the Red Mountain AVA (their website proclaims Hedges the "Guardians of Red Mountain"). They established Hedges Family Estate there in 1987 and began planting their grapes in 1991. The Hedges wines are produced in multiple tiers. The CMS line (Cabernet Sauvignon, Merlot, and Syrah on the red side, Chardonnay, Marsanne, and Sauvignon Blanc for the white) is widely distributed; its high-end flagship is the Hedges Family Estate Mountain, a red Bordeaux blend.

Snipes Mountain AVA

Snipes Mountain, one of Washington's newest AVAs, approved in 2009, is wedged between Red Mountain and Rattlesnake Hills. It's a viticultural region based largely on elevation, with vineyards rooted at 750 to 1,300 feet above sea level. Of its 4,200 acres, just 900 are planted to grapevines, in rocky soils that drain more quickly than the alluvial soils on the Yakima Valley floor. It got its name from cattle baron Ben Snipes, who settled on the mountain in the 1850s.

Col Solare
Chateau Ste. Michelle and Piero Antinori of Italy are partners in Col Solare, an impressive Red Mountain producer.

Just one winery is located in the AVA, Upland Estates, although numerous wineries purchase fruit from it. W. B. Bridgman first planted grapes on Snipes Mountain in 1917, and after Prohibition, he opened Upland—the first winery in Washington east of the Cascades. Upland continued until 1972 when Alfred Newhouse purchased the property. Over the next thirty-five years, Newhouse and his family expanded their Snipes Mountain holdings and those on neighboring Harrison Hill; today, they control some 800 vineyard acres, with Chardonnay (150 acres) and Cabernet Sauvignon (142) the most-planted.

Rattlesnake Hills AVA

Established in 2006, the Rattlesnake Hills AVA, on the southern slopes of the Rattlesnake Hills southeast of the city of Yakima and north of the Yakima River, boasts 1,600 vineyard acres and twenty wineries, most of them small operations.

Hyatt Vineyards, founded in 1983 by Leland and Lynda Hyatt, is one of the oldest in Yakima Valley. They were among the first to adopt Merlot in a big way in the valley; Roza Ridge is their high-end label, Hyatt the value brand. In 2011, Precept Wine of Seattle, the second-largest wine company in Washington, after Ste. Michelle Wine Estates, purchased Sagelands Vineyard in the Rattlesnake Hills AVA from multinational Diageo. Sagelands, the former Staton Hills Winery and, under Diageo, a maker of inexpensive wines, is one to watch now that it's under new ownership.

Naches Heights AVA

Washington's newest AVA, Naches Heights, established in 2011, is located just outside the Yakima Valley appellation, near the city of Yakima. Only 37 acres of vineyards are planted in the 13,000-acre AVA. Unlike most Washington growing areas, Naches Heights, ranging from 1,000 to 2,000 feet in elevation, was not affected by the ancient Missoula floods. Thus, it has lighter, wind-blown loess soils instead of the typical alluvial deposits and, theoretically, will produce distinctive wines. There are no wineries in Naches Heights, although there is potential for substantial vineyard development.

Horse Heaven Hills AVA

South of Yakima Valley, this large, windy AVA on the southern slopes of the Horse Heaven Hills tumbles down to the banks of the Columbia River, an elevation span of 200 to 1,800 feet. It gets plenty of heat during the growing season, and the wind can knock young vines over if windbreaks are not installed. Yet the brisk gusts also greatly reduce frost damage, and they reduce vine vigor so that small berries and small clusters are formed, which produce concentrated wines. The sandy, well-drained soils support a wide range of grapes, including Chardonnay, Riesling, Cabernet Sauvignon, Merlot, Malbec, and Syrah.

Cowboy James Kinney named this area in 1857 after seeing that his herd of horses enjoyed the native grasses on the hillside. It was heaven for the horses. The first vines were cultivated here in 1972, but a planting burst in the 1990s, largely on the tops of three ridges overlooking the river, Canoe Ridge, Alder Ridge, and Zephyr Ridge, helped boost the current planted acreage to 9,450.

Vineyards (twenty-eight) greatly outnumber wineries (six), and many of the plantings are large, but quality can be extremely high. That first 1972 vineyard was the Mercer Ranch, which Paul Champoux leased after serving as its vineyard manager. In 1996, he and his wife, Judy, brought in Quilceda Creek, Andrew Will, Powers Winery, and Woodward Canyon as partners, enabling them to purchase the 175-acre property and rename it Champoux Vineyard. In addition to the partners' single-vineyard bottlings, fruit is sold to several other producers who also designate Champoux on their labels, among them Buty, Fidelitas, Januik, and Three Rivers.

Sineann Winery is an unusual purchaser of Champoux grapes. Owner Peter Rosback's winery is in Oregon's Willamette Valley, where, naturally, Pinot Noir is his mainstay. But Rosback can't resist a great vineyard, so he buys and bottles Merlot and Cabernet Sauvignon from Champoux, as well as grapes from other Columbia Valley locations, and Napa Valley and New Zealand—whatever interests him. Wine wonks salivate over his Pines Vineyard Old Vines Zinfandel, which comes from vines on the Oregon side of the Columbia Gorge, south of The Dalles, believed to have been planted around 1880 by an immigrant Italian stonemason. The Pines Vineyard fell into disuse until viticulturalist Lonnie Wright began reviving the vines in the early 1980s.

Alex and Paul Golitzin of Quilceda Creek are known to be fastidious winemakers, and they're an ideal match for the equally detail-obsessed Paul Champoux. Together they produced four

Wallula Vineyard
This Horse Heaven Hills vineyard, supplier of grapes to several producers, has more than three miles of Columbia River waterfront. On hot days, the water acts as an air conditioner for the vines and provides essential irrigation.

Quilceda Creek Cabernet Sauvignons between 2002 and 2008 that scored the maximum 100 points from the influential Robert Parker's *Wine Advocate*.

Some 30 percent of the wine grapes grown in Washington are from Horse Heaven Hills, largely on the 2,300 acres owned by Columbia Crest Winery, whose parent company is Ste. Michelle Wine Estates. Chateau Ste. Michelle produces Chardonnay, Merlot, Cabernet Sauvignon, and Syrah from its nearby Canoe Ridge estate and also sources from the Columbia Crest vineyard, near Paterson.

Columbia Crest is the state's largest winery, 1.7 million cases per year across four brands—Columbia Crest Reserve, Columbia Crest Grand Estates, Two Vines, and H3—priced between $10 and $45.

Precept Wine of Seattle acquired the 153-acre Canoe Ridge Vineyard in Horse Heaven Hills from Diageo in 2011. Combined with its 800 acres at nearby Alder Ridge Vineyard, Precept has almost 1,000 acres of grapes in the region, which go into the company's numerous wines, the best known being Alder Ridge, Apex, Canoe Ridge Vineyard, and House Wine.

Wahluke Slope AVA

You can count on one hand the number of wineries located in this isolated sub-AVA of the Columbia Valley, bounded by the Columbia River on the south and west, the Saddle Mountains on the north, and the Hanford Reach National Monument on the east. But there are more than twenty vineyards and 6,000 vine acres within the appellation's total 81,000 acres, and Wahluke Slope is an important supplier of Chardonnay, Cabernet Sauvignon, Merlot, and Syrah grapes to wineries throughout the state.

If it weren't for wine grapes and irrigation water, this area of Grant County would be covered in scrub brush—the only vegetation than can naturally survive the hot, dry desert conditions. With irrigation, Wahluke Slope has come to life; the growing-season warmth and abundance of water create the right conditions for growing high-quality grapes. It may be isolated, but Wahluke Slope accounts for approximately one-fifth of Washington grape production.

Most plantings are near the town of Mattawa on the western end of the slope, at elevations of 425 to 1,400 feet. Being a Region III on the UC Davis heat summation scale, Cabernet Sauvignon and Syrah adore it here; winters are moderate and freezes are less common than in more southerly parts of the Columbia Valley.

Butch and Jerry Milbrandt farm ten different vineyards in the Wahluke Slope AVA, as well as several in the Ancient Lakes area. They have worked particularly hard in recent years to match the best clones to each microclimate in their vineyards, and the value of their grapes to wineries has soared as a result. Milbrandt Vineyards launched its own brand in 2007, using its own grapes. The wines are attractively priced, although the star is, not surprisingly, its most expensive: the $50 Sentinel Northridge Red Wine from Wahluke Slope, a blend of Cabernet Sauvignon, Merlot, Malbec, and Petit Verdot.

StoneTree Vineyard on the south slope of Saddle Mountain sells grapes to an all-star winery cast. Named for the petrified tree fossils found in the hills, StoneTree's 257 acres of vineyards were developed starting in 2000, after Tedd Wildman and Mark Wheeler won a twenty-five-year lease from the Washington State Department of Natural Resources. They grow the usual Wahluke suspects—Cabernet Sauvignon, Merlot, and Syrah—and some unusual varieties for this AVA, including Cinsault, Mourvedre, Tempranillo, and Zinfandel.

Wahluke Slope
Pronounced WAH-luke, the AVA is on a large alluvial fan, at elevations of 425 to 1,400 feet. It's one of Washington's warmest AVAs.

Walla Walla Valley AVA

Walla Walla is the Native American term for "place of many waters." Today it means place of many vineyards, wineries, and downtown tasting rooms.

In the early 1990s, there were just six wineries in what was a sleepy farming and college town surrounded by golden wheat fields, onion and asparagus rows, barns, pastures, grain elevators, and the breathtaking Blue Mountains to the east. Today Walla Walla boasts more than one hundred wineries, 1,900 acres of ultra-premium wine grapes, restaurants, wine bars, boutiques, and hordes of visitors during spring, summer, and early fall.

Walla Walla's big wine bang has come via a combination of great ground for wine grapes, early vineyard developers who formed partnerships to do things right the first time, an infusion of talent from California and France, and the motivation of many to turn this remote, rugged, former fur-trapping trading post into a world-class wine region with its own identity.

The Walla Walla AVA, in southeast Washington and northeast Oregon, is one of the few in the country to straddle two states. Approximately 40 percent of the vines in the Walla Walla Valley AVA are located on the Oregon side, but wineries based in Washington need only designate "Walla Walla Valley" on their front labels.

Red wine is the thing in Walla Walla: Bordeaux varieties Cabernet Sauvignon, Merlot, Cabernet Franc, and Malbec; Rhône grapes Syrah, Grenache, and Mourvèdre; and Tempranillo from Spain. One can find Chardonnays and Viogniers from Walla Walla, but plantable land is really too expensive and too scarce for anything but profitable red grapes.

Among the first bonded wineries in the Walla Walla AVA, granted in 1984, were Leonetti Cellar, L'Ecole No 41, Woodward Canyon Winery, Waterbrook, Seven Hills Winery, Walla Walla Vintners, and Dunham Cellars. They still run strong, but now they have much more company—and competition.

When Gary Figgins, a machinist for Walla Walla's Continental Can Company, planted vines in the area in 1974, he was viewed as a quack. It's too cold here, his neighbors said, the weather too inconsistent for regularly ripening grapes. The Columbia Valley's more westerly, and warmer, regions are safer bets, they told him. Figgins persevered, eventually proving that Walla Walla grapes, when planted in the right spots, not only survive, but thrive; his Merlots became instant cult classics. Figgins' home-winemaking buddy, Rick Small of Woodward Canyon, took the plunge in 1981 and has achieved similar success, particularly with his Old Vines and Artist Series Cabernet Sauvignons.

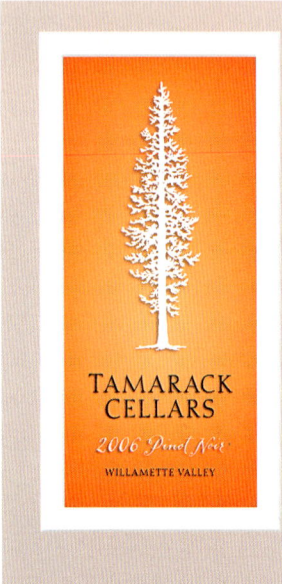

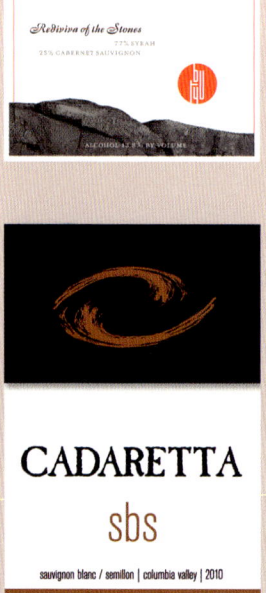

WALLA WALLA VALLEY AVA SNAPSHOT

Vineyard acreage: 1,900 acres (includes Oregon portion)

Most-planted varieties: Cabernet Sauvignon, Merlot, Syrah

Best varieties: Cabernet Sauvignon, Merlot, Syrah

Wineries: 100

Trailblazers: L'Ecole No 41, Leonetti Cellar, Seven Hills Winery, Walla Walla Vintners, Woodward Canyon Winery

Steady hands: Abeja, Amavi Cellars, Buty Winery, Cougar Hills Winery, Dunham Cellars, L'Ecole No 41, Northstar, Pepper Bridge Winery, Reininger Vineyards, Seven Hills Winery, Spring Valley Vineyard, Tamarack Cellars, Three Rivers Winery, Walla Walla Vintners, Woodward Canyon Winery

Superstars: Cayuse Vineyards, K Vintners, Leonetti Cellar

Ones to watch: Cadaretta Wines, Doubleback, Dusted Valley Vintners, Gramercy Cellars, Pursued by Bear

FRENCH INVASION

Washington is a haven for French winemakers who crave the freedom to make whatever wines they wish, from whichever grapes they choose, without strict French government regulation. Winery owners have welcomed these usually university-trained, whip-smart French enologists for their energy, enthusiasm, and new ideas—which are often from the Old World, but apply positively to fruit-driven Washington wines.

Marie-Eve Gilla, winemaker at Forgeron Cellars in Walla Walla, had little chance of landing anything higher than a laboratory job when she graduated from the University of Dijon, so she headed to the United States in 1991. She worked at Argyle Winery in Oregon, then Covey Run, Hogue Cellars, and Gordon Brothers in Washington, before joining Forgeron, where she calls all the winemaking shots. Her French husband, Gilles Nicault—whom she met in Washington—is the on-site winemaker for Allen Shoup's Long Shadows Vintners (see box p. 163).

Renowned French consultant Michel Rolland and University of Bordeaux graduate Philippe Melka, one of Napa Valley's busiest consultants and proprietor of Metisse wines, have brands under the Long Shadows umbrella. Christophe Baron at Cayuse Vineyards, Serge Laville at Spring Valley Vineyard, and Virginie Bourgue, formerly of Bergevin Lane and Cadaretta and now a consultant, are all French-born winemakers with Washington operations.

Then there is Nicolas Quillé, who was born in Lyon, earned master's degrees at Burgundy's University of Dijon and Champagne's University of Reims, and came to the United States in 1997, eventually working for Randall Grahm at Bonny Doon Vineyard. When Grahm separated his Pacific Rim Riesling brand from his flagship Bonny Doon Vineyard in Santa Cruz, California, with the intention to sell it, Quillé found partners in Washington to take it over and relocated the business to West Richland, near Red Mountain, in 2007.

The Den Hoed family, major grape suppliers to Pacific Rim, then invested in a new winery and committed more Riesling grapes to the brand. For it, Quillé makes approximately 200,000 cases a year of Riesling in myriad styles: dry, off-dry, sweet, sparkling, organic, biodynamic, and vineyard-designated. In 2011, Pacific Rim was purchased by the Mariani family, owner of Banfi Vintners in New York and the Castello Banfi estate in Tuscany, with Quillé staying on, and Bill and Andy Den Hoed continuing to supply grapes.

Marie-Eve Gilla
The Forgeron Cellars winemaker and her husband, Gilles Nicault of Long Shadows Vintners, are among several French-born winemakers who have made their home in Washington.

Figgins, Small, and other early Walla Walla vintners, including Marty and Megan Clubb of L'Ecole No 41 and Myles Anderson and Gordon Venerri of Walla Walla Vintners, hedged their bets by purchasing fruit from other areas in the Columbia Valley. They looked to Klipsun and Ciel du Cheval on Red Mountain, Champoux Vineyard in the Horse Heaven Hills, and Sagemoor in the Columbia Valley AVA, among others, to fill grape supply gaps while they nurtured their own vines.

Today Figgins, working with his son, Chris, has converted Leonetti Cellar into an all–Walla Walla–grown brand; Chris is in charge of the separate and relatively new Figgins Estate wine, a Bordeaux-style red.

Ownership of Walla Walla Valley vineyards can be rather incestuous, with various partnerships formed across multiple vineyards. Seven Hills Vineyard, first planted in 1980 by the McClellan and Hendricks families and devoted to red Bordeaux varieties, is a prime example.

Seven Hills, located in Milton-Freewater, was sold in 1994, with Scott Hendricks and Casey McClellan keeping some land for themselves (McClellan retained the Seven Hills Winery name and continues to purchase grapes from his former vineyard). The buyers, Norm McKibben, Bob Rupar, Leonetti's Gary Figgins, and L'Ecole's Clubbs, expanded the vineyard over time to more than 200 acres, largely Cabernet Sauvignon, Merlot, and Syrah. They keep certain sections for themselves and sell fruit from the remaining blocks to two dozen other producers. They own, without question, one of the great vineyards in America.

In 1991, McKibben, who was a partner in Hogue Cellars at the time it was sold to Vincor, planted Pepper Bridge Vineyard on the Washington side of the Walla Walla Valley and founded Pepper Bridge Winery. He and winemaker Jean-Francois Pellet, hired away from Heitz Cellars in Napa Valley, draw grapes from both Pepper Bridge and Seven Hills vineyards for Pepper Bridge wines... yet the story doesn't end here.

McKibben's family, Pellet, and the Goff family planted Les Collines Vineyard in the Blue Mountains foothills between 2001 and 2011 and formed Amavi Cellars. The vineyard and brand are best known for Syrah. Then McKibben and Company established SeVein, an alliance of vineyard owners created to facilitate the development and maintenance of their properties. Clubb, Rupar, Chris and Gary Figgins, and McKibben are the partners, and Seven Hills Vineyard is the SeVein cornerstone, as each partner's winery—Pepper Bridge, Leonetti Cellar, and L'Ecole No 41—harvests grapes from the vineyard. Undeveloped plots are being sold by SeVein to other producers and developed for them; when fully planted, SeVein will be a contiguous, 2,000-plus-acre block.

One SeVein client is Cadaretta Wines, owned by Rick Middleton, whose family has been in the Washington state timber industry since 1898. Cadaretta was launched in 2008, with promising Syrah and Sauvignon Blanc-Semillon wines made from purchased grapes; in that same year, Middleton bought a SeVein parcel, and development of his Southwind Vineyard began, with eleven varieties and twenty-two clones. Cadaretta expects to harvest its first crop from Southwind in 2012.

There are two major types of soils in Walla Walla Valley vineyards: loess (pronounced "luhs"), a wind-blown silt of very fine glacial deposits usually sitting atop rich sedimentary soils, and riverbed cobblestones. Christophe Baron, who grew up in his family's Baron Albert Champagne house, is crazy for the rocks.

As a young man, Baron traveled the world and spent some time making wine in Oregon. He thought he might want to be a Pinot Noir maker, but during a visit to Walla Walla, he spied a field of softball-sized cobblestones that reminded him of the soils of the southern Rhône Valley. In 1996, he purchased the property, in Milton-Freewater, and while the locals laughed at his plans to grow grapes on ground comprised almost entirely of stones, he silenced his critics with his first release of Cayuse Vineyards wines, most of them Syrahs from an area now known as "The Rocks." To his followers, Baron's wines have been nothing short of *incroyable*.

His Syrahs and, more recently, Grenaches, have a wild, gamy character often found in Rhône Valley reds, but is barely discernible in most Washington Rhône-style wines. Baron now owns eight vineyards in Walla Walla, totaling more than 60 acres. All are on cobblestoned ancient river beds, farmed biodynamically, and require special tractors and/or horses to navigate the high-density plantings and narrow rows littered with cobbles.

With vineyard names such as Coccinelle ("ladybug"), En Cerise ("cherry"), and Horsepower, and wines named Bionic Frog, Flying Pig, Impulsivo, Widowmaker, and God Only Knows, Cayuse has both wine quality and storytelling going for it. The wines are sold only through its mailing list, for which there is a wait. That Baron impishly insists that he is a *vigneron* and not a winemaker, and that he owns a *domaine,* and not vineyards, adds to the interest that consumers have in his wines. He is French, and endearingly so.

L'Ecole No 41
Jean and Baker Ferguson transformed this early twentieth-century schoolhouse in Frenchtown, west of Walla Walla, into L'Ecole No 41 Winery in 1983. It's a top-tier producer.

Cayuse Vineyards
Christophe Baron employs Old World methods in his Walla Walla Valley vineyards, including using a horse to plow vineyard rows that are too narrow for tractors.

Charles Smith has Baron to thank for helping him crack the Walla Walla wine business. Smith, a Northern Californian who spent ten years in Scandinavia managing rock bands before moving to western Washington to run a wine shop, happened upon Baron on a visit to Walla Walla. He convinced Smith to move to Walla Walla to make wine—Syrah, specifically—and in 2001, Smith produced his first 330 cases of K Syrah Walla Walla Valley, under the K Vintners banner.

Why K? For no other reason than Smith liked the way the black block letter K looked on a white wine label—bold, sturdy, and a bit like the trunk and arms of a grapevine. A giant K statue, three feet taller than Smith, is anchored in front of his small Walla Walla vineyard and winery, on the outskirts of town. Most of his grapes are purchased, and wines are made under three labels: K Vintners, Charles Smith Wines, and the Magnificent Wine Company, the latter of which he makes for Precept Wine. With names such as Velvet Devil Merlot, Kung Fu Girl Riesling, Boom Boom, and King Coal Syrah, there is no mistaking a Charles Smith wine on the shelf.

Untrained in winemaking but with an innate feel for the craft and an experienced palate, Smith has found an enraptured audience for his wines, which are rich and voluptuous, but surprisingly balanced. He's sussed out quality vineyards beyond the usual suspects, commissioned Danish artist Rikke Korff to design his in-your-face, black-on-white labels, and calls upon his bigger-than-life personality—and head of hair—to help drive wine sales.

Among the Walla Walla wineries going about their business more quietly, letting their wines speak for them, is Abeja. John Abbott, who worked for Pine Ridge Vineyards and Acacia Vineyards in Napa Valley, and Canoe Ridge in Walla Walla, before cofounding Abeja in 2000 with Ken and Ginger Harrington, produces keenly balanced Cabernet Sauvignons and Chardonnays that showcase the elegant side of Walla Walla winemaking.

Northstar is a Merlot-only maker in the Ste. Michelle Wine Estates constellation, bottling a commendable Columbia Valley blend and a focused, cellarworthy Walla Walla Valley Merlot. In 2005, the company also leased the vineyards and winery of Spring Valley Vineyard from Dean and Shari Corkrum Derby (the Corkrums have grown wheat in the Palouse region, north of Walla Walla, for more than a century). Serge Laville is winemaker, and his best effort, among many, is the Merlot-based Uriah blend.

Buty ("beauty") Winery and its sister brand, the Beast, are the enological offspring of Caleb Foster and Nina Buty Foster. Caleb worked for eight years as assistant winemaker at Woodward Canyon, and six more years for other wineries until he and his wife founded Buty in 2000. Their wines—particularly the Columbia Valley Semillon-Sauvignon Blanc-Muscadelle, the Syrah-dominant Rediviva of the Stones from Walla Walla Valley, and the Champoux Vineyard Horse Heaven Hills red—are superb.

Dusted Valley Vintners tops the long list of emerging Walla Walla Valley stars. Wisconsin cheeseheads Chad Johnson and Corey Braunel arrived in the region in 2003 with a winemaking dream, lots of ambition, supportive wives, and very little else. Yet with pluck and advice from generous Walla Wallans, they created a brand that not only has large (for Walla Walla) production volumes of 30,000 cases per year and distribution in thirty states, but also wide critical acclaim. The Dusted Valley Cabernet Sauvignons and Syrahs are as good as any from the region, and the Boomtown second label offers fine value.

There is some celebrity power in Walla Walla, though it's mostly kept under wraps. Actor Kyle MacLachlan (*Desperate Housewives, Sex and the City, Twin Peaks*), a Yakima native, collaborates with Dunham Cellars' Eric Dunham on the Cabernet Sauvignon brand Pursued by Bear. Retired NFL quarterback Drew Bledsoe, who attended Washington State University, owns the 40-acre McQueen Vineyard in Walla Walla and makes the Doubleback Cabernet Sauvignon with Chris Figgins. Master Sommelier Greg Harrington managed wine programs for star chefs Emeril Lagasse and Wolfgang Puck before moving to Walla Walla to make wine. He and his wife, Pam, own Gramercy Cellars, where they produce Cabernet Sauvignon, Syrah, Tempranillo, and various blends.

In 2004, Walla Walla growers established VINEA: The Winegrowers' Sustainable Trust, a program that advocates environmentally friendly and socially responsible viticultural practices in the region. VINEA endorses a number of organic and biodynamic concepts, with an emphasis on low-input growing methods that nurture soil health and encourage biodiversity. VINEA has partnered with LIVE in Oregon (Low Input Viticulture and Enology) to provide third-party sustainable certification through the European organization IOBC (International Organization for Biological Control).

Myles Anderson has contributed much more than fine wines produced in Walla Walla Valley. While sharing winemaking duties with Gordon Venerri at Walla Walla Vintners, he founded Walla Walla Community College's enology and viticulture program in 2000. A certified teacher and educational psychologist, Anderson has helped more than 1,600 students complete winemaking and grapegrowing coursework at the college, where he worked for thirty-one years and oversaw College Cellars, a nonprofit teaching winery, before his retirement.

Lake Chelan AVA

Fifty-mile-long Lake Chelan, the largest glacial lake in the Cascade Range, is in north-central Washington, at the base of the Cascades. At elevations of up to 2,000 feet, the AVA has a cooler climate than most of the Columbia Valley and is suited to early-ripening grapes such as Riesling, Gewürztraminer, Pinot Gris, and Pinot Noir, and cool-climate representations of Syrah and Merlot. Better known for growing cherries and apples, and for the dramatic lakeside scenery that draws water sports enthusiasts from throughout the state, Lake Chelan—which became an AVA in 2009—didn't get its first winery until 2000. The other fifteen that now exist were established in the mid-2000s.

The first modern vineyards were planted in Lake Chelan Valley in 1998, and the first bonded winery, Lake Chelan Winery, was built by the Kludt family in 2000. Those who have followed suit do a booming business in their tasting rooms, thanks to the lake's lure for tourists.

The soils of the 24,040-acre AVA (just 260 are planted to vines) are coarse, sandy glacial sediment with large amounts of quartz and mica. A significant "lake effect" moderates warm temperatures in summer and cold weather in winter, creating even ripening conditions and reducing frost risk.

Tsillan Cellars Winery & Vineyards and Vin du Lac are already accomplished producers in this nascent wine region—Tsillan for Riesling and Italian varieties, Vin du Lac for Cabernet Sauvignon and Cabernet Franc. The proprietors of Nefarious Vineyards have a sense of humor: "We are just a chick, a couple of guys, and a dog striving to blow your mind." Winemakers Dean and Heather Neff, with two young sons, George and Cooper, and a Golden Labrador, Lucy, have vineyards named Rocky Mother (it was difficult to plant in the stony soils) and Defiance, and they produce an exciting Stone's Throw Vineyard Riesling.

According to owners Judy and Don Phelps, Hard Road to Hoe Vineyards' name was inspired not only by the boulders in the vineyard, but also by the story of an entrepreneur who rowed 1930s copper miners across the lake to the Edgemont Lodge for nightly visits with the ladies who worked there. While developing their vineyard, the Phelps have purchased grapes from elsewhere for their wines, the most interesting of which is Iron Bed Red from the Wahluke Slope AVA, a blend of Cabernet Sauvignon, Cabernet Franc, Syrah, and Zinfandel. It seems the miners' wives burned down the Edgemont brothel, with only the iron bed frames surviving the flames.

Bingen Syncline
Syncline Wine Cellars got its name from the Bingen Syncline, a series of 300-foot-high basaltic cliffs rising from the Columbia River in the Columbia Gorge AVA.

Columbia Gorge AVA

The Columbia River splits the Columbia Gorge AVA in two along an AVA-specified 15-mile stretch, with Oregon on its south banks and Washington on the north. The walls of the canyon through which the river churns its way from the Cascade Mountains through Portland, Oregon, and on to the Pacific Ocean, are as high as 4,000 feet, with conifers, oaks, and maples dotting southern hillsides. Views of the roaring river, waterfalls, kite surfers, and Mount Hood are plentiful, and while the Oregon side of the gorge has more cities and amenities, the more barren Washington side is elevated and affords better vistas of the river and its activities.

It's for this reason that Craig and Vicki Leuthold began Maryhill Winery in 2000, constructing their winery on a bluff overlooking the river on the Washington side. Maryhill is now an 80,000-case-per-year producer, making it one of the largest family-owned wineries in the state. The Leutholds make twenty varieties, including the relatively obscure—for Washington—Zinfandel. Most wines are made from purchased Columbia Valley grapes.

James and Poppie Mantone of Syncline Wine Cellars produce wonderfully balanced Rhône-style wines, including Heart of the Hill Mourvèdre from Red Mountain and an aromatic Viognier from Horse Heaven Hills. The Mantones purchase these grapes to supplement those grown on their Steep Creek Ranch, situated on a southern slope on the eastern edge of the Columbia Gorge. West of the vineyard is a series of 300-foot-high cliffs rising from the river, known to geologists as the Bingen Syncline (see above).

PUGET SOUND AVA AND SEATTLE

There are two sides to the Puget Sound coin. The "heads" side is the few who grow their grapes and vinify their wines within the AVA anchored by Seattle—obscure varieties that can withstand rain (between 30 and 60 inches a year) and ripen with minimal sunshine, including Madeleine Angevine, Müller-Thurgau, and Siegerrebe. Land "tails," and you get a multitude of producers who use *Vitis vinifera* grapes (Chardonnay, Riesling, Cabernet Sauvignon, Merlot, Syrah, etc.) from eastern Washington to make their wines in Puget Sound and/or sell them in tasting rooms in Seattle and Woodinville. Large-volume winemakers Chateau Ste. Michelle and Columbia Winery have long been based in Woodinville, joined in recent years by 'boutique' producers and Columbia Valley wineries that have opened tasting rooms in Woodinville and other areas close to Seattle.

It makes sense: the grapes are in eastern Washington, but the population mass, restaurants, wine shops, and tourists are in the west. The success of Chateau Ste. Michelle and Columbia Winery in drawing visitors to their Woodinville tasting rooms paved the way for others to base their operations near Seattle. Betz Family Winery, founded in 1997 by Bob Betz and his wife Cathy, is in the top five on the list of any wine critic's favorite Washington producers. Bob, who worked his way up to vice president of winemaking research in a twenty-eight-year career with Chateau Ste. Michelle, remained in Woodinville after retiring from the company and sources Columbia Valley grapes for his vividly aromatic and soulful Cabernet Sauvignon (Pere de Famille), Merlot (Clos de Betz), Syrah (La Serenne and La Côte Rousse), and Grenache (Besoleil). In mid-2011, the Betzes stunned the industry by announcing they had sold the winery and brand to South African natives Steve and Bridgit Griessel. Betz agreed to remain the winemaker for five years.

Father and son Alex and Paul Golitzin of Quilceda Creek Vintners call Snohomish, 20 miles north of Woodinville, home. Quilceda Creek produces only one variety, Cabernet Sauvignon, and it's always a stunner. Quilceda Creek and a select few other wineries became partners in Champoux Vineyard in the Horse Heaven Hills in 1997, securing access to the grapes. In 2006, the Golitzins acquired a five-acre vineyard next to Champoux and called it Palengat, Jeanette Golitzin's maiden name. From it they produce the Palengat Red Wine, typically Cabernet Sauvignon–dominant with small amounts of Cabernet Franc and Merlot.

Novelty Hill–Januik
This Woodinville winery is indeed a novelty, with a sleek, minimalist design that is unusual for Washington wine country. Here Mike Januik makes the wines for both the Novelty Hill and Januik brands.

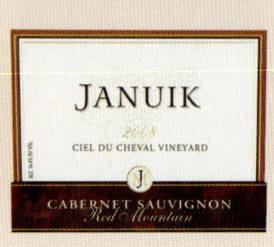

PUGET SOUND AVA SNAPSHOT
Vineyard acreage: **100**
Most-planted varieties: **Madeleine Angevine, Müller-Thurgau, Siegerrebe**
Wineries: **45**
Trailblazers: **Columbia Winery, Chateau Ste. Michelle**
Steady hands: **Brian Carter Cellars, Chatter Creek, Columbia Winery, JM Cellars, Lopez Island Vineyards, Mark Ryan Winery, Novelty Hill, Olympic Cellars, Soos Creek Wine Cellars, Stevens, Wilridge Winery**
Superstars: **Andrew Will Winery, Betz Family Winery, Cadence, Chateau Ste. Michelle, DeLille Cellars/Doyenne, Januik Winery, McCrea Cellars, Quilceda Creek Vintners**

The Golitzins—Alex's uncle was the late, legendary enologist André Tchelistcheff—partnered with Jim Holmes of Ciel du Cheval in the Red Mountain AVA to develop the Galitzine Vineyard, 17 acres planted to Cabernet Sauvignon. The family produces a vineyard-designated wine from Galitzine.

Other top producers based in western Washington include Brian Carter Cellars, Cadence Winery, Chatter Creek, DeLille Cellars, Januik Winery, and Novelty Hill. In addition, forty small producers are located at Woodinville Warehouse Wineries, all within easy distance of each other and providing visitors a great opportunity for tasting dozens of wines.

Chateau Ste. Michelle
The immaculately groomed grounds of Chateau Ste. Michelle and its broad range of well-made—and often exciting—wines draw visitors to Woodinville, north of Seattle.

In Rainier, McCrea Cellars—the first Washington winery to concentrate on Syrah and other Rhône varieties, beginning in 1989 and thus opening the door for other Washington Rhône Rangers—began experimenting with the Spanish grape Tempranillo in 2006. Pleased with his first two barrels, winemaker Doug McCrea started a separate brand, Salida (Spanish for "to exit," as in to end a harvest) Wines, and he produces three Tempranillo-based wines under that label, from grapes grown in the warmer reaches of Yakima Valley.

The Puget Sound AVA starts near Bellingham and extends south past Olympia, including the islands of the sound and the Olympic Peninsula. The Puget Sound Wine Growers Association surmises that grapevines were first planted in the area in 1825. The first documented vineyard was on Stretch Island, in the 1870s. But then Prohibition wiped out any vineyards that existed, and it was only in 1977 that Gerard Bentryn established a

Lopez Island Vineyards
Located in Puget Sound, Lopez Island Vineyards farms its grapes organically. Its rustic winery building was constructed of wood and stones sourced from the island, to minimize environmental impact.

DAVID LAKE

David Lake was the winemaker at Columbia Winery in Woodinville from 1979 until his retirement in 2006, yet his most important contributions to Washington winemaking were his nose for great vineyards and his willingness to take well-informed risks.

At the time of his death in 2009, Lake was widely considered the dean of Washington winemakers. In 1981, he released the state's first vineyard-designated wines, three Cabernet Sauvignons from the Otis, Red Willow, and Sagemoor vineyards. In 1986, he talked grower Mike Sauer into planting Syrah at Red Willow in Yakima Valley, and two years later, Lake bottled Washington's first Syrah. He followed that with the initial bottlings of Cabernet Franc and Pinot Gris.

His path to Columbia Winery, founded in 1962 as Associated Vintners and now owned by E. & J. Gallo, was most unusual. The British-born Lake worked in the English wine trade and earned the Master of Wine title in 1975. He then crossed the pond and enrolled at UC Davis to learn the viticulture and winemaking side of the business. After a stint in Oregon's Willamette Valley, Lake joined Columbia Winery in 1979 and within one year had become its chief winemaker.

Changes in ownership have left Columbia Winery's image less glossy than it was in Lake's heyday, although the company continues his devotion to single-vineyard wines, with Otis Vineyard and Red Willow Vineyard Syrahs, Cabernet Sauvignons, and Merlots remaining the winery's finest.

commercial vineyard on Bainbridge Island, in what would become the Puget Sound AVA. The damp maritime climate encourages the development of mildew and bunch rot in grapes, and the growing season lacks sufficient heat to consistently ripen all but the hardiest of cold-climate European varieties, such as Madeleine Angevine, Müller-Thurgau, and Siegerrebe.

Lopez Island Vineyards, Whidbey Island Winery and San Juan Vineyards also produce those wines, and they import grapes from eastern Washington for use in their Chardonnays, Merlots, Syrahs, and Cabernet Sauvignons. Lopez Island's estate vineyard has been farmed organically since 1986, with oils, soaps, and sulfur used to combat mold and mildew, instead of non-organic chemical fungicides.

Elsewhere in Washington

Ancient Lakes is likely to be the thirteenth AVA in Washington, if the petition submitted to the TTB in 2011 is approved. The region is northeast of Wahluke Slope, near the town of Quincy and Moses Lake. Although there are a dozen wineries here and 1,000 acres of vines, mostly Riesling, Chardonnay, and Pinot Gris, the area, for now, is known for the Gorge Amphitheatre, which presents major musical acts with the Columbia River as a backdrop.

Butch and Jerry Milbrandt of Milbrandt Vineyards, also with important holdings on Wahluke Slope, are doing their best to make the region just as noteworthy for its wines. They grew up in Quincy, in a row-crop-farming family, and in 1998 began planting their Evergreen Vineyard there. It now encompasses 500 acres and is a major supplier of grapes for the Chateau Ste. Michelle & Dr. Loosen Eroica Riesling, and Charles Smith's Kung Fu Girl Riesling and Efeste, as well as Milbrandt's own Rieslings.

Evergreen and other Ancient Lakes vineyards are surrounded by steep cliffs sculpted by Ice Age floodwaters. The material left behind—sand, silt, clay, and hardened calcium carbonate, called caliche—and river-cooled temperatures allow white grapes to retain their natural acidities and minerality. Cave B Estate Winery has cultivated vines in the area since the early 1980s and excels at Syrah and a Bordeaux-style red blend, Cuvée du Soleil. Cameron Fries began planting his vineyard at White Heron two decades ago.

The city of Spokane is northeast of the Columbia Valley AVA, and although few vineyards are planted there, two dozen wineries call it home. Most purchase grapes from the Walla Walla Valley and greater Columbia Valley, although Whitestone Winery, in Wilbur, makes wines from estate-grown fruit from a vineyard 60 miles from Spokane. Winemaker Michael Haig grew up working in his family's vineyard, where he learned winemaking by apprenticing with the wineries who bought his grapes. The first vintage for

White Heron Cellars
Cameron and Phyllis Fries focus on Syrah and red Bordeaux-style wines at their winery above the Columbia River in the Ancient Lakes region of eastern Washington.

Whitestone was 2001 and consisted of a few cases of Merlot. The first full release was in 2002, with Cabernet Sauvignon and Cabernet Franc joining the portfolio.

The Mielke family's Arbor Crest Wine Cellars is located in Spokane, with a vineyard in the Wahluke Slope AVA. Nearby Barrister Winery, named for its attorney owners Greg Lipsker and Michael White (who describe their business as "the little hobby that got out of control"), bottles one of Washington's best Cabernet Francs from purchased Columbia Valley grapes.

Idaho

The sturdy, starchy russet potato made Idaho famous, not only for its prodigious production (the state grows 34 percent of the nation's spuds), but also for aggressive trademarking and promotion by the Idaho Potato Commission. Idaho's russets aren't necessarily better than potatoes grown elsewhere; it's a credit to the commission that its mantra that "warm days and cool nights, ample mountain-fed irrigation, and rich volcanic soils" produce superior potatoes has been so influential. The fact that these conditions are also conducive to producing high-quality wine is just now being promoted in Idaho, often obscured by the long shadows cast by its neighbors to the west, Washington and Oregon.

Outdoor life
Although many Americans associate Idaho with potatoes, trout fishing, and outdoor recreation, the state also has an emerging wine industry.

Until 2007, there was only one appellation in Idaho: Idaho State. That year, the federal government approved the **Snake River Valley AVA** in southwestern Idaho near the state capital of Boise, signaling that Idahoans were getting serious about their wine industry. In 2002, there were only eleven wineries in the state; now there are forty-eight, and the number is certain to grow—even though many Idaho producers, for now at least, rely on grapes grown in Washington State.

The Snake River Valley AVA, where two-thirds of Idaho's wineries are located, encompasses 8,000 square miles and ten counties, with a small portion of it bleeding into eastern Oregon (where just one vineyard is planted). Nestled between the Rocky Mountains and the Snake River, in a high desert with elevations ranging from 1,500 to 3,300 feet above sea level, the AVA is anchored by Ste. Chapelle Winery in Caldwell, Idaho's oldest and largest modern winery, founded in 1976 by Bill Broich and named for a chapel he admired on a visit to Paris.

Traveling in the opposite direction from many, Broich sold Ste. Chapelle and entered the insurance industry, though his winery, designed by Boise architect Nat Adams to mimic that Paris chapel—complete with stained glass windows—is an Idaho icon. So, incidentally, is Adams. Former President George H. W. Bush credits Adams with saving his life: He was one of four fighter pilots flying cover when Bush's bomber was shot down while attacking a Japanese island in 1944.

Now owned by Precept Wine of Seattle, Ste. Chapelle produces 160,000 cases per year of good-value, easy-drinking wines of several varieties. Most Idaho wines are sold to

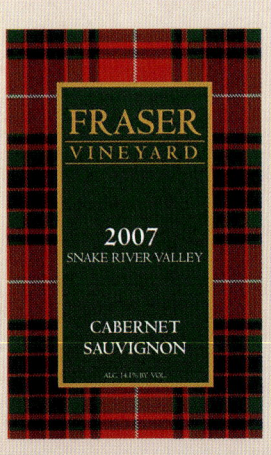
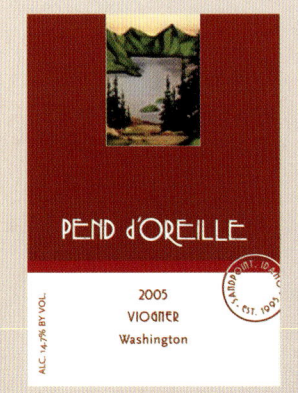

IDAHO SNAPSHOT

Vineyard acreage: 1,600

Most-planted varieties: Chardonnay, Riesling, Viognier, Cabernet Sauvignon, Syrah, Merlot, Malbec, Tempranillo

Best varieties: Chardonnay, Riesling, Viognier

AVA: Snake River Valley

Wineries: 48

Trailblazer: Ste. Chapelle Winery

Steady hands: Pend d'Oreille Winery, Ste. Chapelle Winery, Sawtooth Winery, Snake River Winery, 3 Horse Ranch Vineyards

Superstars: Cinder Wines, Coeur d'Alene Cellars, Fraser Vineyard

SNAKE RIVER VALLEY

Two-thirds of Idaho's forty-eight wineries are located in the Snake River Valley, the state's only AVA.

Idahoans, and at very fair prices. Ste. Chapelle caters to this audience, producing 42,000 cases a year of an off-dry, gentle Riesling and a combined 40,000 cases of what it calls Soft White and Soft Red blends—Chenin Blanc, Sauvignon Blanc, and Muscat Blanc for the whites, and Cabernet Franc, Cabernet Sauvignon, Merlot, and Syrah for the reds. These wines have a touch of residual sugar and 10.5-percent alcohol by volume, making them attractive to those not accustomed to dry wines with firm tannins and high acidity.

Ste. Chapelle can also be more serious, with its Winemaker Series of Dry Riesling, Chardonnay, Merlot, and Cabernet Sauvignon wines, and particularly its luscious Riesling ice wine. Ice wine is produced in years when the growing season is warm enough to ripen the grapes and is followed by temperatures cold enough to freeze the ripened grapes on the vine. The fruit is harvested and pressed while frozen and then fermented, resulting in an unctuous, concentrated dessert wine.

Vineyards in the Snake River Valley are planted in a broad mix of volcanic and sedimentary soils, with the river providing irrigation water. Vines grow on the flanks of ridges, some more than 3,000 feet in elevation, overlooking the river. The AVA's interior location, 600 miles from the Pacific Ocean, insulates it during the growing season, keeping temperatures warm (Boise's highs average 90°F in the summer), with a quick evening cool-down that locks the natural acidity into the grapes. But the fall chill comes early, well before Thanksgiving, and if grapes haven't reached maturity by the time the frost is on the pumpkin, they're pretty much doomed.

While many Idaho vineyards depend on the usual suspects—Chardonnay, Merlot, and Cabernet Sauvignon—recent plantings reflect growers' willingness to test varieties that might be more suitable to local conditions, particularly those that ripen early. Southern Idaho's warm, dry climate is similar to that of the Rhône Valley, and Syrah, Grenache, and

Ste. Chapelle
This Snake River Valley winery is Idaho's oldest and largest, producing good-value wines at the rate of approximately 160,000 cases per year.

Viognier vines show much promise in the Snake River Valley. The same can be said for the Spanish grape Tempranillo; it loves heat and is an early ripener in Idaho.

Fraser Vineyard was Boise's first winery, and its steep, 2,700-foot-elevation plantings in the Snake River Valley afford plenty of sunshine for Cabernet Sauvignon, Merlot, and Petit Verdot. Bill Fraser's first Petite Sirah was released in 2011, and his Viogniers have won numerous medals in Northwest competitions.

Sawtooth Winery, in the Snake River Valley, began life as Pintler Cellars in 1987. Now owned by Precept Wine, Sawtooth makes a wide range of wines at various price points. Its 450-acre Skyline Vineyard is one of Idaho's largest, with all possible exposures hosting myriad varieties, including Cabernet Sauvignon, Cabernet Franc, Merlot, Sauvignon Blanc, and Riesling.

Cinder Wines, owned by the wife-and-husband team of winemaker Melanie Krause and Joe Schnerr, is one of Idaho's nascent superstars. Viognier is the flagship, produced in dry, off-dry, and reserve styles, all of which capture the grape's honeysuckle, pear, and white peach aromas and flavors, enveloped by refreshing acidity. Cinder also produces an exquisite Cabernet Sauvignon–based red blend.

3 Horse Ranch Vineyards also excels at Viognier, as well as a reserve Syrah-Mourvèdre and a reserve Syrah. Owners Gary and Martha Cunningham grow their grapes organically; winemaker Greg Koenig vinifies the wines, a skill he also lends to his family's Koening Distillery and Winery brand.

Hells Canyon Winery's vineyards were planted in 1981 above the banks of the Snake River, overlooking the Owyhee Mountains. Former chef Steve Robertson is owner and winemaker, and his Deer Slayer Syrah is a spicy, balanced wine.

Northern Idaho

Five wineries exist in Northern Idaho, just across the state line from Spokane. Most notable are Coeur d'Alene Cellars and Pend d'Oreille Winery. Coeur d'Alene Cellars has the distinction of being located in Idaho, but producing its wines from grapes grown in the Columbia Valley of eastern Washington.

The Coeur d'Alene area is surrounded by dozens of lakes carved out by Ice Age glaciers. Considering the fishing, hunting, swimming, boating, and hiking tourism business these water bodies and their rivers attract, Coeur d'Alene Cellars owners Kimber Gates and her parents, Charlie and Sarah Gates, decided their winery would be better placed not in Washington, where there is a saturation of producers, but in Coeur d'Alene, where visitors are delighted to discover a tasting room downtown.

Since the Gates started the winery in 2002, they've focused on Rhône-style wines, with an occasional Bordeaux-style red or two thrown in (this is Columbia Valley fruit, after all). Coeur d'Alene Cellars bottles as many as five different Syrahs each vintage from its 3,600-case annual total, including one from the acclaimed Boushey Vineyards in Yakima Valley and an uncommon, for Washington and Idaho, Mourvèdre called simply Mo, from the Horse Heaven Hills.

Pend d'Oreille Winery in nearby Sandpoint, founded by Julie and Stephen Meyer in 1995, also produces wines mainly from Washington grapes, although the Chardonnay and Malbec come from the Snake River Valley AVA. Pend d'Oreille also bottles the insanely popular Huckleberry Blush, a Riesling with 5-percent huckleberry wine added.

A recent grant from the U.S. Economic Development Administration could help boost the growth of Idaho's wine industry. The $100,000 grant fueled a marketing campaign, mapping of the Snake River Valley AVA, and an investigation into the possible creation of new AVAs within the state.

Colorado

Colorado has an excess of natural riches: the saw-toothed, snowcapped Rocky Mountains; evergreen forests; trout-filled streams; cottonwoods and quaking aspens on scenic winding roads; and the Colorado River, which supplies much of the West with its drinking water. Skiing, snowboarding, fishing, and rafting lure visitors, and the largely alpine landscape is a breathtaking setting for major events such as the Food & Wine Classic in Aspen, The Taste of Vail, and the Steamboat (Springs) Wine Festival.

The Rocky Mountain Range
Colorado's two AVAs are located on the west side of the high peaks, although many wineries operate near the major cities of Denver and Boulder, on the east side of the range.

Yet many who attend these fancy food-wine fests have no idea that Colorado produces wines, and some outstanding ones at that. Most wineries are small and family owned (no corporate kingpins here), production volume is low, and most wines are usually sold in tasting rooms and to wineries' wine club members within the state. Some retail stores stock Colorado wines, but restaurants in Denver, the state's largest and most cosmopolitan city, have been slow to embrace the home-team bottlings, relying instead on wines from California, Europe, and elsewhere.

Thus Colorado wines have gone largely unnoticed on a national level, although the state-funded Colorado Wine Industry Development Board is energetically promoting wine country now that there are more than one hundred wineries—up from just five in 1990.

Colorado grape growers are a determined bunch, dealing with harsh winters, snow, and cold nighttime temperatures during the growing season. Most of the state's vines are planted at elevations of 4,000 to 7,000 feet—among the highest in the northern hemisphere. Hard frosts are common, the season is short, and farming risks are high. Balancing the risks are long days of intense solar radiation that boost photosynthesis, the lack of rain from spring through early fall (little fungal diseases), and relatively few pests at high elevations.

With irrigation water accessible from diversions from the Colorado River, agriculture exploded in the area, with apples, pears, peaches, plums, and cherries the major crops. Governor George A. Crawford, founder of the city of Grand Junction in the Grand Valley AVA, planted 60 acres of wine grapes and

Grand Valley & West Elks

The Grand Valley and West Elks AVAs grow the majority of grapes for Colorado's wine production. The area known as the Front Range (not an AVA) includes wineries and some vineyards in and near the cities of Denver, Boulder, and Colorado Springs.

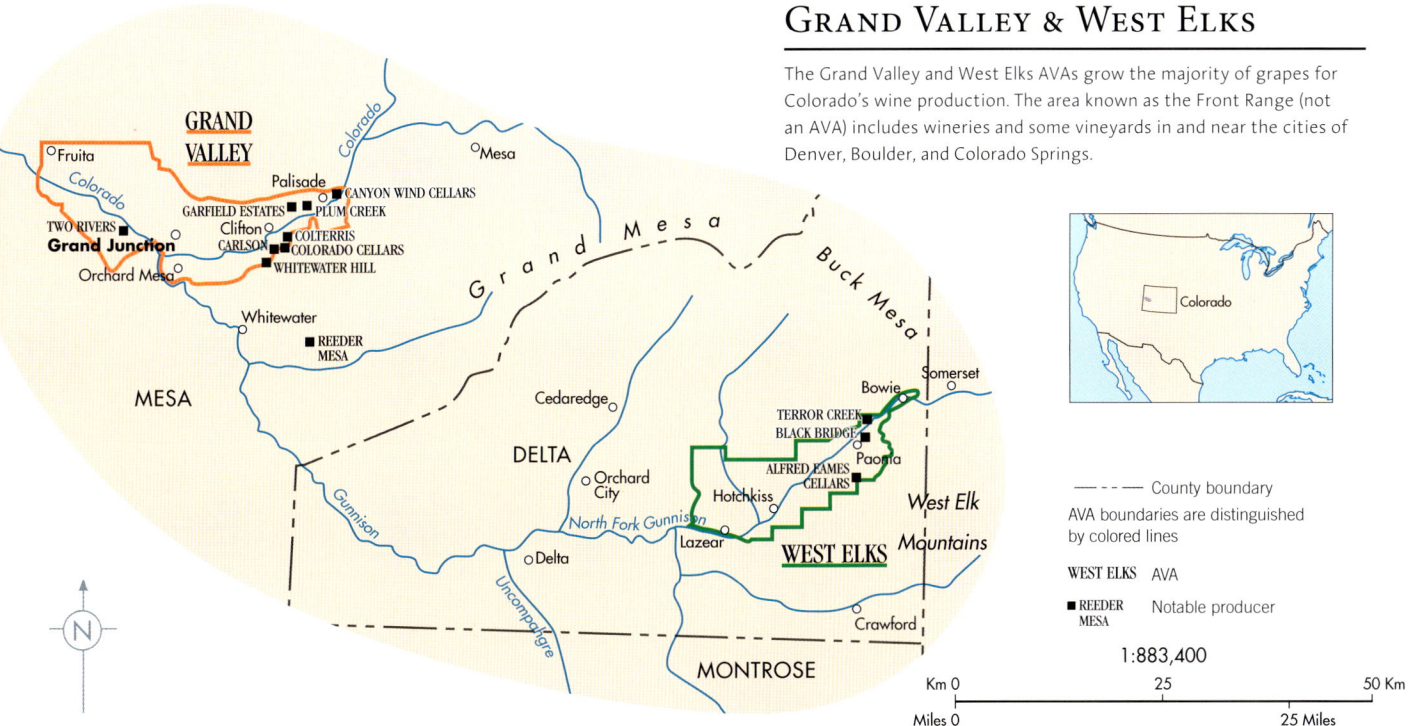

other fruit above Palisade in 1890; by 1909, there were more than a thousand Colorado farms involved in grape growing.

Colorado voluntarily went "dry" four years before Prohibition, in 1916, and the vines were ripped out, not be replanted until the 1970s. The wine industry owes gratitude to a Denver dentist, Gerald Ivancie, for reviving winemaking in the state.

In 1968, Ivancie and his wife, Mary, opened Colorado's first commercial winery since Prohibition, Ivancie Winery, helped by their nine children. For the first few vintages, Ivancie used California grapes to make his wines, but when grape prices soared, he convinced a handful of nearby Palisade farmers to plant vinifera vines from cuttings he had acquired in California. Warren Winiarski was his advisor, before he opened Stag's Leap Wine Cellars in Napa Valley.

With a clutch of kids to put through college, Ivancie sold the winery in 1973 and returned to dentistry; the new owners closed the business in 1975. Ivancie's friend Jim Seewald put together a group of investors and founded Colorado Mountain Vineyards in Golden in 1978, relocating it in Palisade in 1980. It was later sold and renamed Colorado Cellars.

Seewald and his wife, Ann, were instrumental in researching and writing the Grand Valley AVA petition that was approved in 1990. Richard and Padte Turley now own Colorado Cellars, where they produce two dozen different wines, including remarkably pure nongrape fruit wines.

Seven thousand feet is the elevation threshold for wine grapes in Colorado, nearly all of them varieties of *Vitis vinifera*. However, hybrids including Baco Noir, Chambourcin, Marquette, and Vidal show promise because of their cold-climate hardiness. State officials estimate that there are 10,000 acres of land suitable for vinifera in Colorado. A good 25,000 more acres could support hybrid varieties, reducing risks for

COLORADO SNAPSHOT

Vineyard acreage: **1,200**

Most-planted varieties: **Merlot, Cabernet Sauvignon, Riesling, Chardonnay, Syrah**

Best varieties: **Cabernet Franc, Cabernet Sauvignon, Gewürztraminer, Petit Verdot, Riesling**

AVAs: **Grand Valley, West Elks**

Wineries: **100**

Trailblazers: **Colorado Cellars Winery, Plum Creek Winery**

Steady hands: **Black Bridge Winery, Bookcliff Vineyards, Boulder Creek Winery, Carlson Vineyards, Creekside Cellars, Garfield Estates, Guy Drew Vineyards, Plum Creek Winery, Reeder Mesa Vineyards, Sutcliffe Vineyards, Terror Creek Winery, The Winery at Holy Cross Abbey, Two Rivers Winery, Whitewater Hills Vineyards**

Superstars: **Alfred Eames Cellars, Canyon Wind Cellars, The Infinite Monkey Theorem**

One to watch: **Colterris**

Bottling day
At Carlson Vineyards in Palisade, wines are bottled by hand, rather than on an automated line.

Mount Garfield
Grand Valley AVA vineyards are planted along the base of 2,000-foot Mount Garfield, on the eastern edge of the Book Cliff Range.

farmers and increasing statewide production. Viticulturists and enologists at Colorado State University's Orchard Mesa Research Station in Grand Junction have led the way in identifying the best hybrids for the state.

There are two AVAs in Colorado—Grand Valley and West Elks—where the large majority of the state's grapes are grown, and where thirty-five of its one hundred wineries are located. The greatest concentration of production facilities is in and around the Front Range cities of Denver and Boulder, where there are plenty of residents and visitors to sample and purchase wines in city and suburban tasting rooms. These wineries purchase their grapes from Grand Valley, West Elks, and other areas.

Grand Valley AVA

This appellation grows 80 percent of Colorado's wine grapes and produces 50 percent of its wine. Twenty wineries call Grand Valley home, and another fifty or so outside the AVA produce wine from fruit grown within it.

Less than 10 inches of rain falls each year in Grand Valley, so access to irrigation water from the Colorado River is crucial. Based in Palisade, Grand Valley has long been known for its peaches, but wine grapes are now gaining equal status. Vineyards here are planted at elevations as high as 4,720 feet; the last spring frost typically occurs before April 23, with the first fall frost generally in the third week of October.

Still, there is plenty of sunlight and warmth to ripen Merlot, Cabernet Sauvignon, and Syrah grapes, with heat radiating off a dramatic mesa whose cliffs have the flat-topped, 6,000-foot Mount Garfield northeast of Grand Junction as the focal point. The valley that contains the grape-growing area runs east to west and was carved out of the landscape by two rivers, the Colorado and Gunnison, that left deep canyons encouraging air drainage, thus reducing frost damage. During the growing season, this area enjoys warm days and cool nights.

Some wineries bring in grapes or juice from other states in order to have wine to sell in lean vintages, while others, such as Plum Creek Winery in Palisade, are proud that they use 100-percent Colorado-grown fruit, and always have. Plum Creek, a large winery by Colorado standards at approximately 12,000 cases produced annually, was launched in 1984 by attorneys Sue and Doug Phillips. Winemaker Jenne Baldwin, a California native, has been a fixture since 1998. The Plum Creek wines are confidently made, from grapes grown in the Grand Valley and West Elks AVAs. The Grand Mesa Bordeaux-style red is its benchmark wine, and the crowd-pleaser is the Merlot-based, off-dry Palisade Rosé.

At nearby Canyon Wind Cellars, Jay Christianson picked up where his father, Norman, left off in 2007, operating one of the

THE INFINITE MONKEY THEOREM

Ben Parsons is an England-born, Australia-trained, and New Zealand-experienced winemaker who happened to land in Colorado, eventually opening a winery in Denver in 2008 and becoming the state's most talked-about vintner.

Until July 2012, Parsons made his wines in a graffiti-splattered Quonset hut in Denver's Arts District, a location that endeared him mostly to Millennials who embraced their inner urban guerilla-ness by visiting and tasting the wines. With its lack of pretention, and a brand name as intriguing as its location, The Infinite Monkey Theorem became the hottest and hippest wine brand in Colorado.

The Infinite Monkey Theorem gets its name from the theory that a monkey striking typewriter keys for an unlimited time will eventually type the works of Shakespeare. "We are the Shakespeare, not the monkey," notes Parsons. He is unorthodox, innovative, and brash, and he has convinced sommeliers to put his wines on their lists when other Colorado producers have been unable to do so.

Parson's most popular wines—Cabernet Franc, Petite Sirah, Petit Verdot, and the red blend 100th Monkey—are big and voluptuous, sourced from vineyards 200 miles away from Denver. He packages some of his wines in cans and in kegs, the latter of which are sold to restaurants for by-the-glass pours.

Yet success impacts even Quonset hut businesses. In 2012, Parsons moved the Monkey to a 29,000-square-foot facility in Denver, where he has room to grow. He will add production lines for The Infinite Monkey Theorem wines-in-a-can, and a keg-filling station where wineries, distributors, and importers can put their wines into stainless steel casks and deliver them to Denver-area restaurants.

Parsons isn't alone in calling Denver home. On Colorado Winery Row in the

Urban Wine Jungle
Ben Parsons proudly produced his The Infinite Monkey Theorem wines in this Quonset hut on a Denver back street until 2012, when success demanded that he move to roomier digs.

Highlands district, Bonacquisti Wine Company, Verso Cellars, Garfield Estates Vineyard & Winery, and Cottonwood Cellars/The Olathe Winery are a stone's throw away from one another, making it easy for people to visit several tasting rooms in one short walk.

---

few all-estate-grown wineries in Colorado. Norman Christianson began planting the vineyard in 1991, producing wine in 1995. Canyon Wind's 40 acres of vineyards are planted on a bench below the cliffs, in glacially deposited sandstone and cobblestone soils. Cabernet Sauvignon is the flagship grape, followed by Cabernet Franc and Syrah.

In 2007, Canyon Wind produced Colorado's first $100 wine, called IV, a Petit Verdot–driven blend that includes Cabernet Franc, Cabernet Sauvignon, and Merlot. The winds that blow through Debeque Canyon, which gave the winery its name, also inspired a new brand, Anemoi, which debuted in 2011. Jay Christianson and his wife, Jennifer, called their first Anemoi wine Boreas, after a mythical god who was said to have had a violent temper, just as 50-mph winter winds can wreak havoc in the vineyard. The 2009 Boreas—Cabernet Sauvignon, Merlot, Cabernet Franc, and Petit Verdot—is Californian in style, with toasty oak and ripe, forward fruit.

Carlson Vineyards in Palisade, founded in 1988, has had a great run of success with its off-dry Laughing Cat Gewürztraminers and Rieslings, and a Lemberger called Tyrannosaurus Red, named for dinosaur bones found in Grand Valley in the early 1900s. But Carlson's finest wine might be its Cougar Run Dry Gewürztraminer, bone-dry and florally aromatic.

Colterris is a potential star, producing Cabernet Sauvignon from its 19-acre Grand Valley vineyard. It has Napa Valley–trained vineyard manager Tony Fernandez and multiple clonal selections going for it—and the aim of producing rich, Napa Valley-style Cabs.

West Elks AVA

The West Elks AVA is southeast of Grand Valley, straddling Delta and Montrose counties, with its home base the town of Paonia. Vineyards are planted as high as 7,000 feet above sea level and receive more precipitation and colder temperatures than in Grand Valley, making West Elks prime land for Riesling, Gewürztraminer, and Pinot Noir. West Elks soils, with their high organic content, are notably fertile

If any Colorado vintner has achieved California-style cult status, it's Alfred Eames. In one of the first aging caves in the state, Eames takes a decidedly Old World approach to his winemaking, fermenting reds in open vats, aging them in French oak barrels, and leaving them unfiltered. His winery south of Paonia is rustic and functional, reminding one of a cellar in Burgundy. And, indeed, Eames, one of the few to do so successfully in Colorado, produces Pinot Noir from grapes grown in his Puesta del Sol vineyard. His Pinots show best after a few years of cellaring.

Eames also makes Syrah, Tempranillo, and Carmena, based on Carmine—the California crossing with both Cabernet Sauvignon and Carignane genes—using grapes grown by others. He traveled in Europe as a young man and developed a taste for Spanish wine, but he has no formal winemaking training, just instinct. "I've read all the books," he says with a laugh.

One of West Elks' best-known Pinot Noir producers is Black Bridge Winery, with a wine cave constructed out of materials salvaged from a local mining operation. Yet it is Terror Creek Winery that draws the most oohs and aahs, thanks to its situation at 6,400 feet elevation, making it one of the highest vineyards in the United States.

Terror Creek specializes in Riesling, Gewürztraminer, and Pinot Noir, with the white varieties its stars, produced in an Alsatian style—dry, yet with generous fruit character—by Swiss-trained owner and winemaker Joan Mathewson.

Front Range

The Front Range is a geographic region, not an AVA, with a vibrant winemaking community in and around the cities of Denver and Boulder. Producers here purchase grapes, vinify them in industrial-park wineries, and sell them to the thirsty clientele of cosmopolitan Denver and its suburbs.

Boulder Creek Winery in Gunbarrel is such a winery, owned by winemaker Jackie Thompson and her husband, Mike. Their Viognier from Bookcliff Vineyards, Cabernet Sauvignon from Canyon Wind Cellars, and Riesling from Whitewater Hills Vineyards are first-rate, all from Grand Valley–Palisade.

In Boulder, John Garlich and Ulla Merz make their Bookcliff Vineyards wines from their 33-acre vineyard in Palisade and sell grapes to twenty Front Range wineries. Among their most interesting wines are Tempranillo, Petite Sirah, and a Merlot–Cabernet Sauvignon blend, Ensemble.

Elsewhere in Colorado

Those who know their U.S. geography are familiar with the Four Corners, the only place in America where four states meet: Colorado, Utah, Arizona, and New Mexico. In nearby Cortez, in the southwest corner of Colorado, two high-end wineries thrive: Guy Drew Vineyards and Sutcliffe Vineyards.

Both are located in McElmo Canyon, in Montezuma County, where elevations range from 4,500 feet at the Utah border to nearly 10,000 feet on Ute Peak. The high-desert landscape is textbook American Southwest, with sandstone hills, dusty canyons, and ancient Pueblo Indian cliff dwellings.

Guy and Ruth Drew relocated to Cortez from Denver in 1998, transforming a hay farm into a straw-bale-constructed winery and 18 acres of vineyards. They supplement their own dry-farmed grapes with those purchased from other growers. A succulent, unoaked Chardonnay; honeysuckle-scented Viognier; and nicely balanced Cabernet Sauvignon-Syrah blend called Metate are standouts.

Sutcliffe Vineyards is the creation of an Englishman, John Sutcliffe, who came to the United States in 1968. He managed restaurants in New York City before eventually arriving in Cortez in 1992 to farm hay and raise livestock. He planted grapes in 1995, making his first wines in 1999. The Sutcliffe Down Canyon red blend is his signature wine.

The Franciscan fathers who sowed the seeds of California's wine industry never came close to Colorado, but the Benedictines did, establishing the Winery at Holy Cross Abbey in Cañon City, 30 miles west of Pueblo in Fremont County.

The monastery stopped housing monks in 2006, but the winery continues to thrive. Established in 2002, it produces multiple wines, including some made from California grapes; but its best bottles are Bordeaux varieties Cabernet Sauvignon, Cabernet Franc, and Merlot, from Colorado grapes. Winemaker Matt Cookson trained in Napa and Sonoma before joining the winery; Sally Davidson, his former wife and co-owner of The Winery at Holy Cross Abbey, handles the sales and marketing, having honed her skills in California.

Sutcliffe Vineyards
John Sutcliffe (right) chose Cortez, in the southwestern corner of Colorado, to plant Sutcliffe Vineyards. He and his neighbor, Guy Drew Vineyards, are among the state's best producers.

Other Mountain States

The relatively sparsely populated, frontier-like states of Nevada, Utah, Montana, Wyoming, North Dakota, and South Dakota exemplify how winemaking has caught on throughout the United States, although at a small startup level. Agritourism and the move toward eating (and drinking) local goods are alive in states that present major weather challenges for wine producers. Some overcome their climatic limitations by purchasing grapes grown in other states. Such bottlings typically carry the "America" country appellation.

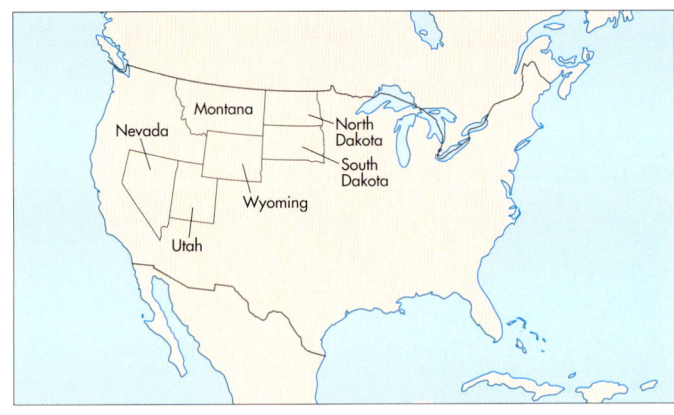

These six mountain states share similar traits: cold winters, springs, and falls; arid summers that demand irrigation; high-desert geography, with altitudes to 6,000 feet; and short growing seasons, which favor early-ripening vinifera and French-American hybrid varieties, as well as nongrape fruit wines. Sub-zero temperatures in winter can kill vines, and hard frosts in spring can damage the vines' tender shoots and buds.

Vintners in these states cross their fingers that their plants survive each winter, and they sometimes have to supplement their own produce with grapes and occasionally wine imported from other states more suited to vinegrowing. They possess fortitude, a pioneering spirit, and business plans that rely on sales of wines, jams, honey, and other items to tourists, local residents, and restaurateurs who embrace homegrown products. "Ferment it, and they will come" is the mantra, and indeed they do, purchasing wines made from grapes, apples, berries, stone fruits, rhubarb, and even jalapeño peppers and pumpkins.

Aficionados may scoff at wines made from elderberries and chokecherries, and sweet grape wines, yet many Americans enjoy these styles, substituting them for Coke or iced tea at dinner. Who's to argue?

South Dakota

With America's first wine collector (and failed vintner) Thomas Jefferson peering down from Mount Rushmore, how could South Dakota not produce wine?

There are seventeen wineries in the state, including a handful near the Black Hills. It was here in 1941, that Gutzon Borglum began carving the faces of U.S. presidents Jefferson, George Washington, Theodore Roosevelt, and Abraham Lincoln on a granite face 5,500 feet sea level near Rapid City in southwestern South Dakota.

Prairie Berry Winery is located there, in tourist mecca Hill City, and is an American success story with a Central European accent. Anna Pésa Vojta and her husband, Jon, settled in the Dakota Territory in 1876, arriving from Moravia (now part of the Czech Republic). Anna made wine from berries and other wild fruits, as did subsequent generations of the family. Now fifth-generation Prairie Berry winemaker Sandi Vojta—a South Dakota State University biology/chemistry graduate—ferments grapes, other fruits, and honey and sells her wines to thirsty visitors to Mount Rushmore and the Black Hills National Park. Her Red Ass Rhubarb and semisweet Frontenac have impressed judges in California competitions; Blue Suede Shoes is an unusual blend of Zinfandel and blueberries.

Prairie Berry has Eldon Nygaard and his wife, Sherry, to thank for opening the doors for South Dakotans to produce wine commercially. In 1996, the Nygaards drafted the state's Farm Winery Act, which made it possible for South Dakotans to turn their crops into saleable wines. The Nygaards' Valiant Vineyards Winery in Vermillion, in the southeastern section of the state, became South Dakota's first bonded winery, opening soon after the act was passed.

Valiant offers a range of options, in all some two dozen grape, fruit, and honey wines, including an American Merlot from grapes purchased from out of state, and Full Throttle, a fortified Cabernet Sauvignon–based wine that is its most popular. The Nygaards also operate Stone Faces Winery in Hill City, where they sell their Prairie Berry wines under the approving gaze of Thomas Jefferson.

North Dakota

North Dakota has received more publicity for being the fiftieth state to claim at least one bonded winery within its borders than

THE WEST | OTHER MOUNTAIN STATES | 191

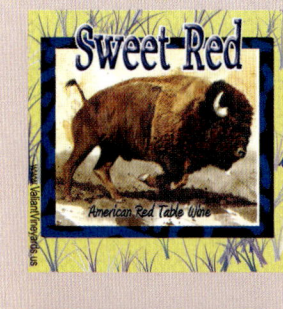
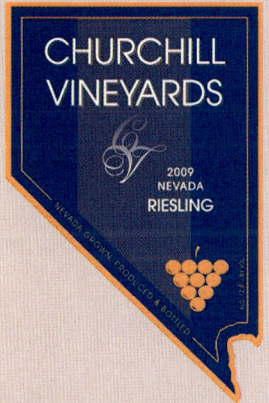

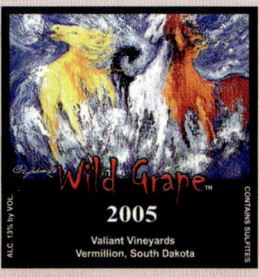

OTHER MOUNTAIN STATES SNAPSHOT

Best varieties: French-American hybrids, Riesling, non-grape fruits

AVAs: None (state appellations only)

Wineries: MONTANA 13; NEVADA 3; NORTH DAKOTA 8; SOUTH DAKOTA 17; UTAH 6; WYOMING 2

Steady hands: MONTANA—Mission Mountain Winery, Ten Spoon Vineyard & Winery; NEVADA—Churchill Vineyards; NORTH DAKOTA—Pointe of View Winery; SOUTH DAKOTA—Prairie Berry Winery, Schadé Vineyard & Winery, Strawbale Winery, Valiant Vineyards Winery; UTAH—Castle Creek Winery, Spanish Valley Vineyards & Winery; WYOMING—Table Mountain Vineyards and Winery

Prairie Berry Winery
South Dakota's bitter cold winters don't support vinifera grapevines, so producers like Prairie Berry Winery in Hill City turn to hybrid varieties and other fruits.

it has for the wines themselves. Considering the harsh climate (anyone who has seen the 1996 film *Fargo,* shot in North Dakota and Minnesota, has a grasp of the frozen tundra landscape), it is remarkable that anyone dares to produce wine in North Dakota.

In 2002, Pointe of View Winery in Burlington, in the north-central part of the state, was the first to do just that; only seven others have followed. Within the continental United States, North Dakota has the coldest winters and shortest growing seasons, and vinifera grapes are viable only in very warm years. Yet Peace Garden State farmers are eager to grow crops that are more lucrative than grains and are exploring cold-tolerant French-American hybrids and other fruits for future wine production.

Pointe of View co-owner and winemaker Jeff Peterson's sweet rhubarb wine is his best seller, and wines made from apples, plums, elderberries, and honey are also successful. His only grape-based wine is Terre Haute Rouge, a semisweet blush wine made from Valiant grapes grown by Souris Valley Vineyard. Valiant, a hybrid developed by the University of South Dakota, is also grown as a table grape.

Maple River Winery ferments fruits, honey, and herbs, but not grapes, west of Fargo. It regularly sells out of its Woodchipper Rhubarb wine (is it a coincidence that the body of a character in *Fargo* was fed though a wood chipper?).

Montana

Thirteen wineries operate in the Big Sky State, with grapevines planted on the western slopes of the Rockies, on sites that provide the vines with optimal exposure to sunlight. Many produce fruit wines, from local cherries, huckleberries, chokecherries, currants, and pears, but there is a band of vintners serious about making wine from vinifera and hybrid grapes.

Mission Mountain Winery is one such producer, and it was the first bonded winery in Montana. UC Davis–trained Tom Campbell Jr. and his father established Mission Mountain in 1984, on the western shore of Flathead Lake in Dayton, south of Kalispell in the western third of the state. Mission Mountain is the largest wine producer (7,000 cases per year) in Montana, and local plantings include Gewürztraminer, Pinot Gris, Riesling, and Pinot Noir.

Like many vintners in mountain regions, Campbell also sources grapes from outside the state. In this case, it's the Rattlesnake Hills AVA in the Columbia Valley of Washington State, where Mission Mountain gets its Chardonnay, Cabernet Sauvignon, Merlot, and Syrah grapes. Campbell has experience making wine in Columbia Valley, and his best bottlings are based on grapes from there, as there is near-certainty that they will achieve physiological maturity every year in the warmer conditions.

Andy Sponseller and Connie Poten have grown grapes organically in Montana since 1998, at Rattlesnake Creek Vineyard, near Missoula. They changed their Rattlesnake Creek brand name in 2005, after receiving a cease-and-desist letter from a Washington vintner who owned the Rattlesnake Ridge trademark. Sponseller and Poten held a competition to choose a new name, going with a Danish wholesaler's suggestion of Ten Spoon Vineyard & Winery—a loose combination of the partners' last names.

Ten Spoon grows hybrids Marechal Foch, Frontenac, Leon Millot, St. Croix, St. Pepin, and LaCrosse organically, and it crafts wines from certified organic vineyards in California, Oregon, and Washington. The flagship wine is Range Rider red, a blend of Marechal Foch, Leon Millot, St. Croix, and Frontenac.

Utah

Wine grapes were planted in Utah in the 1860s, after members of the Church of Jesus Christ of Latter-day Saints (Mormons) settled in the area. But changing Mormon doctrine that banned the consumption of alcohol, and Prohibition, left the state's vineyards and wineries abandoned.

A micro-revival began with experimental vine plantings in the 1970s in the Four Corners region (where Utah, Colorado, New Mexico, and Arizona connect). At elevations of 4,000 feet, vinifera varieties such as Chenin Blanc, Chardonnay, Cabernet Sauvignon, and Merlot flourish in the high desert near Moab, in Grand County in southeastern Utah. Sandy soils in red-rock canyons carved out by the Colorado River and its tributaries, summer days with temperatures hitting 100°F, and vine-refreshing brisk nights make for ideal conditions for grapevines.

The first commercial vineyards were planted in the early 1980s, but because wineries were not permitted in heavily Mormon-populated Utah at the time, the first few harvests were sold to out-of-state producers. In 1988, wineries became legal, and Arches Winery near Moab was the first to open its doors, in 1989. In 2002, Arches was sold to the Fryer family, who relocated it 15 miles north of Moab, at Red Cliffs Lodge, and renamed it Castle Creek Winery. It has 10 acres of Syrah and Cabernet Sauvignon vines and also purchases grapes from others. Best sellers include the blended Outlaw Red and Lily Rose White.

Spanish Valley Vineyards & Winery, founded by the Dezelsky family just south of Moab, has grown grapes in Utah for three decades and produced wine professionally since 1999, from 5 acres of grapes. Gewürztraminer and Riesling are made in off-dry styles; Chardonnay, Merlot, and Cabernet Sauvignon are dry and competent. At the time of writing, the enterprise is up for sale.

Churchill Vineyards
Winter snowfall is typical in Fallon, Nevada, but the spring and summer months are warm enough for Churchill Vineyards to grow Riesling and Gewürztraminer successfully.

Nevada

There are just three wineries in the state famous for legalized gambling, mining, Lake Tahoe (shared with California), and cattle and dairy ranches.

Nevada's first commercial producer (established in 1990) is a one-hour drive from the Las Vegas Strip—Pahrump Valley Winery in Pahrump. Churchill Vineyards in Churchill County, near Fallon, makes Nevada-grown Gewürztraminer, Riesling, and Semillon-Chardonnay, and a California-grown Cabernet Sauvignon. In Minden, close to Lake Tahoe, Tahoe Ridge Winery reaches the tourism market with largely California-grown wines, plus the hybrids La Crosse and Frontenac.

Wyoming

Approximately 70 percent of Wyoming's agricultural income comes from cattle and bison ranching, so wine production is but a single grain in the feed bin. There are two wineries in operation, although other farmers, searching for more profitable crops in trying economic times, are currently trialing wine grapes.

Wyoming winemaking began in 1994, with the opening of Terry Ranch Cellars near the capital city of Cheyenne; the partners later dissolved the business. Patrick Zimmerer, who wrote his University of Wyoming senior thesis on developing vineyards in Wyoming, established one in 2001, and it has grown into the 10-acre Table Mountain Vineyards and Winery in Huntley. Frontenac, Valiant, Marechal Foch, and Marquette are the most suitable grape varieties—and wines—for the challengingly cold Wyoming climate.

Hawaii and Alaska

In 1959, California Cabernet Sauvignons from Napa Valley's Beaulieu Vineyard, Heitz Cellars, and Inglenook were earning kudos as Alaska and Hawaii were becoming the forty-ninth and fiftieth states of the Union. It should come as no surprise that these two states that are physically detached from the other forty-eight are also individualist in their winemaking. Fruit other than grapes plays an important part here. Where else can one purchase a bottle of Maui Splash straight from the tasting room, or sip Wild Salmonberry wine while watching the sun set at 11 PM?

Arctic and tropical climates are not conditions in which wine grapes thrive. Alaska's summer is too short and cold for viticulture. Hawaii, warm and humid year-round, lacks a long winter period in which vines can go dormant, rest for a few months, and then blossom in spring. But both states find ways to produce wine, although they grow very few grapes and tend to rely on the fermented sugars of other fruits for alcohol.

There are no AVAs in Alaska or Hawaii, and some consider the wines produced in these states to be mere novelties. But residents take great pride in their local products, visitors delight in bringing home exotic souvenirs, and a segment of the U.S. population enjoys wines made from fruit other than grapes.

Tedeschi Vineyards
Known for its pineapple-based Maui Blanc and Maui Splash wines, Tedeschi Vineyards on Maui has had some recent success with Chardonnay, Pinot Noir, Syrah, and Carnelian grapes.

Hawaii

Numerous attempts have been made since before Prohibition to grow wine grapes in Hawaii, mostly on Maui and the Big Island (Hawaii). Most have failed, with growers unable to overcome fungal diseases that develop in the humid climate and infect grape clusters with rot. The same year-long, summer-like conditions that draw tourists to Hawaii each year also limit viticulture to only a handful of hybrid varieties, planted at high elevations where there is just enough "winter" to allow the vines to go dormant and breezes to dry clusters from mold-inducing rainfall.

Great wines come from grapevines that have been stressed by the changes of seasons; vine life is too mellow in Hawaii's comfy climate to produce complex grape wines on par with those from the continental United States.

Only two notable wineries have persevered in Hawaii: Tedeschi Vineyards on Maui and Volcano Winery on the Big Island. They rely on disease-resistant hybrid grape varieties such as Symphony and Carnelian, as well as pineapples, raspberries, guavas, and honey. Both producers blend fruit wine with grape wine to achieve a drinkable balance.

Volcano Winery is just outside Volcano National Park on Kilauea, an active volcano on the southeast side of the Big Island. Symphony is the major grape planted here—a UC Davis cross of Muscat of Alexandria with Grenache Gris, which produces fruity white wines that range from dry to sweet, with peach and apricot flavors, and often headily floral aromas.

Planted at 4,000-feet elevation, Volcano's Symphony vines enjoy a short winter dormancy, and the compact clusters of the vine guard against rot development in the inner grapes. The winery makes a number of other fruit-driven wines, including—what else?—Volcano Red, a blend of light red wine (usually made from grape juice concentrate) and

Location, location
Grapevine fungal diseases are a constant problem because of year-round humidity on Hawaii. Planting on open hillsides to take advantage of ocean breezes helps minimize the threat.

purplish-black jaboticaba berries, native to Brazil and grown in the yards of many islanders.

Tedeschi Vineyards, which also bills itself as Maui's Winery, was cofounded in 1974 by Ulupalakua Ranch owner C. Pardee Erdman and Napa Valley's Emil Tedeschi. Ulupalakua, once owned by King Kamehamha III, has been a sugarcane plantation and a cattle ranch, on the slopes of Haleakala, Maui's highest peak (10,023 feet).

Tedeschi and Erdman planted grapes in 1974, at approximately 1,800 feet, in the famously rich Haleakala volcanic soils. To create cash flow while the vines matured, they produced sparkling wine from local pineapples. Soon thereafter, the winery released a still pineapple wine, Maui Blanc; Maui Splash, a pineapple wine with a dash of passion fruit; and a grape-based sparkler, Maui Brut, which the winery says was served at the inauguration of President Ronald Reagan in 1981.

Emil Tedeschi believed that Carnelian, a crossing with Cabernet Sauvignon, Carignane, and Grenache genes, was best suited to Maui's conditions, and some 20 acres of it were planted. Only a few rows remain—lone survivors of the fungal disease *eutypa*.

Tedeschi returned to Napa Valley in 1991 to run his family's Tedeschi Family Winery near Calistoga, and Paula Hegele now manages Tedeschi Vineyards. Recent years have seen the replanting of vinifera varieties, and while the results have been varied, the Rose Ranch Cuvée (a sparkling wine made from Chardonnay and Pinot Noir) and Plantation Red (Syrah with a small amount of Carnelian) have won fans. Still, Maui Splash and Maui Blanc remain Tedeschi's most popular wines, and they can be found in markets across America.

Alaska

Alaskans have never tried to grow grapevines in their state, knowing that it would be nearly impossible to get enough warmth and sunlight to generate sufficient vine photosynthesis in their chilly, if not frozen, conditions. The handful of wineries in Alaska—five at last count—use local fruits and/or buy grape juice from California, Washington, and Canada to ferment into wine.

Denali Winery in Anchorage was the state's first winery, founded in 1997 by Judy Hall. Now owned by Mike and Cathy Bessent, Denali is both a winery that sells its bottles to restaurants, retailers, and consumers, and a make-your-own-wine facility, where regular folks choose grape juice from dozens of varieties grown in California, Washington, Europe, and the Southern Hemisphere and are led through the process of fermenting, clarifying, bottling, and packaging their wines for personal use.

Alaska Wilderness Winery on Kodiak Island specializes in wines made from native-grown produce, including blueberry, salmonberry, raspberry, and rhubarb. Bear Creek Winery in Homer does the same, blending fruit, honey, and sometimes grape wines into sweet, easy-to-drink quaffs.

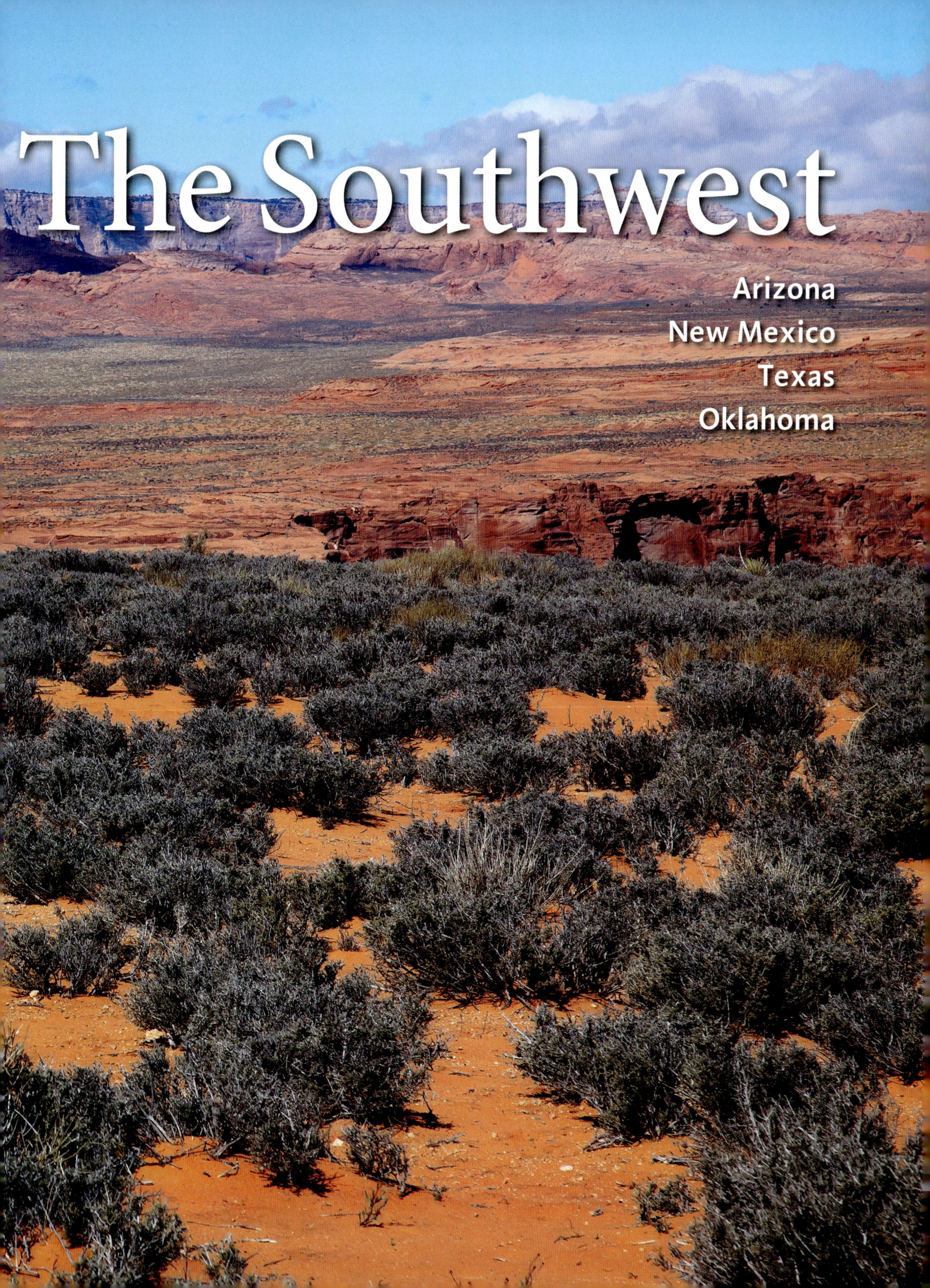

The Southwest

Arizona
New Mexico
Texas
Oklahoma

Arizona

The Grand Canyon State is more than a giant desert, vacation resort, baseball spring training site, and nest for human snowbirds who winter there to escape harsh weather back home. Arizona also has a thriving agricultural industry, growing lettuce, broccoli, cauliflower, citrus, melons, hay, and cotton (the state claims to grow enough cotton each year to make a pair of jeans for every person in the United States). In recent years, wine grapes, and wineries, have become vital contributors to the state's economy, based on the tourism dollars they attract, and the revenue from sales of wines that are shipped directly to consumers in other states.

The Grand Canyon
Approximately 5 million people per year visit Grand Canyon National Park in northern Arizona. On a far smaller scale, yet in rapidly increasing numbers, the state's fifty wineries draw tourists and locals alike to their tasting rooms.

Arizona has three major growing regions, all in the high desert. Elevations of the vineyards planted in Sonoita/Elgin, Willcox, and Verde Valley range from 3,800 to 6,000 feet. Days are hot and arid, yet nighttimes are cool during the growing season, April through November. The porous soils require irrigation and drain quickly after the flash floods that are common, but vines were defenseless against a freak August 2010 hailstorm in Sonoita that stripped them of leaves and developing grape clusters; some vineyards were completed wiped out.

While the total output of the state's wine producers is not large (65,000 cases annually), the growth in the number of wineries has been explosive. In 2004, just ten bonded wineries existed in Arizona; today there are more than fifty, and vineyard plantings have increased to keep up with the demand for Arizona wines. Stars of screen and rock music—filmmaker Sam Pillsbury, and heavy metal rocker Maynard James Keenan—have been lured to Verde Valley north of Phoenix, where the two make some of Arizona's finest wines and draw attention to the industry.

Sonoita AVA

The Sonoita AVA, which includes the towns of Sonoita and Elgin, was established in 1985. It has been favorably compared to Paso Robles, California, for its recent success with Rhône Valley and Spanish grape varieties. The appellation sits at a 5,000-foot elevation and is surrounded by the Santa Rita, Whetstone, and Huachuca mountains. Thanks to the altitude, Sonoita is typically

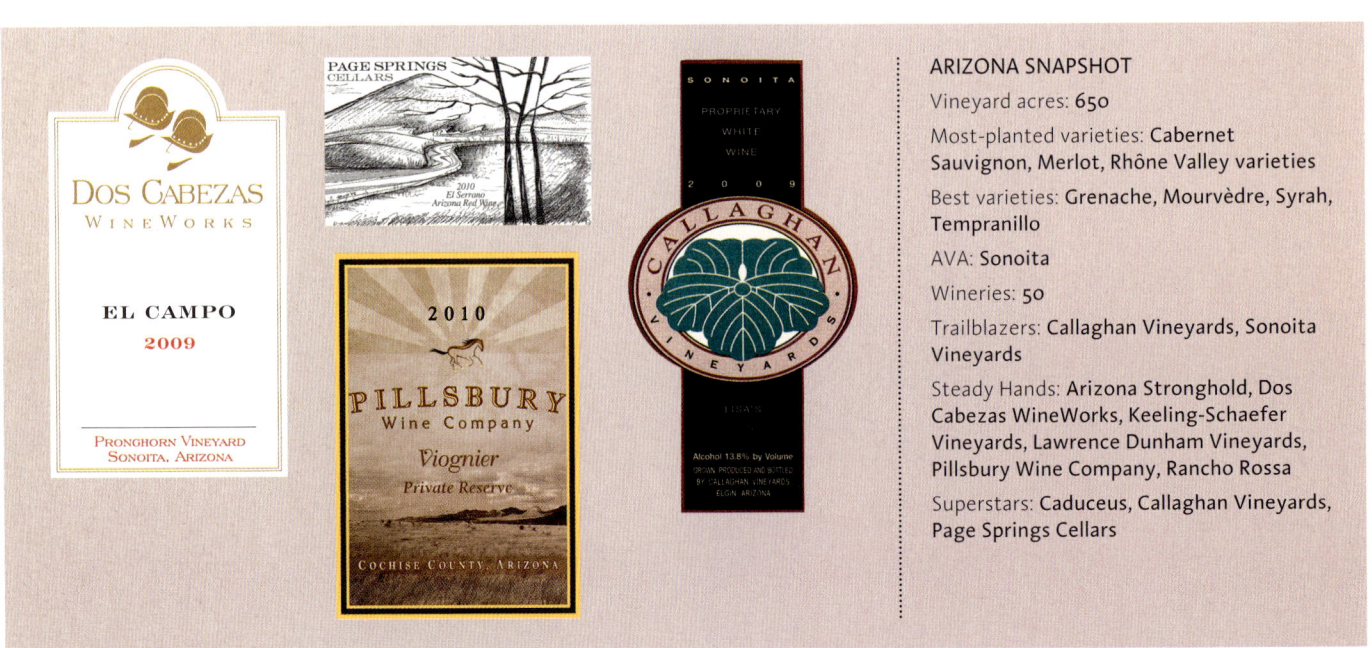

ARIZONA SNAPSHOT

Vineyard acres: **650**

Most-planted varieties: **Cabernet Sauvignon, Merlot, Rhône Valley varieties**

Best varieties: **Grenache, Mourvèdre, Syrah, Tempranillo**

AVA: **Sonoita**

Wineries: **50**

Trailblazers: **Callaghan Vineyards, Sonoita Vineyards**

Steady Hands: **Arizona Stronghold, Dos Cabezas WineWorks, Keeling-Schaefer Vineyards, Lawrence Dunham Vineyards, Pillsbury Wine Company, Rancho Rossa**

Superstars: **Caduceus, Callaghan Vineyards, Page Springs Cellars**

ARIZONA

The state's predominantly high-altitude vineyards and wineries are clustered in the Sonoita AVA and Cochise County in the southeast, and in central Yavapai County.

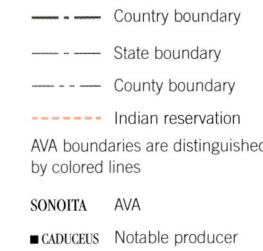

- —··— Country boundary
- —·— State boundary
- —··— County boundary
- ----- Indian reservation
- AVA boundaries are distinguished by colored lines

SONOITA AVA

■ CADUCEUS Notable producer

🔴 Cimarron Vineyards Noted vineyard

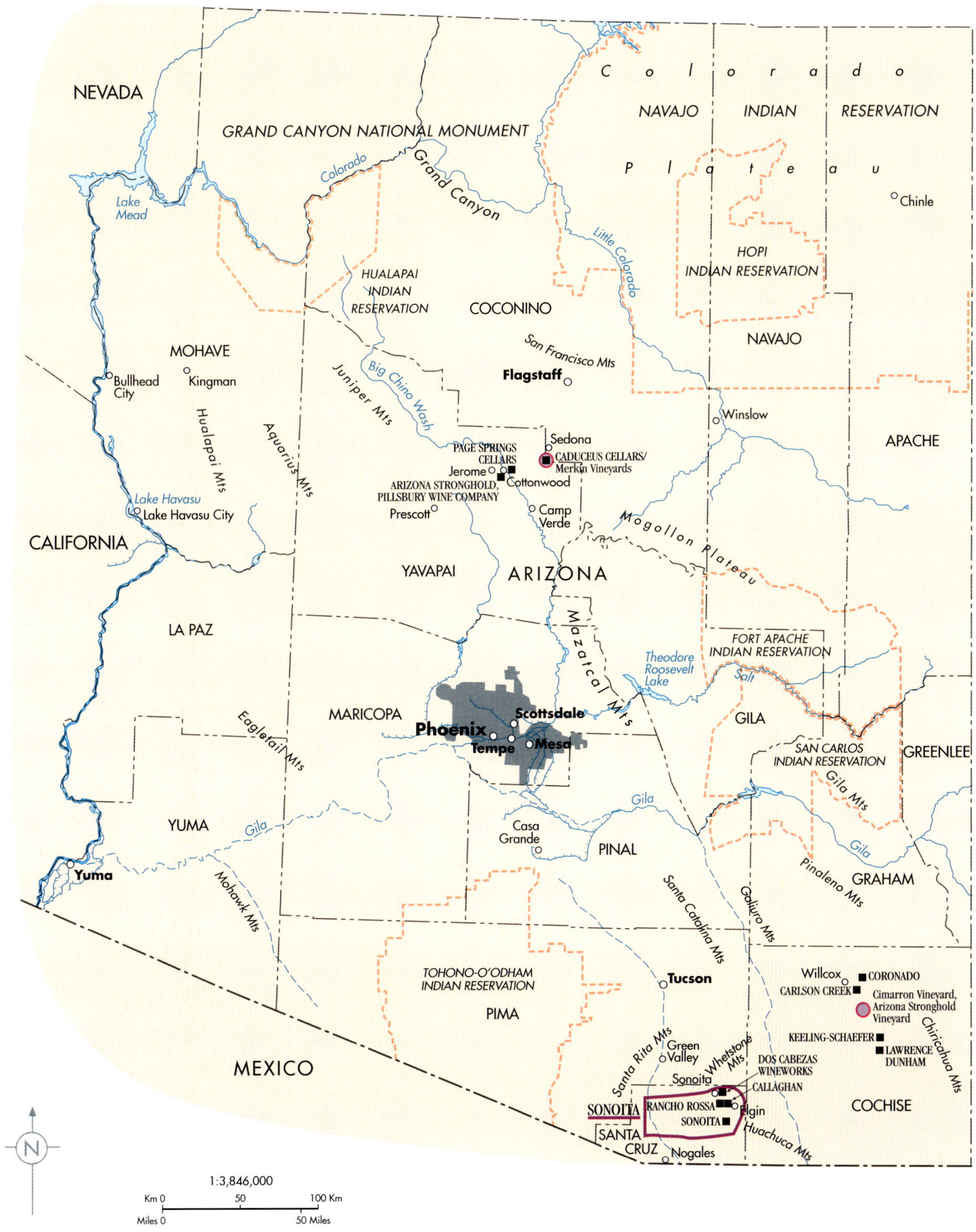

Sonoita Vineyards
Surrounded by mountains, Sonoita's vines are protected from frost and harsh winds; the dry desert conditions during the growing season make it nearly impossible for rot and mold to develop in the grape clusters.

15 to 20 degrees cooler than Tucson, but it is also vulnerable to spring frosts that can injure young shoots and buds.

Dr. Gordon Dutt, a now-retired soil scientist at the University of Arizona in Tucson, suspected that Sonoita's red, rocky soils would be conducive to growing wine grapes, but he worried that the intense summer heat would result in low acidity and pale color in the finished wines. He planted an experimental vineyard in 1973 and was delighted to find that the red wines had deep color and crisp acidity. "We're at an altitude of 5,000 feet, set in rolling grasslands dotted with white oak, and the soil is nearly identical to that of Burgundy, France," he says.

Dutt planted Arizona's first commercial vineyard in 1979 and opened the Sonoita Vineyards winery in Elgin in 1983. Today the winery grows and produces Sauvignon Blanc, Cabernet Sauvignon, Merlot, Mission, Sangiovese, and Syrah.

The winemaking efforts of Callaghan Vineyards in Elgin in the early 1990s drew the attention of U.S. wine critics and opened the door for other vintners. Kent Callaghan and his parents, Harold and Karen, planted their Buena Suerte ("good luck") Vineyard in 1990. Starting with Bordeaux grape varieties, they slowly converted the vineyard largely to Mediterranean grapes, among them Tempranillo, Monastrell, Mourvèdre, and Grenache. Callaghan also makes a Viognier-Riesling white blend called Lisa's and has high hopes for new plantings of Marsanne, Roussanne, Malvasia Bianca, and Grüner Veltliner.

Dos Cabezas WineWorks, founded in Willcox in 1995 by Al Buhl, is now owned by Todd Bostock and his family, of Sonoita (Callaghan was Dos Cabezas' first winemaker). The Bostocks relocated the winery to Sonoita in 2004, near their Pronghorn Vineyard, and sold the Willcox vineyard in 2007 to Arizona Stronghold Vineyards. In addition to using grapes from Pronghorn, Dos Cabezas WineWorks also purchases fruit from Dick Erath's Cimarron Vineyard in Cochise County (see below). Bostock's flagship wine is its El Campo Pronghorn Vineyard, a Mourvèdre-Tempranillo blend.

Callaghan and Dos Cabezas were among the wineries to suffer major vine damage in the 2010 hailstorm. With their crops decimated, they looked to Willcox vineyards for grapes. Some Arizona producers supplement their own grapes with California fruit on a regular basis.

Cochise County

If Sonoita Vineyards is the trailblazer, and Callaghan Vineyards sets the bar for quality, then Dick Erath is the authenticator. The decision by Erath, one of Oregon's Pinot Noir pioneers (he established Erath Vineyards in the Willamette Valley in 1968), to plant wine grapes in Cochise County's Willcox region instantly gave existing vintners validation that they had made the right decision to plant grapes in southern Arizona, and it gave others confidence to purchase land and join the wine game.

Erath, who for years had vacationed in Arizona during Oregon's rainy winters, sold Erath Vineyards to Ste. Michelle Wine Estates in 2005 and moved to southern Arizona. He couldn't resist putting vines on his property, and so established Cimarron Vineyards, planted to Tempranillo, Syrah, Mourvèdre, Sangiovese, Primitivo, and Viognier. No Pinot Noir—it ripens too early there to develop much flavor.

A good portion of Cimarron's grapes go to Dos Cabezas, along with other Arizona producers. Keeling-Schaefer Vineyards, Coronado Vineyards, and Lawrence Dunham Vineyards are also major Cochise County grower/producers. Carlson Creek Vineyard in Willcox is a newcomer to watch, with 2009 plantings the first in what will become an 80-acre estate.

Yavapai County

The Verde Valley in Yavapai County has long been a tourist destination, thanks to its close proximity to Sedona, which offers an eclectic menu of Red Rock Country trails for hiking and biking, ancient Native American dwellings, dramatic canyons, artist colonies, spas, and vortex meditation sites (areas of supposed heightened spiritual and metaphysical energy).

A relatively recent addition to the list is wine tasting and perhaps a sighting of the shaved-headed, tattooed rock-star-turned-vintner Maynard James Keenan. Sedona and the Old West–era towns of Cottonwood, Camp Verde, and Jerome have blossomed with vineyards and wineries in northern Arizona, south of Flagstaff. A study conducted by Northern Arizona University in Flagstaff showed that of the $23 million spent at Arizona wineries in 2010, $18 million were plunked down in Verde Valley.

Keenan, who fronts the bands Tool, Puscifer, and A Perfect Circle, left Los Angeles in 1995 to find a more peaceful life in Jerome. He called on Eric Glomski, former winemaker at David Bruce Winery in California's Santa Cruz Mountains and the most respected enologist in northern Arizona, to show him the ropes. Now they are partners in various projects, and the quality of their wines is exceptional. So are the Napa-like prices, but buyers line up to secure a precious bottle or two of Rhône-style wines with names such as Tazi, Nachise, and Dos Ladrones.

The 2010 film *Blood into Wine* documents Keenan's efforts to establish his Merkin Vineyards and Caduceus Cellars in Jerome, a ghost mine town, with Glomski as his winemaker/mentor. Glomski owns the respected Page Springs Cellars in nearby Cornville, and together they own Arizona Stronghold, a brand

Maynard James Keenan with Eric Glomski
Rock musician Keenan (left) recruited Page Springs Cellars owner Eric Glomski to be the winemaker for his Caduceus wines based in Yavapai County. They are also partners in the Arizona Stronghold brand.

that sources its grapes from the Dos Cabezas Vineyard in Cochise County, which Keenan and Glomski are replanting to mostly Rhône varieties.

Sam Pillsbury is another celebrity vintner in Verde Valley who produces his wines from Cochise County grapes. The New Zealand native responsible for such films as *Free Willy 3* and *The Quiet Earth* owns 40 acres of Syrah, Petite Sirah, Grenache, Mourvèdre, and Malvasia adjacent to Dick Erath's Cimarron Vineyards in Willcox, but his Pillsbury Wine Company is in Cottonwood, and Glomski produces his wines there. The most interesting are the Roan Red (Grenache, Syrah, and Mourvèdre) and Viognier.

New Mexico

In New Mexico, Native American, Hispanic, and Anglo cultures mix in a land of painted deserts, ancient cliff dwellings, and pueblo-style architecture. Some 30 million people visit New Mexico each year, lured by the scenery, Southwestern cuisine, Albuquerque's hot-air balloon festival, Santa Fe's art galleries, and the ongoing space-alien weirdness of Roswell, where in 1947, a flying saucer is alleged to have crashed, with the story hushed up by the U.S. military. Grapevines have a long history here, dating to the seventeenth century, but only recently have wineries become part of the visitor experience.

Santa Fe, New Mexico
Touches of the Native Indian Pueblo architecture of Santa Fe—adobe brick walls, flat roofs, and pine-log beams—are found in many of New Mexico's wineries, juxtaposed against more contemporary designs.

In 1629, Father Gracia de Zuniga, a Franciscan, and Antonio de Arteaga, a Capuchin monk, planted grapevines in the Rio Grande Valley, south of what is now Socorro, New Mexico. They used cuttings from Spain, some 130 years before Father Junipero Serra began establishing California's first vineyards. By the 1880s, the New Mexico Territory had become wine country, with 3,000 acres of grapevines. Prohibition put a stop to wine production, and Rio Grande River flooding damaged or wiped out countless vineyards on multiple occasions.

Only in the late 1970s did the New Mexico wine industry really reemerge, thanks in large part to Europeans who took advantage of the inexpensive land prices in the state. Wine-savvy investors, including the Gruets from France, the Lescombes (with roots in Algeria), and Paolo and Sylvia D'Andrea from Italy, were among those who found their way to New Mexico and began producing wine.

Most vineyards are clustered in the southeast corner of the state, near Ruidoso and Roswell, and in south-central New Mexico, near Las Cruces, Deming, and Silver City. The hot (100-plus degrees), dry summers might seem ill-suited to cultivation of quality wine grapes, but the altitude—ranging from 3,800 to 6,000 feet—delivers tempering nighttime temperatures that are 30 to 40 degrees cooler than in the daytime. Vines are refreshed by this chill-down, and the growing season is lengthened, so that grapes ripen at a steady pace rather than turning to raisins in what would otherwise be a blast furnace.

Numerous varieties are successfully grown in New Mexico. French vinifera varieties including Chardonnay, Sauvignon Blanc, Merlot, Cabernet Sauvignon, and Syrah are planted adjacent to Mediterranean grapes such as Sangiovese and Tempranillo. Trials conducted by New Mexico State University show positive early results with Aglianico, Montepulciano, and Malbec.

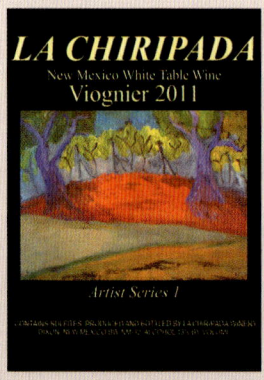
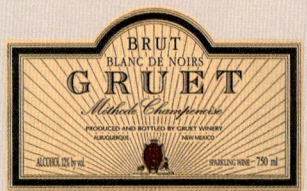

NEW MEXICO SNAPSHOT

Vineyard acres: 1,200

Most-planted varieties: Chardonnay, Sauvignon Blanc, Cabernet Sauvignon, Merlot, Pinot Noir

Best varieties: Gewürztraminer, Riesling, Syrah, Tempranillo, Zinfandel; Chardonnay, Pinot Noir (for sparkling wine)

AVAs: Mesilla Valley (shared with Texas), Middle Rio Grande Valley, Mimbres Valley

Wineries: 42

Trailblazers: La Chiripada, La Vina Winery

Steady hands: Amaro Winery, Casa Rondeña Winery, Guadalupe Vineyards, La Chiripada, Luna Rossa Winery, Milagro Vineyards & Winery, Tierra Encantada Winery, Vivac Winery

Superstars: Gruet Winery, St. Clair Winery/Southwest Wines

Outside New Mexico, the state's winemaking reputation rests heavily on the sloping shoulders of the bottles of Gruet Winery's sparkling wines. Its Brut, Blanc de Noirs, and Brut Rosé are made with traditional Champagne methods but sell for a fraction of the cost, typically retailing for $20 or less. At the higher end, the Gilbert Gruet Grand Reserve and Brut Sauvage Blanc de Blancs are world-class.

Laurent Gruet and his sister, Nathalie, moved to New Mexico when their father, Gilbert Gruet of Gruet et Fils in Champagne, planted an experimental vineyard in Lordsburg in 1983. Finding the area too warm for the Chardonnay and Pinot Noir grapes they had planned to use in their sparkling wines, the Gruets planted a new vineyard near Truth or Consequences, 170 miles from Albuquerque, and they now farm 350 acres of grapes grown at 4,300-feet elevation.

La Chiripada Winery & Vineyard is, with La Vina Winery in La Union, the oldest producer in New Mexico. Founded by the Johnson family in 1977, La Chiripada ("stroke of luck") is snuggled in the Embudo Valley, approximately 40 miles north of Santa Fe. Viognier, Shiraz, and dessert wines are its strong suits.

The **Mesilla Valley AVA** in eastern New Mexico includes a small portion of Texas, near El Paso. Of the AVA's total 280,000 acres, a mere 100 or so are planted to wine grapes. The town of Dona Ana is the heart of the appellation, which is hot and arid during the growing season, with only 10 inches of annual rainfall. Drip irrigation is essential.

The 637,000-acre **Mimbres Valley AVA** is named for the Mimbres River, which millennia ago cut a swath through this southwestern area of New Mexico. West of the Mesilla Valley and just 35 miles from the Mexico border, Mimbres is warmer and drier than Mesilla, with an average of 9 inches of rain a year.

Within the Mimbres Valley AVA is St. Clair Winery, the state's largest facility, with the capability to produce 200,000 cases of wine a year. Its own-brand volume is around 65,000 cases; the winery is also used by other winemakers who don't have their own facilities. Under an umbrella business called Southwest Wines, St. Clair produces several brands, including St. Clair, Blue Teal, and the top-tier DH Lescombes.

The winery is in Deming; its prime vineyard is 47 miles west, in Lordsburg, where it grows Cabernet Sauvignon, Chardonnay, Sauvignon Blanc, Zinfandel, and other varieties. The Rieslings, Gewürztraminers, and Cabernet Francs can be exceptional.

The narrow, elongated **Middle Rio Grande AVA** follows the Rio Grande River as it flows through central New Mexico. Several wineries are located within the AVA, including those near Albuquerque, yet there are few vineyards here. It's rare to find a wine labeled "Middle Rio Grande AVA"; the state appellation "New Mexico" is far more common for any of the state's wines.

Guadalupe Vineyards
The San Fidel vineyard, west of Albuquerque, includes three original vines remaining from the cultivation of wine grapes by Franciscan fathers in the 1600s.

Texas

Everything is big in Texas: ranches, longhorn cattle, steaks, football, egos. Texans are proud and determined—including when it comes to grape growing and winemaking. They have been knocked down time and again by vine diseases, destructive pests, and a climate that can bring drought, hail, high winds, and spring frosts. Yet vintners have remained in the saddle and made Texas the sixth-largest wine-producing state. The winery count has grown from 46 in 2001 to 220; the Texas swagger is justified, and most say that the state's best wines have yet to be made.

The heart of Texas
Rodeos, livestock shows, and barbecue are at the center of Texas culture; winemaking and wine drinking are finding their place too.

In the seventeenth century, before Spanish *padres* constructed missions in California and grew wine grapes, Franciscan fathers planted Criolla (Mission) grapes in Texas, along the banks of the Rio Grande near El Paso. European immigrants arriving in Texas in the mid-nineteenth century began making wine, and Italian Frank Qualia was one of them.

Qualia came to in Texas in 1882, and in 1883 he began producing wine from Black Spanish grapes in Del Rio, southeast of El Paso. His Val Verde (green valley) Winery continued as the state's only commercial winery through Prohibition, producing sacramental and medicinal wines. After Repeal, Frank's son, Louis, took over, and now Louis's son, Thomas, runs Val Verde. Black Spanish (also known as Lenoir or Jacquez) is the only grape grown in the vineyard, and it's used for port-style wines; other varietals are made from purchased grapes.

The nineteenth-century invasion of European vineyards by phylloxera spurred Denison, Texas, horticulturist Thomas V. Munson to action. Munson found that grafting *Vitis vinifera* onto native American rootstock resulted in vines that were resistant to phylloxera. He shipped dormant stem cuttings from Texas to France, and they became the breeding stock for the rootstocks that saved the entire European wine

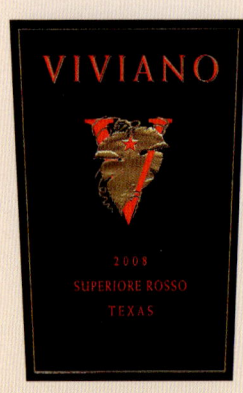

TEXAS SNAPSHOT

Vineyard acres: **4,000**

Most-planted varieties: **Chardonnay, Viognier, Cabernet Sauvignon, Merlot, Tempranillo**

Best varieties: **Black Spanish/Lenoir, Blanc du Bois, Muscat, Sangiovese, Tempranillo, Viognier**

AVAs: **Bell Mountain, Escondido Valley, Fredericksburg in the Texas Hill Country, Mesilla Valley (shared with New Mexico), Texas Davis Mountain, Texas High Plains, Texas Hill Country, Texoma**

Wineries: **220**

Trailblazers: **Llano Estacado Winery, Messina Hof Winery and Resort, Val Verde Winery**

Steady hands: **Alamosa Wine Cellars, Brennan Vineyards, Calais Winery, Flat Creek Estate, Haak Vineyards & Winery, Lost Oak Winery, McPherson Cellars, Messina Hof Winery and Resort, Pedernales Cellars, Spicewood Vineyards, Stone House Vineyard, Texas Hills Vineyards**

Superstars: **Becker Vineyards, Duchman Family Winery, Fall Creek Vineyards, Inwood Estates Vineyards, Llano Estacado Winery**

One to watch: **Fairhaven Vineyards**

Texas

Vineyards and wineries are located throughout the state. The greatest concentration of vineyards are in West Texas, while most wineries are located in Texas Hill Country (see p. 207).

industry. France awarded Munson its Chevalier du Mérite Agricole title for his efforts.

Texas viticulture today is vexed by Pierce's disease, caused by a bacterium that lives in the water-conducting system of plants (the xylem) and is spread from plant to plant by sharpshooter insects that feed on the xylem. Pierce's disease has been controlled to some extent with insecticides, the introduction of predator insects that feast on sharpshooters, and cultivation of varieties resistant to the bugs, such as Blanc du Bois, Norton (Cynthiana), and Black Spanish, but the disease has destroyed many acres of vines, and several Texas vineyards have been replanted since the 1990s because of it.

There are eight AVAs in Texas, with four reigning supreme: Texas Hill Country in central Texas (with two sub-AVAs, Fredericksburg and Bell Mountain), and the Texas High Plains in the west. Wineries also exist in areas without AVA status, including the Gulf Coast region in southeastern Texas and in the northeast, in and around Dallas.

Tourism and wine trails are vital to Texas's wine business and overall economy. In vintages where grapevines suffer yield losses because of damage from hail, thunderstorms, and frosts, some wineries purchase grapes or juice from other states in order to have bottles to sell and to stay in business. However, if Texans had their way, every grape would be grown in the Lone Star State.

Texas Hill Country AVA

This AVA encompasses 15,000 square miles west and northwest of Austin and San Antonio, respectively—Texas-style big. It includes the Fredericksburg sub-AVA and claims more than sixty wine producers but has just 300 acres of vineyards, since many of the state's wineries rely on grapes purchased from the High Plains AVA in West Texas, near Lubbock.

Former cattle rancher Ed Auler and his wife, Susan, own Fall Creek Vineyards near Lake Buchanan and are the architects of the Texas Hill Country AVA. Since planting grapevines beginning in 1975, the Aulers have been leaders in the efforts to improve Texas grape and wine quality and to build retailer and restaurant markets for Texas wines.

A 1991 freeze destroyed most of their vines, and they replanted, but by 2001 Pierce's disease had infected those vines, so the Aulers, like many vintners in the state, began sourcing grapes from other vineyards to hedge their bets. Fall Creek's top wine is Meritus, a Bordeaux-style red blend. The winery is also expert at producing Chardonnay, Chenin Blanc, Viognier, Cabernet Sauvignon, Shiraz, and Tempranillo from estate grapes and others grown in the Salt Lick Vineyard in Hill Country and in the Texas High Plains AVA.

One of the Aulers' growers is Alphonse Dotson, a former defensive lineman for the Oakland Raiders. He began planting grapes on his family's property northwest of Austin in 1997. Although Dotson, a huge man with an even bigger smile, had no previous grape-growing experience, he and his wife, Martha, through trial and error and lots of study, found success at their Certenberg Vineyard in Voca. They sell their Chardonnay, Merlot, and Cabernet Sauvignon fruit and keep their Muscat Canelli grapes for their Certenberg Vineyards Gotas d'Oro ("drops of gold") late-harvest wine.

In **Fredericksburg**, San Antonio endocrinologist Richard Becker and his wife, Bunny, found the log cabin they were searching for to use as a second home; it just happened to come with 180 acres of land. They purchased it without any interest in wine-growing but in 1992, they began planting vinifera where native Mustang grapes were once grown by German settlers. Today the vineyard totals 46 acres and is planted to fourteen varieties. Becker Vineyards also purchases grapes from the High Plains.

R. L. WINTERS AND TEXAS HERITAGE VINES

In East Texas, R. L. Winters grows Chardonnay, Cabernet Sauvignon, and Merlot grapes and ferments them into wine. He happily pours tastes of these wines in his Fairhaven Vineyards tasting room in Hawkins. Yet Winters is most passionate about Texas heritage varieties, which he says could save the state's wine industry if drought conditions such as those endured in 2011 continue.

In 2004, Winters began cultivating Lomanto, Nitodal, and other exotic varieties propagated from T. V. Munson hybrids developed in the late 1800s. Munson bred an estimated three hundred varieties suited for wine production in the southern United States, and several are cultivated in the Thomas Volney Munson Memorial Vineyard on the campus of Grayson County College in Denison.

Winters is intent on establishing the most productive of these grape varieties in his 11-acre vineyard in the Sabine River Valley, and he believes that Lomanto, Nitodal, Extra, Delicatessa, and other Munson breeds can thrive, and make good wines, in drought conditions. He also hopes to convince other Texans to plant these cultivars, as they hold promise for surviving at a time when supplies of irrigation water are dwindling and becoming increasingly expensive.

Texas Hill Country

The vast majority of Texas wineries and tasting rooms are located in the Texas Hill Country AVA, west of Austin.

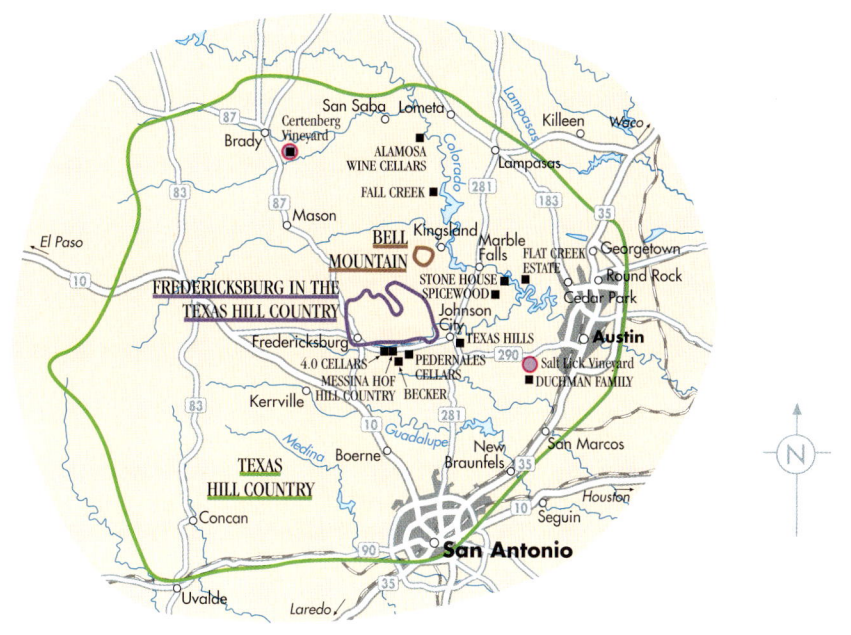

AVA boundaries are distinguished by colored lines

BELL MOUNTAIN AVA

■ FALL CREEK Notable producer
⊙ Salt Lick Vineyard Noted vineyard

Becker is one of Texas's elite brands. All the wines are expertly made, they cover a wide spectrum of prices, and production has grown to nearly 50,000 cases per year, allowing for wide distribution. The Reserve Cabernet Sauvignons are among the state's finest red wines; Prairie Rotie is a medium-bodied, crisp blend of Rhône varieties.

Flat Creek Estate, located east of Marble Falls, is as gorgeous as a Texas wine estate gets, with 20 acres of vine-carpeted rolling hills and another 60 acres that explode with wildflowers in spring. Owners Rick and Madelyn Naber began planting Shiraz, Sangiovese, Tempranillo, Muscat Canelli, Pinot Grigio, Pinot Blanc, and several Portuguese varieties in 2000. The standout wines include Syrah and a seven-variety Sangiovese-based red blend called "Super Texan"—a play on the Italian Super Tuscan category.

One of Texas's most exciting producers is Duchman Family Winery in Driftwood, 30 miles southwest of Austin. Houston doctors Lisa and Stan Duchman purchase Italian grape varieties grown in the Texas High Plains AVA and turn them into new tastes for Texas: red Aglianico, Dolcetto, Montepulciano, and Sangiovese varietals, and whites from Pinot Grigio, Trebbiano, and Vermentino. Duchman (formerly Mandola Estate Winery) also grows Viognier grapes, whose relatively short growing season makes them much better-suited to the West Texas heat than, say, Cabernet Sauvignon.

Angela Moench and her husband, Howard, of Stone House Vineyard in Spicewood, have taken an altogether different path. Angela grew up in Australia's Barossa Valley, and as the daughter of a diplomat, she was introduced to fine wines and gourmet meals at a young age. When the Moenches were living in Houston, they purchased property overlooking Lake Travis near Spicewood. After consulting with experts, they planted the native red grape Norton (Cynthiana)—far more common in Missouri and Virginia—for its resistance to disease and its late bud break, which allows the vines to dodge late-spring freezes. Their Claros Norton is a dry wine, with a superb balance of richness and Norton's high acidity. Scheming Beagle is a port-style Norton.

Wine tourism is big business in Hill Country, and the city of Fredericksburg, settled by German immigrants in the 1850s, is Grand Central Terminal for wine lovers. There are more than twenty wineries and/or tasting rooms on or just off state Highway 290 near Fredericksburg, and 250 inns and guest houses to accommodate tasters. The 70-mile drive from Austin to Fredericksburg makes it easy for visitors to take in the Technicolor wildflower fields, visit the Lyndon B. Johnson National Historical Park in nearby Stonewall, wine, dine, and get a taste of Germany in cowboy country.

With many Texas wineries located off the beaten path, a growing number are setting up shop in Fredericksburg, to grab their share of tourism dollars. In 2011, Messina Hof Winery and Resort in southeast Texas opened a second location, Messina Hof Hill Country, in Fredericksburg. Mendelbaum Cellars is a new tasting room that features wines from Inwood Estates Vineyards in Dallas. 4.0 Cellars, a tasting room/winery collaboration between McPherson Cellars in Lubbock, Lost Oak Winery in Burleson, and Brennan Vineyards in Comanche, opened in April 2012.

4.0 Cellars
Off-the-beaten-path producers Brennan Vineyards, Lost Oak Winery, and McPherson Cellars collaborated on this winery/tasting room near Fredericksburg in 2012, in the Highway 290 tourism corridor.

Texas High Plains AVA

This 12,000-square-mile area covers much of the central and western Texas Panhandle, with Lubbock as the anchor city. Decidedly more important for grape growing (3,500 acres of wine grapes) than winemaking (just eight producers), the High Plains is a supplier of grapes for wineries throughout Texas.

As the name indicates, this AVA lies within the High Plains subregion of the vast Great Plains. The AVA name is apt, as the land is flat as a pancake, with very little vegetation other than agricultural crops, and with elevations of 3,000 to 4,000 feet. Grapevines grow alongside plots of peanuts, cotton, alfalfa, and sorghum, in red sand and clay soils layered over a bed of calcareous caliche, offering excellent drainage. The growing season is semi-arid, with hot summer days and chilly nights. Humidity is quite low and, thus, so is the incidence of mildew and mold on grapes. Yearly rainfall averages a modest 20 inches, and winds of up to 40 miles per hour quickly dry clusters that might happen to get wet.

But High Plains growers must contend with late-spring frosts that can kill the new season's buds, hailstorms that knock developing fruit off the vines, and the occasional tornado that wreaks havoc with more than just grapevines.

To diversify his crops, Neal Newsom converted 100 acres of the family farm in Plains to wine grapes in 1986. He began with Cabernet Sauvignon and then added Tempranillo, Cabernet Franc, Malbec, Sangiovese, and Albariño, among other varieties, to Newsom Vineyards. Dr. Vijay Reddy of Reddy Vineyards farms twenty varieties near Brownfield, including Monastrell, Montepulciano, Aglianico, Tannat, and Cinsault.

Clint and Betty Bingham own the largest vineyard in the AVA, Bingham Family Vineyards in Meadow, with 135 acres, though it is just a small part of their 2,100-acre organic farm (they have eleven children to assist with chores). They started with Viognier and Gewürztraminer, then planted Albariño, Roussanne, Semillon, and Vermentino for white wine production and Cabernet Franc, Cabernet Sauvignon, Dolcetto, Merlot, Monastrell, and Tempranillo for their reds.

Bingham, Newsom, and Reddy are Texas's premier growers and sell their grapes to wineries throughout the state. These farmers have benefited from the advice of Bobby Cox, a consulting viticulturist who planted one of the first commercial vineyards in Texas in 1972 and is the former owner of Pheasant Ridge Winery, near Lubbock.

Fellow pioneers Clinton "Doc" McPherson and Robert Reed began planting experimental varieties in the early 1970s near Lubbock, and they cofounded Llano Estacado Winery there in 1975. Llano's first commercial vinifera vineyard was planted in 1978, and the winery now produces 170,000 cases of wine per year. It is Texas's largest fine-wine producer—only Ste. Genevieve Winery in Fort Stockton bottles more, nearly all of it cheap and cheerful wines sold mostly in grocery stores.

Thanks to the shrewd management of Walter M. Haimann, a former president of Seagram Distillers Company, Llano Estacado gained broad distribution of its wines in Texas and eventually expanded to Europe. The Texas High Plains earned AVA status in 1993, the same year that Haimann hired California winemaker Greg Bruni as vice president and winemaker. The following year, Mark Hyman became VP of sales and marketing, and today, the two manage Llano Estacado.

Bruni, trained at UC Davis, brought much-needed technical skills to Texas. His wines have won numerous awards while competing against California bottles, and they have been served to U.S. presidents and the Queen of England. Most of the grapes are purchased from vineyards in the High Plains and the Chihuahua desert east of El Paso. Bruni's Viviano Superiore Rosso is the flagship wine, a blend of Cabernet Sauvignon and Sangiovese, with a splash or two of other red varieties. A Reserve Tempranillo and unoaked Chardonnay are excellent too.

In 2000, Kim McPherson, son of Clint McPherson, founded McPherson Cellars in Lubbock, after working in California and at his father's Llano Estacado. Established in a former Coca-Cola bottling plant in the Depot District of Lubbock, McPherson Cellars excels at Rhône- and Italian-variety wines made from grapes grown in the High Plains, including Viognier, Roussanne, Sangiovese, and a lovely Syrah rosé.

Southeast Texas

Although it lacks an AVA, Texas's southeast winegrowing region, which extends from Bryan south through Houston, then along the Gulf Coast, has three dozen wineries and a reputation for growing varieties that both can withstand warm temperatures twenty-four hours a day and high humidity and are somewhat resistant to Pierce's disease. Blanc du Bois, a white-wine Muscadine hybrid developed at the University of Florida, and the red-wine Black Spanish grape (also called Lenoir or Jacquez) meet the requirements, and experienced hands can transform these obscure and sometimes scorned grapes into fascinating wines.

If there were a "King of Blanc du Bois," Raymond Haak would wear the crown. At Haak Vineyards & Winery in Galveston County, he produces five styles of Blanc du Bois: dry, semisweet, sweet, reserve, and port-style. The wines share a vibrant quality, with pear, apple, and citrus notes, and sometimes a hint of honeysuckle. Haak also produces a delicious Tempranillo from Reddy Vineyards in the High Plains, as well as fortified dessert wines made in the image of Madeira from the Jacquez grape.

Messina Hof Winery and Resort in Bryan gets its name from Paul and Merrill Bonarrigo's familial roots; his family is from Messina, Sicily; hers from Hof, Germany. The couple began planting their vineyard in 1977 and produced their first commercial wines six years later. The property includes a bed-and-breakfast and a restaurant.

The estate is planted entirely to Lenoir/Black Spanish grapes, which are used in their Papa Paolo port. The Bonarrigos also own vineyards in other parts of the state, including the Texas High Plains AVA, to supply grapes for their 100,000-case annual wine production. The stars include a Private Reserve Cabernet Franc and Paulo Meritage, a Merlot–Cabernet Sauvignon–Petit Verdot blend.

Northern Texas

There are dozens of wineries near Dallas and Fort Worth, in the northeastern section of Texas, and most purchase their grapes from elsewhere in the state. One producer in particular stands out.

Dan Gatlin of Inwood Estates Vineyards is among Texas's most eclectic winemakers. A former retailer—his family owned the Hasty chain of liquor and convenience stores—Gatlin planted five experimental vineyards and cultivated dozens of varieties before determining that Tempranillo and Palomino were most suitable for the terroir. His Cornelious Tempranillo is silky and seductive, in a Pinot Noir style; his Tempranillo–Cabernet Sauvignon blends are robust and structured.

Palomino is the real surprise; while the grape is grown in southern Spain for the production of sherry, it is rare in the United States, and Gatlin deftly blends it with Chardonnay for a lush, honeyed wine.

Brennan Vineyards
The vineyards and winery are located in Comanche, near the junction of the Texas Hill Country and Texas High Plains regions; Viognier and Syrah are the standout wines.

Oklahoma

A territory that would become a state in 1907, Oklahoma was home to Native American tribes including the Cherokee, Choctaw, Chickasaw, and Seminole. A large number of Native Americans continue to reside in Oklahoma, although the state's nickname, the Sooner State, refers to the white settlers who claimed land in the late 1880s, before the U.S. government formalized the opening of the territory to settlement. Oil drilling later made some Oklahoma farmers wealthy, but the Dust Bowl drought of the 1930s and the ongoing threat of tornadoes have limited Oklahoma's agricultural opportunities. Still, makers of wine in Oklahoma remain steadfast in their efforts.

Land of the Great Plains
The state mammal is the American buffalo, or bison, which once grazed the Great Plains by the millions and was a source of food and clothing for Native American tribes. Now buffaloes are found mostly in state parks and reserves.

Oklahoma had just four licensed wineries in 2001, the first among them Cimarron Cellars, established in 1983. Now there are sixty, signaling a significant boom.

In 1908, Oklahoma had an estimated 5,400 acres of grapes and a winemaking culture. However, the Anti-Saloon League and the Woman's Christian Temperance Union campaigned so effectively against alcohol consumption that in 1917, Oklahoma passed a "bone-dry" law, allowing only hospitals, pharmacists, universities, and scientific institutions to use alcohol. The law was overturned the following year, but national Prohibition soon followed, and Oklahoma legislators chose to extend the state ban on alcohol to 1959, twenty-five years after most of the country had begun began drinking legally again.

It was not until the 1980s that Oklahomans got serious about winegrowing again. They've had their challenges: cold, snowy winters; spring freezes; hot, sometimes muggy summers; and vintages like 2011, when many farmers lost most or all of their grapes. Below-zero temperatures in February, 100°F heat in June, and a summer of drought that taxed even the most generous of irrigation systems left the vines, already weakened by the winter freeze, incapable of ripening grapes. Many vintners purchased juice or bulk wine from California to keep their tasting rooms in business.

In typical years, approximately one third of the state's wineries use Oklahoma grapes. The ratio of 80 percent vinifera (Chardonnay, Cabernet Sauvignon, etc.) to 20 percent French-

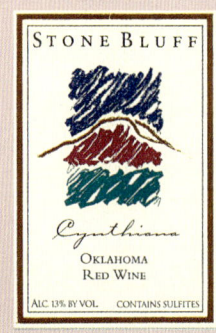

OKLAHOMA SNAPSHOT

Vineyard acres: **800**

Most-planted varieties: **Cabernet Sauvignon, Merlot, Syrah, Riesling**

Best varieties: **Norton/Cynthiana, Syrah, Vidal, Vignoles, Viognier**

AVA: **Ozark Mountain (shared with Arkansas and Missouri)**

Wineries: **60**

Trailblazer: **Cimarron Cellars**

Steady hands: **Chapel Creek Winery, StableRidge Vineyards, Stone Bluff Cellars, Tidal School Vineyards & Winery, Woodland Park Vineyards**

Chapel Creek Winery
Redlands Community College's Chapel Creek Winery in El Reno is a training site for budding winemakers, who produce commercially available wines as part of their education.

American hybrids (Chardonel, Chambourcin, etc.) is likely to change in the aftermath of 2011, because hybrid grapes are far more hardy in cold climates, less thirsty in drought conditions, and remarkably disease-resistant.

Winemaker Annetta Neal and her husband, Don, own StableRidge Vineyards in Lincoln County, on the famous Route 66, which links Chicago and Los Angeles. They are among those who produce wines only from Oklahoma grapes. And they sell their bottlings—Viognier is their best—in a former 1902 Catholic church they've turned into a tasting room.

Tidal School Vineyards & Winery in Creek County is a magnet for those keen to see the historic building constructed during the 1920s oil boom by John D. Rockefeller as a school for the children of his oil workers. Later acquired by another oil baron, J. Paul Getty, the school and site has been transformed into a winery and vineyards and attracts tourists who get their kicks driving Route 66.

The agriculture and research campus of Redlands Community College in Canadian County is where students learn how to become grapegrowers and winemakers. Budding vintners from the college's Chapel Creek Winery have won gold medals at the Oklahoma State Fair for their Norton and Meritage-style red wines.

Oklahoma has no AVA of its own, though its northeastern region shares the **Ozark Mountain AVA** with parts of Arkansas and Missouri. At 3.52 million acres, Ozark Mountain is so large that it gives few clues to consumers who purchase wines labeled with this AVA. The majority of wines made from Oklahoma-grown grapes display the state appellation on their labels.

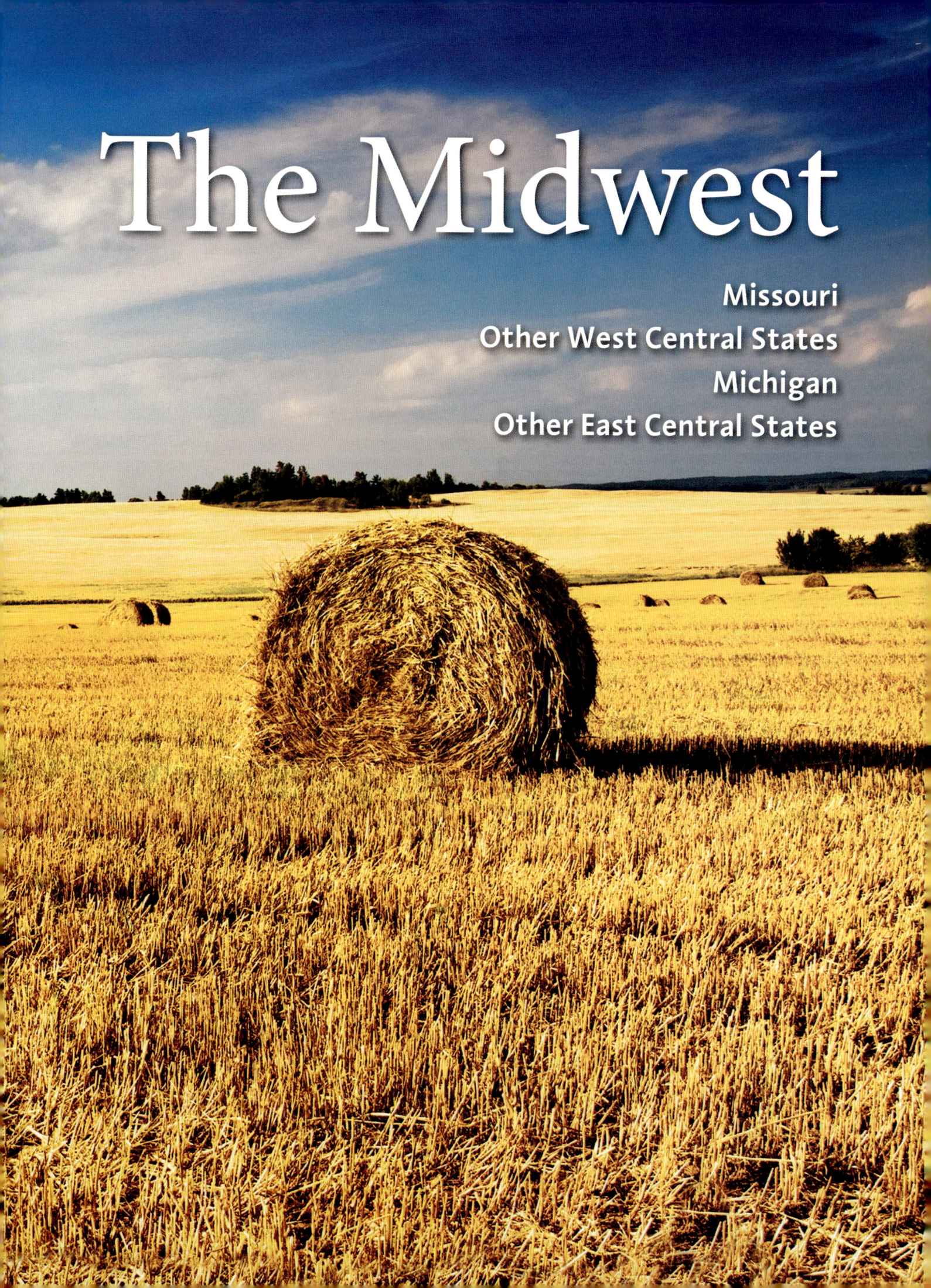
The Midwest

Missouri
Other West Central States
Michigan
Other East Central States

Missouri

"Don't like the weather? Just wait a few minutes and it'll change!"—that's what Missouri vintners say. Icy winters delivered by Canadian Clipper winds; hot, humid summers; spring and summer hurricanes; and day-to-day climatic changes pretty much exclude traditional *Vitis vinifera* grapes such as Chardonnay and Cabernet Sauvignon, which require consistent weather conditions and a long growing season. But the Show Me State produces quality white and red wines, primarily in its southern half, from native and hybrid grape varieties that are far less fussy about where they grow.

Gateway Arch
St. Louis' iconic arch commemorates Thomas Jefferson's nineteenth-century westward expansion of the United States, which also led to the growth of America's wine industry.

The most-planted grape in Missouri is Norton—also known as Cynthiana—and it's an American original, native to the United States and the official state grape. Chardonel, a hybrid crossing of Chardonnay and Seyval Blanc, is second in vine acreage and produces an easy-drinking, if somewhat simple, white wine. The native Concord and the French-American hybrid Vignoles are widely planted, and Chambourcin, a red grape developed in the Loire Valley of France in the late 1950s, is a dependable ripener in Missouri, producing a firmly structured, slightly herbaceous wine with red-cherry notes.

Some of the most compelling Missouri wines, however, are those being made from relatively new hybrid varieties developed at New York's Cornell University. Valvin Muscat, which ferments into a fruity, floral white wine, has become a darling of U.S. wine competition judges. Traminette, a fragrant and spicy white wine reminiscent of one of its parents, Gewürztraminer (the other is Joannes Seyve 23.416), gives Missouri wine buyers an exotic alternative to Chardonel and Seyval Blanc.

The all-things-to-all-people white grape, however, is Vignoles, a French-American hybrid that is wonderfully versatile, capable of producing dry, off-dry, and sweet wines that please a broad range of palates. Stone Hill Winery in Hermann bottles as many as seven different Vignoles wines from one vintage. Its semi-sweet version flies out of the tasting room, assisted, no doubt, by the dazzle of its cobalt-blue bottle.

Yet no Missouri wine grape trumps Norton for star power. Around 1820, Daniel Norton, a Richmond, Virginia, physician, discovered and then began to promote for wine production

MISSOURI SNAPSHOT
Vineyard acreage: **1,600**
Most-planted varieties: **Norton/Cynthiana, Chardonel, Concord, Vignoles**
Best varieties: **Chambourcin, Chardonel, Norton/Cynthiana, Vignoles, Valvin Muscat**
AVAs: **Augusta, Hermann, Ozark Highlands, Ozark Mountain**
Wineries: **114**
Trailblazers: **Mount Pleasant Winery, Stone Hill Winery**
Steady hands: **Adam Puchta Winery, Baltimore Bend Vineyard, Blumenhof Vineyards & Winery, Heinrichshaus Vineyards & Winery, Hermannhof Winery, Jowler Creek Vineyard & Winery, Les Bourgeois Vineyards, Montelle Winery, Mount Pleasant Winery, St. James Winery, Stonehaus Farms Winery**
Superstars: **Augusta Winery, Stone Hill Winery**
One to watch: **Amigoni Urban Winery**

Southern Missouri

Missouri's wine-producing areas are located west and southwest of St. Louis, in the Augusta, Hermann, and Ozark Highlands AVAs. The 3.5-million-acre Ozark Mountain AVA in southern Missouri also includes portions of Arkansas and Oklahoma.

Elmer Swenson
Known as the father of cold-climate viticulture in America, Elmer Swenson crossed French hybrid grapes with native species to create dozens of varieties that could survive harsh winter conditions and produce quality wines. Swenson released the Brianna, La Crosse, St. Croix, St. Pepin, Edelweiss, and other American hybrids, and worked with the University of Minnesota.

a hybrid variety whose ancestry includes *Vitis aestivalis* and *Vitis vinifera* that came to be known as the Norton grape. It made its way to Missouri, acquiring the name Cynthiana along the way, with its vigor and resistance to disease making it ideal for the conditions there.

Norton/Cynthiana usually displays a purple color and aromas and flavors including plum, wild berry, mint, and herbs; chocolate and coffee notes come from oak-barrel aging. Coddling is called for in the vineyard so that when the grapes are harvested, they are balanced in their natural acidity, tannin structure, and fruitiness. The wines benefit from three to four years of bottle age.

It's not hard to comprehend why Norton/Cynthiana is the go-to red grape in Missouri. It suffers few ill effects from -20°F winters, and it is nearly immune to the fungal rot and mold that can destroy other varieties in the moist, warm summers. In 1993, *Gourmet* magazine wine columnist Gerald Asher wrote that Norton is "an indigenous grape that might yet do for Missouri what Cabernet Sauvignon has done for California." Asher was spot-on that Norton would become the state's signature red grape; however, few consumers outside of Missouri and Virginia have ever tasted Norton, because production volumes are small and distribution is limited.

In 2005, there were 50 wineries in Missouri; now there are 114—spectacular growth, indeed, for such a short span of time. But winemaking is not new to Mizzou, and grapes have been cultivated here since the 1850s. In 1900, Missouri was the country's second-largest wine-producing state, behind only California. Then the First World War, Prohibition, and the Great Depression caused farmers to plant other crops, and winemaking came to a near stop. Since the repeal of Prohibition in 1933, Missouri has slowly crawled its way back, and now produces more than a million gallons of wine annually.

The five largest producers—St. James Winery, Stone Hill Winery, Les Bourgeois Vineyards, Crown Valley Winery, and Mount Pleasant Winery—account for some 80 percent of the wine made in Missouri, according to the Missouri Wine and Grape Board. However, the typical winery bottles fewer than five thousand cases per year and sells nearly all its wine in its tasting room.

Missouri has four AVAs, including Augusta, the first federally recognized winegrowing region in the country. The others are Hermann, Ozark Highlands, and Ozark Mountain. Lush, emerald-green vines carpet the rolling hills of Missouri wine country in spring and summer, and many wineries offer vast views of the Missouri River. As summer turns to fall, the explosion of red, orange, and yellow autumn foliage is simply spectacular.

Augusta AVA

On June 20, 1980, Augusta was approved by the Bureau of Alcohol, Tobacco, and Firearms (now the Alcohol and Tobacco Tax and Trade Bureau) as the first American Viticultural Area, eight months before Napa Valley in California became the second.

Located 40 miles west of St. Louis, in the east-central part of the state, the Augusta AVA covers 15 square miles. Over centuries, the winding Missouri River formed alluvial plains of silty loam and clay soils. German settlers discovered in the 1800s that these soils and the temperature-moderating influence of the river were assets for growing wine grapes.

Two such immigrants, brothers George and Frederick Muench, established Mount Pleasant Winery in 1859 in the town of Augusta. They built the cellars in 1881, using wood and limestone from the area, and are said to have shipped their wines throughout the world. Mount Pleasant closed at the start of Prohibition and its equipment was destroyed and vineyards burned to the ground, possibly by government officials. The property began its second life in 1966, when Lucian and Eva Dressel purchased it and brought winemaking back to the old winery.

It changed hands again, but stayed in the family, in 1992, when Chuck Dressel's family purchased Mount Pleasant from his uncle, Lucian. It is the oldest winery in the AVA, with fifteen grape varieties grown on approximately 80 acres. A second tasting room was opened in Branson in 2008, and the Augusta location was renamed Mount Pleasant Estates in 2009. Its Vidal Blanc and Vignoles are consistently good, but the winery is best known for its white, tawny, and vintage port–style wines.

Down the road from Mount Pleasant is Augusta Winery, an unassuming, stone-fronted building founded by Tony Kooyumjian in 1988. Seemingly everything Kooyumjian touches turns to gold medals: Chambourcin, Chardonel, Norton, Seyval Blanc, Traminette, Vidal Blanc, and Vignoles. He is arguably Missouri's most gifted winemaker, coaxing consistently excellent wines from the grapes no matter what the weather gods deliver each vintage.

Kooyumjian purchased Montelle Winery, also in Augusta, from Clayton Byers in 1998, and now works his magic on that brand too. Interestingly, he produces Norton for Augusta Winery, and Cynthiana for Montelle; two names, same grape.

Blumenhof Vineyards & Winery in Dutzow has made a splash with wines made from Valvin Muscat; its Norton/Cynthiana is cleverly named Original Cyn.

Hermann AVA

Like Augusta, the Hermann AVA was first populated by Germans, many of whom had relocated from Philadelphia. The town of Hermann, built on the banks of the Missouri River to resemble a German town in the Rhine Valley, had sixty wineries in operation in the late nineteenth century.

Now, more than one hundred buildings in Hermann are on the National Register of Historic Places. Many a visitor comes for the heritage tours, Oktoberfest, and schnitzel and leaves with a few bottles of wine after unanticipated stops at tasting rooms. Stone Hill Winery, opened in 1847, is the second-largest winery in the state and a magnet for visitors, with its nineteenth-century brick buildings, underground cellars, three tasting rooms, and a restaurant. Its history books tell of it once being the number-two wine producer in the nation and winner of eight gold medals at World Fairs in Vienna and Philadelphia in the 1870s.

The wines produced today by the Held family, which reopened Stone Hill decades after Prohibition, in 1965, range from competent to outstanding; rarely is there a disappointment. Vignoles is Stone Hill's greatest success, in dry to late-harvest styles and everything in between. Two hybrid blends, Steinberg White and Steinberg Red, are extremely popular and fine values, and Stone Hill also bottles two Nortons, including the rare vineyard-designated version, from the Cross J Vineyard.

Some Midwest tasting rooms sell own-label wines made from California grapes. Hermannhof Winery is owned by Californians. The Dierberg family, owner of the Dierberg and Star Lane wine brands in Santa Barbara County, has been a staunch supporter

AMIGONI FAMILY VINEYARDS

At Amigoni Family Vineyards in Centerview, 30 miles east of Kansas City, Michael and Kerry Amigoni are committed to growing members of the traditional European vine family *Vitis vinifera*. Their winegrowing peers fear the Amigonis are living *la vida loca* ("the crazy life").

Michael and Kerry grow Chardonnay, Viognier, Cabernet Sauvignon, Cabernet Franc, and Petit Verdot on 4.5 acres of their 10-acre farm. Despite warnings from others that persnickety vinifera vines cannot tolerate Missouri's harsh winters and moist summers, the Amigonis have already experienced some success with vines planted in 2000.

The Amigoni Estate Cabernet Franc won a Medal of Excellence at the 2011 Jefferson Cup competition, and its Petit Verdot shows promise, particularly as a blending grape. The wines are sold at Amigoni Urban Winery in the West Bottoms district of Kansas City, previously home to the Kansas City stockyards. West Bottoms is an emerging arts and design hub, where "bottoms up" is the theme in the Amigoni tasting room.

Stone Hill Winery
A growing number of Missouri wineries, including Stone Hill in Hermann, harvest their vineyards in the cool of the night so that the grapes arrive at the winery fresh and in pristine condition.

of Missouri wine since 1974, when it purchased Hermannhof and began restoring the 1850s brick structures and ten stone cellars, which were initially built for the brewing of beer. Today Hermannhof produces 15,000 cases of wine a year, and its Tin Mill Brewery is not far away. Tasting room visitors can sample the California wines in addition to the local products.

Ozark Mountain AVA

Six years after the Augusta AVA was formalized in 1980, the U.S. government approved the massive Ozark Mountain AVA, the sixth largest in the United States. The 3.5-million-acre appellation includes parts of southern Missouri, northwestern Arkansas, and northeast Oklahoma and is virtually useless in terms of defining climate and soil characteristics. The Augusta, Hermann, and Ozark Highlands AVAs are all within the Ozark Mountain AVA.

The Missouri portion is centered in Branson, a magnet for lovers of American country music, with concert halls that feature performances by the likes of Dolly Parton, Mel Tillis, the Oak Ridge Boys, and Johnny Mathis. It was a natural for wineries to open tasting rooms nearby, taking advantage of thirsty concert-goers and tourists who flock to Branson. Stone Hill and Mount Pleasant wineries in Hermann and Augusta, respectively, have tasting rooms in Branson.

A handful of wineries in southeastern Missouri, approximately 60 miles from St. Louis, market themselves as being on the "Route du Vin" (State Route WW), which is included in the Ozark Mountain AVA. Cave Vineyard, Chaumette Vineyards, Sainte Genevieve Vineyard, and Twin Oaks Vineyard and Winery are all here, but Crown Valley Winery near the town of Ste. Genevieve draws most of the attention.

Joe Scott began constructing Crown Valley Winery in 2000, modeling the 44,000-square-foot facility after wineries he'd seen in Napa Valley. The first grapes were crushed in 2002, and the winery now bottles 80,000 cases of wine per year—huge for Missouri (although some of the grapes come from out of state). Scott and his family have grown their Crown Valley business to include restaurants, a brewery/distillery, lodgings, a golf club, and—why not?—a tiger sanctuary. Napa Valley does not have tigers.

Ozark Highlands AVA

Ten wineries are located here, and their combined annual production pales in comparison to the 200,000 cases of wine St. James Winery makes each year in the city of St. James.

The AVA encompasses 1.2 million acres in south-central Missouri, and St. James Winery is its locus. Unlike many of the wineries in Augusta and Hermann, St. James is not a resurrection of a pre-Prohibition winery, but rather a startup, by Jim and Pat Hofherr in 1970. Still owned by the Hofherr family, St. James has become the largest Missouri wine producer, and it offers a vast range of hybrid-, native-, and fruit-based wines in dry, semisweet, and sweet versions. The fruit wines are as skillfully made as the higher-end Chambourcins and Vignoles; St. James hedges its bets by producing both a Norton and a Cynthiana.

Other West Central States

Although this region covers a large area, four traits tie vintners together in Iowa, Kansas, Nebraska, and Minnesota: numbingly cold (as low as -25°F) winters and chilly springs; reliance on French-American and U.S. hybrids, and the native Norton, which typically survive such conditions; energetic growers and winemakers who are willing to take risks; and the presence of some remarkable wines that bode well for the future of these emerging winemaking states. Although some vintners continue to bring in juice, an increasing number are looking locally for their grapes.

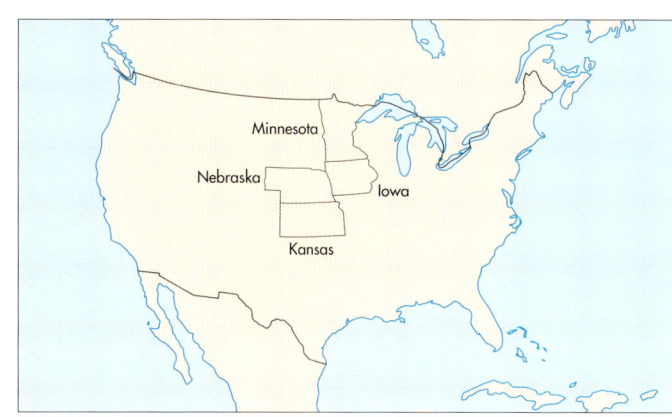

Kansas

Twenty-four wineries are scattered about Kansas, one of those "who knew?" states in relation to winemaking. Farmers were actually quite active in growing wine grapes in the nineteenth century, yet they had a formidable neighbor in hatchet-wielding teetotaler Carrie Nation, leader of the Temperance Movement. Kansas legislated statewide prohibition in 1881, nearly four decades before national Prohibition.

However, many of the vineyards remained intact and well tended, with Kansas growers selling their crops to professional winemakers in neighboring Missouri, as well as to Kansas's enological equivalents of Tennessee bootleggers, until Prohibition took hold in 1920. Kansas's wine industry, like so many others in the country, died. The Kansas Farm Winery Statute, passed in 1985 by the state legislature, opened the door again to commercial winemaking.

Native and hybrid grapes are the lifeblood of Kansas growers: Chardonel, Melody, Seyval, and Vignoles for white wines; Norton/Cynthiana, Chambourcin, and St. Vincent for reds.

Among the most accomplished producers are Les and Michelle Meyer of Holy-Field Vineyard & Winery in Basehor, west of Kansas City. Their Valvin Muscat, Vignoles, Seyval

OTHER WEST CENTRAL STATES SNAPSHOT

Vineyard acreage: IOWA 1,200; KANSAS 350; MINNESOTA 1,500; NEBRASKA 400

Most-planted varieties: Marquette, Frontenac, La Crescent, Chardonel, Chambourcin, Frontenac Gris, Brianna

Best varieties: hybrid—Brianna, Chambourcin, Chardonel, Frontenac, Frontenac Gris, La Crescent, Marquette, St. Croix; native—Catawba, Concord, Norton/Cynthiana

AVA: MINNESOTA—Alexandria Lakes; none in Iowa, Kansas, or Nebraska

Wineries: IOWA 94; KANSAS 14; MINNESOTA 40; NEBRASKA 30

Trailblazers: KANSAS—Smoky Hill Vineyard & Winery; MINNESOTA—Alexis Bailly Vineyard; NEBRASKA—Cuthills Vineyards

Steady hands: IOWA—Cedar Ridge Vineyards, Jasper Winery, Summerset Winery; KANSAS—Holy-Field Vineyard & Winery, Stone Pillar Vineyard; MINNESOTA—Carlos Creek Vineyards, Saint Croix Vineyards, Winehaven Winery and Vineyard; NEBRASKA—Cuthills Vineyards, James Arthur Vineyards, Mac's Creek Winery & Vineyards

Blanc, and Chambourcin bottlings are as good as any in the Midwest, and they bear the Kansas appellation on their labels, meaning the winery purchases few, if any, out-of-state grapes.

Smoky Hill Vineyard & Winery, in the center of the state, was the first winery to open after the Kansas Farm Winery Statute, in 1991. Its production is large enough to supply two tasting rooms, in West Wichita and Wilson, in addition to its home base in North Salina. Wyldwood Cellars—with five sales locations—is Kansas's largest producer, specializing in fruit wines; elderberry is its biggest seller and comes in regular and Reserve styles.

Iowa

There is a Midwestern answer to the rhetorical question of why the chicken crossed the road: To prove to the possum that it could be done. As is the case in Kansas and Nebraska, Iowa winemakers are constantly crossing roads, to show that they too can produce competent wines.

In a state far more widely known as the center of the Corn Belt, the wine industry has grown from 100 acres of grapes and fourteen producers at the turn of the millennium, to more than 1,200 acres and ninety-four wineries in 2012.

Although grapevines are planted throughout Iowa, more acreage is cultivated in the southern half of the state—particularly in Warren County, south of Des Moines—as it typically enjoys slightly warmer temperatures and can support a variety of hybrid and native varieties. In the north, temperatures can drop into the -30s, so it is imperative that cultivars be cold-hardy—and that growers be somewhat lucky in particularly difficult vintages.

Iowans are so serious about grape growing and winemaking that Iowa State University in Ames, and the Iowa Wine Growers Association have embarked on an extensive project, growing and evaluating hybrid varieties at four research stations. The purpose is to identify those grapes that produce high-quality, high-flavor, chemically balanced wines and can also tolerate Iowa's nasty winters.

Some of the newer hybrids developed at the University of Minnesota—Brianna and Marquette for example—have only recently been available to growers (since 2002 and 2006, respectively), so there are no baselines for how they perform in specific terroirs over a period of time, or for the style of wines they will produce.

Thus far, the research team, under the banner of the Midwest Grape and Wine Industry Institute, has reported that varieties that produce aromatic white wines and sparkling wines—Brianna, Frontenac Gris, La Crescent, LaCrosse, and St. Pepin—show promise in Iowa. However, they can be high in both pH and acidity, a precarious imbalance. Methods are being investigated to keep pH and natural acidity in equilibrium, including de-acidification of the wines, and using various yeast strains to produce balanced, palate-pleasing wines.

For red grapes, hybrids grown in Iowa tend to be low in tannins when they're ripe, leaving the wines flaccid and with the likelihood of short life spans. Therefore, stabilizing tannins is another goal of the Iowa project; Frontenac, Marquette, Marechal Foch, St. Croix, and Swenson Red have shown early, positive results.

Wine quality from Iowa is a mixed bag, as one would expect from any emerging Midwest wine region, yet some wineries excel at specific wines. Cedar Ridge Vineyards, located between Cedar Rapids and Iowa City, makes a succulent La Crescent white wine and a light-bodied, semisweet Edelweiss. Jasper Winery in Des Moines has a fondness for Norton, a native variety more common to Missouri and Virginia, and it is experimenting with Noiret, a peppery hybrid developed by Cornell University in New York State.

Summerset Winery in Indianola has a dry Frontenac that does exceedingly well in Midwest wine competitions; its Caba Moch "sangria-style" red table wine is effortless to drink and extremely popular.

Like most Midwest-made wines, the majority of Iowa's bottles are sold to its residents and visitors, with very little of it seeping into other states. There simply isn't enough product for

Saint Croix Vineyards
Temperatures can fall to -30°F in Minnesota vineyards such as these. Grape varieties specially bred at the University of Minnesota to withstand harsh winters, such as Frontenac, Frontenac Gris, Marquette, and other hybrid grapes, are now widely planted in the state.

vintners to seek out new sales opportunities—which is good news for Iowans devoted to drinking locally.

Minnesota

The number of licensed wineries has grown in Minnesota from seven in 1995 to forty today, assisted in large part by the 2007 passage of the state legislature's farm winery law, which allows wineries to operate a restaurant on their premises. Food and wine go hand in hand, and winery visitors who have the option to taste wines with food have an advantage over those who can only swirl, sniff, sip, and spit. Wine makes food taste better, and vice versa.

Grapes bred at the University of Minnesota, including Frontenac, Frontenac Gris, La Crescent, and Marquette—crosses of European varieties with native grapes—can survive temperatures as low as -30°F (not uncommon in snowbound Minnesota) and they also ripen in the state's short summers and resist vine disease. French-American hybrids such as Marechal Foch and Seyval, widely cultivated in other chilly climes, have proved to be only marginally immune to the Minnesota climate.

Alexis Bailly Vineyard in Hastings became the North Star State's first winery in 1978. That same year, the University of Minnesota and Elmer Swenson, the godfather of Minnesota and Wisconsin cold-hardy wine grapes, collaborated to release the Swenson Red and Edelweiss varieties for commercial use, and the state continued to help fund the university's grape research through the early 2000s.

Grape breeder Peter Hemstad was on board in 1996, when the university released Frontenac, now the most popular grapevine in Minnesota and capable of producing blush, red table, late-harvest, and port-style wines. In 2002, La Crescent became available, a white grape variety that can ferment into a wine similar to high-acid Riesling, and in 2006, Marquette made its entrance, a red variety with rounded yet firm tannins.

Saint Croix Vineyards' recent Frontenacs and Marquettes have been gloriously silky and refined, with juicy red-cherry aromas and flavors. Winehaven Winery achieves similar results with its Marquette Reserve.

Despite the explosion of wineries and vineyards, there is just one Minnesota-dedicated AVA, **Alexandria Lakes** near Alexandria in Douglas County. Carlos Creek Vineyards, a large (for Minnesota) producer of myriad wine styles, was the successful petitioner for the AVA and appears to be the lone winery to use it on its labels.

The 2009 establishment of the massive **Upper Mississippi River Valley AVA**, which includes portions of Minnesota, Wisconsin, Iowa, and Illinois, has had little impact on grape sourcing and wine labeling in Minnesota, as the vast majority of vintners use the state appellation on their wines.

Alexis Bailly Vineyard
David Bailly planted this Hastings, Minnesota, vineyard to French-American varieties Léon Millot and Marechal Foch in 1973, and he opened the state's first commercial winery in 1978. His daughter, Nan Bailly, is now the winemaker, and she also works with American hybrid grapes.

Nebraska

Nebraska's wine industry is so young that its oldest commercial winery, Cuthills Vineyards in the northeast section of the state, was founded in 1994; that's yesterday compared to wineries in Europe, and a month ago to California's. There is such rapid growth in the young Nebraska wine industry that it is difficult to say anything definitive except that hybrid grapes are king; the cream hasn't had time to rise to the top; and wines produced one year will likely be significantly better the next, based on experience alone.

Ed and Holly Swanson founded Cuthills Vineyards in 1994, after planting wine grapes beginning in 1985. They converted a 1920s dairy barn in the heart of their seven-acre vineyard, in Pierce County, into a winery and tasting room. The Swansons are committed to producing wines only from Nebraska grapes—no West Coast fruit to muddle the message—and they have an eclectic mix of hybrid and native varieties, including deChaunac, Temparia, LaCrosse, Loralei, Brianna, Petite Amie, and Concord.

Other standout Nebraska wineries include Soaring Wings Vineyard in Springfield, for a sturdy Sunset Red Frontenac and a semisweet Winter White, made from the LaCrosse grape; Superior Estates Winery, for its Traminette; James Arthur Vineyards for its sweet and semisweet versions of Edelweiss; and Mac's Creek Winery & Vineyards, for Brianna and Edelweiss.

With a mere 400 or so acres of wine grapes planted in Nebraska, it's too early to know the state's enological future.

Michigan

Michigan has a longer wine-growing history than most states. In the late 1600s, French explorers made wine from wild grapes growing along what is now the Detroit River. In 1701, at the first permanent French settlement, Fort Ponchartrain, settlers also made wines from these native varieties, and by the mid-1800s, a viable industry was established in Monroe County. Following Prohibition, the industry rebounded quickly and several new wineries opened in the southwest part of the state, where Concord grapes had long been grown for the Welch's Grape Juice Company.

Grand Traverse Bay
Summer and winter, Lake Michigan and the Grand Traverse Bay moderate the climate of the Leelanau and Old Mission Peninsulas, where vineyards produce exceptional Riesling, Gewürztraminer, and Pinot Gris grapes.

Leelanau and Old Mission Peninsulas

The Leelanau Peninsula and Old Mission Peninsula AVAs in northwestern Michigan and the Fennville and Lake Michigan Shore AVAs farther south dominate the state's wine production.

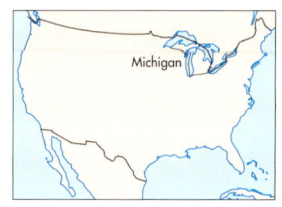

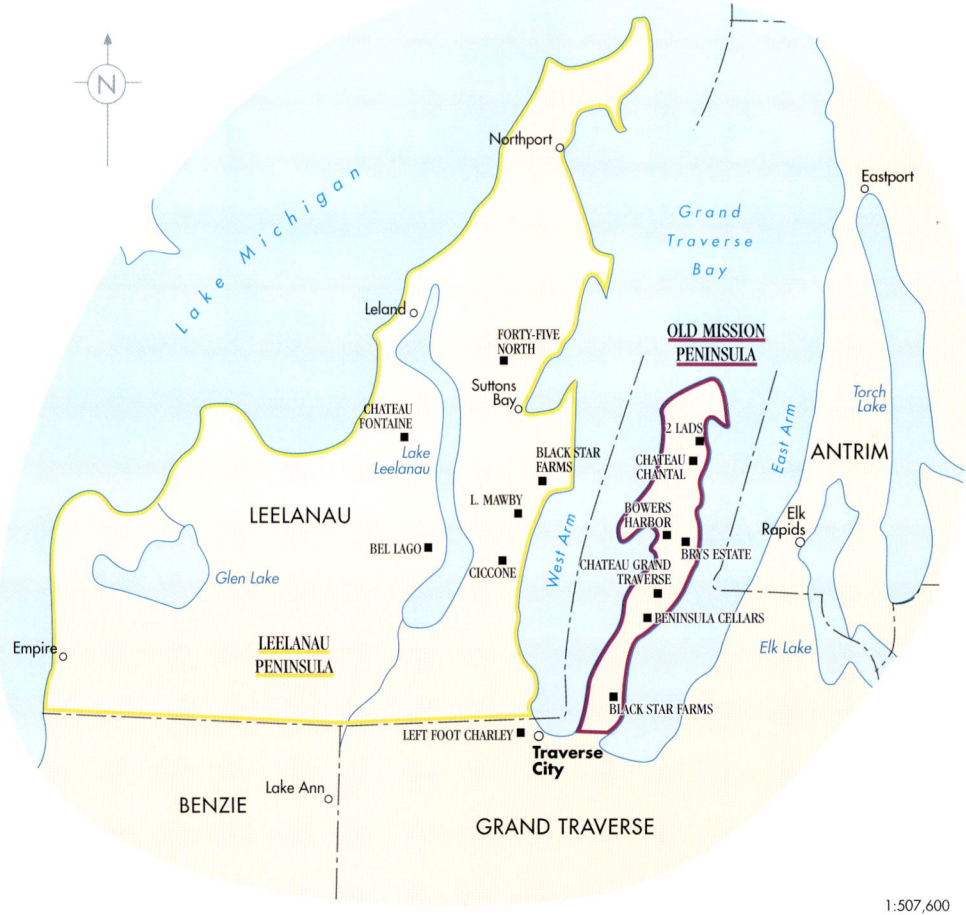

However, other easier-to-grow crops—cherries, peaches, apricots, plums, blueberries, and apples for cider—became more profitable and the number of wineries had dwindled to two by 1970: St. Julian Winery and Warner Vineyards.

A cursory look at the vineyard acreage in Michigan—14,600—might suggest the state is a major wine producer, but 12,600 of those acres are planted to Concord and Niagara grapes used for juice, jams, and jellies. The 2,000 acres of wine grapes may not seem particularly extensive, but the wines produced from them can be very impressive, particularly Alsace and German varietals and sparkling wines. Small yet potentially mighty, Michigan is one of the most vibrant emerging wine regions in America.

Wine-grape acreage has increased more than 60 percent since 2001, with vinifera comprising 60 percent of the total wine-grape plantings. French-American hybrids, including Chambourcin, Marechal Foch, Traminette, Vidal, and Vignoles, make up 35 percent of the vineyard acreage, with native grapes Concord, Niagara, and Catawba at just 5 percent.

Michigan vintners are reliant on varieties that can survive winters as frigid as -35°F and also ripen early in the short, hot summers. Just as in Germany and France's Alsace region, Riesling, Gewürztraminer, Pinot Gris, and Pinot Blanc are the top-tier varieties in Michigan. Its best reds are Cabernet Francs and Cabernet Franc–Merlot blends, which are spicy, elegant, and crisp, rather than rich and voluminous. Pinot Noir is the most-planted vinifera red, although coaxing it into polished wines is a work in progress. The grape is susceptible to bunch rot, and fall rains often compromise wine quality. Yet in warm, dry vintages, Michigan Pinot Noir can be perfectly respectable.

Increasing production of Michigan-grown grapes (thus reducing reliance on California and Washington fruit in difficult vintages) is a mission of Michigan State University's horticulture department. It planted fifty vinifera and hybrid varieties particularly suitable for cool climates at research stations in 2008, and in 2011 began producing experimental wines from them to determine which have solid commercial potential. Albariño, Brianna, Fiano, Grüner Veltliner, Rkatsiteli, and Tocai (Friulano) are among the white grapes being trialed; reds include Dolcetto, Dornfelder, La Crescent, and Lagrein.

Michigan's economy, so heavily reliant on automobile manufacturing, has suffered mightily for more than a decade, but the growth in wineries has been a bright light in the gloom, with seventeen of its eighty-six licensed producers opening since 2010. Wine production in 2011 was a million gallons, and in that year the contribution of the wine industry to the state was $300 million.

Although vineyards and wineries are located throughout the state, the most suitable areas for grapegrowing are within 25 miles of the shores of Lake Michigan. The climate is favorable to aromatic, high-acid white wines; medium-bodied, crisp reds; and sparkling wines. The lake effect, which also protects vines in New York's Finger Lakes region, moderates temperatures in both summer and winter. Breezes from Lake Michigan protect plants from frost in the spring and temper summer days that can be hot and humid. Winter snows blanket the vines, insulating them from freeze injury.

In years when the climate conditions are just right, Michiganders can produce luscious ice wines, made from grapes that are left on the vines until they freeze. The frozen berries, which have intensely concentrated sugars, are pressed and their precious drops of juice fermented into richly sweet yet nervy dessert wines. Riesling and Vidal are good candidates for ice wine, thanks to their high levels of natural acidity, which counterbalance the sweetness, although ice wines can also be produced from red varieties.

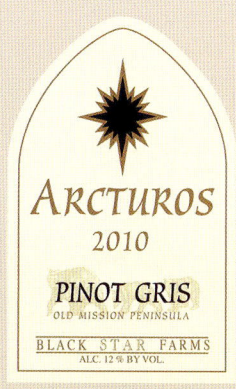

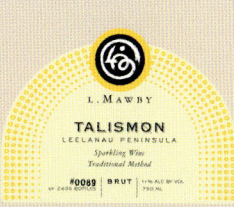
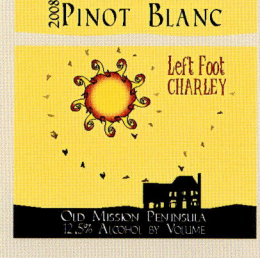

MICHIGAN SNAPSHOT

Vineyard acreage: **3,000**

Most-planted varieties: **Riesling, Pinot Noir, Gewürztraminer, Cabernet Franc, Chardonnay**

Best varieties: **vinifera—Cabernet Franc, Gewürztraminer, Pinot Gris, Riesling; hybrids—Chambourcin, Frontenac, Marquette, Traminette, Vidal, Vignoles**

AVAs: **Fennville, Lake Michigan Shore, Leelanau Peninsula, Old Mission Peninsula**

Wineries: **86**

Trailblazers: **L. Mawby Vineyards, St. Julian Winery, Tabor Hill Winery, Warner Vineyards**

Steady hands: **Bel Lago Vineyard and Winery, Bowers Harbor Vineyards, Brys Estate, Chateau Chantal, Chateau Fontaine, Ciccone Vineyard, Domaine Berrien, Fenn Valley Vineyards, Forty-Five North Vineyard & Winery, Left Foot Charley, Peninsula Cellars, Tabor Hill Winery, 2 Lads Winery**

Superstars: **Black Star Farms, Chateau Grand Traverse, L. Mawby Vineyards**

Chateau Grand Traverse
Although this Old Mission Peninsula winery is best known for its Rieslings, it also harvests and vinifies several other varieties, including Chardonnay, Gewürztraminer, Grüner Veltliner, Gamay Noir, Pinot Noir, Cabernet Franc, and Merlot.

The state's four AVAs are near the eastern shore of Lake Michigan, in two major growing regions. The Northwest region, which grows 51 percent of the state's wine grapes, includes the Old Mission Peninsula and Leelanau Peninsula AVAs; the Southwest region's AVAs, Lake Michigan Shore and Fennville, cultivate 45 percent of Michigan's grapes.

Despite the moderating influence of Lake Michigan, vintners can face stiff challenges. In 2009, the summer was cooler than usual, making it difficult to get full ripeness in their red grapes. In 2010, quality was excellent, but yields were down as much as 40 percent after May frosts damaged developing buds.

Old Mission Peninsula AVA

Old Mission Peninsula is an 18-mile-long finger pointing into the Grand Traverse Bay of Lake Michigan. The anchor, Traverse City, has evolved into a great food and wine town, in addition to the beach-oriented tourist draw it's always been for folks from Detroit and Chicago. Where there is great wine, great food will follow. The scenery along highway M-37, from Traverse City north to the tip of the peninsula, of vineyards hugging the coastlines of the East and West Traverse bays, with their aquamarine waters, is a feast for the eyes spring through fall.

White varieties are perfect for the peninsula, as they tend to ripen earlier than red grapes, which can run out of sunshine and warmth before they reach full maturity. Riesling, Pinot Gris, Gewürztraminer, and other cold-hardy grapes do well in the distinctly continental climate.

Chateau Grand Traverse is the oldest and largest of Old Mission Peninsula's seven wineries, founded in 1974 by Ed O'Keefe and dedicated to vinifera wines. Now overseen by O'Keefe's sons, Eddie and Sean, its small-lot batches raise the quality and complexity bar for all of Michigan. Grand Traverse's Lot 49 Riesling is first-rate, its new Laika Grüner Veltliner very promising, and its Dry Riesling a steely steal.

Black Star Farms has two wineries, a newer one on Old Mission Peninsula devoted to white wines, and the original on Leelanau Peninsula (see below). Of its OMP wines, the Arcturos Pinot Gris is remarkably flavorful, with admirable palate weight; the Arcturos Riesling is medium-dry and juicy.

Eileen and Walter Brys opened Brys Estate Vineyard & Winery in 2004. Relying on estate-grown grapes, they produce several varietals, among them Riesling, Pinot Noir, Merlot, and Cabernet Franc. The spicy Gewürztraminer and fruity Naked Chardonnay are among their best offerings.

Chateau Chantal offers visitors gorgeous views of East and West Grand Traverse bays, and a Proprietor's Reserve Pinot Gris with pleasing citrus and white peach fruit. Stuart Stegenga and his family run Bowers Harbor Vineyards, after converting their farm to wine grapes in the early 1990s. The Block II Riesling has great verve; Langley is a tasty blend of Merlot, Cabernet Franc, and Cabernet Sauvignon.

Pinot Blanc and Manigold Vineyard Gewürztraminer are foundation wines for Peninsula Cellars, owned by the Kroupa family since 1991. 2 Lads Winery has had great success with Cabernet Franc and Merlot. The lads, Cornel Olivier and Chris Baldyga, built a modern glass, metal, and concrete winery that presents a stark contrast to the region's horse barns and old schoolhouses.

After earning acclaim as winemaker at Peninsula Cellars, Bryan Ulbrich left in 2007 to focus on his own brand, Left Foot Charley. The winery is in Traverse City, in a former state mental hospital building, and while Left Foot Charley is outside the Old Mission Peninsula AVA, Ulbrich purchases OMP grapes for his Rieslings, Gewürztraminers, Pinot Gris, and the exceptional Island View Vineyard Pinot Blanc.

Leelanau Peninsula AVA

Established in 1982, the Leelanau Peninsula AVA encompasses 75,000 acres in Leelanau County. It is one peninsula west of Old Mission and enjoys the moderating lake effect of Grand Traverse Bay and Lake Leelanau.

Larry Mawby of L. Mawby Vineyards in Suttons Bay was among the AVA petitioners here, and after more than three decades (his first crush was 1978), he is still going strong, producing high-quality, traditional-method sparkling wines at several different sweetness levels. Under the M. Lawrence label, his tank-fermented bubblies have names such as Sex and Wet—solid sellers in the tasting room, for obvious reasons. Northwestern Michigan is ideal for sparkling-wine viticulture, with early-picked grapes high in acid and low in sugar.

L. Mawby is one of nineteen wineries in the AVA. Black Star Farms, whose partners bought an equestrian facility in 1997 and named it for the star in the marble floor of the manor house, is also in Suttons Bay. In addition to the winery, Black Star Farms has a distillery, creamery, and inn. While its sister winery on Old

Larry Mawby
Larry Mawby, rarely seen without his hat and Hawaiian-style shirt, uses the traditional method to produce some of Michigan's finest sparkling wines. A second fermentation of the wines in the bottle, and aging them in contact with the spent yeast for three years or more, adds complexity to the finished wines.

> **PAPA DON'T PREACH; HE MAKES WINE**
>
> There is one product the superstar Madonna supports without demanding an endorsement fee: Ciccone wines. That's because her father, Silvio "Tony" Ciccone, owns Ciccone Vineyard & Winery in Suttons Bay on the Leelanau Peninsula.
>
> Madonna Louise Ciccone grew up in Bay City, Michigan, and after she left home to become the Material Girl, actress, author, and one-time wife of Sean Penn and Guy Ritchie, her dad planted vines and built a winery.
>
> Established in 1996, Ciccone Vineyard & Winery has 14 acres planted to more than a dozen varieties. The wines are well made and win awards. Although Tony released a Madonna collector's series of wines from the 2005 vintage, his website makes no mention of his famous daughter.

Mission Peninsula concentrates on white wines, the reds, including the Arcturos Cabernet Franc and A Capella Pinot Noir, are vinified on Leelanau Peninsula.

Lake Michigan Shore and Fennville AVAs

St. Julian Winery and Warner Vineyards, both in Paw Paw, collaborated on the application seeking AVA status for Lake Michigan Shore. Their work was rewarded in 1981, and the 1.28-million-acre AVA stretches from the southwestern corner of Michigan north to the Kalamazoo River, and east toward Kalamazoo city. Fennville is a sub-AVA of Lake Michigan Shore.

Eighteen wineries are scattered throughout the area and they, like those in northwest Michigan, benefit from the moderating influence of Lake Michigan. St. Julian, the state's oldest winery, began life in 1921 in Ontario, Canada, founded by Mariano Meconi. After Prohibition, he moved the winery to Detroit, then to Paw Paw. Meconi's daughter, Julia, married Apollo "Paul" Braganini, and Braganini and his two brothers operated the business in the 1950s and 1960s. Paul's son, David, took over in 1977 and continues to oversee St. Julian's annual 106,000-case production. The Braganini Reserves are its top-shelf bottlings.

Tabor Hill Winery in Buchanan, founded in 1968, has had multiple owners and winemakers over the years—not uncommon in the industry. Now owned by the Upton family of Whirlpool washing machine fame, Tabor Hill has become particularly expert at Gewürztraminer and Traminette, the latter a crossing of the Gewürztraminer grape with Joannes Seyve. Traminette is a hardier, more disease-resistant variety than Gewürztraminer, but it delivers similar spicy, rose-petal aromas and lychee flavors.

The Welsch family's Fenn Valley Vineyards in Fennville sub-AVA does a fine job with Riesling and the red blend Capriccio—Chambourcin, Chancellor, Cabernet Franc, and Merlot.

Other East Central States

Surrounding Michigan on the west and south, and with lakes Superior, Michigan, and Erie providing a temperature-moderating effect, Illinois, Indiana, Ohio, and Wisconsin can cultivate both hybrid and vinifera varieties. Here, the French-American hybrids Seyval Blanc, Marechal Foch, and Baco Noir co-exist with the European varieties Chardonnay, Riesling, and Cabernet Franc. Catawba, which has been grown in Ohio since the early 1800s, continues to be made into blush and sparkling wines.

Illinois

They don't call Illinois the Prairie State for nothing: It is largely treeless flatlands and rolling hills, with carpets of corn, soybeans, and grain once one gets away from the cities and suburbs. Chicago, the third most populous city in America, is also one of its windiest, as Lake Michigan gusts are powerful enough to knock pedestrians off their feet. Although wind and the cold winters of the prairie are enemies of grapevines, in southern Illinois, particularly in the Shawnee Hills AVA, warmer temperatures and wind protection allow hybrid and vinifera grapes to prosper. Several Illinois wineries call the Chicago area home, because that's where the population is, but Shawnee Hills is the state's agricultural wine country, and its crops are sold to winemakers throughout the state.

One such buyer is Lynfred Winery, founded in 1979 by Fred and Lynn Koehler in the Chicago suburb of Roselle, west of O'Hare International Airport. Lynfred, the first winery to open in Illinois since Prohibition, has no vineyards and purchases grapes from the West Coast, as well as southern Illinois. It does an admirable job of bottling quality wines that draw crowds to the tasting room. Lynn died in 1984, but Fred forged ahead; in 1985, his Chardonnay won top awards in competitions in

OTHER EAST CENTRAL STATES SNAPSHOT

Vineyard acreage: ILLINOIS 1,200; INDIANA 600; OHIO 1,500; WISCONSIN 750

Most-planted varieties: Concord, Niagara, Chardonnay, Marechal Foch, Riesling, Traminette, Chambourcin, Vidal Blanc

Best varieties: vinifera—Cabernet Franc, Chardonnay, Riesling; native—Baco Noir, Catawba, Concord, Frontenac, Norton; hybrid—Chardonel, Chambourcin, Marechal Foch, St. Croix, Traminette, Vidal, Vignoles

AVAs: ILLINOIS—Shawnee Hills, Upper Mississippi River Valley; INDIANA—Ohio River Valley; OHIO—Grand River Valley, Isle St. George, Lake Erie, Loramie Creek, Ohio River Valley; WISCONSIN—Lake Wisconsin, Upper Mississippi River Valley, Wisconsin Ledge

Wineries: ILLINOIS 101; INDIANA 64; OHIO 150; WISCONSIN 70

Trailblazers: ILLINOIS—Baxter's Vineyards/Nauvoo Winery, Lynfred Winery; INDIANA—Huber's Orchard, Winery & Vineyard, Oliver Winery; OHIO—Ferrante Winery, Firelands Winery, Meier's Wine Cellars; WISCONSIN—Wollersheim Winery

Steady hands: ILLINOIS—Alto Vineyards, Blue Sky Vineyard, Fox Valley Winery, Galena Cellars, Prairie State Vineyards; INDIANA—Easley Winery, French Lick Winery, Oliver Winery; OHIO—Breitenbach Wine Cellars, Debonné Vineyards, Kinkead Ridge, St. Joseph Vineyard, Valley Vineyards; WISCONSIN—Cedar Creek Winery, Door Peninsula Winery, Simon Creek Vineyard & Winery, Weggy Winery

Superstars: OHIO—Ferrante Winery; WISCONSIN—Wollersheim Winery

Chicago and Nevada. Fred passed away in 2011 at age eighty-four, and his family continues to run the business.

Although it's not unusual for many of Illinois' over one hundred wineries to use grapes from out of the state, those who vinify Illinois fruit only take particular pride in that. They look to sturdy hybrid varieties such as Chambourcin, Seyval, Vignoles, Chardonel, and Vidal Blanc, producing them in styles ranging from dry to very sweet to sparkling. Other vintners prefer the much-lower risk of making wine from apples, berries, and other fruits.

The **Shawnee Hills AVA**, located in the foothills of the Shawnee National Forest, is home to the majority of Illinois vineyards. Unlike most of the state, the portion south of Carbondale was not covered by ancient glaciers, which ground the landscape into the prairies. The AVA's hilly ridges of free-draining limestone and sandstone soils, elevations ranging from 400 to 1,000 feet, and paucity of late-spring and early-November frosts add up to a long, stable growing season and encourage full grape maturity.

Alto Vineyards in Alto Pass was the first post-Prohibition commercial winery in the Shawnee Hills, launched in 1981 by Guy Renzaglia (who also founded the Rehabilitation Institute at Southern Illinois University in Carbondale). Chardonel and Chambourcin are arguably Alto's best wines, and its Chambourcin-based Porto di Guido, named for Renzaglia (who died in 2010), is a consistent gold-medal winner in the fortified-wine category. Nearby Blue Sky Vineyard has had a run of success with its Chambourcin and Vignoles wines.

Prairie State Winery, located west of Chicago in Genoa, purchases the majority of its grapes from southern Illinois. Former school teachers Rick and Maria Mamoser opened Prairie State Mercantile in 1998, selling Illinois-made goods, including wine. A decade later, they opened the winery, and their Cabernet Francs are excellent, produced in a lean, tangy style.

Indiana

The Hoosier State's icons include the Indianapolis Motor Speedway and Indy 500; the Jackson 5; David Letterman; Bobby Knight's heyday as the Indiana University basketball coach; and the 1986 hoops movie, *Hoosiers*. In 2000, home-grown Indiana wine barely registered a tick, with only a dozen producers. Now there are sixty-four, and more on the way, as the locavore movement toward locally made foods has segued into "locapour" wines.

Indiana's largest winery, Oliver Winery, bottles nearly 300,000 cases of wine per year at its facility near Bloomington. The state's first commercial winery after Repeal, founded in 1972, Oliver purchases most of the grapes used for the Oliver label from other states. Its higher-end Creekbend Vineyard label is devoted to Indiana grapes, among them Chardonel, Pinot Gris (the wine is labeled Pinot Grigio), Valvin Muscat, Chambourcin, and, surprisingly, Cabernet Sauvignon, a notoriously late ripener.

Founder William Oliver, an Indiana University law professor and home winemaker, was a driving force in the passage in 1971 of the Indiana Small Winery Act, which allows growers to produce and sell their own wines. Oliver Winery opened the following year.

Seven generations of the Huber family have farmed the same piece of land in Starlight, in the southeastern part of the state, not far from Louisville, Kentucky. Huber's Orchard, Winery & Vineyard grows 65 acres of wine grapes plus other fruits meant for wine production. It's truly a diversified business, with a distillery, pick-your-own fruits and vegetables, café, ice cream and cheese shop, and a farm park with animals. Wine production is admirably focused on estate-grown grapes, including Cabernet Franc, Malbec, and Seyval Blanc.

The white hybrid wine Traminette, developed by Cornell University, is the star of a marketing campaign launched in 2011 by the Indiana Wine and Grape Council and Purdue University. "Try on Traminette" seeks to introduce consumers to the variety, which has the floral, spicy character of Gewürztraminer, but the vines can withstand temperatures as low as -15°F. Easley Winery in Indianapolis, like many in Indiana, produces Traminette in a semidry style, with approximately 3 percent residual sugar, and also as sweet, sparkling, and ice wines.

Ohio

In the 1820s, Nicholas Longworth, a lawyer from the Cincinnati area, planted Catawba grapes in the Ohio River Valley. The variety, native to North America and tough enough to handle cold winters, produced a light, semisweet wine, and by 1860, Ohio led the nation in wine production. But disease decimated vineyards, and the Civil War left few men available to tend the vines. Viticulture relocated north, between Cleveland and Toledo, near the southern shores of Lake Erie, where cooler temperatures reduced the threat of mildew and rot in the grapes.

Prohibition halted wine production in the early twentieth century, and most of the land was developed into homes and businesses. It took until the early 1960s for vineyards to return, planted to disease-resistant hybrid varieties and vinifera grapes including Chardonnay and Riesling.

Ohio has five AVAs: **Lake Erie** (shared with New York and Pennsylvania, and where the highest concentration of Ohio wineries is located, at fifty) and the **Isle St. George** and **Grand River Valley** sub-AVAs within it; **Ohio River Valley** (shared with Kentucky, West Virginia, and Indiana), and **Loramie Creek**.

Approximately half of Ohio wineries grow their own grapes; the remainder acquire them from growers in Ohio and other states. The wines of Debonné Vineyards in the Grand River

Ferrante Winery
Those doubting that Ohio can produce quality wine should review the numerous awards won by Ferrante Winery, in both regional and national competitions.

Valley, started by the Debevec family in 1971, are estate grown; the vineyard excels at Riesling and Vidal ice wine.

Debonné's neighbors, Art and Doreen Pietrzyk of St. Joseph Vineyard, have cultivated wine grapes since 1972 and planted vinifera vines in 1986. Their well-made Chardonnays, Rieslings, Pinot Noirs, and Syrahs (the last labeled Shiraz) demonstrate that European varieties can flourish in Ohio, if they are planted in appropriate soil and climatic conditions and farmed with quality, not quantity, in mind.

Ferrante Winery & Ristorante is Ohio's rock-star wine producer; it operates a restaurant as well. Also located in the Grand River Valley sub-AVA of the Lake Erie AVA, Ferrante has had great success with a wide variety of wine types, including Chardonnay, Cabernet Franc, Gewürztraminer, Pinot Gris (labeled Pinot Grigio), and Vidal Blanc and Cabernet Franc ice wines. Its Golden Bunches Dry Riesling, which is actually off-dry, with a range of 1.0 to 1.5 percent residual sugar, goes head to head with New York and Michigan Rieslings in wine competitions and wins a healthy share of gold medals.

Established in 1937 by Anna and Nicholas Ferrante near Cleveland, Ferrante Winery began with native labrusca grapes. Their sons relocated the winery to its current site in Harpersfield Township in 1979, and Anna and Nicholas's grandchildren, brothers Nick and Anthony Ferrante, are the winemaker and vineyard manager for this overachieving winery.

Wisconsin

Wisconsin is the land of large-scale beer brewing (Pabst, Miller, and Schlitz all started here), cheese making (the state ranks first in U.S. production), Green Bay Packers "cheeseheads," and one of the best university fight songs in America, "On, Wisconsin!" The official state beverage is milk, so some might be surprised to learn that Wisconsin has a healthy wine industry too, with seventy producers.

Southwestern Wisconsin has the distinction of being part of the country's largest AVA, the **Upper Mississippi River Valley**, which also includes northwestern Illinois, southeastern Minnesota, and northeastern Iowa. The AVA covers nearly 30,000 square miles, averaging 120 miles east to west, and 225 miles north to south—so huge that it is virtually meaningless in helping consumers identify where grapes are grown and, by extension, the likely style of wine made from them (the ultimate goal of the AVA system).

However, within that monster is the **Lake Wisconsin AVA**, a "mere" 44 square miles in size, covering Columbia and Dane counties in south-central Wisconsin. The AVA is one of the few areas in the Upper Mississippi River Valley that has glacially deposited, gravelly soils, which are conducive to growing premium-quality wine grapes.

A new AVA was approved in 2012, **Wisconsin Ledge**, comprising 3,800 square miles in Door, Kewaunee, Manitowoc, Sheboygan, Ozaukee, Washington, Dodge, Fond du Lac, Calumet, Outagamie, and Brown counties. The "ledge" is a limestone-dominant escarpment that extends from eastern Wisconsin to New York State and into Canada. Lake Michigan, Lake Winnebago, and Green Bay have a warming effect that can extend the growing season to as many as eight weeks longer than other regions in Wisconsin. The Wisconsin Ledge AVA petition states that the growing season in the AVA near Sheboygan, on Lake Michigan, is 184 days; in Baraboo, which is slightly south and in the center of the state, away from the lake, the growing season is on average 56 days shorter. The more time grapes spend on the vine without frosts and freezes, the more flavor, color, and body they develop when they're harvested and vinified.

The largest grouping of wineries in Wisconsin Ledge is in Door County, a popular vacation spot and home to top-notch fruit-wine producer Door Peninsula Winery (its peach wine is perfection) and Simon Creek Vineyard & Winery, which relies largely on grapes purchased from out of state. Steve DeBaker of Trout Creek Winery in Brown County did the heavy lifting to get the AVA petition researched and written.

But the Badger State's finest producer is, with little argument, Wollersheim Winery in Prairie du Sac, within the Lake Wisconsin AVA. Wollersheim, perched on a hill overlooking the Wisconsin River, has a history any winery in America would be happy to have, and today it produces pure, honest, and, for the most part, outstanding wines, from grapes grown in Wisconsin and elsewhere.

Hungarian immigrant "Count" Agoston Haraszthy began planting grapevines at what is now Wollersheim in the 1840s.

Unable to reconcile himself to the damage his vines suffered in the harsh winters, Haraszthy headed to California and a shot at its Gold Rush action in 1849. By 1857, he had begun planting some of California's first European grape varieties in the town of Sonoma and built Buena Vista Winery. Haraszthy returned to Europe in 1861 and later that year reportedly brought back with him 100,000 vines, which he sold to fledgling wineries, becoming the viticultural version of Johnny Appleseed.

Upon Haraszthy's departure from Wisconsin, another immigrant, German Peter Kehl, took over the property during the Civil War and planted native varieties and his beloved Riesling, laying the vines on the ground and covering them with dirt to protect them from Wisconsin's winters. Following Kehl's death, his son, Jacob, continued making wine, selling it in small barrels to customers as far away as Maine. Jacob Kehl died in 1899, and the family converted the farm to more traditional crops twenty years before Prohibition.

By 1972, the property had fallen on hard times. Bob and JoAnn Wollersheim purchased it, replanted the hillside to wine grapes, refurbished the underground wine cellars, and named the business Wollersheim Winery. They hired winemaker Philippe Coquard from the Beaujolais region of France in 1984; Coquard later married the Wollersheim's daughter, Julie, and the couple operates the winery today.

A semidry Seyval Blanc wine the Wollersheims named Prairie Fumé became wildly popular, and a dry rosé produced from another hybrid grape, Marechal Foch, bearing the name Prairie Blush, followed. Foch is also the foundation for Wollersheim's Domaine Reserve red wine.

The winery, in certain cold, dry years, makes a delicious, estate-grown ice wine from St. Pepin grapes, one of many cultivars Bob Wollersheim experimented with in order to find the most suitable grapes for the conditions. He died in 2005.

Coquard does not hesitate to purchase out-of-state grapes for wines he cannot produce with his own fruit. Wollersheim has been tremendously successful with its Rieslings, which typically come from Washington State grapes, as do the Chardonnays and Pinot Noirs. New York State was the source of Seyval for the 2010 vintage of Prairie Fumé.

In 1990, Wollersheim acquired the Stone Mill Winery in Cedarburg and renamed it Cedar Creek Winery (it's located within the Wisconsin Ledge AVA). Coquard produces those wines as well, following the Wollersheim formula of mixing their own grapes with those imported from other states.

Wollersheim Winery
In Prairie du Sac, Sauk County, Wisconsin, barrels of wine age in the Wollersheim cellar, which excels at Marechal Foch–based wines and Rieslings.

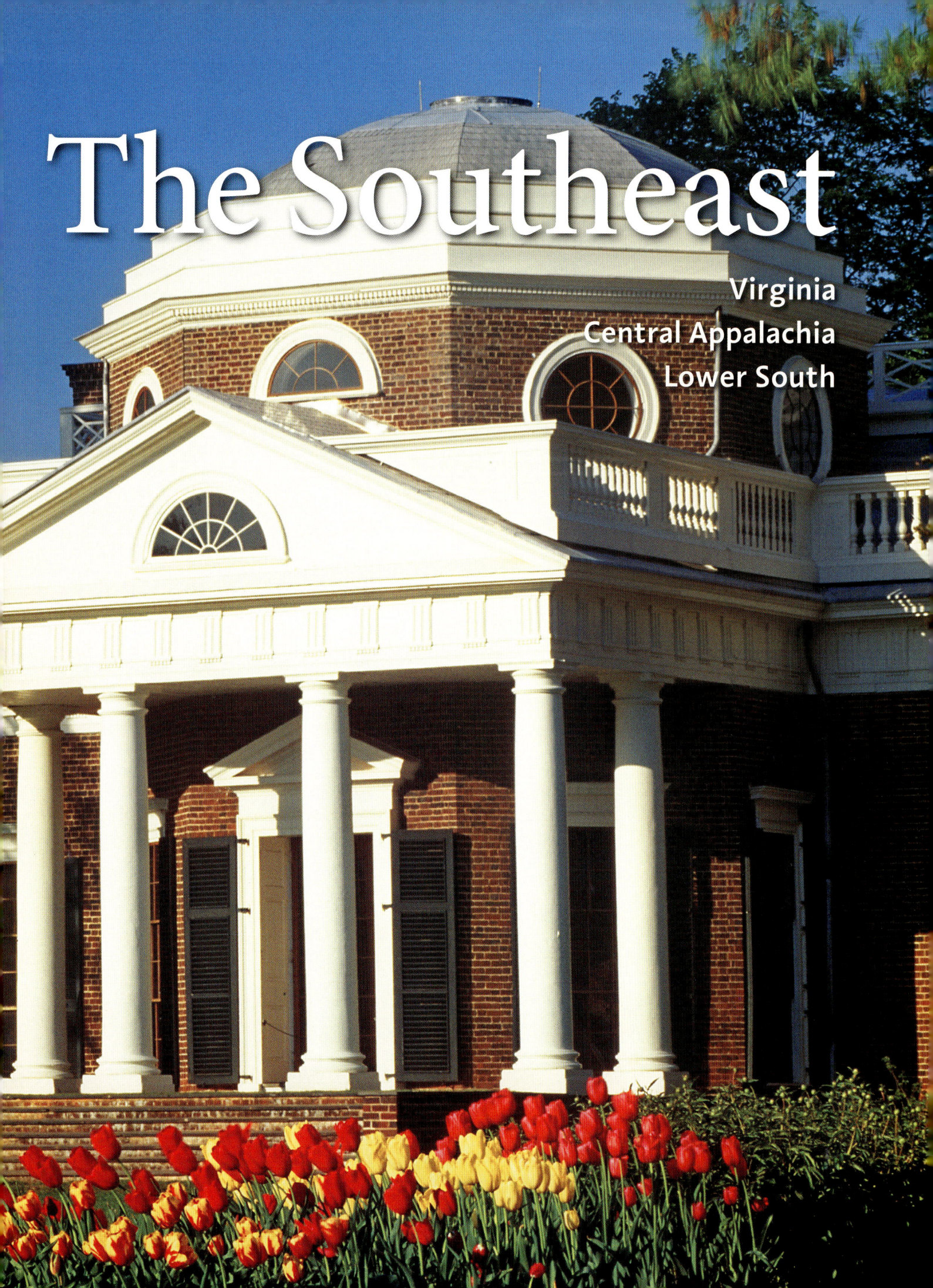

The Southeast

Virginia
Central Appalachia
Lower South

Virginia

In the resting place for departed U.S. presidents, based on the success the Virginia wine industry has come to experience in the past two decades, Thomas Jefferson must be toasting his Virginia homeland with flutes of Thibaut-Janisson Blanc de Chardonnay. Jefferson, America's third president, Virginia governor from 1779 to 1781, and master gardener, attempted to grow *Vitis vinifera* grapes and produce European-style wines at his beloved Monticello estate. He failed miserably, though not for lack of trying.

Monticello Vineyards
Beginning in 1985, the Thomas Jefferson Foundation began restoring the third president's unproductive vineyard at Monticello; wines are produced from these vines and sold at Monticello, pictured on the previous page.

Jefferson did not have what Virginia vintners have today: modern science and research; the ability to counter phylloxera and other vine-killing pests; broad choices of grape varieties and rootstocks; and the understanding that grape varieties will thrive only in soils and climatic conditions suited to them. Jefferson's taste for clarets (the British term for the red wines of Bordeaux) among other wines, led him to plant Bordeaux grapes in the wrong place and in the wrong era.

Today there are 3,200 vineyard acres and two hundred wineries in Virginia, making it the fifth-largest wine-producing state in the United States. Its wine industry has an annual $360 million economic impact on the state each year, when wine sales, tourism, employment, taxes, and other related factors are totaled. Governor Bob McDonnell, elected in 2009, rapidly established himself as an ardent supporter of the commonwealth's wine industry. However, the state limits governors to serving one term; it remains to be seen if McDonnell's replacement in 2013 will continue to support winemaking and grape growing as integral components of the Virginia economy.

Virginia wineries reap the rewards of visitors who come to tour Monticello, Colonial Williamsburg, and Civil War battlefields, then discover that there are wineries nearby. Although some producers set a low quality bar in unabashed pursuit of tourism profits, a growing number of Virginia vintners are focused on quality first and visitors second—and some don't encourage them at all, having the advantage of selling everything they make to a loyal customer base.

Still, many Virginia wineries live and die by walk-ins, because, as encouraging as it has been of the wine industry, the state of Virginia requires that all wines be sold to retail shops and

VIRGINIA SNAPSHOT

Vineyard acres: **3,200**

Most-planted varieties: **Chardonnay, Merlot, Cabernet Franc, Cabernet Sauvignon, Viognier, Petit Verdot, Norton**

Best varieties: **Cabernet Franc, Cabernet Sauvignon, Chardonnay, Norton, Petit Manseng, Petit Verdot, Viognier**

AVAs: **Monticello, Northern Neck George Washington Birthplace, North Fork of Roanoke, Rocky Knob, Shenandoah Valley, Virginia's Eastern Shore**

Wineries: **200**

Veritas Vineyard & Winery
Andrew and Patricia Hodson founded Veritas in 2002, at the foot of the Blue Ridge Mountains near Afton. They are particularly passionate about Sauvignon Blanc and Cabernet Franc.

VIRGINIA

Virginia has six AVAs, but many wineries are located outside their boundaries or instead label their wines "Virginia."

restaurants by wholesalers, the middlemen (unlike some other states). Small wineries unable to secure wholesale representation must rely only on tasting-room sales, so it is important for them to be located near large cities and tourism hubs.

The Old Dominion's winemaking history is as rich as it comes. Virginia was one of the first wine-producing colonies, and the settlers at Jamestown entered into law in 1619 a provision that each male resident would plant and tend at least ten grapevines so that the colony could produce wine and ship it back to Britain. But their efforts were unsuccessful.

Much later, Jefferson struggled for more than thirty years to make wine from his vineyards, going so far as to bring in grape-grower Filippo Mazzei from Italy to advise on the planting of the Monticello vineyard. Alas, the vines either died of disease or were destroyed by stampeding horses. It has only been since the early 1990s that Virginia has become known not just for its wines, but for good, sometimes great, wines.

The key to this resurgence has been the ability of winegrowers to deal with the hot, humid conditions of the growing season and the fungal diseases that come with them. It starts with planting varieties on the sites best suited to them, and realizing that European vinifera vines can withstand pests such as phylloxera only if grafted onto phylloxera-resistant American rootstocks. Grapes with thick skins and loose clusters offer the most protection from berry-invading mildew and rot, and planting on hillsides exposed to breezes provides much-needed air circulation to dry out any moisture on the fruit. Spring frost, rain during the growing season, and even the occasional hurricane, also influence which vine varieties should be planted where.

The 2011 harvest season was particularly difficult, with as much as 12 inches of rain falling on developing grapes in a one-week period. Excessive moisture causes berries to swell with water, diluting their juice; it is difficult to produce concentrated wines under such conditions.

If one variety had to be designated as Virginia's "best" for wine, critics would likely proclaim it to be Cabernet Franc which, in skilled hands, makes a lean, elegant red wine with gentle herbal notes and palate-cleansing acidity. But Jenni McCloud, proprietor of Chrysalis Vineyards, would not just say, she would shout, that Norton is not only Virginia's grape, it's America's grape. Virginians have also fallen for Petit Verdot, an inky, dark-fruited wine that has bold flavors and a tannic grip more in line with California and Washington State reds than the high-acid Cabernet Francs and Merlots of the commonwealth.

Breaux Vineyards
This 400-acre estate in the northern tip of Virginia is visually representative of the state's vineyards: lush and green from spring through summer, with scenic views of the Blue Ridge Mountains. Humidity is a perennial problem.

For white wines, Virginians are particularly proud of their Viogniers, produced from the Rhône Valley grape known for its floral, honeysuckle aromas and rich pear, peach, and tropical fruit flavors. Most Virginia Viogniers are lighter and less unctuous than those from the northern Rhône, with more delicate perfume and a bent toward crispness over depth and complexity. Less widely planted, yet just as successful, is Petit Manseng, a vinifera grape from southwest France that has the welcome punch of ripe fruitiness and crackling acidity. It is made in styles dry, sweet, and everything in between.

There are six AVAs in Virginia—Virginia's Eastern Shore, Northern Neck George Washington Birthplace, Monticello, North Fork of Roanoke, Rocky Knob, and Shenandoah Valley, with Middleburg pending—but many of the state's best producers aren't located within them. Thus, it is easier to find wineries not by AVAs but by the broader geographical regions referred to here. The state appellation "Virginia" is used on labels by those who blend fruit from more than one region into their wines; those whose grapes are not grown within an AVA (see "Northern Virginia Region," below); and those who figure that consumers have no clue where the Shenandoah AVA is (there is a similarly named AVA in California), yet do understand "Virginia."

Northern Virginia Region

There is a large concentration of wineries in Northern Virginia, where close proximity to Washington, D.C., and its international community of wine drinkers makes for a sophisticated customer base. Dulles International Airport, 30 miles west of the White House, is a convenient departure point for out-of-staters who want to rent cars and drive to wine country, where they will discover gorgeous views of the Blue Ridge Mountains, vine-carpeted hillside wine estates, and dozens of tasting rooms.

In early 2012, there were no AVAs in northern Virginia, despite a number of sites that could qualify if someone researched and drafted the petition to the Alcohol and Tobacco Tax and Trade Bureau. In 2009, Boxwood Estate Winery in Middleburg did just that, proposing a **Middleburg AVA** that would comprise 198 square miles in and around the towns of Middleburg, Purcellville, and Delaplane in Loudoun and Fauquier counties, known for horse husbandry, fox hunts, and high-level equestrian training. Boxwood's marketing-savvy executive vice president, Rachel Martin, submitted the AVA petition; the decision was still pending at the time of going to press.

Boxwood has spared no expense in developing its vineyards, constructing a modern winery and establishing tasting rooms in downtown Middleburg and Reston in Virginia, and in Chevy

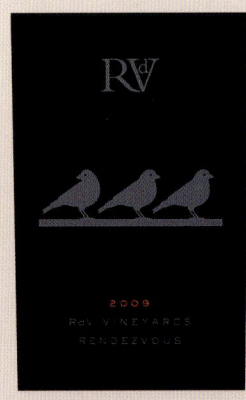

NORTHERN VIRGINIA REGION SNAPSHOT

Vineyard acres: **1,600 (estimated)**

Most-planted varieties: **Cabernet Franc, Chardonnay, Merlot, Norton, Viognier**

Best varieties: **Cabernet Franc, Cabernet Chardonnay, Norton, Petit Manseng, Sauvignon, Viognier**

AVA: **Middleburg (pending)**

Wineries: **66**

Steady hands: **Breaux Vineyards, Chester Gap Cellars, Corcoran Vineyards, Delaplane Cellars, Pearmund Cellars, Rappahannock Cellars, Tarara Winery**

Superstars: **Boxwood Estate Winery, Chrysalis Vineyards, Linden Vineyards, RdV Vineyards**

Central & Northern Virginia

The largest concentration of Virginia vineyards and wineries is east of the Blue Ridge Mountains, in the northern section of the state, and in the Monticello AVA in central Virginia.

Chase and at National Harbor in Maryland. Boxwood's owners, Rita and John Kent Cooke—football fans know him as the former president of the Washington Redskins, owned by his father, Jack Kent Cooke—and their daughter, Rachel Martin, hired legendary Virginia viticulturist Lucie Morton to design the 16-acre vineyard, with dense plantings of Cabernet Sauvignon, Cabernet Franc, Merlot, Malbec, and Petit Verdot. With Bordeaux consultant Stéphane Derenoncourt advising, Boxwood produces two exceptional red wines: Boxwood, a Cabernet Sauvignon–dominant blend, and Topiary, a Cabernet Franc–Merlot wine.

Boxwood's Middleburg neighbor, Jenni McCloud, founded Chrysalis Vineyards in 1997. She states that Chrysalis was "named symbolically for the rare nectar of fine wine emerging from the barrel as the butterfly emerges from her cocoon." It also signifies McCloud's physical, emotional, and professional transformation from Florida high-tech millionaire to country farmer with a fervent passion for Norton, "the Real American Grape!" as she has trademarked it.

Norton (also known as Cynthiana) makes a wine like no other in the United States. It has a deep purple color and soft, low tannin levels similar to those in Pinot Noir and Gamay, but it also has an abundant black fruitiness and high acidity. Daniel Norton (1794–1842), a Richmond physician who lost his wife and child during childbirth, assuaged his grief by gardening, and he bred what would come to be called the Norton grape. It's not known for certain which grapes the doctor crossed to come up with his hybrid, although DNA analysis has shown that it has genes from both vinifera and the native *Vitis aestivalis*, which early settlers found growing wild on the East Coast. Those same settlers found it made undrinkable wine, which makes Norton's appeal all the more intriguing.

Norton was widely planted in Virginia in the nineteenth century, but the vines were pulled out during Prohibition and replaced by Concord grapes used in the making of jams and jellies. Dennis Horton of Horton Vineyards in Central Virginia brought Norton back to life, planting the variety near Charlottesville and vinifying it starting in 1991.

Horton's Norton has legions of fans, but McCloud is America's "Norton Empress." At Chrysalis, she produces four different Norton bottlings each year and also uses the grape in blended wines. The Locksley Reserve Norton, from McCloud's Locksley Estate, is a fine representation of the variety. It is now made by Alan Kinne, Chrysalis's original winemaker, who left to work in Oregon and California, then returned to the Chrysalis cocoon. McCloud has also planted the European varieties Albariño, Petit Manseng, Viognier, Tempranillo, Graciano, and Tannat, all with encouraging results.

Jim Law has, as much as anyone in Virginia, elevated wine quality standards with his Chardonnays and red blends at Linden Vineyards in Fauquier County. Since the early 1980s, Law has

Luca Paschina
The longtime Barboursville Vineyards winemaker is known for his Bordeaux-style red blend Octagon, and varietals important in his native Italy, including Nebbiolo, Barbera, and more recently Vermentino.

been fine-tuning his vineyards and winemaking, and today he makes Burgundian-like Chardonnays and Bordeaux-style reds from his Hardscrabble Vineyard near the town of Linden.

Subtle oak influence and keen balance are hallmarks of Law's wines: The Chardonnays are vibrant, minerally and long-lived; the Hardscrabble reds have a structured Cabernet Sauvignon frame, with Merlot, Petit Verdot, and Cabernet Franc adding flesh to the bones. The Hardscrabble Vineyard is planted on slopes in granite-based soils, so that the vines' roots dry out after being irrigated or saturated by rainfall. Cabernet loathes having "wet feet"; growers with water-retaining clay soils in other areas struggle to achieve high-quality grapes.

Law had an important influence on Rutger de Vink, one of several Linden disciples who went on to establish his or her own winery in Virginia. De Vink was no ordinary cellar rat. A former Marine who had served in Somalia and earned an MBA at Northwestern University, he soaked up as much as he could from Law in 2001. Then he embarked on a search for land upon which to plant Bordeaux varieties and produce what he hoped would be Virginia's version of a First Growth Bordeaux or a California cult classic like Screaming Eagle.

In 2004, de Vink found his site near Delaplane in Fauquier County. The former sheep ranch met his requirements with its steep, well-drained slopes to keep vine roots dry and as immune as possible from frost, and low-fertility soils, which would prevent the vines from producing new growth at midseason, imparting green, herbal characteristics to the grapes. He planted his vines in 2006—40 percent Cabernet Sauvignon, 40 percent

Merlot, and smaller amounts of Petit Verdot and Cabernet Franc—and hired Eric Boissenot, the important Médoc consultant oenologist, whose clients include First Growth châteaux, to blend his wines.

Starting with the first vintage in 2008, de Vink's RdV has impressed critics, both domestic and foreign, with its precision, complexity, minerality, and ageworthiness. RdV ($88) and the second wine, Rendezvous ($55), are among the highest-priced wines from Virginia, and some locals have scoffed at de Vink's pricing, regardless of wine quality. "Virginians will never pay that much for a wine," they've said—but de Vink isn't necessarily selling to Virginians. He is focused on markets that recognize great wine when they taste it; to learn that it is from Virginia makes the sales story all the more fascinating.

Central Virginia Region

Charlottesville is the bull's-eye on central Virginia's dartboard, a sweet spot for its historical significance and high-quality wines. The **Monticello AVA**, established in 1984 and named for Thomas Jefferson's estate (and site of his disappointing attempts at viticulture), hosts more than half of Virginia's vineyard acreage and twenty-five wineries.

At Monticello, listed on the World Register of Historic Places, Jefferson served European wines from his cellar, still very much part of the tourist experience at Monticello, to friends, fellow politicians, and international dignitaries. He developed his taste for fine wine while serving as ambassador to France, and although he was unable to produce wine of his own, Jefferson will forever be known as America's first wine geek.

Vineyards in the Monticello AVA and the Central Virginia area, in Albemarle, Greene, Nelson, and Orange counties, are cultivated on slopes of the Southwest mountain chain, paralleling the Blue Ridge Mountains.

As originally American as Charlottesville is (by way of England), this region's winemaking success can be in large part credited to Italians. In 1976, Gianni Zonin, whose family has produced wine in Italy since 1821, established Barboursville Vineyards on the former estate of James Barbour, Virginia's governor during the War of 1812. Jefferson designed Barbour's home, which included an octagonal room from which the wings of the house radiated. The mansion was destroyed by fire in 1884, but the winery honored it by naming its finest wine Octagon. A blend of Merlot, Cabernet Franc, Cabernet Sauvignon, and Petit Verdot, Octagon has often been mistaken for a Bordeaux wine in blind tastings.

Barboursville has produced numerous varietals and blends made from French and Italian grapes. In 2010, it released Virginia's first Vermentino, a zesty white Italian varietal that appears to thrive in the hot summers. Digging deeper into its Italian ancestry, the winery also produces a lively Reserve Nebbiolo.

Piedmont native Luca Paschina has been the Barboursville winemaker for two decades. Before him was Gabriele Rausse, sent from Italy by Zonin to plant grapes in 1976. At the time, eastern growers were advised to cultivate sturdy hybrid varieties, to ensure consistent crops in every vintage. But Rausse believed vinifera could succeed in Charlottesville, and he was correct; so correct that he created a Barboursville nursery to supply other wineries with vinifera plant material.

In 1998, Rausse started his eponymous winery in Charlottesville, producing fine Viogniers and Cabernet Sauvignons.

Although there are significant plantings of Merlot in Virginia, the variety shines brighter when it is blended with Cabernet Franc and/or Cabernet Sauvignon. Keswick's Merlot gets a dose

CENTRAL VIRGINIA REGION SNAPSHOT

Vineyard acreage: 1,300 (estimated)

Most-planted varieties: Cabernet Franc, Merlot, Cabernet Sauvignon, Viognier

Best varieties: Cabernet Franc, Cabernet Sauvignon, Chardonnay, Viognier

AVA: Monticello

Wineries: 64

Trailblazers: Barboursville Vineyards, Horton Vineyards

Steady hands: Afton Mountain Vineyards, Blenheim Vineyards, Cardinal Point Vineyard and Winery, Cooper Vineyards, Jefferson Vineyards, Keswick Vineyards, King Family Vineyards, Michael Shaps, Veritas Vineyards

Superstars: Barboursville Vineyards, Thibaut-Janisson

Ones to watch: Ankida Ridge, Trump Winery

DONALD TRUMP: VIRGINIA VINTNER

Vintners' eyes are on Trump Winery—formerly Kluge Estate Winery & Vineyard—which billionaire real estate developer and reality TV star Donald Trump purchased for a relative pittance in 2011. Socialite Patricia Kluge had fallen deep into debt on her grand estate south of Charlottesville, losing the property to her bank. Trump, a friend of Kluge's, stepped in to purchase two tracts totaling approximately 200 vineyard acres, plus the winery, pavilion, and carriage museum, for $6.2 million.

Despite locals' fears that the estate would be turned into a housing development or golf course, Donald Trump and his son, Eric, say they will continue to grow grapes and make wine, restoring luster to what once was a showpiece wine estate. In the winery's heyday, Kluge brought in high-powered winemaking consultants from Champagne (Laurent Champs) and Bordeaux (Michel Rolland). The sparkling wines have been stellar for their $30 price; the flagship wine, New World Red, a Bordeaux-style blend, launched at more than $100 per ornately packaged bottle, never quite recovered from its overpricing.

Upon purchasing Kluge Estate, the Trumps set about renovating the buildings and equipment, and they restarted winemaking, which had ceased in 2010 when the bank shut the facility down. Virginians are eager to see what "the Donald" will do with this new business.

The Trumps have famous new neighbors in Steve and Jean Case of AOL fame. In late 2011, they purchased Sweely Estate in Madison and began renovating and replanting. Lucie Morton and Michael Chaps consult, respectively, on viticulture and winemaking at the former Sweely Estate, now called Early Mountain Vineyards.

Trump Winery
Donald Trump purchased the financially strapped Kluge Estate Winery & Vineyard in Charlottesville in 2011 and renamed it Trump Winery. It's a spectacular property, with great potential for producing outstanding wines.

of both, lending the wine more freshness from Cabernet Franc and structure from Cabernet Sauvignon. Its Viognier, Cabernet Franc, and Cabernet Sauvignon are also noteworthy.

A handful of Virginia wineries produce sparkling wine. The most serious one is arguably Thibaut-Janisson in Charlottesville, a partnership of Frenchmen Claude Thibaut and Manuel Janisson—the latter of Champagne Janisson & Fils in Verzenay, the former an experienced bubbly maker with stints at California's Iron Horse and J wineries. In 2007, they released their first Virginia-grown wine, Thibaut-Janisson Blanc de Chardonnay; it was then and continues to be a delicate, sophisticated wine and a favorite of Virginia sommeliers.

Blenheim Vineyards has two cool things going for it: excellent wines and a famous owner. Rocker Dave Matthews, leader of the Dave Matthews Band, designed and built the winery on his property near Charlottesville in 2000. He doesn't make the wines, and is rarely spotted by visitors to the tasting room, but his name is certainly a draw, particularly for a younger crowd, and the Chardonnays, Viogniers, and Cabernet Francs hold their own with any produced in Virginia.

Horton Vineyards, integral to the reintroduction of Norton grapes to Virginia, is also a pioneer of Viognier there, producing the wine as long ago as the early 1990s when only a few Californians were doing so. Also on Dennis Horton's extensive wine menu is a gutsy Cabernet Franc, with a splash of Tannat blended in for muscle.

Michael Shaps and his business partner, Philip Stafford, own Virginia Wineworks near Charlottesville, the state's first custom-crush winery. There, they lease cellar space and equipment to winemakers who don't have their own, allowing more vintners to get into the game without large capital expenditures. Shaps, one of Virginia's top consulting winemakers, also produces super-premium wines under the Michael Shaps label (look for the Chardonnay and Cabernet Franc) and a value-based Virginia Wineworks range of easy-quaffing wines.

Elsewhere in Virginia

The **Shenandoah Valley AVA** is a long, narrow strip that hugs northern and central Virginia on the west. It includes Frederick, Clarke, Warren, Shenandoah, Page, Rockingham, Augusta, Rockbridge, Botetourt, and Amherst counties in Virginia and Berkeley and Jefferson counties in West Virginia. The Blue Ridge Mountains flank it on the east, the Appalachian and Allegheny plateaus on the west. CrossKeys, Glen Manor Vineyards, and Veramar are the top producers here.

The **Hampton Roads Region** offers an American history lesson. Tucked into the far southeastern corner of Virginia, it includes the colonial towns Jamestown and Williamsburg, with their period architecture and museums. The year-round temperate climate allows for the growing of Cabernet Franc, Cabernet Sauvignon, Chardonnay, Merlot, Seyval Blanc, Vidal Blanc, and Norton. Three producers are located here, including The Williamsburg Winery, established in 1983 by Patrick and Peggy Duffeler. Their flagship is Adagio, a red blend that has scored highly at the *Decanter* World Wine Awards in London.

The **Chesapeake Bay Region** of the Northern Neck and Middle Peninsula is bordered by the Potomac and York rivers. Presidents George Washington, James Madison, and James Monroe were born here, and the small towns harken back to Colonial times. The sandy loam soils and a river-moderated climate encourage growers to plant a dozen varieties, including Cabernet Franc, Cabernet Sauvignon, Chambourcin, Seyval Blanc, Syrah, and Vidal Blanc.

All ten of the region's wineries are located in the somewhat cumbersomely named Northern Neck George Washington Birthplace AVA. Ingleside Winery, a former boy's school (built in 1834) and Civil War garrison, was originally established as a dairy farm by the Flemer family. In the 1940s, Carl Flemer Jr. founded Ingleside Vineyards, and the winery was started in 1980 by his son, Doug Flemer. His Petit Verdots and Sangioveses have won gold medals in California wine shows.

Across Chesapeake Bay is the **Eastern Shore Region**, home to the Virginia's Eastern Shore AVA and three wineries: Bloxom Vineyard, Chatham Vineyards, and Holly Grove Vineyards. Surrounded by the Chesapeake Bay and Atlantic Ocean, vineyards in the AVA are cooled in summer and warmed in winter by ocean breezes; as one would expect; the soils are sandy and offer good drainage, which keeps vine roots dry and healthy. Chatham Vineyards has done well with its Church Creek Petit Verdot, a luscious, full-bodied red.

Within the **Blue Ridge Region** are two AVAs, Rocky Knob and North Fork of Roanoke. Blue Ridge snuggles up against West Virginia in the southwest part of the state, and while there are a handful of vineyards and wineries here, most of them have been slow to reveal their personalities. The exception is Chateau Morrisette, one of Virginia's oldest and largest wineries, with an annual production of 60,000 cases. Its first wines were produced in 1982, by William, Nancy, and David Morrisette, who expanded the winery in 1999, using salvaged timber from the St. Marie River to build its timber-frame building.

The **Southern Virginia Region** has a warm-to-temperate climate suited to Cabernet Franc, Cabernet Sauvignon, Merlot, Chardonnay, and Vidal Blanc. Rosemont Vineyards & Winery in LaCrosse won the 2011 Governor's Cup as the best red wine in the state for its Bordeaux–style blend from this region.

Central Appalachia

Kentucky bourbon, Tennessee whiskey, and backwoods moonshine are the iconic alcoholic beverages of this region, which comprises North and South Carolina, West Virginia, Kentucky, and Tennessee. These states, opposed to wineries since Prohibition, have softened in recent years with the realization that wine-related tourism can be an economic shot in the arm. Civil War buffs, tasters along the bourbon and whiskey trails, fans of NASCAR and college basketball, and others now have the opportunity to visit wineries, and more producers pop up every year.

Kentucky

Prior to the Civil War (1861–1865), Kentucky was said to be the third-largest grape grower in the country. But, Kentucky was the site of some of the bloodiest battles of the war, and its vineyards were abandoned.

After the Confederate surrender in 1865, Kentucky's vineyards were replaced by tobacco fields. Prohibition made commercial winemaking illegal until 1976, when the state passed legislation allowing wineries to operate, and while Kentucky bourbon remains the drink of choice for many, and Kentucky Derby attendees sip bourbon-spiked mint juleps rather than wine, the Bluegrass State is making a winemaking comeback.

Since 2000, the number of Kentucky wineries has rocketed from fifteen to sixty-six. While the total production volume is a mere 100,000 cases per year—even a midsized California or Washington winery makes that much—the spurt in wineries is impressive.

Americans' shunning of tobacco products has much to do with that. In the early 1990s, tobacco crop prices dropped as fewer and fewer citizens smoked, dipped, or chewed tobacco, due to health concerns. With funds from the 1998 Tobacco Master Settlement Agreement with cigarette makers, the state government paid farmers to replace tobacco plants with other crops, including wine grapes, and hired viticulture and winemaking consultants to help growers make the transition.

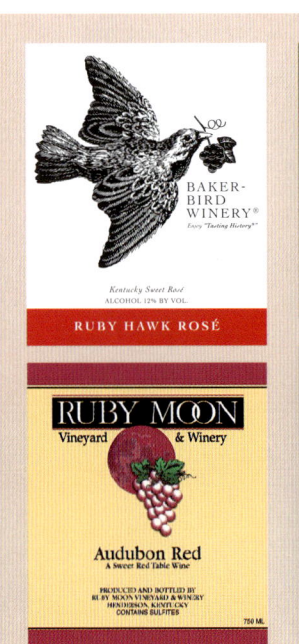
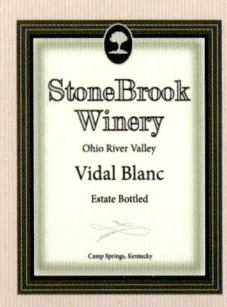
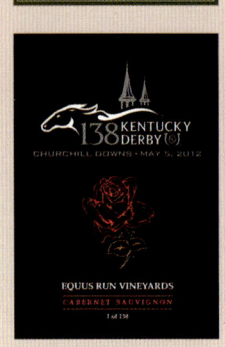

KENTUCKY SNAPSHOT

Vineyard acreage: **300**

Most-planted varieties: **Chardonnay, Cabernet Sauvignon, Cabernet Franc, Chambourcin, Cynthiana/Norton**

Best varieties: **vinifera—Cabernet Franc, Cabernet Sauvignon, Chardonnay, Riesling; native—Cynthiana/Norton; hybrids—Chambourcin, Seyval, Vidal Blanc**

AVA: **Ohio River Valley**

Wineries: **66**

Steady hands: **Acres of Land Winery, Baker-Bird Winery, Chrisman Mill Vineyards, Equus Run Winery, Horseshoe Bend, Jean Farris Winery, Lovers Leap Vineyards & Winery, Prodigy Vineyards and Winery, Ruby Moon Vineyard & Winery, StoneBrook Winery, Wight-Meyer Vineyard & Winery**

French-American hybrids such as Chambourcin, Seyval, and Vidal Blanc grow adjacent to plots of vinifera grapes including Chardonnay, Cabernet Franc, Cabernet Sauvignon, and Petite Sirah. Native varieties Norton (Cynthiana), Concord, and Niagara are also in the viticultural mix. Kentucky's climate hits all extremes, with cold, snowy winters; hot, dry summers; and, in difficult growing years, chilly, damp conditions from bloom to harvest.

Chrisman Mill Vineyards in Nicholasville was established in 1997 by Chris and Denise Nelson. They use only locally grown grapes.

Many of Kentucky's wineries are located in the massive **Ohio River Valley AVA**, which also includes portions of Indiana, Ohio, and West Virginia. Acres of Land Winery, Equus Run Winery, and Lovers Leap Vineyards & Winery are among the top producers in the AVA.

Lovers Leap in Anderson County was established in 1994 by Jerry and Ann Holder; their winery opened in 2001. Now Pam and Logan Leet own Lovers Leap, one of the largest vineyards in the state at 30 acres, planted largely to vinifera vines Chardonnay, Riesling, Cabernet Sauvignon, and Cabernet Franc. Their Norton draws positive attention too.

Much of the University of Kentucky's horticultural research is conducted at Wight-Meyer Vineyard near Shephardsville, south of Louisville, where Jim and Sandy Wight grow more than twenty-one varieties and produce wine from nearly all of them.

Baker-Bird Winery
German immigrants built this Augusta, Kentucky, winery in the mid-1800s. Now Baker-Bird's tasting room, it's one of twenty-two winery buildings on the National Historic Registry.

North Carolina

Largely unnoticed outside the state, the number of wineries in North Carolina has more than quadrupled since 2001, to one hundred, and the state ranks seventh in wine production in the United States. The Tar Heel State tells a tale of two vine species, Native Muscadines and European-style vinifera, and each is important to its developing wine industry. Wineries in the western and Piedmont regions of North Carolina produce wines from *Vitis vinifera* grapes such as Chardonnay, Merlot, and Cabernet Sauvignon. In the south-central part of the state, native *Vitis rotundifolia* Muscadine varieties that can withstand the high humidity of the region dominate viticulture and winemaking.

Yadkin Valley, the state's first AVA (2003), is wedged between the Brushy Mountains and Blue Ridge Mountains foothills, in north-central North Carolina. This green, lush farmland once planted to tobacco has ideal loam and sand soils for wine grapes, and a climate warm and dry enough for European varieties.

With his roots on Tobacco Road, Richard Childress, owner of three NASCAR racing teams, founded Childress Vineyards in Lexington with partner Greg Johns. Their focus is vinifera varieties Chardonnay, Merlot, Cabernet Franc, and Cabernet Sauvignon, produced from Yadkin Valley grapes; the wines are among the finest in the state.

THE MOTHER VINE

Roanoke Island in eastern North Carolina is home to what is believed to be the oldest cultivated grapevine in America, called the Mother Vine. Planted approximately four hundred years ago, the Mother Vine covered 2 acres in 1957, when the Wilson family purchased the property upon which the gnarled Scuppernong, a Muscadine, grows. It has been trimmed back to a quarter acre, its limbs supported by posts and its vines forming a natural arbor.

After accidentally being sprayed with an herbicide by a power company in 2010, the vine was nursed back to health by the Wilsons and viticulture experts from North Carolina State University and the North Carolina Department of Agriculture. Thousands of cuttings have been taken from the Mother Vine and used to plant dozens of North Carolina vineyards.

In 2005, Duplin Winery planted a vineyard with Mother Vine cuttings and in 2008, began producing The Mother Vine Scuppernong, a bottled piece of history from this plot.

Westbend Vineyards in Lewisville is the old-timer in modern-day Yadkin Valley viticulture, founded in 1972 by Jack Kroustalis. Sixty acres of vinifera and hybrid varieties are planted near the banks of the Yadkin River in Forsyth County; the Chardonnays, Sauvignon Blancs, and Cabernet Sauvignons produced by Kroustalis and his crew can be excellent.

Swan Creek is a sub-AVA of the 1.4-million-acre Yadkin Valley, nestled into a southern nook of the mother AVA, in

NORTH CAROLINA SNAPSHOT
Vineyard acreage: 1,800
Most-planted varieties: Muscadine 1,400 acres; vinifera and hybrid 400 acres
Best varieties: Cabernet Sauvignon, Chardonnay, Muscadine
AVAs: Haw River Valley, Swan Creek, Yadkin Valley
Wineries: 100
Trailblazer: Westbend Vineyards
Steady hands: Dobbins Creek Vineyards, Laurel Gray Vineyards, Raffaldini Vineyards, RagAppleLassie Vineyards, RayLen Vineyards, Shelton Vineyards
Superstars: Biltmore Estate, Childress Vineyards, Duplin Winery, Westbend Vineyards

Wilkes, Yadkin, and Iredell counties. Its proximity to the Brushy Mountains gives Swan Creek a distinct soil comprised of schist, mica, and other minerals. There are five vineyards/wineries within the Swan Creek AVA: Raffaldini Vineyards, in Ronda, and Laurel Gray Vineyards, Buck Shoals Vineyards, Shadow Springs Vineyard, and Dobbins Creek Vineyards, in Hamptonville. Raffaldini is noteworthy for its Tuscan-style architecture and Italian varietal wines, including Vermentino, Sangiovese, and Montepulciano.

The Vanderbilt family's Biltmore Estate in Asheville, built in 1895, is a French chateau–design resort in the Blue Mountains, with 250 rooms, restaurants, a spa, and a winery that bottles 200,000 cases annually. Founded in 1970 by Cornelius Vanderbilt's great-great-grandson, George Cecil, the winery began making Muscadine wines, then expanded to Chardonnay, Viognier, Merlot, and other vinifera varieties and now supports its production by purchasing premium grapes from California. The winery says it is America's most-visited, with an estimated million people taking the tour and tasting the wines each year.

Many of them, no doubt, happen upon the winery while visiting this National Historic Landmark for other reasons, but the Napa Valley–like head count is impressive nonetheless.

Muscadines are well suited to the hot, humid Coastal Plain region of southeastern North Carolina. Muscadine types Carlos, Noble, Magnolia, and Scuppernong are resistant to pests and fungal diseases, making them the only viable wine grapes to cultivate here. With their musky aromas and ultrasweet flavors, Muscadines can be an acquired taste for the uninitiated, but many Southerners love their Scuppernong, Carlos, and Noble Muscadine wines.

Located in Duplin County, Duplin Winery is the largest Muscadine-wine producer in the world, bottling 300,000 cases per year. Owned by the Fussell family, Duplin has 49 acres of Muscadines and contracts with fifty growers in Mississippi, South Carolina, and Georgia for an additional 1,200 acres. The majority of the bottlings retain some of the high sugar content of the grapes and, as a result, are very sweet, although dry versions are also made.

According to the U.S. Department of Agriculture's Agricultural Research Service, Muscadines contain more resveratrol, a compound that lowers cholesterol and the risk of coronary heart disease, than any other grape. North Carolina wineries take advantage of this fact to help them sell not only wine, but also Muscadine-based nutritional supplements and skin-care products. The North Carolina market for Muscadine eating grapes is also substantial.

South Carolina

South Carolina's climate is more humid than North Carolina's, so Muscadines are the local grapes of choice. Producers also buy grapes from other states, and they rely on nongrape fruits for the production of sweet wines. In 2012, a law was enacted permitting wineries to use as much as 60 percent out-of-state fruit or juice in their wines—up from 49 percent—to encourage growth in the industry.

There are twelve wineries in South Carolina, most of them located near the tourism hubs of Myrtle Beach and Charleston. The oldest is Carolina Vineyards Winery, which began life in 1985 as Cruse Vineyards and Winery in Chester. Tim and Carrie Walker purchased Cruse in 1999, renamed it Carolina Vineyards Winery, and eventually relocated it to North Myrtle Beach.

Tennessee

The Tennessee Farm Winery Act of 1978 jump-started development of the commercial wine industry in the state, allowing producers to make and sell up to 40,000 gallons of wine a year at the wineries and to have on-site tasting rooms. Tennessee has forty licensed wineries scattered throughout the state and a mere 400 acres of wine grapes. Although state regulations require winemakers to progressively work their way up to using 75 percent Tennessee-grown grapes in their wines, importing grapes and wine from elsewhere is a common practice. Native American varieties dominate at approximately 60 percent of the plantings, followed by French-American hybrids.

Among Tennessee's wineries is Sugarland Cellars in Gatlinburg, which captures the attention of travelers thanks to its location at the entrance of Great Smoky Mountains State Park. Kix Brooks, of the retired Brooks & Dunn country band, owns Arrington Winery in Arrington, 25 miles south of Nashville. He relies on California and Washington grapes for several of his wines—a typical occurrence in Tennessee. Using local grapes, Apple Barn Winery in Sevierville produces a remarkably vibrant and balanced, semisweet Muscadine white, and Century Farm Winery in Jackson makes a lovely Traminette from Tennessee grapes. The state's oldest winery, Highland Manor Winery in Jamestown, opened in 1980, offers native, hybrid, and fruit wines in many styles.

Biltmore Estate
George Vanderbilt's 250-room mansion, completed in 1895 in Asheville, North Carolina, is now an 8,000-acre resort that includes vineyards and a winery (below), that produces 200,000 cases per year.

West Virginia

Bitter spring frosts limit most West Virginia grape growing to hardy hybrids. Potomac Highland Winery in the Eastern Panhandle, however, enjoys a warmer climate, and its vines are planted on rolling hills, which helps mitigate frost damage (cold air settles in low spots). As a result the Whitehill family can produce Chardonnay, Riesling, Cabernet Sauvignon, and Cabernet Franc from their own grapes.

Of the state's fourteen wineries, Fisher Ridge Wine Company (1979) is the oldest, and Daniel Vineyards in Crab Orchard is the largest. Dr. C. Richard Daniel began planting the vineyard in 1990 on a former golf course, and he has since experimented with 114 different varieties. He settled on fourteen of them as suitable for winemaking, among them the native Norton grape; French-American hybrids Seyval, Vidal, and Vignoles; and U.S.-bred Brianna, Cayuga, Traminette, Frontenac, and La Crescent.

The 'Mountain State' has varied climates and elevations, and hosts portions of the Kanawha River Valley, Ohio River Valley and Shenandoah Valley AVAs. While West Virginia is not yet known for quality wines, West Virginia University enologists and viticulturists are striving to improve grape and wine quality through research and industry education.

Lower South

Early settlers in the South attempted to grow European *Vitis vinifera* grapes, but the vines were intolerant of the heavy rainfall and stifling humidity, and fungal infections and Pierce's disease killed most of them. Hybrid varieties were popular for a time, but they, too, struggled. Native grapes thrived, however, and they remain a backbone of Southern wine production today. As the buckle of the Bible Belt, the Deep South remains wary of alcohol consumption. Many counties and parishes remain "dry" long after the end of Prohibition, but winemaking survives, although on a small scale.

Georgia

Georgia grows nearly 50 percent of the country's peanuts and is home to its most famous peanut farmer, President Jimmy Carter. The state's farmers also pride themselves on their juicy peaches—so adored that the late Hall of Fame baseball player Ty Cobb was nicknamed "The Georgia Peach."

But wine grapes are far more difficult to grow in Georgia's climate than peaches, and the majority of vineyards are planted to dependable, climate-adapted Muscadines that typically produce aromatically musky, sweet wines. Yet there is some serious winemaking going on with vinifera grapes too.

The prize of Georgia's viticultural territory is Dahlonega in Lumpkin County, an hour's drive from Atlanta. Unlike most of the South, Dahlonega supports the growth of European varieties Chardonnay, Viognier, Merlot, and Cabernet Sauvignon. Situated on a southern slope of the Blue Ridge Mountains, Dahlonega basks in extended afternoon sunlight and has a more temperate climate than the north slopes of the Tennessee Valley. Vinifera also benefits from the 1,000- to 1,850-foot elevations of Dahlonega, which expose grape clusters to moisture-evaporating breezes. The sandy loam soils are quick-draining and keep vine roots relatively dry; Muscadine varieties can thrive in heavier soils and don't seem to mind having wet feet.

Frogtown Cellars in Lumpkin County is the star producer in Georgia, with excellent vinifera wines made from 44 acres of estate grapes. Craig and Cydney Kritzer opened Frogtown in 1999 and now grow twenty-five varieties. Their Propaganda wine, a Bordeaux-style blend of Merlot, Cabernet Sauvignon, and Petit Verdot, has wowed West Coast critics and sommeliers;

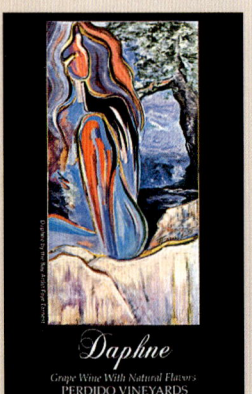
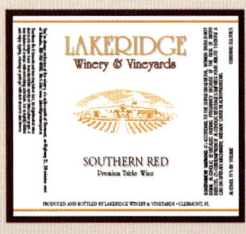

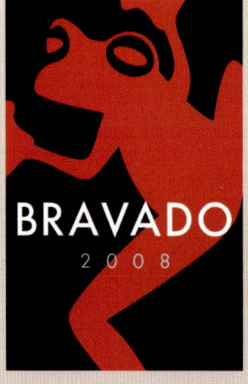

LOWER SOUTH SNAPSHOT

Vineyard acreage: GEORGIA 300; FLORIDA 1,000; ALABAMA 455 (wine and other grapes); MISSISSIPPI 570 (wine and other grapes); LOUISIANA 70 (wine and other grapes); ARKANSAS 500 (wine and other grapes)

Most-planted varieties: Muscadine (Carlos, Noble, Scuppernong)

Best varieties: Blanc du Bois, Muscadine, Norton/Cynthiana

AVAs: Mississippi Delta (Louisiana, Mississippi, Tennessee), Ozark Mountain (Arkansas, Missouri, Oklahoma)

Wineries: GEORGIA 25; FLORIDA 18; ALABAMA 11; MISSISSIPPI 4; LOUISIANA 6; ARKANSAS 5

Steady hands: GEORGIA—Chateau Elan, Habersham Vineyards, Three Sisters Vineyards, Tiger Mountain Vineyards; FLORIDA—Lakeridge Winery & Vineyards, San Sebastian Vineyards; ALABAMA—Perdido Vineyards, Southern Oak Wines; MISSISSIPPI—Old South Winery; LOUISIANA—Feliciana Cellars Winery, Pontchartrain Vineyards; ARKANSAS—Cowie Wine Cellars

Superstar: GEORGIA—Frogtown Cellars

Audacity, a Sangiovese–Cabernet Sauvignon blend, is most unusual for the South, and a dead ringer for a Super Tuscan from Italy. In the Kritzers' own words, their off-dry and sweet Muscadine wines are meant "for the Southern palate." Frogtown's Dahlonega neighbors include Blackstock Vineyards & Winery, Three Sisters Vineyards, and Wolf Mountain Vineyards & Winery.

Chateau Elan in Braselton, in northern Georgia, is a 3,500-acre vineyard estate, winery, resort, and convention center. As Georgia's largest wine producer, it offers a mix of Muscadine and vinifera bottlings. John and Martha Ezzard of Tiger Mountain Vineyards, in the town of Tiger, planted the first modern vinifera plantings in the state in 1995. They now grow Cabernet Franc, Malbec, Mourvèdre, Tannat, Touriga Nacional, Viognier, and Norton and are best known for their Petit Manseng white wines.

Florida

The Sunshine State is aptly named, but its subtropical climate plays havoc with vinifera and most traditional hybrid varieties. Spanish explorers found the wild grapevines known today as Muscadines here, and Floridians have produced wine from them ever since. In the 1940s, the University of Florida began breeding disease-resistant varieties, among them Conquistador and Blanc du Bois, that added more complexity in the finished wines. They are now the backbone of the state's winemaking industry.

Lakeridge Winery & Vineyards opened in Clermont in 1989. There longtime winemaker Jeanne Burgess works wonders with Blanc du Bois and Crescendo, a hybrid-grape sparkling wine. She is also the winemaker at sister winery San Sebastian in St. Augustine, reportedly the site of the first wine made in what would become the United States, in 1562.

Alabama

Jim Eddins has grown Muscadine in southern Alabama since 1972, selling the fruit to a Florida winery until 1978. When the owner died, Eddins was stuck with grapes that had no home, so he started his own winery, Perdido Vineyards, in 1979—the first in Alabama since Prohibition. The northern part of the state is warmer and more conducive to growing wine grapes other than Muscadines. Near Anniston, Southern Oak Wines produces a commendable Norton from its White Oak Vineyards.

Mississippi

Mississippi has three strikes against it in the winemaking game: Southern Baptist–based objections to alcohol consumption, strident state alcohol laws, and the lowest median income in the country. Many Mississippians can't afford to purchase wine, let alone travel to tasting rooms and soak up the wine country vibe. But five wineries have hung tough, producing Muscadine-based wines; the trouper is Old South Winery, founded in 1979 by veterinarian Scott Galbreath.

Louisiana

In 2005, Hurricane Katrina devastated the Gulf Coast, altering the culture and landscape forever. Near Baton Rouge, in the Mississippi Delta AVA, a few dogged vintners continue to produce Muscadine wines, among them Pontchartrain Vineyards and Feliciana Cellars Winery. Pontchartrain has succeeded with Blanc du Bois, the Florida hybrid, which can withstand the humid climate without much threat of mildew or rot and produces a fresh, floral white wine.

Arkansas

Arkansas has just five wineries, although that number could grow as Concord vines are replaced by wine grapes. A star of the still-small show is Cowie Wine Cellars in the Arkansas River Valley, known not only for its hybrid, Muscadine, and fruit wines, but also for owner Robert Cowie's Arkansas Historic Wine Museum. He proudly displays a collection of a hundred church bells there too; this is the Bible Belt, after all.

Lakeridge Winery & Vineyards
In the muggy climate of Clermont, Florida, Lakeridge successfully grows hybrid (Blanc du Bois and Stover) and Muscadine (Carlos and Noble) grapes for its annual production of 80,000 cases of wine.

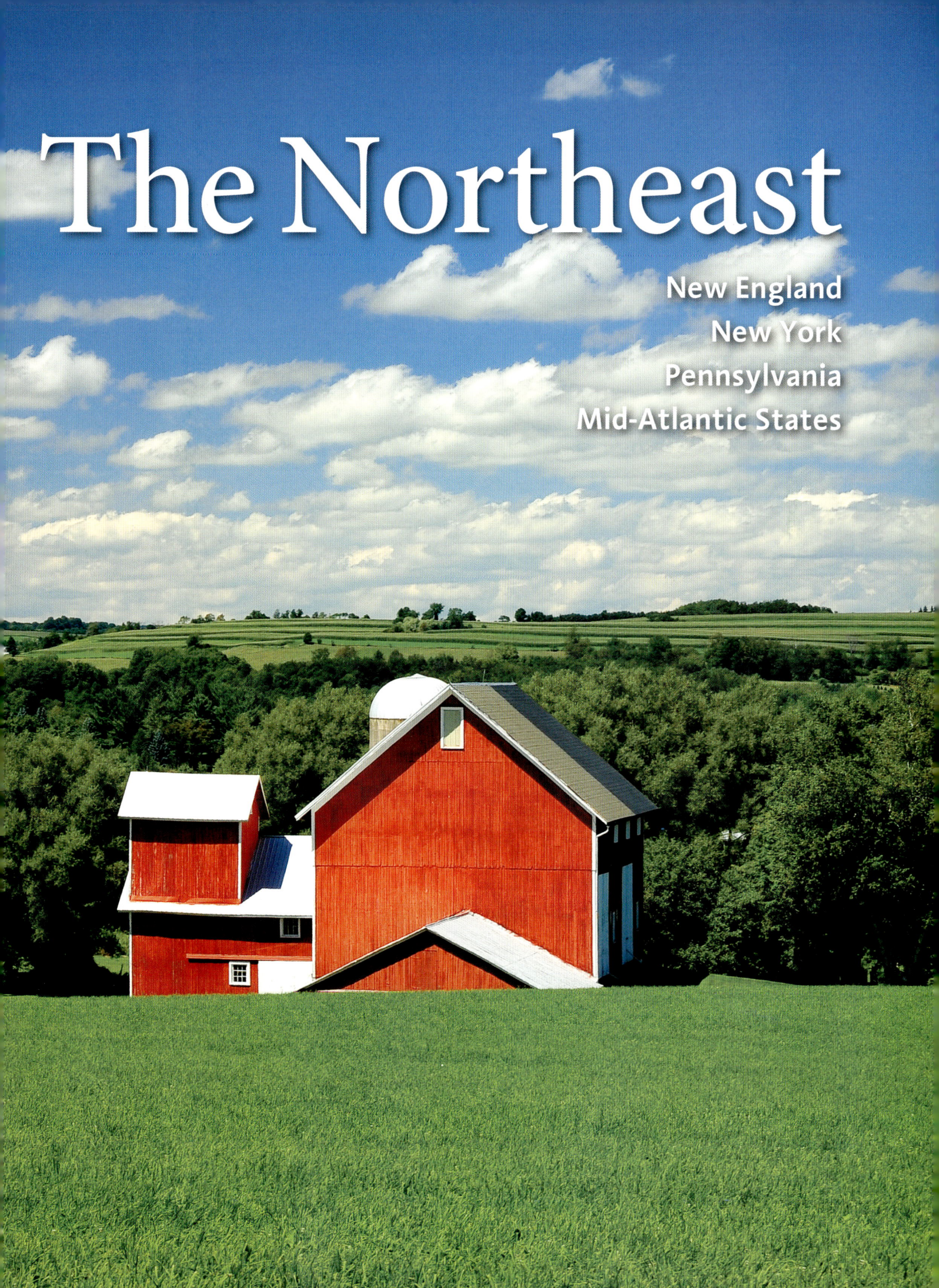

The Northeast

New England
New York
Pennsylvania
Mid-Atlantic States

New England

Despite lush, rolling hills; forests; bountiful farms; and spectacular fall colors—scenery common in many U.S. wine regions—rural New England is not a hospitable place for wine grapes. Apples, cranberries, blueberries, and stone fruits produce prolifically and are fermented into ciders and fruit wines that are popular with many. However, while the growing season is too short to support most *Vitis vinifera* vines, vintners in Connecticut, Maine, Massachusetts, New Hampshire, Rhode Island, and Vermont have hybrids on their side.

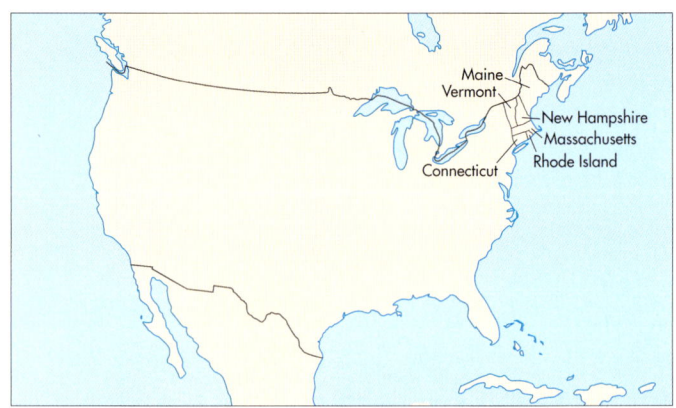

Successful breeding of cold-hardy, early-ripening varieties at the University of Minnesota and Cornell University in New York State has given New Englanders hybrid options such as Cayuga White, La Crescent, and Seyval Blanc for white wines, and Frontenac, Marquette, and St. Croix for reds. In skilled hands, these varieties of grape can be vinified into interesting and rewarding wines.

New Englanders have embraced grape growing as a viable component of their diversified farms. It's common for vintners to produce fruit, hybrid, and vinifera wines, hedging their bets for the inevitable climatically troublesome years. Many wineries purchase out-of-state grapes as extra insurance, and that tactic was important in 2009, when rain-induced rot destroyed up to 90 percent of the crop in some vineyards. Some wineries stayed in business only by bottling and selling wine made from grapes grown elsewhere.

In **Connecticut**, commercial wine production wasn't permitted until 1978, so the existence of twenty-five wineries today is notable. The state's southern areas are the warmest, and thus more hospitable to vinifera grapes. Haight-Brown Vineyard in Litchfield is Connecticut's oldest winery, established soon after the 1978 passage of the Connecticut Winery Act. Hopkins Vineyard in New Preston is part of a farm that has been in existence for more than two hundred years; its stock in trade is sparkling wine. Sharpe Hill Vineyard in Pomfret makes the popular Ballet of Angels, a semidry blend of Cayuga White, Riesling, Seyval Blanc, and Vidal Blanc.

Lincoln Peak Vineyard
Lincoln Peak is Vermont's largest grower of wine grapes—at a mere 12 acres of La Crescent, Marquette, and other cold-hardy varieties. A strawberry stand near Middlebury was converted into the tasting room.

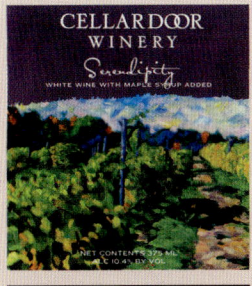

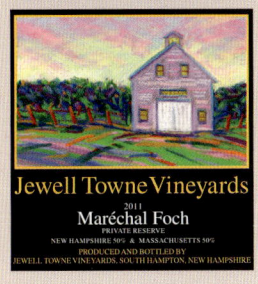

NEW ENGLAND SNAPSHOT

Vineyard acreage: CONNECTICUT 400; NEW HAMPSHIRE 30; RHODE ISLAND 200; VERMONT 120; MASSACHUSETTS 500; MAINE 30

Most-planted varieties: Cayuga White, Seyval Blanc, Vidal Blanc, Marechal Foch, Marquette

Best varieties: Cayuga White, Frontenac, Marechal Foch, Marquette, La Crescent, Riesling, Seyval Blanc, St. Croix, Vidal Blanc

AVAs: CONNECTICUT—Western Connecticut Highlands; MASSACHUSETTS—Martha's Vineyard; MASSACHUSETTS AND RHODE ISLAND—Southeastern New England

Wineries: CONNECTICUT 25; NEW HAMPSHIRE 17; RHODE ISLAND 10; VERMONT 15; MASSACHUSETTS 36; MAINE 23

Steady hands: CONNECTICUT—Chamard Vineyards, Haight-Brown Vineyard, Hopkins Vineyard, Priam Vineyards, Sharpe Hill Vineyard, Stonington Vineyards, Sunset Meadow Vineyards; NEW HAMPSHIRE—Candia Vineyards, Flag Hill Vineyards, Jewell Towne Vineyards; RHODE ISLAND—Newport Vineyards, Sakonnet Vineyards; VERMONT—Lincoln Peak Vineyard, Shelburne Vineyard; MASSACHUSETTS—Travessia Urban Winery, Westport Rivers Winery; MAINE—Blacksmith Winery, Cellardoor Winery

---

Retired emergency room physician Dr. Peter Oldak is the father of **New Hampshire** winemaking. He converted his hobby-gone-wild vineyard/winery to commercial status in 1994, and his Jewell Towne Vineyards in South Hampton produces wines from such obscure varieties as Landot Noir and Valvin Muscat; Oldak coaxes the Alden table grape into a light-bodied, crisp red wine. His most complex wine is an unctuous Vidal Blanc ice wine.

Newport, **Rhode Island**, is the country's yachting capital, and nearby Sakonnet Vineyards is a large, by New England standards, wine producer, at 30,000 cases per year. Vidal Blanc, Gewürztraminer, and its Eye of the Storm rosé are Sakonnet's most confident wines.

Vermont, renowned for its maple syrup, also has a star wine producer in Lincoln Peak Vineyard. It excels at Frontenac Gris, La Crescent, and Marquette, and its Black Sparrow white blend is a top seller. Gail and Ken Albert at Shelburne Vineyard in Shelburne have had a string of successes with their cherry-bomb Marquettes.

In **Massachusetts**, Westport Rivers Winery, founded in 1986 by the Russell family, is run by brothers Rob and Bill Russell. Their Chardonnays and Rieslings have avid followers, but the RJR Brut sparkler is the flagship. Travessia Urban Winery in New Bedford is a new producer dedicated to making wines from Massachusetts-grown grapes; it's one to watch.

Maine's lobsters, L.L. Bean outfitters, and the Kennebunkport retreat of U.S. presidents Bush, father and son, will always have top billing, but the state's wine industry should not be ignored. Two dozen wineries brave the cold conditions, finding success largely with fruit wines. Cellardoor Winery in Lincolnville is the most recognized producer, with a range of wines vinified from West Coast grapes, and some using local grapes and nongrape fruit. Serendipity, its maple-syrup-infused Riesling dessert wine, is a surprisingly delicious example of enological ingenuity.

Jewell Towne Vineyards
Just-picked clusters are transported to Jewell Towne's winery in New Hampshire, located on the shores of the Powow River in South Hampton. Each day during the harvest, a dozen or so volunteers assist with the picking and processing of the grapes.

New York

New York City is acknowledged as the nation's trendsetter in finance, fashion, theater, dance, and art. Its cosmopolitan status is also reflected in world-class restaurants whose wine lists offer opportunities to taste wines from around the world. With the rise of the locavore movement, city sommeliers are increasingly including New York State wines on their lists and urban wineries are popping up in Manhattan and Brooklyn. But New York City is only a tiny corner of the state.

Wineries arrive in the Big Apple
The majority of New York's vineyards are located in the northwestern and southeastern parts of the state, but even the big city has a burgeoning wine industry.

Venture away from the Big Apple, and urbanization gives way to suburbs and then countryside. The electricity of the big city loses wattage the farther north, east, or west one goes, into the winegrowing regions of the Finger Lakes, Hudson Valley, Long Island, Lake Erie, and the Niagara Escarpment, where the current runs at a gentle buzz.

New York was among the first states to produce commercial wines. Brotherhood Winery, in the Hudson River Region AVA, opened in 1839, making it the oldest continuously operating winery in the United States. Great Western Winery, also known as Pleasant Valley Wine Company, arrived in the Finger Lakes area in 1860 and established itself as a producer of native-grape wines and, later, popular sparkling wines made from the American Catawba grape.

Not long after, Gold Seal Vineyards (1865), Eagle Crest Vineyards (1872), The Taylor Wine Company (1880), and Widmer's Wine Cellars (1888) established roots in the Finger Lakes, making sparkling and dessert wines. Prohibition and the Depression halted New York's winemaking march, but the parade restarted in the 1960s and early 1970s, with the arrival of such producers as Benmarl Winery in the Hudson River Region, Johnson Estate Winery on the southeastern shore of Lake Erie, and Bully Hill Vineyards and Dr. Konstantin Frank's Vinifera Wine Cellars in the Finger Lakes.

The real winery boom in New York began with the Farm Winery Act of 1976, which made it easier for small, family-run wineries to enter the business. Since 1976, the number of New York wineries has leapt from 19 to 320, in the process creating new jobs, increased tax revenues for the state, and an explosion in wine-based tourism. New York now is the third-largest wine-producing state, trailing only California and Washington State.

The Farm Winery Act came soon after the Taylor and Great Western wineries changed their grape sourcing from native varieties to *Vitis vinifera*. This left hundreds of grape growers holding worthless contracts for their fruit; the Farm Winery Act gave them the opportunity to produce wine from their own grapes and sell their wines themselves, without a distributor middleman.

Cornell University in Ithaca is the East Coast equivalent of California's UC Davis, a hub for teaching and research in enology and viticulture. At the New York State Agricultural Experiment Station in Geneva, Cornell has successfully bred French-American

NEW YORK SNAPSHOT
Vineyard acreage: 34,000
Most-planted varieties: Concord, Riesling, Niagara, Vidal Blanc, Merlot, Chardonnay
Best varieties: Cabernet Franc, Gewürztraminer, Merlot, Riesling, Vidal Blanc
AVAs: Cayuga Lake, Finger Lakes, Hudson River Region, Lake Erie, Long Island, Niagara Escarpment, North Fork of Long Island, Seneca Lake, The Hamptons Long Island
Wineries: 320

Dr. Konstantin Frank
The Ukrainian immigrant stunned naysayers in the 1950s by demonstrating that vinifera vines could survive in the cool, wet Finger Lakes region.

NEW YORK STATE

From Long Island in the southeast to Lake Erie and Niagara Escarpment in the northwest, New York has tremendous diversity in climate, soils, wine varieties, and the styles it can produce.

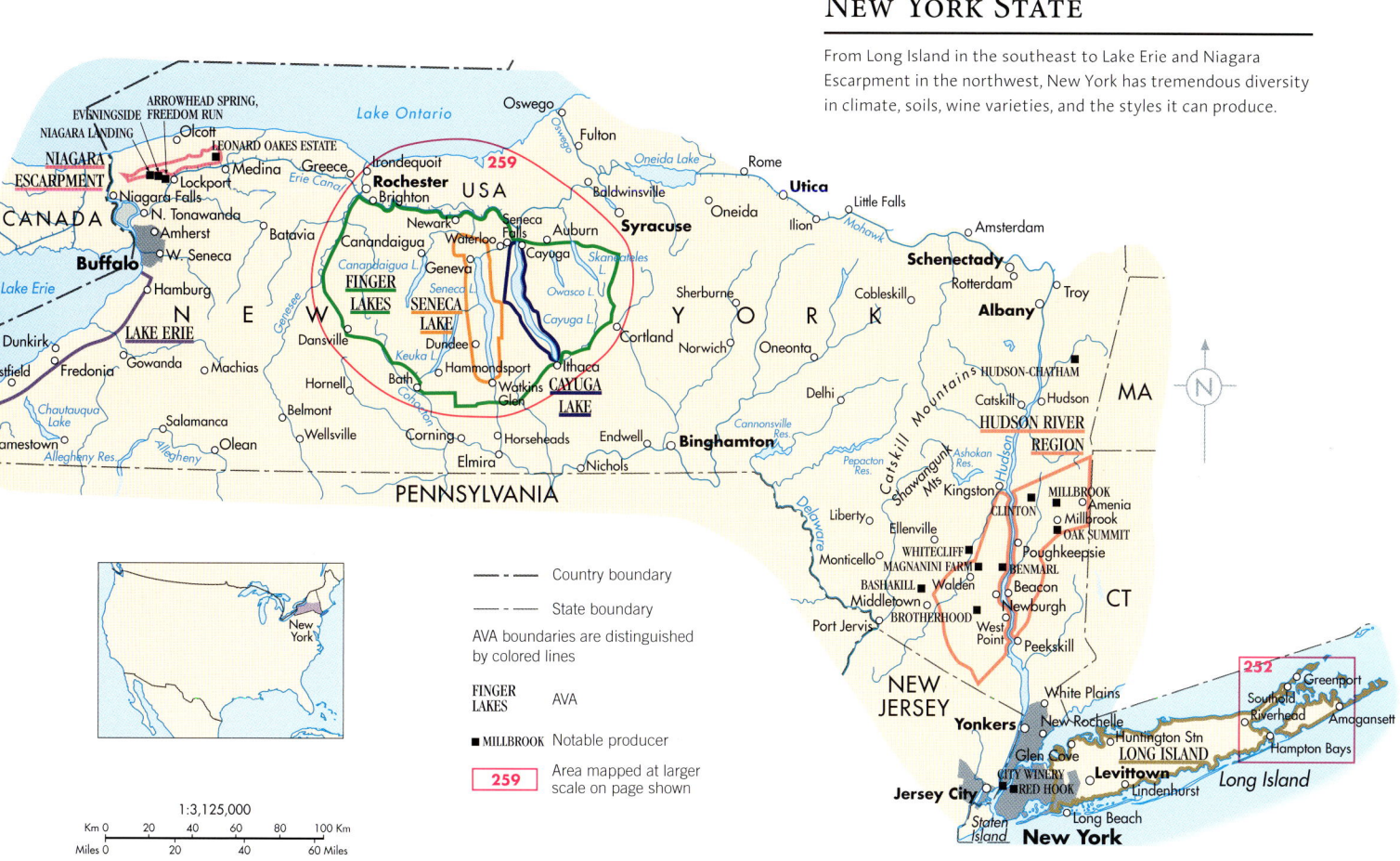

hybrid grapes to withstand the cold, wet, and windy climates of the East and Midwest and to resist the fungal diseases encouraged by the humidity. Many of these hardy hybrids can produce wines that have the flavor characteristics of European vinifera wines.

Of Cornell's recent hybrid creations, the most promising for cold-climate conditions include Noiret, which makes a tart red wine with aromas of black pepper and violets; Corot Noir, a heavier, edgier red wine; and Valvin Muscat, which typically produces a perfumed (think citrus blossoms), fruity white wine. Cayuga White, Chardonel, and Traminette—all light-skinned grapes—have also been highly successful when fermented into wine.

Canandaigua Winery was the birthplace of what is now Constellation Brands Inc., the giant in the global wine, beer, and spirits field, with more than thirty production facilities throughout the world. Now based in nearby Victor, Constellation owns dozens of wine brands, among them Robert Mondavi Winery in Napa Valley, Clos du Bois in Sonoma County, and Hogue Cellars in eastern Washington. Founded in 1945 by Marvin Sands, Constellation is currently operated by his sons, Robert and Richard Sands. Lower-end wine brands Arbor Mist, Taylor New York Desserts, Manischewitz, Richard's Wild Irish Rose, and Paul Masson are produced in Canandaigua, at the site of the original Sands winery.

The New York Wine & Grape Foundation, a nonprofit organization funded by the state, administers multiple programs, including grape and wine research, and marketing and legislative consultation. While its most obvious role is that of cheerleader for New York wineries and vineyards, it also works behind the scenes to lobby for the interests of the industry. The foundation, for example, was instrumental in winning the right of wineries to ship their wines directly to consumers, bypassing wholesalers. It's also a partner in the New York Wine & Culinary Center in Canandaigua, a gateway for visitors to explore the state's wine and food providers via tastings and classes.

In all of New York's viticultural areas, large bodies of water play a crucial role in creating conditions beneficial for growing wine grapes. As it is in other northeastern states, New York's climate is harsh in winter, hot and muggy in summer; lakes and oceans moderate the extremes, providing warming air during cold months and cooling breezes during the growing season. Two of the Great Lakes (Erie and Ontario), the Atlantic Ocean (including Long Island Sound), the lower portion of the Hudson River, and the largest of the Finger Lakes (Canandaigua, Keuka, Seneca, and Cayuga) buffer cold and hot temperatures and reduce the risk of winter injury and spring and fall frosts.

LONG ISLAND AVA

Long Island is often called New York's Bordeaux, as it excels in the red grape varieties Cabernet Franc and Merlot. Extending 100 miles east of New York City, the island splits into the North Fork and South Fork (the latter being home to the Hamptons, populated every summer by celebrities), with vineyards and wineries clustered in the eastern tips of the two forks. Formerly an area of family-owned farms and fishing villages, it has become an attractive, bucolic place for people of means to become farmers and grape growers.

Channing Daughters Winery
This Long Island producer has a penchant for wines made from Italian (Friulano, Malvasia Bianca, and Sangiovese) and German (Blaufränkisch and Dornfelder) varieties.

Long Island

Long Island, the AVA, extends 120 miles into the Atlantic Ocean and has two sub-AVAs within it, the upscale Hamptons, and the more rural North Fork of Long Island.

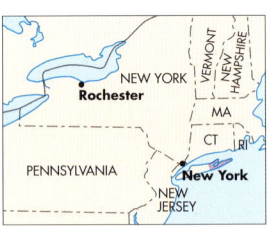

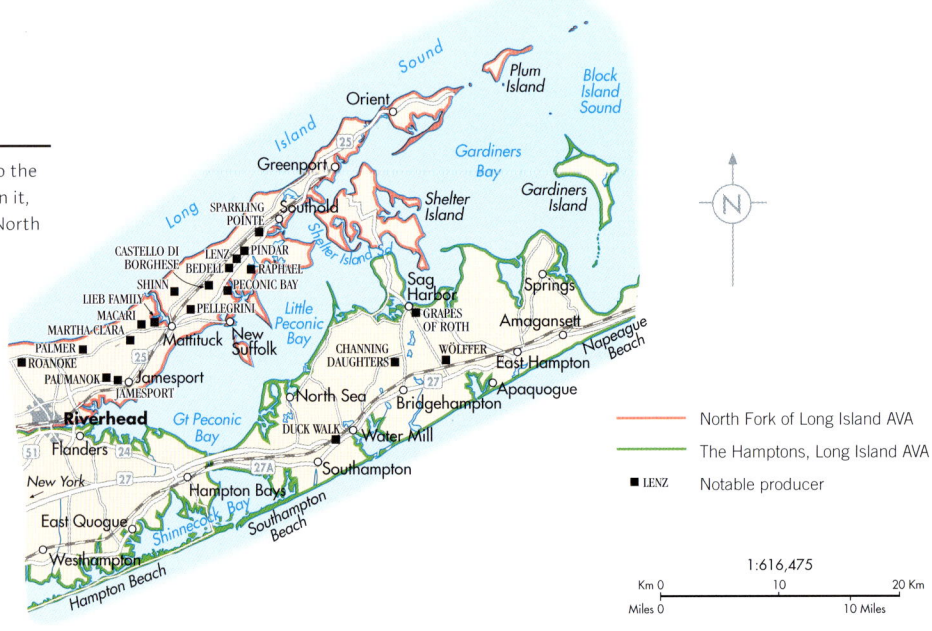

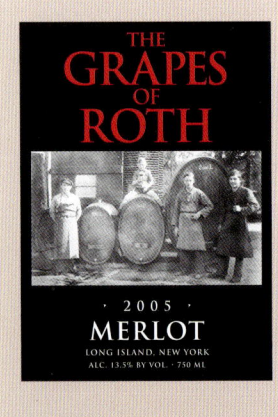
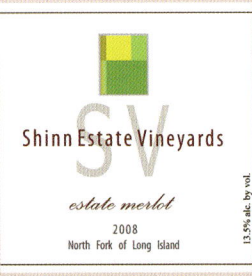

LONG ISLAND AVA SNAPSHOT

Vineyard acreage: 3,000

Sub-AVAs: North Fork of Long Island, The Hamptons Long Island

Most-planted varieties: Chardonnay, Sauvignon Blanc, Cabernet Franc, Merlot, Cabernet Sauvignon

Best varieties: Cabernet Franc, Chardonnay, Merlot, Riesling, Sauvignon Blanc

Wineries: 56

Steady hands: Bedell Cellars, Castello di Borghese, Lenz Winery, Lieb Family Cellars, Martha Clara Vineyards, Peconic Bay Winery, Pellegrini Vineyards, Pindar Vineyards, Sparkling Pointe

Superstars: Channing Daughters, Grapes of Roth, Paumanok Vineyards, Roanoke Vineyards, Shinn Vineyards, Wölffer Estate

One to watch: Macari Vineyards

Peconic Bay separates the two forks, which are flanked by the Atlantic Ocean (South Fork) and Long Island Sound (North Fork). These bodies of water help moderate temperatures, cold or hot, throughout the year, allowing for a long grape-growing season. In the Finger Lakes region in the northern part of New York, spring arrives later and winter comes earlier than here, and Long Island's wider maturation window allows late-ripening varieties such as Merlot and Cabernet Sauvignon to reach maturity before vines begin their winter sleep.

Since the early 1990s, vineyard acreage has increased in the Long Island AVA and its two sub-AVAs, North Fork of Long Island and The Hamptons, Long Island; nearly all of the growth has been in vinifera vines, with hybrids and native grapes almost nonexistent. The majority of vineyards are on the North Fork; the South Fork's land can certainly support grapes, but high-end houses and vacation homes are far more profitable uses of real estate in the Hamptons.

Because the vineyards and wineries are located at the eastern tips of its forks, in close proximity to the ocean, they get some cooling breeze relief in the summer months. The warm temperatures generally persist until early November. Some rain usually falls during the growing season, but Atlantic winds quickly dry out the grape clusters, preventing rot development, and there are long stretches of dry, warm weather in between (the hamlet of Cutchogue, in the heart of the North Fork of Long Island AVA, claims to be "the sunniest spot in New York State").

Long Island's soils were formed in glacial outwash till from the retreat of glaciers ten thousand years ago. Moderately fertile and with excellent drainage to wick away summer rainfall, the soil naturally limits canopy growth, allowing the plants to devote most of their energy to ripening their fruit. The relatively benign conditions accommodate myriad vinifera varieties: the widely planted Chardonnay and Merlot and, in lesser acreage numbers, Sauvignon Blanc, Riesling, Viognier, Gewürztraminer, Pinot Gris, Grüner Veltliner, Albariño, Chenin Blanc, Semillon, Friulano, Pinot Blanc, Cabernet Franc, Cabernet Sauvignon, Petit Verdot, Malbec, Carmenere, Blaufränkisch, Dornfelder, Syrah, and Pinot Noir.

Generally, the wines of Long Island walk a tightrope between California fruitiness and European structure and elegance—a quality shared with Washington State wine. And, like Washington, Long Island's modern winemaking history is short compared to California's: It began in 1973, when Alex and Louisa Hargrave planted the island's first vineyard in Cutchogue; two years later they opened the doors to Hargrave Vineyard's winery. Since then, Long Island growers and vintners have negotiated a steep learning curve, and the growth continues.

It helps to have a trained, well-traveled winemaker to lead the way. Roman Roth, who was born to a winemaking family in Germany and trained in enology there—and with winemaking experience at Saintsbury winery in California and Rosemount

Shinn Estate Vineyards
This North Fork winery produces some of New York's finest Sauvignon Blanc, Chardonnay, Merlot, and Cabernet Franc wines, from organically farmed grapes.

Estate in Australia under his belt—arrived in the Hamptons in 1992 to manage start-up Sagpond Vineyards. During the next several years, Roth oversaw the expansion of Sagpond into Wölffer Estate Vineyard, where he is now winemaker and technical director.

Wölffer is in the Hamptons on the South Fork of Long Island, and was owned by international businessman and fellow German Christian Wölffer until his death in 2008. Roth's meticulous winemaking efforts and deep viticultural knowledge have long been reflected in Wölffer's Chardonnays, Merlots, and Cabernet Francs, which have track records for aging beautifully. Roth's Fatalis Fatum, a blend of Merlot, Cabernet Franc and Cabernet Sauvignon, is a dead ringer for a classic Bordeaux, with an appealing savory character and solid structure.

Roth spreads his experience around, serving as the consulting winemaker for several Long Island wineries, among them Martha Clara Vineyards and Roanoke Vineyards. As if that weren't enough work, he also has his own brand, The Grapes of Roth, for the production of high-end Riesling and Merlot.

Not coincidentally, Roanoke Vineyards on the North Fork is owned by Wölffer viticulturist Richard Pisacano and his wife, Soraya. Pisacano, who has worked in Long Island's vineyards for three decades, and Roth form a formidable team at Roanoke, which produces Bordeaux-style red blends and single-variety Merlots and Cabernet Francs. Cabernet

URBAN WINERIES

There's barely a patch of suitable dirt in New York City on which to grow grapevines, yet that hasn't prevented fine wine from being made in some of New York's hippest neighborhoods. Three upscale winemaking facilities built since 2008—one in Manhattan and two in Brooklyn—have city slickers taking the subway for a trip to "wine country."

In 2008, nightclub superstar Michael Dorf (Knitting Factory) opened City Winery in downtown Manhattan as a combination winery, wine bar, restaurant, and live music venue. There fledgling vintners who purchase a membership produce their own wines (guided by professionals) from grapes purchased throughout the country and trucked to New York in refrigerated bins. The staff produces City Winery house wines that are poured in the bar— many from stainless steel kegs—and the retail wine list is upscale and international in scope.

In the same year, Brooklynite Mark Snyder of Angels' Share Wine Imports opened Red Hook Winery in Brooklyn. Named for the neighborhood in which it is located, Red Hook has two Napa Valley winemakers— natural-wine guru Abe Schoener of Scholium Project and cult modernist Robert Foley of Switchback Ridge and Robert Foley Wines— producing wines from Long Island–grown grapes. Schoener and Foley don't collaborate; each produces his wines from grapes grown in the same vineyards, but with different methods. Snyder's goals: To bring Long Island wines to the attention of New York City sommeliers and to identify Long Island terroir as it is expressed by winemakers with wildly divergent styles.

Brooklyn Winery debuted in 2010 as a wine bar, private-event space, and make-your-own winery. Owners Brian Leventhal and John Stires also offer dishes to pair with the wines they produce at the winery from purchased grapes and a focused list of domestic and imported wines.

City Winery
A winery, wine bar, restaurant, and concert venue, City Winery in downtown Manhattan brings wine country to the urban masses— part of a nationwide trend.

Roman Roth
The German-born, well-traveled Roth settled on New York's Long Island in 1992, where he directs winemaking at Wölffer Estate and has his own brand, Grapes of Roth. His Rieslings and Merlots are European in style, refined and cellar-worthy.

Sauvignon is not a predictable maturer on Long Island, but a portion of Pisacano's 10-acre vineyard reliably ripens Cabernet Sauvignon, largely because it is sheltered from northerly winds by the Roanoke Bluff and gets plenty of sun exposure.

Forty-seven of Long Island's fifty-six wineries are on the North Fork. The region is a harmonious mix of Long Island pioneers and newcomers, and a few changes of ownership have brought some social sizzle.

Thirty-year-old Bedell Cellars has been owned by Michael Lynne since 2000, when he purchased the property from the Bedell family. Lynne, a movie executive who produced *The Lord of the Rings* trilogy and the *Austin Powers* films (among many others), has maintained continuity with the early days of Bedell by retaining founding winemaker Kip Bedell. Bedell works with winemaker Rich Olsen-Harbich, who wrote the North Fork of Long Island AVA petition, which was approved in 1986.

All the grapes are grown on the Bedell Estate in Cutchogue. The flagship wine is Musée, a red blend of Merlot, Cabernet Sauvignon, and Petit Verdot produced only in the best vintages. Bedell's steel-tank-fermented Viogniers are lush in pear, white peach, and honeysuckle aromas and flavors.

At what is now Martha Clara Vineyards in Riverhead, Robert Entenmann (of Entenmann baked goods fame) took a potato field and converted it into a thoroughbred horse farm. Later he added vineyards and hired Wölffer's Roth to make the wines. Not surprisingly, the Martha Clara Riesling is pure and precise, arguably the best wine from this winery, which is named for Robert's mother, Martha Clara.

Take a couple who met while working in Berkeley, California, restaurants, transplant them to Long Island with land to plant a vineyard, and you get an estate that uses organic and biodynamic farming techniques in order to bring harmony to the vines and clarity to the wines. Now married, Barbara Shinn and David Page planted Shinn Estate Vineyards on the North Fork in 2002, two years after they began preparing the soil. Today their 20-acre vineyard teems with life: waves of clover, vetch, and dandelions grow between vine rows; beneficial insects and honeybees hum as one; bantam chickens and rabbits roam about; and earthworms wriggle in every shovelful of upturned earth—a sign of healthy soils.

That Shinn and Page can grow grapes this way in a region where wet conditions force others to use chemicals to combat rot and mildew is a marvel. Their wines—best efforts typically are the Sauvignon Blancs, Chardonnays, and Merlots—are bright and, indeed, focused, just as the couple is on nonintervention in the vineyard.

Paumanok Vineyards was founded by Charles and Ursula Massoud in the early 1980s. Their oldest son, Kareem, is now the winemaker, working in a renovated turn-of-the-century barn outfitted with tanks and barrels. Ursula is German, so naturally, Paumanok produces Riesling (in three styles). Chenin Blanc and Merlot are also standouts.

Channing Daughters Winery's winemaker, James Christopher Tracy, is a San Francisco native who isn't afraid to experiment. Although Long Island is best known for Bordeaux-style red wines made from Merlot and Cabernet Franc, Tracy looks to northern Italy for his winemaking inspiration.

His Sauvignon Blancs and Chardonnays are superbly made, but the roller-coaster thrills come from his (Tocai) Friulano, Malvasia Bianca, Barbera, Sangiovese, Blaufränkisch, and Dornfelder wines, and exotic blends such as Mosaico (Pinot Grigio, Chardonnay, Sauvignon Blanc, Muscat Ottonel, Friulano, and Gewürztraminer).

Hargrave Vineyard became Castello di Borghese after Marco and Ann Marie Borghese's purchase of the property and winery from Alex and Louisa Hargrave in 1999. Louisa remains in the wine business as a consultant and writer; she and Alex deserve credit for creating the first commercial wines on Long Island, and the market for them. Her book *The Vineyard: The Perils and Pleasures of Creating an American Family Winery* should be read by anyone thinking about planting a vineyard and/or producing wine.

Long Island is home to three accomplished producers of sparkling wines: Lenz Winery, Lieb Family Cellars, and Sparkling Pointe. Each employs traditional Champagne production methods, in which the still wines undergo a second fermentation in the bottle, which creates the bubbles (carbon dioxide) and allows the wine to remain in contact with the spent yeast cells for up to several years, thus increasing complexity and richness.

HUDSON RIVER REGION AVA

The Hudson River carves a dramatic path from the Adirondack Mountains some 300 miles south through New York State and joins the ocean beyond Manhattan. Ninety miles north of New York City is the Hudson Valley, an area of pastoral beauty—with family farms, horse ranches, quaint towns, and mansions built in the nineteenth century by Rockefellers and Roosevelts—as well as the producer of some of America's finest foie gras. French Huguenots planted the first grapevines here in 1677, and wine production began soon thereafter. However, it has only been since the early 1990s that the words "quality" and "winemaking" appeared in the same sentence in reference to the region.

The Hudson River Region AVA, established in 1982, basically hugs the banks of the Hudson River from White Plains to north of Poughkeepsie, under the shadows of the Shawangunk and Catskill Mountains.

Previously known as a maker of French-American hybrid wines and of wines produced from grapes purchased from growers on Long Island and in the Finger Lakes region, the Hudson River Region AVA is ever so slowly, yet reliably, moving toward classic European wine grapes, including Chardonnay, Cabernet Franc, and even Pinot Noir, grown at home. The leader of the movement is John Dyson, proprietor of Millbrook Vineyards & Winery in Millbrook, in Dutchess County.

Millbrook's Proprietor's Special Reserve Chardonnay and Proprietor's Special Reserve Cabernet Franc are exceptional wines, clearly the best in the AVA. Dyson also owns famed Pinot Noir producer Williams Selyem, in Sonoma County, California, and recent Millbrook Pinots have shown promise (bonus: a visit to the Millbrook tasting room just might yield a bottle of Williams Selyem).

Dyson, a former state agriculture commissioner and the creator, with Dr. Richard Smart, of the Smart-Dyson trellising system, has planted dozens of varieties in an attempt to determine which grapes can withstand both the severe winters of the Hudson Valley and the humid summers, which promote fungal disease in the fruit; most have been crossed off his list. Winter injury—sometimes fatal—is possible during January and February deep freezes, and spring frosts can destroy an entire crop. In fact, even Dyson, who would prefer to grow all his own grapes, sources Merlot from Long Island because the variety can't withstand these conditions.

In the Hudson River Region, more than anywhere else in New York where vinifera is cultivated, putting the right grape varieties in the right spots is essential in order to reduce risks of crop loss.

Brotherhood Winery
Billing itself as "America's Oldest Winery," founded in 1839 by French Huguenot immigrant Jean Jacques, Brotherhood is a magnet for visitors and a maker of credible wines.

The Hudson River Valley
The Hudson River, which flows north to south through nearly all of eastern New York State, provides warmth to grapevines during the harsh winters in the Hudson River Region AVA (top).

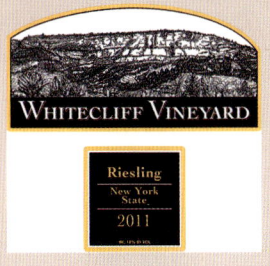
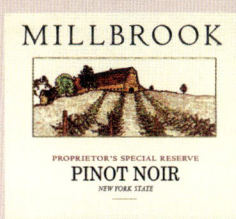
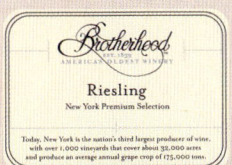

HUDSON RIVER REGION AVA SNAPSHOT

Vineyard acreage: **430**

Most-planted varieties: **Chardonnay, Seyval Blanc, Baco Noir**

Best varieties: **Baco Noir, Cabernet Franc, Chardonnay, Pinot Noir**

Wineries: **33**

Trailblazer: **Brotherhood Winery**

Steady hands: **BashaKill Vineyards, Benmarl Winery, Clinton Vineyards, Hudson-Chatham Winery, Magnanini Farm Winery, Oak Summit, Whitecliff Vineyard & Winery**

Superstar: **Millbrook Vineyards & Winery**

Whitecliff Vineyard & Winery
Yancey and Michael Migliore's Hudson Valley winery sits in the heart of their 26-acre vineyard, in which they grow twenty grape varieties.

For those without the right spots, cold-hardy hybrids such as Cayuga White, Seyval Blanc, Baco Noir, Marquette, and Noiret can produce high-quality, interesting wines. BashaKill Vineyards in Sullivan County has emerged as one of the more competent hybrid-wine producers in the area. Established by Paul Deninno in 2005 in the scenic Catskills, BashaKill bottles Cayuga White, Noiret, Marquette, and various blends.

BashaKill is one of the region's newest wineries. Its oldest, Brotherhood Winery in Washingtonville, was founded in 1839 by a French Huguenot immigrant named Jean Jacques and has operated continuously ever since. Tourism has trumped serious winemaking there over the years, and Brotherhood, which is listed on the National Register of Historic Places, has gotten a lot of mileage out its tag line, "America's Oldest Winery."

Most visitors are eager to pay for winery tours, visit the museum, and grab a bite at the Vinum Café, but current owner Cesar Baeza—one of many proprietors since Brotherhood's birth—has moved winemaking away from grapey *Vitis labrusca* wines to vinifera varieties. Although it's a work in progress, Baeza has done well of late with a blanc de blancs sparkler, a Riesling, and a ruby port–style wine.

John Dyson
Long before he purchased California's iconic Williams Selyem winery in 1998, Dyson founded Millbrook Vineyards & Winery in his hometown of Millbrook, New York, in 1979. Dyson is a former New York State Commissioner of Agriculture and Commissioner of Commerce, developed the "I Love NY" advertising campaign, and, with Australian viticulturist Dr. Richard Smart, devised the popular Smart-Dyson grapevine trellis system.

FINGER LAKES AVA

The Finger Lakes is the most diverse of New York's viticultural areas, with more than thirty varieties planted (65 percent labrusca, 20 percent hybrid, and 15 percent vinifera). Established in 1982, the AVA covers all or parts of thirteen counties and more than 2.5 million acres of land, although just 9,000-plus are in vineyards. Since its federal approval, the AVA has been subdivided into two sub-AVAs, Seneca Lake and Cayuga Lake; Keuka Lake might one day be a third nested AVA within the Finger Lakes appellation.

There are eleven Finger Lakes, ranging in depth from 300 to 650 feet and each extending south from the region's "palm" north of Geneva. These long, narrow fingers were gouged out by ancient glaciers moving south from Hudson Bay, leaving limestone and other mineral deposits behind, soils conducive to growing high-acid varieties such as Riesling.

Four of the lakes play key roles in grape growing—Seneca (the "middle finger"), Cayuga, Keuka, and Canandaigua—with vines planted in shale soils on the hills sloping down to the lakes. The steep hillsides and the lakes prevent cold air from settling over vineyards, thus discouraging frost. But there is no protection from growing-season rains, as growers found in 2011, when they had to work especially hard to eliminate mold from their sodden grapes.

Riesling rules in the Finger Lakes, and other cold-hardy white grapes thrive as well. Red varieties, however, are a roll of the dice. Many vintners have tried mightily to produce Pinot Noir, yet only a few have succeeded. Merlot, once trumpeted as the Finger Lakes' best red, has become a side player, an unreliable ripener with a propensity for producing weedy wines. Cabernet Franc can be brilliant when the grapes are harvested at the opportune moment and vinified by expert hands. This Bordeaux variety matures early and can produce wines that have bright red-fruit flavors, subtle yet complex herbal aromas, and light to medium body. Neutral oak barrels are the appropriate aging vessels, as toasty new oak can obliterate Cab Franc's delicacy.

Hybrid grapes bred specifically for the conditions can produce very respectable wines, although they are largely ignored by wine aficionados who equate Finger Lakes with Riesling, Riesling, and more Riesling. True, Cayuga, Vignoles, and other hybrid varieties have a reputation for being made into sweet, dull wines that please the masses, but a growing number of winemakers are fermenting them to dryness and treating them with respect.

Viticulture and winemaking began here with native and hybrid grapes, including Concord, Catawba, and Cayuga, but *Vitis vinifera* is the present and the future. Ukrainian immigrant Dr. Konstantin Frank was the first to demonstrate that vinifera vines, which he planted on the shores of Keuka Lake, could not only survive but thrive in the chilly, damp conditions. He established Dr. Konstantin

Keuka Lake
Dr. Konstantin Frank was the first to plant vinifera grape varieties in the Finger Lakes, on Keuka Lake, which does not have its own AVA, but likely will one day.

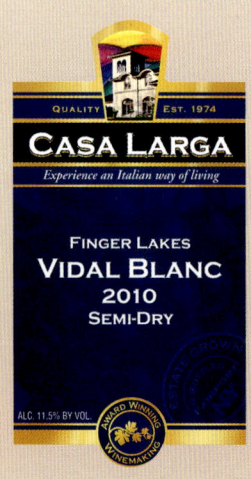

FINGER LAKES AVA SNAPSHOT

Vineyard acreage: **9,124**

Most-planted vinifera varieties: **Riesling, Chardonnay, Gewürztraminer, Pinot Noir, Cabernet Franc, Merlot**

Best varieties: **Cabernet Franc, Chardonnay, Gewürztraminer, Riesling**

Sub-AVAs: **Cayuga Lake, Seneca Lake**

Wineries: **104**

Trailblazer: **Dr. Konstantin Frank's Vinifera Wine Cellars**

Steady hands: **Casa Larga, Chateau Frank, Heron Hill Winery, Hunt Country Vineyards, Keuka Spring Vineyards, McGregor Vineyard**

Superstars: **Dr. Konstantin Frank's Vinifera Wine Cellars, Ravines Wine Cellars, Sheldrake Point**

Frank's Vinifera Wine Cellars in 1962, and its wines are now widely distributed throughout the United States.

Unfortunately for consumers, many of the Finger Lakes' finest wines, among them Cabernet Franc, sparkling wine, and ice wine, are unavailable outside New York State because production volumes are typically small, in the hundreds rather than thousands of cases. Wineries usually sell everything they make in their tasting rooms, to wine club members, and to area restaurants that cater to the tourists visiting the region.

With exceptions, restaurants in New York City have been curiously slow to embrace local bottles, paying far more attention to wines from California, Oregon, Washington, and abroad. Yet Finger Lakes wines, Rieslings in particular, are the darlings of some sommeliers in San Francisco and Los Angeles; not only are they exotic alternatives to German and Washington Rieslings, their food-friendly natural acidity is something few California winemakers can boast about.

THE FINGER LAKES

Eleven lakes shaped like elongated fingers draw warm air into vineyards in winter and cooling breezes in summer, providing an ideal climate for growing aromatic white varieties such as Riesling and Gewürztraminer, and the red Cabernet Franc.

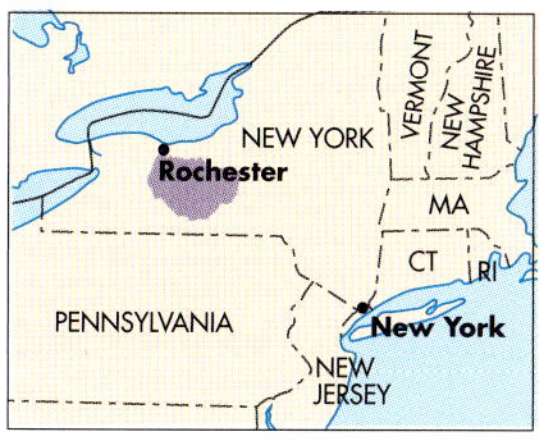

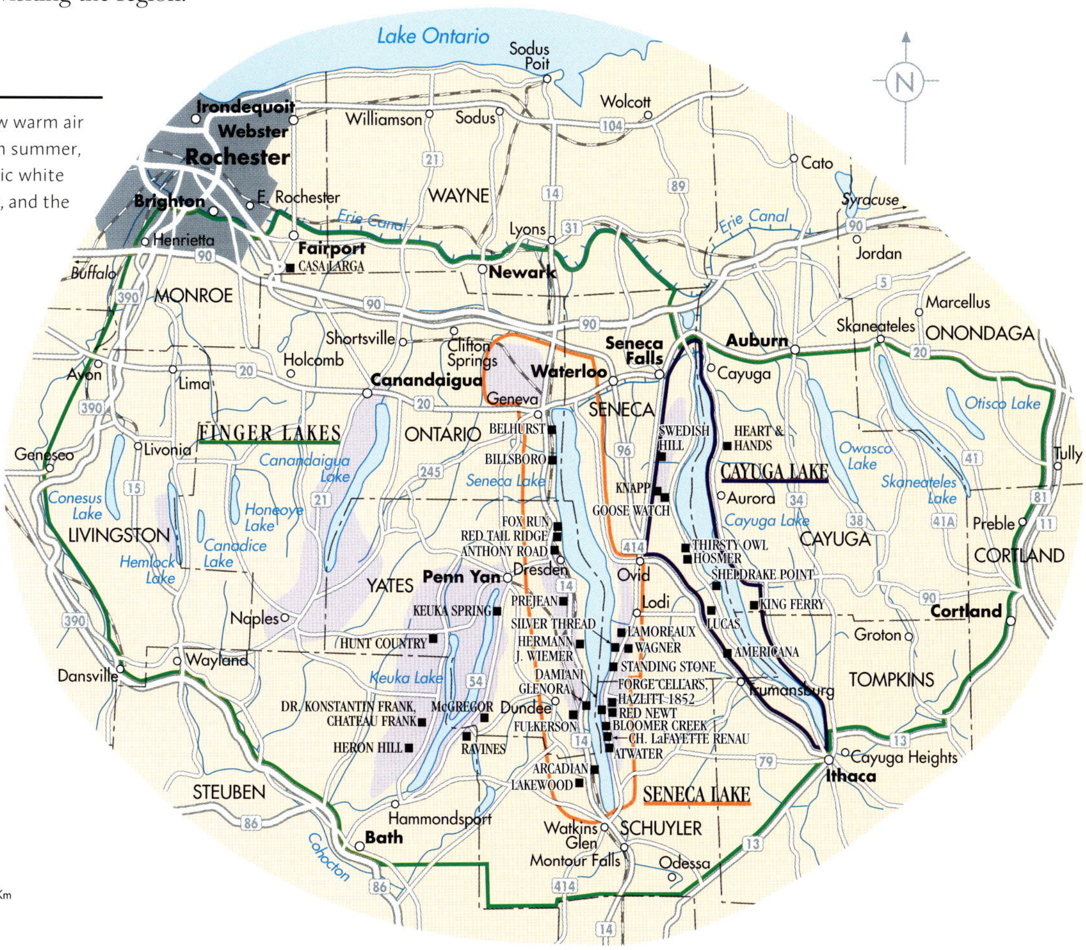

—·—·— County boundary

AVA boundaries are distinguished by colored lines

FINGER LAKES AVA

■ RED NEWT Notable producer

Vineyards

Km 0 — 50 Km

Miles 0 — 20 Miles

LIQUID GOLD

New York excels in ice wines: luscious dessert wines made from grapes that are harvested after they have frozen on the vine. In their ice-cube state, the grapes have a Brix (sugar) level of 35 to 40 degrees; dry table wines are made from grapes usually picked at 23 degrees Brix or slightly higher.

By leaving the clusters on the vines until they freeze, usually in December, vintners harvest grapes with very little juice. What scant amount exists is highly concentrated in sugar, acidity, and flavor, and yields equally concentrated wines.

Riesling and the French-American hybrid Vidal are commonly used for ice wines, with the occasional Cabernet Franc version. While ice wines are hugely rewarding on the palate, producing them comes with risk. Leaving grapes on the vine this long makes them susceptible to disease, devastating rains, and sweet-toothed critters. And in warm vintages, the grapes may not freeze, and a valuable crop turns to useless mush on the vines.

"Iced wines" are those produced by freezing the grapes at the winery, rather than allowing them to freeze naturally on the vine. The New York Ice Wine Festival, held in Fairport every year, is limited to the state's traditionally produced ice wines.

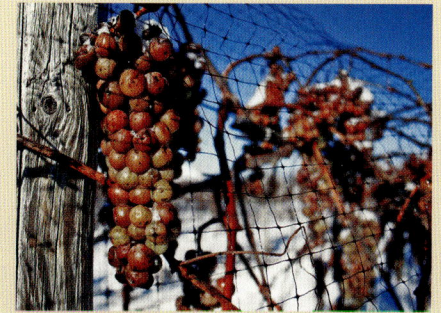

Casa Larga Ice Wine
In particularly cold years, Finger Lakes wineries such as Casa Larga produce ice wine, leaving grapes to freeze on the vines, then pressing out their precious little juice.

Seneca Lake AVA

The largest and deepest of the Finger Lakes, Seneca Lake is 35 miles long and reaches depths of 634 feet. The region became an AVA in 2003, long after Hermann J. Wiemer arrived from Germany in the 1960s to produce Riesling. Rigid and restrained—just like his wines—Wiemer firmly believed Riesling was the Finger Lakes' best grape, and it's no wonder: His mother's family has produced wine in Germany's Mosel region for three hundred years, and his father, Josef, was in charge of the Agricultural Experiment Station in Bernkastel, responsible for restoring the Mosel's vines after the Second World War.

In 2007, Wiemer sold the winery to a group of investors that included Wiemer's assistant winemaker, Fred Merwarth. Merwarth hasn't skipped a beat, using ambient-yeast fermentations to amplify the vineyard characteristics of his Rieslings from Magdalena Vineyards, HJW Vineyard, and Josef Vineyard. Floral aromas, brisk acidity, and impeccable balance are the trademarks of Wiemer wines.

Seneca Lake
Fox Run Vineyards' grapevines are planted along the Seneca Lake shore; snow helps insulate the dormant vines from injury in below-freezing temperatures.

Anthony Road Wine Company is one of the most consistent producers in the Finger Lakes, making a wide range of wines to please all palates. The excitement is at the high end, where owners John and Ann Martini and longtime winemaker Johannes Reinhardt bottle outstanding dry and off-dry Rieslings and Gewürztraminers. Reinhardt, whose family has been in the wine industry in Germany since 1498, makes his strongest statement with the Martini-Reinhardt Selection Riesling Trockenbeeren, a gloriously rich and balanced sweet wine that is also precious because of its extremely limited production and price ($100 per half-bottle).

Red Tail Ridge, owned by former E. & J. Gallo (California) researcher Nancy Irelan and her husband, Mike Schnelle, is the state's "greenest" winery, constructed largely of recycled materials and stone found in the vineyards and with a geothermal heating/cooling system. All supplies used at the winery come from within a 500-mile radius, and drainage ditches, drain tiles, and an irrigation pond minimize storm runoff. Red Tail Ridge produces the requisite Riesling; a lean, elegant Pinot Noir; and more daring varietals such as Blaufränkisch and Teroldego.

Belhurst Castle
This Seneca Lake inn and spa, originally built as a private residence in the late 1880s, also has a winery, which produces admirable Rieslings from Finger Lakes grapes.

SENECA LAKE AVA SNAPSHOT

Vineyard acreage: 4,000 (estimated)

Most-planted varieties: Riesling, Gewürztraminer, Cabernet Franc, Merlot; Chardonnay (for sparkling wine)

Best varieties: Cabernet Franc, Gewürztraminer, Riesling

Wineries: 50

Trailblazer: Hermann J. Wiemer Vineyard

Steady hands: Atwater Estate Vineyards & Winery, Belhurst Estate Winery, Billsboro Winery, Chateau La Fayette Reneau, Damiani Wine Cellars, Fox Run Vineyards, Fulkerson Winery, Glenora Wine Cellars, Hazlitt 1852 Vineyards, Lakewood Vineyards, Lamoreaux Landing Wine Cellars, Prejean Winery, Red Newt Cellars, Standing Stone Vineyards, Wagner Vineyards

Superstars: Anthony Road Wine Company, Hermann J. Wiemer Vineyard, Red Tail Ridge, Tierce

Ones to watch: Arcadian Estate, Bloomer Creek, Forge Cellars

David and Debra Whiting founded Red Newt Cellars and its adjacent bistro in 1998, he as winemaker, she as chef. Their Rieslings, bottled in varying levels of sweetness, and some vineyard-designated, have been top-notch since day one, all produced from purchased grapes grown on Seneca and other Finger Lakes. The Sawmill Creek Vineyard Riesling and Curry Creek Vineyards Gewürztraminer are made in small lots to showcase specific sites; the Glacier Ridge Vineyards Cabernet Franc is among New York's best of that variety.

In 2011, Deb Whiting died of injuries suffered in an automobile accident; Dave, who was also injured, has carried on with both the winery and bistro, with friends and colleagues keeping the businesses running during Dave's grieving/healing period.

The Finger Lakes' most-talked-about wine and, according to some, its finest, is Tierce, a dry, slatey, lime- and tangerine-tinged Riesling reminiscent of a Clare Valley Riesling from Australia. This taut gem is blended each vintage from Riesling lots made by winemakers Peter Bell of Fox Run Vineyards, Johannes Reinhardt of Anthony Road, and Dave Whiting of Red Newt Cellars. They bring their components to the table after each harvest, and through trial-and-error tasting, come up with the final Tierce blend. It's a stunning and age-worthy wine.

Less talked about, but just as exciting, is the work being done with the Saperavi grape by Marti Macinski at Standing Stone Vineyards. Taking a cue from McGregor Vineyard on Keuka Lake, Macinski planted Saperavi, a Republic of Georgia grape variety, in 1994, with hopes that its inky color and intense dark-fruit flavors would boost the color and complexity of her Pinot Noirs. Alas, that particular marriage didn't work out, but Saperavi did, as a stand-alone varietal.

Standing Stone's one acre of Saperavi yields an average of 6 tons each vintage, and 1,000 gallons of wine. It's not a lot, and for now the wine is a curiosity, but if others pick up on it, Saperavi, with its early ripening and fierce resistance to cold and disease, could lift the red-wine game in the Finger Lakes.

Cayuga Lake AVA

Forty-three-mile-long Cayuga Lake was the first Finger Lakes sub-AVA, established in 1988.

Bob Madill, partner, general manager, and winegrower for Sheldrake Point Vineyard, is one of New York's most energetic promoters of the wine industry there, and winner of the 2009 Unity Award from the New York Wine & Grape Foundation for his contributions. Sheldrake Point's wines are estate-grown, made from its 43-acre vineyard on the western shore of Cayuga Lake. The winery, which opened its tasting room in 1998, is a skilled producer of Riesling and Pinot Gris; its 2008 Late Harvest Riesling earned "Best Sweet Riesling in the World" honors at the Canberra (Australia) International Riesling Challenge.

Heart & Hands Wine Company, on the east side of Cayuga Lake, is one of the few wineries in the Finger Lakes to produce a thrilling Pinot Noir. Tom Higgins and his wife, Susan, founded Heart & Hands in 2006 for the express purpose of producing Pinot, and they also bottle small amounts of Riesling. Tom trained with Pinot Noir specialist Josh Jensen at Calera Wine Company in California; he returned to his native Finger Lakes area to meticulously source vineyards capable of growing grapes with a balance of ripe fruit and refreshing acidity and an absence of unripe green character—a Finger Lakes cold-climate curse.

He found the grapes he wanted in two low-yielding vineyards, Sawmill Creek on the east side of Seneca Lake and Hobbit Hollow on the west side of Skaneateles Lake, and from them, he produces a suave Burgundian Barrel Reserve Pinot Noir. In 2011, Tom and Sue Higgins planted their own vineyard overlooking Cayuga Lake.

Sheldrake Point Winery
The winery's vineyards on Cayuga Lake are cooled and warmed, depending on the season, more slowly than the surrounding land, which lengthens the growing season and protects against late-autumn frosts.

When the vines are mature, perhaps in 2014, they should be able to boost production from the current 1,500 cases per year.

Dave and Cindy Peterson are so ardent about Cayuga Lake that they have two wineries in the AVA: their flagship, Swedish Hill, and Goose Watch Winery. Swedish Hill was established in 1986 to take advantage of the grapes the couple grew in the region; production now totals more than 70,000 cases annually, with sparkling wines a specialty. Goose Watch opened in 1997 and makes Pinot Grigio, Viognier, Merlot, and exceptional hybrid varieties such as Diamond and Traminette.

CAYUGA LAKE AVA SNAPSHOT

Vineyard acreage: **600 (estimated)**

Most-planted varieties: **Riesling, Chardonnay, Cayuga White, Vidal Blanc, Pinot Noir**

Best varieties: **Chardonnay, French-American hybrids, Pinot Noir, Riesling**

Wineries: **25**

Steady hands: **Americana Vineyards & Winery, Goose Watch Winery, Hosmer Winery, King Ferry Winery, Knapp Vineyards Winery, Lucas Vineyards, Thirsty Owl Wine Company**

Superstars: **Heart & Hands Wine Company, Sheldrake Point Winery, Swedish Hill Vineyards**

Keuka Lake Region

Keuka is not an AVA, but it likely will be one day. The groundbreaking Dr. Konstantin Frank's Vinifera Wine Cellars is here, in Pulteney, and it is credited with igniting the fine-wine explosion in the Finger Lakes. Dr. Frank grafted European *Vitis vinifera* vines onto North American *Vitis labrusca* roots, and the results were convincing: German and Alsace varieties could withstand the frigid, wet conditions, thanks to the warming effects of Keuka and other Finger Lakes.

Dr. Frank turned winemaking operations over to his son, Willy, who handed the baton in 1993 to his own son, current winery president Fred Frank. His Rieslings, Gewürztraminers, and brut sparkling wines win more than their share of competition medals, and his Rkatsiteli is a spicy and refreshing white wine whose roots are in the Republic of Georgia.

Ravines Wine Cellars' Morten Hallgren concentrates on dry wines, particularly Rieslings, from purchased grapes. His Argetsinger Vineyard Riesling is dry as a bone, gravelly, and built for cellaring. Hallgren, a Dane who grew up in Provence, France, made wines in West Texas; the Biltmore Estate in Asheville, North Carolina; and Dr. Konstantin Frank's Vinifera Wine Cellars before he and his wife, Lisa, founded Ravines in 2000.

Although Riesling is typically fermented in stainless steel tanks, Hallgren ages some of his Riesling lots in neutral oak barrels. This gives the wines a more textured mouthfeel, without imparting any toasty aromas or flavors.

In 1971, the McGregor family began planting vinifera and hybrid grapevines on a bluff overlooking Keuka Lake. Today the McGregors farm a patchwork quilt of varieties, including the usual suspects, Riesling, Gewürztraminer, Chardonnay, and Cabernet Franc; the slightly less usual Cabernet Sauvignon, Merlot, and Sangiovese; the hybrids Muscat Ottonel, Cayuga White, and Vignoles; and the distinctly unusual for the United States: vinifera varieties Saperavi and Sereksiya Charni.

These two red grapes are native to the Republic of Georgia, and from them McGregor produces an insanely popular blend called (presumably causing much offence to Georgians) Black Russian Red. The wine has intense body and bold black- and red-fruit aromas and flavors, but the tannins are mellow and the acidity brisk. At just 150 cases or so produced each vintage, Black Russian Red has become the Finger Lakes' cult-wine counterpart to Napa Valley's Screaming Eagle Cabernet Sauvignon, although it is sold at a fraction of the price.

Keuka Lake
Whereas other Finger Lakes are singularly long and narrow, Keuka is Y-shaped, with a stem that splits into eastern and western forks.

NIAGARA ESCARPMENT AVA

This AVA is part of the greater Niagara region, shared with Ontario, Canada, and famous for its ultrarich ice wines that have a bracing snap from the high natural acidity in the grapes. The Niagara Escarpment AVA encompasses 18,000 acres, but just 400 are planted to wine grapes. The escarpment itself is an eons-old limestone ridge that runs for nearly 700 miles, beginning near Rochester, New York, and extending west through southern Ontario, Michigan's Upper Peninsula, and eastern Wisconsin. The ridge traps air warmed by lake waters and protects vineyards from drastic temperature swings.

To most people, the word *Niagara* means the famous falls on the United States–Canadian border, where East Coasters honeymoon and thrill seeking types go over the falls in barrels (with most surviving, despite the possibility of a deadly crash). This region has long been recognized for the ice wines produced in Ontario, on the Canadian side; now the U.S. side is producing ice wines to rival them.

Lake Ontario to the north, the Niagara River to the west, and the escarpment itself to the south work together to protect grapevines. Ice wine is the "house wine" in Niagara Escarpment, with Leonard Oakes Vidal Blanc ice wine and Niagara Landing Vidal Blanc ice wine winning multiple gold medals in U.S. competitions. Ice wines are produced from grapes left to hang on the vines until they freeze; they are then harvested and pressed of the scant amount of succulently sweet juice left in the grapes, then fermented (see box p. 259).

Arrowhead Springs Vineyards does a fine job with Pinot Gris and Chardonnay grapes grown in the AVA, and its red wines—Cabernet Franc, Malbec, Pinot Noir, and Syrah—are surprisingly fruity. Eveningside Vineyards' Chardonnay and Sauvignon Blanc, Leonard Oakes' Estate Chardonnay, and Freedom Run Winery's Estate Meritage and Estate Reserve Cabernet Franc demonstrate that this region isn't only for ice wine devotees.

The Niagara Escarpment
The limestone ridge, shown (above) from the Canadian side, traps air warmed by the waters of Lake Ontario and the Niagara River, protecting vines from drastic temperature changes and winter injury.

NIAGARA ESCARPMENT AVA SNAPSHOT
Vineyard acreage: **400**
Most-planted variety: **Vidal Blanc**
Best varieties: **Chardonnay, Vidal Blanc**
Wineries: **8**
Steady hands: **Arrowhead Spring Vineyard, Eveningside Vineyards, Freedom Run Winery, Leonard Oakes Estate Winery, Niagara Landing Wine Cellars**

LAKE ERIE AVA

The New York portion of the Lake Erie AVA has 20,000 acres of vines, more than 90 percent of them Concord grapes used for juice and bulk wine. The AVA extends into Ohio and Pennsylvania, making it one of the largest in the country, at more than 42,000 acres. Grapes were first cultivated here in the early nineteenth century, and some wineries survived Prohibition by legally selling grapes to home winemakers, and illegally selling wine to consumers in Canada. After Repeal, the region didn't bounce back, and in 1967, there were fewer than twenty wineries.

More recently, Lake Erie wineries have begun planting vinifera grapes in an attempt to improve wine quality. Near the shores of Lake Erie, in deep, heavy clay soils flecked with glacial deposits, vines are being planted that can withstand the Arctic air masses that flow directly over the region. French-American hybrid and European varieties are being cultivated in the New York portion of the AVA, and the jury is out on whether these plantings will be successful.

Elsewhere in New York

The state's remaining wine production is focused in two emerging areas in northern New York, Thousand Islands and Champlain. Cold-climate grape varieties developed in Minnesota that withstand winter temperatures down to -30°F have sparked interest in the two regions, previously thought too cold to support wine grape production.

North of Albany, the Lake Champlain Valley would be an inhospitably frigid area for grapevines were it not for protection provided by the Adirondacks and the Green Mountains of Vermont. Hybrid Minnesota-bred varieties such as Brianna, La Crescent, and Lacrosse (white grapes) and Frontenac, Léon Millot, and Marquette (reds) are sturdy enough to ripen in the cold conditions.

Just five small wineries operate in the region: Amazing Grace Vineyard and Winery, Elf Farm Winery & Cider Mill, Hid-in-Pines Vineyards, Stonehouse Vineyards, and Vesco Ridge Vineyard.

The Thousand Islands region, along the St. Lawrence Seaway and bordering Ontario, Canada, is home to eight wineries: Coyote Moon Vineyard, Hunt Country Vineyards, Otter Creek Winery, River Myst Winery, Thousand Islands Winery, Tug Hill Vineyards, Venditti Vineyards, and Yellow Barn Winery.

Coyote Moon in Clayton, owned by the Randazzo family, hit it big in major California wine competitions in 2010 and 2011 with its Marquette, Brianna, and River Run wines. River Run, particularly a Catawba-based rosé, has caught the fancy of judges throughout the United States.

Thousand Islands Winery in Alexandria Bay is also a top producer; its Frontenac is first-rate, with a vivid red-cherry aroma and flavor and a refreshing, high-acid finish.

Harvest in Lake Erie AVA
High-yield Concord grapes have been the staple in the Lake Erie region, but hybrid and European varieties are now being trialed.

The lake effect
New York State vineyards of the Lake Erie AVA benefit from the temperature moderation provided by this large body of water (above right).

Pennsylvania

William Penn is said to have planted European grapevines near what would become Philadelphia in 1683, but they died. It was only in 1968 that Pennsylvania's wine industry got a foothold, with the passage of the Limited Winery Act, which gives producers the right to produce wines in regulated quantities and sell them at a limited number of retail locations. The law enabled wineries to bypass wholesalers and the Pennsylvania Liquor Control Board's monopoly stores—which were largely uninterested in local wines—and sell on their own.

Paradocx Vineyard
At Pennsylvania's Paradocx Vineyard, nets are draped over the vines to prevent birds from devouring the nearly ripe grapes. The nets are lifted to allow workers to train the vines and harvest the clusters.

And sell they have, to such a degree that there are now 145 licensed wineries in the state, producing enough vinifera, hybrid, and native-grape wines to rank Pennsylvania seventh in U.S. wine production.

Penn Shore Vineyards and Presque Isle Wine Cellars, both in the Lake Erie AVA in northwestern Pennsylvania, were the first wineries to obtain licences under the Limited Winery Act. The Lake Erie region, shared with New York and Ohio and a major source of Concord, Catawba, and Niagara grapes for Welch's jams and juices, has also emerged as a reliable supplier of Riesling and Vidal Blanc grapes used to produce ice wine. Mazza Vineyards' Vidal Blanc ice wine is consistently exceptional.

The southeast and south-central regions of Pennsylvania, near Philadelphia and Lancaster, are where the majority of the state's wineries are located. The warmer, more moderate climate than that in the chilly Lake Erie AVA encourages the cultivation of European vinifera varieties, plus hybrids and native labruscas. Diversity is the name of the game here.

With the 1990s plantings of early-ripening clones from Dijon, France, vintners in the Lehigh Valley AVA in southeastern Pennsylvania, are having notable success with Chardonnay.

Chaddsford Winery
Picnicking and musical performances are components of Chaddsford's "Wine Bar Weekends" in Pennsylvania's Brandywine Valley. The winery, housed in a red Colonial-era barn, produces excellent Bordeaux-style red wines.

Pinnacle Ridge Winery
Located in the Lehigh Valley AVA, this winery excels with several varieties, particularly the French-American hybrid Chambourcin, produced in three styles.

Cabernet Franc and Chambourcin are also staples. Lehigh Valley's Pinnacle Ridge Winery, in Kutztown, is a quality leader in Chardonnay, and it also produces three versions of Chambourcin, two dry and one sweet, all with the variety's typical red-cherry fruit and crowd-pleasing, silky tannins.

Eric and Lee Miller founded Chaddsford Winery in the Brandywine Valley, south of West Chester, in 1982. Chaddsford is Pennsylvania's largest wine producer (approximately 30,000 cases per year) and most celebrated. Its bailiwick is Bordeaux-style reds, and its Merican Cabernet Sauvignon-Merlot-Cabernet Franc blend is stellar. The winery also honors the native Niagara grape by producing a balanced, semisweet version, and its Chambourcins are among the best in Pennsylvania.

Eastern Pennsylvania

Three of the state's five AVAs are shared with other states, but the Lancaster and Lehigh Valley AVAs are wholly within Pennsylvania.

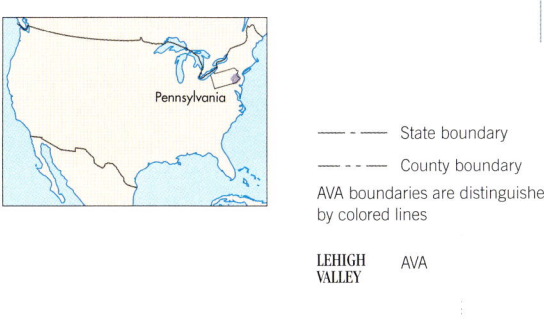

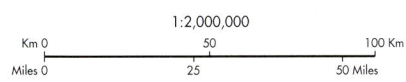

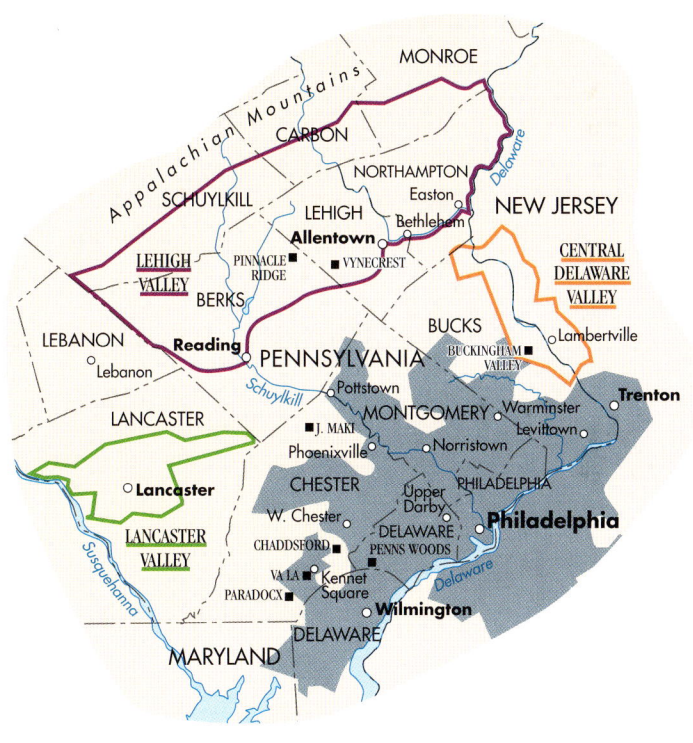

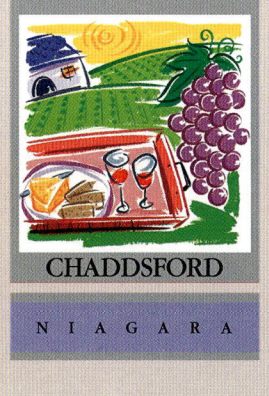

PENNSYLVANIA SNAPSHOT

Vineyard acres: 3,000

Most-planted varieties: Cabernet Franc, Merlot, Chambourcin, Vidal Blanc, Seyval Blanc, Catawba, Niagara

Best varieties: Cabernet Franc, Chambourcin, Chardonnay, Vidal Blanc

AVAs: Central Delaware Valley (shared with New Jersey), Cumberland Valley (shared with Maryland), Lake Erie (shared with New York and Ohio), Lancaster Valley, Lehigh Valley

Wineries: 145

Trailblazers: Penn Shore Vineyards, Presque Isle Wine Cellars

Steady hands: Briar Valley Vineyards & Winery, Buckingham Valley Vineyards, French Creek Vineyards, Mazza Vineyards, Paradocx Vineyard, Penns Wood Winery, Presque Isle Wine Cellars, Va La Vineyards, Vynecrest Vineyards

Superstars: Chaddsford Winery, Pinnacle Ridge Winery

Mid-Atlantic States

Surrounded by the Chesapeake and Delaware bays, Maryland, New Jersey, and Delaware bask in generally warm, breezy summers and are well suited to vinifera. The moderating effects of the bays make this a "sweet spot" on the East Coast, where it's less rainy and less humid than in Virginia and North Carolina to the south, and not as cold as Pennsylvania to the north. Chardonnay, Cabernet Sauvignon, and Riesling star here, with southern Italian and Mediterranean varieties flourishing in the hottest pockets, and Seyval and Chambourcin best in colder regions.

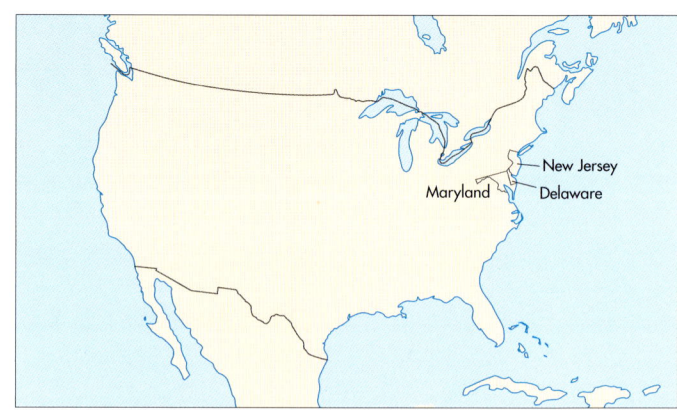

New Jersey

New York's southern neighbor has cultivated grapes and produced wine since Colonial times—though only since the mid-1990s have the adjectives "fine" and "premium" entered the Jersey wine lexicon. A dozen or so of the state's 46 wineries are committed to producing vinifera wines as good as those made in New York and on the West Coast, and they hope others will take their lead.

Alba Vineyard in Warren County earns kudos for its Chardonnays, Gewürztraminers, and Rieslings. Tomasello Winery in Atlantic County, with roots going back to 1933, produces outstanding wines, both dry and sweet, and Unionville Vineyards in Hunterdon County makes impressive Chardonnays. Heritage Vineyards in Glouchester County is known for BDX, a Cabernet Sauvignon-led blend.

The majority of top producers are in the Outer Coastal Plain AVA, which covers 2.25 million acres in southeastern New Jersey (Warren Hills in the northwest and Central Delaware Valley in the southwest are the state's other AVAs). Outer Coastal Plain soils are sandy and well drained—crucial to cultivating quality grapes. The growing-season climate is similar to that of northern Napa Valley, with plenty of warmth to ensure full maturation of the fruit.

Forty varieties are grown in New Jersey, including natives and hybrids, but quality-minded vintners say they must drill down to only those grapes that thrive in the conditions and eliminate the underperformers. White varieties have generally fared better than reds, although Barbera, Nebbiolo, Lagrein, and Teroldego have New Jersey vintners excited by their potential.

In a monumental triumph for New Jersey wineries and consumers, legislation was signed in 2012 allowing for the direct shipment of wines to consumers. It also allows for the licensing of new wineries, a process that had been in limbo while legislators debated their alcohol sales issues.

Delaware

In this tiny state, breweries greatly outnumber wineries, of which there are just three. Nassau Valley Vineyards in Lewes, founded in 1993, was the state's first farm winery and it is a producer of competent Chardonnay, Cabernet Sauvignon, Seyval Blanc, and fruit wines.

Maryland

In 2001, Maryland's main claim to wine fame was that it was home to Robert M. Parker Jr., the most powerful wine critic in the world. But there were eleven wineries too. One of them, Boordy Vineyards, dates to 1945 and was founded by *Baltimore Sun* newspaperman Philip Wagner after he began planting French hybrid grapes in his nursery in the 1930s, then selling cuttings to farmers across the country upon the repeal of Prohibition.

By 2012, the industry had blossomed to fifty-two wineries, producing not only the French hybrids Wagner advocated, but also vinifera varieties such as Chardonnay, Merlot, Cabernet Sauvignon, and Syrah. Rob Deford purchased Boordy in 1980 and has kept it an industry leader, replanting the vineyard and installing state-of-the-art equipment in the winery.

Black Ankle Vineyards, established in 2002 by Ed Boyce and Sarah O'Herron in Mount Airy on Maryland's Eastern Shore, is the state's version of a cult winery. Voluminous rainfall hasn't deterred the couple's viticultural efforts, with breezes from Chesapeake Bay helping to prevent mildew development in the grape clusters. Black Ankle Vineyards (located on Black Ankle Road, which is said to be named for the black mud one's feet sink into during the rainy season), produces 3,500 cases of vinifera wines per year, including some made with the Spanish white wine grape Albariño. Its blended vinifera reds, including Slate and Crumbling Rock, are frequent winners of the Governor's Cup.

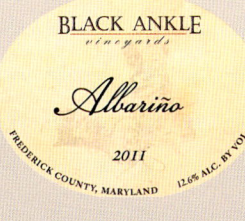

MID-ATLANTIC STATES SNAPSHOT

Vineyard acreage: **NEW JERSEY** 1,045; **DELAWARE** 35; **MARYLAND** 600

Most-planted varieties: Chardonnay, Chambourcin, Cabernet Franc, Cabernet Sauvignon, Seyval Blanc, Riesling

Best varieties: Cabernet Sauvignon, Chardonnay, Seyval Blanc, Syrah, Riesling

AVAs: **NEW JERSEY**—Central Delaware Valley, Outer Coastal Plain, Warren Hills; **MARYLAND**—Catoctin, Cumberland Valley (shared with Pennsylvania), Linganore

Wineries: **NEW JERSEY** 46; **DELAWARE** 3; **MARYLAND** 52

Trailblazer: Boordy Vineyards

Steady hands: **NEW JERSEY**—Amalthea Cellars, Bellview Winery, Cape May Winery, Hawk Haven Vineyards, Hopewell Valley Vineyards, Mount Salem Vineyards, Tomasello Winery, Unionville Vineyards; **DELAWARE**—Nassau Valley Vineyards; **MARYLAND**—Basignani, Boordy Vineyards, Bordeleau, Elk Run Vineyards, Knob Hall Winery, Little Ashby Vineyards, Serpent Ridge, Sugarloaf Mountain Vineyard, Woodhall Wine Cellars

Superstars: **NEW JERSEY**—Alba Vineyard, Heritage Vineyards; **MARYLAND**—Black Ankle Vineyards;

Black Ankle Vineyards
This stellar Maryland wine producer employs organic and biodynamic growing techniques, which include applying compost in place of chemical fertilizers, never using herbicides, and choosing biodiesel fuel to power its tractors.

Index

Page numbers in bold indicate maps; numbers in italics refer to captions. Only primary treatments of grape varieties are indexed.

A bacela Winery, **154**, *154*, 155, 156–57
Abbott, John, 176
Abeja, **165**, 172, 176
Abreu, David, 88
Abreu Vineyards, **67**
Acacia Vineyards, **45**, 51, **55**, 176
Acres of Land Winery, 240, 241
Adam Puchta Winery, 214, **215**
Adams, Leon, 161–62
Adams, Nat, 182
Addamo Estate, 123
Adelaida Cellars, **111**, 112, 113
Adelsheim, David, 148, 152
Adelsheim, Ginny, 148
Adelsheim Vineyard, 148, 149, **150**, 152
Aetna Springs, **55**
Afton Mountain Vineyards, **235**, 237
Ahern, Albert "Abbey," 68
Ahlgren Vineyard, **97**
Airfield Estates, **165**
Airlie Winery, **150**
Alabama, 245
Alamosa Wine Cellars, 204, **207**
Alaska, 195
Alaska Wilderness Winery, 195
Alban, John, 116–17
Alban Vineyards, **116**, 116–17
Alba Vineyard, 268, 269
Albert, Gail, 249
Albert, Ken, 249
Alcohol and Tobacco Tax and Trade Bureau (TTB), 12, 13, 38, 42, 181, 216, 234
Alderbrook Winery, **29**
Alder Ridge Vineyard, **164**–65, 170
Alder Springs, 25
Alexana Winery, *12*
Alexander, Cyrus, 31
Alexander, Glenn, *34*
Alexander, James, 2
Alexander Mountain Estate, **29**, 31–32, *32*
Alexander Valley AVA, **23**, 28, **29**, 31–32, **38**
Alexander Valley Vineyards, **29**, 31, 32
Alexandria Lakes AVA, 219, 222
AlexEli Vineyard and Winery, **150**
Alexis Bailly Vineyard, 219, 222, *222*
Alfred Eames Cellars, **185**, 186
Alicante Bouschet, **4**
Allied Domecq, 84, 144
Allied Lyons, 84
Almaden Vineyards, 4, 108, 109, 136
Alma Rosa Winery & Vineyards, **124**, 126
Alpha Omega Winery, **71**
Alta Mesa AVA, 137, 138
Alto Vineyards, 226, 227
Alvarez, Cheryl, 135
Alvarez, Victor, 135
Alysian Wines, **38**, 39, 40
Amador County, 132–33
Amador Foothill Winery, **130**, 132
Amalthea Cellars, 269
Amapola Creek Winery, **45**, 47, 48
Amaro Winery, 202
Amavi Cellars, 172, 173
Amazing Grace Vineyard and Winery, 265
Ambassador's 1953 vineyard, *48*
Americana Vineyards & Winery, **259**, 262
American Canyon Vineyard, **45**
American Viticultural Area (AVA) system, 6, 12
American Wine Growers, 162
Amerine, Maynard, 53, 119
Amigoni, Kerry, 217
Amigoni, Michael, 217
Amigoni Family Vineyards, **215**, 217, *217*
Amigoni Urban Winery, 214, 217
Amity Vineyards, **150**, 153
Amizetta Estate Winery, **55**
Ampelos Cellars, **111**, 127–28
Anakota, **29**, 32, 34
Anam Cara Cellars, **150**, 153
Ancien Wines, 85, 87
Ancient Lakes, 181, *181*
Anderson, Joy, 167
Anderson, Myles, 173, 176
Anderson's Conn Valley Vineyards, **55**
Anderson Valley AVA, **23**, 22–24
Andrew Murray Vineyards, **124**
Andrew Will Winery, **147**, **160**–61, 162, 168, 170, 178
Anemoi, 188
Angels' Share Wine Imports, 254
Ankida Ridge, **233**, 237
Anne Amie Vineyards, **150**
Annie Green Springs, 4
Antelope Valley of the High California Desert AVA, **140**, 142
Anthony Road Wine Company, **259**, 260, 261
Antica Napa Valley, **55**, 83, *83*, 84
Antinori, Albiera, *83*
Antinori, Alessia, *83*
Antinori, Allegra, *83*
Antinori, Giovanni di Piero, 84
Antinori, Piero, 79, *83*, 84, 163, 168, 268–69
Apex, 170
Apple Barn Winery, 243
Applegate Valley AVA, 146, **147**, **154**, 154, 155
A. Rafanelli Winery, **29**, 35, 36
Araujo, Bart, 59
Araujo, Daphne, 59
Araujo Estate Wines, **58**, *58*, 59–60
Arbor Crest Wine Cellars, **160**–61, 181
Arbor Mist, 251
Arcadian Estate, **259**, 261
Archery Summit, 149, **150**
Arches Winery, 192
Argetsinger Vineyard, 263
Argyle Winery, 149, **150**, 152, 173
Arizona, 198–201, *199*
Arizona Stronghold, 198, **199**, 200, *201*, 201
Arkansas, 245
Arkansas Historic Wine Museum, 245
Armida Winery, **29**
Armstrong, Bill, 115
Armstrong, Liz, 115
Arrington Winery, 243
Arrowhead Spring Vineyard, **251**, 264
Arrowood, Alis, 48
Arrowood, Richard, 31, 47, 48
Arrowood Vineyards & Winery, **45**, 46, 48, 120
Arroyo Grande AVA, **111**, **116**, 116–18
Arroyo Seco AVA, 102, **103**, 106, 106–7
Arteaga, Antonio de, 202
Artesa Winery, **45**, 51, **55**
Asher, Gerald, 216

Asseo, Stephan, 114–15
Associated Vintners, 161–62, 180
Association of African American Vintners, 20
Astrale e Terra, **55**, 83
Atkin, Janice, 126
Atkin, Robert, 126
Atlas Peak AVA, 54, **55**, 83–84
Atlas Peak Vineyards, 84
Atlas Peak Winery, 84, 86
A to Z Wineworks, **150**
Atwater Estate Vineyards & Winery, **259**, 261
Aubert, Mark, 34
Aubert Wines, 34
Au Bon Climat, **119**, **121**, **122**, 122, 126
Auction Napa Valley, 75, 89
Augusta AVA, 214, **215**, 216–17, 218
Augusta Winery, 214, 217
Auler, Ed, 206
Auler, Susan, 206
AVA. See American Viticultural Area
AWC Vienna competition, 62
Azalea Springs Vineyards, **58**, 61

B abcock Vineyards & Winery, **124**, 126
Baeza, Cesar, 257
Bailly, David, *222*
Bailly, Nan, *222*
Bainbridge Island Vineyards & Winery, **160**–61, 181
Baker, Jeremy, 40
Baker-Bird Winery, 240, *241*
Baldacci Vineyards, **77**
Baldwin, Deborah, 115
Baldwin, Jenne, 187
Baldwin, Justin, 115
Baldyga, Chris, 224–25
Baltimore Bend Vineyard, 214, **215**
Balzer, Robert Lawrence, 18
Bancroft Ranch Vineyard, **55**
Banfi Vintners, 49, 173
Banke, Barbara, 26, 123
Barbour, James, 237
Barboursville Vineyards, **235**, *236*, 237
Bargetto Winery, **90**, **97**, 98
Barnard Griffin, **164**–65, 168
Barnett Vineyards, **55**, 65
Baron, Christophe, 173, 174, *174*, 176
Barra, 23
Barrett, Bo, 59
Barrett, Heidi Peterson, 75, 88
Barrett, Jim, 4, **58**, 59
Barricia Vineyard, 44
Barrister Winery, 181
Bartholomew Park Winery, **45**
Bascaules, Philippe, 70
Baseler, Ted, 163
BashaKill Vineyards, **251**, 257
Basignani, 269
Baugher, Eric, 100
Baxter's Vineyards, 226
Bay Area, 90–101
Bear Creek Winery, 195
Beast, 176
Beatty Ranch Vineyard, **55**
Beaux Frères, 149, **150**, 153
Beaulieu Vineyard, 4, *57*, *70*, 71, 70–71, 72, 73–74, 105
Becker, Bunny, 206
Becker, Richard, 206
Becker Vineyards, 204, 206–7, **207**
Beckmen, Steve, 125
Beckmen, Tom, 125
Beckmen Vineyards, **124**, 124, 125

Beckstoffer, Andy, 27, 73–74
Beckstoffer To Kalon Vineyard, 60, **73**
Beckstoffer Vineyards, **71**, 73–74
Bedell, Kip, 255
Bedell Cellars, **252**, 252, 255
Bedell Estate, 255
Bedford Winery, **121**
Bedrock Vineyards, 37, **45**
Bedrock Wine Co., 46
Behrens Family Winery, **55**, 65
Belhurst Estate Winery, **259**, *261*, 261
Bell, Peter, 261
Bel Lago Vineyard and Winery, **222**, 223
Bella Oaks Vineyard, **71**, 72
Bella Vineyards, **29**, 35
Bella Vista Cilurzo Vineyard & Winery, 140
Bell Mountain AVA, 204, **205**, 207
Belloni Vineyard, 44
Bellview Winery, 269
Benches at Wallula Gap, The, 163, **164-165**
Bendick, Carrie, 135
Bendick, Josh, 135
Benedict, Michael, 126
Benessere, **67**, 68
Benevides, Robert, 48
Benito Dusi Ranch, **111**, 113
Ben Lomond Mountain AVA, **97**, 98, 101
Benmarl Winery, 250, **251**, 257
Benmore Valley AVA, **23**, 27
Bennett, Ted, 25
Bennett Lane, **58**, 59
Bennett Valley AVA, 28, **45**, 49
Benovia, **38**, 42
Benton Lane Winery, **147**
Bentryn, Gerard, 179, 181
Benziger, Bruno, 48
Benziger Family Winery, 42, 43, **45**, 46, 48
Bergevin Lane, 173
Berglund, Rod, 39
Bergstrom, 149, **150**
Beringer Brothers, 53, 156
Beringer Vineyards, 4, 26, **29**, 32, 34, 50, 51, **55**, 57, 67, 68, 81, 131
Bernards, Ken, 85
Bernardus Vineyards & Winery, 102, **103**, 107
Bernstein, Arlene, 85
Bernstein, Michael, 85
Bessent, Cathy, 195
Bessent, Mike, 195
Bethel Heights Vineyard, **150**, 153, *159*
Betz, Bob, 178
Betz, Cathy, 178
Betz Family Winery, **160**–61, 168, 178
Bevan Cellars, **45**, 49
Bewley, Stuart, 25
Biale, Aldo, 82
Biale, Bob, 82
Bialla, Linda, *84*
Bialla, Vito, *84*
Bialla Vineyards, **55**, 83, **84**
Bien Nacido Vineyard, **120**, **121**, 121–22, *123*
Big Break Vineyard, **90**
Big River Vineyard, 44
Bingham, Betty, 208
Bingham, Clint, 208
Bingham Family Vineyards, **205**, 208
Biodynamic Wine Guide 2011 (Waldin), 158
Bjelland, Paul, 156
Bjelland Vineyards, 156
Bjornstad Cellars, **38**, 49

Black Ankle Vineyards, 268, 269, *269*
Black Bridge Winery, **185**, 186, 189
Blackbird Vineyards, **55**, 81
Blackburn family, 109
Black Sheep Winery, **130**
Blacksmith Winery, 249
Black Star Farms, **222**, 223, 224, 225
Blackstock Vineyards & Winery, 245
Blackstone Winery, **45**
Blaney, Michael, 118
Bledsoe, Drew, 176
Blenheim Vineyards, **235**, 237, 239
Bloch, George, 35
Bloomer Creek, **259**, 261
Blosser, Bill, 148
Bloxom Vineyard, **233**, 239
Blue Ridge Region, 239
Blue Sky Vineyard, 226, 227
Blumenhof Vineyards & Winery, 214, **215**, 217
Boeger, Greg, 134
Boeger, Sue, 134
Boeger Winery, **130**, 134
Bogle, Warren, 139
Bogle Vineyards, **130**, 139
Boissenot, Eric, 237
Boisset, Jean-Charles, 53
Boisset Family Estates, 53
Bokisch, Liz, 139
Bokisch, Markus, 139
Bokisch Vineyards, **130**, 137, **139**, 139
Bonaccorsi, 126
Bonacquisti Wine Company, 188
Bonarrigo, Merrill, 209
Bonarrigo, Paul, 209
BOND, **73**, 74, 75
Bonny Doon Vineyard, *13*, 13, 96, **97**, 98, 101, *101*, 173
Bonterra Vineyards, 22, **23**, 25
Bookcliff Vineyards, 186, 189
Bookwalter Winery, **164**–65
Boomtown, 176
Boone's Farm, 4
Boordy Vineyards, 268, 269
Bordeleau, 269
Borden Ranch AVA, 137, 138, 139
Borger, Marcia Mondavi, 76, 88, 88
Borghese, Ann Marie, 255
Borghese, Marco, 255
Borglum, Gutzon, 190
Borgue, Virginie, 173
Bosché Vineyard, **71**
Bostock, Todd, 200
Bouchaine Vineyards, **45**, 51, 52–53, **55**
Boulder Creek Winery, 186, 189
Bourgue, Virginie, 173
Boushey, Dick, 166
Boushey Vineyards, 166, 184
Bowers Harbor Vineyards, **222**, 223, 224
Boxwood Estate Winery, 234, **235**, 236
Boyce, Ed, 268
Bradley, Erich, 48
Braganini, Apollo "Paul," 225
Braganini, David, 225
Brandborg, **154**, 157
Brandborg, Sue, 157
Brandborg, Terry, 157
Brander, Erik, 125
Brander, Fred, 125
Brander Vineyard, 125
Brandlin, **58**, 59
Brandt, Jared, 93, *94*
Brandt, Tracey, 93, *94*
Brannan, Samuel, 73
Brassfield Estate, **23**, 27

Braunel, Corey, 176
B. R. Cohn Winery, **45**, 48
Breaux Vineyards, **234**, 234, 235
Breggo Cellars, 22, **23**
Breitenbach Wine Cellars, 226
Brejoux, Pierre, 4
Brennan Vineyards, 204, **205**, 207, 209
Brewer-Clifton, **111**, 126, 127–28
Brian Carter Cellars, **147**, **160**–61, 178, 179
Brianna, 7
Briar Valley Vineyards & Winery, 267
Brick House Vineyard, 149, **150**, 153
Bridgehead Vineyard, **90**
Bridgeview Vineyards and Winery, **154**, 154–55
Bridgman, W. B., 169
Bridlewood Estate Winery, 18, 120, **124**, 124, 136
Brittan, Robert, 152
Brittan Vineyards, **150**, 152
Broadley Vineyards, **147**
Broich, Bill, 182
Bronco Wine Company, 19, 89, 136
Brooklyn Winery, 254
Brooks, Kix, 243
Brotherhood Winery, 250, **251**, 256, 257
Brounstein, Al, 61–62
Brounstein, Boots, 62
Brown, Byron "Ken," 120
Brown, Thomas Rivers, 62
Brown Estate, **55**, 87
Brown-Forman, 24, 25
Bruni, Greg, 208
Brutocao Cellars, 23
Bryant Family Vineyard, **55**, 88
Brys, Eileen, 224
Brys, Walter, 224
Brys Estate Vineyard & Winery, **222**, 223, 224
Buckingham Valley Vineyards, **267**, 267
Buck Shoals Vineyards, 242
Buehler Vineyards, **55**
Buena Suerte Vineyard, 200
Buena Vista Winery, 30, 36, 44, **45**, 51, 52, 53, 229
Buhl, Al, 200
Bully Hill Vineyards, 250
Bunnell Family Cellar, **164**–65
Buoncristiani Family Winery, 87
Burgess, Jeanne, 245
Burgess Cellars, **55**
Burr, Raymond, 48
Bush, George H. W., 182
Buttonwood Farm Winery, **124**
Buty Winery, **164**–65, 170, 172, 176
Byers, Clayton, 217
Byington Winery, **97**
Bynum, Davis, 39–40
Byron Vineyard & Winery, 120, **121**, 122

C abernet Franc, 6
Cabernet Sauvignon, *6*, 6
Cabral, Bob, 40
Cadaretta Wines, 172, 173, 174
CADE, **55**, 63, 64
Cadence Winery, **160**–61, 168, 178, 179
Caduceus Cellars, 198, **199**, 201, *201*
Cahn, Deborah, 25
Cain, Jonathan, 48
Cain Vineyard & Winery, 65
Cakebread, Rosemary, 69
Cakebread Cellars, 26, 57, 70, **71**

INDEX | 271

Calais Winery, 204
Caldwell Vineyards, 87
Calera Wine Company, **103**, *108*, 108, *109*, 153, 262
California, 18-145, **19**, **140**
See also regions by name
California Association of Winegrape Growers, 20
California Certified Organic Farmers, 126
California Coolers, 25
California Shenandoah Valley AVA, **130**, 131, 132
California State Viticulture Commission, 39
California Sustainable Winegrowing Alliance, 20
Calistoga AVA, 54, **55**, **58**, 58–60, **67**
Callaghan, Harold, 200
Callaghan, Karen, 200
Callaghan, Kent, 200
Callaghan Vineyards, 198, **199**, 200
Callaway, Ely, 143, *143*, 144
Callaway Coastal, 144
Callaway Vineyard and Winery, **140**, 143, *143*, 144
Camarda, Chris, 162
Cambianica, Santo, 142
Cambria Estate Winery, **121**, 122, 123
Cameron Winery, **150**
Campbell, Adam Godlee, 153
Campbell, Joe, 153
Campbell, Pat, 153
Campbell, Patrick, 49, 137
Campbell, Tom, Jr., 192
Canandaigua Winery, 251
Canberra International Riesling Challenge, 262
Candia Vineyards, 249
Canoe Ridge Vineyard, **164–65**, 170, 176
Canyon Wind Cellars, **185**, 186, 187–88, 189
Cape May Winery, 269
Capiaux, Sean, 64
Cappelli, Marco, 134, *135*
Cappelli Ranch, **130**, 135
Captûre Wines, 32, *34*
Cardinale, **73**
Cardinal Point Vineyard and Winery, **235**, 237
Cargassachi, **111**, 127–28
Carignane, *4*
Carla's Vineyard, **90**, 96
Carli, Alessio, 109
Carlisle Vineyards, 37
Carlos Creek Vineyards, 219, 222
Carlson Creek Vineyard, **199**, 201
Carlson Vineyards, **185**, 186, *186*, 188
Carlton Winemakers Studio, **150**
Carmel Valley AVA, 102, **103**, 107
Carmody McKnight, **111**, 115
Carneros Creek Winery, 51, 53
Carneros Lake Vineyard, **45**
Carolina Vineyards Winery, 242
Carol Shelton Wines, 35, 36, **38**, 143, 144
Carter, Jim, 144, *144*
Carter, Mark, 60
Carter Cellars, 58, **58**, 59, 60
Carter House Inn, 60
Casa Larga, 258, **259**, *259*
Casa Nuestra Winery, **67**
Casa Rondeña Winery, 202
Casa Santinamaria, 44
Case, Jean, 238
Case, Steve, 238
Castello di Amorosa, *20*, 54, **58**, 59, *60*, 60
Castello di Borghese, **252**, 252, 255
Castle Creek Winery, 191, 192
Castle Vineyards, **45**
Castoro Cellars, **111**, 113
Catalina Island Conservancy, 141
Cathedral Ridge Winery, **147**
Catoctin AVA, 269
Cavatappi, **147**
Cave B Estate Winery, **160–61**, 181
Cave Vineyard, **215**, 218
Caymus Vineyards, 57, 63, 70, *71*, **71**, 71, 88, 105
Cayuga Lake AVA, 250, **251**, 258, **259**, 262
Cayuse Vineyards, **164–65**, 172, 173, 174, *174–75*
Ceàgo Vinegarden, **23**, 25, 27
Cecil, George, 242
Cedar Creek Winery, 226, 229
Cedar Mountain Winery, **90**
Cedar Ridge Vineyards, 219, 220
Cedarville Vineyard, **130**, 134, 135
Ceja Vineyards, **45**, 51, **55**
Celilo Vineyard, **160–61**, *162*
Cellardoor Winery, 249
Central Coast AVA, **19**, **90**, 93, 108, 110, **140**, 144
Central Coast Wine Services, **121**, 122
Central Delaware Valley AVA, **267**, 267, 269
Central Valley, 4, 136–39
Central Virginia Region, 237, 239
Century Farm Winery, 243
Certenberg Vineyard, 206, **207**
C.G. Di Arie Vineyard & Winery, **130**, 134, 135
Chacewater, **23**
Chaddsford Winery, *266*, **267**, 267
Chadwick, Eduardo, 76
Chalk Hill AVA, 28, **29**, **38**, 39, 41
Chalk Hill Estate Vineyards & Winery, **38**, 40, 41, 128
Chalone AVA, 102, **103**, 105–6
Chalone Vineyard, 102, **103**, 104, 105
Chalone Wine Group, 105–6, 117–18
Chamard Vineyards, 249
Chambers, Patti, 36
Chambers, Ray, 36
Chambourcin, *8*, 8
Chamisal Vineyards, **116**, 117
Champagne Taittinger, *50*
Champoux, Judy, 170
Champoux, Paul, 170
Champoux Vineyard, **164–65**, 170, 173, 178
Champs, Laurent, 238
Channing Daughters Winery, **252**, *252*, 255
Chapel Creek Winery, 210, *211*
Chappellet, Donn, 88
Chappellet, Molly, 88
Chappellet Vineyard & Winery, **55**, 57, 69, *87*, 88
Chardonnay, 6
Charles B. Mitchell Vineyards, **130**
Charles Coury Winery, 148
Charles Krug Winery, 34, 57, *67*, **67**, 67–68
Charles Smith Wines, 176, 181
Charter Oak Winery, 47, **67**
Chase, Don, 79
Chasseur, **38**, 39
Chateau Boswell, **67**
Chateau Chantal, **222**, 223, 224
Chateau du Lac, 26
Chateau Elan, 244, 245
Chateau Fontaine, **222**, 223
Chateau Frank, 258, **259**
Chateau Grand Traverse, **222**, *224*, 224
Château Julien, **103**
Chateau LaFayette Reneau, **259**
Chateau Montelena, 4, 28, *58*, **58**, 58–59, 71, 72, 79
Chateau Morrisette, **233**, 239
Chateau Ste. Michelle, **160–61**, 162, 163, 164, 167, 168, *168–69*, 170, 178, *179*, 181
Chateau St. Jean, 31, **45**, 46, 48
Chatham Vineyards, **233**, 239
Chatter Creek, **160–61**, 178, 179
Chaumette Vineyards, **215**, 218
Chehalem, 149, **150**, 152
Chehalem Mountains AVA, 146, 149, 153
Chellini, Mike, 69
Cherokee Vineyard Association, 137–38
Chesapeake Bay Region, 239
Chester Gap Cellars, 234, **235**
Chien Wines, **111**
Childress, Richard, 241
Childress Vineyards, 241
Chiles Valley District AVA, 54, **55**, 87
Chimney Rock, **77**, 77
Chinook Wines, **164–65**, 166, 167
Chouinard Vineyards and Winery, **90**
Chrisman Mill Vineyards, 240, 241
Christian Brothers, 72, 86, 121
Christianson, Jay, 187–88
Christianson, Jennifer, 188
Christianson, Norman, 187–88
Christine Woods, **23**
Christopher Creek, **38**
Chrysalis Vineyards, 233, 234, **235**, 236
Chumeia Vineyards, **111**
Churchill Vineyards, 191, *193*
Ciccone, Madonna Louise, 225
Ciccone, Silvio "Tony," 225
Ciccone Vineyard & Winery, **222**, 223, 225
Ciel du Cheval, **164–65**, 168, 173, 179
Cienega Valley AVA, **103**, 108, 109
Cilurzo, Audrey, 143
Cilurzo, Vincenzo, 143
Cilurzo Winery, 143
Cimarone Estate Winery, **124**, 129
Cimarossa, **55**, 64
Cimarron Cellars, **199**, 210
Cimarron Vineyards, 200–201
Cinder Wines, 182, **183**, 184
Cinnabar Winery, **97**
City Winery, **251**, *254*, 254
Claiborne & Churchill, **116**, 117, 118
Clarksburg AVA, **130**, 139
Clary Ranch, 43
Claudia Springs Winery, 22, **23**
Claypool, Les, 48
Claypool Cellars, 48
Clear Lake AVA, **23**, *26*, 27
Clements Hills AVA, 137, 138, 139
Clendenen, Jim, *119*, *122*, 122–23, 126
Clews, John, 79
Cliff Lede Vineyards, **77**, 77
Clifford Bay, 128
Clifton, Steve, 128
Cline, Fred, 96
Cline, Matt, 96
Cline, Nancy, 96
Cline Cellars, **45**, *96*, 96
Clinton Vineyards, **251**, 257
Clore, Dr. Walter, 161, 166, 167
Clos de la Tech, **97**, 98
Clos du Bois, **29**, 32, 251
Clos du Val, **77**, 77, 79
Clos LaChance, **97**, 98
Clos Pegase, **58**, 59
Clos Pepe Vineyards, **124**, 126, 127–28
Clubb, Marty, 157, 160, 173
Clubb, Megan, 173
Coastlands Vineyard, **29**
Cobb, Buck, 132
Cobb, Ross, 43
Cobb Wines, **29**, 42, 43
Coca-Cola, 65, *136*
Coccinelle, 174
Cochise County, 200–201
Coeur d'Alene Cellars, 182, 184
Cohn, Bruce, 48
Cohn, Jeff, 94, 107
Coit, Lillie Hitchcock, 69
Cold Creek Vineyard, 164
Cole Ranch AVA, 22, **23**
Colgin Cellars, **55**, 88
College Cellars, 176
Collins, Neil, *115*
Collins Vineyard, **67**
Colorado, 185–89
Colorado Cellars, **185**, 186
Colorado Mountain Vineyards, 186
Colorado Wine Industry Development Board, 185
Col Solare, 163, **164–65**, 166, 168, *168–69*
Colson, Alex, 35
Colterris, **185**, 186, 188
Columbia Crest Winery, 163, **164–65**, 170
Columbia Gorge AVA, 146, **147**, 157, **160–61**, 162, *164*, 177
Columbia Valley AVA, 146, **147**, 157, **160–61**, 160, 162, 163, 164, **164–65**, 167, 173
Columbia Winery, **160–61**, 162, 178, 180
Concannon, James, 94
Concannon Vineyards, **90**, 93, 94–95
Concord, 7
Conn Creek Winery, **71**
Connecticut, 248
Connecticut Winery Act, 248
Constant, **58**, 61
Constellation Brands, 46, 51, 70, 76, 88, 115, 120, 136, 139, 166, 251
Continuum Estate Vineyard, **55**, 76, *88*, 88
Contra Costa County, 96
Conway, Gary, 115
Cooke, Jack Kent, 236
Cooke, John Kent, 236
Cooke, Rita, 236
Cookson, Matt, 189
Coombsville AVA, **19**, 54, **55**, 87, *89*
Cooper, Dick, 133
Cooper Garrod Vineyard, **97**
Cooper Mountain Vineyards, **150**
Cooper Vineyards, **130**, **233**, 237
Copain Winery, **38**, 39, 43
Copeland, Gerret, 53
Copeland, Tatiana, 53
Coppola, Eleanor, 70
Coppola, Francis Ford, *34*, 70, 119
Coquard, Julie, 229
Coquard, Philippe, 229
Corbett Canyon, 136
Corcoran Vineyards, 234, **235**
Corison, Cathy, *68*, 69
Corison Winery, **67**, 68, 69
Corley, Chris, 82
Corley, Jay, 82
Corley, Kevin, 82
Corley, Stephen, 82
Cornell University, 250–51
Coronado Vineyards, **199**, 201
Cosentino Winery, **73**
Cosumnes River AVA, 137, 138–39
Cottonwood Cellars, 188
Coturri, Phil, 48–49
Coturri, Red, 48–49
Coturri, Tony, 48–49
Coturri Wines, **45**, 48–49
Cougar Crest, **164–65**
Cougar Hills Winery, 172
Coury, Charles, 148
Covelo AVA, **19**, 22
Covey Run, **164–65**, 173
Cowie, Robert, 245
Cowie Wine Cellars, 244, 245
Cox, Bobby, 208
Coyote Moon Vineyard, 265
Crabb, Hamilton Walker, 57, 73
Crane Family Vineyards, **55**
Crawford, George A., 185–86
Creekbend Vineyard, 227
Creekside Cellars, 186
Cresta Blanca, 95
Creston Manor Winery, **111**
Crete, Michael, 25
Crimson Wine Group, 32
Cristom Vineyards, 149, **150**, 153
Cronin Vineyards, **97**
Crooked Vine Winery, **90**
Croser, Brian, 152
Cross J Vineyard, 217
CrossKeys, **233**, 239
Crown Valley Winery, **215**, 216, 218
Cruse Vineyards and Winery, 242
Crushpad, 48, 93
Cucamonga Valley AVA, **140**, 143
Cumberland Valley AVA, 267, 269
Cunningham, Gary, 184
Cunningham, Martha, 184
Curry Creek Vineyards, 261
Curtis Winery, **124**
Cuthills Vineyards, 219, 222
Cuvaison Estate Wines, 57, **58**, 59
Cynthiana (Norton), 7, **7**

D'Andrea, Paolo, 202
D'Andrea, Sylvia, 202
Dalla Valle, Gustave, 75
Dalla Valle, Naoko, 75
Dalla Valle Vineyards, **73**, 74, 75
Damiani Wine Cellars, **259**, 261
Daniel, Dr. C. Richard, 243
Daniel, John, Jr., 70, 80–81
Daniel Vineyards, 243
Darioush, **55**
Dark Star Cellars, **111**
Darms Lane Wine, **55**
Dashe, Mike, 94
Dashe Cellars, 35, **90**, 93, 94
David Bruce Winery, **97**, 98, 100, 201
David Hill Winery and Vineyard, **150**
Davids, Bob, 126–27, *127*
Davidson, Sally, 189
Davies, Hugh, 61
Davies, Jack, 61
Davies, Jamie, 61
Davis, Jill, 36
Davis, John Marsh, 34
Davis, Rob, 31
Davis Bynum, **38**, 39–40
Davis family, 132
de Brye family, 47
de Coelo Vineyard, **38**, 42
Deaver Vineyard, **130**, 131, 132, 133
DeBaker, Steve, 228
Debevec family, 228
Debonné Vineyards, *226*, 227–28
Defiance, 177
Deford, Rob, 268
Dehlinger, **38**, 39
Dekker, Corry, 64
De La Montanya Winery, **38**, 48
Delaplane Cellars, 234, **235**
Delaware, 268
Del Dotto Vineyards, **55**
Delicato Family Vineyards, 107
DeLille Cellars, **147**, **160–61**, 162, 168, 178, 179
DeLoach Vineyards, **38**, 39, 53, 91
Del Rio Vineyards, **154**, 155, *156*
DeMara, Dyson, 148
Demeter Certified Biodynamic, 158
Denali Winery, 195
Deninno, Paul, 257
Derby, Dean, 176
Derby, Shari Corkrum, 176
Derenoncourt, 27
Derenoncourt, Stéphane, 27, 236
DeRose family, 109
DeRose Vineyards, **103**, 108, *108*, 109
Desert Wind Winery, **164–65**, 166
Devaux, Guy, 72
Devendorf, J. F., 107
de Villaine, Aubert, 52
de Villaine, Pamela, 52
de Villiers, Marq 108
Devil's Gulch Ranch, 39, **90**, *91*, 92
de Vink, Rutger, 236–37
Dezelsky family, 192
Diablo Grande AVA, **19**
Diageo, 51, 71, 94, 105, 118, 169, 170
Diamond Creek Vineyards, 57, **58**, 61–62
Diamond Mountain District AVA, 54, **55**, **58**, 61–62
Diamond Terrace, 61
Diamond T Vineyard, **103**, 104, 107
Dickerson Vineyard, 44
Diel, Armin, 163
Dierberg, Jim, 129, 217–18
Dierberg, Mary, 129, 217–18
Dierberg Estate Vineyards, **124**, 126, 129, 217–18
Dildine, Mike, 37
Dina, Dino, 64
Dobbins Creek Vineyards, 242
Doerner, Steve, 153
Dolan, Paul, 24
Dolce, 75
Domaine Berrien, 223
Domaine Carneros, **45**, 50, *50*, 51, **55**
Domaine Chandon, **55**, 80, *81*, 81
Domaine de la Romanée-Conti, 52
Domaine de la Terre Rouge, 132, 133
Domaine Drouhin Oregon, 149, **150**, 152
Domaine Eden, **97**
Domaine Laurier, 40
Domaine Serene, 149, **150**, 152, *152*, 153
Domaine Ste. Michelle, 163
Domenici family, 46
Dominus Estate, 40, **45**, **55**, *80*, 81
Doña Marcelina Vineyard, **124**
Donkey & Goat, **90**, 93, *94*
Donum Estate, **45**, 51, 52
Door Peninsula Winery, 226, 228

Doré, Dick, 121
Dorf, Michael, 254
Dos Cabezas Vineyard, 201
Dos Cabezas WineWorks, 198, **199**, 200, 201
Dos Rios AVA, **19**, 22
Dotson, Alphonse, 206
Dotson, Martha, 206
Doubleback, 172
Double L, **103**, 104
Doumani, Carl, 77, 79
Doyenne, 178
Drake Estate Vineyard, 40
Draper, Paul, 98, *100*, 100
Dressel, Chuck, 216
Dressel, Eva, 216
Dressel, Lucian, 216
Drew, Guy, 189
Drew, Ruth, 189
Drew Family Cellars, 22, **23**
Dr. Konstantin Frank's Vinifera Wine Cellars, *250*, 250, *258*, 258–59, **259**, 263
Drouhin, Robert, 151
Drouhin-Boss, Véronique, 152
Dr. Stephens Estate Wines, **55**
Dry Creek Valley AVA, 28, **29**, 35–36, **38**
Dry Creek Vineyard, **29**, 35–36, 139
Duchman, Lisa, 207
Duchman, Stan, 207
Duchman Family Winery, 204, **207**, 207
Duckhorn, Dan, 69
Duckhorn, Margaret, 69
Duckhorn Vineyards, 23–24, **67**, 68, 69
Duck Walk Vineyards, **252**
Duffeler, Patrick, 239
Duffeler, Peggy, 239
DuMOL, **38**, 39
Duncan Peak, **23**
Dundee Hills AVA, *12*, 146, 149, 152, *159*
Dunham, Eric, 176
Dunham Cellars, **164–65**, 172, 176
Dunn, Lori, 63
Dunn, Randall, 63, 71, 163
Dunnigan Hills AVA, **19**
Dunn Vineyards, 63, 71, 163
Duplin Winery, 241, 242
Durell Vineyard, **45**
Durney Vineyard, **103**
Dusted Valley Vintners, 172, 176
Dutch Henry Winery, **58**
Dutt, Dr. Gordon, *200*, 200
Dutton, Joe, 39
Dutton, Steve, 39
Dutton, Tracy, 39
Dutton, Warren, 39
Dutton Estate, **38**, 41
Dutton-Goldfield Winery, **38**, 39, 41, 91, 92
Dutton Ranch, 39
Duxoup Wine Works, **29**
Dyer, Bill, 80
Dyer, Dawnine, 80
Dyer Vineyard, **58**, 61, 80
Dyson, John, 40, 109, *256*, *257*
Dyson, Kathe, 40

Eagle Crest Vineyards, 250
Eames, Alfred, 188–89
Early Mountain Vineyards, 238
Easley Winery, 226, 227
Eastern Shore AVA, 239
Eastern Shore Region, 239
Easton, 133
Easton, Bill, 133
Eberle, Gary, *110*, 114
Eberle Winery, *110*, **111**, 112, *113*, 114
E. B. Foote Winery, **147**, 161

Eddins, Jim, 245
Edmeades, Donald, 24
Edmunds, Steve, 94
Edmunds St. John, **90**, 93, 94
Edna Valley AVA, *110*, **111**, 115, **116**
Edna Valley Vineyard, **116**, 116–18
Edwards, Merry, 40
Edward Sellers Vineyards & Wines, **111**, 112
Ehlers, Bernard, 69
Ehlers Estate, **67**, 68, 69
Eisele Vineyard, **58**, 59
Elan Vineyards, **55**, 83
El Dorado AVA, **130**, 131, 134–35
El Dorado County, 134–35
Elf Farm Winery & Cider Mill, 265
Elizabeth Spencer Wines, **23**
Elk Cove Vineyards, **150**, 153
Elke Vineyards, **23**
Elk Run Vineyards, 269
Elliston Vineyards, **90**
El Mocho Vineyard, **90**
Elyse Winery, **55**
Emeritus Vineyards, **38**, 41
En Cerise, *174*
ENTAV, 9
Entenmann, Martha Clara, 255
Entenmann, Robert, 255
Envy Estate Winery, **58**, 60
Enz Vineyards, **103**, 109
Eola–Amity Hills AVA, 146, 149, 153
Eos Estate Winery, **111**
Epoch Estate Wines, 115
Equus Run Winery, 240, *241*
Erath, Dick, 148, 200–201
Erath Vineyards, 148, 149, **150**, 201
Erdman, C. Pardee, 195
Erickson, Andy, 133
Erna Schein, **55**, 65
Eroica, 163, *164*
Escalle, Jean, 91
Eschen Vineyard, **130**
Escondido Valley AVA, 204, **205**
Eshcol, 82
Estancia, 102, **103**, 104
Esterlina Vineyards, **23**
Estrella River Winery, 112, 114
Etude Winery, **45**, 51, **55**, 153
Etzel, Michael, 153
Evan's Ranch, **124**
Evening Land Vineyards, **29**, 42, 43, **111**, 126, 128, 149, 153
Eveningside Vineyards, **251**, 264
Evenstad, Grace, 152
Evenstad, Ken, 152
Evergreen Vineyard, 181
Evesham Wood, **150**
Eyrie Vineyard, The, 149, **150**
Ezzard, John, 245
Ezzard, Martha, 245

Failla Wines, **29**, 42, 43
Fairhaven Vineyards, 204, **205**, 206
Fair Play AVA, **130**, 131, 134–35
Falcone, John, 125, 141
Fallbrook Winery, **140**, 145
Fall Creek Vineyards, 204, 206, **207**
Fanucchi Vineyards, **38**
Farella Vineyard, 87
Far Niente, **73**, *73*, 74, 75, *82*
Farrell, Gary, 40
Favia, 132, 133
Favia, Annie, 133
Fay, Nathan, 79

FAY Vineyard, **77**, *78*, 79
Feliciana Cellars Winery, 244, 245
Fenestra Winery, **90**, 93, 95
Fenn Valley Vineyards, 223, 225
Fennville AVA, 223, 225
Ferguson, Baker, *174*
Ferguson, Jean, *174*
Ferguson Block, 52
Fernandez, Elias, 79
Fernandez, Tony, 188
Ferrante, Anna, 228
Ferrante, Anthony, 228
Ferrante, Nicholas, 228
Ferrante, Nick, 228
Ferrante Winery & Ristorante, 226, 228, *228*
Ferrari-Carano Vineyards & Winery, **29**, 35
Ferrer, Gloria, 50, *52*
Ferris Wheel Vineyard, 157
Fess Parker Ashley's Vineyard, **124**, 128
Fess Parker Winery, 124
Fetzer, Barney, 24, 25
Fetzer, Ben, 25
Fetzer, Bobby, 25
Fetzer, Daniel, 25
Fetzer, Jacob, 25
Fetzer, Jim, 25, 27
Fetzer, John, **25**, 25
Fetzer, Kathleen, 24, 25
Fetzer, Patti, **25**, 25
Fetzer Vineyards, 22, **23**, 24–25, *25*
Ficklin, David, 136
Ficklin, Peter, 136
Ficklin Vineyards, **19**, 136
Fiddlehead Cellars, **111**, 127–28
Fiddletown AVA, **130**, 131, 132
Fidelitas Winery, **164–65**, 166, 167, 168, 170
Fields, Walter, 132–33
Fieldstone Winery, **29**
Figgins, Chris, 173, 176
Figgins, Gary, 157, 160, 172–73
Figgins Estate, 173
Filippi Winery & Vineyards, **140**, 143, 144
Finger Lakes AVA, 250, **251**, 258–59, **259**
Firelands Winery, 226
Firepeak Vineyard, *110*, **116**, 118
Firesteed Wines, **150**
Firestone, Adam, 125
Firestone, Andrew, 125
Firestone, Brooks, 124–25
Firestone, Kate, 124–25
Firestone, Leonard, 124–25
Firestone Vineyard, **124**, 124–25, 128
Fisher Ridge Wine Company, 243
Fish Eye, 136
Fish Friendly Farming, 89
Flag Hill Vineyards, 249
Flanagan Family, **45**, 49
Flat Creek Estate, 204, **207**, 207
Flemer, Carl, Jr., 239
Flemer, Doug, 239
Flora Springs Winery, **67**, 70, 74, **88**
Florentine Guild of Winemakers, 84
Florida, 245
Flowers Vineyard & Winery, **29**, 42, 43
Foley, Courtney, 128
Foley, Lindsay, 128
Foley, Robert, 60, 64, 254
Foley, William, 41, 48, 125, 128, *128*
Foley Estates Vineyard & Winery, **124**, 126, 128

Foley Family Wines, 128
Folonari, Ambrogio, 163
Folonari, Giovanni, 163
Food & Wine Classic in Aspen, 14, *15*, 185
Food Alliance, 158
Foppiano, Louis M., 40
Foppiano Vineyards, **38**, 39
Foppiano Winery, 40
Forge Cellars, **259**, 261
Forgeron Cellars, **164–65**, 173, *173*
Forgerson Vineyard, 179
Gallagher, Patricia, 4, *4*
Galleano family, 144
Foris Vineyards, **154**, 155
Forman Vineyard, **67**
Forni, Antonio, 68
Fortino, 97
Fort Ross–Seaview AVA, **19**, 28, **29**, 42, **43**, *43*
Fort Ross Vineyard & Winery, **29**, **43**, 43
Forty-Five North Vineyard & Winery, **222**, 223
Foster, Caleb, 176
Foster, Carol, *34*
Foster, Markquand, 68
Foster, Mike, *34*
Foster, Nina Buty, 176
4.0 Cellars, **207**, 207, *208*
Foursight Wines, 22, **23**
Foxen Winery & Vineyard, **121**, *121*, 122, 123, *126*
Fox Run Vineyards, **259**, **260**, 261
Fox Valley Winery, 226
Franciscan Oakville Estate, 57, 71
Francis Ford Coppola Winery, **29**, 34, 34
Frank, Dr. Konstantin, *250*, 250, *258*, 258–59, 263
Frank, Fred, 263
Frank, Jeanie, 59
Frank, Willy, 263
Frank, Yort, 59
Frank Family Vineyards, **58**, 59
Franscioni, Gary, *105*, 105
Franscioni, Rosella, 105
Franzia, Fred, 89, *136*
Franzia Brothers, *136*, 136
Fraser, Bill, 184
Fraser Vineyard, *182*, **183**, 184
Frazier Winery, 87
Fredericksburg in the Texas Hill Country AVA, 204, **205**, 206, **207**
Freedom Hill Vineyard, **150**
Freedom Run Winery, **251**, 264
Freeman, Charles, 68
Freeman Vineyard & Winery, **38**, 39, 42
Freemark Abbey, **67**, 68, 69, 120
Freestone Hill Vineyard, **38**, 39
Freestone Vineyards, **38**, 42, 43
Frei Brothers Winery, 35, *136*
Freixenet, 50
French Creek Vineyards, 267
French Hill, **130**
French Lick Winery, 226
Frescobaldi family, 76
Frey Vineyards, **23**
Frick Winery, **29**
Fries, Cameron, 181, *181*
Fries, Phyllis, *181*
Fritz Underground Winery, **29**
Frog's Leap Winery, 70, **71**
Frogtown Cellars, 244–45
Frontenac, 8
Front Range region, 189
frost damage, *114*
Fryer family, 192
Fulkerson Winery, **259**, 261
Furth, Fred, 41, 128
Furth, Peggy, 41
Fussell family, 242
Futo, **73**, 88

Gabriele Rausse Winery, **235**, 237
Gainey family, 125
Gainey Vineyard, **124**, 125
Gainey Winery, *125*, 127–28
Galante, Jack, 107
Galante Vineyards, **103**, 107
Galbreath, Scott, 245
Galena Cellars, 226
Galitzine Vineyard, 179
Gallagher, Patricia, 4, *4*
Galleano family, 144
Galleano Winery, **140**, 143, 144
Gallegos, Victor, 126–27
Gallo, Bob, 18
Gallo Winery, E & J, 4, 18, **19**, 38, 69, 118, *136*, 136, 139, 180, 260
Gallo, Ernest, 18, *136*, *136*
Gallo, Gina, 18
Gallo, Joseph, 18
Gallo, Julio, 18, *136*, 136
Gallo, Matt, 18
Gallo Family Vineyards, 35, **38**, *136*
Gallo Family Wines, **29**, 30, 35, 47, 95, 120
Galloni, Antonio, 88
Gamache, Bob, 167
Gamache, Roger, 167
Gamache Vintners, **164–65**, 166, 167
Garetto, Johnny, 53
Garfield Estates Vineyard & Winery, **185**, *186*, 188
Gargiulo Vineyards, **73**, 74
Garlich, John, 189
Gary Farrell Vineyards & Winery, **38**, 39, 40, 121
Garys' Vineyard, **103**, *105*
Gates, Charlie, 184
Gates, David, 37
Gates, Kimber, 184
Gates, Sarah, 184
Gatlin, Dan, 209
Gauer Ranch, 31–32
Gavilan Range, 108
Geisenheim Research Institute, 9
Gelles, David, 168
Gelles, Patricia, 168
Georges III Vineyard, **71**
Georgia, 244–45
Gerrie, Paul, 153
Geyser Peak Winery, **29**, 30, 32
Ghielmetti Vineyard, **90**, 95, *95*
G. H. Mumm, 4
Gier Winery, 86
Gilla, Marie-Eve, 173, *173*
Glacier Ridge Vineyards, 261
Glen Ellen Vineyards and Winery, 48
Glen Manor Vineyards, **235**, 239
Glenora Wine Cellars, **259**, 261
Glomski, Eric, 201, *201*
Gloria Ferrer Caves & Vineyards, **45**, 51, **52**
Goelet, John, 79
Goff family, 173
Goldeneye, 22, **23**, 23–24
Goldfield, Dan, 39, 92
Gold Seal Vineyards, 250
Goldstein Ranch, 46
Golitzin, Alex, 170, 178–79
Golitzin, Jeanette, 178
Golitzin, Paul, 170, 178–79
Goodchild Vineyard, 123
Gooseross Cellars, **55**, 81
Goose Watch Winery, **259**, 262
Gordon Brothers, 173
Gordon Estate, **164–65**
Goss, Norman, 117
Gott, Cary, 133
Grace Family Vineyards, **55**, 67

Gracie Hill Vineyard, 145
Graff, Richard, 105
Grahm, Randall, *13*, 101, *101*, 173
Gramercy Cellars, **164–65**, 172
Grand River Valley AVA, **226**, 227, 228
Grand Valley AVA, **185**, 186, *187*, 187–88
Granite Springs, 130
Grapes of Roth, The, *252*, 252, *253*, 255
Grape varieties, 6–8
Grassini Family Vineyards, **124**, *129*, 129
Graves, David, **51**, 51, 52
Graziano Family, 22, **23**
Great Western Winery, 250
Green, Patricia, 153
Green & Red Vineyard, **55**, 87
Greenough family, 117
Green Valley of Russian River Valley AVA, 28, **29**, **38**, 38–39, 41
Greenwood Ridge Vineyards, 22, **23**, 24
Gregory Graham, **23**, 27
Grey Stack Vineyards, 49
Greystone, 82
Grgich, Miljenko "Mike," 59, *72*, 72
Grgich, Violet, 72
Grgich Hills Estate, 59, 70, **71**, *72*, 72
Griessel, Bridgit, 178
Griessel, Steve, 178
Groth Vineyards & Winery, **73**, 74
Gruet, Gilbert, 202, 203
Gruet, Laurent, 202, 203
Gruet, Natalie, 202, 203
Gruet Winery, 9, 202, 203
Guadalupe Vineyards, 202, *203*
Guenoc Valley AVA, **23**, 27
Guffy, Dave, *85*, 86
Guillet, Jim, 133
Gullett, Suzy, 133
Guilliams Vineyards, **55**
Gundlach Bundschu Winery, **45**, 47–48
Gur-Arieh, Chaim, 135
Gur-Arieh, Elisheva, 135
Guthrie, Wells, 43
Guy Drew Vineyards, 186, **189**, *189*

Haak, Raymond, 209
Haak Vineyards & Winery, 204, **205**, 209
Haas, Jason, 114, *115*
Haas, Robert, 114, *115*
Habersham Vineyards, 244
Hacienda del Rio, 40
Hafner Vineyard, **29**
Hagafen Cellars, **55**
Hahn, Nicky, 104 Hahn Estates, 102, **103**, 104
Haig, Michael, 181
Haigh, Fred, 30
Haigh, Isabelle, 30
Haight-Brown Vineyard, 248, *249*
Haimann, Walter M., 208
Hall, Craig, 69
Hall, Judy, 195
Hall, Kathryn, 69
Hallcrest Vineyards, **97**
Hallgren, Lisa, 263
Hallgren, Morten, 263
Hall Wines, **67**, 68, 69
Halter Ranch Vineyards, **111**, 112
Hamacher, Eric, 152
Hamacher Wines, 149, **150**, 152
Hames Valley AVA, 102, **103**, 107
Hampton Roads Region, 239

Hamptons Long Island AVA, 250, 252, 253
Handley Cellars, 22, **23**
Hanford Reach National Monument, 171
Hanna Winery, **29**, 32, **38**
Hanzell Vineyards, **45**, 46, 47
Happy Canyon of Santa Barbara AVA, **111**, 119, 120, **124**, 124, 129
Happy Canyon Vineyard, 129
Haraszthy, Agoston, 30, 44, 53, 228–29
Hard Road to Hoe Vineyards, 177
Hardscrabble Vineyard, 236
Hargrave, Alex, 253, 255
Hargrave, Louisa, 253, 255
Hargrave Vineyard, 253, 255
Harlan, Bill, 75
Harlan Estate, 70, **73**, 74, 75, 88, 133
Harrington, Ginger, 176
Harrington, Greg, 176
Harrington, Ken, 176
Harrington, Pam, 176
Harrison Hill Vineyard, **164–65**
Hartford Family Winery, **38**, 41, 43
Hartley Ostini Hitching Post Winery, **124**, 124
Hartwell Vineyards, **77**, 77
Hart Winery, **140**, 143
Harvey, Kevin, 100–101
Harvey, Scott, 132
Harvey, Terri, 132
Haserot, Craig, 48
Hawaii, 194–95
Hawk and Horse Vineyards, **23**
Hawk Haven Vineyards, 269
Haw River Valley AVA, 242
Hazel Talley Vineyard, 117
Hazlitt 1852 Vineyards, **259**, 261
HdV, 51, 52, **55**
Hearst, George, 46
Hearst, William Randolph, 46
Heart & Hands Wine Company, **259**, 262
Heartbreak Grape, The (de Villiers), 108
Heather's Vineyard, 153
Heck, Adolph, 40
Heck, Gary, 40
Hecker Pass, **97**
Hedges, Anne-Marie, 168
Hedges, Tom, 168
Hedges Family Estate, **147**, **164–65**, 166, 168
Hegele, Paula, 115
Heinrichshaus Vineyards & Winery, 214, **215**
Heitz, David, 72
Heitz, Joe, 72
Heitz Wine Cellars, 57, **67**, 68, 72, 88, 173
Held, Betty, *2*, 217
Held, Jim, *2*, 217
Heller Estate, **103**
Hells Canyon Winery, **183**, 184
Hemstad, Peter, 222
Hendricks, Scott, 173
Hendry Ranch Wines, **55**
Hennessy, 80
Henry, Scott, 156
Henry Estate Winery, **154**, 156
Herbert Vineyard, 135
Heritage Vineyards, 268, 269
Hermann AVA, 214, **215**, 216, 217–18
Hermannhof Winery, 214, **215**, 217–18
Hermann J. Wiemer Vineyard, **259**, 261
Heron Hill Winery, 258, **259**
Herzog, Jacques, 81
Hess, Donald, 86
Hess Collection Winery, 26, **55**, 85, 86

Heublein, 70, 73, 109
Hewett Vineyards, 70, **71**
Hid-in-Pines Vineyards, 265
Higgins, Susan, 262
Higgins, Tom, 262
Highland Manor Winery, 243
High Plains AVA, 206
High Valley AVA, **23**, 27
Hill, Holly, 135
Hill, Tom, 135
HillCrest Vineyard, 148, **154**, 154, **155**, 155, 156
Hill Family Estate, **55**, 81
Hills, Austin, 72
Hinzerling Vineyard and Winery, **164–65**, 161
Hiram Walker & Sons, 144
Hirsch, David, 28, 42
Hirsch Vineyards, 28, **29**, 42, 43
Historic Vineyard Society, *4*, 37, 46
HJW Vineyard, 260
Hoage, Jennifer, 115
Hoage, Terry, 115
Hobbit Hollow, 262
Hodson, Andrew, *232*
Hodson, Patricia, *232*
Hoed, Andres, 163
Hoed, Andy Den, 163, 173
Hoed, Bill, 163, 173
Hofherr, Jim, 218
Hofherr, Pat, 218
Hogue, Gary, 166–67
Hogue, Mike, 166–67
Hogue Cellars, **164–65**, 166–67, 173, 251
Holbrook, Cory, 120
Holdenried family, 27
Holder, Ann, 241
Holder, Jerry, 241
Holloran Vineyard Wines, 150
Holly Grove Vineyards, **233**, 239
Holly's Hill Vineyards, **130**, *130*, 134, 135
Hollywood & Vine, **55**, 65
Holmes, Jim, 168, 179
Holy-Field Vineyard & Winery, 219–20
Home Ranch Vineyard, 32
Honig Wine, **71**
Hooker, "Fightin' Joe," 46
Hope Family, **111**, 112
Hopewell Valley Vineyards, 269
Hop Kiln Winery, **38**
Hopkins Vineyard, 248, 249
Hoppes, Charlie, 167
Horse Heaven Hills AVA, **147**, **160–61**, 162, 164, **164–65**, 165, 170
Horsepower, 174
Horseshoe Bend, 240
Horton, Dennis, 236, 239
Horton Vineyards, **235**, 236, 237, 239
Hosmer Winery, **259**, 262
House Wine, 170
Howell Mountain AVA, 54, **55**, 63–64
Huber family, 227
Huber's Orchard, Winery & Vineyard, 226, 227
Hudson-Chatham Winery, **251**, 257
Hudson River Region AVA, 250, **251**, *256*, 256–57
Hudson Vineyard, 40, **45**, 51, 52, **55**
Hundertwasser, Friedereich, 79
Huneeus, Agustin, 163
Hunt Country Vineyards, 258, **259**, 265
Husch Vineyards, 22, **23**, 24
Hyatt, Leland, 169
Hyatt, Lynda, 169

Hyatt Vineyards, **164–65**, 166, 169
Hybrid grapes, 7–8
Hyde, Larry, 52
Hyde Vineyard, 40, **45**, 51, 52, **55**
Hyman, Mark, 208

Ice wines, **11**, 259
Idaho, 182–84
IFOAM (International Federation of Organic Agriculture Movements), 158
Illinois, 226–27
Ilsley Vineyards, **77**, 77, 79
Indelicato family, 107
Indiana, 227
Indiana Small Winery Act, 227
Indiana Wine and Grape Council, 227
Infinite Monkey Theorem, The, 186, **188**, 188
Inglenook Winery, *4*, 57, 70, **71**, 73, 80–81, 82
Ingleside Winery, **233**, 239
International Pinot Noir Celebration (IPNC), 148, 149, 153
Inwood Estates Vineyards, 204, **205**, 207, 209
IOBC (International Organization for Biological Control), 176
Iowa, 220–21
Iowa Wine Growers Association, 220
IPNC (International Pinot Noir Celebration), *148*, 149, 153
Irelan, Nancy, 260
Iron Horse Vineyards & Winery, **38**, 39, 40, *41*, 41, 239
Ironstone Vineyards and Winery, **130**
Island View Vineyard, 225
Isle St. George AVA, 226, 227
Italian Swiss Colony, 34
Ivancie, Gerald, 186
Ivancie, Mary, 186
Ivancie Winery, 186

Jackson, Jess, *26*, 26, 32, 120, 123, 128
Jackson Family Wines, 31–32, 48, 49, 68, 102, 104, 106, 107, 120, 123, 128
Jacques, Jean, *256*, 257
Jacuzzi, Giocondo, 96
Jacuzzi, Valeriano, 96
Jacuzzi Family Vineyards, 96
Jade Lake (Chateau Montelena), *58*, 59
Jahant AVA, 137, **138**, 139
James Arthur Vineyards, 219
James Arthur Winery, 222
Jamesport Vineyards, 252
Janisson, Manuel, 239
Januik, Mike, *178*
Januik Winery, **160–61**, 168, 170, *178*, 179
Jasper Winery, 219, 220
Jaxon Keys, **23**
J. Carey Cellars, *128*
JC Cellars, 36, **90**, 93, 94, 107
J. Christopher Wines, **150**
J. Davies, *58*, 61
Jean Farris Winery, 240
Jefferson, Thomas, *2*, 82, *232*, *233*, 237
Jefferson Vineyards, **235**, 237
Jeff Runquist Wines, **130**, 133
Jekel Vineyards, 104
Jemrose Vineyards, **45**, 49
Jensen, Diana, 100, *101*
Jensen, Josh, 108–9, *109*, 262
Jensen, Rob, 100, *101*
Jeramaz, Ivo, 72
Jeriko Estate, 22, **23**, 25

Jessie's Grove Winery, **130**, 137
Jessup Cellars, **55**, 81
Jewell Towne Vineyards, 249, *249*
J. Lohr Vineyards & Wines, **97**, 102, **103**, *106*, 106, **111**, 112, 113
J. Maki Winery, **267**
JM Cellars, 168, 178
Jocelyn Lonen Winery, **55**
John Daniel Society, 81
John, Duval, 163
Johns, Greg, 241
Johnson, Chad, 176
Johnson Estate Winery, 250
Johnson family, 203
Jonata, 124
Jones, David, 134
Jones, Earl, *154*, 156–57
Jones, Hilda, *154*, 156–57
Jones, Jeanne, 134
Jones, Tom, 142
Jordan, John, 31
Jordan, Judy, 40
Jordan, Sally, *31*
Jordan, Tom, *31*, 31, 40
Jordan Vineyard & Winery, **29**, *31*, 31, 32, 40
Jory soil, 151, **151**
Josef Vineyard, 260
Jose Lopez Vineyard, **140**
Joseph Filippi Winery & Vineyards, **140**, 143, 144
Joseph Phelps Vineyards, 42, 57, 59, **67**, 68
Joseph Swan Vineyards, **38**, 39
Jowler Creek Vineyard & Winery, 214, **215**
J. Pedroncelli Winery, **29**, 35
J. Rochioli Vineyards, **38**, 39
Judgment of Paris (1976), *4*, 4, 68
Justin Vineyards & Winery, **111**, 112, 115
J Vineyards & Winery, 39, 40, 239

Kaiser Aetna, 143
Kansas, 219–20
Kansas Farm Winery Statute, 219, 220
Kapcsandy, Lou, 81, *81*
Kapcsandy Family Winery, **55**, 81
Karlsen, Dan, 104
Karly Wines, **130**, 132
Kathryn Kennedy Winery, **97**, 98
Kautz Family Winery, **130**
Keeling-Schaefer Vineyards, 198, **199**, 201
Keenan, Maynard James, 198, 201, *201*
Keever Vineyards, **55**, 81
Kehl, Jacob, 229
Kehl, Peter, 229
Keller Estate, 43
Keller, Thomas, 54
Ken Brown Wines, 120, **124**
Kendall, Jane, 26
Kendall-Jackson, **23**, 26, 27, 30, 34, **38**, 49, 102, 107
Kendric Vineyards, 91
Kenneth Volk Vineyards, 120, **121**
Kent, David, 94–95
Kentucky, 240–41
Kenwood Vineyards, **45**, 46, 48, 49
Ken Wright Cellars, 149, **150**, 153
Kenzo Estate, 88
Kestrel Vintners, **164–65**, 166, 167
Keswick Vineyards, **235**, 237, 239
Keuka Lake, 258, *263*
Keuka Lake Region, 263

Keuka Spring Vineyards, 258, **259**
King Estate, 146, **147**, 151
King Family Vineyards, **235**, 237
King Ferry Winery, **259**, 262
Kinkead Ridge, 226
Kinne, Alan, 236
Kinney, James, 170
Kiona Vineyards and Winery, **164–65**, 166, 168
Kistler, Steve, 42
Kistler Vineyards, **38**, 39, 42
Klein, Mia, 64
Klinker Brick Winery, **130**, 137
Klipsun Vineyard, **164–65**, 168, 173
Kludt family, 177
Kluge, Moses, 238
Kluge, Patricia, 238
Kluge Estate Winery & Vineyard, *238*, 238
Knapp Vineyards Winery, **259**, 262
Knight, Thomas, 32, 34
Knights Bridge, **29**, 32
Knights Valley AVA, 28, **29**, 32, **34**, **38**
Knob Hall Winery, 269
Koehler, Fred, 226–27
Koehler, Lynn, 226
Koenig, Greg, 184
Koening Distillery and Winery, 184
Komar, Dave, *34*
Kongsgaard, **55**
Kooyumjian, Tony, 217
Korbel Champagne Cellars, 30, **38**, 39, 40
Korff, Rikke, 176
Kosta Browne, **38**, 39
Koth family, 139
Kraemer, Ann, 133
Kramer Vineyards, **150**
Krankel, Manfred, 88
Krause, Melanie, 184
Kritzer, Craig, 244–45
Kritzer, Cydney, 244–45
Kroenke, Stan, 75
Kronos Vineyard, **67**, **68**, 69
Kroupa family, 224
Kroustalis, Jack, 241
Krug, Charles, **56**, 57, 66, 68
Krug, Dr. Jan, 83
Krug's Home Vineyard, **56**
Krupp Brothers Estate, **55**, 83
Krupp Vineyard, **55**
Kuleto Estate, **55**, 128
Kunde, Louis, 48
Kunde Family Estate, *44*, 44, **45**, 46, 48
Kutch, Jamie, 43
K Vintners, **164–65**, 172, 176
Kynsi Wines, 117

Labeling, 13
La Chiripada Winery & Vineyard, 202, 203
Lachs, Jonathan, 134–35
La Crema, 23, **38**, 92
La Crescent, **8**, 8
Lacroute, Bernard, 153
Lacroute, Ronni, 153
Ladera Vineyards, **55**, 63, **64**
La Encantada, **124**, 126
Laetitia, **116**, 117, 118
La Follette Wines, **29**, 49
Lafon, Dominique, 128, 153
Lafond, Pierre, 120, 126
Lafond Winery, **124**, 126
Lagier, Stephen, 85, *86*
Lagier Meredith Vineyard, **55**, 85, 86
Lail, Robin, 80–81
Lail Vineyards, 81
La Jota Vineyards, **55**, 63
Lake, David, *180*, 180

Lake Chelan AVA, **160–61**, 162, 164, 165, 177
Lake Chelan Winery, 177
Lake County, 26–27
Lake County Winegrape Commission, 26
Lake Erie AVA, 226, 250, **251**, 265, **265**, 266, 267
Lake Michigan Shore AVA, 223, 225
Lakeridge Winery & Vineyards, 244, **245**, *245*
Lake Wisconsin AVA, 226, 228
Lakewood Vineyards, **259**, 261
Lambert, Jerry, 36
Lambert Bridge Winery, **29**, 35, *36*
Lamborn Family Vineyards, **55**, 63
Lamoreaux Landing Wine Cellars, **259**, 261
Lancaster Estate, **29**, 32
Lancaster Valley AVA, **267**, 267
Landmark Vineyards, **45**, 48
Langtry, Lillie, 27
Langtry Estate, **23**, 27
La Rinconada, 124, 126
Larkmead Vineyards, **58**, 59
La Rochelle Winery, 93
Las Alturas Vineyard, **103**, 105
Las Amigas Vineyard, **45**, **55**
Las Brisas Vineyard, **45**, 53
Las Lomas Vineyard, *138*
Lasseter, John, 48
Lasseter, Nancy, 48
Lasseter Family Wines, **45**, 48
Las Ventanas, 117
Latcham Vineyard, **130**
Latour, Georges de, 70–71
Laube, James, 56
Laurel Glen Vineyard, **45**, 46, 48, 49, 137
Laurel Gray Vineyards, 242
Lava Cap Winery, **130**, 134
L'Aventure Winery, **111**, 112, 113, 115
Laville, Serge, 173, 176
La Vina Winery, 202, 203
Law, Jim, 236
Lawrence Dunham Vineyards, 198, **199**, 201
Lawson, Rob, 81
Lazy Creek Vineyards, **23**
Le Bon Climat, **121**, 123
L'Ecole No 41 Winery, 157, 160, **164–65**, 168, 172, 173, *174*
Ledson Winery and Vineyards, 45
Leducq, Jean, 69
Leducq, Sylviane, 69
Leducq Foundation, 69
Lee, Dan, 104
Lee, Donna, 104
LEED (Leadership in Energy and Environmental Design), 64, 69, 158
Leelanau Peninsula AVA, **222**, 223, 225
Leet, Logan, 241
Leet, Pam, 241
Left Foot Charley, **222**, 223, 225
Legacy Estates Group, 120
Lehigh Valley AVA, 266–67, **267**
Lemelson Vineyards, 149, **150**, 153
Lemon, Ted, *42*
Lenz Winery, 252, *252*, 255
Leonard Oakes Estate Winery, 11, **251**, 264
Leona Valley Winery, **140**
Leonesse, **140**, 143
Leonetti Cellar, 157, 160, **164–65**, 172, 173
Leone Valley AVA, 142
Les Bourgeois Vineyards, 214, **215**, 216

274 | INDEX

Les Collines Vineyard, **164–65**, 173
Lescombes family, 202
Les Pierres Vineyard, **45**
Lett, David, 148
Lett, Jason, 148
Leuthold, Craig, 177
Leuthold, Vicki, 177
Leventhal, Brian, 254
Le Vigne Winery, 111
Lieb Family Cellars, **252**, 252, 255
Lime Kiln Valley AVA, **103**, 108, 109
Limerick Lane Cellars, **38**
Limited Winery Act, 266
Lincoln Peak Vineyard, 248, 249
Linden Vineyards, 234, **235**, 236
Lindquist, Bob, 122
Lin family, 143, 144
Linganore AVA, 269
Linne Calodo Cellars, **111**, 112
Lioco, **38**, 43
Liparita Cellars, **55**
Lipsker, Greg, 181
Little Ashby Vineyards, 269
Littorai Wines & Estate Winery, 23, **38**, 42, 42, 43
LIVE (Low Input Viticulture and Enology), 158, 176
Livermore, Robert, 94
Livermore AVA, **90**, 94–95
Llano Estacado Winery, 204, **205**, 208
L. Mawby Vineyards, **222**, 223, 225
Locksley Estate, 236
Lockwood Vineyard, **103**
Lodi AVA, **130**, 137–39
Lodi Rules for Sustainable Winegrowing, 139
Lohr, Jerry, 107, 115
Lokoya, **55**, 86
Lombarda Cellars, 68
Lombardo, Giovanni Napoleon, 134
Lompoc Wine Ghetto, 128
Londer Vineyards, 22, **23**
London, Jack, 46
Long Island AVA, 250, **251**, 252–55
Long Meadow Ranch, **55**
Longoria, Richard, 126
Longoria Wines, **111**, **124**, 126, 128
Long Shadows Vintners, 163, **164–65**, 173
Longworth, Nicholas, 2, 227
Loosen, Dr. Ernst, 163, 164
Lopez Island Vineyards, **160–61**, 178, 180, 181
Loramie Creek AVA, 226
Loring Wine Company, **111**, 126, 127–28
Los Alamos Vineyard, 119
Los Angeles County, 142
Los Carneros AVA, 28, **45**, **50**, 50–53, 54, **55**, 90
Lost Oak Winery, 204, **205**, 207
Louisiana, 245
Louis M. Martini Monte Rosso Vineyard, **45**, 46, 47
Louis M. Martini Winery, 18, 46–47, **67**, 68, 69, 133, 136
Louis Roederer, 4, 24
Lovers Leap Vineyard & Winery, 240, 241
Lowden Hills Winery, **164–65**
Lucas, George, 91, **92**
Lucas Vineyards (CA), **130**, 137
Lucas Vineyards (NY), **259**, 262
Luna Rossa Winery, 202
Luna Vineyards, **55**
Lyncourt Vineyards, **124**, 128, 128
Lynfred Winery, 226–27

Lynmar Estate, **38**, 39
Lynne, Michael, 255
Lythgoe, Nigel, 115

Macari Vineyards, **252**, 252
MacCready, Barbara, 135
MacCready, John, 135
Macinski, Marti, 261
Mackey, Clay, 167
MacLachlan, Kyle, 176
MacMurray Ranch, **38**, 136
MacRostie Winery, **45**, 51
Mac's Creek Winery & Vineyards, 219, 221
Madder Lake, 27
Madera AVA, **19**
Madill, Bob, 262
Madonna, 225
Madonna Estate, **45**, **55**
Madroña Vineyard, **130**, 134
Madrone Ranch, 46
Magdalena Vineyards, 260
Magnanini Farm Winery, **251**, 257
Magnificent Wine Company, 176
Magoon, Orville, 27
Mahoney, Francis, 53
Mahoney Ranch, **45**, **55**
Maine, 249
Maison Bleue Family Winery, **164–65**, 166, 167
Maison Deutz, 118
Malbec, Denis, 32, **34**, **81**, 81
Malbec, May-Britt, 32, **34**
Malibu–Newton Canyon AVA, **140**, 142
Malibu Trancas Canyon Vineyard, 142
Malibu Vineyards, **140**, 140
Ma Mere, **121**, 123
Mamoser, Maria, 227
Mamoser, Rick, 227
Manchester Ridge Vineyard, 23, 24
Mandola Estate Winery, 207
Manigold Vineyard, 224
Manischewitz, 251
Mantone, James, 177
Mantone, Poppie, 177
Maple Creek, **23**, 24
Maple River Winery, 192
Marcassin Vineyard, 29, **34**, 42, 43, 88
Marechal Foch, 8
Margerum, Doug, 129
Margerum Wine Company, **124**, 129
Mariani family, 173
Marimar Estate, **38**, 41
Marimar Torres, 39
Marin County, 91–92
Marita's Vineyard, 87
Markham Vineyards, 64, **67**
Mark Ryan Winery, 168, 178
Marks, Susan, 134–35
Mark West Wines, **38**
Marquette, 8
Marshall, James, 130
Marston Family Vineyard, **55**
Martha Clara Vineyards, **252**, 252, 253, 255
Martha's Vineyard, **73**
Martha's Vineyard AVA, 249
Martin, Rachel, 234, 236
Martin family, 155
Martinelli Vineyard, 29, **38**
Martinelli Winery, **38**, 42, 43
Martin Ray Winery, **38**
Martini, Ann, 260
Martini, John, 260
Martini, Louis M., 46, 47, 69
Martini, Louis P., 69
Martini, Michael, 47, 69
Maryhill Winery, **160–61**, 177
Maryland, 268

Massachusetts, 249
Masson, Paul, 98
Massoud, Charles, 255
Massoud, Kareem, 255
Massoud, Ursula, 255
Mastantuono Winery, 111
Masút Vineyard and Winery, **23**, 25
Matanzas Creek Winery, 40, **45**, 46, 49
Mathewson, Joan, 189
Matrix Winery, **38**
Matthews, Dave, 239
Matthews Estate, **147**, **160–61**
Mauritson Family Wines, **29**, 35, 36
Mawby, Larry, **225**, 225
May, Cliff, 74
Mayacamas Vineyards, **55**, 85, **86**, 86, 132
Maybach, **73**, 88
Mayo Family Winery, **45**
Maysara Winery, 149, **150**, 152
Mazza Vineyards, 266, 267
Mazzei, Filippo, 233
Mazzocco Winery, **29**
McClellan, Casey, 173
McCloud, Jenni, 233, 236
McCrea, Doug, 179
McCrea, Eleanor, 69
McCrea, Fred, 69
McCrea, Peter, 69
McCrea, Willinda, 69
McCrea Cellars, **160–61**, 162, 168, 178, 179
McDonnell, Bob, 232
McDougall Vineyard, 39
McDowell Valley AVA, 22, **23**
McGinley Vineyard, **124**, 129
McGregor family, 263
McGregor Vineyard, 258, **259**, 261
McGuire, Bruce, 126
McIntyre, Hamden, 82
McIver, Bill, 49
McIver, Sandra, 49
McKibben, Norm, 157, 173
McKinlay Vineyards, **150**
McKnight, Marian, 115
McMinnville AVA, 146, 149, 152
McNab Ridge Winery, **23**, 24, 25
McPherson, Clinton "Doc," 208
McPherson, Jon, 144
McPherson, Kim, 208
McPherson Cellars, 204, **205**, 207, **208**, 208
McQueen Vineyard, 176
Meador, Doug, 106, 107
Meador, LuAnn, 106
Meconi, Julia, 225
Meconi, Mariano, 225
Meier's Wine Cellars, 226
Melka, Philippe, 163, 173
Melville Vineyards & Winery, **124**, 126, 127–28
Mendelbaum Cellars, 207
Mendocino AVA, 22, **23**
Mendocino County, 22–25
Mendocino Ridge AVA, 22, **23**, 24
Mendocino Wine Company, The, 24
Mendocino Winegrape and Wine Commission, 24
Mercer Estates Winery, **164–65**, 166, 167
Mercer Ranch, 170
Meredith, Carole, 85, **86**
Meridian Vineyards, **111**, 114
Merkin Vineyards, **199**, 201
Merlot, 6
Merritt Island AVA, **130**
Merry Edwards Wines, **38**, 39
Merryvale Vineyards, **67**

Mer Soleil, 102, **103**, 105
Merus, 128
Merwarth, Fred, 260
Merz, Ulla, 189
Mesilla Valley AVA, 202, 203, 204, **205**
Messina Hof Hill Country, **207**, 207
Messina Hof Winery and Resort, 204, **205**, 207, 209
Meteor Vineyard, 87
Mettler Family Vineyards, 137
Meunier, Isabelle, 128, 153
Meunier, Lafon, 128
Meuron, Pierre de, 81
Meyer, Julie, 184
Meyer, Les, 219–20
Meyer, Michelle, 219–20
Meyer, Robbie, 129
Meyer, Stephen, 184
Meyer Family Cellars, 22, **23**, 24
Michael Shaps, **235**, 237, 239
Michael, Sir Peter, 34
Michael-David Vineyards, **130**, 137
Michael-David Winery, 139
Michael Mondavi Family, **45**, 55
Michaud, Michael, 106
Michaud Vineyard, **103**, 106
Michel-Schlumberger, **29**
Michigan, 222–25
Middle Rio Grande Valley AVA, 202, 203
Middleton, Rick, 174
Midnight Cellars, **111**
Midwest Grape and Wine Industry Institute, 220
Mielke family, 181
Migliore, Michael, 257
Migliore, Yancey, 257
Milagro Vineyards & Winery, 202
Milano Family Winery, **23**
Milat Estate Winery, **67**
Milbrandt, Butch, 171, 181
Milbrandt, Jerry, 171, 181
Milbrandt Vineyards, **164–65**, 171, 181
Millbrook Vineyards & Winery, 40, **251**, 256, **257**, 257
Mill Creek Vineyards and Winery, **29**
Miller, Eric, 267
Miller, Lee, 267
Miller, Marshall, **120**
Miller, Nicholas, **120**
Miller, Stephen, **120**
Mimbres Valley AVA, 202, 203
Miner Family Vineyards, **73**, 74
Mineral Springs Ranch, 153
Minnesota, 221
Miraflores Winery, 134, 135
Mirassou, Steven Kent, **94**, 95
Mirassou Vineyards, **94**, 95, 136
Mission Arcángel San Gabriel, 142
Mission Mountain Winery, 191, 192
Mission San Diego de Alcalá, **145**, 145
Mission San Francisco de Solano, 28, 30
Mission San Rafael Arcángel, 91
Mission Santa Barbara, 119
Mississippi, 245
Mississippi Delta AVA, 244, 245
Missouri, 214–18
Moët & Chandon, 4, 80, **81**
Moët-Hennessy, 80
Mohr-Fry Ranch, **130**
Mokelumne Glen Vineyards, **130**, 139

Mokelumne River AVA, 137, 138, 139
Moller-Racke, Anne, 52
Molnar, Peter, 27
Momtazi, Flora, 152
Momtazi, Moe, 152
Momtazi, Tahmiene, 152
Momtazi Vineyard, 152
Mondavi, Cesare, 68, 137
Mondavi, Marc, **67**, 68
Mondavi, Margrit, 76, 88
Mondavi, Michael, 76, 88
Mondavi, Peter, Jr., **67**, 68
Mondavi, Peter, Sr., **67**, 68
Mondavi, Robert, 35, 57, 68, 73–74, **76**, 76, 88, 137
Mondavi, Rosa, 68
Mondavi, Tim, 76, **88**, 88
Mondavi Corporation, 76, 102, 120
Mondavi To Kalon Vineyard, **73**, 73–74, 76
Montana, 192
Monte Bello Winery, 98
Monte Rosso Vineyard, 46–47, 47, 69
Montelle Winery, 214, **215**, 217
Monterey AVA, **97**, 102, **103**, 104
Monterey County, 102–7
Monte Sereno, 117
Montevina Vineyard, **130**, 132–33, 133
Monticello AVA, 232, **233**, 234, **235**, 237
Monticello Cellars, **55**
Monticello Vineyards & Winery, 82, **232**, 233
Montinore Estate, **150**
Mont La Salle Winery, 86
Moore, Jim, 139
Moorman, Sashi, 42, 128
Moraga, Vicente, 143
Moraga Vineyards, **140**, 142
Morelli Lane Vineyard, **38**
Morgan Winery, 102, **104**, 104
Morlet, Luc, 34
Morlet, Nicolas, 34
Morlet Family Vineyards, 34
Morrisette, David, 239
Morrisette, Nancy, 239
Morrisette, William, 239
Morton, Lucie, 236, 238
Mosaic Vineyards, **29**
Mosby Wines, **124**
Moshin Vineyards, **38**, 39
Mother Vine, 241
Moueix, Christian, 80, 80–81
Mount Aukum Winery, **130**, 134, 135
Mount Eden Vineyards, 40, **97**, **97**, 97, 98
Mount Harlan AVA, **103**, 108, 108–9
Mount Palomar Winery, **140**, 143
Mount Pleasant Estates, **215**, 217
Mount Pleasant Winery, 214, 216–17
Mount Salem Vineyards, 269
Mount Veeder AVA, **45**, 54, **55**, 61, 85–86
Mount Veeder Vineyards, **55**, 86
M. Perelli-Minetti Winery, **71**
Mueller Winery, **38**
Muench, Frederick, 216
Muench, George, 216
Mumm Napa, 70, **71**, 72
Munson Memorial Vineyard, Thomas Volney, **205**, 206
Munson, Thomas V., 204, 206
Murrieta's Well, **90**
Muscadine, 7
Myers, Kathleen Heitz, 72

Naber, Madelyn, 207
Naber, Rick, 207
Naches Heights AVA, **160–61**, 162, 164, **164–65**, 165, 169
Naches Heights Vineyard, **164–65**
Nalle Vineyards, **29**, 35, 36
Napa County Resource Conservation District, 72
Napa Green program, 89
Napanook Vineyard, **55**, 81
Napa Valley Agricultural Preserve, 61
Napa Valley AVA, **45**, **55**, 54–89, **58**, **67**
Napa Valley Mexican-American Vintners Association, 20
Napa Valley Reserve, 75
Napa Valley Vintners (NVV), 20, 89
Napa Wine Company, **73**
Naples Winter Wine Festival, 14
Narrows Vineyard, The, **23**
Nassau Valley Vineyards, 268, 269
Native American grapes, 7
Nation, Carrie, 219
National Organic Program, 158
Nauvoo Winery, 226
Navarro Vineyards, 22, **22**, **23**, 25
Neal, Annetta, 211
Neal, Don, 211
Nebraska, 221
Nefarious Vineyards, 177
Neff, Cooper, 177
Neff, Dean, 177
Neff, George, 177
Neff, Heather, 177
Neff, Lucy, 177
Nelson, Chris, 241
Nelson, Denise, 241
Nestlé's Wine World Estates, 34
Nevada, 193
New England, 248–49
New Hampshire, 249
New Jersey, 268
Newhouse, Alfred, 169
Newlan Vineyards, **55**
New Mexico, 202–3
Newport Vineyards, 249
Newsom, Neal, 208
Newsom Vineyards, **205**, 208
Newton, Sir Peter, 60, 65
Newton, Su Hua, 65
Newton Vineyard, **55**, 60, 62, 65
New Vineland, **111**, 128
New York Ice Wine Festival, The, 259
New York State, 250–265, **251** See also regions by name
New York State Agricultural Experiment Station, 250–51
New York Wine & Culinary Center, 251
New York Wine & Grape Foundation, 251, 262
Neyers, 96
Niagara, 7, 7
Niagara Escarpment AVA, 250, **251**, 264
Niagara Landing Wine Cellars, **251**, 264
Nicault, Gilles, 163, 173, 173
Nichelini, Anton, 87, 134
Nichelini Winery, **55**, 87, 134
Nicholas, Nick, 153
Nicholas, Sheila, 153
Nickel, Beth, 75
Nickel, Gil, 75
Nickel & Nickel, **73**, 74, 75
Niebaum, Gustave, 70, 82

INDEX | 275

Niebaum Coppola, 70
Nielson, Uriel J., 120, 121
Nielson Vineyard, 122
Niner Vineyards, **111**, 112
Niven, Catharine, 117–18
Niven, Jack, 117–18
Niven, John, 118
Norman Vineyards, **111**, 112, 113
North Carolina, 241–42
North Coast AVA, **19**, 90, 91
North Dakota, 190, 192
Northern Neck George Washington Birthplace AVA, 232, **233**, 234, 239
Northern Sonoma AVA, 28, **29**, 38
Northern Virginia Region, 234, 236–37
North Fork of Long Island AVA, 250, 252, 253, 255
North Fork of Roanoke AVA, 232, **233**, 234, 239
Northstar, 168, 172, 176
North Yuba AVA, **19**, 131
Norton (Cynthiana), 7, 7
Norton, Daniel, 214, 236
Novak, Beth, 68–69
Novak, Jack, 68–69
Novak, Lindy, 68–69
Novak, Mary, 68–69
Novelty Hill, 160–61, **178**, 179
Novitiate Winery, 100, 101
Nth Degree, 94
Nugent Vineyard, 52
NVV (Napa Valley Vintners), 20, 89
Nygaard, Eldon, 190
Nygaard, Sherry, 190

Oak Knoll District of Napa Valley AVA, 54, **55**, 82
Oak Knoll Winery, **150**
Oak Summit, 251, 257
Oakville AVA, 54, **55**, **71**, **73**, 73–75
Oakville Experimental Vineyard, 74
Oakville Ranch Vineyards, **73**, 74
Obsidian Ridge Vineyard, **23**, 27
Occidental Vineyard, **29**, 42, 153
OCSW (Oregon Certified Sustainable Wine), 158
Officer, Mike, 37
O'Herron, Sarah, 268
Ohio, 227–28
Ohio River Valley AVA, 226, 227, 240, 241
Ojai Vineyard, 122, **140**
O'Keefe, Ed, 224
O'Keefe, Eddie, 224
O'Keefe, Sean, 224
Oklahoma, 210–11
Olathe Winery, The, 188
Old Hill Vineyard, 44, **45**
Old Mission Peninsula AVA, **222**, 223, 224–25
Old South Winery, 244, 245
Oldak, Dr. Peter, 249
Oliver, Raymond, 68
Oliver, William, 227
Oliver's, 117
Oliver Vineyard & Winery, 226, 227
Olivet Lane Vineyard, **38**, 40
Ollivier, Cornel, 224–25
Olsen-Harbich, Rich, 255
Olympic Cellars, 178
Optima Wine Cellars, **38**
Opus One, **73**, 74, 76
ORCA (Oregon Chardonnay Alliance), 152
Oregon Certified Sustainable Wine (OCSW), 158
Oregon, 146–159, **147**
See also regions by name

Oregon Winegrowers Association, 156
Orfila Vineyards & Winery, **140**, 145
Original Grandpere Vineyard, **130**, 132
O'Riordan, Jane, 133
Orleans Hill Winery, **130**
Orogeny Vineyards, 41, 91
O'Shaughnessy, Betty, **63**, 63–64, 86
O'Shaughnessy Estate Winery, 55, **63**, 63–64, 86
OTCO (Oregon Tilth Certified Organic), 158
Otis Vineyard, 164–65, 180
Otsuka, Akihiko, 100
Otter Creek Winery, 265
Outer Coastal Plain AVA, 269
Ovid, **55**, 88
Owen Roe, 149, **150**
Ozark Highlands AVA, 214, **215**, 216, 218
Ozark Mountain AVA, 210, 211, 214, **215**, 216, 218, 244

P & M Staiger Vineyard, **97**
Pacheco Pass AVA, **97**
Pacheco Ranch Winery, **90**, 91
Pacific Rim, 101, 163, 173
Paderewski, Ignacy Jan, 115
Pagani Ranch Vineyard, 37, 44, **45**
Pagani Winery, **49**
Page, David, 255
Page Springs Cellars, 198, **199**, 201
Pahlmeyer, Jayson, 84
Pahlmeyer, **55**
Pahrump Valley Winery, 193
Paicines AVA, **103**, 108, 110
Paige, Dave, 152
Palengat, 178
Palmaz Vineyards, 87
Palmer, Jim, 142
Palmer Vineyards, **252**
Palmina, **111**, 126, 128
Paloma Vineyards, 65
Panther Creek Cellars, **150**, 152, 153
Papapietro Perry Winery, **29**, 35
Paradigm Winery, **73**
Paradise Ridge Winery, **29**, 47
Paradocx Vineyard, **266**, **267**, 267
Paraduxx Wines, **55**
Paragon Vineyard, **116**, 117–18
Paraiso Vineyards, 102, **103**, 104
Parducci, Adolph, 24
Parducci, John, 24
Parducci, Rich, 24
Parducci Wine Cellars, 22, **23**, 24
Parker, Robert, Jr., 56, 88, 153, 170, 268
Parsons, Ben, 188, 188
Paschal Winery & Vineyard, **154**
Paschina, Luca, **236**, 237
Paso Robles AVA, **110**, 110, **111**, 112–15, 113
Paso Robles Wine Country Alliance, 112
Passalacqua, Tegan, 37
Pasternak, Mark, **91**, 91, 92
Patchett, John, 57
Patianna Organic Vineyards, 22, **23**
Patricia Green Cellars, **150**, 153
Patterson, Ellie, 98
Patterson, Jeff, 98
Patz & Hall, 42, **45**, 52, 55
Paul Dolan Vineyards, 22
Paul Hobbs Winery, **38**, 39, 46, 49

Paul Masson, 4, 251
Paumanok Vineyards, **252**, 255
Peachy Canyon, **111**, 113
Pearmund Cellars, 234, **235**
Peay Vineyards, **29**, 34, 42, 43
Peconic Bay Winery, **252**, 252
Pedernales Cellars, 204, **207**
Pedroncelli Winery, **29**, 35
Peirano, **130**
Peju Province Winery, 70, **71**
Pellegrini, Bob, 40
Pellegrini, Ida, 40
Pellegrini, Vincent, 40
Pellegrini Family Vineyards, **38**, 39, 40
Pellegrini Wine Company, 40
Pellegrini Winery & Vineyard, **252**
Pellet, Jean-Francois, 173
Pend d'Oreille Winery, 182, 184
Peninsula Cellars, **222**, 223, 224–25
Penn, William, 266
Penner-Ash Wine Cellars, 149, **150**, 153
Penn Shore Vineyards, **266**, 267
Pennsylvania, 266–67
Pennsylvania Liquor Control Board, 266
Penns Wood Winery, **267**, 267
Pepper Bridge Vineyard, 164–65, 173
Pepper Bridge Winery, 157, 172, 173
Perdido Vineyards, 244, 245
Perrin, Cesar, 114, **115**
Perrin, Francois, 114, **115**
Perrone, Osea, 98
Perry Creek Winery, **130**
Petaluma Gap region, 43
Peter Michael Winery, 32, 32, 34, 129
Peterson, Cindy, 262
Peterson, Dave, 262
Peterson, Jeff, 192
Peterson, Joel, 44, **46**, 46, 137
Peterson family, 60
Peterson-Nedry, Harry, 151–52, 153
Pey, Jon, 92
Pey, Susan, 92
Pey-Marin, **90**, 91
Pezzi King Vineyards, **29**
Pfeiffer, Harold, 121
Pfendler Vineyards, 43
Pheasant Ridge Winery, 208
Phelps, Don, 177
Phelps, Judy, 177
Phelps Creek Vineyards, **147**, 157
Philip Staley Vineyards & Winery, **29**
Philip Togni Vineyard, **55**
Phillips, David, 139
Phillips, Doug, 187
Phillips, Jean, 75
Phillips, Michael, 139
Phillips, Sue, 187
phylloxera, 2, 9, 204
Pickberry Vineyard, **45**
Pico, Pío, 143
Piedrasassi, 42, **111**, 128
Pierce's disease, 9, 9, 143
Pietra Santa Winery, **103**, 108, 109
Pietrzyk Art, 228
Pietrzyk, Doreen, 228
Pillar Rock, **77**
Pillsbury, Sam, 198, 201
Pillsbury Wine Company, 198, **199**, 201
Piña Cellars, **71**
Pindar Vineyards, **252**, 252
Pine Mountain-Cloverdale Peak AVA, **23**, 28, **29**, 32

Pine Ridge Vineyards, **77**, 77, 176
Pines Vineyard, 170
Pinnacle Ridge Winery, **267**, **267**, 267
Pinnacles Vineyard, **103**
Pinot Gris, 6
Pinot Noir, 7
Pinot Noir Pioneer Club, 153
Pintler Cellars, 184
Pisacano, Richard, 253
Pisacano, Soraya, 253
Pisoni, Gary, 105
Pisoni and Lucia, 105
Pisoni Vineyards & Winery, 102, **103**, 105
Pleasant Valley Wine Company, 250
Plum Creek Winery, **185**, 186, 187
PlumpJack Winery, 64, **73**, 74
Pointe of View Winery, 14, 191, 192
Point Reyes Vineyards, **90**, 91
Polaris Wines, **55**, 79
Pon, Ben, 107
Pontchartrain Vineyards, 244, 245
Ponzi, Dick, 148
Ponzi, Luisa, 152
Ponzi, Nancy, 148
Ponzi Vineyards, 148, 149, **150**, 152, 153
Poole, John, 143
Pope Valley, 88
Porter Creek Vineyards, **38**
Portet, Bernard, 79
Portteus Winery, 164–65
Poten, Connie, 192
Potomac Highland Winery, 243
Potter Valley AVA, 22, **23**, 24–25
Powers Winery, 164–65, 170
Prager Winery & PortWorks, **67**
Prairie Berry Winery, 190, 191, 191
Prairie State Mercantile, 227
Prairie State Vineyards, 226
Prairie State Winery, 227
Precept Wine, 169, 170, 176, 182, 184
Prejean Winery, **259**, 261
Presque Isle Wine Cellars, 266, 267
Preston, Lou, 35
Preston Vineyards, **29**, 161
Pretty-Smith Vineyards & Winery, **111**
Priam Vineyards, 249
Pride Mountain Vineyards, **55**, 64, **65**
Pritchard Hill, 87, 88, **88**, 88
Prodigy Vineyards and Winery, 240
Progeny Winery, 86
Prohibition, 2–4, **3**
Pronghorn Vineyard, 200
Provenance Vineyards, 70, **71**
Puget Sound AVA, 160–61, 162, 178–81
Puget Sound Wine Growers Association, 179
Pura, Randy, 106
Purisima Mountain Vineyard, 125
Pursued by Bear, 172, 176

Quady, Andrew, 136, 155
Quady, Herb, 155
Quady, Laurel, 136
Quady North, **154**, 155
Quady Winery, **19**, 136
Qualia, Frank, 204
Qualia, Louis, 204
Qualia, Thomas, 204
Quilceda Creek Vintners, **147**, 160–61, 168, 170, 178

Quillé, Nicolas, 173
Quintessa, 49, 70, **71**
Quivira Vineyards and Winery, **29**
Quixote, **77**, 77, 79
Qupé, **121**, 122

Raffaldini Vineyards, 242
RagAppleLassie Vineyards, 242
Ramey, David, **40**, 40, 51–52
Ramey Wine Cellars, **38**, 40, 42
Ramona Valley AVA, **140**, 145
Ram's Gate Winery, **45**
Rancho de Philo, 143
Rancho El Jabalí, **124**, 126
Rancho La Cuna, **119**
Rancho Rossa, 198, **199**
Rancho San Ignacio, 115
Rancho Sisquoc Winery, **121**, 121
Randazzo family, 265
Rapazzini Winery, **97**
Raphael, **252**
Rappahannock Cellars, 234, **235**
Rattlesnake Creek Vineyard, 192
Rattlesnake Hills AVA, 160–61, 162, 164, 164–65, 165, 166, 169
Rausse, Gabriele, 237
Ravenswood Winery, 35, 44, **45**, **46**, 46, 137
Ravines Wine Cellars, 258, **259**, 263
Ray, Martin, 98
RayLen Vineyards, 242
Raymond Burr Vineyards, **29**, 48
Raymond Vineyard & Cellar, 53, 57, **71**
RdV Vineyards, 234, **235**
Red Car Wine Company, **38**, 42, 43
Reddy, Dr. Vijay, 208
Reddy Vineyards, **205**, 208, **209**
Redhawk Winery & Vineyard, **150**
Red Hill Douglas County AVA, 146, **147**, **154**, 155, 157
Red Hills AVA, **23**, 27
Red Hill Vineyard, **154**, 157
Red Hook Winery, 251, 254
Redlands Community College, 211, 211
Red Mountain AVA, 160–61, 162, 164, 164–65, 165, 166, 167–68
Red Newt Cellars, **259**, 261
Red Tail Ridge, **259**, 260, 261
Red Willow Vineyard, 164–65, 166, **167**, 180
Redwood Creek, 136
Redwood Valley AVA, 22, **23**, 24–25
Reed, Robert, 208
Reeder Mesa Vineyards, **185**, 186
Regan Estate Vineyards, 90
Regusci Winery, **77**
Reinhardt, Johannes, 260, 261
Reininger Vineyards, 164–65, 172
Remick Ridge Vineyards, **45**, 48
Renteria Wines, **55**, 86
Renwood Winery, **130**, 132
Renzaglia, Guy, 227
Replogle, Fran, 95
Replogle, Lanny, 95
Retzlaff, **90**
Revana Family Vineyard, **67**
Reverie, **58**, 61
Rex Hill, 149, **150**
Rhode Island, 249
Rhys Vineyards, **97**, 98, 101
Ribbon Ridge AVA, 146, 149, 153
Rich, Marta, 109

Richard Dinner Vineyard, **45**, 49
Richard Longoria Wines, **111**, 126, 128
Richard's Wild Irish Rose, 251
Ridge Lytton Springs, **29**, 35
Ridge Monte Bello Vineyard, **97**, 99, 98–100
Ridge Vineyards, **29**, 32, 36, 37, **97**, 98, **99**, 100, 113, 132
Ridgeway Family Vineyards, 43
Riedel, Georg, 151
Riesling, 6
Rincon Vineyard, **116**, 117
Rios-Lovell Estate Winery, 90
Ristow Estate Winery, 55
Ritchie Creek Vineyard, **55**, 58
Ritchie Vineyard, **38**, 40
River Junction AVA, **19**
River Myst Winery, 265
River Road Vineyards, **38**
River Run Vintners, **97**
Riverside County, 143–44
ROAR Wines, 102, 105
Roanoke Vineyards, **252**, 252, 253
Robert Biale Vineyards, 47, **55**, 82
Robert Craig Winery, **55**, 63, 86
Robert Foley Vineyards, 63, 64
Robert Foley Wines, 254
Robert Hall Winery, **111**, 112, 113
Robert Keenan Winery, 55
Robert Mondavi Corporation, 76, 102, 120
Robert Mondavi Private Selection, 104
Robert Mondavi Winery, 51, 57, 68, 69, 70, 72, **73**, 73–74, **74**, 76, **79**, 85, 88, 137, 251
Robert Sinskey Vineyards, 52, **77**, 77
Robertson, Steve, 184
Robert Stemmler, 52
Robert Talbott Vineyard & Winery, 102, **103**
Robert Young Clone, 31
Robert Young Estate Winery, **29**, 31, 32
Robledo Family Winery, **45**
Rochioli, Joe, 39, 40
Rochioli, Tom, 40
Rockpile AVA, **19**, 28, **29**, 30, 36
Rockpile Ridge Vineyards, 36
Rockpile Winery, **29**, 35, 36
Rock Wall Wine Company, **90**, 93, 94, 96
Rocky Knob AVA, 232, **233**, 234, 239
Rocky Mother, 177
Rodgers Creek Vineyard, 40
Rodney Strong Vineyards, **38**, 39, 40
Roederer Estate, 22, **23**, 24
Roguenant, Christian, 118, 142
Rogue Valley AVA, 146, **147**, **154**, 154–55, 156
Rolland, Michel, 60, 163, 173, 238
Roll International, 115
Rombauer Vineyards, **67**
Rosa D'Oro, **23**
Rosback, Peter, 170
Rosella's Vineyard, **103**, 105
Rosemary's Vineyard, **116**, 117
Rosemont Vineyards & Winery, **233**, 239
Rosemount Estate, 253
Rosenblum, Kent, 94, 137
Rosenblum, Shauna, 94
Rosenblum Cellars, 47, **90**, 93, 94, 96, 137
Rosenthal, George, 142
Rosenthal: The Malibu Estate, **140**, 142
Roth, Roman, 253, **255**, 255

276 | INDEX

Rothschild, Baron Philippe de, 76
Rothschild, Philippine de, 76
Roudon-Smith Winery, **97**
Round Pond Estate, 70, **71**
Rouzaud, Jean-Claude, 24
RoxyAnn Winery, **154**
Rubicon, 70
Ruby Moon Winery, 240
Rudd Estate, 40, **73**, 74
Rued Vineyards, **38**, 39
Rupar, Bob, 173
Rusack, Alison Wrigley, 125, *141*, 141
Rusack, Geoff, 125, *141*, 141
Rusack Santa Catalina Island Vineyards, **140**
Rusack Vineyards, **124**, 124, 125, **140**, 141, *141*
Russell, Bill, 249
Russell, Rob, 249
Russian Hill Estate Winery, **38**
Russian River Valley AVA, 28, **29**, **38**, 38–41, 51
Russian River Valley Winegrowers group, 38
RustRidge Ranch & Winery, **55**
Rutherford, Thomas, 70
Rutherford AVA, 54, **55**, **67**, **71**, 70–72, **73**
Rutherford Dust Restoration Team, 72
Rutherford Hill, **71**
Ryan, Jim, *108*
Rynders, Tony, 152

Sable Ridge Vineyards, **45**
Saddleback Cellars, 60, **73**
Saddle Rock–Malibu AVA, **140**, 142
Sagelands Vineyard, **164–65**, 169
Sagemoor Vineyard, **164–65**, 173
Sagpond Vineyards, 253
Saint Croix Vineyards, 219, *220*, 222
Sainte Genevieve Vineyard, **215**, 218
Saintsbury, 23, **45**, *51*, 51, **55**, 253
Sakonnet Vineyards, 249
Salado Creek AVA, **19**
Salamandre, **97**
Salida Wines, 179
Salmon-Safe, 158
Salt Lick Vineyard, 206, **207**
Samsara, **111**, 128
San Antonio Valley AVA, 102, **103**, 107
San Antonio Winery, **140**, 142
San Benito AVA, **103**, 108–9
San Benito County, 108–9
San Bernabe AVA, 102, **103**, 107
San Bernabe Vineyard, **103**, *107*, 107
San Bernardino County, 143–44
San Diego County, 145
Sands, Marvin, 251
Sands, Richard, 251
Sands, Robert, 251
Sanford, Richard, 120, 126
Sanford, Thekla, 120, 126
Sanford & Benedict Vineyard, 119, 120, **124**, 126
Sanford Winery, 120, **124**, 126
San Francisco Bay AVA, **19**, **90**, 93–94
San Francisco International Wine Competition, 157
Sangiacomo Vineyard, **45**, 51, 52
San Juan Vineyards, **160–61**, 181
San Lorenzo Vineyard, 32
San Lucas AVA, 102, **103**, 107
San Luis Obispo County, 110–18
San Pasqual Valley AVA, **140**, 145
San Pasqual Winery, 145
San Sebastian Vineyards, 244, 245
Santa Barbara County, 119–29
Santa Barbara County Vintners' Association, 20
Santa Barbara Winery, 120, 126
Santa Catalina Island Company, 141
Santa Clara Valley AVA, **90**, **97**
Santa Cruz Mountains AVA, **97**, 97–101
Santa Cruz Mountain Vineyard, **97**
Santa Lucia Highlands AVA, 102, **103**, 103, 104–5
Santa Maria Valley AVA, **111**, 117, 119, 120, **121**, 121–23
Santa Rita Hills AVA. *See* Sta. Rita Hills AVA
Santa Ynez Valley AVA, **111**, 119, 120, **124**, 124–25, 126
Santino Winery, 132
San Ysidro District AVA, **97**
Saracina Vineyards, 22, **23**, 25
Sarah's Vineyard, **97**
Sattui, Dario, *60*
Saucelito Canyon Vineyard, **116**, 117
Sauer, Mike, 166, *167*, 180
Sausal Winery, **29**, 32
Sauvignon Blanc, 6
Savannah Chanelle Vineyards, **97**
Sawmill Creek Vineyard, 261, 262
Sawtooth Winery, 182, **183**, 184
Saxum Vineyards, **111**, 112, 114
Sbarbaro, Andrea, 34
Sbragia Family Wines, **29**, 35, 47, 64
Scaggs, Boz, 85
Scaggs, Dominique, 85
Scaggs Vineyard, **55**, 85, 86
Scarecrow, **71**
Schadé Vineyard & Winery, 191
Scharffenberger Cellars, 22, **23**
Scheid Vineyards, **103**, 104
Schnelle, Mike, 260
Schnerr, Joe, 184
Schoener, Abe, 254
Schoenfeld, Daniel, 42
Schoenfeld, Marion, 42
Scholium Project, 254
Schonewald, George, 69
Schrader Cellars, **58**, 88
Schram, Jacob, 61, 66
Schramsberg Vineyards, 57, **58**, 61, *62*, 66, 91
Schug Carneros Estate, **45**, 51
Schweiger Vineyards, **55**
Scott, Joe, 218
Scott Harvey Wines, **130**, 132
Screaming Eagle Winery and Vineyards, 70, **73**, 74, 75, 88, 133, 236, 263
Sean Thackrey, **90**, 91, 92
Sea Smoke Cellars, 126–27
Sea Smoke Vineyard, **124**, *127*, 127–28
Seaver, Nancy, 62
Seaver, Tom, 62
Seaver Vineyards, **58**, 61, 62
Seavey Vineyard, **55**
Sebastiani, August, 48
Sebastiani, Samuele, 47–48
Sebastiani Vineyards, **45**, 46, 47–48, 128, 133
Sebastopol Vineyards, 39
Seewald, Ann, 186
Seewald, Jim, 186
Seghesio, Edoardo, 32
Seghesio Family Winery, 32, **38**
Selyem, Ed, 40
Seneca Lake AVA, 250, **251**, 258, **259**, 260–61
Seps Estate, **58**, 59
Sequoia Grove, 70, **71**
Serpent Ridge, 269
Serra, Junipero, 119, *145*, 145, 202
SeVein, 173–74
Seven Hills Vineyard, **147**, 157, **164–65**, 173
Seven Hills Winery, 172
Seven Springs Vineyard, **150**, 153
Seyval, 8
Shadow Springs Vineyard, 242
Shafer, Doug, 79
Shafer, John, 79
Shafer Vineyards, *57*, **77**, 77, *79*, **150**
Shake Ridge Vineyard, **130**, 133
Shannon Ridge, **23**, 27
Shaps, Michael, 239
Sharp, Benjamin, 32, *34*
Sharp, Tara, 32, *34*
Sharpe Hill Vineyard, 248, 249
Shaw Vineyard, *44*, 44, **45**
Shawnee Hills AVA, 226, 227
Shea, Dick, 153
Shea Vineyard, **150**, 153
Shea Wine Cellars, 153
Shelburne Vineyard, 249
Sheldrake Point Winery, 258, **259**, *262*, 262
Shelton Vineyards, 242
Shenandoah Valley AVA, 232, **233**, 234, **235**, 239
Shenandoah Vineyards, **130**, 132
Sherman, William "Tecumseh," 46
Shinn, Barbara, 255
Shinn Estate Vineyards, **252**, 252, *253*, 255
Shoup, Allen, *163*, 163, 173
Sichel, Bettina, 49
Sichel, Peter M. F., 49
Siduri Wines, 23, **38**, 49
Sierra Foothills, 130–35
Sierra Foothills AVA, **19**, **130**, 131
Sierra Madre Vineyard, **121**
Sierra Mar Vineyard, **103**, *105*, 105
Sierra Pelona Valley AVA, **140**, 142
Sierra Vista Vineyards & Winery, **130**, 134, 135
Signorello Estate, **55**
Silverado Vineyards, **77**, 77
Silver Oak Cellars, **29**, 32, **73**
Silver Thread Vineyard, **259**
Simi, Giuseppe, 30
Simi, Pietro, 30
Simi Winery, **29**, 30, 32, 40
Simon, Kay, 167
Simon Creek Vineyard & Winery, 226, 228
Sineann Winery, 170
Sine Qua Non, 88
Sionneau, Lucien, 76
Sisson, Robert, 31, 39
Six Sigma, **23**, 27
Skyline Vineyard, **183**, 184
Sky Vineyard, **55**, 86
Skywalker Ranch, **90**, 91, *92*, 92
Sleepy Hollow Vineyard, **103**, 104, 107
Sloughhouse AVA, 137, 138, 139
S.L.V., 79
Small, Rick, 160, 172–73
Smart, Dr. Richard, 256, *257*
Smith, Charles, 66, 176
Smith, Claudia, 104
Smith, James Berry, 114
Smith, Justin, 114
Smith, Marcia, 80–81
Smith, Rich, 104
Smith, Stu, 66
Smith and Hook Ranch, 104
Smith-Madrone Vineyards & Winery, **55**, 57, 65, *66*, 66
Smoky Hill Vineyard & Winery, 219, 220
Smothers, Tommy, 48
Snake River Valley AVA, 146, 157, **183**, 182–84
Snake River Winery, 182, **183**
Snipes, Ben, 168
Snipes Mountain AVA, **160–61**, 162, 164, **164–65**, 165, 166, 168–69
Snoqualmie Winery, **164–65**, 166, 167, 168
Snows Lake, **23**, 27
Snyder, Mark, 254
Soaring Wings Vineyard, 222
Soberanes Vineyard, **103**, 105
Sobon, Leon, 132
Sobon Wine, **130**, 132
Sodaro, Deedee, *89*
Sodaro, Don, *89*
Sodaro Estate Winery, 87, *89*
Sojourn Cellars, **45**, 48
Sokol Blosser, Susan, 148
Sokol Blosser Winery, 148, 149, **150**, 158–59, *159*
Solano County Green Valley AVA, **19**, **90**
Soles, Rollin, 149, 152
Solis Winery,**97**
Solomon Hills Vineyard, **121**, 121–22, 123
Sommer, Richard, 148, 154, *155*, 156
Sonoita AVA, *30*, 198, **199**, 200
Sonoita Vineyards, 198, **199**, *200*, 200
Sonoma Coast AVA, **19**, *28*, 28, **29**, **38**, 38, 42–43, **90**
Sonoma Coast Vineyards, **38**, 43
Sonoma County, 28–49
Sonoma County Vintners, 20
Sonoma-Cutrer Wines, **38**
Sonoma Mountain AVA, 28, **45**, 48–49
Sonoma Mountain Estate, 48
Sonoma Stage, 43
Sonoma Valley AVA, 28, 44, **45**, 46–48, **55**, **90**
Soos Creek Wine Cellars, 178
Soquel Vineyards, **97**
Sorenstam, Annika, 94
Soter, Tony, 60, 69, 153
Soter Vineyards, 149, **150**, 153
Souris Valley Vineyard, 192
South Carolina, 242
South Coast, 140–45
South Coast AVA, **140**, 140
South Coast Winery & Spa, **140**, 143, *144*, 144
South Dakota, 190
Southeastern New England AVA, 249
Southern California, **140**
Southern Oak Wines, 244, 245
Southern Oregon AVA, 146, **147**, **154**, 154
Southern Oregon, 154–59
Southern Virginia Region, 239
Southwest Wines, 202, 203
Southwind Vineyard, 174
Souverain, **29**, 34, 72
Spañada, 4
Spangler Vineyards, **154**, 155
Spanish Valley Vineyards & Winery, 191, 192
Sparkling Pointe, **252**, 252, 255
Spencer Roloson, 27
Spenker, Joseph, 137
Spicewood Vineyards, 204, **207**
Sponseller, Andy, 192
Spotts family, 69
Spottswoode Estate, 57, 67, **67**, 68–69, 153
Springhill Cellars, **150**
Spring Mountain District AVA, 54, **55**, **58**, 65–66, **67**
Spring Mountain Vineyard, **55**, 57, 65, 66
Spring Valley Vineyard, **164–65**, 172, 173, 176
Spurrier, Steven, 4, 85
StableRidge Vineyards, 210, 211
Stafford, Philip, 239
Stagecoach Vineyard, **55**, 83
Staglin, Garen, 72
Staglin, Shari, 72
Staglin Family Music Festival, 72
Staglin Family, 69, 70, **71**, 72, 133
Stags Leap District AVA, 54, **55**, *57*, **77**, 77–79
Stags Leap Winegrowers, 77
Stag's Leap Vineyard, 79
Stag's Leap Wine Cellars, 4, 26, 54, 57, **77**, 77, *78*, 79, 84, 163, 186
Stags' Leap Winery, **77**, 77, 79, 152
St. Amant Winery, **130**
Standing Stone Vineyards, **259**, 261
Stare, David, 35
Sta. Rita Hills AVA, **111**, 119, 120, **124**, 124, 126–28
Star Lane Vineyard, **124**, 124, 129, 217
Starr, Pam, 69
State Lane Vineyard, 81
Staton Hills Winery, 169
St. Charles Vineyard, **97**
St. Clair Winery, 202, 203
St. Clement Vineyards, **55**, **67**
Ste. Chapelle Winery, 182–83, **183**, *184*
Steele, Jed, 26, 27, 121
Steele Wines, **23**, 26, 27, 121
Steep Creek Ranch, 177
Ste. Genevieve Winery, 208
Stegenga, Stuart, 224
Steiner Vineyard, **45**
Steltzner Vineyards, **77**
Ste. Michelle Wine Estates, 79, 84, **147**, 163, 169, 170, 176, 201
Stephen Ross Vineyards, **116**, 117
Stephen Ross Wine Cellars, 117
Sterling family, 40
Sterling Vineyards, 51, 57, **58**, 59, 60, 65
Steven Kent Winery, 93, *94*, 95
Stevenot Winery, **130**
Stevens, 178
Stewart, Leland "Lee," 34
St. Francis Winery, **45**, 46, 48
St. Helena AVA, 54, **55**, **58**, **67**, 67–69, **71**
Stimson Lane, 163
Stires, John, 254
St. James Winery, 214, **215**, 216, 218
St. Joseph Vineyard, 226, 228
St. Julian Winery, 223, 225
St. Innocent, **150**
Stoller Vineyards, 149, **150**, 158–59
Stolpman Vineyards, 42, **124**, 124, 128
Stone Bluff Cellars, 210
Stonebrook Winery, 240
Stone Corral, 117
Stone Faces Winery, 190
St
Stone Hill Winery, 214, **215**, 216, 217, *218*
Stone House Vineyard, 204, **207**, 207
Stonehouse Vineyards, 265
Stone Mill Winery, 229
Stone Pillar Vineyard, 219
Stone's Throw Vineyard, 177
Stonestreet Winery, **29**, *32*, 32
StoneTree Vineyard, **164–65**, 171
Stonington Vineyards, 249
Stony Hill, **67**, 69
Storrs Winery, **97**
Storybook Mountain, **58**, 59
Strawbale Winery, 191
Strebl, Mary Lee, 72
St. Supéry Dollarhide Ranch, 88
St. Supéry Vineyards & Winery, 70, **71**
Stubbs, Mary, 92
Stubbs, Tom, 92
Stubbs Vineyard, 91
Stuckey, Wendy, 164
Stuhlmuller Vineyards, **29**, 32
Sugarland Cellars, 243
Sugarloaf Mountain Vineyard, 269
Suisun Valley AVA, **19**, **90**
Sullivan Vineyards, **71**
Summerset Winery, 219, 220
Summers Winery, **58**, 59
Summit Lake Winery, **55**
Sunset Meadow Vineyards, 249
Sun Valley Center for the Arts Wine Auction, 14
Superior Estates Winery, 222
Sutcliffe, John, *189*, 189–90
Sutcliffe Vineyards, 186, 189, *189*
Sutter, John, 130
Sutter Home Winery, 4, **67**, 131, 132
Swan, Joe, 39
Swan Creek AVA, 241–42
Swanson, Ed, 222
Swanson, Holly, 222
Swanson, W. Clarke, 135
Swanson Vineyards & Winery, **71**, 74, *135*, 135
Swedish Hill Vineyards, **259**, 262
Sweely Estate, 238
Swenson, Elmer, *216*, 222
Switchback Ridge Wines, **58**, 59, 60, 254
Sycamore Vineyard, **71**
Syncline Wine Cellars, **160–61**, *162*, 177, *177*
Syrah, 7

Taber, George, 68
Tablas Creek Vineyard, **111**, 112, 114, *115*, 116–17
Table Mountain Vineyards and Winery, 191, 193
Tabor Hill Vineyards, 223
Tabor Hill Winery, 223, 225
Taft Street Winery, **38**
Tahoe Ridge Winery, 193
Talbott, Audrey, 104
Talbott, Robert "Robb," 104, 107
Talbott, Robert, Sr., 104
Talbott Vineyards, 104, 107, 153
Talley, Brian, 117
Talley, Don, 117
Talley Vineyards, **116**, 117
Tamarack Cellars, **164–65**, 172
Tangent, **116**, 117, 118
TAPAS (Tempranillo Advocates, Producers and Amigos Society), 157
Tarara Winery, 234, **235**
Tari, Pierre, *4*
Taylor, Jack, 85
Taylor, Mary, 85
Taylor New York Desserts, 251
Taylor Wine Company, The, 250

INDEX

Taz Vineyards, **111**
Tchelistcheff, André, 31, 61, 70, 71, 161–62, 179
Tedeschi, Emil, 195
Tedeschi Family Winery, 195
Tedeschi Vineyards, **194**, 194, 195
Tefft Cellars, **164–65**
Teldeschi Vineyard, **29**, 44
Temecula Valley AVA, **140**, 143–44
Tempest Vineyard, 153
Tempranillo, **157**, 157
Tennessee, 242–43
Tennessee Farm Winery Act of 1978, 242
Ten Spoon Vineyard & Winery, 191, 192
Tepusquet Vineyard, 123
Terlato Wine Group, 120, 126
Terra de Promissio Vineyards, 43
Terra d'Oro, **130**, 132, 133
Terra Valentine, **55**, 65, **65**
Terre Haute Rouge, 192
Terre Rouge Wines, **130**
Terrien, Michael, 27
Terror Creek Winery, **185**, 186, 189
Terry Hoage Vineyards, **111**, 115
Terry Ranch Cellars, 193
Testarossa Winery, **97**, 98, 100, **101**
Texas, 204–9, **205**
Texas Davis Mountain AVA, 204, **205**
Texas High Plains AVA, 204, **205**, 206, 208
Texas Hill Country AVA, 204, **205**, 206–7, **207**
Texas Hills AVA, 204, **207**
Texoma AVA, 204, **205**
Thackrey, Sean, 92
Theodore Gier Winery, 86
Thibaut, Claude, 239
Thibaut-Janisson, 237, 239
Thirsty Owl Wine Company, **259**, 262
Thomas Coyne Winery, **90**, 93
Thomas Fogarty Winery & Vineyards, **97**, 98
Thomas George Estate, **38**, 39, 41
Thomas Jefferson Foundation, 232
Thomas Road Vineyard, 39
Thompson, Claiborne, 118
Thompson, Fredericka Churchill, 118
Thompson, Jackie, 189
Thompson, Mike, 189
Thornhill, Tim, 24
Thornhill, Tom, 24
Thousand Islands Winery, 265
3 Horse Ranch Vineyards, 182, **183**, 184
Three Palms Vineyard, **58**, 69
Three Rivers Winery, 128, **164–65**, 170, 172
Three Sisters Vineyards, 244, 245
Thurston Wolfe Winery, **164–65**, 166, 167
Tidal School Vineyards & Winery, 210, 211
Tierce, 261
Tierra Encantada Winery, 202
Tiger Mountain Vineyards, 244, 245
Tinaquaic Vineyard, **121**, 123
Tin Cross Vineyards, **29**
Tin Mill Brewery, 218
Titus Vineyards, **67**, 68
Tobin James Cellars, **111**
To Kalon Cellar (Mondavi), 76
To Kalon Vineyard, 56, 60, **71**, **73**, 73–74
Tolmach, Adam, 122

Tolosa Winery, **116**, 117
Tomasello Winery, 268, 269
Tom Eddy Wines, **58**, 59
TOR, 64
Torii Mor Winery, **150**
Tracy, James Christopher, 255
Tracy Hills AVA, 96
Trailside Vineyard, **71**, 72
Traminette, 8
Travers, Bob, 85, 86
Travers, Elinor, 85
Travessia Urban Winery, 249
Treana, **111**, 112
Treasury Wine Estates, 51, 79
Trefethen, Catherine, 82
Trefethen, Eugene, 82
Trefethen, Janet, 82
Trefethen, John, 82
Trefethen Family Vineyards, 55, 62, **82**, 82
Trentadue Winery, **29**
Tres Sabores Winery, **71**
Trinchero, Louis "Bob," 4, **131**, 131
Trinchero Family Estates, **67**, **133**, 133
Trinchero Napa Valley, 68
Troon, Dick, 155
Troon Winery, **154**, 155
Trout Creek Winery, 228
Truchard Vineyards, **45**, 51, 52, **55**
Trump, Donald, 238, 238
Trump Winery, **235**, 237, 238, 238
Tsillan Cellars Winery & Vineyards, 177
Tsujimoto, Kenzo, 88
TTB (Alcohol and Tobacco Tax and Trade Bureau), 12, 13, 38, 42, 181, 216, 234
Tualatin Estate Vineyard, **150**
Tubbs, Alfred, 59
Tudal Winery, **67**
Tug Hill Vineyards, 265
Tula Vista Ranch, 52
Tulocay Winery, **55**
Tunnell, Doug, 153
Turley, Helen, 34, 81, 88
Turley, Padte, 186
Turley, Richard, 186
Turley Wine Cellars, 37, **67**, 96, **111**
Turnbull Wine Cellars, **73**
Twain-Peterson, Morgan, 37, **46**, 46
Twin Oaks Vineyard and Winery, **215**, 218
2 Lads Winery, **222**, 223, 224–25
Twomey Cellars, 23, **38**, **58**, 59
Two Rivers Winery, **185**, 186
Two Rock Vineyard, 38
Tychson, John C., 68
Tychson, Josephine, 68
Tyee Wine Cellars, **150**

UC Davis Heat Summation Scale, 51, 53
Ulbrich, Bryan, 225
Umpqua Valley AVA, 146, **147**, **154**, 155–57
Unionville Vineyards, 268, 269
United Vintners, 4
Unti Vineyards, **29**, 35
Upland Estates, **164–65**, 169
Upper Mississippi River Valley AVA, **222**, **226**, 228
Upton, John, 69
Upton, Sloan, 69
Upton family, 225
Utah, 192
Uvaggio, 137

Vail Ranch, 143
Vail, Walter, 143
Vajda, Katherine, 95

Va La Vineyards, **267**, 267
Valiant Vineyards Winery, **190**, 191
Vallejo, Mariano G., 30, 44
Valley of the Moon Winery, **45**
Valley View Winery, **154**
Valley Vineyards, 226
Val Verde Winery, 204, **205**
Vanderbilt, Cornelius, 242
Vanderbilt, George, 243
Van der Kamp Vineyard, **45**, 49
Vanneque, Christian, 4
Van Ruiten Family Vineyards, **130**, 137
Varner Vineyards, **97**, 98
Vashon, 162
Vavasour, 128
Veeder, Peter, 85
Venditti Vineyards, 265
Venerri, Gordon, 173, 176
Venge, Nils, 60
Venge Vineyards, 59
Ventana Vineyards, 102, **103**, 106–7, 153
Veramar, **235**, 239
Veritas Vineyard & Winery, **232**, **235**, 237
Verite Wines, **29**
Vermont, 249
Verso Cellars, 188
Vesco Ridge Vineyard, 265
Viader, **55**
Viansa Winery, **45**
Vidal Blanc, 8
Viento Wines, **147**, 157
Viera, Ramon, 62
Vignes, Jean-Louis, **141**, 142
Vignoles, 8
Villa Creek, **111**, 112
Villa Mt. Eden, 121
Villa Pillo, 40
Villa San-Juliette Winery & Vineyards, **111**, 115
Viña Concha y Toro, 25
Viña Errázuriz, 76
Vina Robles, **111**, 112
Vincor, 166, 173
Vin du Lac, 177
VINEA: The Winegrowers' Sustainable Trust, 158, 176
Vine Cliff Winery, **73**
Vineyard: The Perils and Pleasures of Creating an American Family Winery, The (Hargrave), 255
Vineyard 29, **67**
Vinifera Development Corporation, 73
Vinifera Wine Cellars, 250
Vino Noceto, **130**, 132, 133
Vin Roc Wine Caves, **55**, 83
Vintner's Village, 167
Virginia, 232–39
Virginia's Eastern Shore AVA, **232**, **233**, 239
Virginia Wineworks, **235**, 239
Vista Verde Vineyard, **103**, 109
Vitis labrusca, 7
Vitis rotundifolia, 7
Vitis vinifera, 6
Vivac Winery, 202
Vivier, Stéphane, 52
VML Winery, **38**
Vogelzang Vineyard, **124**, 129
Vojta, Anna Pésa, 190
Vojta, Jon, 190
Vojta, Sandi, 190
Volcano Winery, 194
Volk, Kenneth, 115, 120
Volker Eisele, **55**, 87
von Strasser, Rudy, 62
von Strasser Winery, **58**, 62
V. Sattui Winery, 60, **67**
Vynecrest Vineyards, **267**, 267

Wagner, Charles "Charlie," 71, 105
Wagner, Charlie, **71**, 105
Wagner, Chuck, **71**, 71, 105
Wagner, Joe, **71**, 105
Wagner, Philip, 268
Wagner Vineyards, **259**, 261
Wahluke Slope AVA, **160–61**, 162, **164–65**, 165, **171**, 171
Wahldin, Monty, 158
Walker, Carrie, 242
Walker, Tim, 242
Wallace, Rob, 155, 156
Walla Walla Valley AVA, 146, **147**, **160–61**, 162, **164–65**, 165, 172–76
Walla Walla Vintners, **164–65**, 172, 173, 176
Wallula Vineyard, 163, 170
Walter Clore Wine and Culinary Center, 167
Ward, Dick, 51, **51**, 52
Warner Vineyards, 223, 225
Warren Hills AVA, 269
Warrick, Ken, 115
Washington, 160–81, **160–61**
See also regions by name
Washington State Wine Commission, 161, 163
Wasson Brothers Winery, **150**
Waterbrook, **164–65**, 172
Waters, Alice, 50
Waters Ranch, 84
Wathen, Bill, 121
Wattle Creek Vineyard, **23**, 24, **29**
Weggy Winery, 226
Weisinger's of Ashland Winery, **154**
Wellington Vineyards, **45**
Welsch family, 225
Wente, Carl H., 94
Wente, Carolyn, 94
Wente, Karl, 94
Wente Family Estates, 106
Wente Vineyards, **90**, 93, **93**, 94, 105
Westbend Vineyards, 241, 242
West Elks AVA, **185**, 186, 188
Westerly Vineyards, 125
Western Connecticut Highlands AVA, 249
Westover Vineyards, **90**
Westport Rivers Winery, 249
Westrey Wine Company, **150**
West Sonoma Coast Vintners, 42–43
West Virginia, 243
Wetlaufer, John, 81
Wetmore, Charles, 94, 95
Wetzel, Harry, 31
Wetzel, Maggie, 31
Whaler Vineyards, **23**
Wheeler, Mark, 171
Whetstone Wine Cellars, 87
Whidbey Island Winery, **160–61**, 181
White Heron Cellars, **160–61**, 181
White Oak Vineyards, 245
White, Michael, 181
Whitecliff Vineyard & Winery, **251**, **257**, 257
Whitehall Lane, **67**, 68, **71**
Whitehill family, 243
Whitestone Winery, **160–61**, 181
Whitewater Hills Vineyards, **185**, 186, 189
white Zinfandel, 4, **131**, 131
Whiting, David, 261
Whiting, Debra, 261
Widmer's Wine Cellars, 250
Wiemer, Hermann J., 260
Wiemer, Josef, 260
Wight, Jim, 241
Wight, Sandy, 241

Wight-Meyer Vineyard & Winery, 240, 241
Wild Hog Vineyard, **29**, **38**, 42, 43
Wild Horse Valley AVA, 54, 87–88
Wild Horse Winery & Vineyards, **111**, 115, 120
Wildhurst Vineyards, **23**, 27
Wildman, Tedd, 171
WillaKenzie Estate, 149, **150**, 153
Willamette Valley AVA, 146, **147**, 149, 151–52, **154**
Willamette Valley Vineyards, 146, 149, **150**
Willcox, 200
William Harrison Vineyards and Winery, **71**
William Hill Winery, 36
Williams, Burt, 40
Williams, John, 168
Williamsburg Winery, The, **233**, 239
Williams Selyem, 23, **38**, 39, 40, 108, 109, 256
Wilridge Winery, **164–65**, 178
Wilson Creek Vineyards, **140**, 143
Wilson Vineyard, **29**, **130**, 139
WindWalker Vineyard and Winery, **130**
Wine Advocate, 88, 170
Wineglass Cellars, **164–65**
Wine Group, The, **19**, 70, 94–95, 136
Winehaven Vineyards, 219
Winehaven Winery, 222
Wine Institute, 20
Winery, Curtis, 125
Winery at Holy Cross Abbey, The, 186, 189
Winery Lake Vineyard, **45**, **55**
Wing, Stelham, 86
Wing Canyon Vineyard, **55**, 86
Winiarski, Warren, 4, 77, **78**, 186
Winkler, Albert, 53, 119
Winkler Scale, 51, 53
Winters, R. L., **206**, 206
Wisconsin, 228–29
Wisconsin Ledge AVA, 226, 228, 229
Witness Tree Vineyard, **150**
Wolf Blass Winery, 164
Wolfe, Dr. Wade, 167
Wölffer, Christian, 253
Wölffer Estate Vineyard, **252**, 252, 253, **255**, 255
Wolf Mountain Vineyards & Winery, 245
Wolfskill, Joseph, 142
Wolfskill, William, 142
Wollersheim, Bob, 229
Wollersheim, JoAnn, 229
Wollersheim Winery, 226, 228–29, **229**
Wong, Vanessa, 34
Woodbridge by Robert Mondavi, 76, **130**, 137
Woodhall Wine Cellars, 269
Woodinville Warehouse Wineries, 179
Woodland Park Vineyards, 210
Woodside Vineyards, **97**
Woodward, Phil, 105
Woodward Canyon Winery, 160, 162, **164–65**, 170, 172, 176
Wright, Ken, 152, 153
Wright, Lonnie, 170
Wrigley, William, Jr., 141
Wurtele, Angus, 65
Wurtele, Margaret, 65
Wyldwood Cellars, 220
Wyoming, 193

Yadkin Valley AVA, 241, 242
Yakima Valley AVA, **160–61**, 162, **164–65**, 165, 166–67
Yamhill-Carlton AVA, 146, 149, 152–53
Yamhill Valley Vineyards, **150**
Yavapai County, 201
Yeaman, Becky, 167
Yellow Barn Winery, 265
Yorba, 132, 133
York, Andrew, 115
York Creek, **55**
York Mountain AVA, 110, **111**, 112, 115
York Mountain Vineyards, **111**, 115
Yorkville Cellars, 22, **23**, 24
Yorkville Highlands AVA, 22, **23**, 24–25
Young, Fred, 31
Young, Jim, 31
Young, JoAnn, 31
Young, Robert, 31
Young, Susan, 31
Young's Vineyard, **130**
Yount, George Calvert, 57, 70, 80
Yountville AVA, 54, **55**, **73**, 80–81
Y. Rousseau, 86
Yverdon Winery, 65

Zaca Mesa Winery & Vineyards, 120, 122, **124**, 124
Zahtila Vineyards, **58**, 59
ZAP (Zinfandel Advocates & Producers), 157
Zayante Winery, **97**
ZD Wines, 57, **71**
Zeitman, Ben, 132
Zellerbach, James D., 47
Zenaida Cellars, 113
Zerba Cellars, **147**, 157
Zimmerer, Patrick, 193
Zina Hyde Cunningham Winery, **23**
Zinfandel, **4**, 7
Zinfandel Advocates & Producers (ZAP), 157
Zinfandel Heritage Vineyard, 74
Zocker Wines, **116**
Zonin, Gianni, 237
Zuniga, Gracia de, 202

Acknowledgments

We are grateful to the many people who so generously contributed their time and expertise to this book. In particular, we'd like to thank the following:

California Wine Institute; Katherine Camargo (researcher); Doug Caskey, Colorado Wine Industry Development Board; Robert Champion Jr., Texas Department of Agriculture/Wine Division; Cornell University; Terry Hall, Napa Valley Vintners; Linda Jones, Michigan Grape and Wine Industry Council; Lodi Winegrape Commission; Missouri Wine and Grape Board; Tai-Ran Niew (researcher); Oregon Wine Advisory Board; Paso Robles Wine Alliance; Sonoma County Vintners; Jim Trezise, New York Wine & Grape Foundation; University of Minnesota; Virginiawine.org; Washington Wine Commission; Gary Werner (researcher); Wineries of Old Mission Peninsula.

Photocredits

i: Olena Mykhaylova/Veer; ii: bbourdages/Veer; iv–v: Andrea Johnson Photography, http://andreajohnsonphotography.com; vi–vii: M. J. Wickham; x: AZP Worldwide/shutterstock; 1: compassandcamera/iStockphoto; 2: Stone Hill Winery; 3: Imagno - ullstein bild / The Granger Collection; 4: Bella Spurrier; 5: Mike Officer, Carlisle Winery; 6: Jason Tinacci. Courtesy Napa Valley Vintners.; 7 top: Randall Tagg Photography; 7 bottom: Stone Hill Winery; 8 top: University of Minnesota, David L. Hansen; 8 bottom: Kim Stimeling; 9: Edward Hellman; 10: Jonathan Oakes; 12: Andrea Johnson Photography, http://andreajohnsonphotography.com; 13: Courtesy Bonny Doon Vineyard; 15: Food & Wine/Riccardo Savi; 16–17: Stacie Stauff Smith Photography/shutterstock; 18: Johan Elzenga/Veer; 20: Jim Sullivan; 21: compassandcamera/iStockphoto; 22 top: Navarro Vineyards; 25 top: Courtesy of Saracina Vineyards; 25 bottom: Michael Wright Studio; 26 top: Hannah Henry Photography. Courtesy of the Lake County Winegrape Commission; 26 bottom: Jackson Family Wines; 27: Arpad Molnar; 28 top: Marie Hirsch; 28 bottom: Flowers Vineyard and Winery; 30: Sonoma County Vintners; 31: Avis Mandel (circa 2009); 32: Jackson Family Wines/George Rose; 33: M. J. Wickham; 34 top: Chad Keig for Francis Ford Coppola Presents; 34 bottom: Olaf Beckmann; 36: Lambert Bridge Winery; 37: Lawrence Piggins. www.temperedlight.com; 40: Andy Katz Photography; 41: L.G. Sterling/Iron Horse Vineyards, 2011; 42: Littorai Wines; 43 top: Courtesy of Fort Ross Vineyards; 43 bottom: David Cobb; 44: Timm Eubanks; 46: Peter Griffith; 47: Courtesy of E&J Gallo Winery; 48: Debra Kruth; 49: Kenwood Vineyards; 50 top: Adeline & Grace Photography. Courtesy of Hospitality de los Carneros; 50 bottom: John McJunkin, 2009; 51: Saintsbury 2012; 52: Gloria Ferrer Caves & Vineyards; 54: compassandcamera/iStockphoto; 56: Rocco Ceselin; 57: Russ Widstrand Photography; 58: Chateau Montelena; 60: Jim Sullivan; 62: John McJunkin Photography; 63: Briana Marie Photography; 64: Pat Stotesbery, Ladera Vineyards; 65: M. J. Wickham; 66: J. Gittes; 67: Duncan Garrett; 68: Tia Gavin; 70: Diageo Chateau & Estate Wines; 71: Tyler Jacobsen ©2012 Wagner Family of Wine; 72: Grgich Hills Estate; 73: Randall Cordero, Far Niente; 74: Courtesy of Robert Mondavi Winery; 75: Mark Defeo/Far Niente; 76: Courtesy of Robert Mondavi Winery; 78: Courtesy of Stag's Leap Wine Cellars; 79: Sandy Ilsley, Ilsley Vineyards; 80: Erhard Pfeiffer; 81 top: Eric Wolfinger; 81 bottom: Rustin Domingos; 82: Bret Lyman; 83 top: Waser. Courtesy of Antica Napa Valley; 84: Vito Bialla; 85: The Hess Collection; 86 top: Carole Meredith; 86 bottom: Bob Travers, Mayacamas Vineyards; 87: Chappellet Vineyard & Winery; 88: Jason Tinacci; 89 top: Richard Kramer, Sodaro Estate Winery, Napa, Ca.; 89 bottom: Jason Tinacci/Napa Valley Vintners; 90: Bargetto Winery, Santa Cruz Mountains; 91: Courtesy of Devil's Gulch ; 92: Anne Merrifield. Provided courtesy of Skywalker Vineyards LLC; 93: Wente Vineyards; 94 top: Tom Hood Photography, 2001. Hood is Good. ; 95 bottom: John Benson; 95: Cendrine McNeil; 96: Cline Cellars; 97: Courtesy of Mount Eden Vineyards; 99: Heidi Nigen/Ridge Vineyards; 100: Jamey Thomas ; 101 top: Alex Krause; 101 bottom: From the archives of the California Province of the Society of Jesus; 102: Courtesy Monterey County Vintners & Growers Association; 104: Morgan Winery; 105: Richard Green; 106: Mel Gerst; 107: DFV Wines; 108: Don Barnes; 109 top: Ed Porto Graphic Design; 109 bottom: Courtesy of Calera Wine Company; 110 top: Courtesy of Eberle Winery; 110 bottom: Kirk Irwin; 112: Courtesy of Paso Robles Wine Country Alliance; 113: Ron Bez, Courtesy of the Paso Robles Wine Country Alliance; 114, 115: Tablas Creek Vineyard; 118: Baileyana Winery; 119: Kirk Irwin; 120: Chris Leschinsky; 122: Kirk Irwin; 123: Chris Leschinsky; 125: Andy Katz Photography; 127: Bob Holmes; 128: Brent Winebrenner; 129: Grassini Family Vineyards; 130: Brown Cannon III; 131, 133: Trinchero Family Estates; 135: Chris Cutler; 136: Courtesy of E&J Gallo Winery; 137: Randy Caparoso; 138: Lodi Winegrape Commission; 139: Elizabeth Bokisch; 140: James Palmer, Malibu Vineyards; 141: Christine Photography, Courtesy fo Rusack Santa Catalina Island Vineyards; 143: Callaway Vineyard and Winery; 144: Justin Hulse; 145: Brett Shoaf/Artistic Visuals; 146 top: yourmap/iStockphoto; 146 bottom: Oregon Wine Board; 148: Thad Westhusing; 149, 151: Jason Tomczak; 152: Domaine Serene Vineyards; 154: Courtesy of Abacela; 155: HillCrest Vineyard; 156: Del Rio Vineyards; 157: Courtesy of Abacela; 158–59: Bethel Heights Vineyard; 159: Doreen L. Wynja; 160: Ocean Photography/Veer; 162: 2008 David Lloyd Imageworks; 163: Long Shadows Vintners; 164: David Gn/Veer; 167: Washington State Wine Commission; 168–69: Kevin Cruff; 170: Washington State Wine Commission; 171: Andrea Johnson Photography, http://andreajohnsonphotography.com; 173: Courtesy of Fogerson Cellars; 174: Kirk Hirota; 175: Tyson Kopher; 176: David Lloyd Imageworks; 178 top: Benjamin Benschneider; 179: Chateau Ste. Michelle; 180 top: Brent Charnley; 180 bottom: Courtesy of Columbia Winery; 181: White Heron Cellars; 182: Aurora Open/Veer; 184: Courtesy of Ste. Chapelle ; 185: bluerabbit/Veer; 186: Carlson Vineyards; 187: Colorado Wine Industry Development Board; 188: Marni Mattner; 189: Colorado Wine Industry Development Board; 191: Rodger Slott, Flashbox.us. Provided by Praire Berry LLC; 193: Debbie Frey; 194, 195: tony novak-clifford 2011; The Southwest; 196–97: billperry/Veer; 198: Andy Dean/Veer; 200: Jim Kelso; 201:Ron Newkirk Photography, www.ronnewkirk.com; 202: Mcelroyart/iStockphoto; 203: Antonio Trujillo; 204: Mcelroyart/iStockphoto; 206: Fairhaven Vineyards; 208: Steve Rawls. www.greendogpictures.com; 209: Texas Department of Agriculture/Wine Division; 210: codyphotography/iStockphoto; 211: Ed Zweiacher; The Midwest; 212–213: rsool/shutterstock; 214: rudi1976/Veer; 216: University of Minnesota, David L. Hansen; 217: Kenny Johnson; 218: Stone Hill Winery; 220: Saint Croix Vineyards; 221: Dan Nordstrom; 222: Randomphotog/iStockphoto; 224: Chateau Grand Traverse; 225: Brian Confer; 228: Ron Emser; 229: Courtesy of Wollersheim Winery; The Southeast; 230–231: spirit of america/shutterstock; 232 top: Montes-Bradley/iStockphoto; 232 bottom, 233: Steven Morris; 236: Jon Golden Photography; 238: Jason Keefer. http://jasonkeefer.com; 241: Dinah Bird, Ph.D.; 243: The Biltmore Company; 245: Lakeridge Winery; The Northeast; 246–247: Jorge Moro/shutterstock; 248: Chris Granstrom, Lincoln Peak Vineyards; 249: Jewell Towne Vineyards; 250 top: Veni/iStockphoto; 250 bottom: Dr. Konstantin Frank Wine Cellars; 252: Daniel Gonzalez/Gonzo Photo Studio; 253: Shinn Estate Vineyards; 254: Sabrina Lantos; 255: Bill Miles; 256 top: David Deng/Veer; 256 bottom: Randall Tagg Photography; 257 top: T. Ligamari; 257 bottom: David Bova, Millbrook Winery; 258: Dr. Konstantin Frank Wine Cellars; 259: Christopher Cornett; 260, 261: Randall Tagg Photography; 262: Jan Regan; 263, 264 top and bottom: Randall Tagg Photography; 266 top: Caryn and Paul Dolan; 266 Courtesy of Chaddsford Winery; 267: Kim Stimeling; 269: Melissa L. Schulte

Every effort has been made to trace the owners of copyright photographs. Anyone who may have been inadvertently omitted from this list is invited to write to the publishers who will be pleased to make any necessary amendments to future printings of this publication.